DYNAMIC ASSESSMENT

DYNAMIC ASSESSMENT

An Interactional Approach to Evaluating Learning Potential

Edited by

CAROL SCHNEIDER LIDZ
United Cerebral Palsy Association of Philadelphia and Vicinity

Foreword by J. P. Das

THE GUILFORD PRESS
New York   London

To my parents
Elsie Sussman Berg and Isadore Schneider

© 1987 The Guilford Press
A Division of Guilford Publications, Inc.
72 Spring Street, New York, N.Y. 10012

Printed in the United States of America

Last digit is print number: 9 8 7 6 5 4 3 2 1

Library of Congress Cataloging in Publication Data

Dynamic assessment.

    Includes bibliographies and index.
    1. Learning ability—Testing.   2. Intelligence tests—
Evaluation. 3. Cognition in children. 4. Transfer
of training. 5. Mentally handicapped children—Testing.
I. Lidz, Carol Schneider.
LB1134.D96   1987   371.2′6   86-19375
ISBN 0-89862-695-1

Contributors

JOHN D. BRANSFORD, Ph.D., Department of Psychology, Vanderbilt University, Nashville, Tennessee

ANN L. BROWN, Ph.D., Center for the Study of Reading, University of Illinois–Urbana–Champaign, Champaign, Illinois

MILTON BUDOFF, Ph.D., Research Institute for Educational Problems, Cambridge, Massachusetts

M. SUSAN BURNS, Ph.D., Department of Education, Tulane University, New Orleans, Louisiana

JOSEPH C. CAMPIONE, Ph.D., Center for the Study of Reading, University of Illinois–Urbana–Champaign, Champaign, Illinois

VICTOR R. DELCLOS, Ph.D., Department of Education, Tulane University, New Orleans, Louisiana

SUSAN E. EMBRETSON, Ph.D., Department of Psychology, University of Kansas, Lawrence, Kansas

REUVEN FEUERSTEIN, Ph.D., Hadassah–WIZO–Canada Research Institute, Jerusalem, Israel; and School of Education, Bar Ilan University, Ramat Gan, Israel

TED S. HASSELBRING, Ed.D., Department of Special Education, Vanderbilt University, Nashville, Tennessee

MOGENS REIMER JENSEN, Ph.D., Department of Psychology, Yale University, New Haven, Connecticut; and Hadassah–WIZO–Canada Research Institute, Jerusalem, Israel

SHLOMO KANIEL, Ph.D., Hadassah–WIZO–Canada Research Institute, Jerusalem, Israel; and School of Education, Bar Ilan University, Ramat Gan, Israel

KEVIN J. KEANE, Ph.D., Private practice, New York, New York

PNINA S. KLEIN, Ed.D., School of Education, Bar Ilan University, Ramat Gan, Israel

CAROL SCHNEIDER LIDZ, Psy.D., Clinic Team Services, United Cerebral Palsy Association of Philadelphia and Vicinity, Philadelphia, Pennsylvania

JUDITH S. MEARIG, Ph.D., Graduate Program in School Psychology, St. Lawrence University, Canton, New York

JOEL MEYERS, Ph.D., Department of Educational Psychology and Statistics, State University of New York, Albany, Albany, New York

NORRIS MINICK, Ph.D., Center for Psychosocial Studies, Chicago, Illinois; and University of Chicago, Chicago, Illinois

YAACOV RAND, Ph.D., Hadassah–WIZO–Canada Research Institute, Jerusalem, Israel; and School of Education, Bar Ilan University, Ramat Gan, Israel

TREVOR E. SEWELL, Ph.D., College of Education, Temple University, Philadelphia, Pennsylvania

DENIS H. STOTT, Ph.D., Department of Psychology, University of Guelph, Guelph, Ontario, Canada

CATHERINE THOMAS, Ph.D., Division of Special Education, New Jersey Department of Education, Trenton, New Jersey

DAVID TZURIEL, Ph.D., Hadassah–WIZO–Canada Research Institute, Jerusalem, Israel; and School of Education, Bar Ilan University, Ramat Gan, Israel

NANCY J. VYE, Ph.D., Department of Psychology, University of Western Ontario, London, Ontario, Canada

Foreword

A foreword should enhance the appreciation of a book's content. To serve that purpose, I wish to discuss three issues which are relevant to the foundations of dynamic assessment and to its symbiotic relationship to intervention and enrichment.

The inadequacy of "static" tests of intelligence and the consequent need for dynamic assessment, which would explore the potential of the child for learning, is the *first issue* that permeates the content of many chapters in this book. The type of learning discussed in the book is cognitive, not motor. Since a list of numerous cognitive skills can be constructed, not all kinds are to be given equal importance. But then what *kinds* or classes of cognitive skills are of concern for the teacher, coach, or "mediator" who must intervene between the material to be learned and the learner? Consequently, what underlying processes are to be trained? This is the *second issue* addressed in this volume. The purpose of training or intervention is to bring about transfer, and the farther it is, the more desirable does it become. But how far is far transfer? For example, what is considered *far* by an experimental psychologist who is trying to teach a mentally retarded subject a rehearsal strategy for rote learning of a list of items may be *near,* almost inconsequentially near, for the social activist who is preparing them to live a productive life! The situation is similar to an analogy borrowed from another discipline. It has been remarked that an anthropologist's century is a paleontologist's moment! So, how far is far and what are the conditions that facilitate far transfer is the *third issue* which requires some discussion; again, several chapters have made references to transfer. Let me discuss the three issues one at a time.

The folly of intelligence tests has been written about over and over again. Intelligence tests are static measures of ability, often one general ability, and do not predict the ability to learn. Authors of all theoretical persuasions and points of view agree with this general comment about standardized intelligence tests. Lidz, in her Introduction, cites Jensen's research on Mexican-Americans and Anglo-Americans—the former group were lower in a test of intelligence, but nevertheless no different from the Anglos in learning rate. Lidz, of course, quotes Feuerstein's research on learning potential that is not predicted from IQ insofar as disadvantaged children are involved. Feurstein is the proenvironment social activist of a philosophical persuasion different from Jensen's.

Every new movement needs a theoretical guru or icon. Dynamic assessment has found one in Vygotsky. His message is summarized in the following quotation: "What children can do with the assistance of others might be in some sense even more indicative of their mental development than what they can do alone. . . . " (Vygotsky, 1978, p. 85).

Children learn by interacting with adults and with other children. All higher forms of cognitive activity are learned and performed in the context of one's culture. In this sense, learning, thinking, and problem solving are instances of higher mental activities which have a social origin. Once we accept this, it is easy to see why the ability to learn generally or to learn to solve a problem should be tested while the child has an opportunity to interact with one or more adults. If the child has not had the opportunity for extensive verbal interactions with adults because of his or her social conditions, then as a prerequisite for assessing ability, such experiences should be provided. Active interactions of this sort modify not only the content of thinking but its structure. Vygotsky's notion of zones of proximal development has its origin in this general assumption of intellectual growth through interactions; so has Luria's research on the development of language in children, as well as that on the effect of instruction on logical inferencing in neoliterates (Luria, 1979). This is evident in the following quotes from Luria.

"The 'cultural' aspect of Vygotsky's theory involved the socially structured ways in which society organizes the kinds of tasks that the growing child faces and the kinds of tools, both mental and physical, that the young child is provided to master those tasks" (p. 44). Furthermore, subjective knowledge and cultural heritage blend together. To me, it makes a lot of sense; in Vygotsky's concept of development, ontogenetic and cultural factors blend together; or to borrow from Popper and Eccles (1978, p. 359)—the subjective world of the individual and the history of its culture come together. "The tools that man uses to master his environment and his own behavior did not spring fully developed from the head of God. They were invented and perfected in the long course of man's social history" (Luria, 1979, p. 44).

Vygotsky has been discussed in several chapters (see Minick for an excellent discussion). The notion of "zone of proximal development" has led some of the contributors to operationalize it and to measure it objectively. In one of these attempts, the measure is the number of prompts required for solving a problem or for transferring the skill to solve a new problem. The idea is a neat one, and this prosthetic device has been used previously (see Siegler, 1976); but Vygotsky might not agree that counting the number of prompts is by any means a measure of the "zone." It measures how much aid was needed by the individual to solve a problem—but what determines the amount of aid needed?

We must go back to a consideration of the social origins of intelligent behavior in order to answer that question. The infant's cognitive development from its day of birth, is shaped by interaction with adults. Studies on infant behaviors, such as reaching and tracking, show complex cognitive processes behind these apparently simple motor activities. If infants are given an opportunity to reach fast versus slow moving objects, they develop a scheme which makes them adjust their reaching behavior; but when the speed is too fast as judged by the infants, they may not even attempt to reach the moving object. To give an example of another competent behavior, consider the beginnings of speech and language. In observing early verbal communication between mothers and their infants, the social origin of language and the critical role playing by the mothers in promoting communication with infants become all the more apparent. The ingenious recordings of mother-infant communication made by Treaverthen convinced me that language, the powerful tool for accessing human knowledge, as well as being the tool that determines the way we think, bears the mark of early experience. Hence it is prone to all the cognitive handicaps which exist due to socio-cultural disadvantages.

Perhaps, that is one reason why the replacement of static assessment by dynamic assessment will not eliminate the harmful effects of social disadvantage on the cognitive competence of children. Rather, compensatory training or intervention programs *may* offset some of the deleterious influences of early disadvantage on later competence.

Thus we come to consider intervention or training of the dynamic kind. Assessment alone has a limited value unless it can guide intervention. The type of training recommended, though, depends on what has been assessed. And it is here that we need to delineate a cognitive structure, a model of mental functions which provides a framework for both assessment and subsequent intervention. Do we have a theoretical framework, then, for determining which cognitive functions should be selected for assessment?

The Feuerstein device for assessing learning potential contains various tasks which have an apparent similarity with nonverbal tests of intelligence and with memory problems. Another example of dynamic assessment is provided in the work of Carlson and Wiedl (cited in Lidz's Introduction)—the material comprises the familiar Raven Progressive Matrices (which, by the way, is also used by Feuerstein). A sympathetic critique of their material may agree with the view that the object of assessment is to demonstrate learning potential; but how much is the learning potential independent of the material that is being learned? It seems to me that some clear statements should be made for the reasons for selecting the cognitive processes or scholastic products, such as reading and comprehension (Campione & Brown, this volume) that are involved in assessment. Otherwise, the unsympathetic critic may get the idea that in assessing potential, the test is being taught; in Feuerstein's case, the accusation may be made that he is teaching intelligence tests that are usually given for recruiting Israeli soldiers. Of course, that is not his aim, and both he and I agree that the basic cognitive processes that underlie assessment and training tasks should be understood (see Snart, 1985).

Given the choice, I would include the three major cognitive processes underlying information coding, attention, and planful behavior (Das, 1984a, 1984b; Das, Kirby & Jarman, 1975, 1979) and obtain dynamic assessments for each kind of processing. I would specially opt for dynamic assessment in the case of developmentally delayed, culturally disadvantaged, and learning-disabled children. Then I can prepare individualized intervention programs that will help the child develop the areas of processing in which he or she was found to be weak.

The knotty issue is transfer. Because several chapters in this book have mentioned transfer or generalization, the problem merits discussion. Near, far, and very far transfers have been distinguished, and the farther the transfer, the more desirable is the training program which facilitates or promotes it. An example of very far transfer is as follows (Das, 1985a). Children who were at least 2 years behind their peers in reading were found to have deficiencies in successive processing. A remedial program which emphasized successive processing, but also involved simultaneous processing, planning, and organizing one's activities, as well as attending to relevant features in a problem, was given to these children. Improvement was not only noticed in performing the various processing tasks but also in word-attack skills. The program did not include training in reading nor did it contain material typically related to reading. What did the reading-disabled children learn from the remedial exercises which were subsequently transferred to word reading? Most certainly, they learned neither a common content nor a common procedure. Rather they learned the *principle* of processing the information in the training tasks appropriately, and it is this principle which was transferred to the word-reading task. I have suggested that whereas near transfer can occur on the basis of similarity between the old and the new task, far transfer depends on the eduction of a principle (Das, 1985b). More intelligent children are apt to observe that apparently different tasks may require the same processing; less intelligent children are less likely to notice this. Therefore, the extent of transfer must depend on intelligence to some degree. The relation between IQ and transfer is supported by more than one author in this book.

I have a hunch that there is an IQ threshold below which the eduction of an underlying process does not occur. The threshold can be fixed around IQs of 70 to 75. There is common agreement as Campione and Brown have shown, with the notion that far transfer is hard to come by in the mentally retarded. Could this limitation be attributed to an IQ threshold? Furthermore, could we use the occurrence of far transfer as not only a criterion for the success of dynamic assessment followed by enrichment training, but as a means of separating the truly retarded from what the Soviet psychologists call the temporarily retarded? The temporary retardation may have been brought on by disadvantageous social, cultural, and educational conditions, and is shown in children's performance on standardized, albeit static, tests of intellectual competence.

In concluding the foreword to this book, which will become an important milestone as research on dynamic assessment makes progress, I shall make two personal observations. First, the vast disparity between the majority and the disadvantaged minority children in their level of performance in intelligence or achievement tests should be recognized. It should not be minimized and explained away by dynamic assessment. We should accept both the existence of social inequalities, and the gap in cognitive competence between the haves and the have-nots in America, without being bothered by the question, "which one causes which." Second, there is justifiable optimism in being able to reduce or remove the temporary retardation detected by standardized intelligence tests. The sooner we can institute cognitive remedial programs, the better; but as Feuerstein has so compellingly demonstrated with disadvantaged Israeli adolescents, it is never too late!

J. P. Das, Ph.D.
University of Alberta

REFERENCES

Das, J. P. (1984a). Intelligence and information integration. In J. Kirby (Ed.), *Cognitive strategies and educational performance* (pp. 13–34). New York: Academic Press.

Das, J. P. (1984b). Aspects of planning. In J. Kirby (Ed.), *Cognitive strategies and educational performance* (pp. 35–50). New York: Academic Press.

Das, J. P. (1985a). Global and specific remediation of reading problems. In G. d'Ydewalle (Ed.), *Cognition, information processing, and motivation* (pp. 665–679). Amsterdam: North-Holland.

Das, J. P. (1985b). Remedial training for the amelioration of cognitive deficits in children. In A. F. Ashman & R. S. Laura (Eds.), *The education and training of the mentally retarded* (pp. 215–244). London: Croom Helm.

Das, J. P., Kirby, J., & Jarman, R. F. (1975). Simultaneous and successive syntheses: An alternative model for cognitive abilities. *Psychological Bulletin, 82* (1), 87–103.

Das, J. P., Kirby, J., & Jarman, R. (1979) *Simultaneous and successive cognitive processes.* New York: Academic Press.

Luria, A. R. (1979). *The making of mind* (M. Cole & S. Cole, Eds.). Cambridge: Harvard University Press.

Popper, K. R., & Eccles, J. C. (1978). *The self and its brain.* New York: Springer-Verlag.

Siegler, R. (1976). Three aspects of cognitive development. *Cognitive Psychology, 8,* 481–520.

Snart, F. (1985). Cognitive-processing approaches to the assessment and remediation of learning problems: An interview with J. P. Das and Reuven Feuerstein. *Journal of Psychoeducational Assessment, 3,* 1–14.

Vygotsky, L. S. (1978). *Mind in society.* Cambridge: Harvard University Press.

Contents

III. ISSUES AND IMPLICATIONS

CONCLUSION

Index   497

INTRODUCTION

Historical Perspectives

CAROL SCHNEIDER LIDZ

As with most ideas, the notion of assessment based upon direct teaching intervention is not new. Psychologists have long expressed dissatisfaction with traditional models of assessment and have called for change. What is new is that there finally are realizations of the ideas that IQ tests do not reveal meaningful information about learning ability, that assessment needs to link diagnosis with treatment, that the outcome of assessment should be an array of interventions with potential for direct application to instruction, and that children can be taught to become more competent learners.

Dynamic assessment has finally been taken seriously and has captured the interest and imagination of both researchers and practitioners. This interest is largely attributable to the 1979 publication by Reuven Feuerstein of *The Dynamic Assessment of Retarded Performers*, and to the numerous workshops and presentations by Feuerstein and his colleagues in this country and, in fact, around the world. There is a problem, however. Like many good ideas, there is the danger of fadism, of a quick rise in interest, failure to take hold and infiltrate the establishment, followed by demise and "Monday morning quarterbacking" about what went wrong (Bradley, 1983). If dynamic assessment is a good idea, and we believe it is, then care must be taken to temper premature enthusiasm with well-worked-out theory and adequate empirical investigation. This is the mission of this book. Now that the interest of psychologists has been sparked and their attention gained, it is time for a text to summarize the work that has been accomplished and is in process, and to present the foundations upon which future developments can be based. Most of this work is in a preliminary stage. The intent is to inform the reader about how various researchers and practitioners are attempting to realize the goals of dynamic assessment and to provide a representative sample of work in process, primarily in the western hemisphere.

Two words are of primary importance to the definition and conceptualization of dynamic assessment: activity and modifiability. The examiner and learner are both active; the examiner is an active intervener who monitors and modifies the interaction with the learner in order to induce successful learning. The learner is prodded, directed, and reinforced into a role of active

Carol Schneider Lidz. Clinic Team Services, United Cerebral Palsy Association of Philadelphia and Vicinity, Philadelphia, Pennsylvania.

3

seeker and organizer of information. The product of the assessment is modifiability or change in the cognitive functioning of the learner, presumably positive change. Dynamic assessment, then, is an interaction between an examiner-as-intervener and a learner-as–active participant, which seeks to estimate the degree of modifiability of the learner and the means by which positive changes in cognitive functioning can be induced and maintained. The emphasis here needs to be on cognitive functioning, because the focus of dynamic assessment as used here is on the parameters associated with and thought to underlie intelligence. These interventions typically take place within a test–teach–retest model.

Dynamic assessment is not intended as a replacement of current approaches, but as an addition to currently available procedures. Dynamic assessment can provide hypotheses that respond to unique questions, information that is simply not derivable from other measures. When other approaches can yield information sufficient to respond to referral issues and are appropriate for the child and decisions to be made about the child, these procedures will suffice. When the questions concern modifiability and the need for ideas for intervention, then dynamic assessment is the procedure of choice. Dynamic assessment differs from other approaches to evaluation by direct teaching in its focus on cognitive functions and the attempt to modify these functions; this contrasts with procedures that primarily manipulate academic content.

The work of the contributors to this book represents milestones in the development of the theory and practice of dynamic assessment. Most of this has been accomplished, or at least reported, in the 1970s and 1980s. However, dynamic assessment has a history that extends considerably further back. This history will be reviewed, and, in so doing, the work of researchers other than the chapter authors who have made significant contributions will be described. The chapter contributors will speak for themselves. While the organization of this overview proceeds by decades, it should be clear that this has been done merely to facilitate organization, and that the actual course of events does not always fall neatly within the framework of 10-year divisions.

Historical Review

The 1920s to 1930s

As early as the 1920s, psychologists and others espoused ideas about optimal approaches to the assessment of intelligence that sounded very much like dynamic assessment. For example, Buckingham (1921) concluded that "[a] measure . . . either of the rate at which learning takes place or of typical products of learning will constitute a measure of intelligence" (p. 272), and, later, in the same publication:

> it seems to me that whatever definition we may give to intelligence in the abstract, we are justified from an educational point of view in regarding it as ability to

learn, and as measured by the extent to which learning has taken place or may take place. (p. 273)

In a similar statement, Penrose (1934) suggested that "the ideal test in the study of mental deficiency would be one which investigates the ability to learn" (p. 49).

Dearborn (1921) was even more explicit in his observations and recommendations: "Theoretically, it would follow that measurement of the actual progress of representative learning would furnish the best test of intelligence . . . most tests now in common use are not tests of the capacity to learn, but are tests of what has been learned" (p. 211). And later, "individual tests involving actual learning rather than results of learning are needed" (p. 211). These ideas are echoed well into the 1980s.

Later in the decade, DeWeerdt (1927) reported one of the first practice effects studies. She anticipated much of what had been noted at much later times. First, DeWeerdt cited the basic assumption of traditional intelligence measures, that of the subjects' equal exposure to environmental conditions; she then suggested that

> Since all education is directed toward the improvement of the individual, it is quite possible that a more direct method than the intelligence test for investigating the capacity for improvement under school conditions may be found. (p. 548)

DeWeerdt conducted a study of the effects of practice and enhanced motivation on academic-like tasks. She did not find a general improvability factor, but found the variable of improvability to be fairly task specific. Her results also showed second-day scores to be more reliable indicators of initial ability than the more erratic first-day scores. Most importantly, she concluded that "other measures of the individual beside the one-time test are needed for classification purposes. The practice test is a dynamic test, a measure of the ability to improve under specific training" (p. 557).

Although practice as an intervention did not realize the hopes of those espousing it as a solution to assessment limitations, the motivational basis for dynamic assessment in the dissatisfaction with static measures can be seen to have its roots at least as far back as the first third of this century. Perhaps the most influential of these roots in terms of current thinking about dynamic assessment derives from the work of Andre Rey (1934; Osterrieth, 1945; Rey & Dupont, 1953), a Swiss psychologist, who published most of his work between the 1930s and 1950s. Rey was Feuerstein's mentor, and Feuerstein continued to incorporate some of Rey's measures as part of the Learning Potential Assessment Device (Feuerstein, 1979).

The 1940s

During the 1940s, and earlier, there were signs of concern with some of the issues related to current theoretical developments culminating in dynamic assessment. Woodrow (1946) accepted a single-factor definition of intelligence and therefore drew a distinction between intelligence and learning ability. He also viewed intelligence as an indicator of past acquired knowledge, and discussed learning ability in terms of improvement with practice. Ironically, his research is supportive of dynamic assessment in a backhanded way by showing low associations between practice and measures of intelligence. (Practice, however, has been found to be effective for psychomotor tasks e.g., Fleishman & Hempel, 1955). Woodrow interpreted his findings as a demonstration of the difference between learning ability and intelligence. However, his results can also be interpreted as a demonstration of the lack of effectiveness of practice alone as a modifier of intelligence.

Simrall (1947), as did Woodrow, questioned the equation of intelligence with learning ability, but more clearly distinguished between these entities in terms of how they were measured; in this way it was demonstrated that, despite popular definitions equating learning and intelligence, intelligence tests were not designed to measure learning:

> Intelligence is almost always measured as an average score made by an individual on a number of tests which have been performed once. . . . An intelligence test . . . is not intended to be a direct measure of learning because the opportunity to practice the performance required by the test items is prohibited. Indeed, previous practice of the test renders the measure obtained unreliable and invalid. . . . Retention, not learning, is measured by intelligence tests. (p. 29)

Simrall's research supported her hypothesis of the lack of relationship between measures of intelligence and learning ability (equated with practice).

McPherson (1948), writing in the 1940s, reviewed research as far back as 1919 that included attempts to assess retardates with direct learning experiences. These studies were experimental in nature, and not intended for the derivation of assessment instruments. However, McPherson concluded, as had Woodrow and Simrall, that there was a "lack of covariance of intellectual status and learning behavior," and suggested that "the determination of the nature of learning is essential to a sound educational and clinical manipulation of the subjects" (p. 252). She became even more specific and closer to dynamic approaches in recommending that studies of learning ability not only optimize motivation for the subjects "but will undoubtedly involve the introduction of variations from time to time during the practice. . . . Investigation of learning in situations comparable to those in which the subnormal functions daily is demanded" (p. 253).

The 1950s

COACHING STUDIES

During the 1950s, specific attempts to assess the effects of direct teaching on assessment results reached a peak, although the history of coaching extends back at least to the 1920s (Vernon, 1954). A large portion of the studies of the 1950s on the effects of coaching were carried out in Great Britain. Representative of this literature were the reports of the symposium on the effects of coaching and practice on intelligence tests (Dempster, 1954; James, 1953; Vernon, 1954; Wiseman, 1954; Yates, 1953). These researchers were not concerned with trying to find ways to improve intelligence or assessment, or with optimizing results for low performers. They were primarily responding to commercialization of coaching and were trying to arrive at an opinion and official recommendation regarding the effects of these efforts. Coaching was seen as an attempt to equalize the familiarity of the 10-year-olds taking the British Eleven Plus examinations.

Wiseman and Wrigley (1953) (and Wiseman, 1954), in their review of the literature on practice versus coaching, cited a number of studies that showed significant improvement with practice for brighter children (higher initial scorers), but not for lower scoring children. Studies yielded conflicting results regarding the benefits of coaching over practice alone, some showing greater improvement with coaching and some revealing no advantage. In general, these British researchers focused on the brighter students of age 10 who were candidates for the Eleven Plus examination.

In the Wiseman and Wrigley (1953) study, the practice group was administered a different standardized IQ test every week for 6 weeks with no feedback regarding results or discussion of the tests. The coaching group was taught by regular classroom teachers, using commercially published materials that included exercises for IQ-like test items. It was characteristic of these studies to provide no details regarding the specifics of coaching; in fact, in this study no guidelines were provided to the teachers carrying out the coaching procedures. The practice group made the most gains, 11 points, as compared to the 6-point average gain of the coached group and 4.5-point gain of the controls (test–retest only). No statistical significances were reported, but the authors considered these to be "extremely small" gains (Wiseman, 1954, p. 5). When the data were analyzed according to initial IQ, there was a positive association between IQ and gains from practice, with subjects with higher IQs making the greater gains. Lower IQ subjects benefited more from coaching than from practice.

Yates (1953) described the results of coaching studies carried out at his foundation. In the largest study, coaching and practice yielded similar gains of 6 points, both about 3 points above the controls. He concluded that these were "meagre dividends" (p. 153).

James (1953) did not describe results of formal research, but informally shed some light on the nature of coaching, as commonly carried out by British classroom teachers. Primarily, coaching involved review and discussion of errors on items similar to those on the IQ test, assurance that instructions were understood and followed, and provision of practice in working out sample problems. There is no talk of cognitive functions, styles, or strategies, although it is likely that some of the better teachers included principles of problem solution in their instructions. In an informal, uncontrolled study, James reported a rise of 4.3 points for boys and 5.5 points for girls in IQ scores following coaching. Although James argued strenuously for coaching over practice, his results did not support the superiority of his choice.

Dempster (1954) reported the results of a 1951 study of 8 weeks with three groups: practice, coaching, and controls. Controls gained 1.7 points for boys and 2.4 for girls; the practice group gained 4.5 and 5.5 points, respectively, and the coaching group gained 8.9 and 9.8 points, respectively. Correlations for all groups between the first and last tests exceeded .9. Dempster then did a coaching only study in 1952 that yielded smaller gains, and a 1953 study that yielded results closer to his 1951 gains, when coaching procedures were modified.

Vernon (1954), whose own research on coaching (1952) reported the largest gains (11 points), concluded in his summary and comments on the symposium that, despite differences in gains across various research projects, the evidence was sufficiently suggestive that practice and/or coaching did make a difference to children with borderline IQs. In the case of the British classification tests, a sizable proportion of the children would have had a chance of selection for an academic track who would not have otherwise qualified. However, he also concluded that, on the average, the size of the gains was limited, although for many individuals, gains were large. Vernon also made some interesting observations about the nature of the coaching/practice interventions. First, he said that "it appears that later tests are slightly more reliable and have slightly better predictive validity than early ones" (p. 58). He also noted that "[s]ome types of test items are much more susceptible to practice or coaching than others" (p. 58). Those items that appeared more susceptible were verbal similarities and, in general, nonverbal tasks. Virtually all of these studies relied on gain scores, and Vernon did note some of the problems of using these as measures of change—for example, the large standard deviations that led to unreliability for small groups (under 100), and the lack of uniformity of measuring units across research projects. In his review of non-British practice and coaching studies from the 1920s on, Vernon observed that the earlier studies yielded larger gains. He attributed these differences in results to differences between tests, units of measurement, and test sophistication of the subjects; he also noted differences regarding "aptness" of the coaching. In agreement with more current research, Vernon concluded that children with higher initial scores tended to profit more from practice, whereas those with lower initial scores demonstrated greater response to coaching.

Heim and Watts (1957) attempted to control for some of the methodological problems characterizing earlier coaching research. However, their results were confounded by the large interschool differences for their subjects, which exceeded the intergroup differences. Their results were therefore reported as tentative and suggestive. These authors found that the largest improvement was in response to discussion of errors, and that the results of coaching alone or in combination with practice were in all cases superior to practice alone; personality variables were observed to contribute to outcome, but were not a measured or controlled variable. These authors defined coaching as "working through with subjects problems which closely resemble, but are not identical with, the problems comprising the test. The children are encouraged to take an active part, to offer suggestions, to ask questions, and to explain solutions" (p. 201). Discussion of errors was a separate treatment group.

Ortar (1959), from Hebrew University in Jerusalem, described her approach to coaching, which more closely resembled and reflected the concerns and work of Feuerstein, that is, an attempt to increase the validity of assessment of children from a variety of cultures and early cognitive experiences. Yates, of Great Britain, in his introduction and commentary to Ortar's article, noted that, in contrast to her concerns, "[t]hose local authorities in this country which approve or promote a certain amount of coaching for, or practice in, objective tests prior to the Eleven Plus examination are not seeking to enable educationally deprived children to compete on equal terms with those who have enjoyed vastly superior schooling. They are merely endeavoring to ensure that all children are acquainted with the particular form of examination that has been devised for them" (Ortar, p. 137). That is, the goal of the British researchers was increased test reliability, not assessment of cognitive modifiability.

Ortar noted the ambiguity of the definitions and descriptions of coaching in the literature and the lack of information on the types of experiences that were or were not effective in producing gains. Her interest was clearly to determine educability, or learning potential. She had observed that the children she assessed were more validly assessed by verbal than nonverbal tests for a criterion of school success, and that it was failure to understand the principles of the task that appeared to reduce their success with the nonverbal material. Ortar devised a training task called the Triangles Test, which was similar to the Arthur Stencil Test. The type of coaching provided included explanation of principles and discussion of errors. The test was standardized on 397 Israeli children between the ages of 6 and 14, and the concurrent validity criterion was teacher judgment regarding academic and practical ability. Her research showed a large increase in correlation between coached versus noncoached results and teacher judgment, although no data regarding significance were reported. Ortar explained the great susceptibility of nonverbal measures to coaching by the more adequate training provided by most schools in language.

Messick (1981), in his review and discussion of the coaching literature on Scholastic Aptitude Test scores for the Educational Testing Service, also noted the imprecision of the term "coaching," which has a range of meanings "from short-term cramming and simple practice on sample items at one extreme to long-term instruction aimed at knowledge and skill development at the other" (p. 22), although most coaching for "aptitude" tests emphasized practice and familiarization. Messick in fact accepted a broad definition of coaching to include "any intervention procedure specifically undertaken to improve test scores, whether by improving the skills measured by the test, by improving the skills for taking the test, or both" (p. 26). Such a definition does not allow an answer to the question: is coaching effective? It is necessary to be considerably more precise regarding the nature of the coaching and to elaborate in detail regarding the issue of effectiveness—that is, for what?

Finally, Anastasi (1981a, 1981b) provided a general overview and critique of the coaching literature. She noted three reasons for controversy and confusion in this area: misconceptions regarding the nature of tests, ambiguity regarding the definition of coaching, and methodological problems characterizing the coaching research. Of special note was Anastasi's comment on validity: "We can say that a test score is invalidated only when a particular experience raises the score without appreciably affecting the behavior domain that the test samples" (1981a, p. 1087). It was this distinction that Anastasi applied in her evaluation of the effects of three types of assessment intervention experiences: orientation (practice or familiarization), coaching, and instruction in broad cognitive skills. First, familiarization consistently leads to an increase in retest scores, and is seen as effective in reducing the effects of differences in prior experience related to the test; such familiarization can be accomplished with relatively brief interventions. With regard to coaching, Anastasi noted that the closer coaching was to actual test content, the less it was likely to generalize to criterion measures; in general, coaching studies have shown little or no concern for generalizability. She also noted the considerable variance in definitions of coaching experiences, which often extended from practice and familiarization to remediation of basic skills. Anastasi expressed a positive impression of the results of attempts to improve intelligence and felt that, although these were still in an exploratory stage, results were promising. She concluded that, whereas test familiarization increased validity and coaching reduced validity, training in broad cognitive skills would not affect test validity, but "should improve the trainee's ability to cope with subsequent intellectual tasks" (1981a, p. 1092).

NONCOACHING RESEARCH OF THE 1950S

There were two contributions to the history of dynamic assessment during the 1950s that were independent of the coaching studies. These were the procedures proposed by Haeussermann (1958) and Volle (1957). However, also during this time, theoretical groundwork for dynamic assessment was laid by Piaget's suggestions of the changeability of intelligence and development of a process orientation in assessing intelligence (Meltzer, 1984). Haeussermann, who worked primarily with severely orthopedically handicapped children, developed a complex, nonstandardized assessment that involved exploration and probing to attempt to determine at what level and by what means a child not otherwise assessable could respond. Much later, Jedrysek, Klapper, Pope, and Wortis (1972) attempted a standardization and simplification of Haeussermann's methods in an instrument that could well be the first quasi-dynamic assessment test commercially available to practitioners: the *Psychoeducational Evaluation of the Preschool Child*. This procedure assesses the child across a number of functions appropriate for most preschool curricula. It differs from other procedures in the response to failure of an item. When the child makes an error, a series of probes are administered to determine at what level the child can succeed. This procedure does not, however, provide a test–teach–retest experience for the child, and there are both practical and technical problems, but it remains the first serious attempt to go beyond acceptance of the child's first products with an exploratory response by the examiner. Nevertheless, it remains focused on products and retains most of the static qualities of traditional measures.

On a smaller scale, but more dynamic in nature, was the proposal for testing the limits on the Wechsler Intelligence Scale for Children (WISC) Verbal scale by Volle (1957). Volle acknowledged the common practice of school psychologists of exploring beyond the child's initial response to verbal items in attempts to derive an impression of the nature of errors. He proposed both a standard and an alternate scoring for information, comprehension, and arithmetic subtests. The examiner first asked the questions as written in the manual; if the child made an error that communicated confusion or misunderstanding, the standard phrasing was just repeated; if the child continued to err, the question was rephrased and/or simplified as suggested in his article. Volle offered no data, only a single case description, to illustrate his approach, and he did not discuss the implications for such manipulations as he proposed.

The 1960s

The 1960s can be characterized as a time of isolated efforts to devise direct measures of learning that attempted to assess educability. These were performance tests, administered within a test–teach–retest model.

Schucman (1960) devised such a procedure for severely retarded children between the ages of 5:1 through 11:1. She felt existing tests were beyond the abilities of these children, and hypothesized that "the child's educability can be inferred from his responses to learning situations which require abilities on which education depends, namely, to learn from instruction, to transfer the training, and to retain the learning" (p. 1). The children were tested, trained, retested with different forms of the same measures, and retested after delays of one hour, one week, and 7 weeks to assess retention. Several pilot studies were carried out to determine the most appropriate and effective materials. Schucman's final battery included five tests, all nonverbal: a two-buttons test (imitative ability and memory), a buzz test (size discrimination), a music box test (brightness discrimination), a light test (shape discrimination), and a three-buttons test (brightness discrimination). Training involved demonstration by the examiner, imitation by the child with examiner cues, and prevention or correction of errors. The children were trained to a criterion of three correct consecutive responses on each task. The criterion measure for the procedure was teacher rating of learning ability. These tests were able to discriminate among IQ levels within the severely retarded group, and did reflect learning effects for these subjects; transfer and retention scores were the most sensitive reflectors of IQ. As has been found by other investigators, posttraining scores were more stable than initial test scores, and these posttraining scores were also better predictors of teacher ratings.

Mackay and Vernon (1963) devised a battery of nine tests for cognitively normal children between the ages of 8:9 and 10:11, administered as a group measure. They were concerned with increasing the ability of standard intelligence tests to predict "capacity to make scholastic progress" (p. 177), and it was these authors who appeared to be the first to speak in terms of "acquisition of new mental skills" (p. 177), although they did not elaborate this idea. They also saw such tests as having the potential to generate remedial strategies. However, although their tests involved learning to a greater extent than measures devised by most previous researchers, they were not accompanied by training other than repetition and practice. Mackay and Vernon cited earlier use of performance testing by the U.S. Navy and Army, which used a test–teach–retest format, and noted that these measures "added appreciably" to the predictive validity of the test battery used in those studies (p. 178). However, these authors, as others, continued to accept traditional views of intelligence, and concluded only that learning ability was different from intelligence. Although they did question the existence of a general intelligence factor and sought to enhance the assessment of intelligence with learning ability measures, they did not suggest that intelligence itself might be better assessed by means of direct performance measures. Their research involved a small number (36) of middle-class British children, and the specific tests were as follows: language learning, number substitution, verbal instructions learning, verbal information learning, word memory, geometrical form learning, perceptual detail learning, symbol maze learning, and a group concept formation test. The results of this research were discouraging, particularly with the younger subjects. There were inconsistencies in results involving the new measures, and the results did not contribute to any significant degree to the predictive ability of the more traditional measures.

Supportive of the studies of Jensen (1961, 1963, 1966, 1969), using paired associate learning, Semler and Iscoe (1963) compared black and white children, ages 5 through 9. They found that, despite significant IQ differences between these groups, differences disappeared in paired-associate results by age 9. Similar to research described above, there were negligible associations between paired-associate learning and IQ, adding to the literature suggesting that learning and IQ measures assess different variables.

A. R. Jensen was among the first of the cognitive researchers to address the differences in results on traditional measures of members of ethnic minorities with proposals for dynamic alternatives. As early as 1961 and as late as 1968, Jensen concluded that currently available measures were inadequate estimations of the abilities of low-socioeconomic-status (SES) minority children and that higher level cognitive functions (Level II) were the most susceptible to environmental experiences.

In 1961 Jensen referred to the disproportionate number of Mexican-American children who became classified as slow learners on the basis of data obtained from tests normed on Anglo-Americans. Jensen's research investigated the utility of "direct measures of present learning ability," which he described in contrast to "static measures of achievement acquired in the past" (p. 148). He went on to justify such an approach by the observation that standard approaches to assessment were often "quite inappropriate for children who have not had much exposure to the Anglo-American culture of the normative group" and concluded that "[i]t would seem that a better way to measure learning potential, or to decide whether a child is inherently a slow learner, would be to give the child a standard task and observe how fast he learns it" (p. 148).

The three learning tasks devised by Jensen were measures of immediate recall (learning the names of objects to be used in the other tests, and recalling as many as possible after brief exposure; the objects were reexposed until all were recalled, and the child's score was the total number of unrecalled objects until the criterion of total recall was reached); serial learning (learning the order of objects placed under a series of boxes; the child could lift the box to check the correctness of his or her response, and the score was the number of errors until criterion); and, finally, paired-associate learning (one of a pair of objects was fastened to the outside of a box, with its mate covered by the box; the child had to learn which object was inside the box). In his 1960 research, Jensen compared fourth- and sixth-grade children from low-SES Anglo- and Mexican-American backgrounds, as well as those with higher versus lower IQ scores on a static measure. The main result of this study was a significant difference in favor of low-IQ Mexican-American subjects when compared with low-IQ Anglos. In fact, low-IQ Mexican-Americans performed as well on the learning tests as did those of high IQ in both the Mexican-American and Anglo-American groups (1960, p. 156). Whereas the standard IQ did accurately discriminate between fast- and slow-learning Anglo children, it was not a successful discriminator among the Mexican-Americans. Jensen concluded that "the findings of this study are consistent with the hypothesis that the distribution of basic learning abilities in Mexican-Americans is not substantially different from that in the Anglo-American population of comparable socio-economic level" (1960, p. 156). He also offered as a hypothesis for why the Mexican-Americans, despite adequate learning ability, do poorly in school the idea that they "have not acquired in their environment the kinds of knowledge, habits, and skills that provide the basis for school learning" (p. 157).

In 1963 Jensen compared the performances of predominantly white, middle-class, junior high school children who obtained retarded, average, and gifted levels of IQ scores on a direct learning task that involved associative learning. In presenting the rationale for this study, Jensen wrote: "Only when we can safely assume that the children whose IQs we wish to measure have had quite similar opportunities for learning the kinds of knowledge and skills measured by IQ tests can these tests be said to reflect 'learning' ability" (p. 124). After performing with standard instructions, the retarded group received an additional series of special conditions as follows: verbal reinforcement by the experimenter (informed when correct), stimulus naming (subject named each stimulus aloud as it appeared), stimulus naming with learning (same as previous condition plus continued naming of stimulus as the subject proceeded with the task), and delayed response following reinforcement (when the correct choice was made, a delay before continuing was forced before the subject was allowed to proceed; however, this was done only with two subjects). One particularly interesting result of this study was that the two fastest learners had IQs of 147 and 65, although there were generally high correlations between IQ and the direct learning measures. However, what was found was significantly more variability among the retarded learners on the direct learning measure, and all of the "misclassifications" were from the retarded group; although there were no average or gifted children who performed as low as the average retarded child on the learning measure, "the retarded group spanned the entire range of learning ability in this school population, as measured by this test" (1963, p. 137). As a result of these findings, Jensen hypothesized that, on the one hand "[t]here are probably a number of relatively independent 'dimensions' comprising learning ability" (1963, p. 137), and, on the other, that "the normal and fast learners in the retarded groups are not really retarded in a primary sense, but are children who, at some crucial period in their development, have failed to learn the kinds of behavior which are necessary as a basis for school learning and for the acquisition of the kinds of knowledge and skills tapped by IQ tests" (1963, p. 138). Many of the slow learners profited markedly from the verbal reinforcement condition. Also of relevance was the finding of no significant racial, sex, or ethnic differences on the learning tasks.

Following these demonstrations of the inadequacy of standard measures as reflections of learning ability of low-SES low achievers, Jensen became interested in looking at the components of intelligence and the environmental ingredients that appeared to relate to successful performance on static measures of both intelligence and achievement. In 1966 (and 1968) Jensen speculated that, although 80% of the variance of intelligence appeared to be biological, the remaining 20% was manipulable and should be addressed by psychologists. He also concluded that low-SES children, particularly those in the 70–90 IQ range, would be "the most susceptible to an IQ boost" (p. 99). Jensen saw verbal mediation and mediational processes as among the essential components that differentiated adequate from inadequate achievers. In order to have adequate mediational processes, Jensen hypothesized the necessity for adequate vocabulary and level of arousal for the employment of these processes, leading to spontaneous use as a strategy for problem solving. In his 1969 publication, he speculated that Level II (conceptual) abilities were more susceptible to experiential factors than Level I (associative), and warned that "caution must be observed in obtaining and interpreting test results from low-SES children. It appears . . . that middle class children perform about the same on Level I learning tasks whether they are tested individually or as a group. . . . low SES children, on the other hand, seem to perform considerably worse in the group situation than when tested individually" (1969, p. 31).

During the late 1960s, challenges to traditional approaches to assessment of intelligence became more profound and discussions of basic issues and underlying assumptions began to appear. Articles by Zigler and Butterfield (1968) and Bortner and Birch (1969) were particularly influential. However, in the realm of comparative psychology and animal research, two quotes from Maier and Schneirla (1964) are to the point:

> In order to get at the process of learning, learning ability as such must be isolated. Thus far we have primarily measurements of performance . . . with but little knowledge of the processes and abilities which go to make up the composite score. (p. 369)

and later, in the same publication:

> the observation of a pattern of behavior during development gives no clue as to which process is responsible for certain changes which may appear from time to time. (p. 374)

This serves as a reminder that correlation is not cause, and that, despite impressive predictive ability of IQ tests for school achievement, there is no necessary conclusion that what is being measured is "intelligence."

Zigler and Butterfield (1968) were responding to the frequent use of IQ tests as the primary program evaluation instrument for judging the effectiveness of preschool education and the fact that diverse programs yielded similar degrees of improvement. They observed that "the use of a change in an IQ test score as an indicator of change in a child's level of cognitive functioning carries with it the assumption that this score is a relatively pure measure of the formal aspects of the child's cognitive structure" (p. 1). They proposed that, alternatively, IQ test results were a function of three factors: formal cognitive processes, informational achievements, and motivation. Whereas later researchers chose to focus on delineation of formal cognitive processes in their critiques and proposals for changes in the measurement of intelligence, Zigler and Butterfield investigated the factor of motivation. These authors presented research on a small number of low-SES preschool children to assess the effects of optimization of motivational factors on IQ test results. Optimization involved maximization of success experiences and encouragement to respond. By varying control group experiences, the authors separated out the motivational variables and demonstrated a significant rise in IQ associated with the optimized test conditions. These results support the conclusions of both Feuerstein (1979) and Bortner and Birch (1969), whose writings attributed a significant degree of depressed IQ scores in disadvantaged groups to factors of performance rather than capacity; and Feuerstein (1980) focused his remedial approach on the needs and motivations of the low-performing child in addition to attempting to modify deficiencies of process and content.

Two studies appeared in 1969 that both summarized conclusions that were suggested by past research and pointed the way toward areas of increased focus of the future. These were the investigation of Dubin, Osburn, and Winick, which demonstrated the failure of manipulation of speed and practice variables per se to allow their black subjects to close the gap with their white subjects on an aptitude test (although their low-SES whites and high-SES blacks did improve with practice on two of the four tests), and the study by Gordon and Haywood, whose "culturally deprived" subjects showed positive improvement in response to verbal enrichment.

The 1970s

The work of Feuerstein, Budoff, Campione and Brown and Stott all converged in the 1970s. Because these authors are each represented by chapters in this text, their work will not be further elaborated in this section, but they do need to be kept in mind when thinking of the 1970s. Haywood (1970; Haywood Filler, Shifman, & Chatelanat, 1975) was one of the first to bring the theories and procedures of Feuerstein and his coworkers to the attention of the American public. It was also in the 1970s that Vygotsky's (1978) proposed "zone of proximal development" was realized in assessment procedures developed by Campione and Brown.

An impetus for questioning and rethinking assessment practices in the United States was provided by Great Society legislation of the mid-1960s, continuing in its effects through the 1980s. Demands on program evaluation and assessment of low-SES minority children created a situation that parallels that confronting Feuerstein in Israel during and after the second World War. Here were thousands of children who did not appear dull when left to their own devices, yet who, as a group, obtained low scores on measures purporting to tap intelligence. It became necessary to blame either the tests or the children, and there were proponents for each of these alternatives. Feuerstein's theory in fact offers a resolution somewhere in the middle by suggesting that, while most of these children are not inherently dull, they are nevertheless performing dully in relation to certain types of problem-solving demands, and it is not simply that the measures make them appear limited; new measures are then needed to provide a nudge to this dull performance, with the eventual goal of permanent modification of the performer. However, this is skipping ahead to the end of the decade, when Feuerstein's (1979) book brought his ideas and procedures into the public domain. There were other happenings of the 1970s that warrant mention as well.

During the 1970s, publications could be categorized into three basic groups: expressions of dissatisfaction with assessment practices with suggestions for modifications in the direction of dynamic assessment (hearkening back to the 1920s), development of assessment procedures with dynamic qualities, and continuation of isolated research supportive of a dynamic assessment approach either directly or by implication.

In the first category of expressions of dissatisfaction, Hutson and Niles (1974; and Hutson, 1974), Ross (1976), and Waugh (1970) looked to trial teaching as a "missing link" in the assessment of schoolchildren. Such dissatisfaction with IQ testing and medical model approaches to diagnosis also led to the development of diagnostic–prescriptive teaching. However, this direction is related to dynamic assessment primarily in terms of sources of dissatisfaction with existing models as well as in terms of advocacy of an interactive alternative with implications for remediation. Here the similarity ends, because diagnostic–prescriptive teaching is by definition content oriented and is not concerned with intelligence per se; it responds primarily to the "what" questions of assessment (what to teach), rather than the more process-oriented "how" questions. The examiner in a diagnostic–prescriptive approach is concerned with determining what is effective for teaching the child as static organism, not with changing the capacity of the organism to respond. In dynamic assessment, the child is not merely to be defined and optimally matched, but also to be changed in the direction of increased effectiveness as a learner.

In the second category of development of assessment approaches with dynamic qualities, two groups of researchers stand out: Kratochwill and Severson, and Ozer and his associates. Severson (1976) proposed a procedure called Process Learning Assessment (PLA), which was essentially a trial teaching procedure, but was dynamic in terms of attempts to modify "the teaching environment until the child is learning as optimally as possible" (p. 1). Severson cited two unpublished studies that demonstrated the superiority of a direct teaching reading task over IQ in predicting later reading achievement, as well as his study with Sewell (Sewell & Severson, 1974) (see Chapter 16, this volume), which showed a diagnostic teaching procedure to be equal to WISC IQ in predicting achievement, and superior to IQ specifically in predicting arithmetic achievement. Severson (1976) and Kratochwill and Severson (1977) were primarily concerned with determining the nature of task and instructional variables that enhanced learning. They therefore manipulated such aspects of instruction as print size, loudness, and type of reinforcer. These authors viewed these variables as affecting learning via motivation and affect. They did not address intrachild cognitive processes or strategies. Their approach did, however, intervene directly in the learning process, placing the examiner in an active, interventionist relationship with the child.

Ozer, a neurologist, and his associates (Ozer, 1978; Ozer & Richardson, 1974; Ozer, Richardson, Tannhauser, & Smith, 1970) utilized dynamic-like approaches within their comprehensive multidisciplinary team assessment. This represents a clinical, rather than a research, approach to the issues of dynamic assessment, because Ozer and his colleagues were not interested in examining the nature of their procedures per se, but in applying what they intuitively believed were optimal procedures to learn about the child's functioning. Referred children were brought in for a half-day's evaluation, which included examination by a neurologist, educational diagnostician, social worker, and nurse, and conducted in front of and with the participation of the child's parent and teacher. The assessment focused on "how the child succeeds" (Ozer et al., 1970, p. 162). Of particular relevance is the "neurological developmental observation," or NDO, during which the neurologist noted what he had to do to elicit certain behaviors from the child, such as focusing of attention, ability to trace geometric figures against a distracting background, means of learning new information, and skill with motor tasks. The mother was also asked to teach the child a task (learning a phone number and dialing it on a toy phone), and her interaction and strategies and their effects were observed. If ineffective, new strategies were modeled for and tried by the parent. The educational evaluation involved diagnostic teaching focusing on determining the child's preferred channels, processes, and reinforcements, as well as establishing normative levels; most importantly, the assessment aimed at modification and enhancement of the child's approach to learning. Unfortunately, the information regarding the exact tasks used or precise functions assessed is not explicit in the publications. Ozer and Richardson (1974) did elaborate the details of the NDO, which is a 15-minute attempt to simulate the learning process. The examiner manipulates four variables: programming (breaking down the task), varying modality, focusing, and feedback. The only purpose was to generate ideas or strategies that appeared to help the child learn.

There were a number of research studies throughout the 1970s that supported or related to basic concepts of dynamic assessment. The research of Rohwer is an example of the numerous studies appearing during this time that responded to the implications of Jensen's interpretation of research suggesting genetic limitations in conceptual intelligence of blacks as a group. Because there is an entire chapter that will discuss this topic (see Chapter 16, this volume), only Rohwer's research will be reviewed here.

Rohwer began his work in association with Jensen, but then continued with his own investigations of the relationship between verbal mediation and learning ability and departed considerably from Jensen's later (1980) observations and conclusions. Rohwer was interested in the issue of the determinants of school success and their relationship with variables other than ability to learn, such as ethnicity, SES, and IQ (Rohwer, 1971). He thus challenged both the equation of IQ with ability to learn and the postulation of IQ as an explanatory variable vis-à-vis school achievement. Rohwer (1971) defined learning ability as "the capacity for acquiring, retaining, and producing new information" (p. 192). He and his associates selected learning tasks similar to those of Jensen, favoring paired-associate learning as paradigmatic of much of the learning demands of the classroom (unfortunate, if true).

In a 1971 study using a paired-associate task, Rohwer, Ammon, Suzuki, and Levin documented significant differences between low-SES black children and high-SES white children on both the Peabody Picture Vocabulary Test and Raven Matrices, but not on the paired-associate test. These researchers also found that, whereas IQ differences between these ethnic/SES groups increased with age, differences in paired-associate learning deceased. Furthermore, in a 1971 study (Green & Rohwer) with all black children, the authors found parallel differences between these racial/SES groups that others have found between racial groups when race and SES are confounded, that is, significant differences in IQ but not in paired-associate learning.

Rohwer (1971) took issue with Jensen's two-level model of learning ability and with Jensen's conclusions of an ethnic/SES difference in Level II (conceptual) ability. He disagreed with the description of paired-associate learning as a Level I task, pointing to the need for transformations of input as necessary to success on this task.

In attempting to explain the reason for the lower school success of low-SES black children in the context of what appeared to be ability to learn equal to higher SES white children, Rohwer (1971) postulated "learning tactics," with spontaneous verbal elaboration as one of the critical tactics. Rohwer and his associates (1971) showed that, although the low-SES black children did not improve on a paired-associate retest with practice alone, they showed marked improvement with elaboration training. Rowher (1971) concluded that "the development of tests to measure learning proficiency and learning style is crucial for obtaining an understanding of the phenomena encompassed by the topic of 'Race and School Achievement' " (p. 208).

Camp's (1973) study with severe dyslexics compared the association of static psychometric measures with learning rate during tutorial reading sessions (based on cumulative error curves) and gains in reading achievement. The psychometric tests were not significantly related to either learning rate or reading achievement, whereas learning rate was significantly associated with reading achievement. Although more within a trial teaching framework, this research serves as a validation of a dynamic versus static approach to assessment.

In 1974 Haywood and Switsky replicated the Gordon and Haywood (1969) evidence that low-functioning children were able to respond at levels higher than previously thought if exposed to appropriate interventions, and that these interventions could be brief enough to incorporate into assessment procedures. Haywood and Switsky provided an enriched presentation of verbal similarities (additional exemplars) to low- and average-IQ children and found a significantly positive effect on reasoning scores of the low-IQ subjects, but no effect on those with average IQ scores. Under these enriched conditions low-IQ children demonstrated the ability to abstract as well as to generalize this skill to similar but unenriched material.

Finally, a significant body of research spanning from the late 1970s into the 1980s that was directly related to dynamic assessment was carried out by Carlson and Wiedl. Carlson, of the University of California at Riverside, and Wiedl, of Mainz, Germany, have collaborated on a series of research projects primarily with German children that explore the effectiveness of specific dynamic assessment procedures (Bethge, Carlson, & Wiedl, 1982; Carlson & Wiedl, 1976, 1978, 1979, 1980). These authors began calling their approach "testing-the-limits," but later used the term dynamic assessment. The Carlson and Wiedl research is most significant as a demonstration of the validity of a dynamic approach to assessment in their evidence of the effectiveness of interventions that promote internal cognitive processes and strategies as compared to those that merely provide direct exposure or simple reinforcement. These authors view their research methodology as suggestive of remedial strategies in addition to providing an alternative approach to cognitive assessment.

In their 1976 study with normal second- and fourth-grade children, Carlson and Wiedl compared six conditions during the course of administering and then readministering the Raven Coloured Matrices: 1) standard instructions; 2) verbalization during and after solution (the children were asked to describe the stimulus pattern before searching for the response, and then to explain their reason for their selection); 3) verbalization after solution (explanation of choice only); 4) simple feedback; 5) elaborated feedback (by the examiner, regarding reasons why the child's choice was correct or incorrect, and discussion of the principles of the task): and 6) elaborated feedback plus verbalization during and after solution. Significant results were found for second, but not fourth graders, which favored conditions 2, 5, and 6, with 5 and 6 the strongest. Furthermore, the differences between groups were attributable to changes in the reasoning, and not simple pattern completion or pattern completion through closure items of the Raven.

In 1978 Carlson and Wiedl repeated their procedure with children with learning difficulties (age range 8:4 to 12:9; WISC mean IQ 70.8). The results were similar to the 1976 study in the superiority of the conditions involving verbal descriptions prior to response selection and in the attribution of change to reasoning rather than perception.

In 1979 Carlson and Wiedl introduced the personality variable of introversion (neuroticism)–extraversion and the cognitive style variable of impulsivity–reflectivity into their study. The subjects were again normal second and fourth graders in German schools. Virtually the same results were found as before for the second graders. This time, conditions 2 and 6 reached significance for fourth graders as well. Also, the more impulsive second and fourth graders did more poorly on the Raven, but, for the second graders, this effect was reduced under conditions 2 and 5. Neuroticism interacted differently with the conditions; neuroticism, not impulsivity, correlated positively with test results under condition 2, but impulsivity, not neuroticism, correlated with Raven scores under condition 6. The authors also found significant interactions with intellectual strengths (verbal versus nonverbal) in that the Raven with standard instructions correlated highest with nonverbal IQ scores, subjects with higher nonverbal IQs profited the most from feedback conditions, and those with higher verbal IQs profited the most from verbalization without feedback. This suggests that children who lack well-developed verbal skills require feedback as an optimizing condition, which could lead to the speculation that the feedback provides a verbal model from which the children may be able to develop their own verbal skills.

In 1980 Wiedl (described in Carlson & Wiedl, 1980) again looked at the impulsivity variable, and found the performance of impulsives, not reflectives, to change under conditions of verbalization before and after solution, and examiner elaboration. In a 1980 study by Wiedl and Carlson (also described in Carlson & Wiedl, 1980), the results with handicapped learners (average age 10:10) supported the results of the previous study with this population in finding positive effects under conditions 6 and, with repeated testing, condition 5; no effects were found this time for condition 2, and no differences in effects were found for low- (70 and below) versus high- (90 and above) IQ groups. In all these studies, mere test repetition does not lead to significantly improved results on reasoning items.

In the first study with American children (Dillon & Carlson, 1978), the authors compared just three conditions: standard administration of the Matrices and a Piaget-based measure, verbalization during and after, and verbalization during and after plus examiner elaboration. These subjects were ages 5 through 10, from three ethnic groups: Anglo, black, and Mexican-American. The results were the same for the two measures. In all cases, the intervention conditions were superior to the standard instructions. The verbalization condition alone did not become significant until age 9 to 10; the elaboration feedback plus verbalization condition was effective for all ages and ethnic groups. Differences between ethnic groups also markedly declined under the dynamic conditions from near significance to clearly no difference under dynamic conditions.

These authors have also dealt with the very difficult and important issue of the criterion in validity studies of dynamic assessment. They (Carlson &

Wiedl, 1980) demonstrated that, whereas a static IQ measure was the best predictor of school achievement, the dynamic procedure was the best predictor of an adapted teaching condition (groups differentiated by IQ and self-regulation; teaching emphasizing verbalization, scanning, and self-correction).

Thus, Carlson and Wiedl and their associates have been able to present evidence supportive of the validity of dynamic assessment and its usefulness as a nondiscriminatory approach. They have also provided some insight into the nature of the changes taking place in the learner (improvements in reasoning ability and self-regulation); and a later study by Bethge, Carlson, and Wiedl (1982) demonstrated the effects of dynamic assessment on visual scanning, test anxiety, and negative orientation.

In their 1980 publication, Carlson and Wiedl tried to integrate their empirical findings with an information-processing theory that suggested four factors of problem solving: structures (epistemic, heuristic, and evaluative), processes (analysis and synthesis), components (procedural characteristics, operators, and orientation), and levels (practical with actual physical activity, direct perception, indirect perception, and conceptual knowledge). They saw their findings as interpretable in terms of affecting heuristic structures, analytic processes, procedural characteristics of increased planfulness, reflectivity, exactness, flexibility, and sharpening of responses, as well as both operator and orientation components and the level of conceptual knowledge.

At the beginning of this section it was noted that the primary publications of Feuerstein, Budoff, Stott, Campione and Brown, and others all converged during the 1970s. Kratochwill (1977) remarked on these attempts to formalize and standardize what psychologists had previously incorporated as "extras" in their assessment procedures. He applauded efforts to develop learning potential procedures and emphasized the need for further research and development.

The 1980s

Out of the "resurgence of interest in the concept of intelligence" of the 1970s emerged what Anastasi (1981b) described as "a new concept of intelligence" (p. 6). Characterizing IQ as "that particular horror" (p. 6), often misinterpreted as a trait rather than as a score ("and a poor kind of score at that" [p. 6]), descriptive rather than explanatory, vague in assumptions, excessive in meaning, and fuzzy in implication, Anastasi granted only that traditional intelligence tests provided useful information predictive of both academic and occupational activities. She also noted that one major contribution from Piagetian research was the notion of qualitative changes and differences in intelligence across the life span, suggesting that what intelligence tests measure should vary with developmental level. Finally, as indicated in the above section discussing coaching research, Anastasi found attempts to view intelligence as modifiable and improvable as promising; however, she did not specifically address measures that purport to induce and assess such changes except to differentiate between coaching and procedures that modified broad cognitive skills (i.e., involved "education") and suggested that, whereas the former reduced test validity, the latter did not.

In the same year as Anastasi's publication discussing alternatives to traditional measures of intelligence, Glaser (1981) described the social-educational zeitgeist of the late 1970s and 1980s in terms of a

> shift from a selective system to a system that can be helping, adaptive, and instructionally oriented; the necessity for attaining and assessing high levels of competence; and the presence of a social attitude more willing and scientifically able to unpack the factors of mental abilities and to test the limits of their instructability. (p. 925)

Glaser cited Vygotsky's concept of the zone of proximal development and suggested that "tests can assess levels of learning that might possibly be attained. Accomplishing the latter could orient effective instruction toward teaching children what their development has lacked so far, so that the tested level is interpreted as a possible stepping stone to a higher level" (p. 934). Glaser looked to metacognitive skills as candidates for inclusion in such test content.

Thus, these authors, whom many would consider pillars of assessment development, are suggesting that the time is ripe for changes such as those attempted by dynamic assessment, and are supportive of the direction and nature of the changes represented by dynamic approaches.

The most significant work of the 1980s thus far has been the continuing development of the work both of Feuerstein and of Brown, Campione, and their associates (see Chapters 1, 3, and 14, this volume) as well as the research of a number of other investigators. Carlson and Wiedl (1976, 1978, 1979, 1980; Bethge et al., 1982) span the late 1970s to early 1980s with their significant studies that validate some basic premises of dynamic assessment. Meltzer and her associates (Children's Hospital, Boston, 1984a, 1984b) are producing process-oriented assessments of cognitive and educational skills, that, although not dynamic throughout, do include some dynamic-like characteristics. Ionescu (Ionescu & Jourdan-Ionescu, 1983; Ionescu, Jourdan-Ionescu, & Toselli-Toschi, 1983; Ionescu, Radu, Solomon, & Stonescu, 1974) in Canada has also produced relevant research. The work of these and others will be discussed in terms of their contributions to dynamic assessment trends.

Meltzer and associates (Children's Hospital, Boston, 1984a, 1984b) are developing two process-oriented measures: the Survey of Cognitive Skills (SCS) and the Survey of Educational Skills (SEDS), for children of upper elementary and junior high school age. The SCS is of greatest relevance to this discussion. It attempts to assess three components of problem solving: efficiency of strategy selection, methods of strategizing, and styles of strategizing, with a general concern for the child's ability to determine the appropriateness of a strategy, and to shift as needed. There are sets of both linguistic and nonlinguistic subtests. The examiner observes and rates the student during the process of problem solution, using dimensions of impulsivity/reflectivity, trial-and-error/systematic strategies, analytic/integrative styles, and ability to shift approaches. The nonlinguistic subtests include series completion, categorization, and matrix completion. The linguistic subtests include category shift (picture sort), sequential reasoning, and similes/classification. Although the authors purport only to assess processes of problem solution and do not describe this as a dynamic measure, there is a dynamic-like aspect to the assessment of series completion in the nonlinguistic subtests. This procedure moves from presentation of the task in multiple-choice format to a probe/prompt/question stage (structured questions to elicit the student's awareness of critical task dimensions) to the opportunity to self-correct. This search for prerequisites of learning and consideration of the child's ability to change, although not explicitly induced by the examiner, is a significant deviation from traditional static approaches.

In their 1983 publication Ionescu and Jourdan-Ionescu criticized traditional measures of intelligence for being static, for neglecting the underlying mechanisms of cognitive functioning, for allowing handicapping conditions to interfere with results, for lack of information relating to educational programming, and for cultural bias. Using the Kohs blocks, according to a procedure described in 1974 (Ionescu et al.), Ionescu and his associates conducted research that found great differences among their subjects' ability to respond to intervention. Within a train–test model, these investigators compared the effects of three degrees of intervention: enlargement of the model, dividing the model into four parts, and verbal aid in addition to the first two steps. The Ionescu et al. (1983) approach differs from the test–train–retest models in its omission of a pretest; the model is to train during the course of testing, and the objective is similar to that of Budoff, which seeks to identify gainers as pseudoretarded, in contrast to the more "truly" retarded nongainers.

The 1980s have already witnessed the publication of extended applications of dynamic assessment beyond disadvantaged and educable mentally retarded (EMR) populations to both deaf and reading-disabled students. Application to deaf students is covered elsewhere in this volume (see Chapter 13). In a descriptive case study, Cioffi and Carney (1983) attempted to incorporate the characteristics of dynamic assessment as described by Feuerstein (1979) into assessment of word recognition and passage reading. Their approach consisted of "preteaching difficult vocabulary, activating prior knowledge, developing necessary concepts, providing direction for reading, revealing system and structure in text, and requiring an articulation of what is learned" (p. 768). This is merely a description of how a dynamic approach to reading might be carried out; there are no research results or effects reported.

One recent attempt to deal with validity issues of learning potential, or dynamic assessment led to discouraging results. Popoff-Walker (1982) compared IQ, adaptive behavior, and learning potential test results of normal and EMR third-grade students. The learning potential measure was Budoff's training procedure for the Raven Progressive Matrices (see Chapter 6, this volume), which, however, had been developed for use with adolescents, not with children as young as those in this study. In this study, although both groups profited from training, the EMR–normal gap on initial Raven scores was not narrowed by the training procedure and there was no significant difference between training and practice groups. The author hypothesized that the lack of individualization of training may have accounted for the relative lack of progress of the EMR group. Analysis of gains did show consistently more improvement with training than practice, although this difference was not significant. Adaptive behavior was not related to learning potential, as measured in this study.

Goals Of This Volume

The theory of dynamic assessment raises anew the issue of the relationship between intelligence and learning ability, which has at times been ignored, but never adequately resolved. Estes (1981) pointed to at least one very critical obstacle to resolution: the differences in approaches to measurement. Measurement of learning ability is typically carried out within a context of experimental research and requires time for observation of effects. Intelligence is typically treated as a trait and studied via correlation; furthermore, "intelligence tests tap performance during a short interval of time within which the amount of learning that goes on may be assumed negligible" (p. 121). Although it may be unlikely that there would ever be a direct and simple relationship between intelligence and learning ability as separate entities, it can only be said that the relationship remains undetermined, and that differences found or assumed in the past can be largely attributed to methodology. Dynamic assessment is clearly attempting to bridge this gap, and the implication of research such as that cited by Estes is that demonstration of learning ability, with or without assumptions about intelligence, requires time for demonstration of effects.

Both Mearig (1984) and Hamilton (1983) observed that dynamic assessment, despite its promise, has not been widely adopted by psychoeducational diagnosticians. Hamilton (1983) attributed this to factors such as additional time requirements, perception by professionals of the procedures as yielding information that is insufficiently different from traditional procedures, lack of adequate development of the procedures, or simple inadequate dissemination of information. Mearig (1984) saw a discrepancy between the concepts of the Feuerstein model, which she specifically addressed, and the views of American psychologists, whom she perceived as having

> a continuing reliance . . . on a premise of innate intelligence . . . a tradition of . . . emphasis on classification of children according to their intelligence test scores . . . a tacit acceptance . . . that social class differences will coincide with differences in intellectual functioning . . . a conscious or unconscious assumption that children classified as retarded cannot share in a regular curriculum . . . [and]

relatively little experience of many school psychologists in actually teaching children. (p. 3)

In view of these remarks by Mearig and Hamilton, this book has four primary goals. The first is to provide a sourcebook that will serve to further disseminate knowledge that is available about dynamic assessment, which, together with Feuerstein's basic text describing the Learning Potential Assessment Device (1979), will provide a foundation for and increased awareness of this approach to assessment. Second, it is agreed that dynamic assessment is in an early, formative stage, and therefore is not ready for full acceptance by practitioners. This text strives to move the formulations about dynamic assessment further along, attempting to expand the theoretical bases and to present existing validity data. Third, readers will have a survey of work currently in progress in the United States and Canada. Fourth (and foremost), it is hoped that there is much in this book that will stimulate readers to conduct further research and develop their own thinking about the usefulness and relevance of dynamic assessment procedures. A careful reading of these chapters should fully convince readers that there is genuinely new and additional information that can be contributed by dynamic approaches to psychological assessment.

The chapter authors represent the major theorists and sample the major researchers in the area of dynamic assessment. Although there is some overlap and some necessary redundancy as each author reviews concepts related to the issues discussed, each chapter offers a unique point of view or point of departure regarding the central concern of improving assessment of problem learners within a dynamic assessment model.

The authors grouped in the section on theoretical and empirical foundations more accurately span theory, application, and research. These authors virtually all have specific procedures that they have developed. However, these particular authors have also been the major researchers in the area and offer the most significant "hard" data on the topic of dynamic assessment. It is therefore their contributions to research that led to this particular grouping.

In Chapter 1, Feuerstein, Rand, Jensen, Kaniel, and Tzuriel present a major expansion of the theoretical basis for the Learning Potential Assessment Device, and discuss how their approach differs from other dynamic assessment procedures. Their chapter offers these authors' basic parameters for conducting a dynamic assessment.

In Chapter 2, Budoff discusses some of the basic issues of conducting a dynamic assessment, and reviews his massive body of research that supports the use of learning potential assessment for both nondiscriminatory evaluation, and a means of more accurately determining the capacity of the individual to profit from experience.

In Chapter 3, Campione and Brown describe their approach to dynamic assessment, which represents their interpretation of Vygotsky's zone of potential development. They review their extensive research, which relates their procedures to academic achievement and to the cognitive processes of the problem learner.

Minick, in Chapter 4, reviews and discusses Vygotsky's theories as they relate to dynamic assessment. He argues that researchers who have emphasized the quantitative aspects do not accurately reflect Vygotsky's concern with the qualitative aspects of assessment.

In Chapter 5, Embretson responds to the issue of how to apply psychometrics to dynamic assessment, or, rather, what psychometrics are appropriate for application to this approach. She reviews and discusses reasons for the inappropriateness of existing psychometrics, and looks to latent trait theory for some possible answers.

The chapters on application present a variety of responses to the same question: how to extend dynamic assessment per se and for use with populations other than the adolescents for whom the procedures were first designed.

In Chapter 6, Budoff presents his specific learning potential assessment procedures.

In Chapter 7, Rand and Kaniel present the group administration procedure for the Learning Potential Assessment Device, and review research with this group measure that offers evidence of validity not only for the LPAD as a group measure, but for the LPAD as a dynamic procedure per se.

In Chapter 8, Stott, a pioneer in the development of thinking leading toward dynamic assessment, elaborates the conceptual foundations of his approach, as well as his specific procedures for the young, low-functioning, school-age child. Stott has also been involved in intervention programming for children classified as retarded on static measures, and, in his chapter, he provides case material from this research. Of particular interest is his elaboration of styles and habits of functioning that he believes low performers adapt that obscure their cognitive capacity (compare this with Feuerstein's cognitive deficiencies).

In Chapter 9, Mearig describes her proposal for a literal downward extension of the Learning Potential Assessment Device for use with children between the ages of 5 and 8.

In Chapter 10, Tzuriel and Klein address the 5- to 6-year-old with their novel tasks, designed to reflect the theoretical orientation of the LPAD, but not duplicating the actual instruments. The authors also describe the results of their research using their procedure.

In Chapter 11, Lidz and Thomas present a third alternative to assessment of young children, specifically, children between the ages of 3 and 5. These authors, again within the Feuerstein et al. model, provide a dynamic extension of a frequently used static preschool test, the Kaufman Assessment Battery for Children, and also present their initial validity data.

In Chapter 12, Vye, Burns, Delclos, and Bransford describe and present data on their series of research projects at Vanderbilt University that involve a continuum of assessment services model, spanning from static measures to graduated prompts to mediated assessment. The authors present in detail their dynamic research procedure for children between the ages of 4 and 5 in the perceptual domain, using both the graduated prompt and mediated assessment approaches.

In Chapter 13, Keane applies the LPAD to the deaf population. He both reviews research and reports his own efforts to apply dynamic procedures, making the point that the deaf represent a disadvantaged group who have experienced benign neglect from society, and have yet to realize their cognitive potential.

The chapters in the final section of issues and implications bridge dynamic assessment to the future. These chapters help the reader to consider how dynamic assessment can fit into the current assessment repertory, and issues to consider in attempting to conduct a dynamic assessment.

In Chapter 14, Jensen and Feuerstein review and elaborate the theoretical foundations and procedures of the Learning Potential Assessment Device, and present the updated and expanded list of criteria for a mediated learning experience. The authors discuss the roles of school professionals and implications for necessary changes in the educational system that would be compatible with a dynamic approach to assessment.

In Chapter 15, Meyers offers a model for training psychologists to perform dynamic assessment. His model incorporates elements from a variety of approaches, and is not linked to any one procedure. Meyers does specifically relate dynamic assessment to diagnostic teaching (compare and contrast Feuerstein's views regarding diagnostic teaching).

In Chapter 16, Sewell considers the potential of dynamic assessment as a nondiscriminatory procedure. He sees the focus of dynamic assessment on intervention strategies rather than on classification as a major improvement over static measures.

In Chapter 17, Lidz discusses the concept of cognitive deficiencies. She differentiates among cognitive structures, styles, processes, and strategies, and offers a revised and reorganized listing that attempts to reflect current research in the area; she also reviews research relating cognitive deficiencies to academic achievement.

The concluding chapter, by Bransford, Delclos, Vye, Burns, and Hasselbring, comments on and reacts to the presentations of the contributors, and offers their own ideas on current practices and future directions of dynamic assessment.

I invite the reader to be stimulated, informed, interested, and challenged by the presentations in this book.

I would like to acknowledge the comfort and support offered by my friends and colleagues at United Cerebral Palsy Association, and my husband, Howard (who also contributed original drawings), and to mention how delightful it has been to work with Sharon Panulla and the editorial staff of The Guilford Press.

REFERENCES

Anastasi, A. (1981a). Coaching, test sophistication, and developed abilities. *American Psychologist, 36*(10), 1086–1093.

Anastasi, A. (1981b). Diverse effects of training on tests of academic intelligence. In B. F. Green (Ed.), *New directions for testing and measurement: Issues in testing—Coaching, disclosure, and ethnic bias* (No. 11). San Francisco: Jossey-Bass.

Bethge, H., Carlson, J. S., & Wiedl, K. H. (1982). The effects of dynamic assessment procedures on Raven Matrices performance, visual search behavior, test anxiety and test orientation. *Intelligence, 6*, 89–97.

Bortner, M., & Birch, H. G. (1969). Cognitive capacity and cognitive competence. *American Journal of Mental Deficiency, 74*, 735–744.

Bradley, T. B. (1983). Remediation of cognitive deficits: A critical appraisal of the Feuerstein model. *Journal of Mental Deficiency Research, 27*, 79–92.

Buckingham, B. R. (1921). Intelligence and its measurement: A symposium. *Journal of Educational Psychology, 12*, 271–275.

Camp, B. W. (1973). Psychometric tests and learning in severely disabled readers. *Journal of Learning Disabilities, 6*(7), 512–517.

Carlson, J., & Wiedl, K. H. (1976). Applications of "testing-the-limits": Towards a differential testing approach employing the Raven Coloured Matrices. *Trier Psychologische Berichte, 3*, 1–80.

Carlson, J. S., & Wiedl, K. H. (1978). Use of testing-the-limits procedures in the assessment of intellectual capabilities in children with learning difficulties. *American Journal of Mental Deficiency, 2*(6), 559–564.

Carlson, J. S., & Wiedl, K. H. (1979). Toward a differential testing approach: Testing-the-limits employing the Raven Matrices. *Intelligence, 3*, 323–344.

Carlson, J. S., & Wiedl, K. H. (1980). Applications of a dynamic testing approach in intelligence assessment: Empirical results and theoretical formulations. *Zeitschrift für Differentielle und Diagnostische Psychologie, 1*(4), 303–318.

Children's Hospital, Boston (1984a). *Survey of Cognitive Skills (SCS)*—Experimental edition. Boston: Author.

Children's Hospital, Boston (1984b). *Survey of Educational Skills (SEDS)—Experimental edition.* Boston: Author.

Cioffi, G., & Carney, J. J. (1983). Dynamic assessment of reading abilities. *The Reading Teacher, 36*, 764–769.

Dearborn, W. F. (1921). Intelligence and its measurement. *Journal of Educational Psychology, 12*, 210–212.

Dempster, J. J. B. (1954). Symposium on the effects of coaching and practice in intelligence tests. III. Southampton investigation and procedure. *British Journal of Educational Psychology, 24*, 1–4.

DeWeerdt, E. H. (1927). A study of the improvability of fifth grade school children in certain mental functions. *Journal of Educational Psychology, 18*, 547–557.

Dillon, R., & Carlson, J. S. (1978). The use of activation variables in the assessment of cognitive abilities of three ethnic groups: A testing-the-limits approach. *Educational and Psychological Measurement, 38*, 437–443.

Dubin, J. S., Osburn, H., & Winick, D. M. (1969). Speed and practice: Effects on black and white test performances. *Journal of Applied Psychology, 53*(1), 19–23.

Estes, W. K. (1981). Intelligence and learning. In M. P. Friedman, J. P. Das, & N. O'Connor (Eds.), *Intelligence and learning* (pp. 13–23). New York: Plenum Press.

Feuerstein, R. (1979). *The dynamic assessment of retarded performers: The Learning Potential Assessment Device, theory, instruments, and techniques.* Baltimore: University Park Press.

Feuerstein, R. (1980). *Instrumental enrichment: An intervention program for cognitive modifiability.* Baltimore: University Park Press.

Fleischman, E. A., & Hempel, W. E., Jr. (1955). The relation between abilities and improvement with practice in a visual discrimination reaction task. *Journal of Experimental Psychology*, *49*(5), 301–312.

Glaser, R. (1981). The future of testing: A research agenda for cognitive psychology and psychometrics. *American Psychologist*, *36*(9), 923–936.

Gordon, J. E., & Haywood, H. C. (1969). Input deficit in cultural-familiar retardates: Effect of stimulus enrichment. *American Journal of Mental Deficiency*, *73*, 604–610.

Green, R. B., & Rohwer, W. D., Jr. (1971). SES differences on learning and ability tests in black children. *American Educational Research Journal*, *8*, 601–609.

Haeussermann, E. (1958). *Developmental potential of preschool children*. New York: Grune & Stratton.

Hamilton, J. L. (1983). Measuring response to instruction as an assessment paradigm. *Advances in Learning and Behavioral Disabilities*, *2*, 111–133.

Haywood, H. C. (Ed.). (1970). *Social-cultural aspects of mental retardation*. New York: Appleton-Century-Crofts.

Haywood, H. C., Filler, J. W., Jr., Shifman, M. A., & Chatelanat, G. (1975). Behavioral assessment in mental retardation. In P. McReynolds (Ed.), *Advances in psychological assessment* (Vol. 3). San Francisco: Jossey-Bass.

Haywood, H. C., & Switsky, H. N. (1974). Children's verbal abstracting: Effects of enriched input, age, and IQ. *American Journal of Mental Deficiency*, *78*(5), 556–565.

Heim, A. W., & Watts, K. P. (1957). An experiment on practice, coaching, and discussion of errors in mental testing. *British Journal of Educational Psychology*, *27*, 199–210.

Hutson, B. A. (1974). Psychological testing: Misdiagnosis and half-diagnosis. *Psychology in the Schools*, *11*, 388–391.

Hutson, B. A., & Niles, J. A. (1974). Trial teaching: The missing link. *Psychology in the Schools*, *11*(2), 188–191.

Ionescu, S., & Jourdan-Ionescu, C. (1983). La mesure du potentiel d'apprentissage: Nouvelle approche dans l'evaluation des déficients mentaux. *Apprentissage et Socialisation*, *6*(2), 117–124.

Ionescu, S., Jourdan-Ionescu, C., & Tosselli-Toschi, M. (1983). Nouvelles directions dans l'utilisation d'un test d'intelligence (Cubes de Kohs)—Potential, d'apprentissage, différences inter-culturelles, organicité cérébrale, activité de l'hemisphère droit, traitment de l'information. *Enfance*, *4*, 363–380.

Ionescu, S., Radu, V., Solomon, E, & Stoenescu, A. (1974). L'efficience de l'aide au test des cubes de Kohs-Goldstein, administré chez les déficients mentaux. *Revue Roumaine des Sciences Sociales—Serie de Psychologie*, *18*(1), 75–92.

James, W. S. (1953). Symposium on the effects of coaching and practice in intelligence tests. *British Journal of Educational Psychology*, *23*, 155–163.

Jedrysek, E., Klapper, A., Pope, L., & Wortis, J. (1972). *Psychoeducational evaluation of the preschool child*. New York: Grune & Stratton.

Jensen, A. R. (1961). Learning abilities in Mexican-American and Anglo-American children. *California Journal of Educational Research*, *12*(4), 147–159.

Jensen, A. R. (1963). Learning ability in retarded, average, and gifted children. *Merrill-Palmer Quarterly*, *9*(2), 123–140.

Jensen, A. R. (1966). Verbal mediation and educational potential. *Psychology in the Schools*, *3*, 99–109.

Jensen, A. R. (1968). Social class and verbal learning. In M. Deutsch, I. Katz, & A. R. Jensen (Eds.), *Social class, race, and psychological development*. New York: Holt, Rinehart, and Winston.

Jensen, A. R. (1969). Intelligence, learning ability and socioeconomic status. *Journal of Special Education*, *3*(1), 23–33.

Jensen, A. R. (1980). *Bias in mental testing*. New York: The Free Press.

Kratochwill, T. R. (1977). The movement of psychological extras into ability assessment. *Journal of Special Education*, *11*(3), 299–311.

Kratochwill, T. R., & Severson, R. A. (1977). Process assessment: An examination of reinforcer effectiveness and predictive validity. *Journal of School Psychology*, *15*(4), 292–300.

Mackay, G. W. S., & Vernon, P. E. (1963). The measurement of learning ability. *British Journal of Educational Psychology*, *23*(Pt. 2), 177–186.

Maier, N. R. F., & Schneirla, T. C. (1964). *Principles of animal psychology*. New York: Dover Publications, Inc.

McPherson, M. W. (1948). A survey of experimental studies of learning in individuals who achieve subnormal ratings on standardized psychometric measures. *American Journal of Mental Deficiency*, *152*, 232–254.

Mearig, J. S. (1984). *Feuerstein's dynamic assessment in American school psychology*. Unpublished manuscript, St. Lawrence University, Canton, N.Y.

Meltzer, L. (1984). Cognitive assessment and the diagnosis of learning problems. In M. D. Levine & P. Satz (Eds.), *Middle childhood: Development and Dysfunction*. Baltimore: University Park Press, 131–152.

Messick, S. (1981). The controversy over coaching: Issues of effectiveness and equity. In B. F. Green (Ed.), *New directions for testing and measurement: Issues in testing—Coaching, disclosure, and ethnic bias* (No. 11). San Francisco: Jossey-Bass.

Ortar, G. R. (1959). Improving test validity with coaching. *Educational Research*, *2*, 137–142.

Osterrieth, P. A. (1945). Le test de copie d'une figure complexe—Contribution à l'étude de la perception et de la mémoire. *Archives de Psychologie*, *30*, 206–356.

Ozer, M. N. (1978). The assessment of children with learning problems: A planning process involving the teacher. *Journal of Learning Disabilities*, *11*(7), 422–426.

Ozer, M. N., & Richardson, H. B. (1974). The diagnostic evaluation of children with learning problems: A "process" approach. *Journal of Learning Disabilities*, *7*(2), 82–88.

Ozer, M. N., Richardson, H. B., Tannhauser, M. T., & Smith, C. D. (1970) Diagnostic evaluation of children with learning problems: An interdisciplinary model. *Clinical Proceedings, Children's Hospital, Washington, D.C.*, *26*(6), 161–178.

Penrose, L. S. (1934). *Mental defect*. New York: Farrar and Rinehart.

Popoff-Walker, L. E. (1982). IQ, SES, adaptive behavior, and performance on a learning potential measure. *Journal of School Psychology*, *20*(3), 222–231.

Rey, A. (1934). D'un procédé pour évaluer l'educabilité (quelques applications en psychopathogie). *Archives de Psychologie*, *24*, 297–337.

Rey, A., & Dupont, J. B. (1953). Organization de groupes de points en figures géométriques simples. *Monographies de Psychologies Appliquée*, 1953, No. 3.

Rohwer, W. D., Jr. (1971). Learning, race, and school success. *Review of Educational Research*, *41*(3), 191–210.

Rohwer, W. D., Jr., Ammon, M. S., Suzuki, N., & Levin, J. R. (1971). Population differences and learning proficiency. *Journal of Educational Psychology*, *62*(1), 1–14.

Ross, A. O. (1976). *Psychological aspects of learning disabilities and reading disorders*. New York: McGraw-Hill.

Schucman, H. (1960). Evaluating the educability of the severely mentally retarded child. *Psychological Monographs*, *74*(14, Whole No. 501).

Semler, I. J., & Iscoe, I. (1963). Comparative and developmental study of the learning abilities of black and white children under four conditions. *Journal of Educational Psychology*, *54*, 38–44.

Severson, R. A. (1976). *Environmental and emotionally-based influences upon the learning process*. Paper presented at the American Psychological Association Convention, Washington, DC.

Sewell, T. E., & Severson, R. A. (1974). Learning ability and intelligence as cognitive predictors of achievement in first-grade black children. *Journal of Educational Psychology*, *66*(6), 948–955.

Simrall, D. (1947). Intelligence and the ability to learn. *Journal of Psychology, 23,* 27–43.

Vernon, P. E. (1952). Practice and coaching effects on intelligence tests. *Education Forum, 23.*

Vernon, P. E. (1954). Symposium on the effects of coaching and practice in intelligence tests. V. Conclusions. *British Journal of Educational Psychology, 24,* 57–63.

Volle, F. O. (1957). A proposal for "testing the limits" with mental defectives for the purpose of subtest analysis of the WISC verbal scale. *Journal of Clinical Psychology, 13*(1), 64–67.

Vygotsky, L. S. (1978). *Mind in society: The development of higher psychological processes.* (M. Cole, V. John-Steiner, S. Scribner, & E. Souberman, Eds. and Trans.) Cambridge, MA: Harvard University Press.

Waugh, R. (1970). On reporting the findings of a diagnostic center. *Journal of Learning Disabilities, 3*(12), 30–35.

Wiseman, S. (1954). Symposium on the effects of coaching and practice in intelligence tests. IV. The Manchester experiment. *British Journal of Educational Psychology, 24,* 5–8.

Wiseman, S., & Wrigley, J. (1953). The comparative effects of coaching and practice on the results of verbal intelligence tests. *British Journal of Educational Psychology, 44,* 83–94.

Woodrow, H. (1946). The ability to learn. *Psychological Review, 53,* 147–158.

Yates, A. (1953). Symposium on the effects of coaching and practice in intelligence tests. I. An analysis of some recent investigations. *British Journal of Educational Psychology, 23,* 47–162.

Zigler, E., & Butterfield, E. C. (1968). Motivational aspects of changes in IQ test performance of culturally deprived nursery school children. *Child Development, 39*(1), 1–14.

THEORETICAL AND EMPIRICAL FOUNDATIONS

1

Prerequisites for Assessment of Learning Potential: The LPAD Model

REUVEN FEUERSTEIN, YAACOV RAND, MOGENS REIMER JENSEN,
SHLOMO KANIEL, AND DAVID TZURIEL

The concept of dynamic assessment has recently become a catchword for a variety of approaches to the measurement and assessment of the level of cognitive functioning of the low-achieving individual. As a mental construct, dynamic assessment is used in contrast to the construct of "static measurement," which is used to describe conventional psychometric approaches and techniques. Dynamic assessment is a novel approach, especially when viewed as an applied system, despite the fact that, as a philosophy, it has been with us for awhile (Cronbach & Furby, 1970; Vygotsky, 1934/1962). As a technique, however, it has not, as yet, found full acceptance. It is sufficient to read through some of the more recent scientific, experimental, and popular publications to see how few, if at all, are the references made to the concept of dynamic assessment. Yet there are few among those who are concerned with and involved in the measurement and diagnoses of cognitive processes who do not show deep disenchantment with the present state of the art, and few who do not point to the imperative and urgent need to either abolish totally the use of static measures, substituting different techniques, or at least drastically change their structure.

This generalized malaise experienced by all those confronted with the need to assess large masses of low-functioning populations has given rise to a variety of solutions, which will be the object of our discussion in this chapter. In other instances, however, disenchantment with present practices has turned into a passive response, characterized by withdrawal from use of conventional tests without substituting more adequate approaches. This has been the case in a number of instances where educational systems have set extreme limits

Reuven Feuerstein, Yaacov Rand, Shlomo Kaniel, and David Tzuriel. Hadassah–WIZO–Canada Research Institute, Jerusalem, Israel; and School of Education, Bar Ilan University, Ramat Gan, Israel.

Mogens Reimer Jensen. Department of Psychology, Yale University, New Haven, Connecticut, and Hadassah–WIZO–Canada Research Institute, Jerusalem, Israel.

in a more or less official way to the use of psychometric devices. This was also recently the case in Israel, where an especially established committee suggested that static group tests, which had been used for the purpose of school admission and advancement to higher grades, shall not only no longer be mandatory, but should become prohibited from use in the school system. However, by this prohibition, it is as if only the first part of the verse of the psalm "move away from the evil" has been fulfilled, while the second part— "and do good"—is ignored.

There is a danger that by merely contenting oneself with discontinuation of psychometric practices without filling the vacuum produced with a more adequate approach, what may be chosen instead may prove to be worse than the discontinued practices. By way of illustration, we would consider it an extremely dangerous alternative to substitute teacher evaluations based on achievement test scores for IQ tests. A change in this direction could result in grave injustices to many students. In certain cases the attempted abolition itself is doomed to failure because of the lack of a more appropriate technique. Both professionals and their clients prefer to continue to use a method that may be known to be inappropriate but that at least permits action, rather than totally giving up the practice of assessment as a way to guide the educational process.

In their review of the Learning Potential Assessment Device (LPAD) book (Feuerstein, 1979), Ramey and MacPhee (1981) posed the question: Can dynamic assessment, or, more specifically, the LPAD, be considered as the new paradigm that is necessary in order to respond to the new needs of assessment? Ramey and MacPhee considered the present prevailing conditions in the field of education as leading to such a revolution, and they therefore suggested that society explore the appropriateness of the "dynamic" construct of assessment as the necessary response. The criteria to which Ramey and MacPhee referred are: the disenchantment with the existing philosophical–theoretical stance underlying the practice of psychological measurement; the existence of environmental conditions of a demographic, sociological, political, and economic nature that create pressure for change in the approach toward the evaluation of intelligence of large masses of population; and, finally, the emergence of a different theoretical view of the concept of intelligence, its structure, and its origins, which will benefit from the existing momentum and will lead to the emergence and implementation of a new paradigm.

In the present chapter, we will attempt to describe briefly the reasons for the disenchantment with psychometric theory and practice, as well as the environmental conditions that make the search for a new paradigm of great urgency. We will conclude with a presentation of the LPAD as a possible alternative solution that responds to the philosophical–ideological and pragmatic needs confronting education today.

Disenchantment with Psychometric Theory and Practice

The search for new approaches to the assessment of cognitive functions of masses of disadvantaged populations is determined directly by the large consensus among behavioral scientists concerned with the inadequacy of both the underlying assumptions and the practical outcome of conventional psychometric tests, their modes of presentation, and the resulting interpretations, as applied to increasingly larger masses of populations in need of assessment. This consensus has increased considerably with the expansion of psychometric practice in the last 50 years to unknown proportions. The primary reason for this is the democratization of the educational system, resulting in the inclusion of populations previously considered ineligible for and inaccessible to education. This has brought into the sphere of assessment those populations for which test instruments have never had to be developed, norms established, or techniques applied. It is only necessary to think of the downward extension of assessment to age 0 as a way of identifying certain characteristics of the newborn or the extension of assessment procedures to individuals previously considered untestable because of extremely low levels of functioning or lack of communication tools necessary for assessment, in order to see the problems posed by the expansion of the assessment process that face the psychometrician. Of necessity, this has required some important changes in the usually accepted tools and modalities of assessment. However, the greatest increase in the target populations has its origins in the massive migrations of culturally different populations requiring assessment once confronted with the new, dominant culture to which they must adapt. This is even more the case when the western, technological culture migrates to the third world; assessment then becomes a necessary tool for the selection of populations to become involved in the technologies exported to the developing countries. This confrontation has created a state of disequilibrium in the well-established, hardwired approaches to and conceptions of the nature of intelligence and in ways used to assess differential cognitive development. Thus, the need to include in the educational process large populations of illiterates as a means of integrating them into the army has produced the use of nonverbal tests, with the assumption that merely changing the language of presentation of the task will permit assessment of the true capacities of individuals whose functioning on verbal tests tended to place them in the lowest levels of cognitive functioning.

The need to produce more adequate ways to assess individuals of different ages, from various cultures, on different levels of functioning, or of different biopsychological conditions has given rise to a very large and diverse number of techniques usually referred to as culture-free, culture-fair, or developmental tests. However, many of these attempts have failed to respond to the very need that brought them into existence because they have totally preserved the assumption of intelligence as a fixed entity, and to a very large extent have made no changes in the nature or presentation of the tasks.

The above-mentioned necessity of changing the structure of assessment is therefore coupled with the need to reformulate our views of intelligence itself. For too long, formulation of the concept of intelligence was either ridiculed by the saying that "intelligence is what the tests measure," or was elegantly avoided in order to be able to be operated upon without being hampered by lack of agreement regarding its definition. To a very large extent, the disenchantment with assessment has been strengthened by the understanding of the insufficiency and the inappropriateness of current definitions of intelligence.

Attempts to Modify Psychometric Practice

The various attempts to modify psychometric practice can be categorized into three general types of approaches:

1. Conservation of the conventional structure of the psychometric tests, its contents, and its modes of application, while changing the interpretation of results in a way that reflects culturally determined differences.
2. Alteration of the tasks in a way that allows consideration of the individual functioning within a cultural and developmental context.
3. Modification of the individual's functioning whenever necessary to facilitate assessment of true capacity above and beyond manifest levels of functioning.

Conserve Conventional Structure/Change Interpretation of Results

The first approach assumes that individuals from minority or culturally different subgroups cannot be reasonably compared to individuals from groups on which the diagnostic tools were devised without appearing as deficient. To overcome this, the recommendation has been made to consider the obtained results within the normative framework of a similar group and to ascribe to the individual a level of functioning according to the rank order within that group. The basic assumption is that cultural difference is mainly responsible for the group's level of functioning and it is therefore necessary to consider the individual's functioning as a reflection of these differences rather than as an inherent deficiency. This approach has been considered progressive for a very long time, and has been viewed as the best means of correcting the injustices produced for certain individuals by conventional psychometric approaches. It soon became clear, however, that this way of relating to the individual helped neither the individual nor the group to which he or she belonged, because the groups for which these specialized norms have been devised have been accepted as functioning on a level of relative deficiency, with the individual member of the group ipso facto becoming evaluated in these terms. This is how the attribution of Level I–type intelligence to the black population by Jensen (1980) became possible, and this is also the danger inherent in all attempts to associate different forms and types of intelligence with specific ethnic subgroups or races.

No one will claim that there are no differences in the ways intelligence manifests itself or deny that individuals may have preferential modes of utilizing their intelligence. However, these differences are not necessarily so much inter- as intragroup related; that is, it is possible to find such differences among members within the particular subgroup. Furthermore, the flexibility and adaptability of individuals may make it possible to choose, whenever necessary, a less preferred and a less economical way of functioning. It is this flexibility that should be the object of research and of assessment, rather than emphasizing the differences considered to be fixed and immutable, as may be implied by the very ingenious and otherwise valid work of Sternberg (e.g. 1984) and Gardner (1983). The attempt made by Mercer (1979) to introduce a corrective device for the low results obtained by individuals from certain groups and to compensate them for a measured degree of deviance from the norm has not done much good for the individuals assessed with the System of Multicultural Pluralistic Assessment (SOMPA), nor has it helped to dissipate the negative stereotyping resulting from their low manifest levels of functioning. The teacher, the caretaker, or even the parent confronted with the adaptive difficulties of the child gains little from the new score in attempts to help the child.

Alter Tasks to Consider Individual's Context

The second way in which an attempt has been made to adapt psychometric approaches to the needs of cultural minorities has been to change the nature of the task. A plethora of attempts were made at very early stages of the psychometric movement that responded to the accepted idea that the modality in which a task is presented, in terms of its language or content, may be unfavorably biased for certain populations whose cultural patrimonium did not foster in them the use of that particular modality. Culturally free and fair tests were shaped from this idea, and were presented in modes considered to be more familiar and more accessible to the culturally different or the socially disadvantaged individual. The culturally free/fair test had as its laudable goal the study of the capacity of the individual through study of the acquisition of contents recognized as belonging to the cultural heritage to which the individual or group belonged. Developmental tests were devised that consisted of tasks considered to be relatively or even completely independent of educational experiences, and that reflected modes of adaptation of the organism linked to development rather than to the impact of the environment.

These attempts represent changes of the task used as true measures of the capacity of the individual above and beyond differences in education or culture. All of these techniques are known to have failed to do justice to the appraisal of individuals and groups, because the culturally different as well as the culturally deprived failed to show a higher level of functioning when confronted with these tasks, and, even when they succeeded in responding to the tasks, this success proved to be irrelevant to their adaptation to the requirements of the dominant culture into which they needed to integrate. There is a great abundance of literature pointing to this failure to solve the problem by using culturally fair and developmental tests, and this may be taken to include tasks derived from the Genevan school as well, as became evident from the senior author's experience with Moroccan children. Many of the genetic tasks such as conservation of volume and other tasks allegedly requiring little education failed to disclose the true, adaptive capabilities of individuals from culturally different or disadvantaged groups, many of whom were labeled as low functioning on a variety of levels ranging from dull-normal through educable retarded following their failure to function according to established criteria.

It seems to us that the major reason for the failure of these sincere attempts to solve the problems involved in psychometric measurement derives from the static nature of these attempts. Changes in the task were meaningless as long as the static goals were preserved. Changes in the nature of the task more often than not reflected a belief that the culturally deprived and socioeconomically disadvantaged individual's intelligence differed not only quantitatively, but also qualitatively from the intelligence of the middle-class child, and that, in order to measure it, it was necessary to appeal to the functions that best characterized this differential functioning. Furthermore, the basic assumptions are that these qualitative characteristics are fixed and immutable and, as is the case for those who consider IQ as the sole and true measure of intelligence, these manifestations of low mental functioning are often considered to represent lower forms of human adaptation. This is certainly the basis for the suggestion by Jensen (1980) to assess the intelligence of black people and other "low functioning" individuals with the help of tasks reflecting a Level I type of intelligence. Level I tasks require simple reproductive mental activities such as digit span, short-term verbal memory, and copying, and are said to be adequately mastered by this population to such an extent that the tasks are equally, and in certain instances, even better performed by the low-functioning individual, compared to those whose higher IQ is evidenced by better functioning on Level II tasks requiring elaborational mental activities. The educational and adaptational significance of the suggested restriction to Level I–type intelligence is clearly stated by Jensen in terms of the educational goals to be set for the individual, who, by virtue of his or her genetico-hereditary endowment, is unable to acceed to the higher mental operations needed in order to function in a modern technological society. The education to be offered to these individuals should be, according to Jensen, geared to their inherited, fixed limitations, since intervention is said not to be able to modify a genetically determined mental characteristic.

Moving from this rather extreme paradigm of choosing simple repro- ductive tasks said to reflect the individual's restricted level of functioning, we may look to the various other suggestions included in the use of culturally fair and free tasks as reflecting views on the stable and immutable charac- teristics of these populations, which can best be measured by using tasks of a practical, concrete nature, implying that they need to be nonverbal, non- conceptual, and nonrepresentational. The fact that the individual has not been challenged with tasks of higher mental processes because he or she was not considered to be able to respond to these demands is in turn often in- terpreted as the very evidence of his or her inability. The history of task adaptation to remediate psychometric inadequacy is replete with a double failure: the failure of the low-functioning individual to function better even on the simplified, concrete, Level I–type task, and the failure of these tasks to reveal the adaptive capacities of these individuals and groups. The basic assumptions of the immutability and measurability of intelligence (and, there- fore, its predictability) are inherent in these approaches. These three inter- related conceptions of human intelligence have resulted in a static approach to its evaluation. If indeed intelligence is immutable, it can be measured. One measure taken at a particular point in time in any given condition will be sufficient to predict the future characteristics of the individual. The major goal of psychometric methods is to design tasks and to shape their ability to detect as precisely as possible these immutable and fixed characteristics of the individual that will best predict his or her future development.

It is no wonder, then, that with such assumptions no real change is produced in the results obtained by changing the norms by which performance is interpreted, or by changing the nature of the task or the modality in which the tasks are presented.

Modify the Individual's Functioning

The third approach that responds to the need to assess culturally different or disadvantaged populations represents the attempt to change the individuals confronted with the psychometric task. The failure of the individual to respond is then dealt with by a dynamic approach defined by the intervention of the examiner, which aims to prepare the individual to cope with this exposure to the task. The "dynamic" construct, which aims to change the individual, can, however, be defined by two terms, describing its goals as either functional or structural.

FUNCTIONAL DYNAMIC ASSESSMENT

The term "functional" refers to a dynamic intervention where the major goal is limited to the enhancement of the individual's functioning as it relates to interaction with the specific psychometric task. A number of models can be included within this functional definition: coaching for tasks or to similar ones, or, what is even more typical, intervention aimed at facilitating the individual's functioning in the proximal zone of his or her potential.

The dynamic approach varies greatly from technique to technique, but what they have in common is the goal of enhancing and modifying the functioning of the individual in an area considered critical at a particular point in the assessment. The dynamic nature of this approach lies in the fact that a new dimension is added to the assessment encounter. The task is not interpreted as an expression of the individual's genetico-hereditary history, nor even related to stages of development, but is instead related to his or her functioning in terms of a certain instituted experience and controlled intervention. The question becomes how much better and how different will the individual's functioning be once the new dimension is added to the constitutional and hereditary determinants of his or her behavior. The unidimensionality of the static approach is meaningfully bypassed in favor of a two-dimensional approach that gives a sense of depth to the concept of intelligence and to the outcome of its interaction with experience.

However, this formulation of dynamic assessment sets limits to the quantity and quality of changes that are the target of the intervention. The test–train–retest model is restricted by the nature of the first "test" and the second retest. Thus, only a limited aspect of the individual's functioning is targeted for change. These limitations will necessarily leave unresolved a number of questions as to who and in what dimension of one's functioning one is best affected by the interventions offered. Thus, the Budoff (e.g., 1969) learning potential assessment, which adheres to such a limited goal, has of necessity defined those who benefited from the "teaching" as gainers as compared to the nongainers for whom intervention did not prove to be beneficial. It is only a short step from this to the search for some stable, fixed, and more pervasive characteristic of the individual, and, indeed, the major investment of Budoff has been the search for such a characteristic. From this point of view, one immediately identifies the limited nature of the concept of modifiability as referring to the functioning of the individual on a particular test rather than in more pervasive aspects of his or her modifiability.

STRUCTURAL DYNAMIC ASSESSMENT

The second definition of the construct of dynamic assessment has at its core the concept of structural cognitive modifiability (SCM). Here, the goal of change to be produced in the assessed individual goes far beyond immediate levels of functioning into the search for changes in the very structural nature of the cognitive processes that directly determine cognitive functioning in more than one area of mental activity. This definition of dynamic assessment has as its basic assumption the belief that the human organism is an open system, accessible to structural change, and that this accessibility exists irrespective of the three determinants usually considered as barriers to change: etiology, stage of development, and degree of severity of condition. This assumption represents a very sharp departure from the accepted mode of thinking, and shifts the full responsibility for the modifiability of the individual from the individual being treated or examined to the mediator. This assumption also distinguishes dynamic assessment from the psychometric model in at least three dimensions: first, the target theoretically includes, until proven otherwise, everybody, irrespective of the etiological determinants of deficiencies, age, or severity of condition; second, the goals of change are structural and not peripheral or fragmental; and third, at least theoretically, initial differences in levels of performance among individuals will not necessarily result in differences in the performance of the individual, but, rather, in the amount and nature of the investment necessary in order to produce the desired changes. This again represents a shift of responsibility from the assessed individual to the examiner.

In what follows, we will briefly further examine these three dimensions, and then be in a position to conceptualize the means by which such goals can be realized. We will begin with a discussion of the legitimate population for dynamic assessment.

The LPAD as a Structural Dynamic Assessment Model

Target Population

The only group of individuals who are not viewed as legitimate targets for dynamic assessment are those who, by virtue of their high and efficient levels of functioning, do not require modification; assessment in this case would be costly and superfluous. All others are theoretically limitlessly eligible to be considered candidates for the potentially beneficial effects of dynamic assessment. However, to be practical, dynamic assessment is most appropriate when the condition of the individual requires a search for the reasons for low performance and the most economical and efficient ways to produce changes in these very conditions. Dynamic assessment then offers an active, modificational approach that refuses to accept the manifest condition of the individual as is, and represents the first and most important step in defining the extent of change that can be hoped for, as well as the means by which such changes can be produced. Thus, a legitimate goal of the LPAD is to modify the cognitive style characteristics of an individual, or his or her preferential mode of functioning in the sense of Sternberg or Gardner, challenging the inference of immutability. Every deficiency, regardless of how deeply entrenched, is considered a legitimate target. Thus, the concept of gainer or nongainer should not make the individual ineligible for this assessment.

Goal of Structural Change

The second element to be considered is the nature of the change that the LPAD, as compared to other dynamic approaches, is designed to achieve. The concept of structural change contrasts with the more restricted goals of other dynamic assessment approaches, which place greater emphasis on affecting peripheral components of the individual's functioning, such as test wiseness or familiarity with content or problem prerequisites, or offer a restricted experience with tasks similar to those that are the criterion for success in the test itself (e.g., Kaufman and Kaufman, 1983). In these latter cases, the nature of the intervention will be limited and will tend to conserve a standardized format in order to assure comparability and reliability. In contrast, the LPAD defines its goal in terms of the assessment of cognitive modifiability of the structure itself, rather than in the peripheral, episodic, fragment-like manifestations of cognition.

The first characteristic of structural change relates to the strong cohesiveness between parts and the whole; thus, any change imposed on a part will necessarily affect the whole, and in this way lend a quality of generalizability and permanence to the experienced change. Intervention aiming at this quality of change is an essential characteristic of both dynamic assessment and the remedially oriented Instrumental Enrichment (IE) program (Feuerstein, 1980).

The second characteristic of a structure is its transformability across constancy. The process of change itself goes through transformations affecting its rhythm, its amplitude, and its meaning. Thus, a process of change that may have proceeded at a low pace and with a low amplitude may transform itself in the course of its development into an unpredictable result. Making such transformability possible will be the task of the interventional component included in the LPAD, where the intervention will serve to elicit such changes for the purpose of assessing the modifiability of the individual, and will be used for the remedial program where the changes will become more permanent.

The third characteristic of a structural change is defined by the self-perpetuating and self-regulatory nature of the initiated change. Changes externally or internally imposed will tend to propagate and perpetuate themselves in an autonomous way, responding to internally or externally perceived transformation by an autoregulatory process.

Production of New Cognitive Structures

The difference between interventional components in the LPAD, as compared to other dynamic assessment procedures such as those suggested by Kaufman or Budoff, or techniques based on Vygotsky, is self-evident. The belief in the possibility of a structural change implies that new cognitive structures can be produced in the individual, and not merely discovered or enhanced when they are within the proximal zone of development. In other words, the goals set by the LPAD for the examinee–learner closely follow the postulates of

SCM concerning human modifiability, and attempt to produce such changes in the samples of behavior emitted by the individual during the assessment, which will then be interpreted as representative of what could become a more permanent behavioral repertoire if and when the conditions necessary for the more permanent and stable forms become apparent. In order to reach this goal, LPAD bases its shift from a static to dynamic approach on four major changes in the psychometrically based model.

NATURE AND STRUCTURE OF TASKS

The first change refers to the nature of the tasks selected for the purposes of dynamic assessment and the way in which they are structured. A number of criteria are used for this purpose. The tasks, first of all, must address higher mental processes. Furthermore, the tasks should be relatively accessible to change; that is, they should use fluid rather than crystallized modes of thinking. Also, they must have an optimal rather than minimal level of complexity in order to reflect the molar nature of the real-life situation, and, by this, offer the necessary prerequisites for further learning. Also, the tasks presented as posttests must permit the detection of even the most minimal changes and register these changes in a way to permit interpretation as predictors of future change. This is achieved by structuring the task according to the LPAD model and by searching for changes through the clinical interview and process orientation of the dynamic approach. The search for cognitive modifiability rather than for the stable characteristics of the individual requires a significant change in the nature and structure of the tasks. Thus, reliability of the task is no longer considered a relevant criterion of the usefulness of the test; instead, the "unreliability" of the task, or the degree to which the task lends itself to produce changes within the examinee, will be the criterion for its selection.

RESHAPING OF TEST SITUATION

The second change implied by the LPAD as a dynamic assessment is the radical reshaping of the test situation from a rigidly standardized procedure to a flexible, individualized, and intensely interactive process among the three partners involved: the task (may be changed according to need), the examinee (modified in response to the mediated learning experience of the interaction), and the examiner (changes his or her orientation according to the detected transformations in the examinee's functioning or in the functions involved in the task itself). It is at this stage that the list of deficient functions serves the examiner as a guide for targeting intervention efforts, and the cognitive map serves to determine changes in the nature of the task.

SHIFT TO PROCESS ORIENTATION

The third change is the shift from a product to a process orientation. The test task, which includes fluid processes, the test situation, which permits close observation of the cognitive behavior of the examinee, and the use of the cognitive map, which permits better understanding of the processes underlying the functioning of the individual and the changes produced in his or her structure, all provide a wealth of conceptual apparatuses to support the examiner's ability to develop a prescriptive approach.

MODALITIES FOR INTERPRETING RESULTS

The fourth departure from the conventional psychometric approach and, to a large extent, from other dynamic techniques, are the modalities for interpretation of the results. Interpretation focuses on the peaks in the functioning of the individual, which may appear in an unpredicted way during the course of the assessment, standing out in a kind of splendid isolation from otherwise low functioning. Rather than discarding these incidents as random or chance, or, at best, as learned or even overlearned behavior and therefore irrelevant to the assessment, peaks in performance are to be considered as indications of the capacity of the individual. The responsibility for explaining their appearance, or rather, their lack of more pervasive presence falls upon the evaluator; the examiner must generate hypotheses concerning the source of these peaks and reasons for their inconsistency and discontinuity. Has this behavior appeared because of variations in the modality of input or output? Is it accounted for by variations in the level of complexity? Is the observed peak behavior the product of intervention? Are there changes observed following the appearance of a peak? In other words, the peak performance is a subject of study, analysis, and attempts to capitalize on it by inducing recurrence, and by producing insight into the conditions of its appearance in order to evaluate its generalizability and adaptive significance.

The second component of the interpretation of results is the attempt to locate the origins of success or failure and to attribute to them a specific weight in the evaluation of the intelligence of the individual and his or her modifiability. This is made possible by using the deficient functions that are analyzed during the process-oriented assessment as reflecting the cognitive structure of the individual's functioning, and the cognitive map, which permits the location of the functions. Thus, a decision that the reasons for failure are due to deficiencies in the input or output phase of the mental act, with the elaborational phase being intact, will be meaningfully different from a conclusion that elaboration was the source of the failure. How different would be the evaluation of the individual if we would discover that the failure could be attributed to his or her low degree of familiarity with the content of the task, or to the language of presentation of the task in relation to his or her inability to learn his or her own language or to elaborate operations involved, or attributed to his or her incapacity to use the level of abstraction necessary to solve the problems involved? In the first instance, there is no way to incriminate intelligence for the observed failure, no more than it would be possible to incriminate the cultural anthropologist for failing to understand the language of a tribe he or she has never studied. In the second case, the intelligence of the individual, at least as presented at the moment of the registration of failure, is certainly more incriminable, although still possibly modifiable.

The third component, and the one most central to the LPAD, is the elaborate way of profiling the individual's modifiability by assessment in three distinct areas in which change is simultaneously desired and possible: the domain in which the change has occurred, the quality of the achieved change, and the change in the amount and nature of intervention required for the production of the structural modification. This profile makes it possible to consider not only the individual's modifiability, but to specify areas of strength, qualities of achieved change, and the amount of initial intervention necessary to produce the changes. The change can be conceptualized as happening in four distinct parts: the deficient cognitive function requiring correction, the acquisitions made by the examinee in specific content areas or operations, the changes in the affective component (which relates to amount and nature of motivation and shifts from extrinsic to intrinsic sources and feelings of competency), and, finally, the changes in the degree of efficiency of the individual's functioning across the functions assessed. The aspects of motivation and feelings of competency are particularly important targets for change, since they represent the energetic sources of behavior that, more than anything else, are responsible for the extent to which the individual will use the newly acquired prerequisites of cognitive behavior in adapting to new situations. Generalization and transfer should not be considered to be related solely to the development of cognitive components, but may well be enhanced or obstructed by the energetic investment of the individual. These four parts represent the changes observed in areas where change is found to be necessary in terms of the baseline of the individual's functioning either as described by previous evaluations or as observed during the course of the LPAD.

The question of the permanence of the observed change is of relevance to how much of the change observed in the deficient function is still observable over time. For example, impulsivity in input and output level is known to affect negatively the cognitive functioning of low achievers and is a definite target of intervention of the LPAD. The mediation of regulation of behavior, which is a pivotal parameter of a mediated learning experience (MLE), uses representational anticipatory behavior, conceptual tempo, and insight by imposing a latency period between perception of the stimuli, instruction, and response. Permanence in the control over impulsivity may be accompanied by generalization over a greater diversity of tasks. Generalization and transformability describe the qualities of achieved change that are extremely important to assess since it is enhancement of these qualities that is the real reason for the investment in the LPAD. Permanence, generalization, and transformability of the acquired functions represent the autoplasticity and flexibility of human experience directly responsible for modifiability.

The question of the progressive independence of the individual from the mediational interaction with the examiner concerns the extent to which there is a decrease in the amount and nature of the mediation required in order to make the examinee produce a particular response or undergo a certain type of change in cognitive structure. Vygotsky (1978), in suggesting the use of a dynamic approach, formulated this particular aspect of change by urging those who evaluate children to see to what extent the assessed child is able to do alone the next day what he or she was able to do during the assessment with the help of the adult. Vygotsky considered this to be the major way to assess the child's capacity, and it is with this particular thought that Vygotsky opened the era of dynamic assessment. In the LPAD the profile of modifiability is meaningfully enriched by the conceptualization of the decrease in dependence of the child on the MLE process, which is interpreted as the major sign of the structural nature of the produced change.

The decrease in the child's dependence can be defined in terms of the quantity of intervention necessary for successful functioning, or it can be even better defined in terms of the distance between the intervention and the achieved product. The concept of distance can be evaluated on a continuum between zero (when the contribution of the mediator is maximal) and maximum (when the production is executed entirely by the examinee). Zero distance is best illustrated when the examiner directs the hand of the examinee as he or she draws a figure, or when the examiner offers the beginning of a word as a clue to be either completed or repeated. Minimal distance, on the other hand, is when the role of the examiner as mediator is restricted to stating a general instruction. There are many points between these two extremes. Thus, the instruction to "do here what you did there" leaves a very important part of the work to the examinee; by the same token, as instruction using a categorical superordinate concept such as "compare three parameters: color, size, and direction" is at a far greater distance from the outcome, and, therefore, more independent of the mediator than when the child is told, "here it's red; here, it's small; and, here, it's upside down." A hierarchy of MLE interaction on this continuum can be established, which is applied to diverse tasks, that permits consideration of the nature of the mediational interaction necessary to produce a given result. For example, it becomes possible to respond to the question: Has the individual whose level of functioning did not enable him or her to draw a square without help or to name an object without having the direct assistance of the mediator become able, by the end of the assessment, to do more complex drawings without more assistance than the offering of encouragement or the pointing out of the task to be done? Such a decrease in dependence would be a strong indication that the kinds of changes to be anticipated after intensive and appropriate intervention will produce the characteristics of structural change described in the earlier sections of this chapter.

Significance of LPAD Profile for Structural Cognitive Modifiability

The diagnostic, prognostic, and prescriptive significance of a profile of modifiability based on the three areas of domain, quality, and level of independence lies in their contribution to the theoretical, as well as applied, aspects of SCM. First, and foremost, this is the means of turning assessment into a meaningful source of planned and guided instruction that aims to modify the individual's levels of functioning by reshaping his or her cognitive structure through exposure to adequate amounts of MLE. Imagine an individual who, despite the fact of climbing up to a hierarchically higher level of independence, continues to be mediated at a level of concrete, sensory-based activities. This is all too frequently the case in special education. How many of these children spend years coloring shapes already prepared for them, or linking numbered dots to form shapes, when no demands are made for independent thinking or creativity? We have seen a 13-year-old boy whose prolonged exposure to such experiences has totally hampered his willingness to engage in free drawing of any kind. The ability to decide on the basis of the child's profile to what level of dependence or independence to address intervention is therefore of the greatest importance for any kind of educational or didactical decision. During the LPAD session, the experienced dynamic examiner will vary the mediational interaction in accordance with the carefully observed and interpreted changes in the examinee. The examiner monitors his or her own behavior as carefully as that of the examinee so as not to exceed the child's need to achieve. Intervention that does exceed the child's need may come only as a function of the "transcendence" principle of MLE, but is rarely applied to low-level types of activities.

The profile of modifiability, along with the other conceptual tools of LPAD such as the list of deficient functions, the cognitive map, and the MLE, lend to LPAD the characteristics that make it unique among other existing dynamic procedures. Purely on an external level, the other dynamic approaches differ from the LPAD in their attempts to affect the product by changing the task. The LPAD tries to modify the individual, and then to assess his or her cognitive structural modifiability. In this case, neither the task nor the individual's performance is the target of the assessment, but, rather, the processes by which certain critical aspects of cognitive structure can be modified.

At a deeper level, the LPAD differs from other dynamic approaches in the theoretical assumption concerning human modifiability, which is not considered to be a phase-specific facilitation of this unfolding process that accesses the proximal zone of development, but, rather a more or less sharp departure from a predicted and anticipated course of development. The goal is not merely enhancement, retrieval, or reinforcement of existing functions, but the formation of new structures, and through this formation, the affecting of the cognitive structures of the individual in a pervasive way, permitting his or her adaptation to situations that become increasingly complex and unfamiliar.

It is in this sense that the LPAD may be viewed as representing a dimension of the scientific revolution that can be witnessed in a variety of areas concerning the human condition.

In his paper on the theory of relativity, Sinott (1981) attempts to compare developmental theories to the theory of life span development on a series of parameters characterizing prerelativistic versus relativistic views of the world. In the following, we will describe a selected number of these parameters and relate them to the LPAD in its theoretical and applied aspects. In comparing the prerelativistic to relativistic views on the issue of measurement, Sinott pointed to the fact that according to a prerelativistic, Newtonian view, rigid measurement tools for the assessment of development can be produced. In contradistinction to this, the relativistic view considers that adequate measures can be devised only when the measure is flexible and "measured flexibility" is taken into account. It is not difficult to identify in this view the basic contention of the LPAD that the very concept of measurement is not an adequate term and is an even less acceptable practice for the evaluation of human capacities. The concept of human modifiability as a constant and continuous phenomenon leaves very little place for the reiterative process underlying the concept of measurement.

This is further reinforced when the concept of stages of development is discussed—and we would add the concept of levels of functioning to this. The prerelativistic view considers the subject as attaining a stable stage (level) or manifesting a stable personality trait, in contrast to the relativistic view, where the subject is in a mutable state. Stages are artificial abstractions, and it is better to speak about states in which the individual exists that are modifiable rather than about an individual who *has* traits. The additive nature of experience postulated by a prerelativistic view is restricted, according to the relativistic approach discussed by Sinott, to limited cases, whereas experience generally has differential effects. This is again consistent with the theory of MLE as determining differential consequences of the experienced effects on the individual. The basic component of the psychometric measurability and predictability assumption—that it can offer an exhaustive view of the human being—is paralleled by the prerelativistic concept "that no region of events exists which can not be known." This contrasts with the relativistic view paralleled by SCM, which states that unknowable regions of events do exist, and human development is therefore unpredictable, and static measures inadequate. This analysis of metatheories derived from the theory of relativity is helpful in placing the SCM theory within the broader framework of scientific developments.

The LPAD shares with the psychometric movement the need to use test tasks as means of evaluating the cognitive behavior of individuals and groups, rather than using real-life situations for observations of behavior and achievement. This latter solution, which is postulated by some educational psychologists and referred to as diagnostic teaching, seems to us to represent a real danger when dealing with disadvantaged, low-functioning, and low-achieving individuals, irrespective of the determinants of their condition. To use observational criteria for the assessment of intelligence of these individuals, equating manifest levels of functioning with capacity, is to doom them to their low levels of functioning. However, what proponents of LPAD reject most in the psychometric approach is the static use of this model, with all it entails in terms of assumptions of immutability and predictability. The LPAD shares with other dynamic procedures the need to go beyond the tasks and the products of the examinee, but differs from these approaches in the unwillingness to share the restricted goals that preserve the assumptions of stable and immutable traits that limit intervention to attempts to make manifest only that which is supposed to exist as potential. Within the LPAD model, modifiability is viewed as a process of change, not merely in some peripheral aspects of human behavior, but in those structures that themselves become generators of growth and further change.

Summary

In this chapter, we have attempted to highlight some of the characteristics, both theoretical and practical, of the LPAD specifically, as well as offering guidelines for the construction and application of dynamic assessment procedures in general. Further elaborations and applications of the values of the theory of SCM and its applications in the form of the LPAD, IE, and environmental modifications are described in Chapters 7, 9, 11, and 14 of this volume.

REFERENCES

Budoff, M. (1969). Learning potential: A supplementary procedure for assessing the ability to reason. *Seminars in Psychiatry, 1*, 278–290.

Cronbach, L. J., & Furby, L. (1970). How we should measure "change"—Or should we? *Psychological Bulletin, 74*, 68–80.

Feuerstein, R. (1979). *The dynamic assessment of retarded performers*. Baltimore: University Park Press.

Feuerstein, R. (1980). *Instrumental enrichment*. Baltimore: University Park Press.

Gardner, H. (1983). *Frames of mind*. New York: Basic Books Inc.

Jensen, A. R. (1980). *Bias in mental testing*. New York: The Free Press.

Kaufman, A. S. & Kaufman, N. L. (1983). K-ABC. *Kaufman Assessment Battery for Childen*. Circle Pines, MN: American Guidance Service.

Mercer, J. (1979). *Technical manual: SOMPA*. New York: Psychological Corporation.

Ramey, C. T., & MacPhee, D. (1981). A new paradigm in intellectual assessment? *Contemporary Psychology, 26*(7).

Sinott, J. D. (1981). The theory of relativity: A metatheory for development? *Human Development, 24*, 293–311.

Sternberg, R. J. (1984). Mechanisms of cognitive development: A componential approach. In R. J. Sternberg (Ed.). *Mechanisms of cognitive development* (pp. 163–186). New York: W. H. Freeman & Co.

Vygotsky, L. S. (1962). *Thought and language* (E. Hanfman and G. Vakar, Trans.). Cambridge, MA: M.I.T. Press. (Original work published 1934)

Vygotsky, L. S. (1978). *Mind in Society: The development of higher psychological processes*. (M. Cole, V. John-Steiner, S. Scribner, & E. Souberman, Eds. and Trans.). Cambridge, MA: Harvard University Press.

2

The Validity of Learning Potential Assessment

MILTON BUDOFF

The problems of misclassification and of using IQ to assign minority group children to special classes, whether they are called educable mentally retarded, perceptually or neurologically impaired, or by other imaginative euphemisms related to recent legislation, refuse to disappear. Despite more than four decades of documentation and debate about the shortcomings of the IQ test as a measure of intelligence among children from non-middle-class and/or non-Western backgrounds, the individually administered IQ test remains the primary instrument used to determine the eligibility of these children for placement in special classes. The potentially stigmatizing effect of this placement has been suggested, especially for the "mildly retarded" (Meyerowitz, 1967), although a research review by MacMillan, Jones, and Aloia (1975) failed to unequivocally substantiate this effect.

IQ tests measure the degree to which children can demonstrate that they have spontaneously acquired from their natural environment the skills and knowledge that cumulatively predict academic success. The plausible assumption is made that a child who learned informally at the same rate at his or her chronological-age peers prior to entering school will continue to learn at that rate, formally and informally, both in and out of school. However, this assumption is violated because children from non-middle-class homes do not have as equal and frequent access to appropriate school-preparatory experiences. They may learn differently and in ways that are not consonant with the middle-class bias evident in school curricula. This experiential discrepancy results in lower IQ scores and in perception of these children as less intelligent.

Children from poor and/or nonwhite homes disproportionately score at below-average levels, often in the mentally retarded ranges, on tests that purport to measure intelligence. This IQ difference has been explained in terms of handicaps that poor and/or nonwhite children bring to the testing situation. For example, they are said to be fearful and intimidated by the testing process, have low expectations for success, are often insensitive to speed requirements, are poor test takers, and may find the content of the items unfamiliar.

Milton Budoff. Research Institute for Educational Problems, Cambridge, Massachusetts.

Yet, many of these same low-IQ children are competent problem solvers in their nonschool environments, showing mastery of the skills, knowledge, and strategies necessary to maintain a successful community and family adjustment. In other words, these children often have learned from the relevant experiences in their community and function more successfully than their IQ scores and record of school achievement indicate (see, e.g., President's Committee on Mental Retardation, 1970).

The American Association for Mental Deficiency manual (Grossman, 1983) describes two criteria for diagnosing an individual as mentally retarded: intellective competence (i.e., IQ) and adaptive behavior. However, for school-age children, adaptive behavior is often defined by school adequacy, since this is the focal concern of this developmental stage. In any event, the most potent scholastic outcome predictor is IQ. Thus, the dual criterion for classification is not operative for school-age children, a problem Mercer (1973) sought to address.

What is required for the low-IQ child are measures of capacity that depend minimally on demonstrated school failure. These measures must enable us to distinguish low-IQ children who are relatively unintelligent, defined as not readily profiting from experience, from those who are relatively competent in non-school-related areas of life, and who are, therefore, more able to profit from experience. By the narrow application of the IQ criterion, the latter child is frequently misclassified as mentally retarded because of the lack of formal measures to test the hypothesis that low IQ indicates a pervasive failure to learn and to profit from experience.

Several approaches have been utilized in the past to address this problem. Jastak (1949) argued that evidence contrary to the diagnosis of mental retardation is provided by any single subscale score on an intelligence test that exceeds the prescribed level for mental retardation (i.e., the third percentile). If the child's scores fall uniformly below the third percentile, the child is diagnosed as mentally retarded. Jastak argued for an extensive battery of tests that would allow the child to demonstrate competence on a wide variety of tasks, expecting the falsely identified low-IQ child to perform above this cutoff on some tasks. The difficulty with this formulation is that the tasks chosen as indices of ability to perform more adequately should relate to later school or occupational success. All tasks in intelligence test batteries are not equally predictive of the ability to reason and conceptualize. Perceptual and perceptual–motor tasks, which do relate to early school success, do not relate to success on junior high and high school subjects, and their relationship to postschool success remains unexplored.

The earliest and longest standing approach involved the search for "culture-free" (Davis & Eells, 1953) and "culture-fair" (e.g., Cattell, 1940) tests. Although sophisticated approaches to test construction were employed in developing these tests, increased awareness of the poor performances on the IQ test items of well-adjusted children and adults from non-Western cultures

provided further support for those who argued that tests reflect the socialization process and that test items should tap culturally relevant content. Since
intelligence is not a purely biological phenomenon, although biology certainly
contributes, intelligence tests are measuring the extent to which the individual
has integrated and can express the knowledge of the culture. These tests
cannot be culture free, although they can be constructed to be culturally more
fair. The attempts to identify measures of general ability that are biologically
based are doomed to failure because the construct of intelligence or intelligent
functioning cannot be considered independently of sociocultural influences.

Mercer (1973) approached the problem of minimizing misclassification
by addressing the cultural argument differently. She proposed that the norms
for distinct cultural groups must reflect the average performance levels of
competent persons from that group. Her notion of pluralistic assessment was
developed to require adjustment of the attained Wechsler Intelligence Scale
for Children–Revised (WISC-R) scores to reflect the normative levels of black
and Chicano children separately. Mercer also included a measure to assess
the child's adaptive behavior in the home, neighborhood, and community,
which is presented in an interview format to the child's mother or mother
substitute. Although utilizing the WISC-R as the measure of IQ, the Adaptive
Behavior Inventory provides evidence of the child's competent functioning
outside the school. Low adaptive behavior scores, taken together with low
IQ, would indicate mental retardation. High IQ with low adaptive behavior
scores would indicate maladjustment from the vantage point of the community
and family. This combined measure is used to determine whether the child
is mentally retarded.

Pluralistic assessment, however, does not solve the problems inherent in
the use of IQ tests, even while undoubtedly minimizing misclassification of
children into educable mentally retarded (EMR) status. It does not address
the major problem of providing useful diagnostic–prescriptive information
so that a child-appropriate educational program can be developed. Although
these children might now be placed in regular classes, the fact that they were
singled out for assessment because of poor academic performance in the
regular class means that the assessment has not influenced their educational
situation. Although the student is not considered mentally retarded, his or
her learning situation is not altered.

The Logic of Learning Potential Assessment

This author and his associates have developed learning potential assessment
as an alternative strategy to assessment of cognitive functioning. Rather than
restricting testing to the child's present ability to respond to information
already acquired, learning potential assessment embeds training in a test–
train–retest sequence. The student first views and attempts solution of the
reasoning problems in a traditional format. Subsequently, either in a group

or alone, the child is shown how the problems may be solved and is offered problem-relevant training. Following the training, the child is retested.

The intent of learning potential assessment is to obtain an estimate of general ability derived from reasoning problems of suitable difficulty, which the child has had an opportunity to learn how to solve, and which permit a comparison with the low scholastic aptitude score (e.g., Binet or WISC Verbal IQ). If the child can demonstrate, following a short period of training on a nonverbal reasoning task, that he or she can perform at a level approximating average peer performance, we interpret this to indicate that he or she is not mentally retarded. This reflects our definition of intelligence as the ability to profit from experience.

The learning potential test–train–retest assessment paradigm minimizes the artificiality of the test situation by helping the child to become familiar with the test content in a context calculated to enhance the child's sense of competence. That is, the child is taught to understand how to think about solving the problems when the content of the problems may be unfamiliar and the appropriate strategies or information requested may not be readily apparent. Without this competence boost, the child tends not to perform optimally, implicitly expecting failure (Zigler & Butterfield, 1968). The essence of this assessment strategy, then, is to impose some control on the potentially negative effects of expectations related to school performance.

When the results of the learning potential assessment indicate competencies on reasoning tasks that describe the child's potential for higher level school attainment, the school-based professionals are challenged to seek ways to translate this evidence into an individualized educational plan that will allow the child to maximize the demonstrated capabilities.

We argue, then, that training-based assessment rather than assessment of the current level of functioning of students of cultures or subcultures that emphasize verbal and thinking modes different from those implicit in urban Western cultures will allow these students the opportunity to demonstrate that they can perform as expected when they understand the demands of the tasks. The training embedded within the testing process allows these students to understand the requirements of the test task and to respond to the test demands more effectively. Training helps equalize the differences in experience and elicits more competent performances. This is similar to the use of training embedded within an assessment for vocational performance. A work sample approach to testing potential proficiency on a vocational task is a real-life analog to this training-based assessment approach, since its logic is based on the premise of lack of initial opportunities with the task. The tester wants to assess the time required to attain a criterion of proficiency and the quality of the performance demonstrated by the student, assuming a roughly asymptotic level of proficiency. In the testing situation, the students who experience difficulties in school, whether from rural Morocco or inner-city America, require educational programs in school that are more appropriate to helping them make a transition to a society that explicitly and implicitly values certain capabilities, (e.g., causal abstract verbal explanations). When practitioners accept a low IQ score as signifying an immutable, diminished, biologically based capability, demonstrating that these lower IQ persons can function more optimally when the assessment paradigm is altered challenges this biological hypothesis. The need is to increase attention to and consideration of styles of thinking and contexts within which to apply these thinking styles.

Since 1964, when the first of our papers (Budoff & Friedman) coined the term "learning potential assessment" for the American literature, we have been working with training-based assessment measures. We have demonstrated that many children with a prior history of failure in school and the usual low IQ score that accompanies such failure have the ability to work with abstract reasoning problems that are basically nonverbal in their response demands, as well as with challenging nonverbal curricula. It is likely they can also work more successfully with verbally based materials, but their language store is usually impoverished, compared to their higher IQ peers from the same socioeconomic backgrounds (Harrison, Greenberg, & Budoff, 1975), and they clearly demonstrate difficulties in verbally explaining what they demonstrate they understand nonverbally (Budoff, Meskin, & Harrison, 1971). Their cognitive modifiability is not only evident in learning new strategies, as Feuerstein (1980) argued, but also in better melding the requirements of the curriculum to their need to more consciously relate the strategies they can learn to the processes involved in learning. They can perform better than their school history indicates when their educational program becomes more sensitive to the processes involved in learning. The work of the classroom teacher therefore needs to focus not only on conveying content and concepts, but on how these students can learn more effectively. Students can learn the strategies, but they also need to be reminded to use them in their everyday learning. Their problems derive primarily from their failure to learn to apply these strategies spontaneously. Consequently, they have been under- or improperly educated using curricula that stress abstract, verbal–analytic, and expressive skills, rather than the experiential learning capabilities that reveal their competence. The consequence is that educators play into these students' demonstrated weaknesses without helping them learn to integrate the processes of abstraction, which reinforces both the student's and the teacher's sense of their incompetence.

This paper reviews our past work using learning potential assessment procedures. This approach differs from other dynamic assessment techniques in which it is difficult to distinguish the contribution the tester makes to improved student responses from what the student actually understands and can apply. The fluidity of "dynamic assessment" procedures can work against the client because the student may perform more competently with the uncontrolled cues offered by the examiner than he or she can when it is necessary to apply these skills in the learning situation. This is the situation that originally gave rise to the use of standardized administration techniques for testing. Unsophisticated testers, unfortunately, were trained to administer them rotely and mechanically. The experience became impersonal and unfriendly, and fed into these children's fears, further impeding their performance. The learning potential assessment procedures described in Chapter 6 use relatively standardized training procedures and clearly demonstrate the power of training-based assessment to help practitioners develop programs more appropriate to the needs of their low-IQ, low-achieving students. These procedures also provide evidence of the students' ability to profit from these specially designed instructional programs.

Measurement of Learning Potential

Learning potential assessment was developed as a response to the controversy regarding misclassification of many low-achieving children as educable mentally retarded (Budoff & Friedman, 1964). Measures of learning potential have been available in the American literature since 1961 (e.g., when Miller and Griffith [1961] sought, unsuccessfully, to train mildly retarded subjects on a similarities type of task). Feuerstein used training-based assessment with French-speaking Jewish children from small Moroccan villages during this same time. Russian psychologists have also used various informally administered training-based assessment procedures for some considerable period of years (Luria, 1961). Haywood, Filler, Shifman, and Chatelanat (1975) reviewed the various applications of training-based assessment to the mentally retarded.

We sought to demonstrate the validity of training-based assessment by addressing validity at two levels. After ascertaining the reliability of the procedure and its items, we first sought to demonstrate concurrent validity by relating the learning potential instrument to measures such as WISC or Binet IQ scores or learning scores from a variety of learning tasks. Subsequently, construct validity was studied by examining the differential effects of the EMR student's responses to the training-based assessment on various types of dependent measures, such as social–demographic, personality, vocational aspiration, social interactive, level of responsibilities accorded in the family, and various language-related tasks. In Chapter 6, we describe the learning potential measures, and present details of the relatively standardized testing and training procedures. In this chapter, we review studies of validity at both levels, which also describe the correlates of learning potential status.

The Problem of the Criterion of Learning Potential Status

In its original conception, learning potential measurement was concerned with the extent to which the initially poor performance of IQ-defined educable mentally retarded (EMR) students could be improved by problem-relevant instruction on nonverbal reasoning tasks. The hypothesis was that many residents of an institution for the mentally retarded, as well as students in special classes for the retarded, could profit from such instruction and perform more effectively on the reasoning task because they had been misclassified as mentally retarded on the basis of the IQ score. The initial thrust of this work was concerned with developing a standardized procedure that would demonstrate whether optimized procedures in testing would yield less biased estimates of ability to profit from experience, or intelligence.

During our early work, three patterns of response were identified on the first measure, the Kohs Learning Potential Task (KLPT) for those students whose IQ scores fell within the EMR range (50–79 IQ). *High scorers* demonstrated excellent understanding on the nonverbal task prior to training. *Gainers* performed poorly on the pretest administration, but improved their scores markedly following instruction. *Nongainers* performed poorly initially and did not profit from the instructional procedure. Gainers were defined on the KLPT as those students whose posttraining score was four or more designs higher than their pretraining score. This was three times the mean gain evidenced by a practiced but nontrained sample. Nongainers failed to attain this criterion. A few institutionalized individuals seemed to understand how to solve these nonverbal problems prior to training and solved difficult 3×4 and 4×4 patterns. When student samples were drawn from adolescent-age community special classes for the educable mentally retarded, larger numbers of students solved the difficult nonverbal puzzles prior to training. Proceeding from easier to harder items, they were able to learn how to solve the problems that higher IQ students performed. These students with low IQs were labeled high scorers, and most clearly represent instances of misclassification as mentally retarded (Budoff, 1967; Budoff & Friedman, 1964).

When work was begun with the Raven Learning Potential Test (RLPT), the same learning potential categories were defined, but, by that time, the conception of learning potential had experienced some development. Reliance on gain or improvement following training posed difficulties because of a lack of an anchoring point. To what did improvement refer? Did the child who solved no block designs prior to training but who solved four simple 2×2 puzzles following training possess more of the ability we characterize as learning potential than the child who solved more difficult block problems initially but who failed to improve his or her scores following training? Conceptually and empirically, we found difficulties in this formulation, which was based solely on a gain score without reference to pretraining level. Therefore, for the first studies with the RLPT, we began to work with a norm-referenced criterion. High scorers were defined as those students scoring at or above a criterion set at two-thirds SD below the mean score for the child's chronological age group prior to training. Gainers were defined as those who were below this level before training, but who attained this level following training. Nongainers' scores following training remained below the cutoff point. The cutoff point was taken as equivalent to an approximation of a 90 IQ, which set a more stringent criterion of mental retardation than the customary cutoff of more than 1 SD. This was done to demonstrate, more dramatically than necessary perhaps, that many students in special classes for the mentally retarded were competent nonverbal problem solvers when testing conditions were optimized. One difficulty with this solution was that the cutoff point was arbitrarily established. The problem of defining an appropriate criterion of LP status for the RLPT remained poorly resolved for a considerable period of time.

More recently, we have continued to use the norm-referenced criterion, but have chosen to abandon the previous trichotomous definition of LP status. Our past work clearly demonstrated that high scorers, gainers, and nongainers constituted a linear continuum of ability. Consequently, in our most recent analyses, we have used the following three scores as continuous variables in regression analyses to define three types of performance derived from the LP assessment.

Pretraining scores reflect the present functioning ability of the child on the task, and these scores correlate with verbal and performance IQs. Like IQ scores, they correlate also with such socioeconomic indicators as size of family, degree of intactness of family, race (black, white), and English language competence.

The *posttraining score* includes three major components. First, it reflects the initial level that the subjects demonstrate on the pretest. Second, the repeated administration adds an effect due to repeated exposure to the test materials (practice). The third component of the posttraining score is the effect of training. When the systematic contribution of practice is controlled by incorporating a nontrained group in the research design, the practice effect can be estimated by noting any increments in the test–retest score of the nontrained group. Whereas low-IQ children tend to gain little without specific instruction (Babad & Budoff, 1974), the third component, final level of attainment that potentially able children show, regardless of their initial score, is the most crucial. Following suitable training, many low-IQ children will function at a level similar to the child from more privileged circumstances (Babad & Budoff, 1974; Corman & Budoff, 1973b). This posttraining score, regardless of pretraining level, represents the child's optimal level of performance following an optimizing procedure. It permits a comparison between his or her presently low level of functioning, as indicated by IQ, and his or her potential level of functioning. This posttraining score is hypothesized to be related to performance on tasks or curricula that permit the child to operate in areas of conceptual or cognitive strength, as opposed to areas of weakness such as the verbal–conceptual domain to which IQ scores relate. It is assumed that an educational planner can use this evidence of conceptual strength to help the child upgrade his or her skills in the verbal–conceptual areas, so that the IQ-based prognosis of failure can be reversed.

A third score is the *posttraining score adjusted for pretest level.* This residualized score indicates the child's responsiveness to training, and, by extension to the classroom, it is hypothesized to indicate the student's amenability to instruction, given suitable school experiences.

The following sections summarize studies that indicate the validity of learning potential assessment for seven domains of variables. The major portion of these data was derived from studies in which the KLPT was the criterion task and the learning potential status trichotomy, derived from the gain score criterion, was used. When the study used other learning potential tasks, or when the posttraining score was used as a continuous variable, this information will be indicated. Sections that follow present data relevant to the social, demographic, and psychometric correlates of learning potential status using the Kohs and Raven procedures, the educational implications of learning potential (LP) status, its relation to learning tasks, and various motivational and cognitive style variables. Also, the life circumstances of the subjects as viewed by the students is presented, as well as their mothers' views of their capabilities. Finally, the application of LP procedures to a Spanish-speaking population is discussed.

Social, Demographic, and Psychometric Correlates of Improved Performance following Training

Kohs Learning Potential Test (Budoff & Corman, 1974)

The purpose of this study was to determine the contributions to LP variance of demographic and psychometric factors related to an improved posttest performance on the Kohs Block Designs by psychometrically defined EMR adolescents and to compare these factors with IQ scores on the Stanford–Binet and Wechsler Intelligence Scale for Children (WISC).

The sample consisted of 627 EMR students from nine cities and towns in Massachusetts. Seventy-five percent ($n = 471$) were students in segregated special classes in public schools. Most of the remainder ($n = 134$) were residents of state institutions for the retarded; 22 were participants in a community workshop. The subjects ranged in age from 8 to 40 years, with a mean of 14.55 years (SD $= 2.75$) at the time of initial testing. Fifty-nine percent were males, 38% were white, and 79% had fathers who were manual laborers or menial service workers. Stanford-Binet IQ scores were obtained for 535 subjects; those scores ranged from 65 to 98, with a mean of 68.81 and standard deviation of 10.26.

Data on the following variables were collected from school or institutional records: place and date of birth, father's occupation, race, family size and degree of intactness, number of diseases, age at entry into special class, and WISC and Stanford–Binet IQs. Raven Progressive Matrices (without training) were group administered by project staff, to be used as a criterion measure. The KLPT was administered individually to each subject.

A number of stepwise multiple regression analyses were performed against four main dependent variables: Stanford–Binet IQ, pretraining score (K1), immediate posttraining score (K2) corrected by pretraining score, and delayed posttraining score (K3) corrected by the two prior Kohs scores. Partial correlation coefficients indicated that the Stanford–Binet score was more highly related to noninstitutionalization, family intactness, and WISC Verbal IQ than were the pretraining Kohs (K1) scores.

With all variables held constant, factors related to immediate effects of training on the Kohs were: male sex, family size, birthplace outside northeast United States or in a foreign country, and high scores on the Stanford-Binet, Raven Progressive Matrices, and WISC Performance IQ tests. The only factors significantly related to delayed posttest 1 month following training with the Kohs (K3 with all variables partialled out) were WISC Performance IQ and scores on the Raven. WISC Verbal IQ was not found to be uniquely related to any of the three Kohs scores. In several equations where race and social class were used as independent variables, these two factors were not found to be significantly related to Kohs scores.

Scores following training did not elicit systematic differences from children of different racial and social class backgrounds for pretest Kohs, Stanford–Binet, and WISC Verbal IQ scores. When effects of training were considered, posttraining scores on the Kohs procedure were not affected by age or sex. Performance IQ, whether measured by the WISC or the Raven tests, was consistently related to Kohs scores at all three points in time. The continuing positive relationship to WISC Performance IQ reflects the nonverbal nature of the problems on which training occurred. The hypothesis underlying learning potential assessment that verbal skills are independent of and that poor verbal skills may mask general ability to reason was supported by the low partial correlation coefficients involving WISC Verbal IQ. This hypothesis was further buttressed by the increasingly attenuated relationship of Stanford–Binet IQ with the Kohs scores following training. The training-based model of assessment of reasoning ability, or assessment of learning potential, appears to have validity as an alternate, less biased measure of intelligence with poor, low-school-achieving populations.

Raven Learning Potential Procedure (Corman & Budoff, 1973a)

This study examined demographic and psychometric factors related to improved posttest performance on the Raven Progressive Matrices by psychometrically defined EMR children after training was provided. The investigators sought to determine the factors that accounted for the significant portions of the variance of the Raven scores before and after training. The following factors were examined: social class, race, sex, age, number of diseases, family size, degree of family disintegration, birthplace, score on a group IQ test, WISC verbal IQ, performance IQ, and length of time interval between pretest and posttest.

The sample consisted of 403 EMR children who attended segregated special classes in Massachusetts public schools. They ranged in age from about 7 to 15, with a mean age of 11 years (SD = 2). Sixty-two percent were male and 29% were black. Three-fourths of the subjects were from working class families. The mean Stanford–Binet IQ score was 70.95, with a standard deviation of 7.77.

Data on the following variables were collected from school records: place and date of birth, father's occupation, race, degree of family intactness, number of older and younger siblings, number of diseases, and IQ scores on the WISC, Stanford–Binet, and one of several group intelligence tests. Raven Progressive Matrices were group administered by project staff before and after subjects received training. Kohs Block Designs, with training interpolated, were individually administered to 130 of the subjects with training.

For the total sample, improved performance on the Raven after training was found to be uniquely related to male sex and WISC Performance IQ. Age was found to be positively related to initial performance, but was not significantly related to performance on the total test after training. Scores on the total Raven test before and after training were found to be free of influence by race, social class, and verbal IQ when the total sample was considered. The predictive power of the Kohs score on the total Raven posttest was similar to the predictive power of the Raven score on Kohs scores after block design training.

Differential Sensitivity of Learning Potential Training

As part of testing the validity of the Series Learning Potential Test (SLPT), the responses of IQ-defined bright–normal, dull–average, and subnormal (EMR) samples was examined in two studies. In the first study, the SLPT was administered three times, with the training in problem-relevant strategies interpolated following the second administration, to separate the effects of practice and coaching. Both low-IQ groups gained more than the high-IQ group from the training, but showed no gain from practice. The dull–normal IQ group gained more than the other groups from repeated administrations without training, (i.e., simply from practice). In the second study, the validity of the SLPT in predicting teacher ratings of school achievement was compared to the validity of a group IQ test. Whereas the predictive powers of the SLPT and IQ scores were of the same magnitude for the entire sample and for the bright group, the SLPT was superior to IQ in the dull–average and subnormal groups. In both studies, substantial proportions of EMR subjects reached the average reasoning level of their nonretarded peers following the short training session.

Educational Implications of Learning Potential Status

Learning on a Minimally Verbal Curriculum

Budoff, Meskin, and Harrison (1971) developed a model for testing the educational significance of learning potential scores. They adapted an educational unit, developed by the Elementary Science Study of Education Development Center (1966), that taught simple electrical concepts by allowing the student to manipulate flashlight batteries, bulbs, and copper wires. The investigators formulated a minimally verbal test to evaluate how much the students knew about electrical circuits prior to the course, and then retested them following exposure to the unit. On this test, the students could demonstrate their understanding by pointing to electrical circuits mounted on pegboards to indicate which bulb would light in one section. In a second section, they merely had to indicate whether the bulb specified in the circuit on the pegboard would light or not, and, if so, whether it would be brighter, dimmer, or of the same brilliance as the standard unit of electricity. This format was repeated in a written version that involved simple questions on printed diagrams that closely resembled the actual circuits and, in another section, that utilized schematic or symbolic representations of these circuits.

The evaluation of the laboratory science classes supported the argument that high-learning-potential students are educationally rather than mentally retarded. That is, whereas the level of scores on the evaluation instrument did differentiate between the special and regular class students prior to teaching, special and regular class children could only be differentiated on the basis of their LP status, not their class placement, following teaching.

The deficiencies in thinking of the special class students became evident from the verbal reasons offered for their empirical choices to the 16 pegboard problems. The verbalizations offered for correct answers were coded as to whether they were descriptions of the setups or whether they offered some causal explanation for the choice. The statements were qualitatively weighted for adequacy of response. Learning potential status predicted the level of verbal scores across special and regular class samples when the adequacy of response was considered without regard to whether the explanations were coded as descriptive or causal. The special class high scorers performed as well as any regular class subgroup; special class gainers and nongainers scored well below all regular class groups on the causal explanation variable.

The critical difference between the abilities of the regular and special class students emerged when adequacy and type of response were considered together. There were no differences between special and regular class subjects in giving prescriptive reasons, but there were marked differences in providing causal explanations for their choices. Thus, even though special class high scorers were correct on the pegboard items as often as any regular class LP group, they gave a good causal reason for only 29% of their responses, and *every* regular class LP group exceeded this percentage.

These data indicate that special class children are capable of learning empirically as well as regular class children, especially low-achieving, nonretarded peers. However, they demonstrate marked difficulties when they are required to explain the reasons for their responses. On this latter measure, all the special class LP groups performed poorly, especially in offering causal explanations for their correct choices.

The contrast in the findings for the empirical or nonverbal and the verbal modes of response would seem to reconcile the differences evident between a judgment of competence based on the LP assessment and that on more traditional evaluation procedures. The nontraditional LP approach showed clear differentiations within populations of children who are said to be limited in their ability. The measure, based on their verbal explanations, suggests that these children's difficulties may lie in explaining problems that they understand empirically. Their verbal performance agrees with the IQ-defined deficits. However, the ability the more able students demonstrated when the verbal demand was minimized was similar to that of educationally retarded children of higher IQs.

Mainstreaming Using a Remedial Learning Center (Budoff & Gottlieb, 1976)

Considerable attention has been directed toward the inadequacies of special classes as a source of primary educational intervention for educable mentally retarded children (Budoff, 1972; Christoplos & Renz, 1969; Dunn, 1968; Kaufman, Agard, & Semmel, 1986; Lilly, 1970; MacMillan, 1972). Dissatisfaction with segregated facilities for mildly retarded children has occurred for a variety of reasons. First, the efficacy studies have failed to demonstrate that special classes provide an education superior to regular grade placement for these children. Second, there has been increasing concern with the effects of labeling and, concomitantly, with the frequent misclassification of children from low-income and/or minority group backgrounds as mentally retarded.

Concurrently, the school's increased capability to deliver individualized programs for children with special needs, coupled with its socializing value as a source of normalizing experiences, has resulted in a rapid move away from special classes in favor of integrated educational placements as a primary delivery system for children in need of special education services. Many school administrators have abandoned their special class programs and replaced them with resource rooms, learning centers, itinerant tutors, diagnostic–prescriptive teachers, and the like. Children are being removed from segregated classes and placed into regular grades, most often with specialized educational support. However, there is relatively little evidence available to attest to the effects of reintegrating EMR children into regular classes after they have spent one or more years in a special class. An important newly published study of mainstreaming (Kaufman et al., 1986) discusses these issues and reports results of a large-scale study of regular, resource, and segregated classes using a broad array of variables including child background, intraschool, and intraclassroom variable domains.

Although it is necessary to ascertain the effectiveness of integrated and segregated class placements and the instructional conditions in those placements that will maximize their effect, this goal is not sufficient. We also need to be able to specify characteristics of children that would enable them to succeed in a particular class placement. A child variable we hypothesized as necessary to success in an integrated educational replacement was the student's learning potential status (Budoff & Gottlieb, 1976). Thirty-one children between the ages of 93 and 168 months participated in this experiment. The children had all attended segregated special classes in one of three inner-city schools for at least 1 year prior to their participation in the study. In order to compare the academic and social growth of EMR children in regular classes, special class students were randomly assigned to regular classes ($n = 17$) or retained in special class ($n = 14$).

The experimental treatment was a remedial learning center (RLC), now typically called a resource room. The RLC consisted of a double-sized classroom, staffed by three teachers (one experienced teacher and two first-year teachers); the class accommodated approximately 20 children at a time. Each session of 20 children contained no more than one third of the former special class students. The remainder were regular class children referred by their classroom teachers because they needed special educational help, either remedial or enrichment, or because they could serve as tutors to the mentally retarded children. Students attended the RLC for approximately 40 minutes per day, 5 days a week, although some former special class students spent larger portions of each day there, depending on their educational needs. The RLC was organized as a series of activity stations, with sectors devoted to mathematics, reading, and so on. The major instructional emphases were on mathematics and social–emotional development.

The results of our study indicated no significant differences in achievement, motivation, cognitive style, or teachers' perception of behavior between the reintegrated and segregated children after 2 months in the integrated placement. Major positive effects of the integrated placement were evident by the close of the school year. In contrast to the segregated students, the integrated students showed marked differences in scores in the motivation and cognitive style domains. Examination of the means of the separate measures in the motivation domain after 1 school year indicated that the integrated students felt more positively about their prospects in school, expressed an increased sense of control vis-à-vis their environment, and tended to view their own capabilities as students more positively than when they were still in special class. Integrated children also displayed more reflective behavior than the segregated pupils.

At both points of data collection, both prior to and 1 year after placement, the more able students, by the LP criterion, had higher achievement scores and demonstrated more reflective behavior than their low-able LP classmates. There was also support for the predicted aptitude by treatment interaction. After 1 year in the integrated placement, the more able LP students thought that others regarded them more positively when they were mainstreamed than when they were segregated, whereas the less able LP special class students reported others' attitudes toward them were more favorable when they were in the segregated condition. These results, which provide further validating evidence for the utility of the test–train–retest LP assessment procedure, are particularly significant because they predicted outcomes in two different educational treatments.

Learning Potential and Paired-Associate Learning

A number of studies have compared the learning performance of LP groups on meaningful picture paired-associate tests. With a relatively easy task composed of only six pairs of dissimilar pictures, the scores of high scorers and gainers were combined and compared to the scores of nongainers. No differences were found between learning potential groups in three samples: older (chronological age [CA] 17–23) and younger (CA 10–13) institutionalized samples and a community special class sample (CA 9–17) (Budoff, 1965). With a minimal information load, Kohs LP groups were not differentiated on the usual paired-associate learning task.

When the information load was increased to 10 dissimilar picture pairs and the samples were composed of community special class students ranging in age roughly from 7 to 15 years, the findings were more variable. Gainers learned faster than nongainers with whom they were matched on CA, IQ, and pretraining Kohs block performance (Budoff, 1965). Similarly, White (1968) found that gainers learned faster than nongainers, with gainers performing comparably to high scorers when LP status was defined by the Raven. No differences, however, were found between Kohs LP–defined gainers and nongainers by Glaser (1966, personal communication) or Frank and Riley (1969), but the samples were not matched by starting level. The latter study did find high scorers to be superior to the other groups when LP status was defined by the Raven procedure.

When the information load of the picture paired-associate task was increased to 18 items, clear differences appeared among LP groups. Analyses of the differences in number of errors indicated that the high scorers learned with significantly fewer errors than the gainers and nongainers. There were no differences between the latter two groups. Although the mean differences were significant, there was considerable overlap of performance among the groups, with one nongainer performing better than all other subjects. It appears likely that, with minimal information load, LP groups do not differ in ability to learn a picture paired-associate task. When the load is increased moderately (to 10 items), there may be a point at which nongainers are outperformed by gainers, who perform comparably to high scorers. However, beyond this point, under conditions of overload (18 items), the performance of the gainers breaks down so that they no longer differ from nongainers, and both groups learn more slowly than high scorers.

Mankinen (1972) trained children differing in LP status to embed each of 23 picture pairs in a sentence. One week following training, they were retested on an alternate series of picture pairs. High scorers whose perform- ance had improved markedly immediately following training also learned the new series with few errors. Gainers made fewer errors immediately after training, but learned less efficiently 1 week following, a pattern that was similar to that displayed by the nongainers. Nongainers, however, made more errors in both posttraining trials, although they did show marked reduction in errors.

Learning Potential in Relation to Personality Variables

Given the hypothesis that the more able LP student is educationally, not mentally, retarded, and that the improved response following training reflects increased cognitive ability, we hypothesized that the more able students by the learning potential criterion should be more able to manage and control their behavior, cope more effectively with stress, report better adjustment, and understand and plan more realistically for their future than the less able LP nongainers. We developed the following series of studies to examine this.

LEARNING POTENTIAL AND SELF-CONCEPT

An adaptation of the Laurelton Self Concept Scale (Guthrie, Butler, & Gor- low, 1961) and the Bialer–Cromwell Locus of Control Scales (Bialer, 1961) was administered to 172 psychometrically defined EMR students; the results were factor analyzed (Harrison & Budoff, 1972a, 1972b). Most apparent was the significant negative correlation between maladjustment and Kohs per- formance. Various components of maladjustment, however, showed differ- ential patterns of correlation with successive Kohs administrations. Neurotic anxiety correlated negatively with Kohs performance on the first two tests, and then dropped from significance. Acting out correlated negatively with only the first performance on the Kohs. Friendliness, on the other hand, was increasingly positively correlated with Kohs performance on successive tests, and suggested that inability to relate intimately interfered with the acquisition of Kohs skills. This finding may indicate that those of lower intellectual capacity have more difficulty making friends.

Other correlates of a poor Kohs performance and/or poor gain scores on successive administrations were bravado, mischievousness, obedience, and depressed self-criticism. Correlates of a generally good Kohs performance were feelings that others think well of one's physical capabilities, the fantasy that one will succeed in adversity, and high motivation for achievement.

The most intellectually disabled children (by the Kohs LP criterion) in this population also reported themselves to be the most emotionally and socially handicapped. Children who projected the fantasy of self-worth and those who felt that they could succeed interpersonally under difficult odds did better and improved more on the Kohs LP tasks than those who lacked such fantasies. A pattern of peer rejection and obedience at home seemed to be major correlates of poor Kohs LP performance as well.

LEARNING POTENTIAL AND LEVEL OF ASPIRATION

When aspiration level of gainers and high scorers was compared in an experimental situation in which actual performance was controlled, and success and failure conditions manipulated, gainers' aspirations tended to reflect their actual performance (Harrison, Singer, Budoff, & Folman, 1972). Nongainers' aspirations, however, tended to be distorted under a condition of failure, and most especially when they had previously experienced success.

LEARNING POTENTIAL AND SUCCESS–STRIVING VERSUS FAILURE–AVOIDANCE

Forty-eight special class EMR students from an urban and a suburban school who had been administered the Kohs LP test were classified as having failure-avoidant or nonfailure-avoidant (success-striving) behavioral styles according to the relative difficulty of a block design they were willing to construct following successful completion of an initial subject-chosen design. This designation was made by asking the student in an individual session to select one of the block designs with which he or she was already familiar. Those whose choices tended to be easier than the designs they had successfully completed during the posttraining LP session were considered to be failure–avoiders, and those whose choice of designs were at or above their highest correct solution were categorized as success–strivers. The prospect of failure, per se, did not seem to govern choice behavior on this task.

Discrimination learning efficiency was determined with a two-choice simultaneous discrimination problem under one of two concretized feedback conditions: positive feedback (student received token for correct responses) or negative feedback (student forfeited tokens for incorrect responses). The results revealed no discrimination learning differences among LP groups who were success–strivers. The performance of failure-avoidant nongainers, however, was strikingly inferior to that of failure-avoidant gainers and high scorers. The results indicated that nongainers were not of uniformly poor learning ability relative to gainers and high scorers, and that the performance of all three groups was partly determined by behavioral styles, which may be somewhat independent of actual learning ability (Mankinen, 1968).

LEARNING POTENTIAL AND RESPONSE TO FRUSTRATION

On a behavioral measure of response to frustration, Budoff and Pines (1971) reported a tendency toward less disruption following a mild stressor (mirror tracing of a six-pointed star) among the more able LP special class students than among less able nongainer peers. The criterion task was the Pins and Collars subtest of the Crawford Small Parts Dexterity Test. The students were required to place a small steel pin in a narrow hole and a collar on top of the pin, using a pair of tweezers. Facility on the task is easily disrupted by tension.

Learning potential status predicted rate of performance on the motor task. There was support for the hypothesis that high-able (LP) students (high scorers and gainers) would cope with stress more adequately than low-able (LP) nongainer students. The performance of high scorers and gainers was similar during all three phases of the experiment. Performance among the nongainer group, however, differed. Nongainers performed erratically during the prefrustration phase and showed a markedly delayed response to frustration. They demonstrated marked proficiency early in the postrecovery phase, but were unable to maintain this, and their performance slowly deteriorated; they seemed unable to maintain their initial appearance of adequacy (Budoff & Pines, 1971).

RESPONSE TO A QUESTIONNAIRE AND SENTENCE COMPLETION TEST REGARDING FRUSTRATION (BUDOFF & PINES, 1971)

A questionnaire and sentence completion test that consisted of hypothetical frustrating situations in the areas of school, peer, and parental relations was administered to EMR groups of nongainers, gainers, and high scorers as defined by the Kohs LP procedure. The responses to each of these measures were analyzed along two dimensions: active or passive, and positive or negative. The activity described in the response was defined by its relation to the source of the frustration. If an act was directed toward the source, it was coded as active. If an act was directed toward oneself or away from the frustrator, it was coded as passive. The positive–negative dimension refers to the social acceptability of the act or the emotion involved. The two dimensions were combined into the following scoring categories: active–positive (acting in a socially acceptable way toward the frustrator); active–negative (acting in a socially unacceptable way toward the frustrator); passive–positive (withdrawal from the frustrator through acting in a socially acceptable way); and passive–negative (withdrawal from the frustrator in a socially unacceptable way).

The sample of 27 special class adolescents, subdivided by learning potential status ($n = 9$ per group), was used for each of the measures, which were administered individually during several sessions in a long series of contacts by the same examiner (Pines). All subjects were residents of a low-income housing project. They ranged in age from 10 years, 7 months to 16 years, 7 months, and in IQ from 69 to 90.

Special class gainers and high scorers gave many fewer responses coded in the passive categories than the nongainers and many more coded "active–positive." Gainers give the fewest passive and most active–positive responses. The results in the quadratic comparisons were due to the effects of the nongainers, since there were no differences between high scorers and gainers.

There were few active–negative responses that were given by any group, and no systematic differences on this variable by LP status.

High scorers and gainers give their more passive–negative responses to peer and family rather than school situations, unlike the nongainers, who were most negative toward school. Gainers and high scorers responded more positively to school situations than did nongainers.

A subsidiary question of this study concerned the consistency of responses across the open- and closed-ended conditions. It has been observed that nongainers tend to be inconsistent verbal responders in an interview situation, especially as the questions become more specific. The situations were presented to elicit these two types of responses in order to systematically test this observation.

When the discrepancies in the coded choices given to the open- and closed-ended questions were summed over each subject's responses to the 15 questions, high scorers and gainers gave the fewest discrepant choices, while nongainers' responses tended to be more discrepant. This finding of discrepant responding across the two modes of response to the same situation indicates that the nongainer tends to be an inconsistent responder. By contrast, the gainer and high scorer tends to maintain consistency even if, as in the forced-choice situation, they realize that there is another answer they prefer. The nongainer seemingly either did not care if answers were changed, did not even realize that another answer was given, or offered more flippant verbal responses.

When five frustration situation sentence completion items were presented in a format covering four content areas (school, peers, mother, and father), the major hypothesis was again supported. Membership in an LP status group was associated with differing types of responses. As with the questionnaire, nongainers' completions were more often passive–negative when compared to high scorers. High scorers gave more active–negative and active–positive responses than nongainers. When gainers' responses were compared with those of the high scorers and nongainers, the significant quadratic components indicated that gainers gave fewer passive–negative and more active–positive responses than the high scorers and nongainers. Again, these effects seem mainly attributable to the deviant pattern evidenced by the nongainers. There was relatively little difference between high scorers' and gainers' means.

LEARNING POTENTIAL AND TASK DISSONANCE

The Stroop Color Word Test was administered to determine whether special class adolescents differing in Kohs LP status would also differ in coping with the mild interference task dissonance of having to report the colors when the color names are printed in an ink of a conflicting color. The prediction was that the more able (LP) students would manage the interference on the color–word task more effectively than the nongainers. The only significant finding was the trend for this prediction to be supported. High scorers were less susceptible to interference effects than the nongainers, but there were no significant differences in performance. The groups did differ, however, in a personality characteristic: the ability to inhibit response to a conflictual stimulus and to respond adequately with minimum time delay.

LP AND RIGIDITY IN THE EMR ADOLESCENT

Lewin (1936) argued that retardates, as compared to normal children of the same mental age (MA), were characterized by a lessened permeability in the boundaries between cognitive regions. Kounin (1941) extended this position by stating that the degree of rigidity in these boundaries was a positive monotonic function of chronological age. This argument generated the prediction that, with MA held constant, older retardates would suffer from greater cognitive rigidity than younger retardates, who would in turn be more rigid than normal children. This prediction was supported by a series of five experiments (Kounin, 1941). Zigler (1962) argued that the differences in performance that Kounin demonstrated may be largely accounted for by motivational factors.

We used the LP procedure to elicit different levels of performance on a nonverbal task within homogeneous populations of EMR students and included many of the conditions cited by Zigler to maximize the child's understanding and participation (Budoff & Pagell, 1968). Twenty special class gainers and 20 nongainers between the ages of 12 and 17 were selected. Mean CA was 14:6; mean Binet IQ of both groups was 72.8. The MA control group consisted of a sample of 20 fourth-grade children of average IQ. Twenty ninth graders of average IQ served as CA controls. All four groups were selected from working-class backgrounds, as determined by father's occupation and parents' educational level. Each of the groups contained 10 boys and 10 girls. The groups were further subdivided into socially deprived and nondeprived categories after consultation with teachers and school records.

Two measures of rigidity were employed: a simple "marble-in-the-hole" game, Zigler's adaptation of the problem used by Kounin (1941), and an adaptation and extension of Kounin's concept-switching task in which 27 cards could be sorted for three concepts (shape—circle, star, and square; color—red, green, and yellow; and number of figures—one, two, and three). Two sessions were held with each subject individually. At the first session, simplified versions of the two experimental tasks were presented in a supportive atmosphere that would minimize apprehensiveness. Within 1 week, the experimentor presented the two experimental tasks. When the concept-switching task was presented, the child was told a candy bar would be provided for each concept sorted successfully. Seven trials were allowed for each concept sort.

The CA normals spent markedly less total time on the marble task than the MA normals ($p < .01$), nongainers ($p < .01$), and gainers ($p < .05$). The gainers tended to spend less time than nongainers and MA normals (.10

$> p > .05$). There were no differences between nongainers and MA normals in mean time. The CA normals also required the fewest trials to switch concepts. The gainers required fewer trials than the nongainers ($p < .05$), but the MA normals did not differ from either the gainers or nongainers, the mean score falling between these two groups. Ranking the means, the CA normals grouped for the three concepts most rapidly (mean = 1.15 trials per concept), followed by the gainers (1.90), MA normals (2.47), and nongainers (3.30). All three of the latter groups required significantly more trials to switch concepts than did the CA normals.

An analysis was performed to determine the order of the difficulty for attaining the three concepts: color, shape, and number. The mean number of trials required was 1.83, 1.86, and 2.58, respectively. The number concept was significantly more difficult to attain than color or shape. When the number of children in each group who attained each concept sort was tabulated, fewer nongainers sorted for shape than members of the three other groups, and fewer nongainers and MA normals sorted for the number concept. Students from socially deprived backgrounds spent more time on the marble task, supporting Zigler's social reinforcement hypothesis. However, there were no differences in performance on the concept-switching task which could be ascribed to level of social deprivation.

LEARNING POTENTIAL AND IMPULSIVITY

Mankinen (1970), using an adaptation of Kagan's (1965) Matching Familiar Figures task as a measure of impulsivity with white and black adolescent special class students, reported that the more able (LP) subjects (high scorers and gainers) demonstrated less impulsivity, matching more figures correctly than the less able nongainers.

The Special Class Student's World Inside and Outside of School

Learning Potential and Students' Self-perceptions

A major issue in this research program was to determine the extent to which students in special segregated classes who responded differently to the learning potential procedure differed from their classmates who also had school achievement problems. My associates and I explored these differences by addressing their views of their life situation in wholistic terms. The views of low-achieving regular class and EMR special class adolescents from a white, low-income, urban inner city district were compared by administering an interview individually to each student that examined their perceptions of:

1. Their social interests and activities
2. Their familial obligations and relationships
3. Their vocational aspirations and expectations
4. Their attitudes and feelings about school

All the students were also administered the learning potential procedure. We were concerned with distinguishing the factors that seemed related to the presumed mild mental retardation of the special class students, or their life circumstances—their economically poor family backgrounds and history of poor achievement in school.

The samples consisted of all the non-brain-damaged students in three EMR special classes ($N = 46$) and regular class controls ($N = 33$) drawn from the low academic tracks of the same urban, low-income junior high school serving predominantly white children. Special and regular class students differed significantly in IQ (mean = 69.97 and 92.31, respectively) and chronological age (CA) (mean = 14:42 and 13:18, respectively). Learning potential groups also differed significantly in IQ, in accordance with previous findings on large EMR samples (Budoff, 1970). High scorers and gainers had higher IQs than nongainers. The groups did not differ significantly in social class background when the principal wage earner's occupation was rated. Evidence for the academic difficulties of the low-achieving, regular class sample were reflected by their low grade point average for their four major academic subjects (<2.0, when A = 4, B = 3, C = 2, D = 1, and F = 0). All students were interviewed individually in a 1-hour session. The results are discussed first in reference to the regular versus special class comparisons, and then by learning potential status across the two groups. The results are given in abstracted form; fuller reports are available from the author.

SOCIAL INTERESTS AND ACTIVITIES

There were few differences reported in the social interests and activities of these two samples. Regular and special class students' activities and interests lacked variety, and, except for athletic interests, tended to be unstructured and focused on an interpersonal, belonging dimension rather than knowledge oriented. The special class students tended to report themselves as more socially isolated and as peripheral group members.

Among the special class students, the more able on the LP assessment reported themselves to be more socially isolated, engaged in more passive activities or in athletics, did not belong to peer groups, disliked group activities, and said they did not desire to change their situation. The less able (nongainer) students reported more active social involvements with their peers. However, data from this and other studies indicate that nongainers tended to give socially desirable responses that did not reflect their actual behaviors (Folman & Budoff, 1972).

FAMILIAL OBLIGATIONS AND RELATIONSHIPS

Special class students tended to report they spent their free time with their families rather than with friends. Both special and regular class students reported they were given responsible roles at home; the regular class students tended to report more responsibility in the home.

Nongainers reported themselves most alienated from their parents, and desired increased physical contacts, although not verbal interactions. High scorers and gainers, to a lesser degree, reported spending their free time outside the family, although they reported good relations with their families. High scorers reported having good relations with their mothers, and desired better relations with their fathers (Folman & Budoff, 1972).

VOCATIONAL INTERESTS AND ASPIRATIONS

Special class members were able to get and hold jobs to the same extent as the regular class adolescents. However, they displayed a lack of initiative in obtaining jobs that may have been attributable to their stigmatized status. Regular class students had realistically higher job aspirations and expectations than did special class students.

Within the special class sample, high scorers and gainers aspired to low-level jobs and clearly sought to minimize risk of failure, and expressed little involvement in their present low-skilled jobs. The nongainers expressed desires regarding unrealistic jobs but lowered their statements of aspirations when asked what jobs they expected to attain to the level of their special classmates (Folman & Budoff, 1971).

ATTITUDES TOWARD SCHOOL AND SCHOOLING

The interview results indicated that:

1. Fewer special than regular class students saw a relationship between their present schooling and their future lives.
2. Although the majority of both groups aspired to finish high school and to continue their education, more regular class students expected to do so.
3. More regular than special class students tended to take personal responsibility for their failures in hypothetical locus of control questions, while special class students tended to blame themselves for their actual school failures.
4. Although most of the adolescents in both groups saw themselves as comparable or poorer students than their siblings, chronological age peers, friends, and classmates, more special class pupils saw themselves as better academically than their classmates.
5. Special class students tended to say they expended much effort in their schoolwork and tended to see their schoolwork as being the best they could do, while the regular class students expressed more lackadaisical attitudes toward their schoolwork.

Within the special class sample, LP status was related to the following academic variables. Like their regular class peers, the more able LP students: (a) related school to their future adult job situation; (b) exhibited less discrepancy between their academic aspirations and expectations; (c) reported being given more responsible roles in hypothetical classroom situations; (d) exhibited an internal locus of control in both success and failure situations; and (e) reported putting more effort into their schoolwork. There were no differences in the special class students' self-perceptions of their scholastic ability.

SUMMARY

In sum, the child segregated into a special class and not participating in the general stream of life in junior high school or high school is susceptible to the stigmatizing effects of this placement, no matter how devalued school may be in the social and value context of his or her community. Although our findings indicate few major differences in the response of special and regular class students from a low-income, inner-city white community, the most able (LP) special class students do indicate some distress in their lives: they tend to isolate themselves or may be isolated socially except for athletic activities; they have low vocational aspirations, although they desire more success in school and brighter prospects as adults. There is evidence in these data, in short, that they felt stigmatized, "different," and have difficulty coping with their special status.

These data offer further support for the broad range of differences within the psychometrically homogeneous special class population, and evidence in support of the hypothesis that the more able (LP) students' perceptions of themselves tend to agree with those of their regular class peers, when both samples are drawn from the same low socioeconomic areas. (See also Appendix 4 in Kaufman, Agard, & Semmel, 1986, for descriptions of very different clusters of IQ-defined EMR students.)

Learning Potential and Mother's Perceptions of Child's Placement in an EMR Class

Another source of data regarding the competence of children outside of school is the perception of the child's parents. The mothers of 27 males who had been placed in a special class and who had been examined with the LP procedure were interviewed in their homes. The sample was unbalanced: 20 of the children were gainers and 7 were nongainers. Three-fourths of the gainers' mothers thought their children learned less and were slower than their nonspecial class peers. However, 6 of the 20 thought that the reasons for the learning problems were "environmental" or external to the child and family; 5 thought the children's limitations were only in special areas of study or academic performance. The parents on the whole did not relate the child's failure in school to success in life (steady job, happy marriage, etc.). Three-fourths of the gainers' mothers anticipated that their children would "outgrow" their learning problems, and only 1 predicted that her child would not. Nineteen of the 20 thought their children would marry, in contrast to the nongainers' mothers, of whom 4 of the 7 anticipated that their children would marry.

The emotional reactions of the mothers of gainers and nongainers to their child's placement in special class also differed, with gainers' mothers exhibiting more surprise and upset at the time of placement, and many maintaining feelings that the placement was inappropriate. Of the nongainers' mothers, 5 of the 7 said the placement "confirmed their suspicions," and none said they thought the placement inappropriate.

Gainers' and nongainers' mothers also differed in their physical descriptions of their children, with gainers' mothers less often describing their children as "different in a negative way," and nongainers' mothers more often wanting play supervision for their children. Informal peer group play was more successfully achieved by gainers, 16 of whom were said to see friends daily. Four nongainers saw their friends rarely or said they had none.

Learning Potential and Postschool Adjustment

Additional powerful support for the learning potential argument can be drawn from data that indicate that the more able (LP) students from the special classes will attain economic and social independence as adults to a greater degree than the nongainers. There was a significant relationship between LP status and military service classification, with a higher proportion of gainers having qualified. Of those students who had worked during the high school years, gainers tended to have worked for a longer period of time. The more able (LP) persons were more likely to report having a special group of friends, a higher rate of participation in high school groups, and dating experience. They were also more likely to live away from home and to have a driver's license.

As another index of adult adjustment, the status of the persons in the original institutional studies tested with the Kohs Learning Potential Test (Budoff, 1967; Budoff & Friedman, 1964) was determined. These persons were surveyed from 7 to 10 years following the original data collection, and it was found that the more able (LP) students were no longer in residence, whereas the less able remained at the institution, having been judged by the staff as less capable of establishing economic and social independence (Budoff, 1971).

Summary and Conclusions

Investigations at the Research Institute for Educational Problems have demonstrated the applicability and validity of learning potential assessment with low-income, black, white, Spanish-speaking, and moderately and severely mentally retarded children. The training-based procedure has also been demonstrated to be effective in discriminating high-risk kindergarten children in the German Democratic Republic (Frohriep, 1978) and among Israeli Hebrew- and Arabic-speaking students (Babad & Bashi, 1978).

In a lengthy set of studies over the past 16 years, mainly using a test-train-retest design, we have demonstrated that training-based assessment among low-IQ-defined special class students using relatively standardized test administration and training procedures has identified marked differences in understanding of Jensen's nonverbal Level II conceptual reasoning tasks following training. Students who demonstrated improvement in performance after 1 hour of training were also characterized by marked differences over a broad range of variables. For example, children who demonstrated competence on the LP task tended to score higher on other nonverbal or minimally verbal tasks, such as the WISC Performance scale and Raven Progressive Matrices, administered in a traditional format. Personality data, whether behavioral or verbal, suggest a greater sense of personal adequacy in the more able children, greater flexibility on a concept shift task, more flexibility and ability to delay response, ability to manage frustrations more effectively, a view of oneself as less neurotic or maladjusted, the tendency to set aspiration levels consonant with one's performance even under stress of failure, and the feeling that one is not manifestly different socially from one's "nonretarded" peers. However, these students do realistically feel inadequate in academic areas, and seem to be making the more concrete and realistic vocational plans.

The most tenable hypothesis by which to explain these consistent differences between more and less able special class students is to consider the high-able group by the learning potential criterion (high scorers and gainers) as *educationally handicapped*. These are children who have been unable to progress satisfactorily in school for a number of reasons, but who seem to have ability not usually ascribed to them. Those who do not profit from the experience of training on the nonverbal reasoning tasks (nongainers) seem to function on a wide variety of tasks in the way that mentally retarded children are described.

What we have learned subsequent to these early studies is that manipulating the training strategies can probably alter the low-responding student's performance. For example, some nongainers, who were defined by their low improvement scores following the experimenter-designed training, improved their performance markedly on nontrained block designs when the training instructions requested them to design their own block designs, copy them, and then reproduce them from their own drawings. More recent work has demonstrated that when training is embedded within the testing process high-risk kindergarten children and substantially retarded adolescents and adults show markedly improved performance on such tests at the Leiter International Scale, Raven Progressive Matrices, and the Kohs Block Designs (Frohriep, 1978) (Budoff & Hamilton, 1976; Hamilton & Budoff, 1974). Differences in response to the training can be shown to be associated with different rates of progress on an objectives-based curriculum with moderately and severely mentally retarded adolescents and adults (Budoff & Allen, 1978).

What has not been readily available is a methodology by which to translate the results of Budoff's training-based procedures into prescriptive treatment programs for individual clients. In formulating an assessment strategy, the client's strengths and weaknesses should be ascertained in the initial testing contacts or from the referral. These data would be used to develop hypotheses about the client's potential capabilities. Appropriate training and posttest(s) to test the hypotheses would then be designed/selected. Subsequent contacts would be used to test and generate hypotheses, and, finally, formulate a treatment plan. This proposed procedure would maximize the use of expensive professional time. Carefully designed tests with appropriate training would allow the identification of the areas of functioning likely to benefit and the teaching strategies appropriate to the particular person.

There are considerable problems in interpreting the meaning of the gains following training that can be demonstrated in the laboratory or clinic. For example, unless the procedure carefully selects items that do not appear in the posttraining task, it is not possible to claim gains from training that will transfer to similar types of problems. It is even more difficult to gauge the extent to which transfer and generalization to real-life contexts will occur. To demonstrate generalization the client must spontaneously choose options appropriate to particular contexts that vary considerably in their specific circumstances and be ready to reject them in favor of other options should they prove inappropriate. As a profession, we have largely failed to demonstrate how to help our clients attain this ultimate criterion state for complex tasks. There is no evidence that we can accomplish the transfer to spontaneous usage in real-life contexts of the types of higher order skills Feuerstein claims.

Although our earlier research proceeded on the premise of application to classrooms, we were primarily concerned with demonstrating that low-IQ children in special classes for the mentally retarded who responded positively to the training were different from those who did not respond to our training, and that these differences provided evidence of their misclassification as mentally retarded. The misclassification of children into special classes is still a major social problem, especially for minority children. In prescribing treatments for those children who profited from the training, our most successful generalization was that they would respond most effectively to challenging, individualized programs in classrooms. Our understanding of appropriate educational programs for these high scorers and gainers on nonverbal reasoning tasks was best exemplified by the practice of experienced and innovative teachers who would abandon their preconceptions about the child's inabilities and develop appropriate and challenging programs.

The concerns in current practice as reflected in the literature have changed to an increasingly prescriptive stance. Casting training-based assessment in terms that are prescriptive in the specific manner requested for individual education or service plans involves new thinking. Future work must indicate how training-based assessment may be used in clinical practice and translated into treatments that can be administered in schools.

Finally, cognitive education must demonstrate that highly specific training can result in improved performances in applications to real-life situations by the child. Cognitive training, however, is not likely to be successfully integrated into spontaneous use in the person's daily life at any level of sophisticated application unless embedded in experiential applications or a wide variety of appropriate and inappropriate context-specific learnings that provide opportunities for practice and that will allow the student to define when the strategy is effective or ineffective.

At our present level of understanding, the psychologist might best work with teachers and other service personnel to help them understand the optimal approaches to a client when the capacity to profit from challenging mini-experiences can be demonstrated in training-based assessments. The psychologist and the teacher should confer to continually sharpen the focus of the training in the direct service setting. Concurrently, the psychologist will be evaluating these derived prescriptive implications so the training-based assessment and prescriptive treatments derived from it can be also sharpened.

REFERENCES

Babad, E. Y., & Bashi, J. (1978). On narrowing the performance gap in mathematical thinking between advantaged and disadvantaged children. *Journal for Research in Mathematics Education, 9* (No. 5).

Babad, E. Y., & Budoff, M. (1974). Sensitivity and validity of learning potential measurements in three levels of ability. *Journal of Educational Psychology, 66*, 439–447.

Bialer, I. (1961). Conceptualization of success and failure in mentally retarded and normal children. *Journal of Personality, 29*, 303–320.

Budoff, M. (1965). Learning potential among the educable mentally retarded. Progress Report to the National Institute of Mental Health. Mimeographed.

Budoff, M. (1967). Learning potential among institutionalized young adult retardates. *American Journal of Mental Deficiency, 72*, 404–411.

Budoff, M. (1970). Learning potential: A supplementary procedure for assessing the ability to reason. *Acta Paedopsychiatrics, 37*, 293–309. (ERIC Document Reproduction Service No. ED 048 703)

Budoff, M. (1971). *Learning potential and institutional discharge status among adult EMRs.* RIEPrint #33, Cambridge, MA: Research Institute for Educational Problems.

Budoff, M. (1972). Comments on providing special education without special classes. *Journal of School Psychology, 10*, 199–205.

Budoff, M., & Allen, P. (1978). The utility of a learning potential test with substantially mentally retarded students. Application of a formboard version of the Raven Progressive Matrices (Sets A, AB, B). RIEPrint #110. Cambridge, MA: Research Institute for Educational Problems.

Budoff, M., & Corman, L. (1973). *The effectiveness of a group training procedure on the Raven learning potential measure with children of diverse racial and socio-economic backgrounds.* RIEPrint #58. Cambridge, MA: Research Institute for Educational Problems.

Budoff, M., & Corman, L. (1974). Demographic and psychometric factors related to improved performance on the Kohs learning potential procedure. *American Journal of Mental Deficiency, 78*, 578–585.

Budoff, M., & Friedman, M. (1964). "Learning potential" as an assessment approach to the adolescent mentally retarded. *Journal of Consulting Psychology, 28*, 434–439.

Budoff, M., & Gottlieb, J. (1976). Special class EMR children mainstreamed: A study of an aptitude (learning potential) × treatment interaction. *American Journal of Mental Deficiency, 81*, 1–11.

Budoff, M., & Hamilton, J. (1976). Optimizing test performance of the moderately and severely mentally retarded. *American Journal of Mental Deficiency, 81*, 49–57.

Budoff, M., Meskin, J., & Harrison, R. G. (1971). An educational test of the learning potential hypothesis. *American Journal of Mental Deficiency, 76*, 159–169.

Budoff, M., & Pagell, W. (1968). Learning potential and rigidity in the adolescent mentally retarded. *Journal of Abnormal Psychology, 73*, 479–486.

Budoff, M., & Pines, A. (1971). *Reaction to frustration as a function of learning potential status.* RIEPrint #9. Cambridge, MA: Research Institute for Educational Problems. (ERIC Document Reproduction Service No. ED 048 709)

Cattell, R. G. (1940). A culture-free test of intelligence. *Journal of Educational Psychology, 3*, 161–179.

Christoplos, P., & Renz, P. (1969). A critical examination of special education programs. *Journal of Special Education, 3*, 371–380.

Corman, L., & Budoff, M. (1973a). *A comparison of group and individual training procedures on the Raven Learning Potential Measure.* RIEPrint #56. Cambridge, MA: Research Institute for Educational Problems. (ERIC Document Reproduction Service No. ED 086 924).

Corman, L., & Budoff, M. (1973b). *A comparison of group and individual training procedures on the Raven Learning Potential measure with black and white special class students.* RIEPrint #57. Cambridge, MA: Research Institute for Educational Problems. (ERIC Document Reproduction Service No. ED 085 969).

Davis, A., & Eells, K. (1953). *Davis-Eells Games: Davis-Eels Test of General Intelligence or Problem-Solving Ability, Manual.* Yonkers-on-Hudson, New York: World Book Co.

Dunn, L. M. (1968). Special education for the mildly retarded—Is much of it justifiable? *Exceptional Children, 34*, 5–22.

Elementary Science Study of Education Development Center. (1966). *Batteries and bulbs.* (Trial Teaching ed.) Newton MA: McGraw-Hill.

Feuerstein, R. (1980). *Instrumental enrichment: An intervention program for cognitive modifiability.* Baltimore: University Park Press.

Folman, R., & Budoff, M. (1971). Learning potential status and vocational interests and aspirations of special and regular class adolescents. *Exceptional Children, 38*, 121–130. RIEPrint #7. Cambridge, MA: Research Institute for Educational Problems. (ERIC Document Reproduction Service No. ED 048 707)

Folman, R., & Budoff, M. (1972). Social interests and activities of special and regular class adolescents as compared by learning potential status. RIEPrint #36. Cambridge, MA: Research Institute for Educational Problems. (ERIC Document Reproduction Service No. ED 062 752)

Frank, L., & Riley, L. (1969). A further analysis of paired associates learning and learning potential status. *Studies in Learning Potential, 1*, 5.

Frohriep, K. (1978). *Zur Entwicklung, Differehzierungsfähigkeit und Validität eines neuentwickelten Verfahrens zur Diagnostik der Hilfsschulhedürftigkeit-eine verfahrenskritische Untersuchung zur diagnostischen Valenz eines traditionellen verfahrens, eines Dangzeit-Derntests und eines Kurzzeit-Lerntests mit lernproze-orientierlen Auswertungsmöglichkeiten.* Diss. A. APW der DDR, Institut für Päd. Psychol. Berlin.

Grossman, H. J. (Ed.). (1983). *Classification in mental retardation.* Washington, DC: American Association on Mental Deficiency.

Guthrie, G., Butler, A., & Gorlow, L. (1961). Patterns of self attitudes of retardates. *American Journal of Mental Deficiency, 66*, 222–229.

Hamilton, J. L., & Budoff, M. (1974). Learning potential among the moderately and severely mentally retarded. *Mental Retardation, 12*, 33–36. (ERIC Document Reproduction Service No. ED 085 960)

Harrison, R. H., & Budoff, M. (1972a). A factor analysis of the Laurelton Self-Concept Scale. *American Journal of Mental Deficiency*, 76, 446–459.

Harrison, R. H., & Budoff, M. (1972b). Demographic, historical, and ability correlates of the Laurelton Self-Concept Scale in an EMR sample. *American Journal of Mental Deficiency*, 76, 460–480.

Harrison, R. H., Greenberg, G., & Budoff, M. (1975). Differences between educable mental retardates and nonretardates in fluency and quality of verbal associations. *American Journal of Mental Deficiency*, 79, 583–591. (ERIC Document Reproduction Service No. ED 085 973)

Harrison, R. H., Singer, J., Budoff, M., & Folman, R. (1972). Level of aspiration as a function of learning potential status in the educable mentally retarded. *Psychological Reports*, 30, 47–57.

Haywood, H. C., Filler, J. W., Jr., Shifman, M. A., & Chatelanat, G. (1975). Behavioral assessment in mental retardation. *Advances in Psychological Assessments*, 3, 96–103, 113–120.

Jastak, J. (1949). A rigorous criterion of feeblemindedness. *Journal of Abnormal and Social Psychology*, 44, 367–378.

Kagan, J. (1965). Individual differences in the resolution of response uncertainty. *Journal of Personal and Social Psychology*, 2, 154–160.

Kaufman, M., Agard, J. A., & Semmel, M. E. (1986). *Mainstreaming: Learners and their environment.* Cambridge, MA: Brookline Books.

Kohs (1923). *Intelligence measurement.* New York: Macmillan.

Kounin, J. (1941). Experimental studies of rigidity: I. The measurement of rigidity in normal and feebleminded persons. *Character and Personality*, 9, 251–273.

Lewin, K. (1936). *A dynamic theory of personality.* New York: McGraw-Hill.

Lilly, M. S. (1970). A training based model for special education. *Exceptional Children*, 37, 745–749.

Luria, A. R. (1961). An objective approach to the study of the abnormal child. *American Journal of Orthopsychiatry*, 31, 1–14.

MacMillan, D. L. (1972). Motivational style; An important consideration in programs for EMR-labeled children. *Journal of School Psychology*, 10, 111–116.

MacMillan, D. L., Jones, R. L., & Aloia, G. (1975). The "mentally retarded" label: Libelous or legendary? *American Journal of Mental Deficiency*, 79, 241–261.

Mankinen, R. (1968). *Discrimination learning of EMRs, as a function of learning potential and striving orientation.* RIEPrint #17. Cambridge, MA: Research Institute for Educational Problems.

Mankinen, R. (1970). The relationship of an impulsivity measure to LP status. *Studies in Learning Potential*, 1, 12.

Mankinen, R. (1972). Learning potential status and verbal mediation training with EMR students. *Studies in Learning Potential*, 2, 29.

Mercer, J. R. (1973). *Labeling the mentally retarded.* Berkeley: University of California Press.

Meyerowitz, J. H. (1967). Self-derogations in young retardates and special class placement. *Mental Retardation*, 5, 23–26.

President's Committee on Mental Retardation. (1970). *The six-hour retarded child.* Washington, DC: U.S. Government Printing Office.

White, B. (1968). *An initial validation of Raven's Learning Potential procedure.* Unpublished report, Research Institute for Educational Problems.

Zigler, E. (1962). Rigidity in the feebleminded. In E. Trapp & P. Himmelstein (Eds.), *Readings on the exceptional child.* New York: Appleton-Century-Crofts.

Zigler, E., & Butterfield, E. C. (1968). Motivational aspects of changes in IQ test performance of culturally deprived nursery school children. *Child Development*, 39, 1–14.

3

Linking Dynamic Assessment with School Achievement

JOSEPH C. CAMPIONE AND ANN L. BROWN

Proponents of dynamic assessment methods are concerned with identifying students who are likely to experience academic problems and with providing descriptions of those students' strengths and weaknesses in such a way that remedial programs can be developed. A major stimulus for the interest in dynamic assessment procedures is a dissatisfaction with certain features of standardized "static" tests. In these static tests, children are asked for specific information or are required to solve certain types of problems. The tester provides no help during the testing session. The score individuals attain represents an estimate of their current, unaided level of competence. All too often, the unwarranted inference is made that these scores are a measure of ability level, for example, an IQ score of 70 is seen as relatively permanent and resistant to change. In many cases, particularly when children from culturally different backgrounds are involved, this picture may provide a dramatic underestimate of their potential level of performance under more favorable circumstances.

Dynamic assessment methods aim to go beyond this state of affairs by assessing the operation of basic psychological processes presumed responsible for acquisition of the information requested on standard tests. Some children may not have acquired the information or skills being assessed, but nonetheless may be able to do so quite readily if given the opportunity. The future academic performance of children in this category would be expected to be better than one would anticipate on the basis of their initial, unaided static test performance. To generate this additional diagnostic information, developers of dynamic assessment methods have used a number of different techniques, all of which involve the provision of some form of help to the child. This aid can take the form of modifying the format in which the test is administered (e.g., Carlson & Wiedl, 1978, 1979), providing direct instruction in methods of solving the problems (e.g., Budoff, 1974), or attempting to evaluate directly a set of target processes (e.g., Feuerstein, 1979). The assumption is that performance estimates obtained under these altered condi-

Joseph C. Campione and Ann L. Brown. Center for the Study of Reading, University of Illinois–Urbana-Champaign, Champaign, Illinois.

tions will provide more accurate assessments of individual differences than standard test scores, or will at least supplement the picture they paint.

Although sharing common assumptions, the methods that have been advanced differ in a number of ways, including the goal of the program. Some aim to engineer maximal levels of performance; others seek to measure the magnitude of response to instruction; still others focus on the efficiency of operation of specific cognitive processes. Different program goals have resulted in different methods of conducting the assessment. In this chapter, we outline our own variations on the theme of dynamic assessment. The approach we have adopted has been influenced by two lines of research, one specifying the format of the assessment itself and the second identifying the target processes we seek to evaluate.

A General Framework

Our approach to both assessment and instruction has been heavily influenced by Vygotsky (1978) and neo-Vygotskians currently working in the Soviet Union on the development of assessment techniques for recognizing academic delay (Vlasova & Pevzner, 1971; Zabramna, 1971). Both the Soviet investigators and our team have been influenced by Vygotsky's general view of learning and development and his notion of a "zone of proximal development." We emphasize, however, that the resultant approach is an amalgam of our views on cognition and instruction and Vygotsky's theory; it is in no way meant to represent Vygotsky's original views unchanged (Brown & French, 1979; see Chapter 4, this volume). Vygotsky emphasized that much of learning was mediated through social interactions. Children experience cognitive activities in social situations and come to internalize them gradually over time. At the outset, the child and an adult work together, with the adult doing most of the work and serving as an expert model. As the child acquires some degree of skill, the adult cedes the child responsibility for part of the job and does less of the work. Gradually, the child takes more of the initiative, and the adult serves primarily to provide support and help when the child experiences problems. Eventually, the child internalizes the initially joint activities and becomes capable of carrying them out independently. At the outset, the adult is the model, critic, and interrogator, leading the child toward expertise; at the end, the child adopts these self-regulation and self-interrogation roles. It is this gradual transfer of control that we seek to capture in our assessment and instructional sessions.

Within this context, Vygotsky also described the zone of proximal development, which refers to the distance between the level of performance a child can reach unaided and the level of participation that can be accomplished when guided by a more knowledgeable participant. For a certain child, in a particular domain, this zone may be quite small, the interpretation being that the child is not yet ready to participate at a more mature level than his or her unaided performance would indicate. For another child in that domain, or that child in another domain, the zone of proximal development can be quite large, indicating that with aid, sometimes minimal aid at that, the child can participate much more fully and maturely in the activity than one might suppose on the basis of only unaided performance.

The assessment process suggested by Vygotsky has been quite influential in the diagnostic testing of problem learners in the Soviet Union (Brown & Ferrara, 1985; Brown & French, 1979; Campione & Brown, 1984; Wozniak, 1975). This process involves an initial assessment of competence, followed by instruction on the target task(s). Children with high degrees of readiness (broad zones of proximal development) within that domain should benefit considerably from the intervention, whereas those with less readiness will not perform much better with this help than they did prior to it. As with other approaches, this measure of gain is presumed to possess greater predictive utility than the initial, unaided level of performance.

This framework has guided our work in both assessment and instruction. In this chapter, we will describe three sets of experiments that form part of an overall program of research with two major goals: (a) the development of diagnostic methods of assessing individual differences in students' readiness to perform in traditional academic domains, and (b) the use of the resulting information to guide the design of instructional programs that enhance the academic performance of students exhibiting relatively poor performance. In addition to the Vygotskian influence, these experiments all involve aspects of dynamic assessment. Despite these similarities, the series also differ from each other in important ways. The differences arise because the studies are addressed to different issues within the present enterprise, including some that are primarily of theoretical interest and others that involve both theory and practice. Before proceeding to the specific studies, we will review some of the considerations that influenced our specific choices.

Background

To put the overall research effort into context, we will describe the issues that have attracted our interest over time and the considerations that led us to this particular approach. We have long been concerned with the diagnosis and remediation of weak students' academic problems. To accomplish this diagnosis and remediation, we need: (a) to identify the students likely to experience difficulties, (b) to analyze the academic domain in question in terms of theoretical specification of the skills underlying successful perform-ance, (c) to apply methods of assessing the individual's competence with those skills, and (d) to implement instructional methods for overcoming whatever deficiencies may be revealed through the assessment process.

As with many others, we have been less than optimistic about the role standard ability tests can play in this overall endeavor. In the next sections, we outline several reasons for this concern. The first involves a contrast between two kinds of diagnostic procedures. This is followed by a more detailed analysis of the structure of standard tests. Having then described our reasons for adopting dynamic assessment methods, we distinguish two distinct uses we have made of the term.

Forms of Diagnosis

With regard to diagnosis, there are two levels at which the enterprise can be evaluated, one mainly aimed at *identification* and the second more concerned with *prescription*. In the former case, we might be concerned with identifying the students who are likely to experience difficulties, thus indicating the need for particular attention. A more valuable diagnosis would also be prescriptive; it would specify in detail the reasons for the problem, thus indicating both the need for, and direction of, remedial attempts. Although both identification and prescription are valuable, prescription enables us to work toward the second, instructional goal.

This distinction highlights the strengths and weaknesses of standard intelligence and ability tests. Under some circumstances, they do provide information that contributes to the identification goal (i.e., they can indicate students who are likely to experience problems); however, even this success has its limitations. Of more importance, standard tests have been much less successful at meeting the prescriptive goal. In the next section, we review some hypotheses about the sources of the specific limitations of those tests.

Limitations of Standard Test Procedures

One immediate question that arises is why there is a need for dynamic assessment approaches. Our goal is to link diagnosis and remediation; however, that goal is by no means novel. Standardized intelligence and ability tests were intended to identify individuals with academic problems, and many were designed to provide "profiles" of ability that should allow a somewhat detailed analysis of the strengths and weaknesses of individuals. From such a picture, it should be possible to prescribe interventions tailored to the needs of particular students or groups of students. Such approaches, however, have not yielded much in the way of encouraging results (Brown & Campione, in press; Mann, 1979), and there are several reasons why this might be the case.

PRODUCT-BASED NATURE

Standard tests analyze the student's current level of performance but provide no direct evidence regarding the processes that may have operated or failed to operate to bring about that performance. Therefore, they provide at best a partial view of the testee's status. A nice statement of this point was made by Vygotsky (1978), who noted that static test scores do not provide any information about

> those functions that have not yet matured but are in the process of maturation, functions that will mature tomorrow but are in the embryonic stage. These functions could be called the 'buds' or 'flowers', rather than the fruits of development. The actual developmental level characterizes mental development retrospectively, while the zone of proximal development characterizes mental development prospectively. (pp. 86–87)

It is not that developers of standard tests are unconcerned with process— they do interpret the results in terms of sets of processes—but rather that their approach is to infer the processes underlying test performance from analyses of the structure of the test results themselves. Given their nature, standard tests rest heavily on the assumption that all testees have had comparable backgrounds and opportunities to acquire the information requested. This assumption is particularly suspect for students from minority or disadvantaged backgrounds. With such populations, abilities are quite likely to be underestimated. The result is that the identification goal of the evaluation is jeopardized.

LEVEL OF DESCRIPTION

If we turn to the prescriptive aspects of assessment, there are further problems with the process analyses involved in traditional tests. The "profiles" that result from such tests and that are used as the basis for description and diagnosis are couched in terms of very global aspects of performance (e.g., auditory sequencing) that are not easily theoretically relatable to interesting academic areas and tasks. Such diagnoses at best rest on somewhat vague abstractions from a particular psychological theory and cannot provide the kind of specific information needed to design instructional programs. For example, if auditory sequencing were diagnosed as the problem, it would not be clear how best to intervene. Even if such skills can be developed, it is then left to the student to determine how and when these skills are to be used in academic contexts.

DEGREE OF GENERALITY ASSUMED

Finally, there is a related problem. The profiles that emerge are based on assumptions about the generality of the factors inferred from such tests. The abilities are presumed to be extremely general ones that operate in many, if not all, academic domains. While domain-general skills may well exist, it is also abundantly clear that there are important domain-specific capabilities that underlie successful performance in different domains (e.g., mathematics or reading). The tests available generally do not tap these skills in any meaningful way. Although perhaps obvious, it seems reasonable to argue that if one is interested in assessing skill in the area of math, the assessment should be situated in the context of math problems. Again, the case of such processes as auditory sequencing is illuminating. The potential relevance of these processes to intervention programs rests on very strong theoretical assumptions about the nature of academic intelligence. The factors are presumed to be quite general, with the result that they affect performance in many situations. Improving auditory sequencing, then, would be expected to have widespread effects throughout the system. The analogy is with a muscle system in which practice on different skills strengthens the overall system and thus affords generalized improvement in performance.

STATIC NATURE OF EVALUATION

Although not a necessary feature of standard tests, nonetheless the result of assessment is frequently taken as providing a relatively permanent characterization of the individual in question. The classifications that result, already presumed to reflect "general" academic ability, further tend to be regarded as fixed and unlikely to change over long periods of time. A measured IQ of 70, for example, is frequently assumed to reflect a relatively permanent characteristic of the student in all situations and under all circumstances.

Interpretations of Dynamic Assessment

Because this volume is concerned primarily with issues regarding dynamic assessment, we think it useful at this point to contrast two different ways in which we have used the term. The question is, what is dynamic about dynamic assessment? Although in both cases the important distinction is between static and dynamic properties of the assessment process, they differ in what, within the procedure, is regarded as dynamic—that being assessed, or the assessment itself. In the more traditional usage, the one we have already described, the interest is in assessing the efficiency of operation of the psychological *processes* involved in growth and change. The interest is not so much in evaluating an individual's current state of knowledge or skill as in estimating his or her readiness for change. The contrast is clearly with standard test procedures in which descriptions of individuals are couched in terms of what they currently know about some domain; or alternatively stated, the contrast is between product- and process-based assessments of individual differences.

In the second case, we emphasize the dynamic nature of assessment itself—the notion that any assessment needs to be continuously reevaluated as the student begins to acquire skill within some domain. Again, this is a feature of Vygotsky's treatment of the zone of proximal development. His argument is that instruction creates this zone; hence, with instruction, an individual's zone of proximal development changes, and it becomes necessary to continually update the diagnosis if instruction is to be appropriately directed. The assessment of an individual's zone, or readiness, is assumed meaningful for only brief periods, because one's readiness can itself change with practice and/or instruction. In this vein, we have also attempted to construct situations in which the assessment itself is dynamic rather than static, cases where the evaluator continually refines the diagnosis of the learners as they acquire competence. Thus, we use the phrase "dynamic assessment" to refer to: (a) assessment of process, or of the dynamics of change; and (b) the need to continually change and refine the diagnosis of the individual learner, that is, the dynamic, constantly changing nature of assessment itself.

An Alternative Approach

Our approach to dealing with the limitations of standard test methods involves several features. One is that assessment should evaluate as directly as possible the particular *processes* underlying successful performance. The second is that the assessment should ideally be situated *within a specific domain*, rather than being aimed at "general intellectual functioning." This in turn increases the likelihood that the processes can be specified in sufficient detail that instructional prescriptions can be designed. Finally, we make explicit the assumption that any diagnosis may have a very short half-life, and that *rediagnosis* must be an integral part of any resultant intervention.

Having decided to concentrate as directly as possible on process is only a first step—it is still necessary to specify the process(es) to be evaluated, and then to determine how to situate that assessment.

TARGET PROCESSES

In our work thus far, we have concentrated on the role of quite global learning and transfer processes; the long-term goal is to be much more specific about the factors underlying individual differences in learning and transfer. In initial studies, we looked at the extent to which these global processes were related to overall academic ability. In more recent studies, we have concentrated on learning and transfer processes assessed within specific domains. In effect, we have assumed that estimates of individuals' learning potential and transfer efficiency within some domain provide measures of their readiness to perform in that domain.

This view emerged from a long series of studies with scholastically weak students, frequently labeled as learning disabled or mildly retarded. In that work, we concluded that, in a variety of problem-solving situations, those students had difficulty learning new information (required complete and detailed instruction to do so) and were relatively unlikely to use that information flexibly in new problem situations (Brown, 1974, 1978; Brown & Campione, 1978, 1981, 1984; Campione & Brown, 1977, 1978, 1984; Campione, Brown, & Ferrara, 1982).

METHODS OF ASSESSMENT

Although that conclusion seems reasonable enough, at the time we began this program the bulk of the available evidence did *not* support the position that assessments of learning ability or transfer flexibility would provide much helpful information about individual students (see Campione et al., 1982; Campione, Brown, & Bryant, 1985). The question is how one might reconcile the disparate sets of findings. We have outlined our hypotheses in other sources (e.g., Campione & Brown, 1984), and will summarize them here. The major argument is that, in the studies generating negative findings, the estimates of learning and transfer efficiency (a) were obtained in asocial learning situations; (b) involved only minimal feedback from the evaluator, most frequently simple feedback about the correctness of individual responses; and (c) were situated in arbitrary domains. The metrics of learning and transfer were the amount of time and/or the number of trials needed to bring about learning.

As an example of this research approach, consider some studies reported by Woodrow comparing the learning (Woodrow, 1917a) and transfer (Woodrow, 1917b) performance of groups of retarded and nonretarded children with mental ages of around 10 years. The learning tasks he used involved a geometrical form sorting task in which the children were required to sort five forms into different boxes. They sorted 500 of these a day for 13 days, guided at best by feedback about the correctness of their individual placements. The main index of learning was the increase over time in the number of forms sorted. The transfer tasks consisted of two new sorting tasks (lengths of sticks and colored pegs) and two cancellation tasks (letters and geometric forms). Using these tasks, Woodrow found no differences between the retarded and nonretarded groups in either learning or transfer performance. In these studies, learning and transfer were seen as passive, asocial, extremely general processes that could be tapped in any task domain. These conditions were typical of many studies failing to find evidence that learning and/or transfer processes represented important dimensions of individual differences (see Woodrow, 1946, for a review).

In contrast, the more recent studies, those yielding positive results, are characterized by a concern for structured intervention, often involving complex social interaction. The problems to be learned are set in nonarbitrary domains, that is, ones where there are rules for the students to learn and where it is possible to come to understand why certain responses are appropriate in given situations and not in others. This understanding then serves as the basis for subsequent use of the newly acquired information; that is, principled transfer is possible (Brown & French, 1979; Campione & Brown, 1984). The metric of learning or transfer efficiency is the amount of help needed for a student to acquire a rule or procedure.

Given this analysis, we assumed that if we wished to assess individual differences in learning and transfer that would be of diagnostic significance, we would have to match these latter conditions. The learning should be guided by the adult tester and should involve the acquisition of rules or principles whose application in novel contexts we could subsequently observe. These ideas clearly meshed nicely with those of Vygotsky (1978), and our procedures have become quite similar to those employed by neo-Vygotskians in the Soviet Union.

The studies we have conducted follow the same general format. They begin with an evaluation of children's initial competence. Following this, the children are placed in a mini-learning environment where an adult (or a computer) works collaboratively with them until they are able to solve sets of problems independently. If they are unable to solve a particular problem, they are given a series of hints to help them. The initial hints are very general ones, and succeeding ones become progressively more specific and more concrete, with the last "hint" actually providing a detailed blueprint for generating the correct answer. This titration procedure allows us to estimate the *minimum* amount of help needed by a given child to solve each problem. The metric of learning efficiency is the number of hints required for the attainment of the learning criterion (typically two successive problems solved with no help). Note that the metric here differs from that used by several others interested in dynamic assessment, including Vygotsky, in that it is not *how much improvement* one can bring about through intervention, but rather *how much aid* is needed to bring about a specified amount of learning.

Exactly the same hinting procedure is used on the transfer problems, generating the analogous metric. Note that the index of transfer propensity is thus a dynamic, rather than static, one (Brown, Bransford, Ferrara, & Campione, 1983). That is, we do not measure how many or what types of transfer items individuals can solve on an unaided test (a static measure); rather, we are concerned with how facile they are in coming to deal with related portions of the overall problem space (a dynamic measure)—specifically, how many hints they require to solve the various types of transfer problems. Following these instructional sessions, a posttest is given, and the gain brought about by the instruction determined.

To summarize, we decided to situate our assessment of learning and transfer efficiency in social interactional contexts in which the evaluator would be engaged in the task of teaching the children how to solve sets of problems; the measures of learning and transfer could then be based on students' responses to that instruction.

There is one further point to emphasize. The hints employed were based on a detailed task analysis and were designed such that each one would provide more specific information than the previous one(s). These hints were given in a fixed sequence and were, with one exception, independent of the individual child's responses (the exception was that if the child had already generated the information provided by an early hint, that hint was omitted, and the experimenter gave the next hint in the sequence). The procedure was then *task*, rather than *child*, oriented. This was done because we aimed to produce quantitative data with good psychometric properties; the number of hints as an index is likely to have psychometric properties only if the test administration is standardized as much as possible.

The trade-off is with more clinical procedures in which assessors vary their questions, or prompts, with different children as those children show different approaches to the problems at hand. Such approaches may well provide richer information about the skills and aptitudes of individual children; however, they are less likely to produce strong quantitative data. As we will describe later, we have attempted in some of our more recent studies to modify our procedures in ways that allow us to combine the strengths of the different approaches.

TASK DOMAINS

The next decision involved the selection of a domain in which to embed the teaching. Given an interest in transfer propensity, it is necessary to choose a domain in which rules or principles can be learned and applied to novel types of problems. Because we were also interested in academic skills, we also wished to choose a domain that was known to be related to school performance. In our initial studies investigating the diagnostic utility of measures of learning and transfer, we worked with inductive reasoning problems, variants of progressive matrices problems, and series completion problems, because performance on those tasks is known to be related to scholastic success. Furthermore, enough was known about the structure of those tasks so that it was possible to design a theoretically based teaching, or hinting, sequence. In our work on instruction emphasizing the dynamic nature of the assessment process itself, we concentrated on studies of reading and listening comprehension, skills of considerable academic importance.

Specific Studies

We will summarize the results of three sets of studies. The first two involve the theoretical and diagnostic status of the learning and transfer measures obtained in our adaptation of the zone of proximal development testing procedures. These deal with issues of *concurrent validity* and *predictive validity*. In the first case, we selected students of varying academic ability and assessed their performance as they learned how to solve inductive reasoning problems. Performance on these problems, featured on most ability tests, consistently distinguishes academically successful from less successful students. Our expectation, then, was that learning and transfer indices, obtained in these domains, would be related to assessed ability.

In the case of predictive validity, we wished to go one step further and evaluate the extent to which the dynamic measures would provide diagnostic information beyond that afforded by static ability tests. Although ability test performance was expected to be related to learning–transfer efficiency in these inductive reasoning domains, we also expected that the dynamic measures would provide more information about the future performance of subjects within those domains than would the static tests.

In these studies, instruction is provided, and response to instruction is used as a metric of individual students' readiness to deal with the domain under study. The concern is with how much instruction is needed to bring about a given level of performance.

The third series is more "purely" instructional. The goal here is to maximize the performance of individual students in important academic domains. One key element of the instructional program is the need to continually update the diagnosis of students' current skill levels, rather than to use the initial estimate as a long-term index.

Studies of Concurrent Validity

In these studies, we were interested in the extent to which measures of learning and transfer efficiency, obtained within the context of prototypic ability test items (specifically inductive reasoning tasks) would be related to general ability levels. There are two issues involved:

1. Regarding diagnosis, do either or both measures distinguish lower ability students from those of higher ability? (an identification issue) and
2. Regarding theory, can part of the variance in individual differences in this domain be attributed to learning and/or transfer dynamics? (a qualitative issue)

STUDY 1: CAMPIONE, BROWN, FERRARA, JONES AND STEINBERG (1985)

In this study, we used a variant of the Raven Progressive Matrices task. At the outset, subjects were given a pretest involving the kinds of problems that were to be used in the diagnostic–instructional sessions. Each problem involved a 3 × 3 matrix with the lower-right entry left blank; the subject's task was to select, from a set of six, the pattern that best completed the matrix. The subjects consisted of groups of retarded (mean IQ = 72) and nonretarded (mean IQ = 118) children matched for a mental age of approximately 10.5 years and for performance on the pretest.

During the instructional sessions, students worked at a computer terminal. In the initial phase, they learned to solve problems involving three rules: rotation, imposition, and subtraction. Examples are shown in Figure 3.1. During this, the learning portion of the study, the problems were presented in a blocked format. Each student learned the rotation problems to a criterion, then the imposition problems, and finally the subtraction problems (an easy-to-hard sequence). In the next (maintenance) session, novel exemplars of the same type were presented, but now in a random order. The ensuing (transfer) session included these same problem types interspersed with a set of transfer problems; these required the use of combinations of the

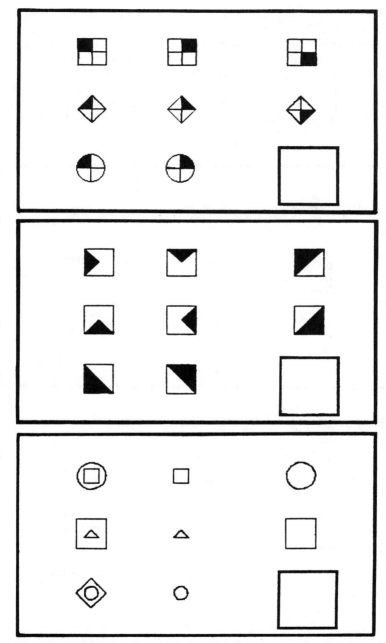

FIGURE 3.1   Examples of the learning problems used in the matrices study. The *top panel* contains a rotation problem, the *middle panel* an imposition problem, and the *bottom panel* a subtraction problem.

original rules (rotation + imposition; rotation + subtraction). Examples are shown in Figure 3.2.

In contrast to the pretest procedure (and the standard procedure used with the Raven), the task here was to *generate* the pattern needed to complete the matrix by issuing a set of pretaught commands using a touch-sensitive screen. Graduated and animated hints were provided via the computer as needed, with an adult reading the hints to the child if necessary and providing general encouragement. The hints were presented in a preset sequence, pro-

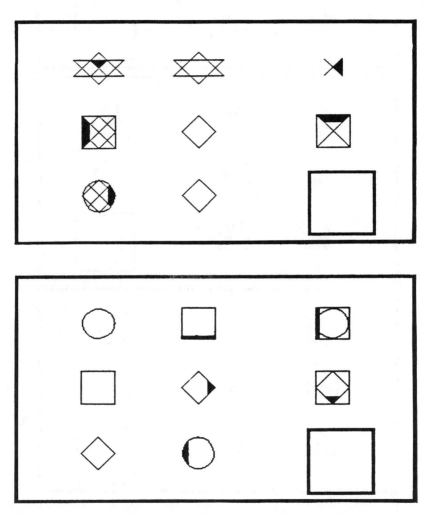

FIGURE 3.2   Examples of the transfer problems used in the matrices study. The *top panel* contains a rotation plus subtraction problem, the *bottom panel* a rotation plus imposition problem.

ceeding from very general hints offering relatively little specific information about the form of the solution to very specific hints, which eventually provided a detailed blueprint from which the child could generate the correct answer. The numbers of hints taken to reach the learning criterion and to solve the maintenance and transfer problems were the metrics of learning and transfer efficiency. A sample hint sequence (for Rotation problems) is shown in Appendix A.

No differences were obtained during the learning phase of the study, possibly because of the matching procedures that equated the groups for both mental age and entering competence. However, group differences were apparent during both the maintenance and transfer phases of the study. Furthermore, those differences tended to increase as the similarity of the training and test contexts decreased. The greater the need for flexibility in applying the learned rules, the larger were the differences between retarded and non-retarded children. Thus, in this study, transfer, but not learning, performance did distinguish the different ability groups.

STUDY 2: FERRARA, BROWN, AND CAMPIONE (IN PRESS)

This study included a different ability range and a developmental factor, contrasting third- and fifth-grade children of average and above-average ability. A second inductive reasoning task, letter series completions, was used. One major difference between the series completion and matrices tasks was that in the series completion case a more detailed examination of "transfer distance" was included. The idea, supported by the results of the Campione et al. (1985) study, was that individual or group differences would be more apparent as the transfer distance, or the difference between the learning and transfer situations, increased. Although there have been some suggestions that, for example, retarded children may show "near transfer," they are quite unlikely to show "far transfer" (e.g., Brown, 1978; Campione & Brown, 1977). A nice general statement of this notion was provided by Gagné (1970) in the course of describing lateral transfer:

> In the case of this kind of transfer, the question of how much appears to be a matter of how broadly the individual can generalize what he has learned to a new situation. Presumably, there are limits to the breadth of generalization, which vary with different individuals. One could perhaps think of a whole range of situations of potential applicability of [some learned rules] that display decreasing degrees of similarity to the situation in which the rule had originally been learned. At some point along this dimension of breadth of generalization, a given individual will fail to transfer his previously learned knowledge. Another individual, however, may be able to exhibit transfer more broadly to a wider variety of differing situations.

Although the idea is an attractive one, there are few relevant data available, one problem being that there has frequently been no objective way of determining transfer distance in the domains that have been investigated. The series completion task was one that lent itself nicely to this task. Specifically, "transfer distance" can be defined in terms of the number of transformations distinguishing the learning problems from the various transfer items. Examples of the learning, maintenance, near-transfer, far-transfer, and very far transfer items are shown in Appendix B.

The child's task is to fill in the blanks with letters that continue the pattern that is determined by a certain periodicity and by certain alphabetic relations (*Next*, the appearance of letters in alphabetical sequence; *Identity*, the repetition of letters; and *Backward-next*, the appearance of letters in reverse alphabetical sequence). On the learning items, the children learned to deal with the Next and Identity relations, and with the periodicities of two and four. *Maintenance* items involve no transformations, but are simply novel exemplars of the same problem types learned originally. *Near-transfer* items involve the same principles (relations and periodicities) learned originally but in different combinations. *Far-transfer* items involve the application of a novel periodicity (three) or relation (Backward-next). *Very far transfer* items involve the use of novel principles in a novel context.

There was an overall effect of ability during the learning phase; high-ability children needed fewer hints to learn the initial problems than did the average-ability group. The transfer data, however, were of more interest. The major finding, as expected, was that group differences increased as transfer distance increased. These results are shown in Figure 3.3, where it can be seen that virtually no aid was required on the maintenance items and very little on the near-transfer items; there were no instances of group differences. However, on the far-transfer and very far transfer items, group differences were highly reliable. The results of a series of correlational analyses revealed the same pattern. Correlations between IQ scores and number of hints taken were nonsignificant for maintenance and near transfer, but reliable when far-transfer and very far transfer performance was considered.

STUDY 3: CAMPIONE AND FERRARA (IN PREPARATION)

The next study involved a comparison of retarded and nonretarded children on the series completion task. The results were quite consistent with those of the first two studies. Group differences emerged on both learning and transfer sessions, with the differences being larger during transfer. As in the previous studies, the nonretarded children performed extremely well on the maintenance series, requiring virtually no help to solve those problems; however, the retarded students did need experimenter-provided hints to deal with those problems. On far-transfer and very far transfer tests, the differences between the groups again increased reliably.

Overall, the results of these three studies establish the concurrent validity of the learning and transfer measures. Groups of children of contrasting ability do differ in terms of their learning, and particularly transfer, performance. Less able children tend to need more help to solve sets of original learning

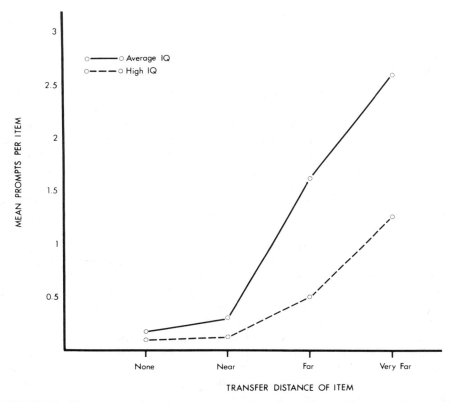

FIGURE 3.3   The mean number of prompts required on the transfer problems as a function of ability and transfer distance.

problems, and then continue to be at a disadvantage when they are required to make flexible use of the rules or principles they have been taught. The greater the amount of flexibility required, the larger the difference between the groups.

The notion of transfer distance does appear to be an important one in terms of diagnosis of group differences. The farther the distance the larger the magnitude of any difference. Furthermore, groups of different ability vary in how "far" they can transfer before they begin to encounter difficulties. In both Studies 1 and 3, where retarded children were involved, those students began to require help even on the maintenance series. Having learned to solve particular sets of problems, they still experienced difficulties when they were asked to solve problems of exactly the same type later in a different context. Children of average and above-average ability, in contrast, handle maintenance (and even near-transfer) items extremely well. It is only when far-transfer problems are given that they begin to need significant amounts of help; and only when these far-transfer problems appear do the average and above-average ability groups begin to differ.

Studies of Predictive Validity

In the next set of studies, we (Bryant, 1982; Bryant, Brown, & Campione, 1983): (a) attempted to extend the previous results to younger children (5-year-olds), and (b) addressed the issue of whether the learning and transfer measures do provide additional diagnostic information about individual subjects beyond their standard ability scores. The ideal way to evaluate predictive validity would be to have measures of initial competence, along with measures of general ability and learning and transfer scores. Then, at some later point in time, we could reassess the students' ability. The question would then be which score(s) best predict later performance—initial competence, general ability, or the learning and transfer indices. In these studies, our general procedure was to give subjects a pretest, learning and transfer sessions, and then a final posttest. The transfer sessions included maintenance, near-transfer, and far-transfer items, again defined in terms of the number of transformations distinguishing the transfer probes from the learning items. The pretest included both evaluations of general ability (subscales from the Wechsler Preschool and Primary Scale of Intelligence [WPPSI] to generate an overall IQ estimate and the Raven Coloured Progessive Matrices) and a task-specific pretest. In the latter, baseline levels of performance on the *items to be included* in the learning and transfer sessions were obtained. The posttest was a read-ministration of this pretest, and our major interest was in the gain that resulted as a consequence of the instruction afforded in the learning and transfer sessions.

Two separate studies were conducted, one involving a simplified version of the matrices task (Bryant, 1982) and the second a simplified version of the series completion task. The major results are shown in Tables 3.1 and 3.2, which portray a series of multiple regression analyses. The first finding to note is that there are significant relations between the ability scores and the learning and transfer metrics, thus replicating the results of the previous studies. Children of higher ability tend to require fewer hints to solve the original sets of problems, and require fewer hints to deal with the transfer problems.

Of more interest are the results of the analyses of the gain scores. In these analyses, the effects of the estimated IQ score and the Raven score were extracted first. In both studies, they did allow a reasonable prediction of the gain score, accounting for around 60% of the variance in that score. Even after the effects of the ability scores were extracted, however, the learning and transfer scores still accounted for significant additional portions of the variance in gain scores; thus, taking the learning and transfer scores into account did provide further diagnostic information about individual chil-

TABLE 3.1.   Multiple Regression Summary Table for Matrices Task

Dependent variable	Independent variable	Correlation (r)	Multiple R	Increment in R²
Training	Information	− .439*	.439	.193*
	Coding	− .043	.587	.152*
Transfer	Information	− .389*	.389	.151*
Residual gain	Estimated IQ	.485*	.485	.235*
	Raven	.472*	.608	.135*
	Training	− .605*	.770	.224*
	Transfer	− .598*	.876	.173*
	Far transfer	− .698*	.884	.014

*Significant at the 5% level.

dren. In the matrices task (Table 3.1), the learning score accounted for an additional 22% of the variance, and the transfer score for an additional 17%. In the series completion task, the learning score did not result in an increase in predictability of gain scores, but the transfer score did account for an additional 22% of the gain variance beyond the ability scores. Alternatively, the simple correlations show that the learning and transfer scores are better predictors of gain score than either of the static ability measures. Finally, within the set of dynamic measures, the tendency is for the transfer measures to be more strongly associated with gain scores than the learning index. This is consistent with the findings from the earlier series where ability group differences were larger on transfer than during learning.

The studies reviewed thus far establish that the dynamic assessment measures do provide diagnostic information about children and can play a role in the *identification* component of diagnosis, but what about the *prescriptive* component? Do the measures suggest any particular sources of problems to which instructional programs might be geared? The answer is, "Yes, to some

TABLE 3.2.   Multiple Regression Summary Table for Series Completion Task

Dependent variable	Independent variable	Correlation (r)	Multiple R	Increment in R²
Training	Block design	− .476*	.476	.227*
	Vocabulary	− .427*	.677	.153*
Transfer	Block design	− .581*	.581	.338*
	Animal house	− .479	.641	.073
Residual gain	Estimated IQ	.521*	.521	.272*
	Raven	.352	.578	.062
	Training	− .461*	.595	.020
	Transfer	− .693*	.745	.221*
	Far transfer	− .558*	.745	.000

*Significant at the 5% level.

extent." Throughout the series of studies, the largest and most consistent effects have concerned aspects of transfer propensity. Transfer measures were most strongly related to ability measures—it was transfer that best discriminated among various ability groups. Transfer flexibility is also the best predictor of gain scores. Our best overall description of differences between more and less successful students would then be in terms of the processes underlying the judicious application of acquired skills to the solution of novel problems. The suggestion is that any program that is designed for use with academically weak students must deal with the transfer issue. It is not sufficient to plan instruction in such a way that rules and principles are learned to some criterion; it is also necessary to attempt to provide these tools in a context that stimulates students' ability to use them with some flexibility.

Although this is a general suggestion, and one that has been around for decades (i.e., teachers are frequently told to "teach for transfer" even if not taught how to do so), what makes it more than a platitude is the fact that some of the instructional principles that are effective at inducing transfer have been identified (e.g., Brown & Campione, 1978, 1981; Palincsar & Brown, 1984) and shown to be effective. These include training in multiple settings; attention to the metacognitive environment of instruction (making the student aware of the skills being taught and of the need to actively monitor and regulate them); and the range of applicability of those skills (teaching the skills in the actual context in which they are to be used, rather than as isolated skills). Furthermore, many programs designed for weak students intentionally *do not* include such components; the idea is that for such students instruction should concentrate on making sure they "know the basic facts," a form of mastery learning that leads to a concentration on drill aimed at perfecting individual skills, quite the opposite of the conclusions we have reached. To buttress this argument, in the section on "Instructional Design" below we review a program of research that has embodied these features and that has produced impressive results. That work has included the general suggestions mentioned here along with more specific suggestions that followed, once the particular domain in question has been specified. Before turning to the instructional work, however, we would like to indicate the ways in which we are attempting to improve the basic assessment procedures.

Current and Future Issues Regarding Assessment

The initial results obtained in our adaptation of Vygotsky's zone of proximal development approach to assessment have been encouraging. Over a series of studies involving different tasks and subjects of widely varying ages and abilities, the learning and transfer metrics have consistently provided useful information about students. They are not only related to ability measures (which are themselves predictive of academic success), but also provide additional information not captured by those tests. They have also consistently led to an emphasis on transfer processes as sources of individual differences, and hence to suggestions about the design of intervention programs aimed at weak students. Our ongoing studies include attempts to improve on the diagnostic properties of the dynamic measures, in terms of both the identification and prescriptive goals. We are also extending the procedures to more academically relevant tasks for both practical and theoretical reasons.

THE ROLE OF PERSONALITY FACTORS

One line of research attempts to improve on the predictive power of dynamic measures by adding information about individuals' attribution styles. The assessment is carried out in a social interactional system where an expert and a novice work together to solve sets of problems. In this situation, students ask for, and are given, help as needed. It is unlikely that their responses in such a social situation are determined by purely "cognitive" factors. On a general level, there appeared to be clear differences between the ways young children (5-year-olds in Bryant's work; Bryant, Brown, & Campione, 1983) and the elderly (French, 1979) responded to the hinting procedures. The elderly appeared threatened by the need for hints and interpreted them as indicating that they were failing on the task; in contrast, the young children appeared more willing to accept the help and still feel that they had solved the problems themselves. There was also some evidence that different children interpreted the input in different ways, some seeking it frequently and others doing everything they could to avoid asking for help so they could in fact be allowed to solve the problems themselves. This, along with some of their spontaneous verbal comments, indicates that children adopt either *learning* or *performance* goals (Dweck & Elliot, 1983; Dweck & Bempechat, 1984) in the task that lead them to react differently to the need for aid. If we could assess those orientations, we should be in a better position to evaluate the children's performance during the assessment sessions. To collect some relevant data, we have redone the Campione et al. (1985) matrices study with a large group of fourth graders. We have also administered to these students a pair of social comparison questionnaires—Crandall, Katkovsky, and Crandall's (1965) Intellectual Achievement Responsibility Scale and Harter's (1983) Perceived Competence Scale: Revised Version. The hypothesis is that, by taking into account an individual's attributions and orientations, more accurate predictions about future performance can be obtained.

We are also attempting to generate richer descriptions of individual students and more detailed and prescriptive pictures of the differences between successful and unsuccessful students. We would like to be able to get rich qualitative descriptions of students' approaches to the problems while maintaining the standardized format that has produced useful quantitative data (i.e., to merge the psychometric and clinical approaches).

One approach that is particularly promising involves having students "talk aloud" about their approaches as they work on the problems. The initial attempt here has shown that fourth graders can handle this requirement quite well, and it appears that adding this component does not materially change the ways in which they approach the problems. (It is also the case that some 5-year-olds provide spontaneous talk-alouds during the testing sessions; the social interactional nature of the assessment process seems to support this nicely. When these talk-alouds do occur, they are quite informative about individual children's approaches and supplement the quantitative data in interesting ways.) Although these data are not fully analyzed, these talk-alouds do appear to provide useful information. For example, successful students tend to spend a considerable amount of time "planning" their moves; they talk about what the answer should look like before they begin to construct their own answer or before they consider the alternatives from which they have to select. Less successful subjects tend to begin their construction activities without fully analyzing the problem; they tend to misclassify problems and proceed in an unsystematic fashion to construct an answer. There are also differences in the ways in which successful and unsuccessful students recover from errors, or from false starts that do not lead to problem solution. We are confident that this information could be used to design more powerful and individually tailored programs of instruction.

EXTENSION TO ACADEMIC DOMAINS

Finally, having shown that our procedures do work, we are extending them to richer and academically more interesting domains—initially, early mathematics. There are several reasons for doing this. First, pragmatically, this domain is one of clear educational significance, and, given that the procedures we have used require a large amount of effort to develop, it makes sense to situate that work in such an area. Assessments of individual readiness are of more immediate interest if obtained in math than if obtained in inductive reasoning domains; and the leap from diagnosis to suggestions for the design of instructional programs is shorter in the case of math.

Second, of more theoretical interest, there already exist a number of detailed analyses of the structure and development of mathematical knowledge. This work makes it possible to obtain a reasonably thorough picture of students' mathematical knowledge before they enter the assessment situation. This is important because it is only when we can assess the quality of an individual's knowledge in some area that we can clearly evaluate the differential contributions of content knowledge and learning–transfer dynamics to the assessment process. For example, some might argue that the differences in learning and transfer efficiency that are uncovered in our studies are actually no more than manifestations of individual differences in content knowledge. Unless we have a good measure of that knowledge, it is difficult to refute that claim. In some current work, Ferrara (Ferrara, Brown & Campione, 1985), as part of her dissertation research, is working on the development of a test of early math knowledge. She is also designing hinting procedures that can be used with simple addition and subtraction problems. With these assessments of knowledge and learning–transfer efficiency in hand, it will be possible to assess the predictive properties of the dynamic measures when students are equated for their entering knowledge.

This leads to the last point. We are interested in devising measures that can predict students' future trajectories. The success of such an enterprise can best be evaluated in an area where there is room for a large amount of improvement; inductive reasoning problems of the type with which we began this research do not serve this purpose well. In contrast, mathematics, even early mathematics, is an area where there is considerable room for improvement; therefore, we can track the progress of students over long periods of time while they are acquiring increasingly sophisticated sets of skills. In this way, stronger tests of the utility of dynamic assessment procedures can be designed.

Instructional Design: The Dynamic Nature of Assessment

In this section, we describe the highlights of a program of research that has concentrated more directly on instruction, and instruction in a particular academic domain. The concentration on a specific domain makes it somewhat easier to specify in more detail the skills distinguishing strong from weak students. The goal was to improve the reading and listening comprehension skills of students experiencing particular difficulties with that task. In the main studies (Brown & Palincsar, 1982, 1986; Palincsar & Brown, 1984), the subjects were seventh-grade students of relatively low overall ability (IQs ranged from 60 to 100, with a mean of around 80) whose reading comprehension scores lagged 1 to 4 years behind those of their age and grade mates.

The general design of the instructional sessions was based on the same Vygotskian principles that guided the development of the assessment procedures. We sought to mirror in the teaching situation the gradual transfer of control of cognitive skills that Vygotsky described. The teacher and students began by working together, with the teacher initially doing most of the work. As the children began to acquire the target skills, they were encouraged to take on more and more responsibility until they were eventually able to employ the skills when working independently.

The specific features of the instruction were based on a considerable amount of prior research indicating that one major difference between skilled and unskilled comprehenders lay in the kinds of active comprehension strategies (both comprehension fostering and comprehension monitoring—see Palincsar & Brown, 1984, for additional description) they brought to the task of reading for meaning. Specifically, good readers, in the course of studying a text, tend to: (a) stop and *summarize* what they have read periodically; (b) formulate *questions* that capture the main idea of what they have just read; (c) attempt to *clarify* any inconsistencies that appear; and (d) *predict* what the author will go on to say. The instructional program that Palincsar and Brown developed was designed to teach these four strategies. Our interest here is with only a portion of the overall program, the way in which assessment of student capabilities is integrated into the overall framework.

If one were to consider the students with comprehension problems and diagnose their competence in the use of the four activities just listed, it would turn out that all would essentially fail the test. There is little evidence of their using these activities without explicit instruction. Furthermore, when asked to engage in the activities, they do so very poorly. We have then a reasonable diagnosis about the sources of their problems. The question is, what do we do about it? How strongly should that diagnosis affect instruction? And how long should that diagnosis be retained? The procedures that Palincsar and Brown developed, termed "reciprocal teaching," provide some insights into these issues.

We do not have the space here to provide the details of their approach. The main point for our purposes is that, in the teaching sessions, the teachers engaged in constant on-line diagnosis and rediagnosis of each student's current level of skill. This was possible because the teaching method forced each student to produce the key activities overtly. When the group was engaged in reading a text, the teacher and students took turns leading a dialogue about the text segment they had just read. The leader of that dialogue was required to summarize what had just been said and formulate a question about the main point of the section. When appropriate, students were also told that they should seek to clarify any inconsistencies or confusions that arose, and to predict what might happen next.

Several features of this interaction are important; they were included to maximize the likelihood that transfer of the target strategies to an array of academic tasks would result. First, note that the students engage in the target activities *in the context of actually reading and understanding texts*. It is also made clear to them what those activities are, why they are useful, and where they can be applied. Furthermore, as the students carry out the activities, the teacher is able to see how well they are executed and diagnose what individuals' current problems, if any, with the particular skills are. In this way, feedback can be provided to each student tailored to particular needs at the moment.

Over time, as student competence increases, the teacher's diagnosis changes, and different types of feedback are provided requiring more advanced responding from the student. In this way, the student is gradually led to master the various activities, until eventually an acceptable level of skill is reached. The teacher begins by doing a large part of the work for the student, but, as the diagnosis changes, progressively more work from the child is required until the teacher can eventually fade out, leaving the student to perform unaided. Our point here is simply that the initial diagnosis (the students do not engage in these activities) needs to be constantly updated, so that the teacher can respond appropriately to the students' needs at any point in time, and thus provide the kind of input necessary to move them one step further toward independent competence.

To see how this works in practice, we can consider a classroom teacher interacting with two remedial seventh graders—her interactions are quite different in the case of Charles, who makes a very weak beginning, and Sara, who has a clear (but inadequate) idea of how to ask questions concerning texts. (Charles: IQ = 70, Reading Comprehension = third grade; Sara: IQ = 84, Reading Comprehension = fourth grade.)

CHARLES

The group is reading a passage about American snakes. Charles has a great deal of difficulty taking his turn leading the dialogue, primarily because he doesn't know how to formulate an appropriate question (see Appendix C): "What is found in the Southeastern snake, also the copperhead, rattlesnakes, vipers—they have—I'm not doing this right." The teacher responds to his difficulty and tells him the main idea: "Do you want to ask something about the pit vipers?" When he still fails to ask an adequate question, she prompts, "What would be a good question about the pit vipers that starts with the word 'why'?" When he still cannot manage it, she models, "How about, 'Why are the snakes called pit vipers?' " After two tries, he copies the teacher's question and she provides praise and encouragement. Even imitating a fully formed question is difficult for Charles initially.

Four days later Charles is still having difficulty asking questions on a passage about spiders. The teacher models one for him, but this time she waits for him to find the main idea himself and attempt to make up a question: "How do they spend most of his time sitting?" The teacher responds, "You're very close. The question would be, 'How does spinner's mate spend most of his time?' Now you ask it." And he does.

Seven days into the procedure, Charles can make up questions with a little help pinpointing main ideas, and by the 11th day he takes his turn as teacher with two questions: "What is the most interesting of the insect eating plants, and where do the plants live at?" After 15 days he produces acceptable questions each time it is his turn to lead the dialogue:

CHARLES: "Why do scientists come to the South Pole to study?"
TEACHER: "Excellent question! That's what the paragraph is all about"

SARA

In contrast to Charles, another student in the group, Sara (see Appendix D), has a clear idea of what kinds of questions occur in schools: "fill in the blanks."

The teacher, preoccupied with Charles, tolerates such questions until the second day and then attempts to take Sara beyond this level:

SARA: "Snakes' backbones can have as many as 300 vertebrates—almost _____ times as many as humans?"

TEACHER: "Not a bad beginning, but I would consider that a question about a detail. Try to avoid 'fill in the blanks' questions. See if next time you can find a main idea question and begin your question with a question word—how, why, when . . ."

On the third day, Sara comes up with a main idea question, but this time she selects a line in the text, "several varieties of snakes live all their lives in the sea," and turns it into a question, "Can snakes live their whole lives in seas?" The teacher again increases her demand and asks, "See if you can ask a question using your own words." For the remainder of the sessions, Sara composes questions in her own words, becoming more and more like the model teacher in her turn.

SUMMARY

The teacher's responses to Charles and Sara are different, and this variation appears to dovetail well with their entering skill levels and rates of improvement. As the teacher diagnoses their growing levels of competence, she asks more and more of Charles and Sara, until they eventually generate good questions with no teacher guidance. Notice that they are never asked to make a large jump, never asked to move quickly to unaided performance. Rather, they are gradually guided to that level, something that can occur only if the teacher continues to update her assessment of their evolving capabilities.

RESULTS OF REPLICATIONS

This program has produced impressive results in a number of replications ranging from experimental studies involving small groups through larger-scale studies involving classroom instruction conducted by teachers with their regular, and frequently large, reading groups. We will highlight some of the major gains here (see Palincsar & Brown, 1984, for more detail). First, throughout the period during which instruction was provided, students took daily tests on their ability to read a science or social studies passage and then answer from memory 10 comprehension questions. Instructed students' performance on these tasks begins at around 30–40% correct and improves steadily until they are consistently scoring 80% correct. Second, there is also evidence that students' newfound skills are being transferred to classroom activities. For example, in one study, all seventh graders in the school (approximately 140) took regular exams, consisting of reading passages and answering comprehension questions, in their science and social studies classes. At the beginning of the intervention, the students in the reciprocal teaching groups scored at around the 15th percentile; by the end they had moved up to above the 50th percentile. Third, students showed evidence of transferring some of the trained skills to laboratory-based tests. There were significant increases in their ability to detect text inconsistencies, generate questions probing the main idea of the passages they read, and write summaries of portions of assigned texts. Fourth, students' standardized reading comprehension scores increased significantly—by an average of just over 2 years.

Although none of the students showed evidence of using the target activities spontaneously at the outset of the studies, and some had extreme difficulty producing them when initially instructed to do so, the teacher was able to monitor the improvement that did occur and provide the kind of practice and feedback needed to continue that improvement. As a result, the students learned to use the skills independently and flexibly, leading to worthwhile improvements in their ability to read and understand texts.

Summary

We have reviewed several lines of research incorporating features of dynamic assessment. In that research we have used dynamic assessment to refer to two distinct sets of activities, one emphasizing the view that assessment attempts should be aimed as directly as possible at the processes underlying successful performance on academic tasks, and the second that the assessment itself should be continuously updated. Our studies conducted thus far have shown that the measures of learning and transfer efficiency that we generate in our adaptation of Vygotsky's zone of proximal development testing procedures do possess both concurrent and predictive validity. They have also indicated that the best predictors of the extent to which individuals are likely to profit from instruction are their initial responses to instruction and (even more sensitive) the extent to which they can transfer their newly learned skills to novel situations.

In the context of instruction, we have argued that, whereas early diagnoses can provide important information about the kinds of educational programs needed with weak students, those diagnoses need to be continuously updated if they are to contribute meaningfully to instructional goals. Diagnosis should not be used to pigeonhole students, but rather to provide information indicating how instruction should change over time.

ACKNOWLEDGMENTS

Preparation of this manuscript and the research reported therein were supported by Grants HD-05951, HD-06864, and HD-15808 from the National Institute of Child Health and Human Development. We would like to acknowledge the considerable input from Nancy Bryant, Roberta Ferrara, and Annemarie Palincsar at various points in the program.

REFERENCES

Brown, A. L. (1974). The role of strategic behavior in retardate memory. In N. R. Ellis (Ed.), *International review of research in mental retardation* (Vol. 7, pp. 55–111). New York: Academic Press.

Brown, A. L. (1978). Knowing when, where, and how to remember: A problem of metacognition. In R. Glaser (Ed.), *Advances in instructional psychology* (Vol. 1, pp. 77–165). Hillsdale, NJ: Erlbaum.

Brown, A. L., Bransford, J. D., Ferrara, R. A., & Campione, J. C. (1983). Learning, remembering, and understanding. In J. H. Flavell & E. M. Markman (Eds.), *Handbook of child psychology* (4th ed.), *Vol. 3: Cognitive development* (pp. 515–529). New York: Wiley.

Brown, A. L., & Campione, J. C. (1978). Permissible inferences from the outcome of training studies in cognitive development research. *Quarterly Newsletter of the Institute for Comparative Human Development, 2,* 46–53.

Brown, A. L., & Campione, J. C. (1981). Inducing flexible thinking: A problem of access. In M. Friedman, J. P. Das, & N. O'Connor (Eds.), *Intelligence and learning* (pp. 515–529). New York: Plenum Press.

Brown, A. L., & Campione, J. C. (1984). Three faces of transfer: Implications for early competence, individual differences, and instruction. In M. Lamb, A. Brown, & B. Rogoff (Eds.), *Advances in developmental psychology* (Vol. 3, pp. 143–192). Hillsdale, NJ: Erlbaum.

Brown, A. L., & Campione, J. C. (1986). Cognitive science and learning disabilities. *American Psychologist, 41*(10), 1059–1068.

Brown, A. L., & Ferrara, R. A. (1985). Diagnosing zones of proximal development. In J. Wertsch (Ed.), *Culture, communication, and cognition: Vygotskian perspectives* (pp. 273–305). Cambridge, MA: Cambridge University Press.

Brown, A. L., & French, L. A. (1979). The zone of potential development: Implications for intelligence testing in the year 2000. *Intelligence, 3,* 253–271.

Brown, A. L., & Palincsar, A. S. (1982). Inducing strategic learning from texts by means of informed, self-control training: *Topics in Learning and Learning Disabilities, 2*(1), 1–17.

Brown, A. L., & Palincsar, A. S. (1986). Reciprocal teaching of comprehension strategies: A natural history of one program for enhancing learning. In J. Borkowski & J. D. Day (Eds.), *Intelligence and cognition in special children: Comparative studies of giftedness, mental retardation, and learning disabilities.* New York: Ablex.

Bryant, N. R. (1982). *Preschool children's learning and transfer of matrices problems: A study of proximal development.* Unpublished master's thesis, University of Illinois.

Bryant, N. R., Brown, A. L., & Campione, J. C. (1983, April). *Preschool children's learning and transfer of matrices problems: Potential for improvement.* Paper presented at the Society for Research in Child Development meeting, Detroit.

Budoff, M. (1974). *Learning potential and educability among the educable mentally retarded* (Final Report Project No. 312312). Cambridge, MA: Research Institute for Educational Problems, Cambridge Mental Health Association.

Campione, J. C., & Brown, A. L. (1977). Memory and metamemory development in educable retarded children. In R. V. Kail, Jr. & J. W. Hagen (Eds.), *Perspectives on the development of memory and cognition* (pp. 367–406). Hillsdale, NJ: Erlbaum.

Campione, J. C., & Brown, A. L. (1978). Toward a theory of intelligence: Contributions from research with retarded children. *Intelligence, 2,* 279–304.

Campione, J. C., & Brown, A. L. (1984). Learning ability and transfer propensity as sources of individual differences in intelligence. In P. H. Brooks, R. D. Sperber, & C. McCauley (Eds.), *Learning and cognition in the mentally retarded* (pp. 265–294). Baltimore: University Park Press.

Campione, J. C., Brown, A. L., & Bryant, N. R. (1985). Individual differences in learning and memory. In R. J. Sternberg (Ed.), *Human abilities: An information processing approach* (pp. 103–126). New York: Freeman.

Campione, J. C., Brown, A. L., & Ferrara, R. A. (1982). Mental retardation and intelligence. In R. J. Sternberg (Ed.), *Handbook of human intelligence* (pp. 392–490). Cambridge, MA: Harvard University Press.

Campione, J. C., Brown, A. L., Ferrara, R. A., Jones, R. S., & Steinberg, E. (1985). Differences between retarded and non-retarded children in transfer following equivalent learning performance: Breakdowns in flexible use of information. *Intelligence, 9*, 297–315.

Carlson, J. S., & Wiedl, K. H. (1978). Use of testing-the-limits procedures in the assessment of intellectual capabilities in children with learning difficulties. *American Journal of Mental Deficiency, 82*, 559–564.

Carlson, J. S., & Wiedl, K. H. (1979) Toward a differential testing approach: Testing-the-limits employing the Raven matrices. *Intelligence, 3*, 323–344.

Crandall, V. C., Katkovsky, W., & Crandall, V. J. (1965). Children's beliefs in their own control of reinforcements in intellectual-academic achievement situations. *Child Development, 36*, 91–109.

Dweck, C. S., & Elliot, E. S. (1983). Achievement motivation. In E. M. Hetherington (Ed.), *Handbook of child psychology* (4th ed.); *Vol. 4: Socialization, personality, and social development* (pp. 642–692). New York: Wiley & Sons.

Dweck, C. S., & Bempechat, J. (1984). Children's theories of intelligence: Consequences for learning. In S. G. Paris, G. M. Olson, & H. W. Stevenson (Eds.), *Learning and motivation in the classroom*. Hillsdale, NJ: Erlbaum.

Ferrara, R. A., Brown, A. L., & Campione, J. C. (in press). Children's learning and transfer of inductive reasoning rules: Studies in proximal development. *Child Development*.

Feuerstein, R. (1979). *The dynamic assessment of retarded performers: The learning potential assessment device, theory, instruments, and techniques*. Baltimore: University Park Press.

French, L. A. (1979). *Cognitive consequences of education: Transfer of training in the elderly*. Unpublished doctoral dissertation, University of Illinois.

Gagné, R. M. (1970). *The conditions of learning* (2nd ed.). NY: Holt, Rinehart, & Winston.

Harter, S. (1983). *Supplementary description of the self-perception profile for children: Revision of the perceived competence scale for children*. Unpublished manuscript, University of Denver, Denver, CO.

Mann, L. (1979). *On the trail of process*. New York: Grune & Stratton.

Palincsar, A. S., & Brown, A. L. (1984). Reciprocal teaching of comprehension-fostering and monitoring activities. *Cognition and Instruction, 1*(2), 117–175.

Vlasova, T. A., & Pevzner, M. S. (Eds.). (1971). *Children with temporary retardation in development*. Moscow: Pedagogika.

Vygotsky, L. S. (1978). *Mind in society: The development of higher psychological processes* (M. Cole, V. John-Steiner, S. Scribner, & E. Souberman, Eds. and Trans.). Cambridge, MA: Harvard University Press.

Woodrow, H. (1917a). Practice and transference in normal and feeble-minded children. 1. Practice. *Journal of Educational Psychology, 8*, 85–96.

Woodrow, H. (1917b). Practice and transference in normal and feeble-minded children. 2. Transference. *Journal of Educational Psychology, 8*, 151–165.

Woodrow, H. (1946). The ability to learn. *Psychological Review, 53*, 147–158.

Wozniak, R. H. (1975). Psychology and education of the learning disabled child in the Soviet Union. In W. Cruikshank & D. P. Hallahan (Eds.), *Research and theory in minimal cerebral dysfunction and learning disability*. Syracuse, NY: Syracuse University Press.

Zabramna, S. D. (Ed.). (1971). *Otbor detei vo vspomogatel'nye shkoly* [The selection of children for schools for the mentally retarded]. Moscow: Prosveshchenie.

Appendix A: A Sample Hint Sequence for a Rotation Problem

HINT 1:   "This problem is called a turning problem. Think about why it might be called that. . . . Do you know how to solve the problem now or do you want another hint?

HINT 2:   "This is row 1. Put picture 1 in the practice box. Touch IN. Touch the picture. Now try to make the picture look like the second picture." (if successful) "You did it. Now make it look like the last picture." (If child cannot make picture 3, PLATO will give hint 2A.)

   HINT 2A: "This is row 1. This is picture 1. Watch how it turns. Watch again. Now you do it." (If child cannot repeat the above demonstration, PLATO will give hint 2B.)

   HINT 2B: "This is row 1. Let's try to make the last picture in the row. Put picture 1 in the practice box. Touch ⌃ . Touch ⌃ again. Good. You have made the last picture in row 1. Now try to make the missing picture."

HINT 3:   "Now let's look at row 2. Put picture 1 of row 2 in the practice box. Now make it look like picture 2." (If child does not respond correctly PLATO will display TOUCH ⌃ .) "You did it. Now make the picture in the practice box look like the last picture in row 2. Now try the problem again." (If child cannot make picture 3 PLATO will give hint 3A.)

   HINT 3A: "Touch ⌃ . Touch ⌃ again."

HINT 4:   "You used the turning rule to make the last picture in rows 1 and 2. The last picture in row 3 is missing. Try to use the same rule to make the missing picture in row 3." (If child cannot do so, PLATO will give hint 4A.)

   HINT 4A: "This is the shape you work with." (PLATO displays appropriate shape.) "Put it in the practice box. Touch the first picture in row 3. Now touch ⌃ . Now touch ⌃ again. That is correct. Touch DONE."

EXPLANATION (given with every original learning problem): "Good. Look at all three rows. The turning rule is used in each row. And you used the turning rule to make the missing picture. You turned picture 1 to get picture 2. Then you turned picture 2 to get picture 3."

In original learning, the child continues to solve rotation problems until he or she can do *two* problems in a row without any hints. Then PLATO will move ahead to the first imposition problem.

Appendix B: Examples of Learning, Maintenance, and Transfer Items

Problem type	Pattern[a]	Sample problem	Correct answer
Original Learning	NN	N G O H P I Q J _ _ _ _	(R K S L)
	NINI	P Z U F Q Z V F _ _ _ _	(R Z W F)
Maintenance (Learned pattern types; new instantiations)			
Near Transfer (Learned relations and periodicities, but in new combinations)			
	NI	D V E V F V G V _ _ _ _	(H V I V)
	NNNN	V H D P W I E Q _ _ _ _	(X J F R)
Far Transfer (New relation, Backward-next; or new periodicity, three letters)			
	BN	U C T D S E R F _ _ _ _	(Q G P H)
	NBNI	J P B X K O C X _ _ _ _	(L N D X)
	NIN	P A D Q A E R A _ _ _ _	(F S A G)
Very Far Transfer (Backward-next as well as Next relations and "period" of two letters, but relations must be sought between strings of letters rather than within a string)			

Instructions: Pretend that you are a spy. You want to send the message in the first line below in a secret code that only your friends will understand. Someone has begun coding the message for you on the second line. Try to figure out the secret code and finish coding the message by filling in the blanks with the letters that follow the code.

S I X S H I P S G O N E

T H Y R I H Q R _ _ _ _   (H N O D)

[a]The letters themselves in the pattern notations refer to the alphabetic relations (i.e., *N* = Next, *I* = Identity, *B* = Backward-next). The number of letters in each pattern notation equals the period.

Appendix C: The Acquisition of Question Asking by a Weak Seventh-Grade Student (Charles)

Day 1

TEXT:

> The water moccasin, somewhat longer than the copperhead, is found in the southeastern states. It lives in swampy regions. It belongs, as do also the copperhead and the rattlesnake, to a group of poisonous snakes called pit vipers. They have pits between their eyes and their nostrils which, because they are sensitive to heat, help the snakes tell when they are near a warm-blooded animal. Another name for the water moccasin is "cottonmouth." This name comes from the white lining of the snake's mouth.

s: What is found in the southeastern snakes, also the copperhead, rattlesnakes, vipers—they have—I'm not doing this right.
T: All right. Do you want to know about the pit vipers?
s: Yeah.
T: What would be a good question about the pit vipers that starts with the word "why?"
s: (*No response*)
T: How about, "Why are the snakes called pit vipers?"
s: Why do they want to know that they are called pit vipers?
T: Try it again.
s: Why do they, pit vipers in a pit?
T: How about, "Why do they call the snakes pit vipers?"
s: Why do they call the snakes pit vipers?
T: There you go! Good for you.

Day 4

TEXT:

> Spinner's mate is much smaller than she, and his body is dull brown. He spends most of his time sitting at one side of her web.

s: (*No question*)
T: What's this paragraph about?
s: Spinner's mate. How do spinner's mate . . .
T: That's good. Keep going.
s: How do spinner's mate is smaller than . . . How am I going to say that?
T: Take your time with it. You want to ask a question about spinner's mate and what he does, beginning with the word "how."
s: How do they spend most of his time sitting?
T: You're very close. The question would be, "How does spinner's mate spend most of his time:" Now, you ask it.
s: How does spinner's mate spend most of his time?

Day 7

TEXT:

> Perhaps you are wondering where the lava and other volcanic products come from. Deep within our earth there are pockets of molten rock called *magma*. Forced upward in part by gas pressure, this molten rock continually tries to reach the surface. Eventually—by means of cracks in the crustal rocks or some similar zone of weakness—the magma may break out of the ground. It then flows from the vent as lava, or spews skyward as dense clouds of lava particles.

s: How does the pressure from below push the mass of hot rock against the opening? Is that it?

t: Not quite. Start your question with, "What happens when?"

s: What happens when the pressure from below pushes the mass of hot rock against the opening?

t: Good for you! Good job.

Day 11

TEXT:

> One of the most interesting of the insect-eating plants is the Venus's flytrap. This plant lives in only one small area of the world—the coastal marshes of North and South Carolina. The Venus's flytrap doesn't look unusual. Its habits, however, make it truly a plant wonder.

s: What is the most interesting of the insect eating plants, and where do the plants live at?

t: Two excellent questions! They are both clear and important questions. Ask us one at a time now.

Day 15

TEXT:

> Scientists also come to the South Pole to study the strange lights that glow overhead during the Antarctic night. (It's a cold and lonely world for the few hardy people who "winter over" the polar night.) These "southern lights" are caused by the Earth acting like a magnet on electrical particles in the air. They are clues that may help us understand the Earth's core and the upper edges of its blanket of air.

s: Why do scientists come to the south pole to study?

t: Excellent question! That is what this paragraph is all about.

Appendix D: Improvement in Question Asking by a More Competent
Seventh-Grade Student (Sara)

Day 2

TEXT:

> The snake's skeleton and parts of its body are very flexible—something like a rubber hose with bones. A snake's backbone can have as many as 300 vertebrae, almost ten times as many as a human's. These vertebrae are connected by loose and rubbery tissues that allow easy movement. Because of this bendable, twistable spinal construction, a snake can turn its body in almost any direction at almost any point.

s: Snakes' backbones can have as many as 300 vertebrates—almost _____ times as many as humans.

t: Not a bad beginning, but I would consider that a question about a detail. Try to avoid "fill in the blank" questions. See if next time you can find a main idea question and begin your question with a question word—how, why, when . . .

Day 3

TEXT:

> There are snakes in nearly all parts of the world. Some snakes prefer warm, arid desert areas. Others prefer leafy forests, fields, and woodlands. Some stay in areas near water and are fine swimmers. Then there are several varieties that live all their lives in the sea.

s: Can snakes live their whole lives in seas?

t: See if you can ask a question using your own words.

Day 4

TEXT:

> The other kind of camel—the one with two humps—is the *Bactrian*. Its home country is the Gobi Desert of northeastern Asia. The Bactrian has shorter legs and longer wool than the one-humped camel. It also has stronger, more rugged feet. This is important because instead of having sand to walk on, the Bactrian camels live in rough and rocky parts of the world.

s: Where is the Bactrian found?

t: Good for you.

Day 6

TEXT:
> When most full-grown spiders want to travel, they have to walk on their eight legs. But some small kinds of spiders, and many young ones, use an easier way. They climb up on bushes, fence posts, or weed stems and spin streamers of silk. When the wind catches the silk and blows it away, each spider tightly holds onto his own streamer. The silk streamer carries him through the air as if it were a parachute or a balloon.

S: I think I have another. When it's traveling, what do they compare the spider to?
T: An interesting question.

Day 11

TEXT:
> The young caterpillar's first meal is its own eggshell. Then it eats a leaf and each day eats more and more food. After a few days, the caterpillar becomes too large for its skin. A new skin forms beneath the first one, the old skin comes open and, like a snake, the caterpillar wriggles its way out of the split skin. Then the caterpillar goes on eating leaves or other kinds of food. When the new skin becomes too tight for the growing body, it again splits and comes off. By then the caterpillar is covered by another skin. This eating and shedding goes on for several weeks. The old skin may be replaced by a new one four or five times. Each time the skin is shed, the size and color of the caterpillar change.

S: Why does the caterpillar's skin split?
T: Excellent question. That was the point of the entire paragraph.

4

Implications of Vygotsky's Theories for Dynamic Assessment

NORRIS MINICK

Development of Dynamic Assessment Procedures

Contemporary efforts to develop dynamic assessment procedures can trace their historical roots to a variety of geographical locations and theoretical traditions, yet they have a common source in the practical problems that arise in evaluating and educating children who perform poorly in school or on more traditional static tests of psychological development or intellectual potential. As Campione, Brown, Ferrara, and Bryant (1984) have noted, attempts to develop dynamic assessment procedures have consistently been motivated by the conviction that static approaches to the assessment of learning ability or learning potential have failed to provide the kinds of information that educators need in order to facilitate the psychological development and the educational advancement of these children (p. 79).

This connection between a direct involvement with these kinds of children and a rejection of traditional static approaches to assessment is not accidental. Historically, static measures of learning potential came into wide use because they were thought to provide a means of selecting personnel for educational, military, and industrial placement in a way that would maximize the return on a given investment in training or instruction. In this context, the difference between an individual's current level of mental functioning and an individual's ultimate potential for learning is often not the primary consideration. The fact that two individuals have a similar potential for development may be less important than the fact that there are differences in the levels of performance they currently manifest. This is not the case where the primary concern is that of helping children realize their full developmental and educational potential. When faced with a child who performs poorly in school, the educator wants to know whether these difficulties are a function of the child's ultimate potential for learning, the child's current level of readiness as defined by previous learning opportunities, or other factors associated with the social context of schooling. Moreover, the educator wants a qualitative assessment

Norris Minick. Center for Psychosocial Studies, Chicago, Illinois, and University of Chicago, Chicago, Illinois.

of the child's current level of functioning and some indication of the kinds of instruction that might facilitate development.

It is the failure of static measures of intellectual potential and development to provide this information that has stimulated work in dynamic assessment. All those involved in the dynamic assessment movement recognize the need to develop assessment devices that provide: (a) direct measures of the child's potential for learning and development, (b) information on the processes that lead to the child's success or failure on cognitive tasks, and (c) information on what might be done to facilitate the child's education and development. Moreover, the procedures that have been designed by those involved in the dynamic assessment movement to provide these kinds of information share a focus on the extent to which the child benefits from attempts by the examiner to facilitate performance. It is these concerns and approaches that provide the common foundation of the work that has been carried out by those associated with the dynamic assessment movement.

If we move beyond these common goals and assumptions to the design of specific assessment techniques, however, two distinct traditions can be distinguished within this movement. The techniques that have been developed by scholars such as Brown and Campione (e.g., Brown & Ferrara, 1985; Brown & French, 1979; Campione et al., 1984) or Budoff (e.g., Budoff & Friedman, 1964; Budoff & Hamilton, 1976) have been designed to provide quantitative measures of a child's learning ability or learning efficiency. These techniques are based on a test-train-retest format. The child is first tested while working alone in order to provide a baseline measure of skills on the experimental task. Subsequently, the examiner provides a controlled protocol of assistance and instruction while the child is working on comparable tasks. Finally, the child is observed while working alone to assess the amount of benefit from this instruction. The product is a quantitative measure of the child's ability to be modified by instruction.

In contrast, although Feuerstein and his colleagues recognize the need to develop quantitative measures of learning potential (Feuerstein, 1979; Feuerstein, Miller, Rand, & Jensen, 1981), they have resisted modifying their own assessment techniques in ways that would allow them to produce these kinds of quantitative measures. For example, Feuerstein (1979) prefers not to test his subjects prior to training in order to establish baseline measures, arguing that the child's failures on these tests makes it difficult for the examiner to involve the child in subsequent cooperative work on similar tasks (p. 321). Similarly, Feuerstein (1979) insists on maintaining flexibility in the examiner's interaction with the child, arguing that the organization and content of the interaction should be determined by the child's need for assistance rather than by an established protocol (p. 100). Feuerstein makes a strong case for the view that these measures are necessary: (a) for developing the positive relationship between the child and examiner that is essential to the teaching–learning process, (b) for identifying the strengths and weaknesses reflected in the child's efforts to carry out the task, and (c) for providing each child with the specific kinds of assistance that are required in order to attain the highest possible level of performance. Without baseline measures or a standard assessment protocol, however, Feuerstein is unable to produce the kinds of quantitative measures that are the focus of the work of Brown, Campione, and Budoff

Thus, although all those involved in developing dynamic assessment techniques recognize the need for both quantitative measures of learning potential and qualitative analyses of the child's psychological processes, important differences exist in current assessment procedures that can only be understood by asking which of these goals dominated the processes through which the procedures were designed and developed. Feuerstein has sacrificed the capacity to provide quantitative measures of learning ability in his effort to gain access to information on the qualitative nature of the child's psychological processes and to information on the kind of assistance that the child needs to attain more adequate levels of performance. Brown, Campione, and Budoff have sacrificed sensitivity to these qualitative factors in their effort to obtain valid, reliable, and quantifiable measures of learning ability. From the educator's perspective, these quantitative and qualitative data complement one another. In designing assessment procedures, however, techniques that maximize access to one type of information often minimize access to the other.

A recognition of the goals, assumptions, and assessment techniques that characterize these two approaches to dynamic assessment is essential to any attempt to understand the significance of Vygotsky's concept of the zone of proximal development (ZPD) for the dynamic assessment movement. In the West, the concept of the ZPD has influenced the development of dynamic assessment techniques primarily through the work of Brown, Campione, and Budoff. These efforts, in turn, were stimulated by similar work in the Soviet Union. Budoff traces his early work in dynamic assessment to a brief discussion of the ZPD in a paper written by Luria (1961), a close collaborator of Vygotsky's in the 1920s and 1930s (Budoff & Friedman, 1964, pp. 434–435). Similarly, the early efforts of Brown and Campione in dynamic assessment were attempts to replicate research that was being carried out in the late 1970s by Luria's colleagues in Moscow (see Brown & Ferrara, 1985; Brown & French, 1979). Thus, in both the West and the Soviet Union, attempts to translate the concept of the ZPD into assessment practice have consistently been associated with the development of procedures that are designed to produce quantitative measures of learning efficiency or learning potential.

In my view, these applications of the concept of the ZPD are inconsistent with Vygotsky's theoretical formulations and with his suggestions concerning how the concept might be used in assessment practice. In outlining the concept of the ZPD, Vygotsky was proposing a new theoretical framework for analyzing the child's current state of development and for predicting the next or proximal level of development that the child might be expected to attain.[1] That is, Vygotsky was concerned not with the quantitative assessment of learning ability or intelligence, but with the qualitative assessment of psychological processes and the dynamics of their development. Thus, despite its historical connections with the work of Brown, Campione, and Budoff, Vygotsky's concept of the ZPD, and the system of theory and research of which it is part, have more direct implications for the kinds of assessment problems that have been addressed in the work of Feuerstein and his colleagues than they have for the task of producing quantitative measures of a child's learning efficiency or learning potential.

Of course, my purpose in developing this argument is neither to criticize the work of Brown, Campione, and Budoff (or that of their counterparts in the Soviet Union) nor to question its significance to the dynamic assessment movement. The validity and the significance of this work has been clearly demonstrated irrespective of any connections it may or may not have with Vygotsky's ideas. On the other hand, the historical association of this work with Vygotsky's concept of the ZPD tends to obscure the very real implications that his concept has for the qualitative assessment of psychological processes and psychological development. As a consequence, my discussion of the significance of the concept of the ZPD for dynamic assessment must begin with an attempt to differentiate Vygotsky's understanding of the concept from that which currently dominates attempts to apply it in assessment practice.

The ZPD: Current Interpretations and Applications in Assessment

Suppose I investigate two children upon entrance into school, both of whom are ten years old chronologically and eight years old in terms of mental development. Can I say that they are the same age mentally? Of course. What does this mean? It means that they can independently deal with tasks up to the degree of difficulty that has been standardized for the eight-year-old level. If I stop at this point, people would imagine that the subsequent course of development and of school learning for these children will be the same, because it depends on their intellect. . . . Now imagine that I do not terminate my study at this point, but only begin it. . . . Suppose I show . . . [these children] various ways of dealing with the problem . . . that the children solve the problem with my assistance. Under these circumstances it turns out that the first child can deal with problems up to a twelve-year-old's level, the second up to a nine-year-old's. Now are these children mentally the same?

When it was first shown that the capability of children with equal levels of mental development to learn under a teacher's guidance varied to a high degree, it became apparent that those children were not mentally the same age and that the subsequent course of their learning would obviously be different. This dif-

---

1. The term "proximal" has traditionally been used in translating the Russian term "blizhaishei" in this context, though the term "nearest" would represent a more literal translation.

ference between twelve and eight, or between nine and eight, is what we call *the zone of proximal development. It is the distance between the actual developmental level as determined by independent problem solving and the level of potential development as determined through problem solving under adult guidance or in collaboration with more capable peers.* (Vygotsky, 1935/1978a, pp. 85–86)

This statement of the concept of the ZPD provided the point of departure for Luria's early proposals concerning the development of dynamic assessment techniques (Luria, 1961, pp. 6–7) and continues to play that role in the work of Brown, Campione, and their colleagues (Brown & Ferrara, 1985, p. 273). Based on a reading of this statement alone, it is not clear whether Vygotsky views the analysis of the ZPD as a means of assessing the child's learning ability or sees it as a means of producing a qualitative assessment of the child's current state of psychological development. However, a more basic thesis is reflected clearly in this statement, specifically, the thesis that *assessment practices that focus entirely on the child's unaided performance fail to tap important differences in mental functioning that can be identified by analyzing how the child responds to assistance from adults or more capable peers.* As I suggested earlier, this thesis is fundamental to all current approaches to dynamic assessment. More significant in the present context, it represents a real and very important link between Vygotsky's concept of the ZPD and the dynamic assessment techniques that have been derived from it.

Nevertheless, if we consider the nature of the psychological characteristics that are thought to be tapped by analyzing the child's collaborative activity or if we consider the methods that are to be used to tap them, we can begin to see the differences between Vygotsky's understanding of the ZPD and that of those who have applied this concept in assessment practice. Once again, the central issue is whether this concept is to be used in producing a quantitative measure of learning ability comparable to traditional IQ measures or in producing a qualitative assessment of the child's current state of development.

In the paper that stimulated Budoff's work in dynamic assessment, Luria (1961) argued that the retarded population includes not only truly "feeble-minded" children but children with secondary retardation caused by factors such as hearing deficits that have interfered with the normal developmental process. Luria suggested that a dynamic approach to assessment based on Vygotsky's concept of the ZPD might prove more useful than more traditional static tests in differentiating truly "feebleminded" children from those with a more substantial but as yet unrealized potential for development.

To clarify this idea, Luria (1961, pp. 6–7) adapted the illustration outlined by Vygotsky in the statement quoted above. Luria asked his readers to consider three children with IQs of 70. When these children work on their own, they perform at similar levels. When they are asked to carry out a task with the examiner's assistance, however, one benefits little from this assistance while the other two perform at significantly higher levels than when working alone. Finally, when each of these children is asked to carry out the task independently following the instruction session, the first child continues to perform at the initial low level, the second drops back to this level from that which had been achieved with assistance, and the third continues to work independently at the higher level.

In this statement, Luria modified Vygotsky's illustration of assessment in the ZPD by introducing: (a) a test following the collaborative work between the child and the examiner, and (b) a third child whose behavior is differentiated from that of the second on the basis of this test. Although they appear to be modest, these modifications are symptomatic of a perspective on the ZPD and its significance for assessment that is very different from Vygotsky's. Luria argued that both the child's ability to work with adult assistance and the extent to which subsequent independent performance improves as a result of that assistance provide information that is useful in differentiating groups of low-IQ children. Implicit in his paper, however, is an emphasis on comparing "pretest" and "posttest" scores, an emphasis on measuring the extent to which the child's independent performance improves as a consequence of the examiner's assistance in the second phase of the assessment process. Thus, the interaction between the adult and child loses the central position it had in Vygotsky's analysis. It is transformed into a training phase in an assessment procedure that is designed to measure how much a child benefits from instruction, a procedure that is designed to differentiate a child's learning ability and ultimate intellectual potential from current performance capabilities.

This view of the ZPD and its application in dynamic assessment has been developed more fully and more clearly in the work of Brown, Campione, and their colleagues. In a recent article, Campione et al. (1984) introduced the concept of the ZPD as a means of assessing "the child's readiness or intellectual maturity in a specified domain" (p. 78). In my view, this statement correctly reflects Vygotsky's perspective on the ZPD. As the authors' move from their discussion of Vygotsky's ideas to their discussion of the application of these ideas in assessment research, however, they begin to treat the analysis of the ZPD as a means of assessing not readiness or intellectual maturity but learning efficiency and transfer propensity.

> We wished to test Vygotsky's assumption that assessments of how students respond to socially structured instruction within some domain of interest would provide important diagnostic information about them. We were interested in both the initial acquisition of information and in its later flexible use. . . . Again, the notion is that, even if all children perform at the same (poor) level initially, the ease with which they acquire relevant information and put it to use will allow us to distinguish children who are likely to experience later problems in that area from children who are not.
> Vygotsky's point is that, while how much a student knows about some area (as assessed on the static test) is a powerful predictor of performance in that

area, *children also differ in how efficiently they learn.* [italics added] (Campione et al., 1984, p. 79)

Following this statement, Campione et al. (1984) discussed early definitions of intelligence that emphasized learning capacity and learning efficiency. They also discussed previous attempts to assess these factors directly by measuring the child's ability to learn. The authors' use of the concept of the ZPD in assessment is then presented as an attempt to succeed where these earlier attempts had failed (1984, p. 80).

Without questioning the importance of this problem or the validity and utility of the attempts of Brown, Campione, and their colleagues to solve it, I would argue that the conceptual connections of this work with Vygotsky's understanding of the ZPD are limited. Like Luria, Budoff, and their colleagues, Brown and Campione share Vygotsky's conviction that analyzing how the child responds to instruction provides diagnostic information that is inaccessible to more traditional assessment procedures. In outlining the concept of the ZPD, however, Vygotsky's point was not that "children differ in how efficiently they learn" (Campione et al., 1984, p. 79) but that children differ in their current state of development in ways that cannot, in principle, be assessed by techniques that are limited to analyzing children's performance when they are working alone.

Vygotsky's Conception of the ZPD

Vygotsky's perspective on the ZPD is reflected clearly in all that he wrote on the topic.[2] However, a good place to begin in the context of the present discussion is Vygotsky's introduction of this concept in his classic monograph, *Thinking and Speech* (Vygotsky, 1934/1986, pp. 203–204).[3] In many respects, this statement of the concept of the ZPD parallels the one that provided the point of departure for the work of Brown and Campione. However, several ideas that are central to Vygotsky's understanding of the ZPD are expressed more clearly in *Thinking and Speech*.

> Psychological research on the problem of instruction is usually limited to establishing the level of the child's mental development. The sole basis for determining

2. To my knowledge, Vygotsky discussed this concept in detail in four papers. The primary source used by Brown and Campione was a paper published in an edited volume of translations entitled *Mind in Society* (Vygotsky, 1935/1978a). This paper was taken from a collection of Vygotsky's papers on education and mental development (Vygotsky, 1935). A second discussion of the ZPD is found in Vygotsky's classic volume *Thinking and Speech* (Vygotsky, 1934/1986, pp. 246–255). A third source is an article entitled "The Problems of Age" that has only recently been published in Russian (Vygotsky, 1984a). The fourth source, entitled "The problem of instruction and mental development in the school age," is also untranslated (Vygotsky, 1956).

3. Vygotsky (1934/1986) and Vygotsky (1934/1962) are both translations of a volume entitled *Myshlenie i Rech'* [Thinking and Speech], which was first published in Russian in 1934. The latter, however, is a much abbreviated edition of the original work, less than half its length. Unavoidably, many arguments critical to understanding Vygotsky's perspectives are not contained in Vygotsky (1934/1962), including much of his discussion of the ZPD.

this level of development is tasks that he solves independently. This means that we focus on what the child has and knows today. Using this approach, we can establish only what has already matured, we can determine only the level of the child's *actual* development. To determine the state of the child's development on this basis alone, however, is insufficient. The state of development is never defined only by what has matured. If the gardener decides only to evaluate the matured or harvested fruits of the apple tree, he cannot determine the state of his orchard. The maturing trees must also be taken into consideration. Correspondingly, the psychologist must not limit his analysis to functions that have matured; he must consider those that are in the process of maturation. If he is to fully evaluate the state of the child's development, the psychologist must consider not only the actual level of development but *the zone of proximal development*. How can this be accomplished?

When we determine the level of actual development, we use tasks that require independent resolution. These tasks function as indices of fully formed or fully matured functions. How, then, do we apply this new method? Assume that we have determined the mental age of two children to be eight years. However, we do not stop with this. Rather, we attempt to determine how each of these children will solve tasks that were meant for older children. We assist each child through demonstration, through leading questions, and by introducing the initial elements of the task's solution. With this help or collaboration from the adult, one of these children solves problems characteristic of a twelve year old while the other solves problems only at a level typical of a nine year old. This difference between the child's mental ages, this difference between the child's actual level of development and the level of performance that he achieves in collaboration with the adult, defines the zone of proximal development. In this example, the zone can be expressed by the number 4 for one child and by the number 1 for the other. Can we assume that these children stand at identical levels of mental development, that the state of their development coincides? Obviously not. (Vygotsky, 1934/1986, pp. 203–204)

Two important aspects of Vygotsky's concept of the ZPD are expressed clearly in this statement. First, Vygtosky distinguished two aspects of a child's current state or current level of mental functioning. Specifically, he distinguished between functions that are fully mature and functions that are currently in the process of maturing. The former are manifested in a child's independent cognitive activity. They can therefore be assessed by using traditional static assessment techniques. The latter are manifested only when the child is working in collaboration with an adult or more competent peer. Their assessment requires an analysis of the child's ZPD. "Identifying processes that have not yet matured but are maturing constitutes the second task of the diagnostics of development. This task is resolved by finding the *zone of proximal development*" (Vygotsky, 1984a, p. 262). Thus, Vygotsky argued that if we are to evaluate not only fully mature mental functions but functions that are currently in the process of maturing, we must analyze not only the child's independent but also his or her collaborative activity.

Second, in measuring both the actual state of a child's development and the child's ZPD, Vygotsky's goal was not to assess learning efficiency or ultimate developmental potential but to obtain a full assessment of the child's current state of development. Vygotsky does not argue that the gardener should assess the fertility of the soil or the genetic quality of the seed in order to predict the garden's ultimate potential for production. He argued that if the gardener is to fully assess the garden's current condition or predict its production in the immediate future, not only fully mature fruits or fruit-bearing trees but those that will soon mature must be considered. Vygotsky saw the application of the concept of the ZPD in assessment as a means for obtaining a more comprehensive picture of the child's current developmental state and for predicting the dynamics of development in the immediate future, that is, in the next or *proximal* phase of the child's development.

It was no accident that Vygotsky looked to the child's collaborative activity in his attempt to evaluate maturing mental functions. Fundamental to much of his theory and research was the concept that advanced human mental processes have their origin in collaborative activity that is mediated by verbal interaction. In his view, it is as part of this kind of social unit that the individual first participates in new forms of mental activity. For Vygotsky, the "maturation" of mental functions involves the individual's mastery of the organization and the mediational means that constitute this collaborative activity. It is through this process and with these mental tools that the individual acquires the capacity to organize and mediate mental activity outside the supporting framework of social interaction, that is, in independent activity (see Wertsch, 1979, 1981, 1985).[4]

Vygotsky saw this process as a general law of the child's cultural or psychological development (1960, pp. 197–198; see also 1956/1981, p. 163).

> For the child . . . development based on collaboration and instruction is the source of all the specifically human characteristics of consciousness. Development based on instruction is a fundamental fact. Thus, a central feature of the psychological study of instruction is the potential the child has to raise himself to a higher intellectual level of development through collaboration. . . . The zone of proximal development . . . *determines the domain of transitions that are accessible to the child.* . . . What lies in the zone of proximal development at one stage is realized and moves to the level of actual development at a second. In other words, what the child is able to do in collaboration today he will be able to do independently tomorrow. (Vygotsky, 1934/1986, p. 206)

This is why Vygotsky saw the analysis of the child's performance in social interaction as so critical to the assessment of maturing mental functions. For Vygotsky, these functions are "manifested" only in the child's collaborative activity because it is here, on the intermental plane (i.e., in collaborative social interaction), that these functions first emerge. The maturing functions

---

4. Vygotsky's views on this process and those reflected in Feuerstein's concept of "mediated learning experience" (1979, pp. 70–74; 1980, pp. 13–36) are compatible. Moreover, the two sets of concepts would seem to have a certain potential for mutual enrichment. This is not, however, an appropriate context for a detailed analysis of these perspectives on the relationship between social interaction and psychological development.

must be assessed through an analysis of the child's collaborative activity because it is only here that they exist, because they have not yet matured and been transformed into intramental or individual functions.[5]

As Wertsch (1984) has pointed out, Vygotsky's "emphasis on the interpsychological origins of intrapsychological functioning means that the potential level in the zone of proximal development cannot be conceptualized, let alone measured, solely in terms of an individual's ability" (p. 12). The maturing functions and the ZPD are *created* in social interaction. Strictly speaking, they are characteristics not of the child as such but of the child engaged in collaborative interaction.

Of course, if the level of a child's performance in the ZPD were entirely dependent on the type of assistance or collaboration provided by the examiner, the analysis of the child's behavior in the ZPD would tell us nothing about the child's current state of development. Vygotsky was convinced, however, that although a child may attain more advanced levels of mental functioning in social interaction than when acting alone, the child's current state of development still limits the kinds of behavior that are possible.

> If I know arithmetic, but run into difficulty with the solution of a complex problem, a demonstration will immediately lead to my own resolution of the problem. If, on the other hand, I do not know higher mathematics, a demonstration of the resolution of a differential equation will not move my own thought in that direction by a single step. (Vygotsky, 1934/1986, p. 204)

Relying on current theory and data, Wertsch (1984) has been able to develop this argument in a much more sophisticated fashion than was possible for Vygotsky. Wertsch has made it clear, for example, that, although the ZPD is defined by social interaction, the kind of social interaction that the child can become involved in is determined by the current level of development. In the same sense that the ZPD is not a characteristic of the child in any simple sense, the assistance and social interaction that are provided to the child do not exist in an environment that can be defined apart from the developmental state of the child. They are, rather, defined and created by the child's needs and capabilities.[6]

Vygotsky, however, had limited empirical data to support his position that the ZPD is defined not only by the assistance or instruction provided to the child but by the child's current state of development. The data he did

5. I am simplifying Vygotsky's perspective to some extent here. In discussions of both play (Vygotsky, 1966/1978b), and thinking (Vygotsky, 1934/1986, chap. 6), Vygotsky's arguments suggest that he assumed that there will be phases in the development of the maturing functions that will be manifested by the child in independent activity before full maturation. Given the complexity of this problem, I have chosen not to deal with it here.

6. Toward the end of his life, Vygotsky developed this idea explicitly in his own work, arguing that it is the "social situation of development" as it is defined by the child's psychological characteristics, rather than an objective environment conceptualized in isolation from these characteristics, that is the source of social and cultural influences on the child's development (Vygotsky, 1984a, 1984b).

have came from Kohler's (1925) classic studies of imitation in chimpanzees. In this work, Kohler distinguished two types of imitation: (a) a mechanical form of imitation associated with the development of meaningless, automatic habits; and (b) a meaningful form of imitation associated with the development of rational, goal-oriented operations. In Kohler's time, comparative psychologists had studied these two forms of imitation extensively and identified many of their distinctive characteristics. What was unique in Kohler's work, and what made it so important to Vygotsky, was his finding that the chimpanzee "can meaningfully carry out through imitation only that which it can carry out independently" (Vygotsky, 1934/1986, p. 205), that meaningful or rational imitation is strictly limited by the ape's level of intellectual functioning.

Vygotsky insisted that imitative processes[7] have a different significance in the psychological development of the chimpanzee and the child (1934/in press, p. 206), but he argued that Kohler's findings on the limitations of meaningful or rational forms of imitation were applicable to both.

> The possibilities of his [i.e., the child's] intellectual potential are not limitless. Rather, they change in a strictly lawful manner in accordance with the course of his mental development such that at each age-stage there exists for the child a definite zone of intellectual imitation connected with the actual level of development. (1984a, p. 263)

And elsewhere:

> We said that in collaboration the child can always do more that he can independently. We must add the stipulation that he cannot do infinitely more. What collaboration contributes to the child's performance is restricted to limits that are determined by the state of his development and his intellectual potential. (1934/1986, p. 204)

Thus, in Kohler's work on imitation, Vygotsky found an empirical foundation for his claim that the upper limits of the ZPD are dependent on the child's current state of development.

Once again, this point was critical to Vygotsky's claims concerning the importance of analyzing the child's activity in the ZPD. If imitation and social learning are represented as purely mechanical processes that involve only the accumulation of skills, associations, and knowledge, the observation of a child's performance in collaborative work can contribute nothing to an analysis of the child's current state of development. This conception of imitation implies that "the imitation of a given intellectual operation can be a purely mechanical, automatic act *that says nothing about the mind of the imitator*"

---

7. When Vygotsky used the term "imitation" in this context, he was referring not to a passive or automatic repetition of observed behavior but to cognitive or rational learning that occurs through social interaction (Vygotsky, 1984a, p. 263). He used the term "imitation" here only to emphasize the connection between his analysis of social interaction and development and Kohler's work on imitation in chimpanzees.

(Vygotsky, 1984a, p. 262). In contrast, Vygotsky argued that "the child can imitate only that which lies within the zone of his own intellectual potential" (1934/1986, p. 204). For Vygotsky, this meant that analyzing the ZPD could play a critical role in assessing the child's current state of development.

Thus, Vygotsky saw the analysis of the ZPD not as a means of assessing learning potential or learning efficiency but as a means of gaining insight into the kinds of psychological processes that the child might be capable of in the next or proximal phase of development and a means of identifying the kinds of instruction or assistance that will be required if the child is to realize these potentials. The fact that the ZPD and the maturing processes that provide its content are defined simultaneously by the assistance that is made available to the child and by the child's actual state of development complicates Vygotsky's conception of the ZPD. It also creates several practical and conceptual difficulties for those interested in applying this concept in assessment practice. However, it is precisely because the ZPD is simultaneously defined by the social environment and the state of the child's psychological development that it has such tremendous implications for psychological theory and educational practice.

The Concept of the ZPD and the Problem of Instruction and Development

In the previous section, I argued that Vygotsky saw the analysis of the ZPD as essential to any full assessment of a child's current state of development. Although this may be an adequate statement of this perspective for purposes of comparison with that which has dominated related experimental work in dynamic assessment, we also want to explore the positive implications of this perspective for dynamic assessment. This requires a clearer understanding of what Vygotsky had in mind when he referred to the current state of development and to mature or maturing functions. To achieve this, we must analyze the concept of the ZPD within the broader framework of Vygotsky's thought.[8]

With one exception (Vygotsky, 1984a), Vygotsky always discussed the concept of the ZPD in connection with the problem of the relationship between instruction and development, a problem that was central to much of Vygotsky's work during the last few years of his life. Vygotsky's concern with this problem was partly a reflection of his long-standing interest in the practical problems of education (e.g., 1935, 1935/1978a, 1983), but this problem also had tremendous theoretical implications for Vygotsky. Instruction is one form of social interaction. For Vygotsky, the analysis of the relationship between instruction and development was one way to approach the more general

8. Because the concept of the ZPD is part of a new system of theoretical constructs that emerged in Vygotsky's thinking between 1932 and his death in 1934, this analysis would ideally include a discussion of the historical development of Vygotsky's thought (Minick, 1985, 1986). In the present context, however, I will limit myself to a discussion of the issues and constructs that were directly connected with the concept of the ZPD in Vygotsky's writing.

problem of the relationship between social interaction and development. Moreover, Vygotsky saw the relatively controlled context of formal school instruction as a natural laboratory for empirical research on this issue. As a consequence, much of the research carried out by Vygotsky and his colleagues during the 1930s focused on the issue of the relationship between school instruction and psychological development (Leont'ev, 1983b; Shif, 1935; Vygotsky, 1934/1986).

The concept of the ZPD was fundamental to Vygotsky's understanding of the process through which instruction had its impact on development. Vygotsky supported the view that social interaction and instruction require appropriate levels of development to be successful, but he rejected the notion that instruction must await the development of all the mental functions that are required for the independent performance of the tasks that provide the content for instruction. To the contrary:

> When instruction in written speech begins, the basic mental functions that underlie it are not fully developed; indeed, their development has not yet begun. Instruction depends on processes that are not yet matured, processes that have just entered the first phases of their development.
>
> This latter point is supported by research in other areas. Instruction in arithmetic, grammar, and natural science do not begin when the appropriate functions are mature. . . . The development of the psychological bases of school instruction do not predate instruction; they develop in unbroken internal connection with it. (Vygotsky, 1934/1986, pp. 198–200)

This concept of the integral relationship between the development of a child's mental functions and the development of social interaction was fundamental to Vygotsky's understanding of the relationship between instruction and development. It was, indeed, fundamental to the whole of his perspective on psychological development.[9] As we have seen, it was in the ZPD that Vygotsky found instruction and the mental functions developing in "unbroken internal connection."

Vygotsky's conception of the relationship between instruction and development is reflected in its most concrete and developed form in his analysis of the development of scientific concepts in formal instruction (1934/1986,

---

9. Although social interaction served as the central explanatory principle for Vygotsky throughout his career, several of his recently published papers make it clear that he was attempting to develop a more general explanatory framework during the last few years of his life (Vygotsky, 1984a, 1984b). In this work, Vygotsky extended his analysis of the relationship between psychological development and social interaction to the relationship between psychological development and forms of socially and culturally organized practice that may or may not involve social interaction. The concept of the ZPD was extended in important ways as part of this process (1966/1978b, 1984a). This explanatory framework provided the foundation for the subsequent development of "activity theory" by Vygotsky's students and colleagues (see Leont'ev, 1975/1978, 1956/1981; Minick, 1985; Wertsch, 1981, 1985).

chap. 6). To understand Vygotsky's perspective on the relationship between instruction and development, or to understand his conception of the ZPD, we must first understand his views of the development of scientific concepts in school and the psychological significance of this process (1934/1986, p. 186).

In their studies of scientific concepts, the immediate question concerning Vygotsky and his colleagues[10] was whether the systems of social and natural science concepts that a child learns in school (e.g., "socialism," "communism," and "capitalism"; "mammal," "reptile," and "amphibian"; or "lever," "force," and "fulcrum") develop in the same way and have the same psychological characteristics as the concepts that the child acquires in a more spontaneous manner in the preschool period (e.g., "brother," "puppy," or "bicycle"). Vygotsky immediately rejected two positions on this issue: (a) the position that scientific concepts are merely transferred from the adult to the child in instruction, that is, the position that they do not develop; and (b) the position that scientific concepts follow the same developmental course as spontaneous concepts (1934/1986, pp. 156–161). Vygotsky argued that those who maintained these positions had failed to see the fundamental differences in the genetic histories of scientific and spontaneous concepts or the implications that these differences might have for their psychological nature and development.

Vygotsky argued that Piaget was one of very few psychologists who had recognized that spontaneous (or everyday) and nonspontaneous (or scientific) concepts had different genetic origins and one of the few who had considered the possibility that their psychological characteristics might differ. Vygotsky argued, however, that Piaget had made three fundamental errors in his analysis of the relationship between spontaneous and nonspontaneous concepts. First, Piaget assumed that it is only spontaneous concepts that reflect the child's own thought, representing nonspontaneous concepts as something introduced from the outside, something foreign to the child's thought. Second, Piaget assumed that there is no mutual influence between these two types of concepts, that because the former represents the thought of the child and the latter the thought of the adult, a barrier exists between them in the child's mind. Third, Piaget represented the relationship between these two types of concepts as external and antagonistic, arguing that the adult's socialized concepts eventually supplant those of the child. Vygotsky rejected each of these assumptions, arguing that (a) nonspontaneous concepts are built on a foundation provided by spontaneous concepts, (b) both types of concepts reflect the characteristics of the child's thought, and (c) there are complex patterns of influence and interaction between them (1934/1986, pp. 162–165).

10. Vygotsky's theoretical analysis of the development of scientific concepts was based primarily on the work of his colleague Zh. I. Shif (1935), although a large group of his students and colleagues was working on this problem at the time of his death (Leont'ev, 1983a, p. 389).

In Vygotsky's view, perhaps the most universal and developmentally significant characteristic of school instruction is its tendency to introduce conscious awareness (*osoznanie*) into many domains of the child's activity. By the time a child has reached school age, for example, the phonemic and grammatical systems of the native language have been mastered and the child is able to use them freely and correctly in verbal communication. In Vygotsky's view, however, the child lacks conscious awareness of these processes. The child uses linguistic rules and sounds but is not aware of them. In learning to write, however, the child is forced to analyze the phonemic organization of the native language. To spell a word, the child must analyze the distinct sounds or phonemes that compose it. Similarly, in the formal study of grammar, the child's attention is directed toward the grammatical rules of the native language.

Vygotsky's understanding of the concept of "conscious awareness" is expressed clearly in the following illustration:

> Conscious awareness is not simply part of the conscious or unconscious. It does not designate a level of consciousness. It designates a different level in the activity of consciousness. I tie a knot. I do it consciously. I cannot, however, say precisely how I have done it. My action, which is conscious, turns out to be lacking in conscious awareness because my attention is directed toward the act of tying, not on *how* I carry out that act. Consciousness always represents some piece of reality. . . . [Here], the actions that I carry out in the process of tying the knot, what I am doing, is not the object of my consciousness. It can, however, become the object of consciousness. (1934/1986, p. 181)

In Vygotsky's view, instruction in writing and grammar shifts the child's attention from what is being communicated to the means of communication. This provides the foundation for the development of the conscious awareness of important aspects of speech and language that is necessary for the development of effective writing skills.

Vygotsky argued that the instruction through which the child learns systems of scientific concepts in school leads to conscious awareness of the semantic aspect of speech in much the same way that instruction in writing and grammar leads to conscious awareness of its phonemic and grammatical aspects. Spontaneous or everyday concepts develop in the process of communicating about things. Here, words function as the means of communication. The adult may explain the meaning of a word to the child, but the purpose of the interaction and the focus of attention is not the system of word meanings but the things, events, or experiences that are the object of the act of communication. The interaction or collaboration that arises between the teacher and the child in the instructional process that leads to the understanding of a given domain of scientific knowledge (e.g., mathematics, geometry, biology, or the social sciences) is based on a qualitatively different form of communication. Here, the word assumes a different function, acting not only as the means of communication but as its object. "The development of scientific concepts *begins with the verbal definition*" (Vygotsky, 1934/1986, p. 155).

It begins with the teacher's definition and explanation of concepts and with the child's attempts to explain and compare them, to reflect on these explanations and comparisons, and to correct them. Instruction in a system of scientific concepts begins with a form of verbal interaction between the adult and child that directs the child's attention to word meanings and to the systematic relationships between word meanings that are fundamental to any organized system of scientific knowledge.

Because of these differences in the organization and purpose of these forms of communication, and because of the different functions that the word assumes in them, there are significant psychological differences between the child's scientific and spontaneous concepts. Conscious awareness of concepts and their relationships appears first in the domain of scientific concepts.

> The child gains conscious awareness of spontaneous concepts at a relatively late point in the developmental process. His abilities for the verbal definition of concepts, his potential for giving a verbal formulation of them, and his volitional use of the concept in establishing complex logical relationships between other concepts are not present in the initial stages of the developmental process. The child knows things; he has a concept of the object. However, what the concept itself represents remains vague for the child. He has a concept of the object and is consciously aware of the object that is represented in the concept. He is not, however, consciously aware of the concept itself; he does not have conscious awareness of the act of thought that allows him to represent the object. In contrast, the development of scientific concepts begins with that which remains most underdeveloped in the spontaneous concept over the whole of the school age. It begins with work on the concept itself; it begins with work on the concept's verbal definition, with operations that presuppose the nonspontaneous application of this concept.
>
> Scientific concepts begin their life at a level that the development of the child's spontaneous concepts has not yet reached. Work on the new scientific concept in the process of instruction requires the very operations and relationships that are impossible for the child of this age. (Vygotsky, 1934/1986, pp. 213–214)

Thus, although there may be systematic relationships between word meanings before scientific concepts emerge, it is through the study of scientific concepts that the child begins to become aware of these relationships, that the child begins to perceive a given concept as a component in a system of interrelated word meanings.

Vygotsky was convinced that the emergence of scientific concepts had profound implications for the development of a child's verbal thought. He illustrated this point empirically through research carried out by his colleagues (e.g., Leont'ev, 1983b; Shif, 1935). Shif (1935) found, for example, that if primary school children were asked to complete a sentence ending in the word "because," they were much more successful when the sentence was based on concepts taken from their studies in social science than when it incorporated terms drawn from everyday experience. That is, they were more likely to meaningfully complete a sentence such as "There is little waste in a socialist economic system because . . . " than they were to meaningfully complete a sentence such as "The boy fell off the bicycle because. . . ." In Vygotsky's view, this reflects the fact that it is in the realm of scientific concepts that a child first begins to act on concepts and their relationships in the conscious, volitional manner that is required by a task of this kind (1934/1986, pp. 210–212).

For Vygotsky, however, the significance of scientific concepts for the development of verbal thinking went far beyond what he and his colleagues were able to demonstrate in their empirical research. In his view, conscious awareness of word meanings and of the relationships between them provides the foundation for profound changes in verbal thought. This idea is reflected in the following statement:

> The key difference in the psychological nature of these two kinds of concepts is a function of the presence or absence of a system. Concepts stand in a different relationship to the object when they exist outside of a system than when they enter into one. . . . Outside a system, the only possible connections between concepts are those that exist between the objects themselves, that is, empirical connections. This is the source of the dominance of the logic of the action, and of syncretic connections of impressions, in early childhood. Within a system, relationships between concepts, relationships that mediate the concept's relationship to the object through its relationship to other concepts, begin to emerge. A different relationship between the concept and the object develops. *Supraempirical connections between concepts become possible.*
>
>   It could be demonstrated that all the characteristics of the child's thought identified by Piaget . . . stem from the extrasystemic nature of the child's [spontaneous] concepts. (1934/1986, p. 234)

Thus, Vygotsky argued that instruction in scientific concepts creates the foundation not only for a new form of concept but for new forms of verbal thought that are associated with it. Vygotsky insisted, however, that the development of scientific concepts and the development of spontaneous concepts were interdependent processes. On the one hand, Vygotsky was convinced that the development of scientific concepts was dependent on the existence of a well-developed form of spontaneous concept. On the other, he was convinced that the emergence of scientific concepts eventually transformed the existing spontaneous concepts. In his words:

> [On the one hand,] the system, and the conscious awareness that is associated with it, is not brought into the domain of the child's concepts from without, it does not simply replace the child's own mode of forming and using concepts; rather, the system itself presupposes a rich and mature form of concept in the child, a form of concept that is necessary so that it may become the object of conscious awareness and systematization. . . . [On the other hand,] the first system, which emerges in the sphere of scientific concepts, is transferred structurally to the domain of everyday concepts . . . it restructures the everyday concept and changes its internal nature from above. (1934/1986, p. 184)

Vygotsky's attempts to characterize the level of development in spontaneous concepts that is necessary to begin formal instruction in scientific concepts were inadequate, a fact of which he was very much aware (1934/1986, p. 242). Nevertheless, he insisted that such a dependence exists. First, although the process of defining and analyzing concepts that lies at the core of instruction in scientific concepts differs qualitatively from the preschooler's use of words in communication, this process is dependent on the child's developed system of everyday concepts. It is through a child's everyday concepts that much of the process of defining and explaining the scientific concept must be carried out. It is these concepts that provide real content for scientific concepts and link them to the child's experience, creating the potential for understanding. Second, Vygotsky argued that specific terms such as "because," "although," "before," and "now" must be mastered as means of communication in the child's spontaneous speech before conscious awareness of them can be gained or they can be used in a system of scientific concepts and scientific thought. Thus, because the relationship of the scientific concept to the object world is mediated through other concepts, its development is inherently dependent on the development of spontaneous concepts.

For precisely the same reason, the emergence of the scientific concept inevitably has an impact on the development of at least certain groups of spontaneous concepts. As we have just seen, the process of defining and analyzing the scientific concept cannot occur unless the child's spontaneous concepts are drawn into this process. As they are drawn into this process, however, they begin to change in important ways.

> *The everyday concept acquires a whole series of new relationships with other concepts as it comes to stand between the scientific concept and its object.* Its relationship with the object is also transformed in this process. (1934/1986, p. 220)

To the extent that the everyday concept is drawn into the system of scientific concepts, and to the extent that a child is forced through school instruction to reflect consciously on its meaning and its relationships to other concepts, the characteristics of word meaning and thought that originate with instruction in scientific concepts will be extended downward to the domain of the everyday concept. Moreover, only to the extent that this occurs will a child's scientific concepts be anything but empty verbalisms.

Vygotsky summarized his analysis of the development of scientific concepts, and linked this analysis to his conception of the ZPD, in the following way:

> We can now state our findings in more general terms. *The strength of the scientific concept lies in the higher characteristics of concepts, in conscious awareness and volition.* This is, in contrast, the weakness of the child's spontaneous concept. The strength of the spontaneous concept lies in spontaneous, situationally meaningful, concrete applications, that is, in the sphere of experience and the empirical. The development of scientific concepts begins in the domain of conscious

awareness and volition. It grows downward into the domain of the concrete, into the domain of personal experience. In contrast, the development of spontaneous concepts begins in the domain of the concrete and empirical. It moves toward the higher characteristics of concepts, toward conscious awareness and volition. The link between these two lines of development reflects their true nature. This is *the link of the zone of proximal and actual development*.

Conscious awareness and volitional use of concepts, the characteristics of the school child's spontaneous concepts that remain underdeveloped, lie entirely within his zone of proximal development. They emerge, they become actual, in his collaboration with adults. This is why the development of scientific concepts presupposes a certain level in the development of spontaneous concepts; within the zone of proximal development, conscious awareness and volition appear with these concepts. At the same time, scientific concepts restructure spontaneous concepts. They help move them to a higher level, forming their zone of proximal development. . . . scientific concepts provide a segment of development which the child has not yet passed through . . . the scientific concept moves ahead into a zone where the corresponding potentials have not yet matured in the child. This allows us to begin to understand that instruction in scientific concepts plays a decisive role in the child's mental development. (1934/1986, pp. 216–217)

With this discussion of the relationship between the development of scientific and everyday concepts, we can begin to understand Vygotsky's perspective on the ZPD in more concrete terms. Several points warrant emphasis. First, the actual level of development, as defined by mature mental functions such as the everyday concept, is not simply a measure of completed developmental cycles. The actual level of development determines the kind of collaborative or intermental activity that is possible at a given state of mental development. Second, the new psychological formations that emerge in the ZPD, that is, maturing functions such as scientific concepts, are not simply brought in from the outside and added to an existing repertoire of functions. On the one hand, they can form only by including existing mature functions in the new systems of psychological activity that are organized in collaborative social interaction. On the other hand, because they incorporate existing functions in new functional systems, maturing functions do not merely supplement but transform mature functions. Third, although the development of the functions that emerge in the ZPD is dependent on existing or mature systems of psychological functions, it is not immanent in them. Scientific concepts and the forms of thinking associated with them are not simply planted in a child's mind from the outside, but they would not develop without the reorganization of the child's psychological activity that occurs in social interaction.

The ZPD and the Diagnostics of Psychological Development

Vygotsky's proposals concerning the use of the concept of the ZPD in assessment practice are closely tied to his conception of the ZPD as the primary locus of change in human psychological development. In the most general terms, Vygotsky believed that by creating and analyzing the ZPD for experimental purposes the investigator gained access to the internal dynamics of the developmental process itself. In this respect, the analysis of the child's activity in the ZPD can be used either as a tool for general developmental research or as a means of analyzing the unique characteristics of this process in a particular child.

Vygotsky focused on the issue of the significance that studying a child's behavior in the ZPD might have for assessment practice in only a single paper (1984a). Here, citing Gesell,[11] Vygotsky began by emphasizing the differences between two basic approaches to the measurement or assessment of psychological development, labeling them "symptomatic" and "diagnostic."

As defined by Vygotsky, a symptomatic assessment focuses on behaviors and characteristics (or complexes of behaviors and characteristics) that are typical of children of a particular psychological type or developmental stage. In contrast, a diagnostic assessment relies on an explicit explanatory theory of psychological development in an attempt to penetrate "the internal causal-dynamic and genetic connections that define the process of mental development" (1984a, p. 265). The goal of a diagnostic assessment is to understand why a child displays specific behavioral, cognitive, or affective symptoms and, where necessary, to develop theoretically motivated and practically useful recommendations for facilitating psychological development.

Vygotsky argued that many commonly used static assessment procedures were symptomatic rather than diagnostic in their approach, specifically mentioning in this connection procedures that were used to measure the child's coefficient of mental development. Vygotsky argued that these tests were used to define and catalogue the external manifestations of psychological development rather than to provide insights into the developmental process itself, and compared this approach to the way medical diagnosis was carried out before extensive knowledge of physiological and disease processes had been developed. He argued that in this early period in the history of medicine, the physician's symptomatic diagnosis of "cough" or "fever" offered the patient little more information than was self-evident to the patient through direct observation and provided little information that could help the physician develop effective approaches to treatment. Vygotsky argued that many of the procedures used in psychological assessment could also be characterized in this way:

> If the child is brought for consultation with the complaint that his mental development is inadequate, with the complaint that he thinks, understands, and remembers poorly, and the psychologist offers a diagnosis of "a low level of mental development" or "mental retardation," nothing is explained, nothing predicted, and the psychologist is no more able to provide any practical assistance than is the physician who offers the diagnosis of a cough. (1984a, p. 268)

---

11. Vygotsky credited Gesell with making this distinction, but did not provide specific references to Gesell's works.

In more general terms, Vygotsky argued that:

> If we are limited to the definition and measurement of the symptoms of devel-
> opment, we can never go beyond a purely empirical statement of what is already
> known about the child. The best we can do is to refine the statement of these
> symptoms and verify their measurement. We will never, however, be able to
> explain the phenomena we observe in the child's development, predict the sub-
> sequent course of development, or indicate what practical measures must be
> taken. (1984a, pp. 267–268)

In Vygotsky's view, the study of child development and the evaluation
of developmental problems required a shift from a symptomatic assessment
to a "clinical diagnostics that is based on determining of the very course of
the developmental process" (1984a, p. 265). Vygotsky believed that the concept of the ZPD was critical to this task.

> The theoretical significance of this diagnostic principle [i.e., analyzing the ZPD]
> is that it allows us to penetrate the internal causal-dynamic and genetic links that
> define the process of mental development. . . . The development of the internal
> individual characteristics of the child have their immediate source in the child's
> cooperation . . . with other people. Thus, when we use this principle of coop-
> eration in establishing the zone of proximal development, we gain the potential
> for directly studying that which most precisely determines the level of mental
> maturation that must be completed in the proximal or subsequent period of his
> age development. (1984a, p. 165)

This is why Vygotsky argued that the analysis of a child's work with adult
assistance might be as significant for assessment purposes as the analysis of
work that is carried out independently.

Conclusion

Vygotsky's conception of the ZPD, together with the system of theory and
research of which it is part, has a great deal to offer developmental psychology
generally and the dynamic assessment movement in particular. The analysis
of a child's activity in the ZPD could be extremely useful in producing a
qualitative assessment of the strengths and weaknesses of a child's mental
activity and in identifying the types of assistance that are needed to move the
child to more advanced levels of development. In many respects, the work
of Feuerstein and his colleagues has demonstrated the utility of this general
approach. Despite the sophistication of Vygotsky's theoretical work in this
area, however, his death in 1934 prevented him from implementing the concept of the ZPD in practical diagnostic work. Fifty years after the concept
was developed by Vygotsky, attempts are now being made to implement it
both in assessment practice and in developmental research (e.g., Rogoff &
Wertsch, 1984). Most of those involved in this effort would agree, however,
that the development and application of the concept is still in its infancy.

The practical task of implementing the concept of the ZPD in diagnostic research will be a long and difficult process. Vygotsky was not in a position to provide a detailed outline for the concept's proper implementation in assessment practice when he was writing, and we are not in a position to do that now. It may be useful, however, to identify some of the problems that may be encountered.

The first point I would emphasize in this connection is that the successful use of the concept of the ZPD in diagnostics will depend on how well we understand the relevant developmental processes and their underlying mechanisms. This is true, of course, of any attempt to assess the qualitative nature of a child's development or to design means to facilitate that development. Feuerstein (1979) has outlined a "cognitive map" of the kinds of psychological processes that he sees as basic to adequate mental functioning and has discussed the concept of "psychological mediation" as a mechanism critical to their development. The success of his work in assessment has been directly linked to these theories concerning the content and mechanisms of psychological development. Vygotsky's theories concerning these mechanisms provide a powerful foundation for applying the concept of the ZPD in assessment practice, but they must be refined and grounded in additional empirical research on the development of specific psychological processes.

Second, in analyzing the ZPD we will have to do more than identify the upper limits of a child's collaborative activity, the task that was often emphasized by Vygotsky in his comments on the analysis of the ZPD for assessment purposes. Identifying the upper limit of a child's ZPD may be a useful means of identifying the kind of psychological functioning a child may be capable of in the immediate future. Feuerstein (1979) has used similar indices in assessing the child's potential for development. Focusing only on this upper limit, however, could be misleading and would nullify much of the potential value of analyzing the child's behavior in the ZPD. Wertsch (1984) has clearly shown that it would be useless to look only at the level of performance attained by a child in collaboration without analyzing the characteristics of that collaboration. To assess the psychological functions that are currently maturing, to predict the proximal stage of a child's development, or to develop programs of education and remediation designed to further that development, the assessment of the ZPD must focus on the qualitative characteristics of the interaction between the adult and child.

Finally, it is important to emphasize that many basic characteristics of traditional approaches to assessment will be altered as dynamic approaches to assessment are developed on the basis of the concept of the ZPD. For example, the relationship between test design and the assessment process as a whole will change. In general, the assessment of qualitative aspects of psychological development through static techniques involves the design of tests that require a given mental process or a given level of development for successful performance. Inherent to this approach are the difficulties that arise in interpreting performance failures because of the fact that successful performance on these tests inevitably involves not only the mental function being assessed but other factors such as memory, attention, and motivation. A dynamic approach to assessment avoids this problem, while creating several others. Where the examiner is allowed to act freely in helping the child carry out a task, assistance will ideally be provided in all domains of psychological functioning necessary for the child to attain a maximum performance level. On a task involving deductive reasoning, for example, the examiner may be forced to provide assistance related to motivation; to metacognitive, analytic, and organizational skills; or to memory and attention. Moreover, it is by analyzing the kind of assistance that the examiner has to provide to bring the child to a given level of performance that the assessment of the child's psychological development is carried out. As a consequence, what might traditionally be viewed as a test of deductive reasoning skills may result in a diagnosis of problems in memory or motivation. Obviously, the relationship between the development of assessment tasks and the assessment process itself will be very different here than it is in more traditional static approaches to assessment. In facing these kinds of problems as we develop dynamic assessment procedures, we will have to rethink many of our basic assumptions about the practice of assessment.

Feuerstein et al. (1981) have argued that to "the extent that assessment is regarded as an integral part of intervention and not as an end in itself, the necessity to understand the nature of the processes that produce cognitive change becomes imperative" (p. 202). In my view, it is here that the work of Feuerstein and his colleages is weakest. Like others working within the dynamic assessment movement, their approach assumes that instruction, social interaction, and other means of organizing and reorganizing the child's psychological activity can play a key role in the process of cognitive development and change. Their understanding of the mechanisms of change, however, remains largely implicit and intuitive. In contrast, with all its faults, the work of Vygotsky and the subsequent work of colleagues and students (see Minick, 1985; Wertsch, 1981, 1985) provides a powerful theoretical framework for understanding the mechanisms in socially organized forms of interaction and activity that can lead to change in the child's psychological functions. In this respect, as a component of Vygotskian developmental theory, the concept of the ZPD has tremendous potential for enhancing our understanding of why certain children experience difficulty in school and for facilitating the development of forms of remediation that may enable them to overcome these difficulties.

REFERENCES

Brown, A. L., & Ferrara, R. A. (1985). Diagnosing zones of proximal development. In J. V. Wertsch (Ed.), *Culture, communication, and cognition: Vygotskian perspectives* (pp. 273–305). New York: Cambridge University Press.

Brown, A. L., & French, L. A. (1979). The zone of potential development: Implications for intelligence testing in the year 2000. *Intelligence, 3*, 255–273.

Budoff, M., & Friedman, M. (1964). "Learning potential" as an assessment approach to the adolescent mentally retarded. *Journal of Consulting Psychology, 28*, 434–439.

Budoff, M., & Hamilton, J. L. (1976). Optimizing test performance of moderately and severely mentally retarded adolescents and adults. *American Journal of Mental Deficiency, 81*, 49–57.

Campione, J. C., Brown, A. L., Ferrara, R. A., & Bryant, N. R. (1984). The zone of proximal development: Implications for individual differences and learning. In B. Rogoff & J. V. Wertsch (Eds.), *Children's learning in the "zone of proximal development"* (pp. 77–92). San Francisco: Jossey-Bass.

Feuerstein, R. (1979). *The dynamic assessment of retarded performers: The learning potential assessment device, theory, instruments, and techniques.* Baltimore: University Park Press.

Feuerstein, R. (1980). *Instrumental enrichment: An intervention program for cognitive modifiability.* Baltimore: University Park Press.

Feuerstein, R., Miller, R., Rand, Y., & Jensen, M. R. (1981). Can evolving techniques better measure cognitive change? *The Journal of Special Education, 15*, 201–219.

Kohler, W. (1925). *The mentality of apes* (E. W. Winter, Trans.). New York: Harcourt, Brace, & Company.

Leont'ev, A. N. (1978). *Activity, consciousness, and personality* (M. J. Hall, Trans.). Englewood Cliffs, NJ: Prentice-Hall. (Original work published 1975)

Leont'ev, A. N. (1981). *Problems of the development of mind* (Progress Publishers, Trans.). Moscow: Progress Publishers. (Original work published 1956).

Leont'ev, A. N. (1983a). *Izbrannye psikhologicheskie proizvedeniia* [Selected psychological works] (Vol. 1). Moscow: Pedagogika.

Leont'ev, A. N. (1983b). Ovladenie uchashchimisia nauchnymi poniatiiami kak problema pedagogicheskoi psikhologii [The mastery of scientific concepts as a problem in pedagogical psychology]. In A. N. Leont'ev, *Izbrannye psikhologicheskie proizvedeniia* (Vol. 1, pp. 324–347). Moscow: Pedagogika.

Luria, A. R. (1961). An objective approach to the study of the abnormal child. *American Journal of Orthopsychiatry, 31*, 1–14.

Minick, N. (1985). *L. S. Vygotsky and Soviet activity theory: New perspectives on the relationship between mind and society.* Unpublished doctoral disseration, Northwestern University, Evanston.

Minick, N. (1986). The development of Vygotsky's thought. Introduction to L. S. Vygotsky, *Collected works: Problems of general psychology* (Vol. 1) (N. Minick, Trans.). New York: Plenum.

Rogoff, B., & Wertsch, J. V. (Eds.). (1984). *Children's learning in the "zone of proximal development".* San Francisco: Jossey-Bass.

Shif, Zh. I. (1935). *Razvitie zhiteiskikh i nauchnykh poniatti* [The development of everyday and scientific concepts]. Moscow: Gosudrstvennoe Uchebno-pedagogicheskoe Izdatel'stvo.

Vygotsky, L. S. (1935). *Umstvennoe razvitie detei v protsesse obucheniia* [The mental development of children in the process of instruction]. Moscow/Leningrad: Gosudarstvennoe Uchebno-pedagogicheskoe Izdatel'stvo.

Vygotsky, L. S. (1956). *Izbrannye psikhologicheskie issledovaniia* [Selected psychological investigations]. Moscow: Academy of Pedagogical Sciences RSFSR.

Vygotsky, L. S. (1960). *Razvitie vysshikh psikhicheskikh funktsii* [The development of the higher mental functions]. Moscow: Academy of Pedagogical Sciences RSFSR.

Vygotsky, L. S. (1962). *Thought and language* (E. Hanfmann & G. Vakar, Trans.). Cambridge, MA: M.I.T. Press. (Original work published 1934)

Vygotsky, L. S. (1978a). Interaction between learning and development. In L. S. Vygotsky, *Mind in society: The development of higher psychological processes* (M. Cole, V. John-Steiner, S. Scribner, & E. Souberman, Eds. and Trans.) (pp. 79–91). Cambridge, MA: Harvard University Press. (Original work published 1935)

Vygotsky, L. S. (1978b). The role of play in development. In L. S. Vygotsky, *Mind in society: The development of higher psychological processes* (M. Cole, V. John-Steiner, S. Scribner, & E. Souberman, Eds. and Trans.) (pp. 92–104). Cambridge, MA: Harvard University Press. (Original work published 1966)

Vygotsky, L. S. (1981). The genesis of higher mental functions. In J. V. Wertsch (Ed.), *The concept of activity in Soviet psychology* (pp. 144–189). Armonk, NY: M. E. Sharpe. (Original work published 1956)

Vygotsky, L. S. (1983). *Sobranie sochinenii: Osnovy defektologii* [Collected works: The foundations of defectology] (Vol. 5). Moscow: Pedagogika.

Vygotsky, L. S. (1984a). Problema vozrasta [The problem of age]. In L. S. Vygotsky, *Sobranie sochinenii: Detskaia psikhologiia* (pp. 244–268). Moscow: Pedagogika.

Vygotsky, L. A. (1984b). Chast' vtoraia: Voprosy detskoi (vozrastnoi) psikhologii [Part two: Problems of child (age) psychology]. In L. S. Vygotsky, *Sobranie sochinenii: Detskaia psikhologiia* (pp. 244–385). Moscow: Pedagogika.

Vygotsky, L. S. (1986). Thinking and speech. In L. S. Vygotsky, *Collected works: Problems of general psychology* (Vol. 1) (N. Minick, Trans.). New York: Plenum. Translation of V. V. Davydov (Ed.). (1982). *L. S. Vygotskii: Sobranie sochinenii* [L. S. Vygotsky: Collected Works] (Vol. 2). Moscow: Pedagogika. (Original work published 1934)

Wertsch, J. V. (1979). From social interaction to higher psychological processes. A clarification and application of Vygotsky's theory. *Human Development, 22,* 1–22.

Wertsch, J. V. (Ed.). (1981). *The concept of activity in Soviet psychology.* Armonk, NY: M. E. Sharpe.

Wertsch, J. V. (1984). The zone of proximal development: Some conceptual issues. In B. Rogoff & J. V. Wertsch (Eds.), *Children's learning in the "zone of proximal development"* (pp. 7–18). San Francisco: Jossey-Bass.

Wertsch, J. V. (1985). *Vygotsky and the social formation of mind.* Cambridge, MA: Harvard University Press.

5

Toward Development of a Psychometric Approach

SUSAN E. EMBRETSON

Dynamic testing is becoming an increasingly important movement among psychologists and educators. In dynamic testing an attempt is made to modify the performance level of an examinee by introducing material or instructions that can aid performance. Dynamic testing is believed to be diagnostically and theoretically superior to standard (static) testing, because it mirrors the learning process. For example, Vygotsky (1978) believed that the sensitivity of an examinee's performance to external aids and cues is theoretically revealing of the examinee's learning potential. Similarly, Feuerstein (1979) believes that dynamic testing is more relevant to diagnosing educational interventions that may be given to the examinee. Examples of dynamic testing studies include Babad and Budoff (1974; Budoff, Chapter 2, this volume), Carlson and Wiedl (1979), Feuerstein (1979, 1980; Chapter 1, this volume), and Campione and Brown (Chapter 3, this volume).

However, psychometricians are typically less than enthusiastic about dynamic testing for several reasons. First, psychometrics traditionally has regarded procedures that modify scores to be coaching, which brings up many concerns about the meaning of the scores. For example, a primary concern about coaching for the Scholastic Aptitude Test has been the possible decrease in test validity (Messick & Jungeblut, 1981), particularly if coaching changes or automatizes the examinee's methods of item solving. Furthermore, score comparability is also an issue, if only some examinees obtain the coaching sequence, as is currently the case for many college admissions tests. Second, many psychometricians do not believe that learning ability is a viable construct. Woodrow's (1938, 1946) research indicating that individual differences in learning (i.e., improvement over practice) were task specific and unrelated to intelligence is often cited as evidence against the learning ability construct. (These findings will be reexamined below.) Third, the measurement of change is beset with so many problems that some psychometricians have suggested abandoning change measures altogether, if possible (Cronbach & Furby, 1970).

In general, the development of psychometric methods for dynamic testing mirrors the dismal view of many psychometricians of the potential of dynamic

Susan E. Embretson. Department of Psychology, University of Kansas, Lawrence, Kansas.

testing. The major relevant work concerning the measurement of change (Harris, 1963), is based on classical test theory. Although classical test theory provided a useful means of conceptualizing issues for several decades, the many advantages of item response theory, based on latent trait models (Lord, 1980), have made classical test theory increasingly obsolete in psychometrics. Unfortunately, the implications of latent trait models for dynamic testing (with some promising exceptions) constitute virtually unexplored territory.

Thus, this chapter cannot present a unified collection of psychometric methods for dynamic testing. Instead, the chapter will attempt to develop some heuristics for psychometrics of dynamic testing. What will be presented here is an outline of some psychometric issues involved in this approach. Perhaps most central to psychometric issues are the goals of dynamic testing. Thus, the traditional topics of scaling the test items and scores, reliability, and validity will be covered only after the possible goals and design of dynamic tests are considered. The few relevant articles on latent traits models for dynamic testing will be presented, as will some relevant issues concerning the measurement of change.

It is hypothesized that a key element in future psychometric methods for dynamic testing is mathematical modeling. First, mathematical modeling is relevant to scaling through item response theory. That is, latent trait models predict the response of a particular person to a specified item. The advantageous properties of latent trait models solve some problems in comparing the changes that result from dynamic testing between persons or groups. Second, mathematical modeling is also relevant to construct validity and reliability, particularly if applied conjointly with a latent trait model. Mathematical modeling can be effective in evaluating the substantive nature of the changes introduced by dynamic testing procedures. Furthermore, mathematical modeling can assess the persistence of any performance change, particularly through growth-modeling approaches (e.g., Bock, 1976).

The importance of the mathematical modeling approach for construct validity became clear with R. J. Sternberg's (1977) componential theory. Component processes that were identified by subtasks or by scoring the stimulus features of items modeled both item difficulty and response time. Then, componential analysis was linked to contemporary psychometric methods by the development of multicomponent latent trait models (Embretson, 1984; Whitely, 1980a, 1980b) and by the emergence of important European research on the linear logistic latent trait model (Fischer, 1973) in the American psychometric literature.

The componential approach has changed the issues that are deemed relevant to testing. At one time, the correlates of the test score provided the major focus of construct validation studies. This approach emphasized the product of a person's encounter with items, rather than the process. Now, however, many psychometricians (e.g., Embretson, 1983; Messick, 1972) view process-oriented studies as relevant to construct validity. Furthermore, process-oriented studies are particularly relevant to dynamic testing, because it is often maintained that a major difference from traditional testing is its emphasis on the process rather than the product (e.g., Feuerstein, 1979, 1980).

The current chapter is organized into five major sections: (a) psychometric issues in designing dynamic testing procedures, (b) scoring the dynamic test, (c) evaluating reliability, (d) evaluating validity, and (e) conclusion and summary. Throughout the chapter, an application of psychometric procedures to the dynamic testing of spatial ability will be presented to illustrate some methods that are described.

Prior to considering psychometric issues, a general definition of dynamic testing is needed. For the purpose of this chapter, dynamic testing attempts to modify the performance level of an examinee by the design of the testing materials or test administration procedures.

Some features of this definition need elaboration. First, as did Feuerstein (1979), this definition distinguishes performance level from capacity. Performance level is the current mental efficiency of the examinee, whereas capacity is the limiting level of development, under optimal conditions. Although performance during or after the dynamic testing procedure may be a better indicator of capacity, it is assumed that capacity remains constant during the testing. Capacity *may* be modifiable, but a more extended intervention, such as the Instrumental Enrichment Program (Feuerstein, 1980) is required. Second, the definition concerns performance *level* rather than other aspects of performance, such as which processes or strategies are changed. Although the changes in processes and strategies may be specified in the design of the dynamic testing procedure, the primary goal is to change the level of performance. Performance changes may provide insights into deficient processes so that assessment may be linked with treatment. Third, although the typical goal is to *increase* performance levels, the definition merely indicates modification. This allows for the possibility of a meaningful decrease in performance, for example, by omitting certain accompanying structures or procedures. Fourth, the design of the dynamic testing materials and procedures can be quite diverse. For example, external aids or hints may accompany the items (e.g., see Chapter 3, this volume), or the examiner may probe and instruct the examinee on his or her approach to problem solving (e.g., Feuerstein, 1979). Fifth, no restriction on the primary test score of interest is implied in the definition. Several possible scores, and some relevant psychometric issues, will be discussed below.

Designing Dynamic Tests: Psychometric Issues

Some recent directions in psychometrics indicate that the design of psychological and educational tests is increasingly becoming a science rather than an art (Embretson, 1985b; Roid & Haladyna, 1982). A major source of change is the increasing connection of tests to psychological or educational theory, such as has been permitted by the cognitive component analysis of aptitude (Pellegrino & Glaser, 1979; R. J. Sternberg, 1981). For example, it has been postulated (Embretson, 1985b) that the test developer can function as an experimenter who manipulates the content and procedures of a task to operationalize specified constructs.

Test design is especially relevant to dynamic testing. Specific materials or procedures are introduced to change performance. The nature of the materials and procedures can be manipulated to operationalize specified constructs. Some current implementations of dynamic testing seem especially well anchored in theory. For example, Campione and Brown (Chapter 3, this volume) interpret Vygotsky's concepts of external aids as hints given for performance in their test. Similarly, Feuerstein (1980, Feuerstein et al., Chapter 1, this volume) based his procedures on a theory that emphasizes mediated learning experiences.

A Model for Test Design

To provide a framework for considering the design of dynamic testing, it is useful to conceptualize construct validation research as concerning two separate issues, construct representation and nomothetic span (Embretson, 1983, 1985a). Dynamic testing may influence both aspects of construct validity. Construct representation refers to the processes, strategies, and knowledge stores that are involved in item responses. Construct representation is studied by task decomposition methods and is explicated by understanding the various components, metacomponents, strategies, and knowledge structures that are involved in solving psychometric items.

Nomothetic span, in contrast, concerns the utility of the test as a measure of individual differences. It is supported by elaborating the pattern, magnitude, and frequency of relationships of the test score with other measures of individual differences, such as criterion scores, group membership, or scores on other tests.

Establishing the nomothetic span of a test through correlational research is standard practice in test development. However, the relationship between construct representation and nomothetic span is crucial to the construct validity of the test and to test design. That is, how do individual differences in performing the underlying cognitive processes influence the test's variance and covariances with other measures?

Figure 5.1 shows the relationship of processing components (C) to ability and external variables. Ability is explained by a weighted combination of the underlying cognitive components, which, in turn, accounts for the predictive validity of the test. In fact, if individual differences in performing the component processes are measured, they can completely replace the ability test score. So, ability is postulated merely to be an intervening variable (MacCorquodale & Meehl, 1948) that is a convenient referent for the particular combination of processing components that are required for solving an item set.

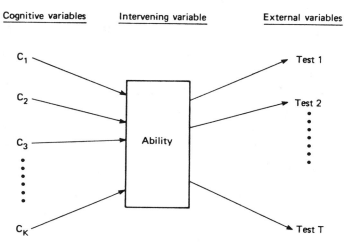

FIGURE 5.1   The relationship of processing components (C) to ability and external variables. (From Embretson, S. E. [1985a]. Multicomponent latent trait models for test design. In S. Embretson (Ed.), Test design: Developments in psychology and psychometrics. New York: Academic Press. Reprinted by permission of the publisher and author.)

The same item type appearing on different tests may not represent the same component competencies. For example, if the vocabulary level of a verbal item is quite low, then nearly all persons will encode word meaning correctly. Thus, individual differences in solving the items will depend primarily on their ability to handle the other operations, but not encoding. Conversely, if the other operations involved in the item are easy, so that even persons with little ability can easily handle the operations, then the test will primarily measure individual differences in encoding word meaning.

A major aspect of test design is manipulating the difficulty of the processing events through item content. Figure 5.2 elaborates the impact of stimulus content, components, and strategies on test scores (Embretson, 1985a). These sources were also indicated in R. J. Sternberg's (1977) componential theory, but the focus in Figure 5.2 is on individual differences and the test score. The various sources are considered important only if they influence individual differences in item-solving accuracy.

A major assumption for the model in Figure 5.2 is that the correct information outcome from several component processes (e.g., C_1) is required to solve the item. The stimulus content of the item (e.g., S_1) influences the difficulty of the component processes. Some items may be solved by more than one strategy. A strategy involves a distinct combination of components that can be executed to solve the item. Figure 5.2 shows that components C_1 and C_2 form strategy St_1 and that C_2 and C_3 form strategy St_2. The total item may be solved by either strategy, given that the decision is made to execute it. The impact of the stimuli, components, and strategies on item solving determines the nature of the ability that is measured by the test score. In

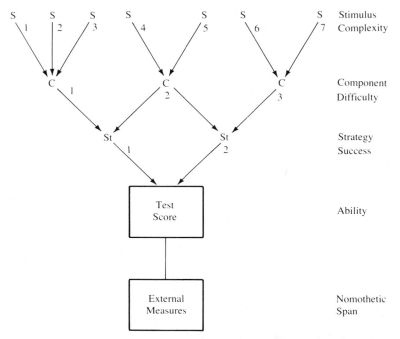

FIGURE 5.2   Impact of stimulus (S) content, components (C), and strategies (St) on test scores.

turn, the nomothetic span of the test is determined by the nature of the ability
that is measured.

    Dynamic testing procedures may change several aspects of processing,
as presented in Figure 5.1. The strategies that are applied to item solving
may be changed by imposing a strategy or training a strategy. For example,
Carlson and Wiedl (1979) imposed a strategy for solving Raven Coloured
Progressive Matrices by requiring examinees to verbalize while taking the
test. Feuerstein (1979), on the other hand, trained examinees in general
strategies and principles to help them profit from experience. The individual
component operations may also be changed. For example, Campione and
Brown (Chapter 3, this volume) give successively more complete hints about
problem components until solution is achieved.

Goals of Dynamic Testing

Why design a dynamic testing procedure? At least three goals for dynamic
testing can be distinguished: (a) to provide a better estimate of the specified
ability construct(s), (b) to measure new abilities, and (c) to improve mental
efficiency. Each of these will be elaborated, in turn, and then some relevant
psychometric issues will be indicated.

PROVIDING A BETTER ABILITY ESTIMATE

The first goal, providing a better estimate of ability, can result from dynamic testing procedures when the test does not measure the same trait for all examinees. Incomparability of performance between examinees can be reduced in several ways. First, irrelevant component processes with respect to the test design specifications can be eliminated by training examinees to a high level of performance. For example, Embretson and Farha (1985) improved estimates of spatial ability by training examinees in three-dimensional folding and rotation tasks. Their data suggested that the procedure eliminated item differences in anchoring the stem figure to the alternatives as a source of task difficulty. Eliminating anchoring as a difficulty factor made the posttest a better measure of rotational processes. Another example is given by Carlson and Wiedl's (1979) dynamic test procedure of verbalization during solution, which reduced the negative impact of personality variables on the Raven test performance.

Second, dynamic testing can improve ability estimates by supplying the outcomes from prerequisite processes for item solving. For example, if the goal is to measure analogical reasoning, definitions could be supplied for those words that the examinee does not know. For such an examinee, performance on the item indicates word knowledge rather than reasoning. The separability of sequentially dependent processes in analogical reasoning has been shown in several studies (R. J. Sternberg, 1977; Whitely, 1980a).

Third, dynamic testing procedures can reduce the number of processing strategies that are employed to solve items by training examinees in the use of a single strategy. That is, examinees may be employing item-solving strategies that utilize qualitatively different components to represent and process information. When subjects use different strategies, different abilities may be utilized to solve items. R. J. Sternberg and Weil (1981) found that the three-term series task depended on spatial ability when subjects used a spatial strategy but depended on verbal ability under a verbal strategy. In such a case, the abilities that are estimated by the total score for an examinee depend on the strategy that was selected. Thus, it is not clear what ability is measured by the items. Another example is Hughes' (1983) study that found that learning rate was a better measure of general ability when all examinees were trained to use the same strategy.

Fourth, dynamic testing procedures can train subjects in decision strategies that are related to the test format, but are unrelated to the constructs that are specified in the test design. For example, Bryden (1979) found that sex differences in a dichotic listening task disappeared when factors such as the allocation of attention, order of report, and decisions concerning whether to report items about which examinees were uncertain were minimized by the testing procedure. Thus, for females the task was measuring executive functioning rather than the intended construct.

To summarize, these examples suggest that ability estimates can be improved by a dynamic testing procedure when the task involves different components, strategies, or executive functions for different examinees. By changing the testing materials or training procedures, the measure becomes a better estimate of the intended ability by eliminating the irrelevant contributors to performance.

In contrast to the traditional psychometric view on coaching, using dynamic testing to improve ability estimates should imply (a) improved internal properties of the test, such as internal consistency or goodness of fit to a latent trait model; (b) increased predictive validity, as a result of the improved estimation of true score on the intended trait; and (c) a change in the impact of various cognitive factors on performance, such as processes, strategies, or executive functions. Studies that examine the possible improvement of ability estimates should assess these categories to evaluate dynamic testing procedures.

For all procedures that attempt to improve ability estimates, score comparability is an issue that must be solved. The norms for the test presented under standard conditions will be inapplicable to the test taken during or after the dynamic testing procedures since the scores of some examinees may change.

Furthermore, the particular score to utilize is also an issue. Perhaps only the score after the dynamic testing procedures is interesting. Thus, new norms must be obtained. In this case there is no point in obtaining a pretest measure. Or, perhaps two scores, reflecting the initial status and change, are desired. In this case, however, rather than "improving ability estimates" a new ability (modifiability) is being measured. This will be discussed below.

MEASURING NEW ABILITIES

The second goal, measuring new abilities, is the goal of several current dynamic tests. The goal is not to improve the estimation of ability but to measure a new ability, such as modifiability. Several investigators have sought to measure modifiability as a trait. For example, Whitely and Davis (1974) measured the modifiability of analogical reasoning from an intervention session. Budoff and his colleagues (Babad & Budoff, 1974; Budoff & Corman, 1974; Chapter 2, this volume) measured modifiability from a "test-train-retest" procedure. A major issue here is the type of scores that may indicate modifiability. Some possibilities are simple gain, residualized gain, and slope (which requires multiple measurements). Some related issues are the extent to which change reflects error of measurement and has predictive validity.

Woodrow's classic work on learning ability may also be seen as an attempt to measure a new ability: learning ability. His intervention consisted of many trials of practice. Woodrow (1938) measured learning ability as amount of improvement over the practice trials. Woodrow's design for modifiability assessment, however, probably represents an extreme case for problems with gain scores. Woodrow studied simple perceptual tasks in which individuals vary little in final levels of performance. Hence, the amount of improvement depends almost totally on initial level. That is, the lower the initial level the more learning. Thus, Woodrow's "learning ability" construct reflected mainly initial performance levels, which was highly task specific for his perceptual tests.

Another approach to modifiability is reflected by Campione and Brown's test (Chapter 3, this volume). They measure modifiability of performance by scoring the number of hints needed to solve a problem that has been failed. The fewer the hints the more modifiable the examinee. A major issue for this approach is the extent to which a new trait is measured by scoring the number of hints. Perhaps this just provides a better estimate of the initial ability.

Feuerstein (1979; Chapter 1, this volume) also assessed modifiability, but in addition sought to pinpoint specific deficiencies that underlie poor performance in the Learning Potential Assessment Device. The issue addressed is which cues, hints, or procedures make a difference in the examinee's performance. A possible "scoring" procedure is to mathematically model performance for an individual across items in which the supplied cues are systematically varied. Which cue leads to the highest level of performance?

Finally, other "new" dimensions that can be measured concern the maximal level of performance that can be reached. For example, the asymptotic level of performance could be estimated by obtaining multiple measurements after intervening experiences. Fitting the multiple data points to hypothesized curves of the modification process could assess slope and upper and lower asymptote. Bock (1976) reviewed several problems in the measurement of growth that are relevant to assessing modifiability. These will be presented briefly below.

IMPROVING ABILITY—MENTAL EFFICIENCY

The third goal is to improve ability (i.e., mental efficiency). Extensive training is required to change the level of mental efficiency on the task. For example, Feuerstein's (1980) Instrumental Enrichment program trains examinees on the input, elaborative, and output processes that he postulates to underlie academic performance. Transfer to both similar and dissimilar tasks has been found.

The major issue for this goal is the continued applicability of the norms, reliability, and validity given for the original test to the individuals who have taken the training program. Some additional psychometric issues are comparing individuals and programs. That is, when is an individual's change more than to be expected from measurement error? Do programs change two or more different traits equally? These comparisons require special scale properties for the test, to be reviewed below.

Scoring the Dynamic Test

Types of Dynamic Test Scores

How should performance be measured to reflect the changes introduced by the dynamic testing procedures or materials? Several types of scores are possible, and they are associated with somewhat different issues for reliability and validity. Furthermore, the different goals for dynamic testing are also related to the appropriateness of the various scores.

SIMPLE GAIN

Simple gain (G), the posttest score Y minus the pretest score X, has seemed the obvious measure of change: $G = Y - X$. However, this index is so beset with problems that some investigators (e.g., Cronbach & Furby, 1970; Lord, 1963) recommended abandoning it altogether. The reliability of gain scores is a special problem, since it depends on the reliability of the initial scores. Lord (1963) pointed out that large individual differences in gain are particularly likely when the pretest and posttest have large measurement errors. Thus, the assessment of reliability is an important issue for simple gain scores.

Further difficulties arise for simple gain scores as a result of their negative correlation with initial status (McNemar, 1969). Lord (1963) showed that, when reliabilities of the pretest and posttest are less than perfect, the regression of scores to the mean results in a negative correlation with initial status. That is, even if there is no average change in score levels, the low scorers tend to gain while the high scorers tend to lose (i.e., they move toward the mean). Since simple gain is negatively correlated with initial status, gain scores are confounded indices of change. Thus, the correlation of simple gain with criterion measurements may reflect the impact of initial status rather than gain.

A last problem with simple gain scores is the inequality of the units for the pretest and posttest. Comparing gains between individuals assumes not only that both tests provide fully equal measurements but that the scores represent equal interval measurements. Raw test scores generally do not have these properties, which consequently limits the measurement properties of simple gain scores.

RESIDUALIZED GAIN SCORES

Cronbach and Furby (1970) recommended that, if change is to be measured at all, residualized gain scores provide the fewest disadvantages. A very simple residualized gain score (G_r) may be computed as follows: $G_r = Y - (b_{y \cdot x} + a)$, where $b_{y \cdot x}$ is the linear regression coefficient for the posttest, Y, regressed on the pretest, X. Thus, residualized gain is the change that is not predicted by the pretest and hence reflects gain that is not linearly dependent on the pretest. A clear advantage of residualized gain is that its predictive validity, if any, will be independent of the initial score levels. However, reliability and the inequality of score units still are important issues for this type of score.

POSTTEST SCORES

If the dynamic test goal is to improve ability estimates, the initial test score may be regarded as misleading or irrelevant to the goals of testing. Hence, it is possible to use the posttest score alone. Thus, the initial pretest and the intervention are regarded as part of the standardized testing procedures, but do not provide any scores of interest. This approach is not typical in aptitude testing, but cognitive psychology experiments often devote considerable effort to bring performance to asymptotic level (under the experimental condition) before obtaining a measure of performance. For example, with the S. Sternberg (1969) task, 50 or 100 practice trials are not uncommon. The basic rationale is to eliminate performance differences due to different strategies or unfamiliarity with the laboratory procedures.

Using the posttest score alone presents no special problems if the test norms, reliability, and validity are based on the dynamic procedure. The standards for traditional tests are readily applicable to this type of dynamic test. However, it is also important to consider the construct validity of the posttest, as compared to the pretest, since the utility of the extended testing time is clearly an issue. That is, does the dynamic testing procedure change the construct representation (i.e., processing components, strategies, and knowledge structures involved in performance) of the test? Does nomothetic span change? That is, does the reliability and predictive validity of the posttest improve over the pretest?

A special issue for the posttest score is whether or not scores for change or the initial test would contribute additional predictive validity. This will be considered below.

If the dynamic test goal is to improve mental efficiency, then the posttest score is the appropriate score. Some assumptions that require empirical support are: (a) the constancy of the trait that is measured (that is, does the test measure the same trait before and after the intervention); (b) that the norms from the original test are still valid, and (c) that the predictions for scores achieved after intervention are valid.

SCORES REFLECTING BOTH INITIAL PERFORMANCE AND CHANGE

Another approach to scoring dynamic tests is to use two scores. For example, initial status on the pretest (X) may be scored in addition to simple gain (G). However, since simple gain is confounded with initial status, it provides a satisfactory assessment only in a very special case. That is, simple gain may be added to initial status in a multiple regression equation to predict criterion variables. Whitely and Dawis (1975) showed that the incremental validity of simple gain, in this case, assesses the predictive validity of modifiability.

Another approach is to use two scores that are uncorrelated to assess initial status and change. An interesting possibility is to use the predicted posttest score Y', as $Y' = b_{y \cdot x}X + a$, along with residualized gain (G_r). These scores will be uncorrelated, and furthermore, the set of two scores is theoretically interesting because their sum is the posttest score. Thus, these two scores represent an orthogonal partitioning of the posttest, that which can be predicted from initial status and that which cannot be predicted, the unexpected gain.

THE COURSE OF THE INTERVENTION

Yet another approach is to score the intervention procedure itself. For example, Campione and Brown (Chapter 3, this volume) score the number of "hints" that are needed to bring task performance to a criterion level. They administer the same set of items three times, in a pretest, with hints, and in a posttest. The fewer the hints, the more modifiable the examinee. The internal structure of the testing procedure, including pretest, is an important issue for this type of score. That is, to what extent does number of hints provide a different index than the initial score?

Another possible approach is to model growth in performance levels with successive amounts of intervention. Rather than "scoring" the test, a growth curve would be fitted to indices obtained under successively greater amounts of intervention. Figure 5.3 (from Bock, 1976) shows a growth curve that is fitted to successive measurements on a single individual. In this example, a child has been placed in an accelerated program with a goal of improving ability. Bock (1976) compared the fit of linear, quadratic, and cubic functions for these scores. Two measurement properties are required for growth curve modeling of an individual's cognitive performance. First, the scale units of the successive measurements must be equal. Second, the measurement error associated with each score at each time must be known. These properties are obtained in tests that are scaled by latent trait models, but are not obtained in tests that are developed by classical test theory. Latent trait models will be discussed more fully below.

Although model fitting for growth, as shown above, apparently has not been implemented as a scoring procedure for dynamic testing, it offers some possible theoretical advantages by assessing several aspects of individual differences. The advantages of curve fitting for comparing individual differences in physical stature have been explored (e.g., Thissen, Bock, Wainer, & Rocke, 1976), but a serious application to mental growth has yet to be attempted. However, concepts of intelligence as mental efficiency, capacity, and current mental functioning could possibly be defined by growth parameters. For example, if latent trait ability scores (e.g., test performance) are plotted against amount of intervention or "hints," the following indices can be obtained from fitting a logistic curve as in Bock (1976): (a) asymptotic level, or the highest score that is obtainable under the intervention design; (b) the intervention

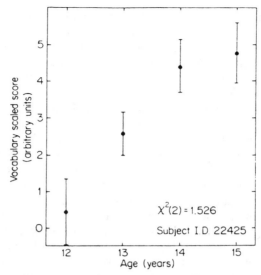

FIGURE 5.3 Growth curve fitted to successive measurements on a child placed in an accelerated program with a goal of improving ability. (From Bock, D. F. [1976]. Basic issues in the measurement of change. In D. N. M. de Gruijter & L. J. T. van der Kamp (Eds.), *Advances in psychological and educational measurement*. New York: John Wiley. Reprinted by permission of the publisher and the author.)

level at which peak growth velocity is obtained, that is, when half of the growth has occurred; and (c) the peak growth velocity. Mental capacity could be measured as asymptotic level and modifiability, perhaps, as the peak growth velocity.

Issues in Scaling the Test

Many designs for dynamic testing require that equivalent measurements be obtained from different item sets. Repeating the same test items after the intervention confounds the effect of item repetition with the effect of the intervention. Thus, more than one form of the test is needed. Unfortunately, it is widely recognized that test parallelism, as discussed in classical test theory (Gulliksen, 1950) cannot be met in practice. Classical test theory focuses on the test score, which is number correct (unless corrected for guessing). For scores from different tests to be equivalent, the tests must meet several conditions of parallelism, including equal means, standard deviations, reliabilities, and validities.

The measurement of change encounters at least three additional difficulties in estimating ability by classical test theory. First, if changes are to be compared between individuals, it must be assumed that raw scores truly represent an interval scale of ability. That is, the distances between the various raw scores must be equal increments in ability. To illustrate the implications for the measurement of change, consider the following example. Suppose the pretest to posttest change for person 1, $Y_{21} - Y_{11}$, equals change for person 2, $Y_{22} - Y_{12}$, as follows: $Y_{21} - Y_{11} = Y_{22} - Y_{12}$. By simply rearranging terms in this equation we can see that equal change implies that the interval between their pretest scores, Y_{11} and Y_{21}, equals the interval between their posttest scores, Y_{21} and Y_{22}, as follows: $Y_{21} - Y_{22} = Y_{11} - Y_{12}$. When equivalent score changes are used to indicate equal change, it is implicitly assumed that the equality holds regardless of the initial score level. Unfortunately, however, classical test theorists, such as Guilford (1954, p. 364), have often noted that "there is insufficient logical or experimental support for believing that obtained scores bear a linear relation to ability." For example, a one-point change at the mean has quite a different implication for individual differences than a one-point change at the extremes.

Wright and Stone (1979) showed how item difficulty levels, spread, and spacing can completely determine the raw score differences between two persons who differ somewhat in true ability. That is, on an eight-item test the score differences could range anywhere from 0 to 8, depending on the difficulties of the items that are selected. For example, if very easy items are selected, the score differences would be 0, since both persons would be likely to get all items correct. However, if the items had difficulties that fell between the two persons' abilities (i.e., below the ability of one person and above the ability of the other), one person could answer all 8 correctly while the other person could answer none of the items, yielding a raw score difference of 8 points! Clearly, it is desired that equal intervals on the true ability scale be distributed equally on the test. Although it has long been known that item difficulty distributions control the raw score distributions and the discriminability between score levels (Ferguson, 1949), classical test theory yielded no means to achieve equal ability discriminations. If change is to be measured, individual differences in change could be observed purely as a function of unequal ability discriminations between the tests.

When scores are compared over two scales involving different item sets, it is even more difficult to assume that raw score differences reflect the same intervals. The distributions of item difficulties may be quite different, thus creating different score distributions. Worse yet, even if the two scales are equated for item difficulty prior to administering dynamic testing procedures, an effective dynamic testing procedure will change the item difficulty distributions on the posttest. For example, if examinees increase their performance levels as a result of dynamic testing procedures, then the posttest items will be less difficult.

A second additional difficulty for change scores is that classical test theory does not readily provide a basis for interpreting performance changes. Classical test theory provides a norm-referenced interpretation of scores in which interpretation depends on score distributions. Scores from two or more measurements, such as pretest and posttest, have similar meanings only if the conditions of parallelism are met (i.e., a high correlation between normative standing on the two measures). If individuals differ in true gain, which is the only reason for measuring individual differences in gain, then the normative standing of individuals is shifting from pretest to posttest. Since the equivalency of the measures depends on the comparability of normative standings, classical test theory provides no way to interpret true individual differences in gain.

A third additional difficulty in the measurement of change is that classical test theory does not allow for systematic differences in measurement error between different gain scores. Classical test theory assumes that measurement error variances are constant between score levels. However, modern test theory (e.g., Lord, 1980) has made clear that extreme scores are measured substantially less reliably if the item difficulties are selected to yield a normal distribution of scores. Too few extremely easy or extremely difficult items will be available for the extreme ability levels. This is a special problem for gain scores because the extreme levels can be expected to change more between alternative forms solely on the basis of measurement error arising from too few appropriate items.

LATENT TRAIT MODELS AND ITEM RESPONSE THEORY

Applications of item response theory based on latent trait models are increasing rapidly in testing. For example, future group testing will increasingly be administered as computerized adaptive tests that require item response theory to equate scores. Furthermore, individual intelligence tests can also be expected to employ item response theory. These tests have often had flexible test content, adapted to the level of the examinee. A recent major test, the British Ability Scales (1982), utilized latent trait models to equate scores across varying test content.

Latent trait models provide a means of equating scores that could not be obtained from the classical test theory approach. It is beyond the scope of this chapter to provide an introduction to latent trait models. The reader is referred to Whitely (1980a) for a brief introduction and to Lord (1980) or Hambleton and Swaminathan (1985) for a more complete treatment. Latent trait models will be discussed here only in terms of how they achieve equating.

Equivalency is accomplished by modeling the encounter of a person with an item from not only the person's ability, but also from one or more parameters that describe each item. A simple latent trait model, the Rasch (1960) model, predicts the probability that person j passes item i as follows:

$$P_{ij} = \frac{\exp(\theta_j - b_i)}{1 + \exp(\theta_j - b_i)} \tag{1}$$

Where $_j$ = the ability of person j
b_i = the difficulty of item i
θ = the ability of person j

By including item parameters into the item response model, estimates for abilities take the difficulties of the items directly into account. Another important aspect of the model is that ability and item difficulty are placed on the same scale. That is, it can be seen that item solving depends on the difference between the person's ability and the item's difficulty (in an exponential function).

Applications of latent trait models typically require several steps. First, a large sample of examinees is administered the items from the item bank to calibrate their parameters. This is similar to the norming procedures for classical tests, except that the focus is on the individual item parameters rather than score distributions. If the Rasch model is used, an item difficulty value will be estimated for each item (b_i). The scale for the item difficulties resembles Z scores. Implementations of the Rasch model typically fix the mean to 0, so that the item difficulties range between -3.00 and 3.00.

Second, once the items are calibrated, the investigator can then select items to constitute a pretest and posttest. Not all individuals need to receive the same items. The investigator can select whatever item subset is most appropriate for each examinee's ability level. For example, in computerized adaptive testing, the items are tailored to the ability level of each examinee. The most informative items for the Rasch model have difficulties at the person's threshold; that is, the person has a .50 probability of passing. If a person has an ability of -2.00, which is a low ability, the most appropriate item has a low difficulty of -2.00 as well. The reader can confirm that these values will yield a probability of .50 in Equation 1 since the exponents will be 0 and e^0 is 1.00. Hence, the numerator equals 1 and the denominator equals 2.

Item difficulties *do not* have to be equated between different item sets. In fact, it is desirable to tailor item difficulties to the ability level of the persons who are tested so as to provide the most information about their ability and the least measurement error.

Third, after the items are selected, they are administered to the target subjects for the particular study. Fourth, ability scores are estimated. If the Rasch model is selected, with only one item parameter, then scoring tables may be prepared in advance for each subset that is selected since raw score is a sufficient statistic. Table 5.1 presents such a scoring table. For each possible raw score on this subset, an ability estimate is given. For another item subset, a different table must be generated. However, these tables are easily generated once the item parameters have been calibrated. Note that the ability estimates also have the same range as Z scores. However, they are anchored to the mean of the item bank (which was set to 0 for the Rasch model).

A maximum likelihood estimate of the ability equivalent for raw scores may be prepared in advance for each item subset that is selected if the item difficulties have been calibrated on a large sample. The criterion for ability

TABLE 5.1. Ability Estimates and Measurement Errors for Raw Scores on a 13-item Test

Raw score	Ability θ_I	Measurement error
1	−2.58	1.06
2	−1.78	.78
3	−1.26	.67
4	− .85	.62
5	− .49	.58
6	− .16	.57
7	.17	.57
8	.50	.58
9	.85	.61
10	1.26	.67
11	1.78	.78
12	2.57	1.05

estimation under maximum likelihood is, given the difficulties of the selected items, to find the ability estimate that would give the observed response patterns behind each raw score the highest likelihood.

CHANGE SCORES IN LATENT TRAIT VERSUS CLASSICAL TEST THEORY

It was indicated above that three special problems arose in classical test theory in measuring change: (a) raw score intervals were not linearly related to ability score intervals and the exact form of the relationship will vary between test forms, (b) no basis existed for interpreting performance changes, and (c) systematic differences existed in measurement errors for different score levels.

First, distances between ability scores are equal for different test forms that are scaled by latent trait models because ability is scaled to be additive to item difficulty in influencing the probability of a response. Additional ability increments yield additive effects on response potential regardless of initial score level.

Equal discriminations between close ability score levels can be achieved by administering the items adaptively. That is, items are selected from a large item bank for an examinee until a specified level of precision is achieved. This level can be approximately equated for all examinees. Adaptive testing is best implemented on computers so that the most informative items may be selected and precision may be calculated.

Second, latent trait ability scores have precise meaning for performance in the domain of items. That is, for any item in the domain, a probability of successful performance can be given using Equation 1. Thus, ability scores and score changes can be interpreted without reference to norms. That is, scores have direct implications for performance in the item domain. If the item bank is sufficiently well defined, criterion-referenced interpretations of ability scores may be given (Whitely & Dawis, 1974). Ability gains may be interpreted directly as increased competency in the item domain. This interpretation contrasts to norm-referenced interpretations in which change depends on replacing some person in a distribution.

Third, latent trait models also yield indices that can be used to adjust change scores for differences in measurement error. Wright & Stone (1979) proposed an index of change that adjusts latent trait ability scores for varying standard errors. It should also be noted in Table 5.1 that standard errors are given with *each ability estimate*. These errors depend on how much information is available about that ability. Information is highest when there are many items at the examinee's level. The index is the difference in ability scores divided by the pooled standard errors from the two tests, as follows:

$$Z = \frac{\theta_1 - \theta_2}{(\theta_1^2 + \theta_2^2)^{\frac{1}{2}}} \tag{2}$$

If the value exceeds a critical level, such as 1.96 for the .05 confidence level, then change is significant.

Lord (1963) indicated that gain scores should be compared to a "no-treatment" condition. One way to investigate this is to compare gain to measurement error. However, the index in Equation 2 may not be fully adequate for no-treatment comparisons considered by Lord (1963) to be desirable for the measurement of change. For example, Whitely and Dawis (1974) found that the mean standardized change index, as indicated above, was not 0 for a practice condition. Since practice is a "no-treatment" condition, some adjustment is required in the posttest abilities. One method that adjusts the scores for practice is to include an index that reflects the preceding item experience in the item parameter. Thus, a solution to an item is more likely when it has been preceded by other items. When this experience is included with the item, then person estimates will be lowered accordingly. Kempf (1977) proposed a "dynamic test model," using latent trait theory, that allowed for practice effects in calibrating items. Although he could not effectively estimate the new item parameters, some recent developments (Mislevy, 1985) with certain constraints are able to separate item calibrations from some practice effects.

Reliability

Stability

Stability refers to the repeatability of a score over varying conditions. Strictly speaking, the repeatability of a *change* score can be assessed only under very special conditions. If the dynamic testing effect resides only in the items or accompanying materials, then scores will decline to the initial level when these are removed. Then, the various procedures can be reintroduced and a replication of the "gain" can be attempted. In general, however, this special condition is not very interesting for dynamic testing. Dynamic testing typically tries to change the examinee so that scores do not revert to their initial level.

Rather than examine the repeatability of a *change* score, it is better to examine the degree to which pretest and posttest(s) are influenced by temporary conditions in the person or situation. However, it is well known that test–retest reliability estimates are influenced by true changes in performance (as a result of practice, for example) as well as temporary factors. Thus, for the test–retest formula, both true changes and temporary error will decrease reliability.

However, a method to separate error arising from temporary conditions and true change has been proposed (Whitely, 1979), and may be applied if at least four test scores are obtained (e.g., pretest and three posttests or continuing instruction over four tests). If score levels are changing over repeated administration of a test, it is possible to use a variant of structural equation models (e.g., Joreskog, 1974) to estimate both the true change variance and the temporary error variance for each test. Whitely (1979) showed how a simplex model can be implemented within a structural equation model to estimate unreliable variance. Table 5.2 shows the means, standard deviations, and correlations between 20 daily administrations of a motor task in which substantial practice effects are observed. The simplex model is appropriate when means and standard deviations are changing over repeated measurements, but the correlations between the measurements have a certain pattern. That is, correlations are generally increasing for later trials and the length of time (or intervention) between measurements decreases their intercorrelation. Table 5.2 shows decreases in means (indicating improvement) and standard deviations for the motor task.

Jones (1970) suggested that the pattern of trial correlations is also revealing about the nature of the change that is occurring. He postulated that a simplex form holds if error components in performance are declining. Thus, individual differences are decreasing, since error variance is decreasing. Furthermore, correlations between adjacent trials (along the diagonal) should be gradually increasing, since error is becoming less important. Another implication is that the correlations between adjacent trials should be higher than for nonadjacent trials because their overlap in error components is greater. Jones' approach may be interesting to apply to dynamic tests with several repeated assessments to assess the nature of the changes that are occurring.

Another method to assess stability is by fitting growth curves to assess the durability of the change. Since this was discussed above, it will not be repeated here.

Equivalency and Homogeneity

The consistency of performance over repeated testing is an important issue for dynamic testing, for all types of dynamic scores. If the quality to be measured is unidimensional, then indices of internal consistency such as Cron-

TABLE 5.2. Means, Standard Deviations and Intertrial Correlations

| Trial | Correlations | | | | | | | | | | Criterion | $\bar{X}$ | SD |
	1	2	3	4	5	6	7	8	9	10			
1	–	.81	.66	.36	.38	.34	.34	.19	.23	.25	.23	97	48
2	–	–	.72	.44	.36	.38	.41	.24	.34	.35	.28	61	27
3	–	–	–	.60	.61	.67	.68	.53	.59	.54	.37	48	18
4	–	–	–	–	.55	.50	.58	.60	.67	.62	.52	47	20
5	–	–	–	–	–	.62	.69	.70	.65	.68	.27	39	14
6	–	–	–	–	–	–	.77	.66	.64	.65	.36	35	10
7	–	–	–	–	–	–	–	.70	.66	.66	.37	32	10
8	–	–	–	–	–	–	–	–	.82	.76	.25	31	10
9	–	–	–	–	–	–	–	–	–	.81	.41	29	8
10	–	–	–	–	–	–	–	–	–	–	.44	26	6

Note. From Whitely, S. E. (1979). Estimating measurement error on highly speeded tests. *Applied Psychological Measurement, 3,* 141–159.

bach's Alpha or fit to a latent trait model should assess the quality of the measurement during or after the test intervention. If the goal is to improve ability estimates, then the internal consistency of the posttest should be greater than that of the pretest. For measurements of the course of intervention, such as number of external aids required for item solution, internal consistency over items can also be measured, using Cronbach's Alpha.

Internal consistency is also relevant to those dynamic testing procedures that attempt to measure new traits. Such procedures implicitly entail the hypothesis that the ability that is measured after the dynamic testing procedure is not the same as that measured by the original test items. This, of course, represents a hypothesis that can be tested by methods such as factor analysis of item (tetrachoric) correlations or fitting a unidimensional versus multidimensional latent trait model (Bock, 1976).

Interestingly, measuring the course of intervention by the number of hints may result not in a new ability but in an improvement of ability estimates over the pretest. Typically, the pretest score is based on items that are scored dichotomously (pass versus fail). Number of hints is a graded response in which originally failed items still receive credit depending on the number of hints required for solution. It could well be that number of hints is a more reliable measure of the original trait. Master's (1982) partial credit latent trait model gives insight as to why. The partial credit model is known to provide less measurement error for an ability with fewer items than the original dichotomous scoring. An application of the partial credit latent trait model to the course of intervention (number of hints) may provide a superior estimate of ability than the original test.

Validity

Two separate aspects of validity, construct representation and nomothetic span (Embretson, 1983), will be discussed for dynamic testing. As indicated above, construct representation research is concerned with identifying the variables that underlie performance, whereas nomothetic span research is concerned with evaluating the utility of a test as measurement of individual differences. The goal of this section, as for the others, is to examine some special issues for dynamic testing rather than to present a comprehensive review.

Construction Representation

COGNITIVE PROCESSES

A major thesis by many proponents of dynamic testing is that the cognitive processes that govern performance change in importance under dynamic testing. For example, Feuerstein (1979) outlined a theory of input, elaboration, and output phases of performance. His dynamic testing procedures change the impact of these processes on performance, particularly for the elaborational phase.

Some specific hypotheses about construct representation should be generated and tested for dynamic testing. The three possible goals of dynamic testing entail somewhat different hypotheses. First, if the goal is to improve ability estimates, for example, it can be hypothesized that cognitive processes that are irrelevant to the intended aptitude construct decrease in importance. Second, if the goal is to measure modifiability, it can be hypothesized that dynamic testing changes general aspects of cognitive processing so as to indicate learning ability. An alternative hypothesis, preferably to be rejected, is that dynamic testing changes only task-specific processes, so as automatize or routinize performance. Third, if the goal is to improve true ability, then it also can be hypothesized that dynamic testing procedures change cognitive processing, but in this case the initially low-ability examinees become more like the higher ability examinees in processing.

Component latent trait models (Embretson, 1984) can be used to test hypotheses about the cognitive components that are involved in performance. A theory of the components must be operationalized into a mathematical model that has values for each item. For the multicomponent latent trait model (Whitely, 1980b), item subtasks operationalize the postulated components, whereas for the linear logistic latent trait model (LLTM) (Fischer, 1983) scores for the items on the complexity of certain stimuli operationalize the components.

The linear logistic latent trait model will be elaborated here, since it is also used to test another aspect of construct representation, the locus of change, to be described below. The linear logistic model is a Rasch-type model, as shown in Equation 1, except that item difficulty (b_i) is replaced by a mathematical model of item difficulty. The mathematical model is very similar to a regression of item difficulty on the scores for the items. Thus, for the linear logistic latent trait model, b_i is replaced by the following:

$$b_i = \sum_k \lambda_k q_{ik} + a \tag{3}$$

where q_{ik} = the score for item i on stimulus complexity factor k

λ_k = the weight of complexity factor k in item difficulty

a = a normalization constant

For example, Embretson and Farha (1985) modeled item difficulty for their DAT figure folding pretest and posttest from a model of five complexity factors that were scored for each item. The factors that were scored included: (a) the maximum number of changes in plane to fold the stem—a given side may need rotation in two directions to create the figure (X_1); (b) the maximum number of surfaces carried in folding the figure (X_2); (c) the number of opposite pairs of markers (X_3); (d) the number of adjacent pairs of markers (X_4); and (e) the number of oblique sides (X_5).

Item difficulty on the pretest was predicted significantly by the following linear logistic model:

$$b'_{pre} = .75\ X_1 + .04\ X_2 - .32\ X_3 + .58\ X_4 - .52\ X_5 - .11$$

whereas the posttest item difficulty was predicted by the following model:

$$b'_{post} = .73\ X_1 + .02\ X_2 - .38\ X_3 - .02\ X_4 - .71\ X_5 - 1.29$$

It can be seen that the weights for the various stimulus factors are nearly identical except for X_4, number of adjacent markers. The significance tests confirmed that the weights for X_4 were significantly different between the pretest and the posttest ($p < .01$). This stimulus factor is postulated to determine the difficulty of the anchoring process of the stem to the alternatives. When its impact on item difficulty is reduced, the posttest becomes a relatively more pure measure of rotational processing.

THE LOCUS OF CHANGE

An important issue for dynamic testing is identifying the locus of change. That is, are changes in performance global, or are they specific to the item or person? Item-specific changes can result when the dynamic testing procedure supplies information or skills that apply only to some items. Person-specific changes result from individual differences in sensitivity to the dynamic testing procedure.

Spada and McGaw (1985) presented four models of change that may be tested with the linear logistic latent trait model. Three models were developed for homogeneous tests (presented in Table 5.3) as follows: (a) global learning effects, that is, all item difficulties change by a constant (g_t) for the occasion t; (b) item-specific effects (the training has unequal effects on different items, so that an item has a different parameter on each testing occasion, b_{it}); and (c) person-specific effects (although the items remain constant, separate abilities for each person are needed for each testing occasion, θ_{jt}). It can be seen in Table 5.3 that the exponent parameters for the linear logistic latent trait model differ for the three models, hence providing different mathematical models of the data.

The models can be compared for goodness of fit to dynamic testing data, using conditional maximum likelihood estimation. For completeness, it seems appropriate to add two models to Spada and McGaw's (1985) set: (a) person- and item-specific changes, when both persons and items are influenced differentially by the dynamic testing procedure (shown as Model IV in Table 5.3) and (b) no change, when both items and persons remain constant (shown as Model V in Table 5.3).

TABLE 5.3.   Latent Trait Models for Change

$$P(X_{ijt} = 1 \mid i,j,t) = \frac{e^{\lambda_{ijt}}}{1 + e^{\lambda_{ijt}}}$$

where: i = item, t = time, j = person
   I.   Global learning:
            $\lambda_{ijt} = \theta_j - b_i + \delta_t$
   II.   Person-specific learning:
            $\lambda_{ijt} = \theta_{jt} - b_i$
   III.   Item-specific learning:
            $\lambda_{ijt} = \theta_j - b_{it}$
   IV.   Person- and item-specific learning:
            $\lambda_{ijt} = \theta_{jt} - b_{it}$
   V.   No change:
            $\lambda_{ijt} = \theta_j - b_i$

The set of models represent alternative hypotheses about the nature of change. Dynamic testing typically assumes that person-specific change is the correct model, since it is the only model that measures something other than the ability on the initial test, without intervention procedures. Interestingly, this model is implicitly *multidimensional* since more than one ability score is obtained for each person (i.e., one for each occasion, such as pretest and posttest). These scores represent different abilities that are not necessarily highly correlated.

An application of Spada and McGaw's (1985) models of learning is Embretson and Farha's (1985) study on the dynamic testing of spatial ability. They found that the best model for their data was person-specific change, thus indicating that somewhat different abilities were measured before versus after their intervention procedure. They interpreted the person-specific change as indicating that the ability that was measured by the posttest eliminated sources of individual differences that were irrelevant to the intended ability construct for the pretest.

Nomothetic span

CRITERION-RELATED VALIDITY
A major motivation for dynamic testing is improved validity for educational criteria. Although the traditional educational criteria (e.g., school grades or achievement) are not necessarily the targets of dynamic testing, the goals of providing measurements that are more diagnostic of specific learning deficits (e.g., Feuerstein, 1979) and of determining how these defects may be remedied entail criteria to be predicted nevertheless.

Since traditional tests provide at least moderate prediction of many educational criteria, the case for dynamic testing is strong if incremental validity is supported. That is, what do the dynamic test scores add to the traditional test scores in prediction? This suggests a multiple regression of an educational criterion on both the traditional and the dynamic test scores.

For example, Embretson and Farha (1985) regressed two measures of test editing performance (for a microcomputer education class) on the spatial ability pretest and posttest (after the intervention). The multiple correlation significantly increased with the addition of the posttest.

The type of dynamic test score that is selected will also influence predictive validity. For example, the zero-order correlations can be compared between the pretest and posttest. In the case of Embretson and Farha's (1985) study, it was found that the posttest was a significantly better predictor than the pretest. However, this is not necessarily the case, even if incremental validity is supported. The incremental validity results from measuring something new or from increasing precision on one or more components. However, the posttest score can have a lower correlation with a criterion than the pretest score if individual differences on important components for the criterion have been substantially reduced.

Even if the posttest alone can be justified theoretically as an appropriate score for dynamic testing, a combination of two scores generally will yield higher predictive validities. If the predicted posttest score and the unpredicted posttest score (i.e., residualized gain) are both entered into a regression, the relative weights will depend on optimizing prediction of the criterion. If just the posttest score is used (the sum of the two scores), their implicit weights in prediction will depend on their relative standard deviations, not their validity.

STRUCTURAL ANALYSIS OF CORRELATIONS AND TRANSFER

Nomothetic span research on the test's correlations with other measures should be influenced heavily by construct representation research. Construct representation research can generate hypotheses about the pattern and magnitude of intercorrelations from an analysis of the component processes involved in the measures. For dynamic testing, if the construct representation is changed by the testing procedures, then different predictions about the correlations of the traditional test score and the dynamic test score can be generated. That is, the dynamic test score should correlate higher with measures of the changed constructs than the traditional test score.

These predictions can be tested by structural equation models (Joreskog, 1974) using several reference measures to reflect the construct changes. Alternative structural models can reflect different theories about the nature of the dynamic test change. For example, suppose that one theory states that the impact of dynamic testing is on elaborational ability, and another states that memory span is also influenced. A model for the first theory would specify that change scores correlate only with the reference tests that measure elaborational ability, whereas the second theory would specify that change scores correlate with both elaborational ability and memory span.

Studies on the transfer of dynamic testing (training) to other tasks could also generate models that can be tested by structural equations. To give an example, suppose that a near-transfer task and an irrelevant task have been identified on the basis of component overlap from construct representation. That is, the construct that is postulated to be changed by dynamic testing is represented on the transfer task but not on the irrelevant task. Each task is administered twice, before and after dynamic testing. Furthermore, the dynamic test is scored by a pretest and a posttest. Structural equation models for observational studies of change (i.e., longitudinal studies) can be applied to test hypotheses about transfer.

Figure 5.4 shows a conceptual organization of the dynamic test and the transfer tasks that can guide structural equation modeling. The arrows indicate the impact of a variable on those that occur at a later time. Three arrows go

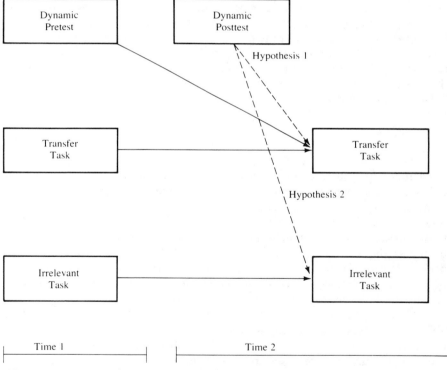

FIGURE 5.4   Conceptual organization of the dynamic test and transfer tasks that can guide structural equation modeling.

to the transfer task at time 2, from the transfer task at time 1, from the pretest, and from the posttest. The central interest is in the contribution of the posttest, controlling for the pretest (i.e., residualized gain). A structural equation coefficient for the posttest impact can be interpreted as a regression coefficient, as the impact of a variable controlling for all others in the equation. However, note that the transfer task at time 1 is also entered into the model. Thus, the impact of the posttest is controlled for initial standing on the transfer test. In other words, the structural weight for posttest represents only that aspect of the transfer task at time 2 that is not predicted from time 1, or residual gain in the transfer task. If transfer has occurred, then the structural coefficient for the posttest predicting should be significant (the broken line shown in Figure 5.4).

The irrelevant task shows the same three predictors as the transfer task, with the same relative controls. In this case, however, the structural coefficient for the posttest is expected to be nonsignificant since the irrelevant task does not contain the component that is supposedly changed by the dynamic testing procedures. Hypotheses about transfer can be tested by comparing model fits when the posttest structural coefficient is set to 0 versus when it is a free parameter, able to have a significant weight.

Testing hypotheses about change by structural equation modeling of longitudinal data is a very active area for methodologists. Dwyer (1983) presented a very extensive overview of model testing for longitudinal studies that may provide some useful prototypes for dynamic testing.

Conclusion and Summary

The goal of this chapter has been to examine the psychometric issues that are relevant to dynamic testing and to explore psychometric methods for scaling the test and assessing reliability and validity. It was noted that at least three goals of dynamic testing can be discerned: (a) improving ability estimates; (b) assessing new constructs, such as modifiability of performance; and (c) improving true ability. The three goals entail different psychometric issues and relevant supporting data.

Dynamic testing often concerns the measurement of change. Possible change scores and their associated psychometric problems were reviewed. Several problems arise from the classical test theory approach, including unequal scale intervals between raw scores, lack of a basis for interpreting performance change, and systematic differences in measurement errors for different score levels. It was shown that the scaling of tests by latent trait models remedies these problems.

Assessing the reliability and validity of dynamic tests also involves some new issues and requires special methods. For reliability, it was shown that classical test–retest methods confound true change with temporary influences on performance. Some methods to assess reliability were presented, but multiple replications are clearly required. In fact, perhaps the modeling of growth rather than change should be a more central focus for reliability studies.

For validity, changing performance levels by dynamic testing procedures makes the assessment of construct representation—the components, strategies, and knowledge structures that underlie test performance—especially important. The three goals of dynamic testing entail different hypotheses about the nature of processing changes. Examples of psychometric modeling methods to assess construct representation were presented. A related issue is the locus of change. That is, does performance increase globally, or is change specific to the items or to the persons? Nomothetic span—assessing the test as a measure of individual differences—also presents some special problems. It was suggested that understanding the specific effects of dynamic testing on cognitive processing of the test can lead to hypotheses about the magnitude and pattern of correlations of the dynamic test score with other measures. An example using transfer tasks as external measures was given.

This chapter must be considered only a rudimentary beginning of psychometrics for dynamic testing. Few psychometric methods have been developed specifically for dynamic tests. However, this chapter shows that the basis for psychometric methods for dynamic tests does exist. If dynamic testing fulfills its theoretical promise, the needed psychometric research will probably be forthcoming.

REFERENCES

Babad, E. Y., & Budoff, M. (1974). Sensitivity and validity of learning potential measurement in three levels of ability. *Journal of Educational Psychology*, *66*, 434–447.

Bock, D. F. (1976). Basic issues in the measurement of change. In D. N. M. de Gruijter & L. J. T. van der Kamp (Eds.). *Advances in psychological and educational measurement*. New York: John Wiley.

British Ability Scales. (1983). London: NFER–Nelson Windsor, Berk S.

Bryden, M. P. (1979). Evidence for sex-related differences in cerebral organization. In M. A. Wittig & A. C. Petersen (Eds.). *Sex-related differences in cognitive functioning: Developmental issues*. New York: Academic Press.

Budoff, M., & Corman, L. (1974). Demographic and psychometric factors related to improvement performance on the Kohs learning potential procedure. *American Journal of Mental Deficiency*, *78*, 578–585.

Carlson, J. S., & Wiedl, K. H. (1979). Toward a differential testing approach: Testing-the-limits employing the Raven's matrices. *Intelligence*, *3*, 323–344.

Cronbach, L. J., & Furby, L. (1970). How we should measure change—or should we? *Psychological Bulletin*, *74*, 68–80.

Dwyer, J. H. (1983). Application of structural equation models to causal inference from longitudinal data. In J. Dwyer, *Statistical models for the social and behavior sciences* (pp. 325–438). New York: Oxford University Press.

Embretson, S. E. (1983). Construct validity: Construct representation versus nomothetic span. *Psychological Bulletin*, *93*, 179–197.

Embretson, S. E. (1984). A general latent trait model for response processes. *Psychometrika*, *49*, 175–186.

Embretson, S. E. (1985a). Multicomponent latent trait models for test design. In S. Embretson

(Ed.), *Test design: Developments in psychology and psychometrics*. New York: Academic Press.

Embretson, S. E. (1985b). The problem of test design. In S. Embretson (Ed.), *Test design: Developments in psychology and psychometrics*. New York: Academic Press.

Embretson, S. E., & Farha, M. (1985, August). *Improving test validity by training spatial visualization skills*. Paper presented at the annual meeting of the American Psychological Association, Los Angeles.

Ferguson, G. A. (1949). On the theory of test discrimination. *Psychometrika, 14*, 61–68.

Feuerstein, R. (1979). *The dynamic assessment of retarded performers: The learning potential assessment device, theory, instruments, and techniques*. Baltimore: University Park Press.

Feuerstein, R. (1980). *Instrumental enrichment: An intervention program for cognitive modifiability*. Baltimore: University Park Press.

Fischer, G. (1973). Linear logistic test model as an instrument in education research. *Acta Psychologica, 37*, 359–374.

Guilford, J. P. (1954). *Psychometric methods*. New York: McGraw-Hill.

Gulliksen, H. (1950). *Theory of mental tests*. New York: John Wiley.

Hambleton, R. K., & Swaminathan, H. (1985). *Item response theory*. Boston: Kluewer-Nighoof Publishing.

Harris, C. (1963). *Problems in measuring change*. Madison: University of Wisonsin Press.

Hughes, O. L. (1983). A comparison of error based and time based learning measures as predictor of general intelligence. *Intelligence, 7*, 9–26.

Jones, M. B. (1970). Rate and terminal processes in skill acquisition. *American Journal of Psychology*, 222–236.

Joreskog, K. G. (1974). Analyzing psychological data by structural analysis of covariance matrices. In D. H. Krantz, R. C. Atkinson, R. D. Luce, & P. Suppes (Eds.), *Contemporary developments in mathematical psychology*. San Francisco: Freeman.

Kempf, W. (1977). A dynamic test model and its use in the microevaluation of instructional material. In H. Spoda & W. F. Kempf (Eds.), *Structural models in thinking and learning*. Bern, Switzerland: Hans Huber Publishers.

Lord, F. M. (1963). Elementary models for measuring change. In C. Harris (Ed.), *Problems in measuring change*. Madison: The University of Wisconsin Press.

Lord, F. J. (1980). *Applications of item response theory to practical testing problems*. Hillsdale, NJ: Erlbaum.

MacCorquodale, K., & Meehl, P. E. (1948). On a distinction between hypothetical answers and intervening variables. *Psychological Review, 55*, 95–107.

Master, G. M. (1982). A Rasch model for partial credit scoring. *Psychometrika, 47*, 149–174.

McNemar, Q. (1969). *Psychological statistics*. New York: John Wiley.

Messick, S. (1972). Beyond structure: In search of functional models of psychological process. *Psychometrika, 37*, 357–375.

Messick, S., & Jungeblut, A. (1981). Time and method in coaching for the SAT. *Psychological Bulletin, 89*, 191–210.

Mislevy, R. (1985). *The dynamic test model revisited*. Paper presented at the annual meeting of the Psychometric Society, Nashville.

Pellegrino, J. W., & Glaser, R. (1979). Cognitive correlates and components in the analysis of individual differences. *Intelligence, 3*, 187–214.

Rasch, G. (1960). *Probabilistic models for some intelligence and attainment tests*. Copenhagen: Danish Institute for Educational Research.

Roid, G. H., & Haladyna, T. M. (1982). *A technology for test-item writing*. New York: Academic Press.

Spada, H., & McGaw, B. (1985). The assessment of learning effects with linear logistic test models. In S. Embretson (Ed.), *Test design: Developments in psychology and psychometrics*. New York: Academic Press.

Sternberg, R. J. (1977). *Intelligence, information processing and analogical reasoning: The componential analysis of human abilities*. Hillsdale, NJ: Erlbaum.

Sternberg, R. J. (1981). The nature of intelligence. *New York University Education Quarterly*, *3*, 10–17.

Sternberg, R. J., & Weil, E. M. (1981). An aptitude-strategy interaction in linear syllogistic reasoning. *Journal of Educational Psychology*, *72*, 226–239.

Sternberg, S. (1969). Memory scanning: Mental processes revealed by reaction time experiments. *American Scientist*, *57*, 421–457.

Thissen, D., Bock, D., Wainer, H., & Rocke, A. F. (1976). Individual growth in stature: A comparison of four growth studies in the U.S.A. *Annals of Human Biology*, *3*, 529–542.

Vygotsky, L. S. (1978). *Mind in society: The development of higher psychological processes* (M. Cole, V. John-Steiner, S. Scribner, & E. Souberman, Eds. and Trans.). Cambridge, MA: Harvard University Press.

Whitely, S. E. (1979). Estimating measurement error on highly speeded tests. *Applied Psychological Measurement*, *3*, 141–159.

Whitely, S. E. (1980a). Latent trait models in the study of intelligence. *Intelligence*, *4*, 97–132.

Whitely, S. E. (1980b). Multicomponent latent trait models for ability tests. *Psychometrika*, *45*, 479–494.

Whitely, S. E., & Dawis, R. V. (1974). The effects of cognitive intervention on latent ability measured from analogy items. *Journal of Educational Psychology*, *66*, 710–717.

Whitely, S. E., & Dawis, R. V. (1975). A model for psychometrically distinguishing aptitude from ability. *Educational and Psychological Measurement*, *35*, 51–66.

Woodrow, H. (1938). The relationship between abilities and improvement with practice. *Journal of Educational Psychology*, *29*, 215–230.

Woodrow, H. (1946). The ability to learn. *Psychological Review*, *53*, 147–158.

Wright, B. D., & Stone, M. H. (1979). *Best test design*. Chicago: MESA Press.

APPLICATIONS TO CURRENT PRACTICE

6

Measures for Assessing Learning Potential

MILTON BUDOFF

Training-based assessment was studied at the Research Institute for Educational Problems in the development of learning potential (LP) assessment procedures as an alternative to traditional IQ testing. This chapter presents the specifics of the test procedures, the various models used in our training-based assessment work, and the applicability of these models to different at-risk populations, including students categorized as educable mentally retarded, moderately and severely mentally retarded, those from language backgrounds other than English, and specific racial or nationality backgrounds. Chapter 2 presents the logic and validity data relevant to learning potential assessment. While some of the materials in this chapter overlap with the materials in Chapter 2, this chapter is focused on assessment procedures and models; Chapter 2, on the logic and validity of the procedures.

The LP assessment approach is based on a conceptualization of intelligence which stresses trainability, or the ability to profit from learning experiences. This approach has addressed problems of trainability by examining the child's general ability to reason when one ensures the child knows the types of materials being examined. It assumes that the effect of the prior and continuing experiences of poor and/or nonwhite children which did not allow them to spontaneously acquire school-relevant skills in their natural environment will be minimized in this assessment. The learning potential paradigm provides subjects with training experiences directly relevant to the reasoning task presented; they are given the opportunity to demonstrate that they can apply their problem-solving ability and to show whether they can improve their performance on the task. The improved performance indicates problem-solving capability not evident when training is not provided as part of the test administration. The usual learning potential assessment paradigm replaces the traditional product-oriented one-session test (e.g., IQ test) with a three-stage procedure which includes a pretest, training session(s), and a posttest.

Milton Budoff. Research Institute for Educational Problems, Cambridge, Massachusetts.

The Instruments

Four instruments developed at the Institute for assessing learning potential are available for general use: procedures based on Kohs Block Designs, Raven Progressive Matrices, the Series Learning Potential Test, and the Picture–Word Game. A Spanish language version is available for two measures (the Raven Progressive Matrices and the Series Test) and a formboard version of the Raven Progressive Matrices is available for use with moderately and severely mentally retarded adolescents and adults.

The Block Design Learning Potential Procedure

Budoff (1967, 1969; Budoff & Friedman, 1964) first measured learning potential using Kohs' (1923) original Block Design Test. Using enlarged designs drawn to the scale of 1-inch cubes for testing and training, Budoff et al. devised a training program that taught strategies useful for solving block design problems. This task was selected because it does not involve verbalization or verbal exchange with the tester, is not associated with school-like work and the subjects therefore have not experienced failure with the task, and involves a large component of reasoning; however, a few basic strategies can be taught that allow the intelligent student to solve quite difficult problems.

Training is directed toward teaching the principles involved in the construction of the block designs. The materials consist of a test series of 15 of the original Kohs Block Designs, including five designs with 16 blocks and a set of 16 one-inch cubes, each with a red, white, blue, yellow and red/white and blue/yellow sides. The designs are arranged in order of increasing difficulty. Design 7 from the Wechsler Adult Intelligence Scale (WAIS) was added. The designs are printed on 5 × 6-inch white cards to double the scale of the original Kohs designs so that the stimulus designs and the block constructions are equivalent in size. This modification was suggested by Goldstein and Sheerer (1941) as a means of simplifying the task. The five coaching designs consist of three four-block designs (C from WISC; 3 and 7 from the Kohs series), and two nine-block designs (5 from the WISC and 8 from the WAIS). The coaching designs are printed in the same format and dimensions as the test designs.

The 15 test designs are administered individually three times: first prior to coaching, and then 1 day and again 1 month following coaching. Kohs instructions for administering the test are used at each session. A sample problem is demonstrated by the examiner. The child has to construct the sample correctly before the remainder of the items are presented. Testing is discontinued after three successive failures.

The coaching procedure emphasizes the following principles:

1. Maximizing of success by the possibility of working down to the simplest elements in the design.

2. Freely offered praise and encouragement.
3. The strategy of motorically checking the construction, block by block, against the design card to encourage an active, planned, and systematic work approach and to allow the subject to see concretely the success he or she is achieving,
4. Emphasis on the concept of two-color blocks as the elements composing the design (e.g., by teaching the process of building a stripe and the concept of orientation of the blocks in a design by constructing a diamond).

The coaching sequence for an item is so designed that the subject has to solve the problem initially from a stimulus card in which the blocks are undifferentiated. If he or she fails to solve the problem, he or she is presented one row of the design at a time. On succeeding presentations, if the subject fails to align the blocks correctly, the blocks are progressively outlined. Five coaching designs were used: three four-block and two nine-block designs.

RELIABILITY AND STABILITY OF THE KOHS LEARNING POTENTIAL TEST

The Kohs Learning Potential Test results in a stable assessment of ability to reason. Correlations of .701 and .835 between pretest and immediate posttest scores were computed from the scores of nontrained samples of EMR institutionalized and community special class adolescents. Correlations obtained between immediate and delayed (1 month) posttraining scores ranged from .89 and .95 with large diverse samples and .866 between immediate posttest and a test 6 months after training with smaller institutionalized samples (Budoff, 1967; Budoff & Friedman, 1964).

The Raven Progressive Matrices Learning Potential Test

Although work with the Kohs block designs procedure demonstrated consistent differentiation of children in special classes for the educable mentally retarded above the age of 12 or 13 years, below these ages there was poorer differentiation; a disproportionate number of subjects, particularly female and black subjects, fell into the nongainer or low-able category (Budoff & Corman, 1973). It was thought that the visual organizational demands of the task may be too difficult for the younger subjects and working with blocks may not sufficiently motivate girls. We therefore decided to develop an additional learning potential measure that would be useful for younger subjects and might evidence fewer biases than those produced by the Kohs measure.

Initially, we explored the utility of Feuerstein's procedure (1968), which uses the Raven Progressive Matrices Test (Series A, AB, and B; Form 1956) in a pre–posttest design with training on double classification problems drawn from Set B. The difficulty was that Feuerstein trained to the six 2 × 2 analogy problems in the B series and then tested responses to them on the posttest.

The improvement demonstrated by trained subjects could be attributed to the trained items (mean increase from 17 to 23 items) (Feuerstein, personal communication, 1967). Also, we found the verbal instructions obtained in Jerusalem to be too vague and nonspecific to provide for a relatively standardized administration. We chose to retain this task, but to design a more explicit training procedure. Two goals were set. The first required that the task discriminate among primary grade, lower class children who had serious school learning difficulties and low IQs. The second goal was to develop a second learning potential procedure for the teenage sample.

The initial experimental plan sought to train understanding of the double classification problems. To make the procedure applicable for the younger student, however, training procedures were added that were relevant to the easier items on Sets A and AB (1956 series), namely, pattern completion and orientation, so as to provide problems within the grasp of young children. Hurtig (1959) and Jacobs and Vandeventer (1971) have shown that double classification problems are too difficult for younger primary-grade children even following training. A factor analysis of the Raven items (Sets A, AB, and B) demonstrated these three subsets, and a larger, more mixed fourth factor, a general visual design orientation (Corman & Budoff, 1975). Item analyses set the order of difficulty of the item types, and training was developed with these factors in mind.

For the teenage students (above 12 years), the hypothesis was that if the double classification training was effective, the subjects would show transfer to 3×3 problems (Raven Series C, D, and E; 1958) for which no specific training was given.

The Raven Progressive Matrices, Sets A, AB, and B (Raven, 1956) and Sets C, D, and E (Raven, 1958), are group administered before and after training. The intervals between training and posttest administrations are uncontrolled because the tests are group administered. The training in the initial version was offered individually in one or two sessions, depending on the child's age and responsiveness. A special answer sheet was designed that allowed the children more space for their answers. The colored matrices booklet (Raven, 1956) is distributed first and completed by the children. Then a separate recording sheet for Series C, D, and E (Raven, 1958) is distributed along with the problem booklet, which presents 3×3 analogy problems in black and white designs. The tests are administered as described by Raven in the manuals. Unlimited time is allowed for each set of items. The class proceeds through the colored matrices one set at a time, waiting for most of the children to complete a set so all may start the next series together. On the C, D, and E series, the children are instructed to continue until they complete the entire book after the start of Set D. Since many of the problems in these series are too difficult for many, younger children are urged to do as well as they can. They are also told that the problems are much too difficult for them and that they should not dwell too long on any one problem if they cannot figure it out, since these problems were meant for much older children and adults. In later versions of the training, the posttest was restricted to Sets C and D. A later version of this training was group administered using 35-mm slides to maintain the students' attention at the chalkboard. In the latest version of this training, no training booklets are used; the students, as a group, work out the correct answer by drawing it in on the chalkboard on the picture projected by the slide.

Throughout the training, a number of principles are followed. First, no problem that appears in the Raven Matrices is presented in the training series. Second, great effort is made to be certain that the child understands the demands being made for performance of the task. Thus, the training procedure is not strictly standardized, but allows for a number of variations to ascertain whether the child understands what is required. Problems are presented in up to three different formats before training is discontinued.

Third, the requirements of the task are demonstrated initially on materials that are pictorial and meaningful (e.g., an incomplete American flag or a Campbell's soup can for pattern completion tasks). Successive problems require the child to deal with geometric forms in order to attune the child to the formats presented in the test.

Fourth, the requirements of the task are concretized in motoric performance, for example, having the child draw the item that completes the pattern in a workbook before looking at the various alternative solutions presented. In the double classification problems, it was found that children could easily derive one attribute at a time, but often did not hold the first attribute in mind while they derived the second. The child's understanding was facilitated by having him or her draw the relevant attributes one at a time, as they were derived. This helped to concretize the elements of the solution process so that many children, after this type of practice, could do the double classification problems mentally with very little difficulty. The child's attention was focused on the elements of the problem since the choices below the problem were covered. When the correct response was drawn, the child's attention was then directed to the choices in the lower half of the page. The solution process throughout this part of the training is verbalized by the examiner.

After the child has done this correctly for a series of items, and the examiner feels that the child understands what is required, the procedure is altered. In the first alteration, the child is asked to solve the problem with the choices covered, and then asked to select the correct choice. After successful handling of this modification, the child continues to solve the problems in the usual mode (i.e., with the choices uncovered). The examiner continues to direct the child's attention to the elements of the problems before the alternative choices are considered. When some children, in their haste, become careless, they are asked to draw the two elements of the correct design for a number of items. When a child has difficulty drawing the designs, the examiner draws them at the child's direction.

The fifth principle followed in individual training is that, during the training on the double classification problems, after the child ceases to draw the alternative and begins doing the problems mentally, on every third problem the child is required to indicate verbally how he or she arrived at this solution. This seems to help the child maintain the quality of the solution process attained by the drawing accompanied by the examiner's verbalization. A minimal verbal response, often in combination with pointing by the child, suffices to indicate to the examiner that the child is solving the problems.

Two studies were conducted to test the effects of training on the Raven Matrices problems. The first (Corman & Budoff, 1973b) was a study in which samples of regular class children from grades 2 to 6 were pretested, trained, and posttested. All subjects were from a low-income, white, urban district. They were pretested on Matrices Series A, AB, and B, and C, D, and E in a class administration. Subjects from each age group were randomly assigned to the trained and nontrained conditions after being ranked on the basis of pretest scores on Sets A, AB, and B. Following completion of individual training, all of the subjects were retested in their own class-size groups, on the same series of problems. The composition of the two groups at each age level was similar in age, group-administered IQs, pretest scores on the Raven Series A, AB, and B, and the number of children who had repeated grades.

Training on problems found in the Raven Matrices Series A, AB, and B did improve the performance of these children. The posttraining scores of all but the 12-year-olds improved to an asymptotic ceiling imposed by lack of additional problems. This training also improved the performance of trained younger children on the 3 × 3 analogy problems of Sets C, D, and E, for which they had not been trained.

For the second study (Corman & Budoff, 1973c), samples of children from special classes for the educable mentally retarded were available from the same inner-city area and suburban communities. These subjects were also trained individually and pre- and posttested in class-size groups.

The trained special class students did not attain the posttraining mean score of the regular class students on Sets A, AB, and B. Following 1 hour of training on the types of tasks found in the Raven Matrices, however, the special class students' scores increased to approximate the pretraining level of the regular class subjects.

The special class students did very poorly on the nontrained 3 × 3 problems, even following training on the 2 × 2 analogies. They simply did not spontaneously transfer the training received on the 2 × 2 analogies to the 3 × 3 problems. This failure led to revisions in the training procedure. Training stimuli and procedures oriented toward application of different appropriate principles for the various types of 3 × 3 problems were developed. These procedures have been pilot tested and revised, and are available for use with students above 12 years of age. Tests of the trained special class and regular class students indicated that trained groups attained higher scores on

Sets C, D, and E. At this point in our work with students in schools, we became increasingly involved with elementary rather than junior high—or high school–age students, and have not used this procedure to any great extent. A further limitation is the lack of appropriate recent American norms for the Matrices test, especially for low-income and minority group adolescents.

RELIABILITY OF THE RAVEN LEARNING POTENTIAL TEST

Test–Retest Reliability. Test–retest reliability on Sets A, AB, and B for regular and special class students has been determined with two independent samples. The sample in Study 1 consisted of second- through sixth-grade nonhandicapped students who resided in a low-income urban area and special class students who ranged in age from 7 to 15 years (mean = 11 years, SD = 2). The majority of both groups were from working class families, and about 25% were black. The sample in Study 2 consisted of normal subjects evenly distributed among grades 1 through 5 in two schools in a large urban community, and special class subjects ages 5½ to 14 years (mean = 10, SD = 2) who attended the same schools from which the normal sample was drawn. In Study 2 about half of both the populations was black. Twenty-eight percent of the nonhandicapped children were from middle-class backgrounds as compared to 5% of the EMR children.

All tests were administered to class-size groups in both studies. The procedures of the studies differed with respect to the interval between pretest and posttest and size of training groups. The time interval between the two test administrations averaged 30 days in Study 1 and about 1 week in Study 2. In Study 1, all subjects were trained individually; in Study 2, nonhandicapped subjects were trained in groups of 6 to 13, and half the trained EMR subjects received training in groups of 5 to 8, with the other half trained individually. Investigations comparing the effects of individual and group training have revealed that, on the average, posttest scores of children trained in groups do not significantly differ from those of individually trained children (Corman & Budoff, 1973b, 1973c).

Test–retest correlations for trained and nontrained nonhandicapped and EMR subjects are presented in Table 6.1. These correlations indicate stability of the distribution of total scores for both nonhandicapped and EMR subjects after training, although the correlation for trained nonhandicapped subjects was somewhat lower in Study 1 than in Study 2. The test–retest reliability, represented by the correlations for nontrained subjects, was high for nonhandicapped children in both studies. For EMR subjects, test–retest reliability was only .514 in Study 1, but was .871 in Study 2. The longer interval between test administrations in Study 1 may partly explain the lower coefficients obtained in that investigation. The low test–retest reliability of the EMR subjects may reflect the highly variable performances of these children. Variability of response appears to be a major problem presented by these children (Baumeister & Kellas, 1968) and provides further justification for

TABLE 6.1. Test–Retest Correlation Coefficients for EMR and Nonhandicapped Subjects in Studies 1 and 2

Subjects	Study 1	N	Study 2	N
Nonhandicapped				
Trained	.605	147	.749	173
Nontrained	.817	84	.839	201
EMR				
Trained	.751	319	.769	110
Nontrained	.514	46	.871	55

training-based models of assessment. That is, variability of response to a task may be reduced considerably and understanding enhanced when the demands of the test are more clearly communicated, especially in a "hands on," physically involving, competence-inducing training experience.

Internal Consistency. Table 6.2 presents the Kuder–Richardson formula 20 (KR 20) reliability coefficients and standard errors of measurement obtained for EMR and nonhandicapped children. The EMR children ranged from 7 through 15 years. The nonhandicapped children were in grades 2 through 6, ranging from 7 through 11 years. The KR20 coefficients in the table indicate a high degree of internal consistency, both before and after training, for nonhandicapped as well as EMR children.

The Series Learning Potential Test

The first entirely group-administered learning potential measure is the Series Learning Potential Test (SLPT), entirely developed at the Research Institute for Educational Problems. This is also a nonverbal reasoning task. Each item presents a horizontal row of cells, each of which contains a stimulus figure. One cell is blank. The subjects must identify from among the multiple choices on the right side the picture that best completes the series. Four concepts may vary in a series: semantic content (meaningful or geometric figures, up to six instances in one item), size (large/small), color (black/white), or ori-

TABLE 6.2. Kuder–Richardson Formula 20 (KR20) Reliability Coefficients on the Raven Progressive Matrices for EMR and Nonhandicapped Subjects in Studies 1 and 2

Subjects	KR20	SEM	N
Nonhandicapped			
Pretraining	.89	2.11	243
Posttraining	.86	1.88	147
EMR			
Pretraining	.88	2.22	399

entation (up/down, left/right). Three concepts may appear on one series and they may vary symmetrically or asymmetrically. Thus, a blank cell may require a large black dog. The child is trained to identify the separate concepts composing a series, to trace the pattern of occurrence for each concept separately by "singing the tune," and to cross out the choices that are inappropriate for a correct solution for that concept. Each concept is traced successively until one choice remains as the correct answer. Thus, the child is directed to check the size of the figure, using the "tune" large, large, small; large, large, small; ——————— , large, small. All the small figures among the answer choices would be crossed out on the answer side of the page. The child does the same with color, "singing the tune" for the concept (black, white; black, white; black, ——————), and then with type of figure. The children are trained on items that only include meaningful pictures.

Two equivalent 65-item forms of the test are used, with items corresponding in concepts but not in specific pictures or their arrangements. The test booklets are titled "The Series Game." None of the 17 coaching items is identical to any of the 130 test items. The test contains several types of items, 40 of which consist of meaningful pictures. Effectiveness of the transfer from the trained principles is measured by two scores. First, improvement in solving the series of 40 meaningful pictures on posttest indicates the child can solve nontrained instances of the trained items. Ten series items use geometric figures to determine whether the child can transfer the strategies learned in training with the meaningful pictures to dissimilar stimuli.

Second, 15 double-classification items are presented in matrix format to test generalization of the strategies learned to problems that require the same reasoning process as the series problems, although the arrangement of the stimuli is quite different, and the strategies may be mediated differently. Five matrices are presented in meaningful pictures, and 10 in geometric symbols.

As developed, the test is considered suitable for children from 7 to 16 years of age. In general, the pretest requires about 30 minutes; the training session on the next day lasts about 30 to 35 minutes. This may vary depending on the extent to which the children require help in understanding the items. The posttest is administered on the day following training, and again later than 1 week following training, and requires about 25 to 30 minutes.

Seventeen series of meaningful pictures are used in the training session. The disposable booklet is entitled "Tricks for the Series Game." The training session is conducted as a group session. The group may range from 5 to 30 children, depending on the children's age or ability level and the class setting. Training emphasizes the following:

1. In each series "something changes," and the child must first identify which aspects of the problem are changing (the concepts)—for example, object, size, or color.
2. The concept that changes in each series has a "tune" or rhythm.

After identifying a concept, the child is shown how to discover and "sing" the tune to himself or herself. The child is encouraged to "sing the tune" beyond the blank cell in the series, and beyond the series itself. The intent is to have the child understand the regularities of the pattern.

3. Most series have more than one "tune." The child must find all the "tunes," but "sing" them one by one. The student learns to simplify the process of solving the problem by identifying each concept and solving it separately.

4. For every "tune" the student crosses out the choices that do not solve the series problem. Nothing needs to be remembered. Remaining choices indicate there are more "tunes" to be "sung."

5. "Tunes" do not necessarily start at the beginning of the series, and they can be "sung" in any direction.

In short, the children learn to identify the concepts composing the series and to simplify the problems by solving each concept separately, using an appropriate "tune." Subjects must overcome the tendency to look at more than one concept at once, ignore irrelevent concepts, and solve them one at a time. For example, big/little is sung by the group, then large/small, and so on.

In compiling the final forms of the test, several issues were considered. First, we wished to select items that showed good discrimination among subjects, as evidenced by the magnitude of the correlation between item and total test score. At the same time, we wished to include items at all levels of difficulty, although very easy and very difficult items have less discriminatory power than items in the middle range. Since the posttraining performance on the Series Learning Potential Test was the crucial score for evaluating learning potential, we wished to have the most discriminatory items in each equivalent pair placed in the posttest. These items were defined as those showing higher internal consistency, a higher gain from pre- to posttest, with each of the wrong choices equally attractive. These issues were addressed by administering equivalent pilot forms of the pretest and posttest to 289 subjects prior to and following training. Of the 289 subjects, 61 were classified as educable mentally retarded and in special classes; 228 attended regular classes in several New England schools. Ages ranged from 7 to 16 years, although most regular class students were in the middle elementary grades. Item analyses evaluated the internal consistency and level of difficulty of each item and the amount of change in percent passed observed for each item from the pre- to posttraining sessions.

The final two forms of the test contain 65 items each. The level of difficulty of both forms is equal; 70.81% for the pretest and 70.97% for the posttest were passed by the pilot test sample. These figures were quite high because of the fact that the majority of the subjects in this analysis were bright, middle-class subjects in regular classes. The average correlation coefficient between item and total test score was .43 for the pretest and .48 for the posttest. The average change in percent passed following training for the items placed in the final pretest form was 8.72%. The average change following training for the items placed in the posttest form was 12.62%. Thus, although the two forms are equivalent in the characteristics of the items and levels of difficulty, the posttest form contains items of greater discriminability that show greater rates of improvement following training.

Following this initial developmental work, the Series Test was used with and without training and with large numbers of children in regular and special classes, ranging in age from 6 to 16 years. The most disturbing feature of the data from these studies was the evidence for both EMR and regular class students that the students attained a de facto ceiling on the test by 8 years of age for both the pre- and posttraining scores, although the latter scores were higher on the average and the scores were not at the actual ceiling for the test. This apparent ceiling restricted the value of the instrument to younger students.

The de facto ceiling at age 8 in these early data necessitated further study of the characteristics of the two forms of the SLPT. A younger sample was utilized to examine the curve of increase in scores. The Series Test was given to first- through fourth-grade students in 79 classrooms in six middle- and working-class Connecticut towns. All students were tested twice. Students were assigned to subsamples that determined the test forms they received and whether or not they were trained between the two test sessions. Other data collected included IQ scores, information on race and social class, and scores on the Gates–MacGinitie Reading Test. All testing took place during one winter and spring.

Analyses of test characteristics (Corman & Budoff, 1973a) showed the KR20 of both pretest forms to be .95 and the interform correlation coefficient between total pretest scores to be .84. Test–retest reliabilities were .87 and .90 for Forms A and B, respectively.

Analysis of variance of Series scores by town indicated that upper-middle-class, mostly white, suburban students had higher mean pretest scores than urban, mostly black, lower socioeconomic status (SES) students. Analysis of initial performance by grade revealed that fourth graders attained the higher scores, third graders the next highest, second graders the next highest, and first graders the lowest.

Trained students achieved a greater mean score increase than nontrained students. Training was found to be most effective for grades 1 through 3, and trained second and third graders in the poor, largely black samples had the largest increase in mean scores. In the middle-class towns, the greatest increase occurred for the first and second graders. Fourth graders appeared to profit least from training, suggesting that the children were operating at the de facto ceiling on the tests.

Results of multiple regression analysis revealed that students who had high IQs, were white, and had fathers with middle-class occupations tended to obtain higher scores on the Series tests both before and after training. *Training, however, was able to boost the mean scores of lower class students to the pretest level of middle-class students in four of the five towns analyzed.* (The exception was an upper-middle-class suburb, where the discrepancy between initial scores of lower and middle-class students was the greatest.)

Correlation coefficients between Series scores and Gates–MacGinitie reading subtest scores showed that scores on these tests were positively related. The correlation coefficients between the Series pretest and posttest scores and the reading comprehension subtest were .471 and .592, respectively. Results of multiple regression analysis, however, indicated that social class and race were related to both subtests as well as to the Series scores, so that the relationship between Series and Gates–MacGinitie scores was reduced to nonsignificance when social class and race were taken into account.

Thus, the Series Test forms are shown to be reliable and equivalent, and training was found to be effective and most useful for first- through third-grade students. The results suggest that, if the scores following training are used as the index of the low-SES child's ability in the primary grades, a more optimistic picture emerges.

The Picture Word Game

The Picture Word Game (PWG) was constructed to provide a nonverbal training-based measure of low-achieving young children's ability (grades K through 5) to work with language-type symbols. The PWG was a modification of the Semantic Test of Intelligence (STI) constructed by Rulon and Schweiker (1953). In the STI the child learns to associate a geometric symbol with a picture of an object or action (e.g., man, woman, runs, pushes). The student must "read" the sequence of symbols, analogous to a sentence, and choose the appropriate picture from a multiple-choice array that best represents the meaning of the sentence. No memory is required for reading the picture-symbol meanings because the current vocabulary of "words" appear on the top of the double facing pages. Therefore, we thought the task might represent a vehicle to examine verbally related competencies in a training-based format without the need to read words or talk about materials, skills in which these children are often deficient.

Gimon, Budoff, and Corman (1974) administered the STI to 76 Spanish-speaking children from low-income families who ranged in age from 6 to 13 years. Results indicated that a ceiling effect occurred with children over 8 years old. STI scores were significantly correlated with vocabulary scores on both the Spanish and English versions of the WISC. The investigators concluded that the tasks used in the STI were related to verbal ability, but that the difficulty level of the test would have to be broadened in order to be useful with normal children spanning a wider age range.

The following principles governed development of the Picture Word Game in broadening difficulty level:

1.   Administration as an untimed measure to minimize the effect of speed on performance and to reduce spurious inflation of variability and consequent reliability.

2.   Increase of the vocabulary (i.e., the number of symbols) from nine "words" in the STI to 16 in the PWG.

3.   Inclusion of the concept of symbols representing numbers in addition to noun and verb representation.

4.   Reduction of the number of items requiring translation from picture to symbol from all to half. The remaining half required a symbol-picture translation. In training and the test our theory was that the students had to see the pictures and the geometric figures as equivalents. An internal measure of the effectiveness of the teaching sequence would be the extent to which the child could utilize the same picture–symbol combination in both directions: to decode the symbols into their pictorial equivalents, and to generate sentences in the "new" language that would explain the picture.

5.   Reduction of the number of items to 60 from the initial 217, so that the PWG could be administered in one class period.

6.   Increase of the number of symbols in the most difficult sentences from four (STI) to five (PWG). It was not possible to construct a meaningful sentence of more than five symbols within this format, when these symbols represented only nouns, verbs, and numbers.

The original form of the Picture Word Game contained 60 items, with odd-numbered items requiring translation from symbol to picture and even-numbered items requiring translation from picture to symbol. The test included 6 one-symbol, 12 two-symbol, 18 three-symbol, 18 four-symbol, and 6 five-symbol items. Vocabulary comprised 16 symbols: five nouns (cat, dog, woman, boy, horse), five intransitive verbs (sit, lie down, walk, stand, run), three transitive verbs (pull, chase, carry), and three numbers (two, three, and four).

A training procedure was developed that could be entirely concluded before administration of the test, rather than embedding training within the test as in the STI. Oral instructions were used in the training instead of relying solely on pantomimed instructions to minimize the sense of artificiality (Gimon et al., 1974).

The training booklet contains 10 of the 16 symbols used in the vocabulary of the test. A page with all the symbols in the vocabulary is attached to the back of the training booklet, so that it can be easily detached and referred to by the student during the training session. The six symbols contained in the test but excluded from training are one noun, one intransitive verb, and the three numbers. The training booklet items are similar to those in the test, and there are slides of each training item. The trainer simultaneously displays the slides and explains the principles of the tasks and techniques for solution to students using the training booklet.

Pilot testing was conducted with a sample of 205 students from a low-income urban school district: 10 first- through fifth-grade classrooms, two classes per grade, evenly divided by sex. The mean age of the sample was 9 years, 2 months, with a standard deviation of 1 year, 7 months.

All students were trained in one class period and tested in class-size groups in a second-class period 3 days following training. A student's score was calculated as the percent of items answered correctly of the total number of test items.

The test showed a high degree of internal consistency reflected in a KR20 reliability coefficient of .95. The mean percent of correct responses for the total sample was 75.5 (SD = 20.8). Despite efforts to make this test more difficult than the STI, a ceiling effect was found for students at or beyond the third grade.

Items were selected for the final test that met three criteria: (a) the difficulty level of test items for the total sample was evenly distributed throughout the test (i.e., approximately equal numbers of easy and moderate-to-hard items were retained); (b) to the extent possible, each item selected showed a gradual increase in difficulty from grades 1 to 5; and (c) the discrimination of each item was not less than .25 for the total sample. These procedures were used in an attempt to produce test scores that would reflect a developmental trend and reduce the likelihood of a ceiling effect on the final test. The revised test consisted of 37 items, including 1 one-symbol, 7 two-symbol, 9 three-symbol, 9 four-symbol, and 11 five-symbol items.

This version was again tested with another sample consisting of 90 students from a low-income urban district. Subjects were evenly divided into five first- through fifth-grade classrooms, one class per grade, and attended an elementary school in the same urban community as the school from which the pilot sample was drawn. Subjects were evenly divided by sex. The mean age of the sample was 8 years, 10 months (SD = 1 year, 9 months).

All students were trained and tested in class-size groups in one class period. All students' scores on the Stanford Paragraph Meaning and Vocabulary Subtests were obtained from their school records. Discrimination indices of almost all items were high, reflected in the high KR20 reliability coefficient of .93. Mean item difficulties revealed that several procedures used to modify the STI were successful in increasing the difficulty level of the PWG when the total sample was considered: (a) items requiring translation from symbol to picture were significantly harder than items that required translation from picture to symbol ($F = 63.64$, 1/85 df, $p < .001$); (b) the difficulty of items increased linearly as the number of symbols increased from two to five ($F = 70.27$, 3/225 df, $p < .01$); and (c) the two most difficult sets of items on the test were items employing the concept of number, which had not been taught and all of which had three or more symbols (mean = 59.3%), and the five-symbol items (mean = 53.4%).

Despite the effectiveness of these procedures, however, mean scores (in terms of percent correct) for each grade again revealed a ceiling effect for children beyond the third grade. Total score means reflected the same dichotomy between grades 1 to 2 and 3 through 5 found on the pilot test despite item selection procedures that retained items with the most marked linear developmental trend. The gap between second and third graders widened as the number of symbols increased from three to four. Items involving number concepts and those requiring translation from picture to symbol also differentiated first and second graders from the rest of the sample.

Mean stanines on the Stanford Comprehension and Vocabulary subtests were relatively comparable among the five grades and revealed that these children's reading skills were in the moderate to low range in relation to national norms. The mean stanine for the total sample was 4.3 ($\pm$ 1.8) on comprehension and 4.1 ($\pm$ 1.4) on vocabulary. Scores on the PWG were correlated with scores on these two subtests to provide evidence of validity of the PWG as a language measure. Coefficients of .37 and .34 were obtained with comprehension and vocabulary, respectively. Although these coefficients are low in terms of concurrent validity, they are similar in magnitude to the validity coefficient of .385 obtained by Rulon and Schweiker (1953) with the STI.

In its present form the PWG appears to be most useful with students up to second-grade levels of achievement. Its use as an indicator of language-related competencies, makes it a distinctive and useful test for young children who experience difficulty in reading, writing, and language arts, perhaps even language delay.

Learning Potential Assessment with Other Populations

Relationship of Race and Social Class to Performance of Average Children on the Raven Learning Potential Measure

In a study examining the differential effectiveness of the group training procedure with intellectually average children from different racial and socioeconomic backgrounds, it was demonstrated that group training was equally effective with black and white children. Group training, however, was shown to be more beneficial for students from middle and high socioeconomic backgrounds than for students from lower class families (Budoff & Corman, 1973).

Learning Potential among the Moderately and Severely Retarded

In light of both the inappropriateness of conventional tests and the trend toward providing educational programs for the moderately and severely retarded, this study explored the hypothesis that a moderately or severely retarded person's learning ability can be predicted more readily from posttraining scores than pretraining or IQ scores, and that IQ scores would correlate highly with pretraining scores, but relate minimally to posttraining scores (Hamilton & Budoff, 1974).

The subjects were 40 institutionalized mentally retarded persons ranging in CA from 12 to 22 years and in Peabody Picture Vocabulary Test (PPVT) IQ from less than 10 to 51. Thirteen demonstration-training items were developed to correspond to each difficulty level on the test for the Extended Kohs Test, which used a train-within-test paradigm. These items were used in the three testing sessions and the training session. During testing, these items were used to demonstrate equivalent design constructions at particular difficulty levels. During the training session, the same items were used to teach the student strategies for solving problems at a given difficulty level. Each student was trained on four of these nontest items: the training item which corresponded to the highest level of difficulty successfully completed during pretraining, followed by the training items which corresponded to the next three difficulty levels.

The Extended Kohs Test was administered individually three times. The experimental variable of training was introduced 6 days following the pretest, at which time the student received an individual training session lasting no more than 30 minutes. On the following day, both the trained and control subjects were retested with the Extended Kohs Test. After approximately 1 month, trained and control subjects were retested with the Kohs to determine the continuing influence of the training experience.

As indicators of predictive validity, a modified version of the Knox Cube Test, which involved reproducing visually presented tapping sequences, was administered approximately 1 week after the delayed posttraining session. A questionnaire was administered to the teachers regarding the learning rates of each student in a teaching situation. Repeated measures analysis of variance revealed that trained students profited from a systematic learning experience more than the nontrained controls. This finding was consistent for higher (mean 41.5) and lower (mean 15.1) IQ groups.

Preliminary evidence suggesting the validity of this training-within-testing procedure was indicated by a significant partial correlation between the Knox Cube scores and posttraining scores, with the effects of pretraining scores removed. It should be noted that Knox scores did not correlate significantly with PPVT raw scores. The teachers' ratings of learning were compared with response to the learning potential category, with agreement on 16 of the 20 students. The hypothesis that predicted the relationships between IQ and pre- and posttraining scores was supported. PPVT data were significantly related to pretraining scores, but were minimally related to posttraining scores when the effects of pretraining scores were removed. The results of this study were supported by a later study by Budoff and Hamilton (1976).

Another study further examined the applicability of the train-within-test

LP assessment model to moderately and severely retarded adolescents (Budoff & Allen, 1978) by examining the differences in response to three modes of presentation of a nonverbal reasoning test, Raven Coloured Progressive Matrices. This study compared the usual book format with a formboard presentation with or without training. For the training procedure that used the formboards, the following alterations were made:

First, the test items were arranged in order of increasing difficulty within the factors described by Corman and Budoff (1974): Simple Continuous Pattern Completion, Discrete Pattern Completion, Continuity and Reconstruction of Simple and Complex Structures, and Reasoning by Analogy. The purpose of presenting the items grouped by factor was to maximize the probability that learning on one item in a factor would transfer to other items similar in form and principle of solution.

Second, the test administration was modified by providing a training procedure with a graded series of clues. After an initial administration without an aid or prompt, if the student failed to complete the item successfully by placing the correct piece in the space, four sets of clues were presented and the student was permitted additional opportunities to complete the design. Initially the trainer verbally explained salient features of the design, concurrently pointing to them. In the next set of clues, the verbal explanation was repeated, and the answer card, which indicated the correct choice, was introduced for a few seconds for perusal by the child and withdrawn. If the child continued to choose incorrectly, verbal explanations were repeated, the answer card shown again, and the trainer modeled the correct solution, but both latter aids were withdrawn. Finally, both the answer card and the trainer's model were left in front of the child while he or she tried to solve the design. At each aid stage, the student had two trials.

What is interesting in the training procedure is that the unaided presentation trial elicited approximately the same correct score as the Raven book or formboards presented according to standard instructions. Simply providing verbal explanation of some critical features of the puzzle's elements elicited an increment in correct scores approximately similar to the unaided administration. Providing an answer card with the verbal explanation provided further enhancement in scores. The more explicit clues provided little further increase in scores. Merely explaining some salient characteristics of the problems approximately doubled the score. Providing answer cards and other more explicit clues provided further enhancement of scores, but was not as potent, cumulatively, as the verbal explanation. This finding is similar to that of Budoff and Hamilton (1976), who reported that simply providing some orienting instructions to the student accounted for most of the benefit of the training procedure.

The introduction of training in the assessment procedure changes a number of features of the test situation for the participant. The most evident change is affective. The person's perception of the situation changes from a purely evaluative one, with the negative affect attached to such situations, to one in which the role of the examiner is perceived as helping the student to achieve competence. This change was reflected in the evident pleasure with which mentally retarded persons approached the training assessment sessions. They enjoyed the contacts and came repeatedly without qualms, although their initial response to testing was usually negative affect and avoidant behavior, supporting Zigler's thesis (1966) of the value of a positive social reinforcement in a context of enhanced competence. The active intervention of the examiner in the role of trainer helped to increase focus on the critical features of the stimulus display, helped to structure an attack on the problem, and encouraged the active testing of hypotheses regarding the critical features of the problem without fear of negative judgment. The procedures stimulated and sustained an active work orientation to the problems.

The largest increment in performance occurred after one helping trial using the train-within-test mode, suggesting the possibility that the more able of these persons may primarily require simple orienting information to solve problems they initially failed. In short, expanding on the salient features of a problem resulted in considerably enhanced problem solving among these low-functioning, substantially mentally retarded adolescents and young adults.

Validation of Learning Potential Measures with Spanish-speaking Children

Spanish-speaking Americans have been overrepresented in special classes for the mentally retarded, and have been inappropriately educated as if they were mentally retarded. The designation of these children as mentally retarded by an IQ score is clearly inappropriate because of both cultural and linguistic differences.

Studies reported in this section compared the relative predictive power of LP and IQ scores on various criterion measures administered to Puerto Rican and Mexican-American students. Instructions for administering the LP procedure in Spanish, which were used with the Puerto Rican sample, are reprinted in Gimon, Budoff, and Corman (1974), and are available on request.

One hundred eighty-eight Spanish-speaking students from two urban school districts in Massachusetts constituted the sample for the first study. The 78 girls and 110 boys ranged in age from 6 years 2 months to 14 years 10 months, with a mean age of 10 years 3 months ($\pm$ 2 years 2 months). Seventy-six were in grades 1 to 3 (mean CA = 8.67 $\pm$ 1.25 years). The students in both schools were similar in age and IQ, and spoke Spanish primarily. However, one school program used Spanish as the primary language of instruction with English as a second language (transitional bilingual model), whereas the other school taught academic subjects in English.

Ninety-two percent of the students were either born in Puerto Rico or their families had migrated from that island. Low socioeconomic status of the subjects was indicated by the mean family size of 6.26 ($\pm$2.38) and mother's mean educational level of 6.46 years ($\pm$2.84).

Students received the following instruments in the order listed: WISC IQ (Performance and Vocabulary); Inter-American General Ability Series (IAGAS) numeric, nonverbal, and verbal subtests; Picture Motivator Scale (Haywood, 1968); and Raven and Series LP. The WISC, IAGAS, and Picture Motivator Scale were administered in both Spanish and English, with language order counterbalanced and each pair of measures given on consecutive days. The LP measures were administered with Spanish instructions on three consecutive days (pretest, one group training session, posttest) with order of the two measures counterbalanced. No group was presented with both LP measures during the same week.

Results indicated that scores on the Spanish WISC Performance scale and the vocabulary subtests in English and Spanish portrayed these Spanish-speaking children as intellectually below average. Many children's scores were in the mentally retarded range. However, showing these low-income Spanish-speaking students how to perform more effectively on a reasoning task in a competence-inducing context resulted in higher scores: their average Raven pretraining score was in the 25th percentile, and rose to the 50th (and above) percentile following training. Raven posttraining scores, together with age, performance IQ, and Spanish WISC Verbal scores, were significant predictors of verbal achievement in Spanish. High verbal achievement in English was related to age, high scores on the English WISC vocabulary test, and extrinsic motivation. The best combination of predictors of nonverbal and numeric achievement in both Spanish and English was provided by the Series post-training LP score, age, and WISC performance IQ. The results are presented in greater detail in Gimon, Budoff, and Corman (1974).

To indicate the broader significance of the learning potential procedure with Spanish-speaking students, better validity criteria are required that permit these children to demonstrate their general capability to reason without the negative effects of language-related learning. Specifically, the experimental paradigm must permit these children to learn concept-appropriate information and principles over time, unlike the achievement criterion, which measures adequacy of past acquisition.

In a second study with a Hispanic population, specifically designed curricula that emphasized learning concepts served to demonstrate this broader capability with low-income IQ-defined EMR students (Budoff, Meskin, & Harrison, 1971). A curriculum unit was developed that taught students concepts of electricity by manipulating flashlight batteries, bulbs, and wires. The electricity unit was translated and taught in Spanish, and the evaluation test was administered in Spanish prior to and following the course. This instrument allowed comparisons at two levels of abstraction within a minimally and maximally verbal mode of response. The minimally verbal sections of the test required responses to actual electrical setups mounted on pegboards (concrete level) and to electrical problems presented as two-dimensional drawings (representational or symbolic level). In the verbal sections of the test the students were asked to explain in Spanish the reasons for their choices on a subset of pegboard items. Responses were scored for verbal–descriptive and verbal–conceptual competence.

The sample selected for this study consisted of 54 Spanish-speaking students in classes equivalent to second through sixth grades. These students were administered the WISC IQ test, the Semantic Test of Intelligence, and Raven Progressive Matrices learning potential assessment in Spanish. After these tests had been given, students participated in the electricity classes as part of their general science requirement. The age range of this group was 6 years 7 months to 13 years 8 months, with a mean age of 9 years 10 months (± 1.9 years). The sample consisted of 32 boys and 22 girls. The mean WISC full-scale IQ in Spanish (86 ± 18) indicated that many would be psychometrically classified as "slow learners" or "educable mentally retarded."

Posttraining scores on the LP procedure significantly predicted postteaching diagram scores and the minimally verbal test of symbolic electrical knowledge. By contrast, the students' scores on three IQ measures (pretraining Raven, WISC Performance IQ, and WISC Spanish Verbal scores) did not significantly predict any of the four postteaching electricity scores. This study is presented in greater detail in Budoff, Corman, and Gimon (1976).

From these studies with Puerto Rican children it was concluded that LP procedures show promise of providing less biased indicator of general ability among Spanish-speaking students than traditional intelligence tests.

Conclusion

This chapter has demonstrated that the technology of training-based assessment, although certainly not fully developed, is neither as novel nor as limited in its availability as has been suggested by Feuerstein, Rand, and Miller (1980). There are developed and validated test-train-retest instruments, even procedures attuned to the working styles of moderately and severely impaired persons that can demonstrate their ability to profit from appropriate test presentations as opposed to the inappropriate tests usually administered (Budoff & Allen, 1978). Clinical work with specific clients requires focused hypotheses that the test-train-retest strategy can support or sharpen. Conclusions relevant to clients can be reached more cost effectively in terms of professional time using these more standardized procedures, and can also allow more specific interpretations of the meaning of the client's posttraining performance.

As this chapter indicates, we have used other assessment paradigms than the test-train-test paradigm to discern ability not evident in the student's school or IQ test performance. In the Picture-Word Game, by its nature, the student was tested once after training since arbitrary symbols were taught. The paradigm for working with moderately and severely mentally retarded persons employed a "train-within-test" model. That is, when the student made a mistake the materials for that item were reviewed at that moment during the course of the "test." In another instance, we tested the hypothesis that students could not learn from the training experience in the usual training situation by employing a procedure in which the student made up his or her own test designs and then copied them from his or her diagrams. A proportion of the "nonlearners" by our first procedure grasped and applied the principles of the assessment materials after this experience.

What must be made clear by this evidence is that the "test-train-test" model is one of many training-based assessment models, and that future work must tap the range of possible approaches that will ensure the student *cannot* perform when we make the diagnostic judgment that he cannot. We have placed the responsibility on the examiner to explore the range of options testing this hypothesis of greater learning potential since this judgment is important in the student's school life. The options explored also permit the examiner to make statements about the conditions under which the student *does and does not* fare well in learning.

The work with learning potential assessment started with a concern for developing a more equitable means of discriminating ability among severely low-achieving school children who had been classified as educable mentally retarded. Later we became concerned with using this assessment paradigm with children from backgrounds of high educational risk. These children, though not officially labeled mentally retarded, also experience considerable difficulty in school and are generally viewed as having limited scholastic aptitude (IQs below 90). Our research suggests strongly that with low-income and/or nonwhite or non-English-speaking students, a training-based assessment process represents a more culture-fair means of measuring general ability to reason or intelligence, when it is defined as the ability to learn and profit from experience.

What was needed was measures that would enable us to test this hypothesis of greater ability when the task was more suitably structured to the particular learning styles and conditions of these students so that the validity of the hypothesis could be tested. This chapter presents the measures we developed in this effort. Subsequent investigations showed the applicability and validity of these learning potential procedures with low-income black, Spanish-speaking, and moderately and severely mentally retarded children. The data relating to the measurement procedures are presented in this chapter; those related to the validity of the learning potential hypothesis are presented in Chapter 2.

REFERENCES

Baumeister, A. A., & Kellas, G. (1968). Intrasubject response. In N. R. Ellis (Ed.), *International review of research in mental retardation* (Vol. 3). New York: Academic Press.

Budoff, M. (1967). Learning potential among institutionalized young adult retardates. *American Journal of Mental Deficiency*, 72, 404–411.

Budoff, M. (1969). Learning potential: A supplementary procedure for assessing the ability to reason. *Seminars in Psychiatry*, 1, 278–290.

Budoff, M., & Allen, P. (1978). The utility of a learning potential test with substantially mentally retarded students. Application of a formboard version of the Raven Progressive Matrices (Sets A, AB, B). RIEPrint #110. Cambridge, MA: Research Institute for Educational Problems.

Budoff, M., & Corman, L. (1973). *The effectiveness of a group training procedure on the Raven learning potential measure with children of diverse racial and socio-economic backgrounds.* RIEPrint #58. Cambridge, MA: Research Institute for Educational Problems.

Budoff, M., Corman, L., & Gimon, A. (1976). An educational test of learning potential assessment with Spanish-speaking youth. *Intraamerican Journal of Psychology*, 10,13–24.

Budoff, M., & Friedman, M. (1964). "Learning potential" as an assessment approach to the adolescent mentally retarded. *Journal of Consulting Psychology*, 28, 434–439.

Budoff, M., & Hamilton, J. (1976). Optimizing test performance of the moderately and severely mentally retarded. *American Journal of Mental Deficiency*, 81, 49–57.

Budoff, M., Meskin, J., & Harrison, R. G. (1971). An educational test of the learning potential hypothesis. *American Journal of Mental Deficiency*, 76, 159–169.

Corman, L., & Budoff, M. (1973a). *The Series Test as a measure of learning potential.* RIEPrint #47. Cambridge, MA: Research Institute for Educational Problems.

Corman, L., & Budoff, M. (1973b). *A comparison of group and individual training procedures on the Raven Learning Potential measure.* RIEPrint #56. Cambridge, MA: Research Institute for Educational Problems. (ERIC Document Reproduction Service No. ED 086 924)

Corman, L., & Budoff, M. (1973c). *A comparison of group and individual training procedures on the Raven Learning Potential measure with black and white special class students.* RIEPrint #57. Cambridge, MA: Research Institute for Educational Problems. (ERIC Document Reproduction Service No. ED 085 969)

Corman, L., & Budoff, M. (1974). Factor structures of retarded and nonretarded children on Raven Progressive Matrices. *Educational and Psychological Measurement*, 34, 407–412.

Corman, L., & Budoff, M. (1975). IQ and learning potential measurements of general intelligence: A comparison of relationships. In D. A. Primrose (Ed.), *Proceedings of the Third Congress of the International Association for the Scientific Study of Mental Deficiency* (Vol. 1). Cambridge, MA: Research Institute for Educational Problems. RIEPrint #55. (ED 086-921).

Feuerstein, R. (1968). Learning potential assessment device. In B. W. Richards (Ed.), *Proceedings of the First Congress of the International Association for the Scientific Study of Mental Deficiency* Surrey, England: Michael Jackson Publishing Co. Ltd.

Gimon, A., Budoff, M., & Corman, L. (1974). Learning potential measurement with Spanish-speaking youth as an alternative to IQ tests: A first report. *Interamerican Journal of Psychology*, 8, 233–246.

Goldstein, K., & Sheerer, M. (1941). Abstract and concrete behavior. *Psychological Monographs*, 53(2, Whole No. 239).

Haywood, H. C. (1968). Motivational orientation of overachieving and underachieving elementary school children. *American Journal of Mental Deficiency*, 72, 662–667.

Hurtig, M. (1959). Experimental study of the possibility of intellectual learning in normal and retarded children. *Enfance*, 371–383.

Jacobs, P. I., & Vandeventer, M. (1971). The learning and transfer of double-classification skills by first graders. *Child Development, 42*, 149–159.

Kohs (1923). *Intelligence measurement.* New York: Macmillan.

Raven, J. C. (1956). *Coloured Progressive Matrices: Sets A, AB, B.* London: H. K. Lewis & Co. Ltd.

Raven, J. C. (1958). *Standard Progressive Matrices: Sets A, B, C, D, and E.* London: H. K. Lewis & Co., Ltd.

Rulon, P., & Schweiker, R. (1953). *Validation of a non-verbal test of military trainability.* Final Report, June, 1953, Department of the Army.

Zigler, E. (1966). Mental retardation: Current issues and approaches. In L. W. Hoffman & M. L. Hoffman (Eds.), *Review of child development research,* (Vol. 2), New York: Russell Sage Foundation.

7

Group Administration of the LPAD

YAACOV RAND AND SHLOMO KANIEL

The chapters in this volume by Feuerstein et al. (Chapter 1) and Jensen and Feuerstein (Chapter 14) discuss extensively the philosophical and theoretical foundations of dynamic assessment and more specifically the Learning Potential Assessment Device (LPAD). The reader is also referred to additional literature for detailed elaboration of both the theory and the applied aspects of the LPAD methodology (Feuerstein 1979; Feuerstein, Haywood, Rand, Hoffman, & Jensen, 1985; Hilliard, 1983; Narrol & Bachor, 1975). Our main focus in this chapter will be the LPAD as a group-administered procedure, and research findings from the use of the group-administered LPAD in educational settings and for educational purposes will be presented.

Theoretical Considerations

Although group administration may be considered an extension of the initial clinical face-to-face LPAD administration, it is important to reiterate some of the characteristic features of the LPAD method deemed essential for an appropriate comprehension of the ongoing interaction during the group administration. The LPAD method is inherently linked to intervention. Consequently, the process of assessment does not relate only to the performance of the subject per se, but encompasses also—and not to a lesser degree—the entire interactional process that takes place during the assessment. Although group testing cannot have all of the characteristic features of the individual LPAD administration (not allowing, for example, the same extent of development of tester–testee relationship), it still differs considerably from the conventional methods, first of all, by activating—prior to the test performance—learning processes, and second by intervention during the testing itself, whenever the tester considers that some basic prerequisites are still not available to the subjects.

The pretesting learning phase is intended to create what may be called a "standardization of comprehension" rather than a "standardization of instructions." The interactional process between the examiner and examinee

Yaacov Rand and Shlomo Kaniel. Hadassah–WIZO–Canada Research Institute, Jerusalem, Israel; and School of Education, Bar Ilan University, Ramat Gan, Israel.

can be compared to a stick at the distal (D) pole of which is the testee, and at the proximal (P) pole is the examiner. In conventional testing, standardization has to be assured at the D pole of the stick. This is an absolutely necessary condition in order to allow comparison to the normative standard. In contrast, LPAD procedures emphasize heavily the other pole (P) of the stick. The examiner aspires to help the examinee to reach a sound comprehension of the nature of the tasks. Instructions are combined with learning in order to assure with all the subjects the existence of the cognitive prerequisites that are a *conditia sine qua non* to appropriate functioning on the test items. This basic distinction between the two types of test administrations, although more salient in individual testing, is maintained in group testing too, despite the fact that group testing does not allow a full assessment of the individual's performance processes or of his or her idiosyncratic difficulties.

Another characteristic of LPAD testing is the connection between the assessment process and the prescribed postassessment interventional procedures. This is related to the fact that both the assessment method and a systematic interventional program are intrinsically linked to the same theoretical and conceptual framework. Conventional methods of assessment do not have specific links with interventional methods. Considering the manifest level of functioning of the individual as reflecting his or her optimal capacities, conventional procedures tend more to a categorization of individuals according to their performance level and to a group-oriented prescription of treatment procedures expressed mainly in classroom organization, institutional placement, and other such prescriptions of a general nature. The LPAD method, by virtue of its orientation to uncover in a highly discriminative way the specifics of the individual's functioning, is in a much better position to prescribe more sophisticated and more differentiated individual-oriented environmental interventions, which will require frequent reassessment in order to allow for readjustment of the intervention procedures. The LPAD is therefore an ongoing process of evaluation rather than a "one-shot" assessment procedure.

LPAD group testing is only a first step of the assessment process and has to be followed in many cases by the more refined individual LPAD testing. The frequency of such a follow-up is contingent upon the specific characteristics and responses of the individual tested and the particular scope of decisions. However, although group LPAD testing does not yield sufficient information for determining the educational and teaching process that the individual needs to experience, it offers many other possibilities that pertain, on the one hand, to the clarification of theoretical assumptions of the procedure and, on the other hand, to broad educational issues such as school organization and classroom composition.

Before presenting more empirical research with the LPAD, it is important to introduce briefly the group LPAD battery of tests, its testing procedures, and its basic characteristics.

Battery Composition and Group Testing Procedures

The usual battery of the group LPAD is composed of the following eight tests:

1. Organization of Dots Test (ODT)
2. Human Figure Drawing (HFD)
3. Complex Figure Test (CFT)
4. Organizer (ORG)
5. Set Variations I (VAR I)
6. Set Variations II (VAR II)
7. Numerical Progressions Test (NPT)
8. Representational Stencil Design Test (RSDT)

Additional tests of the individual LPAD battery can also be adapted and used in a group administration by introducing group learning procedures and didactical devices such as posters.

In most cases, a battery of three to four of the above-mentioned tests is used. Test selection is contingent upon the specific goals of the testing and the particular characteristics of the target population, such as age, rhythm of work, and known level of functioning. The test battery requires little verbalization but varies in the nature of the performance required by the tasks and their level of difficulty. (For a detailed presentation of the tests, see Feuerstein et al., 1985.)

The basic model of the group testing is: (a) demonstration, (b) test, (c) learning, and (d) retest. The *demonstration phase* introduces the subject to the specific nature of the tasks and provides the basic test instructions. The *test phase* determines basic information regarding the individual's level of functioning. This will serve as a baseline for comparative purposes after learning is activated.

The *learning phase* is perhaps the most essential and the one that differs most significantly from the usual testing procedures. The group undergoes a learning process that refers both to the nature of the tasks and to the prerequisites deemed necessary in order to solve them. For example, if the task requires multidimensional analogical thinking, subjects are trained not only to identify the relevant dimensions and to relate to them in an isolated manner but also to integrate them in various configurations, to perceive them in a precise way, and to use them differentially as required by the specific task item. The test items themselves are not used for learning purposes. What is taught are the principles and the strategies that are appropriate for the given problem-solving process. Special attention is given to specific difficulties that individual subjects may encounter. These latter are often used for reiteration of the teaching for the entire group and for reinforcing adequate thinking processes.

The *retest phase* is used to assess the efficiency of the intervention activated during the learning sessions. The difference in performance between test and retest is used as an indicator of the general level of modifiability obtained via an intervention that is similar in many respects to the regular classroom activity. It is also useful in detecting students who may show specific facilities for modifiability or specific difficulties in being modified by group procedures. In order to make such assessment possible, the groups should not exceed 20 students. When larger, it is advisable to split the class into two smaller groups, so that individual communication and observation is possible.

The specific time required for both learning and testing varies from test to test and is contingent upon the nature of the target group, its general rhythm of performance, and its efficiency on the learning procedures. Generally we may divide the tests into two categories: (a) the short ones (HFD, ODT, CFT), requiring about 15–30 minutes for training and 10–15 minutes for performance; and (b) the longer ones (ORG, VAR I, VAR II, NPT, RSDT), which require about 60 minutes for learning and the same amount of time for the testing. In order to allow some individualization of intervention during the course of the assessment, the testing is usually performed by two persons, one who conducts the testing and another who is available to the testees when necessary.

In none of these interventions are ready-made responses provided; the testees must act on their own to activate the adequate thinking processes required for the solution of the tasks.

A few general considerations must be stated regarding the LPAD group testing:

1. Group testing does not replace individual testing. It precedes it as a screening device in order to detect—and refer for further assessment—those students who show pronounced difficulties in performing in a group setting.

2. Group testing is basically used to establish a baseline of the individual's level of functioning, to which his or her further performances can be related and compared.

3. A high level of functioning on LPAD group testing can be interpreted as reflecting performance efficiency that will be even more salient under the more favorable conditions of the individual testing. On the other hand, a low level of functioning on the group testing does not necessarily reflect a low level of the individual's capacities to function adequately. It may be related to specific difficulties in acting under the less favorable conditions of the group setting, in which case higher levels of functioning may still be obtained in an individual setting because of its multivaried possibilities of *intervention*.

4. Group testing should never be used as the sole instrument for decision making for either placement or didactic–pedagogical practices. When

failure is demonstrated on the group testing, additional individual assessment is imperative in order to explore both the reasons and the appropriate means for intervention.

5. Learning is an important element in group administration and it should not be limited to the sheer explanation of the instructions. It must include correction of deficient functions, while using model tasks as instruments to introduce appropriate procedures for data gathering, elaborational processes, and reaction patterns. This group activity may be supplemented during the testing with specific individualized interventions whenever this appears to be necessary.

6. Test item composition should be structured in such a way as to allow the principles and methods of work acquired with one task to be useful in the solution of subsequent tasks. Learning will have to relate to the basic working principles and thinking processes, but the test itself will become progressively more complex and more remote from the situation in which the principles were initially acquired. By this structuring, when implemented systematically, we may obtain even through group testing meaningful information as to the level of modifiability and adaptability of the individual to new and more demanding situations.

Empirical Findings

LPAD group testing has been widely used for a variety of educational purposes and has also yielded meaningful support to structural cognitive modifiability (SCM) theory and its basic assumptions.

LPAD and Structural Cognitive Modifiability

According to the SCM theory, the human organism is to be considered an open system in relation to environmental influences, which not only have considerable impact on the manifest level of functioning of the individual but also influence in a meaningful way the ongoing processes of development as well as the formation of mental and personality structures. These structural modifications are expressed in the individual's interactions with the environment. The selection of stimuli to be acted upon, the assignment of relevancy to situational components, the attribution of relative values and priorities linked to the individual's goals or need systems, the integration of multidimensional information emanating from various sources, the activation of retrieval systems and relation of internally stored information with new impinging external data—all these, and many others, may be induced, reinforced, and modified by environmental intervention. By such intervention, the general level of adaptation of the individual may be considerably altered and meaningfully strengthened.

The human modifiability hypothesis, especially in the area of intellectual functioning, is contested by many. Although behavioral changes are frequently reported as a result of environmental control and manipulation, they relate mostly to more molecular aspects of behavior and little, if at all, to durable modifications that would affect broader operational systems. These latter are considered by many as basically unmodifiable. The antagonistic views concerning the impact of environmental intervention on human functioning are deeply rooted in the long-lasting controversy of nature versus nurture, which will doubtlessly remain a field of debate in the future.

Arguments against the modifiability hypothesis differ in nature and intensity. Even when it is assumed that the environment may play a paramount role in determining the ultimate level of functioning of the individual, special caution is often expressed in relation to the following three issues: (a) age limits, (b) etiological source for the misfunctioning, and (c) the level of functioning on which we have to operate.

The issue of age refers to the question of the existence of barriers or limits to the individual's modifiability imposed by the chronological age of the individual. The notion of "critical age," which was originally introduced in psychology in relation to developmental maturational processes, has also been applied to the development of intelligence and other major human psychological functions.

The issue of etiological factors refers to the question of whether modification is possible regardless of the source of impairment. When the low level of functioning of the individual can be linked to some very distinct etiological factor of organic nature, there is often a particularly strong tendency to assume that the level of functioning of the individual is immutable. Down syndrome is a very good illustration of this approach. The fact that the condition is of chromosomal nature and contains a great number of manifest and well-defined observable physical components facilitates an overgeneralized view that all the impaired functions—including the intellectual ones—are immutable.

The third issue refers to the degree of severity of the individual's impairment. The possibility of modifying normal or superior-functioning individuals is well accepted, and all education and pedagogico-didactical practices are based upon such a conception. However, the controversy increases as the individual's severity of the impairment increases and his level of functioning decreases. According to some claims, the impact of environment is strongest on individuals who function on the upper levels of mental functioning, but decreases or even ceases completely to play any significant role when it reaches the lower levels of functioning. In the latter case, the genetic and hereditary endowment is considered to remain almost the sole determinant of the individual's level of functioning.

The SCM theory, although not denying the importance of genetic endowment and its primordial role as a determinant of human functioning, does not attribute exclusivity to it. It is the combination of both heredity and environment and the interactional processes between them that are the ultimate determinants of the individual's levels of functioning. According to SCM theory, heredity may determine the limits of the developmental framework, but environment will determine to what extent potentials will be activated and materialized and to what extent the individual will make adequate use of what has been acquired through educational intervention. The relationship between heredity and environment is perhaps best summarized by the following inscription found at the Johnston Canyon in Alberta, Canada:

> The shapes you will see in this canyon are always changing. The rock dictates where the creek will run, but the water decides what rock will stay or go, and whether it will go now or later . . .

LPAD Cultural, Test Reliability and Interventional Aspects

In order to illustrate the use that can be made with LPAD group testing for purposes of assessing human modifiability, we would like to refer to a study done on Bedouin children and adolescents (Feuerstein, 1979). Bedouin culture is highly specific and at variance from both the Israeli and the Arab culture. Studies done with Bedouins have shown that they have extreme difficulty with problem-solving behavior when abstract thinking, conceptualization, and other representational behaviors are required (Kugelmas & Lieblich, 1968; Wagner, 1977). Explanatory hypotheses of their low test performance scores refer often to specific cultural elements. For instance, Bedouins show at the onset of adolescence low-average scores on the Raven Standard Progressive Matrices (RSPM) test (mean = 19.2), similar to those of the "mentally deficient" population, whereas their reported scholastic performance is much better and of less variance from their peers in the other cultural settings in Israel. The particularly low scores on the RSPM were tentatively explained as being related to a specific cultural style, namely, a preference to choose responses that are located at the right or the left of spatial extremities. This explanation implies that the cultural behavioral style of the group is predominantly higher in the hierarchy of responses than those determined by the mental rational thinking process. The question remains if this potent culturally determined reaction style can be modified by systematic environmental intervention.

The following study is a combination of LPAD assessment and Instrumental Enrichment (IE) intervention (Feuerstein et al. 1980; Feuerstein & Rand, 1977). The target population consisted of a group of 113 Bedouin boys between 12 and 15 years of age, in sixth (30), seventh (28), eighth (25), and ninth (30) grades. LPAD VAR I, VAR II, and RSDT (for explanation of the tests, see Feuerstein 1979) were administered both pre- and postintervention. Intervention consisted of a 3-hour per week IE program over a period of 2–3 months. The outline of the study was as follows: (a) learning session, (b) LPAD—pretest, (c) IE—intervention, and (d) LPAD—posttest.

The findings showed the following main results:

1. Average scores on the LPAD tests at the pretest level (after the learning session) were significantly superior to the average scores obtained by these same age groups within the Bedouin population.

2. In 10 out of 12 pre–post comparisons (three for each grade) retest scores were significantly superior to the initial pretest scores at the .01 level or better.

3. Posttest scores of the study population on all the tests except for RSDT approach the average scores of the regular Israeli school children as obtained in a variety of other studies. The lower performance on the RSDT may be at least partially attributed to the fact that the RSDT tasks are at a very high level of nonfamiliarity to the Bedouins, who are very rarely required to use representational operations with figural contents. More intensive intervention may be advisable in order to reach higher levels of efficiency.

These findings indicate that intervention, when systematically applied, may overcome powerful and deeply encrusted cultural hierarchies of responses. The LPAD VAR I and VAR II tests, although differently constructed and sequenced, are similar in kind as well as in form of presentation to the analogical thinking tasks of the Raven Matrices. Nevertheless, the culturally determined "choice of extremities" phenomenon did not prevail and at the posttest level performances were significantly better on both the LPAD measures and the RSPM.

A number of studies have yielded reliability data on the tests themselves. Rand (1982) conducted a study on a population of regular (R) and culturally deprived (CD) public school students in Israel of both sexes in grades 4 to 7 at the age of 10 to 14 years (N = R, 195; CD, 226; mean age = 12.7). The first question posed was if the LPAD group measures will distinguish between the two populations. The LPAD VAR I test was used for this purpose; the results for both R and CD school settings are presented in Table 7.1.

Table 7.1 shows that the LPAD VAR I test consistently discriminates between the two populations. Differences are highly significant and corroborate the information made available to us by the school authorities as to the respective levels of scholastic performance. The fact that significant differences are found on all the subtests adds support to the contention that the test is measuring dimensions in a consistent and systematic way.

Reliability data for the LPAD tests (VAR I and VAR II) were obtained on the same population by computing split-half coefficients respectively for both the R and CD populations. Results are presented in Table 7.2, which shows high reliability coefficients for the total scores on both tests (coefficients ranging from .82 to .89). Subtest reliability coefficients, although lower, are all statistically significant, ranging from moderate to high. On both tests (VAR

TABLE 7.1.   LPAD VAR I Test, Means, SDs, t Scores, and Level of Significance for Total Scores, Based upon Fourth, Fifth, Sixth, and Seventh Graders in Regular (R) and Culturally Deprived (CD) School Settings ($N = 421$)

	Population							
	R			CD				Significance
Grades	Mean	SD	N	Mean	SD	N	t Value	($p <$)
4	20.86	5.37	46	13.37	7.14	53	6.04	.001
5	22.32	5.36	61	16.30	6.79	54	5.23	.001
6	24.36	3.58	48	20.52	5.79	53	3.94	.01
7	24.37	4.16	40	18.88	6.13	66	5.55	.001
Total	22.94	4.02	195	17.27	6.78	226	7.96	.001

I, VAR II) reliability coefficients are generally lower in the R population than in the CD population.

In another study done by Rand (1983), split-half coefficients were calculated separately for the LPAD VAR I and VAR II tests, on a population of regular school fifth graders ($N = 122$). Four classes were divided at random into two groups of two classes each, and different learning strategies were employed. Whereas the low learning (LL) group received only a standard explanation as to the test requirements, the high learning (HL) group received additional practical exercises with one task for each subtest similar to the subsequent test items. The split-half coefficients are presented in Table 7.3 for both tests and both administration procedures. The data in Table 7.3 indicate clearly that the total score reliability is high for both tests (coefficients ranging from .82 to .90). Again, subtest reliability coefficients are lower, ranging from moderate to high and statistically significant at the level of .01 or better. The LL groups show generally higher coefficients as compared with

TABLE 7.2.   LPAD VAR I and VAR II, Split-Half Correlations for Total Test and Subtests (A, B, C, D, E) Based Separately upon Fourth, Fifth, Sixth and Seventh Graders of Regular (R) and Culturally Deprived (CD) School Settings ($N = 421$)

	VAR I		VAR II	
Tests	Regular ($N = 195$)	Culturally deprived ($N = 226$)	Regular ($N = 195$)	Culturally deprived ($N = 226$)
A	.56	.67	.55	.80
B	.45	.74	.48	.65
C	.77	.77	.60	.84
D	.60	.60	.69	.60
E	.65	.79	.63	.88
Total	.86	.82	.83	.89

TABLE 7.3.   LPAD VAR I and VAR II, Split-Half Correlations for Total Test and Subtests (A, B, C, D, E) Based upon Regular School Fifth Graders (N = 122) in High-Learning and Low-Learning (LL) Groups

Tests	HL (N = 65)		LL (N = 61)	
	VAR I	VAR II	VAR I	VAR II
A	.51	.63	.81	.75
B	.46	.58	.61	.65
C	.58	.60	.84	.72
D	.68	.69	.58	.64
E	.58	.68	.89	.82
Total	.82	.83	.90	.86

their HL peers. This corroborates the previously reported findings in which coefficients were consistently higher in the lower functioning CD groups than in the R groups.

More recently, a new version of VAR II has been designed that contains items that are more difficult but similar to the first version in the nature of the cognitive processes involved in the solution of the tasks. Table 7.4 presents the correlation matrix between the two tests, obtained from a group of fourth graders in a regular school (two classes, N = 82). Students underwent testing within their regular classes on both versions, with an interval of 2 weeks. The results in Table 7.4 indicate a moderate to high correlation between the different subtests, ranging from .60 to .88, and a correlation of .89 between the two total scores, reflecting high predictability from one version to the other. Both seem to measure similar or identical dimensions of cognitive functioning.

The differential effects of intensity of investment during testing was the object of an extended study done by Tzuriel and Rand (1983) on a population of fourth to ninth graders in both culturally deprived (N = 595) and regular

TABLE 7.4.   LPAD VAR II, Versions One and Two, Pearson Product–Moment Correlation Coefficients, Based upon Regular (R) Fourth-Grade Student Population (N = 82)

Version II	Version I					
	A	B	C	D	E	Total
A	.60	.51	.30	.55	.49	.55
B	.50	.76	.63	.62	.63	.78
C	.53	.68	.66	.59	.66	.77
D	.48	.63	.49	.69	.57	.71
E	.66	.68	.61	.67	.88	.85
Total	.65	.79	.66	.71	.77	.89

(N = 799) schools. Two LPAD tests (VAR I and VAR II were administered respectively to grades 4 to 6 and 7 to 9 under differential learning conditions. The classes were divided at random into the following three groups: A (high learning), B (low learning), and C (no learning). The RSPM test was used as a criterion measure and was administered as a group test in the conventional psychometric manner before (pre) and after (post) the LPAD testing. According to the results obtained at the pretest level on the RSPM, subjects were divided into three categories for each group separately: high (H), medium (M), and low (L). Comparisons of the RSPM scores were made between pretest and posttest groups to assess the differential effects of intervention. Table 7.5 presents the statistical significance of gains obtained by the different groups.

Results in Table 7.5 show that intervention—here defined operationally as having LPAD group testing—significantly raised the performance levels on the static RSPM test for the high- and low-learning groups as compared to the nonlearning controls (A = 10 out of 12, B = 7 out of 12, and C = 2 out of 12). High-learning groups also produced a greater number of significant results than the low-learning groups (10 vs. 7 significant gains). On the other hand, groups with a high initial level of performance on the RSPM were generally less affected by the intervention. Tentative explanations may refer to a ceiling effect or to the inadequacy of the learning procedures for this population, which probably had the basic requirements necessary for performing on the test already in their behavioral repertoire. Further investigation is still required to assess durability of effects over longer periods of time. Clinical observations reported elsewhere (Feuerstein et al., 1979), as well as empirical studies with the IE program, have shown remarkable durability of effects (Rand, Mintzker, Miller, Hoffman, & Friedlender, 1981; Ruiz, 1985), when intervention was massive and occurred over long periods of time.

TABLE 7.5.   RSPM—Statistical Significance of Gains from Pretest to Posttest by Grade Groups (A = Grades 4–6; B = Grades 7–9), Initial Performance Level and Learning Conditions (HL, LL, NO)[a], Based upon Culturally Deprived (CD) (N = 595) and Regular (R) (N = 789) Students

| RSPM initial level | Learning conditions, group A | | | | | | Learning conditions, group B | | | | | |
| | H | | L | | NO | | H | | L | | NO | |
	CD	R	CD	R	CD	R	CD	R	CD	R	CD	R
Low	.01*	.01*	.01	NS	.05	NS	.01	.01	.05	.05	NS	NS
Medium	.05	.05	.01	NS	NS	.05	.01*	.01*	.05	.01*	NS	NS
High	NS	NS	NS	NS	NS	NS	.01	.01	NS	.01*	NS	NS

[a]HL = high learning, LL = low learning, NO = nonlearning.

The significant results obtained in the LL groups may be at least partially ascribed to the learning experience intrinsically inherent in the LPAD procedures themselves. The item order and structure causes continuous learning because the tasks share similar operational principles. By virtue of investing in adequately solving the test problems, efficient strategies and methods are acquired and applied into new, similar situations.

In a similar study done by Rand and Ben-Schachar (1979), the RSPM test was administered to a population of 337 boys and girls in grades 5 to 8, in the usual static manner of administration. One week later, all the groups received LPAD testing (VAR I to fifth and sixth graders, and VAR II to seventh and eighth graders). Each class was also split randomly into two parts: LPAD with learning (L); and without learning (NL). At the end of the study, all subjects were retested with the RSPM as a static measure in order to assess gains. Results indicated that, although some increase was also observable with the NL control groups, the L groups showed a considerable, and statistically significant, increase in their level of performance on the RSPM ($p < .001$), with both VAR I and VAR II.

These studies, as well as many others, provide meaningful support to the human modifiability hypothesis. Significant changes related to environmental intervention were observed with different age groups and with a variety of initially low-functioning levels, including EMR or even trainable mentally retarded students. Findings also suggest that, when massive environmental intervention is activated, efficiency not only will be maintained over time but may even be enhanced (see Rand et al., 1981). This latter phenomenon may be attributed to the use the individual makes of the acquired principles and strategies in real-life situations, reaching out beyond the task-specific setting in which those principles were acquired.

LPAD and Educational Decision Making

LPAD group testing is also widely used for various purposes of decision making in educational organizations such as classroom grouping, and selection for enrichment programs. In many schools, especially with low-functioning students, classes are homogeneously grouped by virtue of their psychometric performance and scholastic achievement. Based upon daily observations, educators very often express doubts as to the merit and legitimacy of such a classification system. They often feel that the low level of the educational goals set forth by the school, the nondemanding requirements, the inadequacy of the school curriculum, inappropriate didactical procedures, as well as the amount and nature of the educational investment play a highly negative role in the development of their students by not allowing them to transcend the preimposed limits set by the school system that are reflected by the homogeneous classroom organization. A study on this issue was done by Feuerstein,

Rand and Hoffman (1979) in an educational residential center in the lower Galilee in Israel. This institution is a vocational high school for both regular (R) and culturally deprived (CD) low-functioning adolescents. After a program of 2–4 years, the graduates become involved in some work or enroll into the Israeli Army. The subjects of this study were the 9th and 10th graders, that is, those who were in their first or second year at this institution. Students of each grade were divided into two distinct classes as follows: 9A and 10A contained the regular, well-functioning students, and 9B and 10B contained students considered to be extremely low functioning.

Educators and school authorities reported consistently low academic and vocational achievement and poor motivation of the students to engage in academic activities. These contrasted considerably with the students' successful adaptation to a variety of nonscholastic activities that demanded high levels of mental functioning. Based upon these observations, school authorities formulated the following two questions:

1. Does the manifest level of functioning of the student reflect fully the student's true abilities, or can it be meaningfully modified?
2. What would be the effects—for both the normal and the low-functioning students—of regrouping classes based upon principles of heterogeneity?

In order to answer these questions, a battery composed of a static measure, the PMA (Thurstone's Primary Mental Abilities) test, and three LPAD tests (VAR II, RSDT and NPT) was administered at the beginning of the school year to the entire 9th and 10th grade population ($N = 126$). Table 7.6 presents the results obtained at the pretest level, before reorganization of the classes took place.

Results in Table 7.6 show that, at the pretest level, A classes were significantly superior to B classes on the PMA static measure, but did not show similar differences on the LPAD measures. Based upon these findings, a regrouping of the classes was performed, taking into account the additional information obtained by the LPAD as well as other students' characteristics reported by the educational staff. Because of some demands of the vocational training program, a group of 10 students of the 10A class continued as a separate homogeneous group. This permitted a comparison with their peers who were merged heterogeneously into the new classes.

Table 7.7 presents the results obtained for the initial groups at the end of the school year after heterogeneous regrouping was implemented. A comparison of pretest to posttest results (from Tables 7.6 and 7.7) yields the following findings:

1. Test scores increased from pretest to posttest on all measures, both static (PMA) and dynamic (LPAD), for all the groups.
2. The results obtained by the B groups in both 9th and 10th grades

TABLE 7.6. Means, SDs, and Statistical Significance for PMA and LPAD Tests: VAR II, RSDT, and NPT at Pretest Level by 9th and 10th Graders of Regular (A) vs. Low-Functioning (B) Students, Based upon Total Study Population ($N = 126$)

Tests	9A ($N = 32$)		9B ($N = 35$)		Significance ($p <$)	10A ($N = 36$)		10B ($N = 23$)		Significance ($p <$)	Maximum score
	Mean	SD	Mean	SD		Mean	SD	Mean	SD		
PMA	165.9	17.8	153.8	14.7	.01	170.28	14.9	154.3	22.6	.01	220
LPAD:											
VAR II	31.5	9.0	26.8	8.1	.05	38.9	10.0	35.8	10.4	NS	58
RSDT	11.2	3.3	10.0	3.4	NS[a]	13.2	3.0	9.2	4.4	.01	20
NPT	29.4	7.2	26.4	6.7	NS	32.7	7.4	29.0	9.6	NS	46

[a]NS = nonsignificant.

TABLE 7.7 Means, SDs, and Statistical Significance for PMD and LPAD Tests: VAR II, RSDT, and NPT at Posttest Level by 9th and 10th Graders of Regular (A) vs. Low-Functioning (B) Students, Based upon Total Study Population ($N = 103$)

Tests	9A ($N = 28$)		9B ($N = 27$)		Significance	10A ($N = 32$)		10B ($N = 16$)		Significance	Maximum score
	Mean	SD	Mean	SD		Mean	SD	Mean	SD		
PMA	189.6	12.7	179.6	13.5	.01	190.5	11.2	183.3	20.3	NS	220
LPAD:											
VAR II	41.6	10.8	35.7	10.8	.05	51.2	9.1	44.8	11.4	NS	58
RSDT	13.0	4.0	13.3	2.6	NS[a]	16.3	2.8	12.8	4.5	.05	20
NPT	34.1	7.8	31.7	7.8	NS	38.3	4.4	36.1	6.2	NS	46

[a]NS = nonsignificant.

were on most measures significantly higher than those obtained by the A groups at the pretest level (the initial 10th graders at the pretest level).

3. Differences between A and B groups remained similar from pretest to posttest but the initial statistically significant difference on the PMA with the 10th graders dissipated and both groups (A and B) performed on a similar level.

4. When the homogeneous 10A group was compared with the heterogeneous group no differences were found between the two on any LPAD measures, and an initial difference on the PMA (6.3 points) on the pretest level dropped to 3.4 points at the posttest level.

The implementation of this study also yielded a meaningful change in the attitudes of the institution's educational staff. Teachers and counselors learned to be more sensitive to their students' achievements in various areas, to attribute to them appropriate meaning, to be more flexible and, finally, to be open to continuous experimentation in order to maximize their students' capacities.

The following study is another illustration of the possible use of LPAD testing as a tool for educational decision making and for changing attitudes within broader educational systems. An urban settlement in the central area of Israel, defined as CD, was interested in selecting the upper 5% of its school population for special enrichment programs, in order to assure future local leadership. The entire school population of fourth to sixth graders ($N = 1300$) of the settlement received LPAD group testing on a test battery composed of the static RSPM and 6 LPAD tests. Some of the tests were repeated at the end of the testing period in order to assess consistency of performance and learning effects. Despite the extended number of hours required for this testing, antagonistic attitudes were not reported for either the teachers or the students. Attendance at testing sessions was very high, with absences for only well-founded reasons such as health or family problems.

Although final results of this study are not yet available, the testing has already been instrumental in several ways: (a) selection of the "gifted" group, which included students from classes considered to function on a low level; (b) prescription of the enrichment programs in order to correct the deficient cognitive functions as revealed by the testing; (c) modification of the educational atmosphere within schools from a self-image of a "backward" school system to one of educational challenge and interventional effort; and (d) modification of the general attitude of the local educational authorities. Prevalent antagonistic attitudes toward investment in testing and in intervention have been dropped, and new programs of this nature have been initiated and are in the process of implementation.

The contention that static and dynamic measures are at least partially measuring different areas of mental activity is supported by the following study by Rand and Kaniel (in press). The following battery of tests was administered to a population of 130 boys and girls, sixth and seventh graders at the ages of 12 and 13 years, in school defined as CD:

1. Static measures: (a) RSPM; (b) MILTA (MIL), a verbal intelligence scale.
2. Dynamic tests: (a) LPAD, VAR I; (b) LPAD, VAR II; (c) LPAD NPT; (d) LPAD ORG.
3. Achievement tests: (a) Hebrew (HEB); (b) English (ENG); (c) mathematics (MAT).

All the tests were administered twice. At the first administration (pretest), all static measures (RSPM, MIL) as well as the NPT and ORG, were administered in the conventional psychometric way. At the second administration (posttest), RSPM and the entire LPAD battery was administered according to the LPAD paradigm. Two-factor analyses were done respectively for all the pretest and posttest measures. Varimax rotated factor matrix yielded two main factors with eigenvalues of 1.00 or higher, and with item loadings within the factor of .50 or higher. The obtained factor composition is presented in Table 7.8.

The findings in Table 7.8 can be summarized as follows:

1. In both factor analyses, static measures differed from the dynamic ones and clustered together with the achievement tests.

TABLE 7.8. Factor Composition of Static Measures, LPAD Tests, and Achievement Tests (Pretest and Posttest) Based upon a Population of Sixth and Seventh Graders in a Rural Public School (N = 130)

	Pretest		Posttest	
Static factor	Dynamic factor	Static factor	Dynamic factor
MIL	RSPM*	MILTA	RSPM†
RSPM*	LPAD	ACH	LPAD
LPAD	VAR I	HEB	VAR I
NP**	VAR II	ENG	VAR II
ORG**		MAT	NPT†
Ach			ORG†
HEB			
ENG			
MAT			

*RSPM yielded high loadings in both factors.

**Administered in conventional static manner.

†Administered in the LPAD manner.

2. LPAD tests (NPT and ORG), when administered in the conventional way, clustered together with the static measures, but when administered according to the LPAD procedures loaded higher on the dynamic factor.

3. The high loading of the RSPM on both factors at the pretest level may be attributed to the combination of the static test administration procedures with a high similarity of the cognitive processes involved in the RSPM, VAR I, and VAR II tests (analogical thinking). When LPAD administration procedures were introduced to the RSPM, it loaded high only on the dynamic factor.

4. The posttest level factor analysis showed clear distinction between the static and dynamic factors. Static tests and the achievement battery formed a product-oriented factor, whereas all the LPAD tests clustered together and formed a process-oriented factor.

These findings indicate that the LPAD tests tap functional dimensions that differ from the psychometric assessment instruments, and are also less correlated with scholastic performance as measured by achievement tests. Therefore, they are efficient instruments for adding information of high value to the understanding of human functioning and of the individual's possibilities to become modified through environmental intervention.

Conclusions

Although the LPAD method is already highly elaborated in terms of test construction, administration procedures, and interpretation of test performance, it still requires extensive scientific research. Its varied purposes, its complexity, and its multidimensionality are highly challenging for scientific inquiry and systematic scrutiny. Such an investment may offer new avenues for development of insight into the mental functioning of the human being. Despite the considerable amount of knowledge we have accumulated, we may still be at the beginning of a long journey.

REFERENCES

Feuerstein, R. (1979). *The dynamic assessment of retarded performers: The learning potential assessment device, theory, instruments and techniques.* Baltimore: University Park Press.

Feuerstein, R. (1980). *Instrumental enrichment: An interventional program for cognitive modifiability.* Baltimore: University Park Press.

Feuerstein, R., Haywood, H.C., Rand, Y., Hoffman, M. B., & Jensen, M. R. (1985). *Learning potential assessment device: Manual.* Jerusalem: Hadassah–WIZO–Canada Research Institute.

Feuerstein, R., & Rand, Y. (1977). *Redevelopment of cognitive functions of retarded early adolescents: Instrumental enrichment.* Jerusalem: Hadassah–WIZO–Canada Research Institute.

Hilliard, A. G. (1982). *The learning potential assessment device and instrumental enrichment as a paradigm shift.* Paper presented at the AERA Conference, New York.

Kugelmas, S., & Lieblich, I. (1968). Relation between ethnic origins and GSR reactivity in psychological detection. *Journal of Applied Psychology, 52,* 159–162.

Narrol, H., & Bachor, D. (1975). An introduction to Feuerstein's approach to assessing and developing cognitive potential. *Interchange, 6,* 2–16.

Rand, Y. (1982). *LPAD tests: VAR. I and VAR. II—Reliability data for group testing and discrimination power.* Paper presented at the IASSMD Conference, Toronto.

Rand, Y. (1983). *LPAD tests: VAR. I and VAR. II—Differential levels of learning and reliability.* Unpublished manuscript, Hadassah–WIZO–Canada Research Institute, Jerusalem.

Rand, Y., & Ben-Schachar, N. (1979). *Differential effects of LPAD learning and static measures.* Unpublished manuscript, Hadassah–WIZO–Canada Research Institute, Jerusalem.

Rand, Y., Feuerstein, R., & Hoffman, M. B. (1982). Structural cognitive modifiability: A holistic (sic) approach to assessment and interventional procedures. Paper presented at the AERA Conference, New York.

Rand, Y., & Kaniel, S. (in press). *Learning potential assessment device: Static measures and achievement tests: A factor analysis.* Jerusalem: Hadassah–WIZO–Canada Research Institute.

Rand, Y., Mintzker, Y., Miller, R., Hoffman, M. B., & Friedlender, Y. (1981). The instrumental enrichment program: Immediate and long-term effects. In P. Mittler (Ed.). *Frontiers of knowledge in mental retardation, Volume I—Social, educational, and behavioral aspects.* Baltimore: University Park Press.

Ruiz, B. (1985). *Cognitive modifiability and irreversibility: A study on the medium-range effects of the instrumental enrichment program* (in Spanish). Publ. No. 4. Ciudad Guayana, Venezuela: National Experimental University of Guayana.

Tzuriel, D., & Rand, Y. (1983). *LPAD testing as an intervention: Differential learning conditions and levels of performance on Raven's standard progressive matrices (RSPM).* Jerusalem: Hadassah–WIZO–Canada Research Institute.

Wagner, J. (1977). *Die intelligenz und psychologische welt von Beduin kinder in der Negev Wueste Israels.* Frankfurt-am-Main, Germany: Peter Land.

8

Relating Learning Styles to Learning Capability

DENIS H. STOTT

Developing Learning Capability in the Retarded

Relegating the Concept of "Intelligence" to History

In the history of our civilization there have been points at which a theoretical barrier to progress is broken down and the way is cleared for outstanding new advances. The realization that the earth was round and not flat encouraged Columbus to set out on his voyage of discovery. The abandonment of the primitive idea that illness and death were due to witchcraft—or the will of a god that must not be interfered with—opened the way for a science of medicine. I believe that the abandonment of the notion that everyone has exactly so much of a mysterious quality called "intelligence" will similarly clear the way for major advances in education, especially in the education of the retarded.

It is only too apparent that there are vast individual differences in mental development and performance, and the new orientation does not attempt to deny or minimize this fact. We may legitimately speak of intelligent or unintelligent behavior, meaning thereby that the act in question was or was not preceded by the thinking necessary to obtain a correct result.

But stupid behavior need not necessarily be—and most often is not—due to the individual's inability to carry out the antecedent thought processes. It may be that no attempt was made to think out the problem. All that can be said is that the requisite thought processes did not occur. Anyone committing a foolish act can think back and recall instances when it was possible to say, "I didn't stop to think" or "That aspect of the matter never occurred to me." An intelligence test does not distinguish between inability and nonuse of capabilities.

Denis H. Stott. Department of Psychology, University of Guelph, Guelph, Ontario, Canada.

The first part of this chapter, "Developing Learning Capability in the Retarded," is a modification of an article first published in the *Journal of Practical Approaches to Developmental Handicap,* *1*(3), 19–31, 1977. The author wishes to thank its Editor, Dr. Roy I. Brown, for his permission to reprint it.

The weakness of an explanation of individual differences in terms of "intelligence level" (i.e., that some people *are* intelligent, some *are* dull, and most are somewhere in between) becomes apparent when we observe people, and ourselves, in everyday life. Those who are intelligent, according to the orthodox theory, ought always to operate intelligently, but this is by no means the case. The academically well qualified—that is, the supposedly intelligent—sometimes behave very stupidly. And the so-called retarded, as exemplified in the case notes below, can use well-thought-out strategies of considerable subtlety within the spheres in which they wish to operate effectively, and are often able to manipulate the adults in charge of them. Because of their handicaps, which, as the case notes will also show, are by no means always of a cognitive character, the retarded are forced to use special strategies. These take into account, and often exploit, their handicaps. With certain types of retardates, notably those with Down syndrome, their needs for effectiveness and for control of their environment seem to be similar to those of normal people. Apart from their intrinsic handicap, the nature and extent of which we know little, they suffer from the environmental handicap of being treated as mental defectives, hence their need to resort to subtle means of effectiveness and control within the limited scope allowed them. Any assumption that another person, even a retarded individual, is less intelligent than oneself often results in being fooled.

What Is "Retarded"?

The reader may at this point begin to wonder why, in view of the above, I persist in using the words "retarded" and "retardate." I do so in their original and literal sense, namely, that the person in question is retarded in the development of those concepts, and hence of the understanding and thinking skills, necessary for independent functioning in the life of our society. It does not necessarily imply mental deficiency, which is a conceptually obsolete term, nor does it imply some mysterious and unchangeable state. A few years ago a worker in a very good normalization program who was addressing my students described a young woman who spoke sensibly and gave every other appearance of normality. Then he added, as if to make his point, "You would never know she was a retardate." It struck me that two centuries ago, when people believed that there existed certain people called witches, gossips of the time might have been heard saying, "You would never know she was a witch." Once, by means of an IQ test or other assessment procedure, an official ascertainment of retardation has been made, we tend to regard the individual in question as a different sort of person; he or she remains a "retardate," despite evidence to the contrary. In fact, such evidence is often ignored or dismissed because of the contradictions it poses. I therefore recommend that the term "retarded" be used only as a characterization of the individual's current level of development and mode of functioning, and this is the way it is used in this chapter.

The Developmental View of Individual Differences

When the performance of a retardate in everyday life is studied without preconceptions about mental deficiency, we usually get an apparently contradictory picture of undoubtedly poor functioning together with surprisingly good functioning in certain areas (most often in the retardate's dealings with people). These contradictions can be explained when we train ourselves to think in terms of the *use* of capabilities. From use comes development, and from nonuse comes retardation. This is central to the developmental theory of individual differences in intelligent behavior. This point of view was well stated by Overstreet (1925), who was a professor of philosophy at the City College, New York. *"The mind is what it does, or better still, the mind becomes what it does.* Give a mind something new to feed upon; give it something new to do; and it becomes a different mind."

Equating "Intelligence" with IQ

Unfortunately Overstreet's commonsense approach was overshadowed by a flood of psychometric zeal. Psychologists designed their tests to conform with the thinking characteristic of Western education—and not surprisingly found that the tests tended to measure exactly what they were designed to measure: the kinds of capabilities involved in academic success. From this, the psychometricians made the inexcusable assumption that the common element in their tests, and also in academic performance, was "intelligence." However, they were awkward about describing what "intelligence" really was, and no generally accepted definition could be found. Eventually there seemed to be general agreement not to enquire further about the nature of intelligence and to settle for the definition that intelligence is simply what intelligence tests measure. This is in fact the attitude taken by Jensen (1969) in his article in the *Harvard Educational Review*.

Misuse of IQ Tests

Very soon the concept of intelligence and of its measurement began to be used to discriminate against immigrants of non-Anglo-Saxon origin. Goddard (one of the "big three," with Terman and Yerkes, who introduced the Binet Test in America) reported in 1912 that 83% of the Jewish, 80% of the Hungarian, 79% of the Italian, and 87% of the Russian immigrants were "feebleminded" (Kamin, 1974). Laughable as such findings may be to us now, it is necessary to ask whether we are not guilty of similar misjudgment of the low performance of blacks and other disadvantaged members of the community, as well as of those who suffer from developmental handicaps. Many authorities have been expressing this view over the past decade. Dunn (1968) has described traditional intelligence testing as "digging the educational graves of many racially and/or economically disadvantaged children." Zigler (1966) was one of the first to challenge the concept of mental deficiency (i.e., extreme "low intelligence") by pointing out that the term is meaningless so long as we do not know what intelligence is. He went so far as to say that, "One can do little in the way of remedial teaching and treatment as long as such difficulties are attributed simply to the lower 'intelligence' of the retarded."

The Active–Modificatory Approach

Feuerstein (1970) identified two contrasting approaches to the education of the retarded that relate to the teacher's beliefs about the possibility of developing the capabilities of retarded students. On the one hand, he describes the passive–acceptant approach, which assumes that the retardate has a limited potential that cannot be changed, and efforts to bring about any advance are therefore useless. This was basically the attitude of Burt (1969), based on his conviction that those at the lower end of the IQ distribution were incapable of logical thought or understanding, and should therefore only be taught mindless, repetitive tasks. The alternative, *active–modificatory* approach, rejects any notion of a potential or ceiling, and calls for exploration of the capacity of the retarded individual.

Study of Inhibition of Mental Growth

It was the author's experiences with delinquent youths, and notably his friendship with two of them (Searle, pp. 81–90, and Potter, pp. 334–341, in Stott, 1950), that brought him to question the assumption of a specific "level of intelligence." They and several other youths in that sample operated at a level determined by their situation. One showed exceptional creativity and oral literary ability, yet was illiterate and regarded by some as a borderline mental defective. The other gave the appearance of being a simpleton and ended up in an institution for mental defectives; yet he was an avid reader of crime fiction, and for years had been not only a very skilled burglar, but had enunciated very clever guidelines for burglarizing.

The realization, as in the case of these delinquents, that some young people could be motivated toward poor mental functioning, even to the level of retardation, led the author to wonder to what proportion of retardates this could apply. It also led to his interest in determining if the process could be reversed. In other words, was it possible to design situations that would stimulate the would-be retardate to develop capabilities to the extent of a normal level of functioning?

The first step was to study and classify the ways in which mental growth could be inhibited. The result was the recognition of 14 faulty styles of learning that were described in the Guide to the Child's Learning Behavior (Stott, 1971, 1978). As the thought-inhibiting types of learning behavior were identified and found to apply to a variety of children, materials were designed to overcome them. The result was the *Flying Start Learning-to-Learn Kit* (Stott,

1971), an experimental edition of which was tested out in a number of Metropolitan Toronto Schools for the Trainable Retarded.

An Experiment in Stimulating Mental Growth

The following experiences in the treatment of retarded children are included in a book on assessment for two reasons. The first is that, without empirical support, theorizing can be dismissed as mere rhetoric—and catchy, but unsupported theories have always been, and remain, a danger in education. To substantiate a theory, the processes have to be demonstrated—in this instance, exactly how some children fail to develop their mental capabilities to the extent that they are assessed as retarded.

The second reason for reproducing the following observations about the disabling learning styles of some children made in the course of a treatment program is that our concepts of assessment are changing. If a child's mental capabilities are assumed to be the expression of a set of innate abilities, the aim of assessment is to attempt to measure the "givens" that establish the limits of the child's attainment. If, on the other hand, we believe that, in large measure, "the mind becomes what it does," assessment must be dynamic in character, that is to say, it must test the child's capacity for "becoming." This involves an exploration of a retarded child's learning-related behavior in order to discover why the normal processes of learning have not occurred, and of the possibility, with appropriate techniques, to teach the child how to learn. The information gained in the course of such an exploratory training program provides the core of a dynamic assessment.

The experiment in question, which consisted of working over the summer months with 16 children nominated by the principal of a school for the retarded and 2 nominated by the supervisor of a nursery for the retarded, has been reported more fully in the original article (Stott, 1977). The first case, that of Peter, is reproduced in its entirety in order to exemplify the nature of the learning-to-learn training program and to demonstrate in detail this boy's response to it. For the rest, all that space in this chapter allows are brief descriptions and discussions of the types of incapacitating learning-related behaviors observed.

RETREAT INTO INCOMPETENCE: PETER

When we first started to work with the 8-year-old Peter, some months before the Project began, he had become so sensitive about his speech defect that he avoided saying anything but an occasional single word. His bewilderment and sense of inferiority spread to his general social relationships and his attitude to learning.

The following paragraphs in quotation marks are taken verbatim from notes made from the beginning of our work with him. The materials cited are examples of items of the *Flying Start Learning-to-Learn Kit* (Stott, 1971), illustrations of which are given in Figures 8.1 to 8.6.

First Day. "Peter put together all the 2-piece puzzles [Figure 8.1A] and he tried to do two of the 4-piece [Figure 8.1B]. He gave up after several tries because one of the pieces did not seem to fit properly. At other times he would look but didn't see any errors with the last piece he had fitted, and when I commented that perhaps it might look better if it was in another position or turned around, he sometimes would still leave it where it was.

"He and I then played the pink Merry-go-round game [Figure 8.2]. At first Peter didn't really understand what to do. He didn't want to wait and listen to instructions, and used a trial-and-error strategy. Initially, he could not see that the thick line had to be on the outer side of the circle. However, after a few trials, he understood because he said "Oh" and continued to fit his pieces together properly. But, once or twice, he reverted to the trial-and-error procedure."

Two Days Later. "I started this session with letting him work on the 4-piece puzzles. And this time, he had no difficulty. He did very well.

"Peter and Gary (his friend) played with the pink Merry-go-rounds together. There was some improvement from the first session. He had no trouble putting the thick line on the outer side of the circle. He wanted to play the game over and over again."

FIGURE 8.1.   *A:* The two-piece puzzles invite the retarded child to commit himself or herself to a very easy task, and give him or her the immediate satisfaction of having made a picture. *B:* The four-piece puzzles need a little more concentration. Because the pictures are cut into uniform rectangles trial-and-error fitting as in an irregular jigsaw will not help. The child has to attend to the picture—but he or she gets immediate reinforcement of every act of attention. (From Stott, D. H. [1971]. *Flying start learning-to-learn kit.* Guelph, Ontario, Brook Educational. Reprinted by permission of the publisher.)

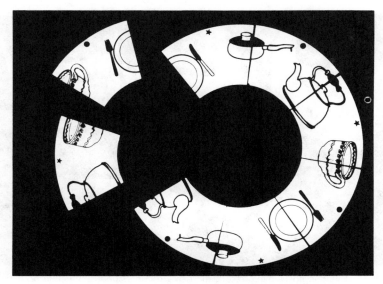

FIGURE 8.2.   The merry-go-rounds train the child to restrain impulsive (nonthinking) responses. Since one player has the "dot" segments and the other the "star" segments each has to await his or her turn; otherwise the circle cannot be completed correctly. (From Stott, D. H. [1971]. *Flying start learning-to-learn kit.* Guelph, Ontario: Brook Educational. Reprinted by permission of the publisher.)

Seven Days Later.   "Peter has a very good strategy when he is playing with the pink Merry-go-rounds. . . . when Gary and he played with the green Merry-go-rounds [one stage harder], he was the first to recognize that there were two bulldozers, two cars, two bicycles, etc."

Two Days Later.   "Gary and Peter started the session with the green Merry-go-rounds. Peter sorts the pieces without being told to do so. He has no difficulty in fitting the correct piece in the circle.

"Then they played with the yellow Mail Boxes [Figure 8.3]. Peter is very good at this. He placed all of his letters correctly. He pays attention to the letters and matches them with the letters on the boxes.

"Peter never seems to tire of working with the games. For instance, when Gary and he were playing with the Merry-go-rounds, he reached for the next set immediately after the set they were working with was completed. He plays with the same sets repeatedly."

Five Days Later.   "Peter did four sets of What's Happening? [Figure 8.4]. He fitted the puzzles together quite well. But he was shy about telling a story of what was happening in the picture. He pointed to certain objects in the picture and told what they were. However, it was difficult to understand what he said because of his speech defect. He works with a good strategy: he is very particular and precise in fitting the pieces together. Every piece

FIGURE 8.3.   The mail boxes reinforce attention and discrimination. If the child posts the letter card in the correct box the other player says "Right." This activity is well within the capability of the typical "trainable" child. (From Stott, D. H. [1971]. *Flying start learning-to-learn kit.* Guelph, Ontario: Brook Educational. Reprinted by permission of the publisher.)

has to fit together perfectly without any overlap. He appears to be a perfectionist.

"Then he did some of the Six-piece Puzzles [Figure 8.5]. Again he was very good at putting the pieces together and making them fit properly."

Two Days Later.   "Peter and Gary played with the Green Mail Boxes. Peter can match the letters very well. He did not make any mistakes when he was mailman. I gave him a few, perhaps eight, to mail initially. When he

FIGURE 8.4.   What's Happening teaches the retarded child to look for meaning in pictures. They fit the pieces by the order of the numbers on their backs, with a number guide if necessary. (From Stott, D. H. [1971]. *Flying start learning-to-learn kit.* Guelph, Ontario: Brook Educational. Reprinted by permission of the publisher.)

FIGURE 8.5.   The six-piece puzzles reinforce a systematic, thinking approach to a task. As in *What's Happening* the order of placing the segments is given by the numbers on their backs. Impulsivity and getting the pieces out of order only make the task more difficult. (From Stott, D. H. [1971]. *Flying start learning-to-learn kit.* Guelph, Ontario: Brook Educational. Reprinted by permission of the publisher.)

had finished mailing them he picked up some more. He never seemed to tire.

"Peter answers when he is spoken to, but with single words. He does not like to say anything if more are required."

Three Weeks Later.   "Today Peter was laughing and talking a bit when he was putting together a picture—a horse. He obviously enjoyed it. After he had completed it he told me he lives on a farm and has a horse."

In the Project Peter was at first reluctant to play with children of his own age, but by the end of an afternoon on the beach he was playing normally and splashing water with the other kids. He learned to "dish it out" as well as take it.

In the instructional sessions he continued the use of the good learning habits he had developed earlier, and he revealed a vivid imagination. In the reading program he mastered all the simple sounds. It is understandable from Peter's poor initial performance on the Flying Start materials that he should have been given an IQ of only 41. It might also have been recorded that he had poor spatial ability. Very soon, however, he developed good motivation, and his new-found desire to succeed prompted him to apply good learning strategies. That he had settled down to a state of mental incompetence was certainly not because of an intrinsic impairment of ability or of motivation.

On the contrary, he set himself high standards, and showed extraordinary persistence at tasks that needed thought.

The effect of the program seems to have been to reverse the retreat into incompetence that originated as a defensive reaction to his speech defect. Children gauge their competence and develop their self-image by measuring their performance in certain standard areas against that of their age peers. We hear children testing each other as to whether they can hop, wink, skip, or count to 100. Not being able to speak properly must be a shattering blow to a child's self-image, which could undermine confidence in coping with learning tasks.

We have also to consider the impression that a severe speech defect in a child makes upon adults who have to teach or assess him or her. A general defense of unresponsiveness in order not to get involved in speaking situations can easily be interpreted as mental subnormality. Used in the testing situation, such a strategy means a low IQ. From this point our expectancies take over. Such expectancies are reinforced—as in three cases in this series—when the child's background is one of severe social disadvantage. Then it is easy to fall into the hallowed diagnostic stereotype of "familial feeble-mindedness."

The 10 children in the sample without physical defects and of normal physical appearance suffered from handicaps of temperament that induced them to adopt strategies for avoiding the challenges of living as normal people in a normal world.

The first of these strategies was the deliberate choice of the role of a retardate. Because of their temperamental restlessness, need for dependence, or timidity, these children found it difficult or too stressful to keep up with other children. It was less frustrating for them to cease to compete in the uneven struggle and to go to the other extreme.

RETREAT INTO A RETARDED DEPENDENCY: MOIRA

The most outstanding instance of this retreat into retardation was that of the four-year-old Moira, who was attending the nursery for the retarded. When we first met her she would not undertake even the simplest of tasks, such as putting together the two halves of a picture (Figure 8.1A). We caught her off guard by asking her to show a much younger child how to do it. Over the coming weeks she alternated between easy mastery of successive Flying Start items and reversions to her retarded role. However, such relapses became increasingly more rare as she learned the delights of playing like a normal child. Within a few months she started on a reading program, and showed a remarkable talent for linking sounds with letters. She was able to enter a normal kindergarten; 5 years later she was functioning as an average student in a regular grade 4/5 class. A detailed account of her habilitation is given elsewhere (Stott, 1976).

Moira's pseudoretardation followed a not-infrequent but seldom recognized pattern: that of playing stupid in order to achieve the privileged position of being ministered to and excused of all responsibility. The role playing is utterly convincing unless one knows the type and can read the counterindications. A psychometrist equipped with an intelligence test falls an easy victim to the strategy. But such children give themselves away to the trained observer by occasionally forgetting to be dull.

THE DEFENCE OF HYPERACTIVITY: ROBERT

The second of the avoidance strategies frequently observed among the retarded is that of restlessness, unruliness, and clowning. Robert, the second child from the nursery for the retarded, would never remain in his seat long enough to finish any task. As with Moira, the treatment strategy of offering a source of fulfillment more attractive than the retarded role was successful. The circle-making puzzles of the Flying Start caught his attention (Figure 8.2), and before long he had learned that the necessary requisites for success in them were to keep in his seat, give attention to detail, and resist distractions. In his original state Robert was a prime example of the now-fashionable "attention–deficit" syndrome; but with him—and probably with many of those thus diagnosed—it was not so much neuropathological as a learned way of life. Like Moira, Robert entered our reading program, quickly mastered the phonic principle, learned to count up to 10, and was able at five years to enter a regular kindergarten.

One may wonder how Robert was ever considered to be retarded. Three factors contributed to this false impression. First, he had the immature speech typical of the young hyperactive child, so that it was difficult to understand him. Second, his hyperactivity at the inception of the Project constituted a real and severe learning handicap; if he had been allowed to develop it as a style of life he would have become one of those "mentally retarded" boys whose mental ability was in fact effaced by their restlessness. Third, he came from a culturally disadvantaged home, his mother being illiterate. With his other handicaps it was easy for a public health nurse to see in him a well-known pattern of familial feeble-mindedness. Again we have to ask how many other young children suffering from a combination of developmental immaturity, temperamental handicap, and a disadvantaged home are assigned the same role, and, once placed in a "retarded" environment, have no option but to play it.

UNFORTHCOMINGNESS: SUSAN AND JOHN

By far the most common handicap of temperament responsible for retardation and educational backwardness is that designated as unforthcomingness (Stott, 1960, 1961). It consists of an undue apprehensiveness of anything strange or supposedly difficult. In extreme cases the child is unwilling to try any problem the solution of which is not obvious. Consequently the child gets no practice in solving problems and never ventures mentally beyond the restricted world of a familiar environment. Indeed, because the children thus afflicted give such a strong impression of "low intelligence," this important form of behavior disturbance has not received the recognition it deserves.

Four of the 10 children of normal physical appearance were victims of unforthcomingness. It was seen in its typical form as a learning handicap in 13-year-old Susan. When given a task she would look as though she did not know where to begin. The teacher always had to make the first move, and then she would join in slowly and cautiously. During the session she would loosen up and become involved in the task. She came to terms with her fear of decision by relying upon stereotyped procedures. In counting, for example, she had always to begin at 1. When asked any direct question, she froze and was unable to produce an answer.

John also had this handicap to a marked degree. Once inside the school building, it was extremely difficult to entice him outside to play. "There might be people out there!" he would say. Although officially assessed as retarded on the basis of an IQ of below 50, he was a boy of undoubted ability. He could read reasonably well, and knew how to sound out unfamiliar words. He could add and subtract, and during the Project began to do multiplication and division. That he thought about the rationale of these processes was shown by the way he overcame his ignorance of the 3-times multiplication table. To find the answer to 3 times 6 he said "twice 6 are 12, so one (on) from 12 is 13, 2(on) from 12 is 14", and so on up to 18.

THE DOWN SYNDROME CHILDREN: TOM

Of all handicapped children, those suffering from Down syndrome are among the most likely to be preclassified as retardates. Because of this assumption, they are exempted from the normal socialization processes. Little is expected of them regarding mental development or coping with the demands of everyday life, and they may be given a jester's license to behave in what for a normal child would be an unacceptable manner. It is interesting to speculate how a normal child would develop if the parents made a similar assumption of mental subnormality and did not expect normal socialization. The result in terms of mental development might resemble what is observed in Down syndrome children. Indeed, the case of Moira, described above, might be viewed as a natural experiment in the effects of offering a child retardation as a mode of life. At the time she was discovered, her mother and all the adult volunteers at the Nursery were reinforcing the helplessness and non-participation by which she was able to control her human environment.

In working with Down syndrome children one cannot help noticing their use of a strategy that takes advantage of their exemption from social pressures. It is as if the child is saying, "I am going to do this if it suits me, and I won't do it if it doesn't suit me." Moreover, Down syndrome children would seem to be endowed with a normal range of motivation. Like ordinary children, some are docile and some are aggressive, some are content with being dependent and others make strong demands for effectiveness and dominance.

Some are even creative within the limited scope allowed them. It is understandable, therefore, that many will seek to take advantage of the role accorded to them, and develop the capabilities that suit them in that role. Often these take the form of skills in human relationships, and an understanding of humor. Because nearly all Down syndrome children have these temptations to exploit their role as retardates, we know little of the range of their mental capabilities.

The above observations are exemplified in 10-year-old Tom. In the classroom and at play he was enthusiastic and imaginative, with a flair for make-believe games. When he agreed to work he showed a high rate of correct response, with good intuitive discrimination and good perception. Like so many Down syndrome children, however, he had a will of his own, and decided when he was going to work and when he was going to act the clown, make excuses for quitting the job, or just be "tired." During the Project he settled down once he was separated from his partner in clowning. He learned to count to 10, and despite a speech problem mastered the sound values of most of his letters.

THE LESSONS OF THE EXPERIMENT

To summarize the experiences of the Project team, it became clear that the children who were categorized and treated as retarded were initially functioning at far below their capabilities. Their handicaps, as we saw them, were physical or temperamental rather than cognitive. Nevertheless, these handicaps had produced a cumulative retardation. It could be seen how a speech defect, an extremely apprehensive temperament, or even being accorded the role and privileges of a retardate, could start a learning-disabling chain reaction. It was noteworthy how, in some instances, the appearance of retardation could be produced by a not-too-severe physical or temperamental handicap compounded by socioeconomic disadvantage. Even the Down syndrome children showed themselves capable of functioning above initial expectations. In the short duration of the Project we could not say that we had reached any child's mental limits, nor could we estimate what these were.

The second conclusion was that each retarded child needed individual study in order to understand both the source of the retardation and the means of reversing the cumulative maldevelopment. Mental retardation should be seen as a result rather than a cause. Instead of a diagnosis in terms of "intelligence level," we need a systematic assessment of the child's learning and problem-solving behavior. Of no observation can we say, "This is intelligence," only that "This is behavior." And despite our present lack of precision in the objective identification of types of behavior, we can at least say, "This is a type of behavior that must be detrimental to learning." If a child is so apprehensive of anything new or supposedly difficult that he or she freezes up before any problem and fails even to attempt a solution, this is behavior that could preclude cognitive processing. Similarly, the child who does not

FIGURE 8.6.   The Matchers further reinforce reflectivity. The child has to find the exact match for the presented card among the row of six. Three criteria have to be taken into account. (From Stott, D. H. [1971]. *Flying start learning-to-learn kit*. Guelph, Ontario: Brook Educational. Reprinted by permission of the publisher.)

take in the information because of inattention, or who makes an impulsive guess without processing the information he or she does get, is not likely to advance in problem solving. Similar behaviors within the testing situation will almost certainly produce low IQs.

It follows that, until we have taught the child to use adequate learning strategies, we have no means of discovering how his or her perceptual or cognitive capabilities may be developed. In short, the diagnosis, to be of value, must consist of a period of work with the child in order to discover whether the incorrect learning strategies can be rectified. We may have to decide that the child is so damaged that the neurological basis for a better behavioral organization does not yet exist, but we are not justified in coming to this conclusion as the result of an interview, test, or observation carried out at any one point of time. We have to give poorly functioning children the benefit of a carefully designed program that modifies their behavior specifically within problem-solving and learning situations. The Flying Start Learning-to-Learn Program may be considered a modest step in this direction, while offering a means of assessing the capabilities uncovered.

Suggested Procedures for Implementation

The "active modificatory" approach to retardation as exemplified here—if it is to become generally adopted—would need to be embodied in standard procedures that can be operated by the teacher–assessor. The first essential is that a record be kept for each child, not only of attainment, but also of growth in learning skills. Since the teacher cannot be expected to maintain a running record of what happens during the whole school day, an hour or so might be set aside, perhaps once a week, for systematically recorded observation. During these periods—possibly with the help of volunteers or students in training to be teachers—observations would be made of each child's learning style, and of the extent to which he or she is able to cope with tasks.

A monthly review conference might be held, which would normally include teachers and the school principal, a school psychologist, and/or a special-education consultant. A major function of such a conference would be to collate observations on those children whose progress was disappointing and to formulate appropriate programs of remediation for them. This was in fact the procedure used in the remedial programs at the Center for Educational Disabilities, except that the conferences took place at the end of each session. One anticipated effect of such procedures would be the development of a wider range of remedial approaches and materials.

Empirical Studies of the Validity of the Concept of Learning Style as a Factor in Attainment

The theoretical position enunciated in the above report was that the primary and immediate reason for poor mental functioning in nearly all children and in most so-called retardates is that they fail to exploit their mental capabilities. Moreover, there is good case evidence, supported by professional experience, that this proposition applies even to some degree to those suffering from genetic anomalies. The word "immediate" is used above to indicate that behind the failure to exploit capabilities there may lie a variety of background reasons, such as constitutional impairments of temperament (excessive fear of failure, impulsivity, and so on) and/or adverse environment. These background handicaps are seen as affecting the child's mental functioning and educational attainments by generating attitudes and behaviors in learning or problem-solving situations that are detrimental to good performance.

The behavioral sets, either of temperamental or cultural origin, that individuals bring into play in learning situations constitute their *learning style*. The validity of this concept depends upon a demonstration that learning style, as thus defined, does indeed affect attainment. To date two studies of this issue have been reported.

The first (Stott, Green, & Francis, 1983) used a seven-item checklist of learning style, reproduced in Table 8.1, which had been developed for the screening of large populations of children. It was the subject of a follow-up study conducted in 62 primary schools in and near London, England, on a cohort of 2,272 five- and six-year-old children. The teachers completed the checklist after the children had been in school only 3 or 4 months, before they had been exposed to formal learning. There was thus no risk that the children's attitudes could have been affected by experiences of success or

TABLE 8.1.   Checklist of Learning Style

	Certainly applies	Applies sometimes	Doesn't apply
1. Shows by his or her answers that he or she is giving attention.			
2. Settles down well at an activity that needs some concentration.			
3. Copes with something new without getting nervous or upset.			
4. Is willing to fall in with the general activities of the class.			
5. Is willing to try on his or her own.			
6. Accepts help when he or she cannot manage a task.			
7. Is an alert child who enters into activities with interest.			

failure in school. A year later their current teachers (in nearly all cases not the same individuals who completed the learning style checklist) assessed the 2,013 children who were still available for attainment in reading, arithmetic, and spoken language. Correlations of these assessments with the children's learning style 1 year earlier were, respectively, .50, .50, and .47, and .54 for the three combined. Because 22% of the children had good learning style (fault score of 0) and a further 13% showed only one minor fault, while relatively few scored 8 or more (out of a total fault score of 14), the distribution was extremely skewed. Thus the above correlations understate the closeness of the relationship between learning style and future attainment. It is a matter of some interest that the above correlations are somewhat better than those between IQ and attainment in young children when there is a similar interval of 1 year between the two assessments (Feshbach, Adelman, & Fuller, 1974).

Figure 8.7 gives a more detailed picture of the relationship between these children's learning styles and their performance in reading. They were divided into three groups of above average ($n = 784$), average ($n = 759$), and below average ($n = 470$) on the basis of the teachers' ratings. It is seen that of the children with a 0 fault score for learning style only between 3% and 4% were below-average, while nearly 70% were above-average readers. At fault scores of 4 and 5 the proportions are about equal, but at higher fault scores the proportion of the below average progressively increases, to the point that at score 14 there are none but poor readers.

Nevertheless it cannot be assumed that the statistical relationship between learning style and future attainment implies causality. Such a conclusion is justified only if (a) a poor learning style always results in poor attainment, (b) the exceptions can be explained or (c) manipulation of one variable results in reliable effects in the other. In effect comparatively few of the cases in the above study were discordant in the sense that their good or fairly good rating

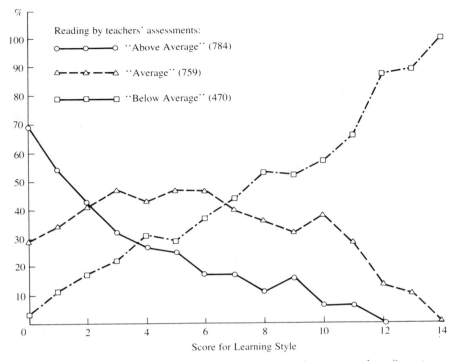

FIGURE 8.7.   Percentage of children at each point of learning style score in each reading category.

for learning style was contradicted by subsequent poor attainment. It was therefore decided, as a further follow-up of the study, to interview the teachers and school principals of these "discordant" children in order to discover why their early promise, in terms of learning style, did not result in adequate achievement.

To obtain a large enough sample of discordant children, "adequate" learning style was defined by a fault score of 3 or less. This produced a sample of 91 children who were discordant in the sense of not achieving the level of achievement predicted by their learning style. It was reduced to a subsample of 51 by selecting those children attending the larger and more accessible schools.

The investigator asked the principals and class teachers to suggest reasons for the failure of the children in question and enquired specifically about possible health handicaps, the children's domestic and cultural backgrounds, social adjustment, temperament, and attendance record. They recorded specific events liable to be detrimental to the child's progress. This excluded general demographic variables such as socioeconomic status, overcrowding, one-parent families, and disadvantaged ethnic group, because these infer only a greater probability of poor attainment and not all children are adversely

TABLE 8.2. Distribution of Principals' and Teachers' Reasons for Discordance between Learning Style and Attainment Assessments

Reasons for discordance	A	B	C	D	E	F	G	H	I	J	K	No other	Total of children affected
A Sensory defects	1	—	1	1	1	3	3	—	—	—	1	—	6
B Health handicaps	—	—	—	2	—	1	2	—	1	—	—	3	7
C Underreactive coping style	1	—	—	—	—	4	4	—	1	2	3	8	15
D Overreactive coping style	1	2	—	—	—	1	2	—	2	—	1	2	7
E Abnormal behavior	1	—	—	—	—	—	2	—	1	1	—	—	5
F Lack of parental encouragement	3	1	4	1	—	2	5	1	2	1	4	1	12
G Severe family stress	3	2	4	1	2	5	—	—	2	1	3	2	15
H Physical deprivation or neglect	—	—	—	—	—	1	—	—	—	1	1	1	3
I English the second language	—	1	1	2	1	2	2	—	—	1	6	—	10
J Incompatible teacher	—	—	2	—	1	1	1	1	1	—	1	—	4
K Long absences	1	—	3	1	—	4	3	1	6	1	—	—	10

affected by them. For example, the breakup of the parents' marriage was accepted as a reason for the child's lack of progress only if it occurred during the interval of 1 year between the assessments for learning style and attainment.

A list of the factors considered to be detrimental to attainment are presented in matrix form in Table 8.2, together with the number of children affected. The effect of each of these hypothesized reasons for failure can be estimated both by their frequency and the number and nature of other possible reasons with which they were associated. There is the complication, however, that some of the listed reasons are interrelated and could be expected to occur in combination. This applies, for example, to sensory defects, health handicaps, lack of parental encouragement, and severe family stress. In addition, children of the disadvantaged families in which these reasons are most likely to occur tend to be inhibited and passive. The strong association between English as the second language and long absences requires an explanation: most of the children in question were Asiatic Indians or Pakistanis, whose parents sometimes withdrew them from school to take them on lengthy visits to their native countries.

Table 8.2 shows that of the behavioral handicaps, the most frequent—with 15 children affected—was underreactive coping style. This included lack of confidence, inhibiting anxiety, lethargy, overdependence, and school refusal. Such behaviors would be expected to result in a poor learning style and in particular be the direct opposite of the third component of good learning style, "Copes with something new without getting nervous or upset." Consequently, it may be wondered why children with these emotional handicaps were placed in the "adequate" learning style category. The answer lies in the overgenerous cutoff score used as a criterion for "adequacy" referred to earlier. The above item was in fact marked for 12 of the 15 underreacting children, but, because they showed few other learning style defects, their scores did not exceed the cutoff point of 3. Similarly, all seven of the overreacting children had been marked adversely on item 2 of the learning style checklist ("Settles down well at an activity that needs some concentration") but likewise did not score more than 3. In short, both these under- and overreacting children were only discordant in terms of the design of the study. Their presence among the discordants strengthens rather than diminishes the predictive value of learning style.

Only one of the 51 children, a Mauritian girl who scored just within the "adequate" learning style category with a rating of 3, was free of all the handicaps listed in Table 8.2. Nevertheless, her principal reported that there had at one time been some family problems. Except for this one doubtful case, all the discordance between learning style and attainment was accounted for. It is thus justifiable to conclude that if a young child evidences a good learning style, his or her attainment in the basic academic skills will, in the absence of certain known detrimental influences, be average or above.

This statement leaves little room for certain traditional explanations of learning failure, namely, low intelligence and specific reading disability (dyslexia). If either of these had been a significant factor in the study cohort, there would have been a number of cases of poor performance that remained unexplained by either defect of learning style or the identified handicaps. As noted, however, there was virtually no unexplained residue.

Severely retarded children would have been identified at or before school entry and referred to some form of special education or care. It is also possible that some of the seven children in the "abnormal behavior" category would later be ascertained to be retarded because the nature of their behavior disturbance was of a type that would be incompatible with thriving in a public school. It is of interest that none of the principals or classroom teachers cited "dullness" as a reason for the academic failure of any child. It is therefore suggested, in conformity with the theme of this chapter, that what passes for "low intelligence" is in most cases either a matter of poor learning style or the inhibition of normal mental functioning by one or more of the physical, temperamental, or social handicaps listed in Table 8.2. This suggestion becomes all the more plausible when it is considered that poor learning style in the form of inattention, failure of concentration, depression, or lack of confidence is also likely to be detrimental to performance in a test of so-called mental ability and that such tests assess the cumulative effects of such factors. Low IQ may consequently be nothing more than evidence of poor learning style.

As regards specific reading disability, if there had been any "dyslexics" in the sample, it should have been possible to identify them as children with a learning style good enough to perform at least at an average level in other areas but with notably poor performance in reading. A search was therefore made within the whole study cohort of 2,013 children for those who were subaverage in reading but average or above in arithmetic and spoken language. There was only one notably poor reader (graded E) who had an above-average (B) rating in one of the other areas, but this child also had an E in the third area, so that the disability in reading was not specific. No subaverage (D + E) readers achieved above-average performance in both of the other areas, and only 1.6% achieved this level in one of them. An additional 4.6% of the poor readers had an average grade in both arithmetic and spoken language, but a percentage of this disorder is to be expected on grounds of probability—that is, there are likely to be a few children of otherwise average capabilities who are somewhat behind in their reading for a variety of reasons.

In the second study of this issue, Birrell, Phillips, and Stott (1985) used the same seven-item checklist in Table 8.1 on a sample of 246 five-year-old indigenous British children in Coventry, England. In this study, academic attainment was measured 2 years later both by teachers' assessments and formal written tests of reading, arithmetic, spelling, and language. The relationship between learning style and attainment was expressed in both prod-

TABLE 8.3.   Relation of Learning Style to Attainments 2 Years Later

	Attainment tests[a]		Teachers' gradings[a]	
	PM	MR	PM	MR
Reading	.53	.55	.48	.52
Number	.39	.41	.43	.46
Spelling	.47	.49	—	—
Language	—	—	.47	.51

Note. Modified from Birrell, H. V., Phillips, C. J., and Stott, D. H. (1985). Learning style and school attainment in young children: A follow-up study. *School Psychology International, 6,* 207–218.

[a]PM = product–moment; MR = multiple regression. The values are negative since the measure of learning style was a fault score. All are highly significant.

uct–moment correlations and multiple regression coefficients. The results are shown in Table 8.3. It is of interest that the effect of style of learning at so young an age as 5 years 3 months (the mean age at which the assessment was made) is maintained even after 2 years of schooling. Contemporary methods of teaching apparently do not do much to overcome the poor learning styles that some children bring into school with them. It will be of interest to observe the success of experimental curricula in which one of the chief goals would be to teach children how to learn.

The implications of the effects of learning style not only on school attainment but also on test performance are too far-reaching to be adequately discussed in this chapter. An ongoing international and cross-cultural study, so far unpublished, has revealed very large differences in learning style scores that parallel ethnic and social class differences in IQ. It may therefore be that, for example, the so-called mental inferiority of blacks may be accounted for by a heritage of environmental disadvantage that has resulted in poor learning-related behavior. This raises the broader issue—so far empirically unexplored—of the determinants of learning style in general.

REFERENCES

Birrell, H. V., Phillips, C. J., & Stott, D. H. (1985). Learning style and school attainment in young children: A follow-up study. *School Psychology International, 6,* 207–218.

Burt, C. (1969). *The Backward Child* (5th ed.). London: University of London Press.

Dunn, L. M. (1968). Special education for the mildly retarded—Is much of it justifiable? *Exceptional Children, 35,* 5–22.

Feuerstein, R. (1970). A dynamic approach to the causation, prevention and alleviation of retarded performance. In H. C. Haywood (Ed.) *Sociocultural aspects of mental retardation.* New York: Appleton-Century-Crofts.

Feshbach, S., Adelman, H., & Fuller, W. W. (1974). Early identification of children with high risk of reading failure. *Journal of Learning Disabilities, 7,* 639–644.

Jensen, A. R. (1969). How much can we boost IQ and scholastic achievement? In "Environment, Heredity, and Intelligence" (Reprint series No. 2). *Harvard Educational Review, 38,* 1–123.

Kamin, L. J. (1974). *The science and politics of I.Q.* New York: John Wiley.

Overstreet, H. A. (1925). *Influencing human behavior.* New York: Norton.

Stott, D. H. (1950). *Delinquency and human nature.* Dunfermline, Fife: Carnegie U.K. Trust.

Stott, D. H. (1960). Should we "segregate" the slow-learning child? *The Slow-Learning Child,* 7, 15–20.

Stott, D. H. (1961). IQ changes among educationally subnormal children. *Special Education,* 50, 11–14.

Stott, D. H. (1971). *Flying start learning-to-learn kit.* Guelph, Ontario: Brook Educational.

Stott, D. H. (1976). Pseudoretardation as a form of learning disability: The case of Jean. *Journal of Learning Disabilities,* 9, 354–364.

Stott, D. H. (1977). Developing learning capability in the retarded. *Journal of Practical Approaches to Developmental Handicap.* 1, 19–31.

Stott, D. H. (1978). *The hard-to-teach child.* Baltimore: University Park Press.

Stott, D. H., Green, L. F., & Francis, J. M. (1983). Learning style and school attainment. *Human Learning,* 2, 61–75.

Zigler, E. (1966). *Mental retardation: Current issues and approaches.* In L. W. and M. Hoffman (Eds.). *Review of child development research, Volume II.* New York: Russell Sage Foundation.

9

Assessing the Learning Potential of Kindergarten and Primary-Age Children

JUDITH S. MEARIG

Feuerstein (1979) originally developed the Learning Potential Assessment Device (LPAD) for retarded adolescents. Although the instruments have been used with younger individuals of varying ages and abilities, they are not appropriate in their present form for most kindergarten–primary-age children, particularly those who are significantly below average in their cognitive development or have serious attention problems. This age span encompasses many important maturational and learning changes, and the range of individual differences is great. Yet it seems logical to apply learning potential assessment theory and techniques as early as possible, so that an orientation of success in learning may be established. Clarke and Clarke (1976) as well as Feuerstein (1979) have documented that adolescence is not too late to effect substantial changes, and the course of cognitive development may be alterable at any time during the life span with increasingly intensive intervention. However, for maximal effectiveness and economy, enhancement of learning seems most logical during the early, most formative stages (Berreuta-Clement, Schweinhart, Barnett, Epstein, & Weikart, 1984; Burns, 1980; Caldwell, 1973; Gray, Ramsey, Klaus, 1981; Hunt, 1961).

The general, yet questionable, practice of relying on standardized tests for classification of young children further argues for the development of a downward extension of the LPAD. If we believe in the potential for improvement in the quality of cognitive development, it may be most productive to use dynamic assessment techniques, careful study of individual learning patterns and cognitive styles of an individual child, experimental teaching with analysis of errors, and criterion-referenced testing. Video recording of these processes can be done unobtrusively in many settings with today's technology. The opportunity provided for repeated observations and observations by more than one person can add significantly to the analysis of the learning process.

For younger children particularly, the goal of dynamic assessment should be to discover *what can be learned with good teaching*. While some children

Judith S. Mearig. Graduate Program in School Psychology, St. Lawrence University, Canton, New York.

may not learn higher cognitive functions even with such teaching, at present a large group who have the potential are going unrecognized with standardized test procedures and traditional teaching methods. The decision about how far a society should go to maximally develop cognitive functioning in this potentially educable but vulnerable group of children ultimately becomes philosophical and political. Feuerstein (personal communication, 1982) noted that what may vary more than children's cognitive potential is the commitment of adults to help them reach that potential. One thing is certain—the traditional emphasis on ability tests to predict learning outcome independent of teaching will have to be relinquished, if dynamic assessment is to be embraced and the commitment to cognitive modifiability is to be realized. Moreover, the importance of classification would dwindle. Traditional, static procedures may serve adult needs for order and ease of communication, and, unfortunately, have come to have funding dependent upon these results. However, it is seldom that there is the sophisticated kind of classification that Hobbs (1975) cites.

Feuerstein's (1979) learning potential assessment automatically includes initial teaching of cognitive functions. However, emerging cognitive abilities of many below-average learners of primary school age can be aided more systematically than usually occurs in the present form of LPAD instrumentation and procedures. What seem appropriately defined as deficient cognitive functions in adolescents may, in fact, be yet-to-be developed functions in many 5- to 8-year-olds. On the one hand, adolescents have more of an experiential background and basic cognitive skill development upon which to build. On the other hand, much younger children will be less likely to have incorrectly or inefficiently developed cognitive functions and the accumulation of negative emotional factors that often accompanies them. Moreover, some deficient cognitive functions in Feuerstein's (1979) list are not relevant for young children and others need to be substituted or added.

The emphasis, then, in dynamic assessment for young children should be on identifying and strengthening *emerging* cognitive functions rather than on correcting deficiencies. We should talk less about "administering" and "examining" and concentrate more on dynamic assessment and teaching techniques to bring out learning potential in young children. The comparison of a child with his or her age peers is a very secondary objective. In dynamic assessment, the artificiality of the distinction between teacher and psychological examiner becomes particularly apparent. In fact, dynamic assessment techniques would be most effective in the hands of teachers who could provide continuity and individualized instruction based on assessment findings. Moreover, if the child is having difficulty learning or executing a task, the psychologist's or teacher's first question should be, "What am *I* doing wrong?" Inability of the child to learn should be the "last resort" explanation. Shaping and sequencing of all steps and the use of successive approximation should be fundamental in dynamic assessment and teaching, and are examples of

behavior modification that can make Feuerstein's approach even more effective for young children. However, some behavior modification procedures
employed today in educational programs are antithetical to the principles of
cognitive modifiability and dynamic assessment. One example is the use of
reinforcement for a correct answer (the product) with little concern about
the process through which the answer was achieved. Feuerstein (1979) stressed
the importance of the child's understanding of responses so that underlying
knowledge can be generalized to future problem solving.

Young Children's Cognitive Functions: Deficient or Emergent?

Cognitive functions in young children should be referred to as emerging rather
than deficient not only because this reflects reality but also because it may
determine the orientation and expectancy of teachers and psychologists. For
example, instead of "jumping in the middle" and attempting to teach a pre-
cursor cognitive skill not previously learned, as may be done with an adolescent when the deficiency is encountered during an LPAD, instruments for
younger children can systematically teach such skills in sequence. Individual
differences still have to be accommodated, but the assessment tasks and the
teaching approaches can reflect cognitive development characteristics known
to be typical in children in the kindergarten–primary age range.

The younger the child, the more closely all aspects of development—
physical, social, emotional, and cognitive—are interwoven (Erikson, 1950;
Kessler, 1966; Palmer, 1983). The assessor and teacher of cognitive development must be sensitive to these interactions. A few of the factors this
author has found that can have significant impact on the direction of cognitive
learning in kindergarten–primary-age children include anxiety generated by
lack of predictability in the child's life, external and internal standards set for
the child, birth position, peer modeling and pressure, sex of the teacher, the
reward system employed, and the degree to which an overall feeling of competence is developing. A child's attitude toward learning is being formed at
this time and, in turn, the child's self-concept may depend largely on his or
her opportunities for success in cognitive activities. Therefore, mediation of
a feeling of competency (Feuerstein, 1980) by those teaching and judging a
child, especially parents and teachers, can be crucial. The early school years
provide the first substantial objective or extrafamily evaluation for most children. Dynamic assessment, with individualized teaching as an integral component, has the opportunity to establish a positive orientation toward learning
that can extend throughout the child's entire school career.

Mussen, Conger, Kagan, and Huston (1984) cited some critical aspects
of early learning, assessment, and teaching that are often neglected when
drawing conclusions about a young child's cognitive potential:

1. A child's performance may fail to reveal his or her actual competence
    because he or she interprets a problem differently than the adult.

An example is response to the question, "Are all the cars in the garages?" when the child is shown more garages than cars. The child often will say, "No," because he or she assumes there would not be garages without cars to go in them. Mussen et al. noted: "Each question—indeed every communication—from one person to another contains hidden, implicit understandings between speaker and listener" (pp. 220, 221). Eventually, the child usually learns the assumptions implicit in the adult's questions, which is one reason cognitive performance may improve with age.

2. We must always ask whether a failure is due to an existing competence not able to be manifest because of some extraneous factor, such as outside noise distracting the child, or to a flaw in the child's actual competence in the cognitive function sampled. This author suggests the following hierarchy: (a) the child is unable to learn meanings, at least not without extremely intensive instruction; (b) the child is unable to focus his or her attention long enough to learn meanings; (c) the child presently does not know meanings, but could learn them; and (d) the child has learned, but cannot remember meanings.

3. If a child has a focusing difficulty, we need to discover how general it is in terms of various materials and settings, as well as the underlying reasons. The range of possible explanations is great.

4. It probably is best to conceive of a child's competence—actual and potential—as applying to limited rather than to very broad domains. (This warning about generalizing has important implications for intelligence testing and interpretation.)

5. From an information-processing approach, we should focus on understanding specific processes rather than attempting to utilize a single comprehensive theory, and be most interested in *how* children come to acquire factual knowledge and to relate different facts, sometimes in an abstract manner.

6. The nature of the information to be learned and remembered can make a difference, as can requirements of the problem-solving process itself—there are many individual differences in children.

In contrast to dynamic assessment of most preschool children, where different kinds of materials are often required to evaluate various aspects of cognitive development, the existing LPAD instruments can be modified for most beginning school-age children. One advantage of modification of a single instrument is continuity, since progress of individual children can be more easily followed longitudinally. Also, the examiner has flexibility within both the regular and simplified LPAD versions in the starting point for children of even older ages. Furthermore, structure is provided for what otherwise might be an extemporaneous attempt to teach beginning stages of a higher cognitive function after discovering a regular LPAD instrument, at least initially, is too advanced. Kindergarten–primary-age children for whom even this downward extension of the LPAD is difficult could use materials developed primarily for preschool children by Tzuriel and Klein or Lidz and Thomas (see Chapters 10 and 11, respectively, this volume).

Some of Feuerstein's (1979) input and output phase–deficient cognitive functions are what this author has long referred to as executional difficulties or, in some cases, what Ginsburg and Gannon (1985) referred to as variations in cognitive style. Dynamic assessment is well suited to consider individual cognitive styles, which are often the deciding factor in whether or not a cognitive skill is actually learned or executed. Unfortunately, executional difficulties or inefficient (for the task presented) cognitive styles may be misinterpreted as reflecting deficits in higher cognitive functions.

What follows is a list of emerging cognitive functions generally considered to be important for kindergarten–primary-age children. It should be noted that, in agreement with Feuerstein's (1979) comments regarding his original group of deficient cognitive functions, this list should not be taken to be complete. It is important that psychologists and teachers continue to scrutinize children's successful cognitive functioning as well as failures in order to attain specificity in understanding the actual dynamics of cognitive processing. Only then can a teacher provide the kind of instruction to help an individual child learn what before he or she could not.

Emerging Cognitive Functions[1]

INPUT PHASE

1. Lessening of an egocentric frame of reference and reduction of the injection into a task of the child's own needs of the moment. (M)
2. Increasing attention span. Growing ability to focus attention unhindered by distractions peripheral to the task or outside distractions. (M, Me)
3. Increasing ability to distinguish critical stimuli from background. (Me)
4. Increasing ability to focus perception; diminishing of blurred and sweeping perception. (F)
5. Learning during a directed task to restrain superfluous conversation—sometimes pertinent, sometimes not, and often egocentered. (Me)
6. Increasing ability to shift focus of attention smoothly from one stimulus configuration or orientation to another. (M, Me)
7. Increasing number of verbal units that can be absorbed or comprehended, as well as of words with no concrete reference. (Me)

1. The letter following each function indicates its source: F = Feuerstein (1979); M = Mussen et al. (1984); Me = Mearig.

8. Sharpening of ability to identify the source of an action rather than attributing it to a superficial association. (Me)
9. Increasing ability to recognize and predict cause–effect relationships and to distinguish such relationships from contiguity or coincidence. (M)
10. Beginning ability to plan exploratory behavior. (F)
11. Growing concept of conservation of constancy. (M)
12. Development of verbal tools and concepts to help discrimination and memory of input stimuli, including objects, events, and relationships. (M, F)
13. Ongoing improvement in spatial orientation. (F)
14. Ongoing improvement in temporal orientation and understanding and estimation of the passage of time. (Me)
15. Growing need for precision and accuracy in data gathering. (F)
16. Developing capacity for considering two or more sources of information at once and in an integrated manner. (F)
17. Growing independence of kinesthetic cues, concrete demonstration, simultaneous visual and auditory cues, and reinforcement of one's own verbalization. (Me)
18. Learning to select out relevant cues in defining a problem. (F)

ELABORATION PHASE

1. Growing ability to enter into mental operations that are flexible and reversible. (M)
2. Maturation of concepts of time and passage of time. (Me)
3. Learning to sequence events in terms of a logical or time progression. (Me)
4. Learning to sequence steps in problem solving. (Me)
5. Making the transition from dependence on the concrete to independent, abstract thinking and generalization. (F, M, Me)
6. Improving manipulation of symbols, including words. (Me)
7. Growing facility in using symbols. (M)
8. Development of spatial orientation and stable systems of reference that later contribute to topological Euclidean organization of space. (F)
9. Learning to identify critical attributes, the dimensions defining a concept that match those most adults agree are critical. (M)
10. Learning to ignore or go beyond initial, simple hypotheses and attend to new and relevant aspects of a problem. (F)
11. Learning that the context of a problem does not have to relate to the child's own life or any other reality; looking at a problem from someone else's vantage point and becoming less egocentric. (M)
12. Becoming flexible in problem-solving approaches and learning to shift codes being used to represent the elements involved. (M)

13. Stabilizing of factors in conservation of constancy, such as size, shape, or quantity, across other dimensions of the perceived object. (M)

14. Beginning strategies for increase in short- and long-term memory-rehearsal, association, clustering, and detecting patterns of organization. (M)

15. Increase in working memory speed so more complex problems can be solved, and growth in ability to hold in memory and manipulate an increasing number of units. (M)

16. Increase in availability of vocabulary, images, schema, and concepts to help memorize, reason, and problem solve, and a transition from images to concepts. (M)

17. Symbolic concepts becoming more readily available for use in thought. (M)

18. Increase in ability to describe concepts in words. (Me)

19. Learning to move to formal qualities of concepts to help in concept sorting—superordinate, functional, relational, and analytic. (M)

20. Developing the concept of class inclusion, ability to reason simultaneously about parts and wholes. (M)

21. Developing the understanding that things can belong to more than one category. (M)

22. Learning to pause and reflect in order to decide the kind of concept involved in a task and to plan a course of action. (F, M)

23. Beginning to elaborate certain cognitive categories as verbal concepts become part of the child's vocabulary on a receptive level and then are able to be mobilized at the expressive level. (F)

24. Moving in problem solving from the superficial and only one approach to thoughtful analysis and looking "beneath the surface." (M)

25. Progressing toward the deductive phase of problem solving and formal or informal application of a rule to solve a problem. (M)

26. Learning spontaneous comparative behavior. (F)

27. Learning to use relational thinking (taller, larger, and so forth). (M)

28. Expanding the mental field (this ability aided by lessening of an egocentric frame of reference); growing ability to decenter to focus attention on several attributes of an object or event simultaneously and to understand relationships between dimensions. (M)

29. Learning to relate one experience to another conceptually, moving beyond an episodic grasp of reality. (F)

30. Learning to process more than one kind of information at once. (F)

31. Beginning to learn the following: pursuit of logical evidence; interiorization; inferential, hypothetical thinking; strategies for hypothesis testing; and planning behavior. (F, M)

OUTPUT PHASE

1. Impulsive responding gradually replaced by reflection, motorically and verbally. (F, M)
2. Diminishing of egocentric communication. (M)
3. Sufficiently thorough learning of responses so they can be elicited or emitted automatically. (M, F)
4. Beginning of projection of virtual relationships. (F)
5. Lessening of trial-and-error responses. (F, M)
6. Improvement of verbal concepts and fluency for communication responses that have been adequately elaborated. (F)
7. Developing of need for precision and accuracy in communicating responses. (F)
8. Growth in *capability* of making precise and accurate responses. (F, Me)

General Principles for Dynamic Assessment with Kindergarten–Primary-age Children

Dynamic assessment is best described in terms of a mediated learning experience (MLE). According to Feuerstein and Jensen (1980):

> Mediated learning experience is that which takes place when an initiated human being, a mother, father, or other care giving adult, interposes himself or herself between the organism and the stimuli impinging on it and mediates, transforms, reorders, organizes, groups, and frames the stimuli in the direction of some specifically intended goal and purpose. The mediating person transmits with the stimuli certain specific meanings by virtue of selecting some stimuli, making them salient as compared with others, and making certain stimuli accessible to the organism in a repetitive, reinforced way as compared to others which are ruled out and rendered dim. . . . *Furthermore, the mediator makes the child focus, not only upon the stimuli selected by him, but on relationships between them, the succession of their presentation, and the relationship of these stimuli to anticipated outcomes such as specific purposes and goals by scheduling, grouping, and organizing the world for the child.* The mediator enriches the interaction between the child and the environment with ingredients that do not pertain to the immediate situation but belong to a world of meanings and intentions derived from generations of culturally transmitted attitudes, values, goals, and means. Through this process of mediation, the cognitive structure of the child is affected. (pp. 409–410)

It is the middle part of this process (italic portion of quotation) with which dynamic assessment as mediation for kindergarten–primary-age children is most concerned. The goals are to make existing competence manifest and, as much as possible, to teach absent cognitive competencies involved in the LPAD instruments. Since each assessment varies with the nature of the child, it is both impossible and inappropriate to devise specific test instructions such as are provided for static procedures. Some general principles to follow in attempting to meet these objectives include the following.

1. Directions must be made clear to the individual child. The examiner must be able to restate quickly or translate so that full understanding of the task is attained. Lapses in the examiner's verbalization, unless for a specific purpose, should be avoided, especially in the case of children who are easily distractible. Lapses that result in loss of the child's concentration can be costly. Language simplification and emphases of important words are very important. Any examples given of verbal mediation, or at times even content, should not be repeated verbatim. The primary requirement for the LPAD examiner–teacher is to be extremely flexible, adapting teaching techniques and specific verbalization to the needs of the individual child on each task, and rephrasing quickly when necessary. The *assessor* literally has to be dynamic. Different children need different kinds of interaction to stimulate their best performance. This is one reason it can be misleading to make predictions of future learning from standardized testing procedures. The assessor must adapt his or her initial teaching to the child's present understanding and cognitive style, realizing that even within one child these factors may vary according to the nature of the task (Ginsburg and Gannon, 1985). Ginsburg and Gannon (1985) pointed out that cognitive style variables are most important in interaction with each other and with situations. They also noted that cognitive style may be taught, and dynamic assessment seems an ideal medium for this teaching process.

2. Some children's focusing may be helped if the examiner points as well as speaks with emphasis. This is especially true for children who have become dependent on visual cues from watching much television.

3. Stimuli to be focused upon often must be exaggerated; critical stimuli must clearly stand out from background. Similarly, the child may need help when shifting focus of attention.

4. For children who have marked difficulty focusing upon the specific task at hand, using separate cards for each problem may help, as on Organization of Dots, The Organizer, and Numerical Progressions. This, of course, is already done on the Matrices and would not be applicable on some other tests. An alternative to the separate pages is a heavy black line separating items, presently used on Numerical Progressions and The Organizer. Mussen et al. (1984) noted that tests and their formats can handicap impulsive children and, since young children with academic problems often are more impulsive, a circular process of failure and diminishing motivation may occur.

5. Tzuriel and Klein (1984) stressed the importance of three dimensions and of manipulation for young children to help them do analytical and other higher order thinking. Children within the age group with which this chapter is concerned are making a transition from the concrete to the abstract. Young children should have the opportunity to manipulate materials *within* the MLE

process. Feuerstein (1979) has pointed out that manipulation of materials may hinder concept learning by retarded children, but this seems most likely to occur in the case of random rather than mediated manipulation. The most important function of MLE in these instances is to make the concrete manipulation purposeful and to provide an effective *transition* from the concrete to the abstract. Manipulation of materials and use of three-dimensional visual aids can be beneficial if they initiate a systematic sequence leading from the concrete to the abstract. This author also has found that many kindergarten–primary-age children still engage naturally in physical manipulation. Deliberately involving them motorically in some tasks may assure that they will not be diverting such movements (and some attention) elsewhere. Finally, carefully observing as well as manipulating three-dimensional objects (the origin of many abstract concepts and symbols) and following a transition sequentially to their various representational levels may be particularly helpful for children who spend much time viewing one-dimensional television.

6. "Trial-and-error" manipulation is not always detrimental in initial learning stages of higher cognitive functions. At the early age levels, a rapid succession of various trial-and-error responses may result in the desired conceptual understanding *after* the correct response finally is achieved, especially if mediation is provided at that point. Similarly, hypothesis testing that results in a few errors may be instructive when these errors then can be analyzed (Bruner, 1963). Feuerstein (1979) asked the child or adolescent to explain why alternative choices were wrong on the Raven Progressive Matrices and the Set Variations, although no manipulation was involved. Another learning technique appealing to 5- to 8-year-old children that might be incorporated in some LPAD assessment as well as classroom teaching procedures is finding errors that others have made.

7. The number of units of information to be dealt with simultaneously should be limited initially and, in some cases, cues should be provided to assist memorization, although the goal of dealing with an increasing amount of information remains.

8. In systematically teaching cognitive processing, the examiner must be careful not to stifle creative thinking, or to give the child the impression there always is only one "right" answer or way to solve a problem. The young child's orientation toward all learning is being formed, and the intensity of the LPAD–MLE teaching approach, whatever orientation to learning it conveys, can have great impact.

9. Mussen et al. (1984) noted that a child's strategy for classifying information depends to a great extent on the materials being classified and his or her familiarity with them. Therefore, this variable should be controlled for in the materials chosen or at least taken into account in the evaluation of the child's performance (see "Associative Recall" section below in this chapter).

10. Similarly, the specific stimulus array shown is important in determining the concepts the child chooses to draw from it. Mussen et al. (1984)

observed that a child's thinking cannot be considered analytical or relational without specifying the stimulus materials presented, since a preferred conceptual response is rarely independent of the material being classified. A child may be analytic with visual stimuli containing subtle analytic cues, but superordinate with verbal representations of these objects. Thus, the child should have familiar objects and ideas to use in order to demonstrate understanding of relational concepts.

11. For young children, the contents through which cognitive processes are taught should not be "neutral," that is, unrelated to the curriculum they are expected to master in school. The rationale is different for older children who have failure associations with certain content and/or more intellectual maturity to apply cognitive skills learned separately to a variety of materials. At present, the reverse often occurs in the early grades. Children are taught content, with concepts being peripheral and assumed to be learned in the course of instruction. The LPAD–Instrumental Enrichment (IE) process could reverse this emphasis. This author believes that an ultimate goal should be the development of a primary curriculum emphasizing problem solving as well as basic reading and mathematical skills. Then cognitive process could be taught simultaneously with content, which seems the most efficient approach. Until this objective is attained, a transition should be made from LPAD cognitive processes to primary-grade subjects.

12. It is important not to let the child become blocked for any period of time. The child may lose any productive steps in problem solving he or she has acquired and may become discouraged.

13. Finally, an LPAD goal for young children equal in importance to gaining access to higher cognitive functions is mediation of competence at a critical time in cognitive learning. M. R. Jensen (personal communication, 1984) noted that if the child perceives incompetence early in learning and begins to anticipate failure, premature closure of effort to succeed will likely occur when subsequent tasks are initially perceived as difficult. The child then will not even absorb all crucial information or consider all problem-solving alternatives. This does not happen only in a one-to-one teaching–learning situation; in fact, it is more frequent and most devastating in a group. Under fear of failure, nonintellectual factors disintegrate first and block effective functioning of intellectual ones (M. R. Jensen, personal communication, 1984).

Modifications of LPAD Instruments for Kindergarten–Primary-age Slow-Learning Children[2]

The order of presentation of instruments should depend on the individual child's known strengths and weaknesses as well as on level and breadth of conceptual difficulty of the instrument. All instruments do not have to be

---

2. Some familiarity with Feuerstein's (1979) LPAD instruments is assumed in this section.

given to a child to obtain valuable information about learning potential. Generally, Organization of Dots and Associative Recall are good instruments with which to begin. Numerical Progressions and the Simplified Matrices were next in level of difficulty for the children this author worked with in the process of determining age appropriateness of the modified materials. The Organizer and the Representative Stencil Design Test were the most difficult. After success on modified versions, children can attempt instruments in the regular LPAD.

M. R. Jensen (personal communication, 1982) described three levels of examiner intervention:

1. No intervention required, or only preparatory action, such as drawing attention to the task, inducing planning behavior, or inhibiting impulsivity.
2. Orienting child toward elements of functioning necessary to solve and complete the task, such as identification, recognition, discrimination, segregation, comparative behavior, representational behavior, visual transport, conservation of constancies, summative behavior, spatial orientation, and/or temporal orientation.
3. Active intervention.
   a. Point to best starting point.
   b. Draw a line to start or complete a figure.
   c. Perform functions together with the child, such as discrimination between elements, comparing elements, summing of relevant information, or sequencing steps toward solution of the task.
   d. For the young age group under discussion, this author would add, teach prerequisite skills and/or the cognitive function itself.

Simplified Versions of Some LPAD Instruments

This section contains the author's modified versions of Feuerstein's (1979) Organization of Dots, Numerical Progressions, Associative Recall, The Organizer, Raven Coloured Progressive Matrices, and the Representational Stencil Design Test instruments. For each instrument, the purpose is to assess the current status of and teach the next few stages of the emerging cognitive functions involved. It will be noted that in some cases slight modifications of the emerging cognitive function statements are made appropriate to the specific instrument. The author is also working on simplified versions of the Complex Figure task, the Plateaux Test, and Verbal Analogies.

Organization of Dots

EMERGING COGNITIVE FUNCTIONS
Input Phase:

1. Increasing ability to focus attention, diminishing of blurred and sweeping perception.

2. Gradual inhibition of impulsive first impressions, and planning of exploratory behavior.
3. Increasing ability to smoothly shift focus of attention from one stimulus configuration to another.
4. Increasing ability to ignore irrelevant stimuli in close proximity to the task.
5. Increasing ability to distinguish the critical stimulus from background.
6. Growing concept of conservation of constancy.
7. Ongoing improvement in spatial orientation.
8. Growing need for precision and accuracy in data gathering.
9. Developing capacity for considering two or more sources of information at once and in an integrated manner.
10. Lessening of trial-and-error responses as part of the learning process itself.

Elaboration Phase

1. Ability to enter into mental operations that are flexible and reversible.
2. Development of spatial orientation and stable systems of reference that later contribute to topological Euclidean organization of space.
3. Learning to ignore and go beyond initial, simple hypotheses and to attend to new and relevant aspects of a problem.
4. Becoming flexible in problem-solving approaches and learning to shift codes being used to represent elements involved in a problem.
5. Stabilizing of factors in conservation of constancy such as size, shape, and quantity across other dimensions of the perceived object.

Output Phase

1. Impulsive responding gradually replaced by reflection.
2. Beginning of projection of virtual relationships.
3. Developing the need for precision and accuracy in communicating responses.
4. Growth in capability to make precise and accurate responses.
5. Improvement in visual transport.

DESCRIPTION OF MATERIALS AND PROCEDURAL GUIDELINES

Children who have not mastered the concepts of square and triangle should be taught these prior to using the printed sheet by the successive presentation and explanation of three-dimensional wooden objects (triangle, square, and rectangle for comparison), then cardboard cutouts, and finally pictures. The concepts can be reinforced kinesthetically, if necessary, by having the child feel the outline of the wooden figures and then trace the completed figures drawn on paper.

Many children will be able to begin with the simplified page of the modified dot configurations. Some may be able to start with the regular form of Organization of Dots but, if there is any doubt, it is best to start with the simplified page in order to ensure a success experience and stabilizing of basic concepts. This version consists of three rows of five single squares or triangles and one row containing both configurations, in one case with the two shapes overlapping. The figures are twice as large as those on the original version by Rev and Dupont (1953), which Feuerstein employed (see Figure 9.1). In the bottom row of each shape, the dots are partially connected, with such cues gradually being faded until only dots are presented. Also, the square is gradually rotated to introduce constancy of shape across positional orientation.

The square and triangle are overlapped only in the last block. Using different colored dots for each of them may in a few cases be necessary to highlight the separate configurations and simplify the task. When the child has completed the page of simple forms successfully, the regular form may be given.

There is no prescribed verbal mediation for this or any other instrument, as indicated earlier. The examiner must say and do whatever will effectively mediate *the particular child's* grasp of the concepts. The examiner also must praise frequently and be precise when communicating what is wrong, in language the child can understand. Because of space limitations, examples of verbal mediation this author has found helpful are given only for Organization of Dots. These were used in trying the instrument modifications for age appropriateness with 12 children in kindergarten, prefirst grade, and educable mentally retarded resource rooms for children who were having serious difficulty in classroom learning. The instruments were also given to an advanced second grader. Examples of these mediations are:

- "Close your eyes and try to see a square."
- "Look for the dots that you could try that would make straight, not slanted, lines, with every line just as long as every other line."
- "You can go through dots (for the triangle) that you already have used for the square, but you cannot stop at any of them."
- "Always look for the square first."
- "It usually helps to start with an outside dot."
- "First, trace where you think the square is with the eraser end of your pencil." (However, the child may have to draw two lines after finding two dots—four seem to be too many bits of information to visualize for some children in this age group.)
- "Watch it—that square is standing on its end."
- "Remember, the lines must go straight from one dot to another; you cannot turn and go another way."
- "Remember, the lines in a square must all be the same length."
- "Move down the square above with your eyes so you can see what you are looking for" (when the child needs to orient himself or herself to dots making up a square standing on end).

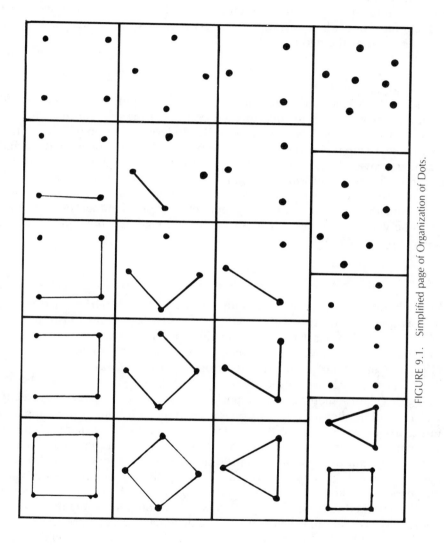

FIGURE 9.1. Simplified page of Organization of Dots.

- "Remember, the lines must come together to make a square—one cannot go off in another direction."

The children who need to go through the preliminary sequence beginning with concrete representation sometimes want to hold the wooden objects next to the printed dots when starting to draw. Also, some children start verbalizing to themselves as they go along.

TO BE RECORDED

The kind of work needed by the child prior to the simplified sheet is recorded as: initial response by the child to each figure and the number and kinds of errors; cognitive functions that seem to be hindering performance; cognitive styles that seem to be retarding performance; the kind of mediation and teaching provided, and the child's response to each component of these. Because the examiner works so hard to be explicit and to choose words carefully so the child will learn, there is rarely sufficient time to write down everything the child says. However, complete responses in their original form could be very important for analysis, so it is strongly recommended that the session(s) be recorded.

COMMENTS

Most children with whom the author has worked could go on to complete the regular sheet of dots with varying degrees of help. Immaturity in some of the elaboration phase cognitive functions became apparent in the last two rows but, even here, all but two kindergartners were able to do at least a few of these with minimal help. An indication that learning was taking place was given when, after having difficulty recognizing the square and completing the triangle, a child sometimes would quickly do the next configuration correctly.

If the child shows impulsivity on this instrument, it is likely to be apparent in classroom activities as well. It is important to remember that such impulsivity may prevent higher cognitive abilities from having a chance to function. If the child can do well on Organization of Dots with minimal help but is having trouble in academic work, factors other than reasoning, possibly language related, should be looked to for explanation. If the child cannot do the Dots well initially but learns with mediation, the same sequential, explicit approach in classroom instruction may be beneficial. Also, work assignments in which impulsivity can easily prevent successful completion should be controlled or avoided. If the teacher does not have much time to work individually with children, written assignments should be as independent as possible of executional difficulties. If the child cannot learn to do the Dots even with mediation and is not overly impulsive, immaturity or serious cognitive limitation may be the explanation. In either case, the teaching process should be tried again at a later date.

Numerical Progressions

EMERGING COGNITIVE FUNCTIONS
Input Phase

1. Increasing ability to recognize and predict cause–effect relationships.
2. Gradual inhibition of impulsive first impressions.
3. Increasing ability to shift focus of attention smoothly from one stimulus orientation or configuration to another.
4. Increasing ability to recognize a pattern.
5. Ongoing improvement in spatial organization.
6. Growing capacity for considering two sources of information at once and in an integrated manner.

Elaboration Phase

1. Ability to enter into mental operations that are flexible and reversible.
2. Completion of transition from dependence on the concrete to independent thinking.
3. Learning to ignore or go beyond initial, simple hypotheses and to attend to new and relevant aspects of a problem.
4. Becoming flexible in problem-solving approaches and learning to shift codes being used to represent the elements involved.
5. Learning to pause and reflect in order to decide the kind of concept involved in a task and to plan a course of action to complete the task.
6. Moving in problem solving from a superficial and/or single approach to thoughtful analysis and looking "beneath the surface."
7. Progressing toward the deduction phase of problem solving and formal or informal application of a rule to solve a problem.
8. Learning spontaneous comparative behavior.
9. Learning to do relational thinking.
10. Expanding the mental field (aided by lessening of an egocentric frame of reference). Learning to decenter, and to focus attention on several dimensions simultaneously with an understanding of the relationships between them.
11. Learning to process more than one kind of information at once.
12. Beginning to learn interiorization.
13. Beginning to learn inferential, hypothetical, "iffy" thinking.

Output Phase

1. Impulsive responding gradually replaced by reflection.
2. Beginning of projection of virtual relationships.
3. Increasing number of responses based on systematic analysis or principles rather than trial and error.

4. Developing of the need for precision and accuracy in responses.
5. Growth in *capacity* to make precise and accurate responses.
6. Improvement in visual transport.

DESCRIPTION OF MATERIALS AND PROCEDURAL GUIDELINES

This instrument (see Figure 9.2) consists of 20 forward and reverse progressions, the first six being straightforward counting with some numbers missing and the last five involving grouping of numbers. In between, there are reverse progressions, counting by twos (odd and even numbers), and counting by fives. This content is much simpler than Feuerstein's (1979) original instrument of 15 progressions in the pretest, 16 in the teaching phase, and 45 in the regular instrument. However, children who complete the simplified version without too much difficulty may go on to at least the first page or two of the original pretest.

Heavy lines are drawn between sequences to help the child focus on the task at hand, although at times it may be helpful for him or her to look back at an already completed sequence for reference. Even with the lines, the writer has encountered a few children who have difficulty focusing on and tracking the numbers and sequence being analyzed, so the examiner must be alert to this possibility. Pointing and/or verbalizing to the child may help.

Children must have some concept of counting and addition to do this instrument, as well as of subtraction of one-digit numbers. As is true of the regular version for older children and adolescents, the purpose of the instrument is not to teach basic arithmetical skills but to develop cognitive functions such as those listed above. However, this author has found that most children in this age group, regardless of assessed overall intellectual and classroom functioning, improve these basic skills when they must analyze the progressions. Cuisinaire Rods also can be used to reinforce counting and relationships among numbers. Going in reverse order on a few progressions without skipping any numbers is an intermediary step to actually transposing numbers.

Children should be encouraged to purposefully scan the numbers, then to verbalize what principle or rule they think is operating, and finally to suggest the missing numbers before writing them down. Some children may have to be given two choices, one right and one wrong, by the examiner as an intermediary step. Justification for the choices should always be discussed. This is a good instrument to practice flexibility and rule-shifting in problem-solving approaches.

If arithmetic rules in school have only been memorized and not understood, the child may have difficulty on Numerical Progressions until mediation helps him or her to understand the logic behind a rule and shift his or her problem-solving orientation more easily. Furthermore, a positional concept such as "before," which the adult is likely to use in mediating reverse sequences, often has to be taught with concrete examples before children can do this manipulation mentally. Even then their approach at first often is to

5	10	15	20	__		
25	20	15	10	__		
20	18	16	14	__	__	
17	15	13	11	__	__	
2	6	10	__	__	__	
1	2	4	1	3	5	1	__
1	4	7	2	5	8	3	__

FIGURE 9.2.   Numerical Progressions task.

count up from one to the number to find what comes immediately before, since the capability to reverse is only beginning to emerge. The adult initially may have to ask the child to recall the number he or she has just said when counting up to find the number immediately before.

TO BE RECORDED

All responses given and the arithmetical processing the child goes through are recorded, whether verbalized or inferred by the adult from the responses themselves.

Associative Recall

EMERGING COGNITIVE FUNCTIONS
Input Phase

1. Increasing concentration ability. Growing ability to focus attention and to take in the total stimulus field, instantaneously or in quick succession of stimuli.
2. Increasing ability to absorb and retain multiple verbal units.
3. Increasing recognition of a whole from its part.
4. Increasing ability to focus, diminishing of blurred and sweeping perception.
5. Increasing ability to smoothly shift focus of attention from one stimulus configuration to another.
6. Development of verbal tools and concepts to help discrimination and memory of input stimuli, including objects and relationships.

7. Developing capacity for considering two sources of information at once and in an integrated manner.

Elaboration Phase

1. Facility in using symbols, progressing from index (part of an object) to symbol (something logically associated with the object) to sign (verbal representation).
2. Increase in availability of vocabulary, images, and concepts to help memorize.
3. Learning to shift codes being used to represent elements involved.
4. Beginning development of strategies for increase in short-term memory; in this instance, rehearsal, association, and symbol representation.
5. Increase in speed and flexibility of memory.
6. Growth in number of bits of information that can be held and manipulated in memory.
7. Transition from images to concepts. Symbolic concepts become more readily available for use in thought and memory.
8. Learning to inhibit or go beyond obvious associations and attend to substitutes and relational associations.
9. Beginning to reason simultaneously about parts and wholes.
10. Beginning to elaborate certain cognitive categories as verbal concepts become part of child's vocabulary at receptive level and are able to be mobilized at expressive level.

Output Phase

1. Verbal responses becoming well enough learned so they can be emitted automatically.
2. Improvement of verbal concepts and fluency for communicating responses that have been adequately elaborated.
3. Developing of need for precision and accuracy in communicating responses.
4. Improvement in visual transport.

DESCRIPTION OF MATERIALS AND PROCEDURAL GUIDELINES

The colored pictures are on foam board so that the basic set of materials are reusable. There are two forms of each version: part–whole and functional reduction. In the part–whole form, a meaningful part of the original object is reduced (see Figure 9.3A); in the functional form, a product or function intimately connected with the original object is substituted and then reduced (see Figure 9.3B). Changes from Feuerstein's latest version of this instrument include: reducing the bits of information to be recalled from 20 to 10; replacing some objects with ones that are more easily recognized and named by young children; drawing the objects larger and in color so visual recognition is not a problem; having two forms of the instrument, in which one set of objects is more basic to a young child's experience than the other; and making all reductions meaningful and consistent in the form of the reduction.

If the goal of this instrument is to assess formation of associations and memory, varying strengths of word novelty should be controlled for. Furthermore, consistency and meaningfulness in the relationship of the object to its partial representation can be important for children still learning the logic of such associations. They also can have some carryover to other reasoning tests such as Verbal Analogies, where clarity concerning the nature of the relationship is of primary importance. Otherwise, the varying complexity of the task for different children may make the intended association and memory skills on this instrument more difficult to analyze.

As in Feuerstein's version, the child first is asked to name each object in the top line of drawings. Then the examiner goes over the names of all the drawings once more. The child next is asked to name objects from the first reduction in the second line. In both of these cases, the other rows of pictures are covered. Then, in the teaching phase, the first three lines are uncovered, the third being a further reduction of these in the second line. The examiner points for emphasis to each object and its two reductions, as the child, if possible, names the object three times. If the child hesitates, the examiner names the objects. Then, the second reduction in order (row three), the first reduction in rearranged order (row four), and the second reduction in rearranged order (row five) are exposed separately for the child's naming. Finally, the original first reduction in the second row is tried again. With all the pictures removed, the child then is asked to recall as many of the objects as possible (free recall). After 10 minutes the child may be asked to do this again (delayed recall), with intervening activity (or lack thereof) clearly noted. In both cases the examiner should encourage the child to continue if the child stops after naming only a few objects.

TO BE RECORDED

All of the child's responses are recorded, so that comparisons of objects recalled can be based on different degrees of part reduction and part versus function, as well as different orderings of the associative elements. Also, immediate and delayed free recall responses can be analyzed for primary recency effects.

COMMENTS

If the child has had trouble recalling the successive reductions, further assessment can be done to identify the nature of the difficulty, such as cues so minimal that the representation is lost, changed order of cues causing a memory overload, or problems in the associative process itself. For children having difficulty with beginning reading, this information could be useful in the selection of instruction methods that would deemphasize their weaknesses.

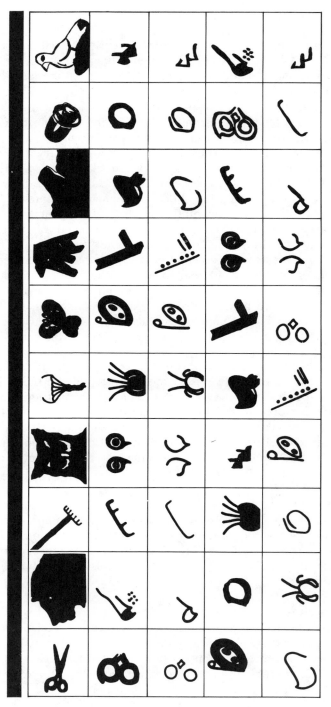

FIGURE 9.3A. Associative Recall task: part–whole form.

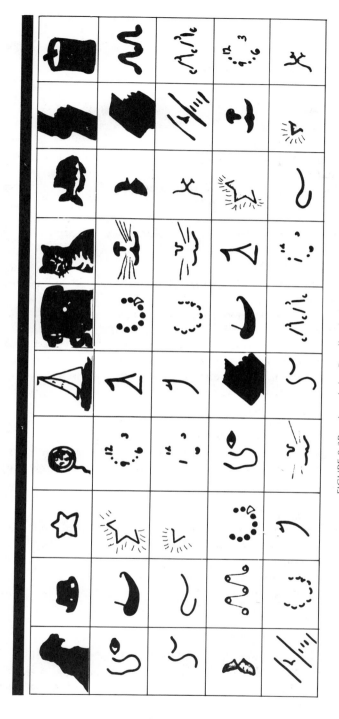

FIGURE 9.3B. Associative Recall task: functional form.

The Organizer

EMERGING COGNITIVE FUNCTIONS

Input Phase

1. Growing ability to sustain focused attention.
2. Increasing ability to shift focus of attention smoothly from one stimulus configuration to another.
3. Development of verbal tools and concepts to help discrimination and memory of input stimuli.
4. Developing capacity for considering two or more sources of information at once and in an integrated manner.
5. Ongoing improvement in spatial orientation.
6. Inhibition of impulsivity and blurred and sweeping perception.

Elaboration Phase

1. Ability to enter into mental operations that are flexible and reversible.
2. Learning to sequence events logically.
3. Improving manipulation of symbols, including words.
4. Development of spatial orientation and stable systems of reference.
5. Learning to ignore or go beyond initial, simple hypotheses and to attend to new and relevant aspects of a problem.
6. Facility in using symbols to stand for objects—in this instance, letters, or the sign of the index–symbol–sign sequence (Kamii & Radin, 1966).
7. Becoming flexible in problem-solving approaches and learning to shift the codes being used to represent the elements involved.
8. Growth in number of units the child can hold in memory and manipulate.
9. Beginning of ability to transpose and transform material mentally.
10. Expansion of the mental field.
11. Learning to process more than one kind of information at once.
12. Beginning to learn interiorization and inferential, hypothetical, "iffy" thinking.
13. Learning to decenter and to focus attention on several attributes of an event simultaneously, with an understanding of the relationships between dimensions.

Output Phase

1. Impulsive responding gradually replaced by reflection.
2. Beginning of projection of virtual relationships.
3. Lessening of trial-and-error responses as part of the learning processes itself.
4. Improvement in visual transport.

DESCRIPTION OF MATERIALS AND PROCEDURAL GUIDELINES

This is a much simplified and shortened version of Feuerstein's practice and test forms of the Organizer. The instrument consists of 12 tasks in which overlapping sets of directions are given for position placement of three or four objects (colors, numbers, names, animals, or vehicles) (Figure 9.4).

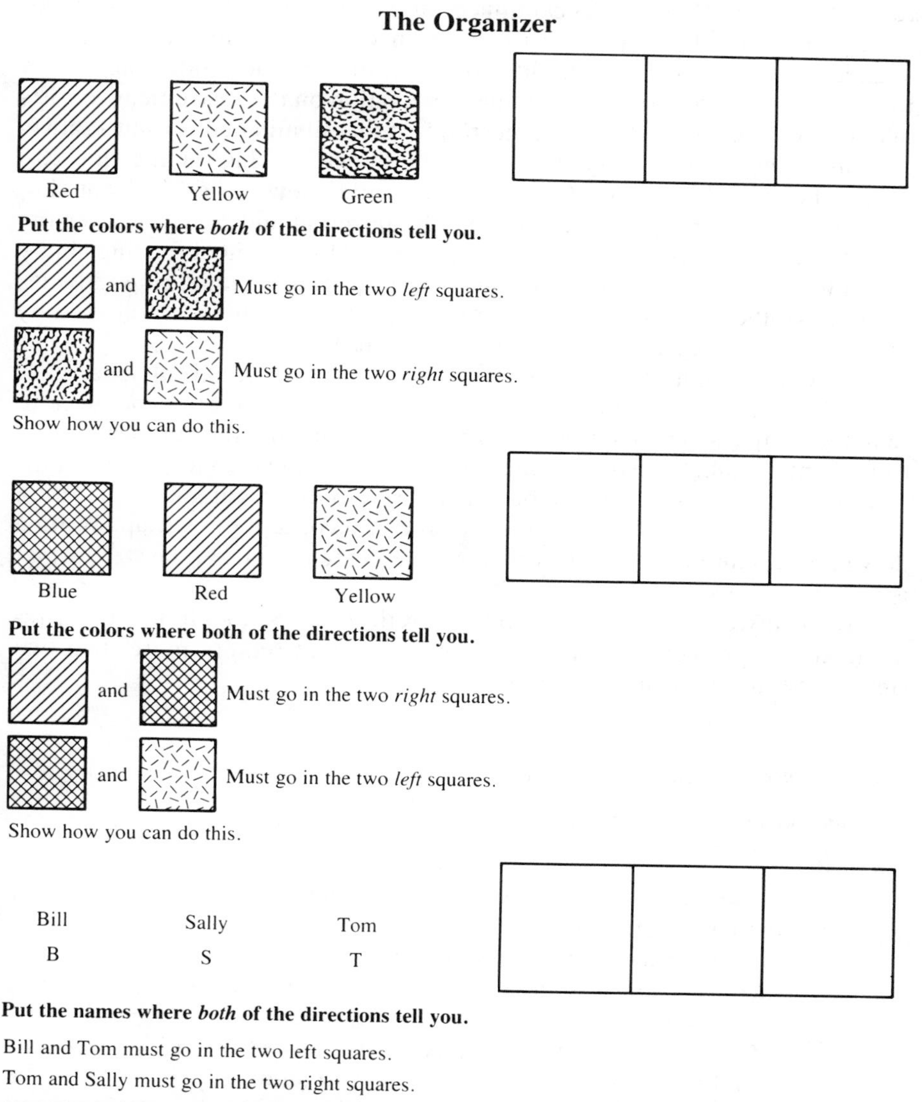

The Organizer

Red   Yellow   Green

Put the colors where *both* of the directions tell you.

and Must go in the two *left* squares.

and Must go in the two *right* squares.

Show how you can do this.

Blue   Red   Yellow

Put the colors where both of the directions tell you.

and Must go in the two *right* squares.

and Must go in the two *left* squares.

Show how you can do this.

Bill   Sally   Tom

B   S   T

Put the names where *both* of the directions tell you.

Bill and Tom must go in the two left squares.

Tom and Sally must go in the two right squares.

FIGURE 9.4.   The Organizer. (*Note:* Lines have been drawn in to indicate color changes but do not appear in the actual materials.)

There are eight tasks with two overlapping directions; for example, red and blue must go in the two left squares; blue and yellow must go in the two right squares. Four tasks have three overlapping directions. Children who can read can go through an index–symbol–sign sequence, as pictures of objects, their names, and then the first letter of their names are used.

If able, the child is asked to read the directions; otherwise, the examiner reads them. The child is also cautioned initially not to pick up the pencil or even point until all the positions have been worked out mentally. The examiner must make sure that "right and left", "outside and inside," and "next to" are clearly understood. The primary mediation on this instrument consists of advising the child to place the object(s) first that simultaneously must satisfy two directions. If necessary, the examiner should do this for the first two steps. The mental transformation required is often new and difficult for children in this age group. Therefore, the Organizer should be given after the child has been successful on other instruments. Also, minimal reading ability is an advantage. If the child can read, helpful preparatory sequencing activities are to have the child find two words out of place in a sentence, followed by arranging words (each on a card) into a sentence.

If the child cannot read, effectiveness of the adult's verbalization becomes particularly important, because the child has to create some verbal cues to retain the objects in memory while transposing them, and the number of units to be kept in mind constitutes one limitation. Positional concepts also must be clear, and the notion that an object can be in both a right and left position requires a clear concept of "middle" as well as a concept of overlap. Writing down the two initial possibilities as was done in the original Organizer format is a transitional step.

Difficulty on this instrument may be reflected in school in mental arithmetic and in problem solving in other subjects that require more than two steps and transposition of materials.

Raven Coloured Progressive Matrices

EMERGING COGNITIVE FUNCTIONS
Input Phase

1. Lessening of an egocentric frame of reference.
2. Increasing attention span.
3. Increasing ability to recognize a pattern.
4. Increasing ability to focus perception, reduce blurred and sweeping perception.
5. Increasing ability to smoothly shift focus of attention from one stimulus orientation or configuration to another.
6. Increasing ability to distinguish critical stimulus from background and to ignore irrelevant stimuli in close proximity to the task.

7. Development of verbal tools and concepts to help discrimination and memory of input stimuli, including objects, events, and relationships.
8. Ongoing improvement in spatial orientation.
9. Growing need for precision and accuracy in data gathering.
10. Developing capacity for considering two or more sources of information at once and in an integrated manner.
11. Learning to select relevant cues in defining a problem.

Elaboration Phase

1. Beginning ability to enter into mental operations that are flexible and reversible.
2. Development of spatial organization and stable systems of reference.
3. Learning how to identify critical attributes.
4. Learning to ignore or go beyond initial, simple hypotheses and attend to new and relevant aspects of a problem.
5. Beginning flexibility in problem-solving approaches and learning to shift codes being used to represent elements involved.
6. Stabilizing of factors in conservation of constancy such as size, shape, and quantity across dimensions of the perceived object.
7. Learning to pause and reflect in order to decide the kind of concept involved in a task and to plan a course of action to complete the task.
8. Moving in problem solving from the superficial and only one approach toward thoughtful analysis and looking "beneath the surface."
9. Learning to decenter—to focus attention on several attributes of an object or its representation simultaneously and to understand relationships between dimensions.
10. Learning to process more than one kind of information at once.

Output Phase

1. Impulsive responding (motorically and verbally) gradually replaced by reflection.
2. Beginning of projection of virtual relationships.
3. Lessening of trial-and-error responses as part of the learning process itself.
4. Improvement in visual transport.
5. Growth in capability to make precise and accurate responses.

DESCRIPTION OF MATERIALS AND PROCEDURAL GUIDELINES

The choices for the first eight Raven colored matrices are reduced to three or four. As in the regular LPAD (Feuerstein, 1979), the child is asked to select the part missing from the matrix and, frequently, to explain why the alternative choices are incorrect. Reducing the number of choices for the missing part of that matrix reduces a tendency toward blurred and sweeping perception and the number of bits of information to be processed simultaneously. In order to do the task on this instrument, the child must first clearly understand the concepts of same and different. The Columbia Mental Maturity Scale (Burgemeister, Blum & Lorge, 1972) may help the child to move gradually from perceptions of straightforward and concrete similarities and differences to more abstract comparisons and extractions of similarities. In the reduced matrices version, figures vary in only one dimension for a while. A black line with an arrow below the row of figures may be helpful at first to reinforce directionality. Figures that can easily be seen in reverse should not be used when assessing young children. Also, some children need initially to draw lines from their choice to the matrix, reinforcing the visual transport.

The children with whom the author tried the materials usually could give reasons why the other choices were wrong, sometimes spontaneously after they were asked about the first few. However, verbalization ability must be taken into account here; the examiner may have to supply words when the child cannot but indicates his or her reasons through physical gestures.

Representational Stencil Design Test

EMERGING COGNITIVE FUNCTIONS
Input Phase

1. Lessening of an egocentric frame of reference and the injection of the child's own needs of the moment into a task.
2. Increasing ability to recognize a pattern.
3. Increasing ability to recognize and predict cause–effect relationships.
4. Learning to control impulsive exploratory behaviors; more reflection.
5. Learning from any errors that are made.
6. Increasing ability to smoothly shift focus of attention from one stimulus orientation or configuration to another.
7. Increasing ability to distinguish critical stimulus from background and, among completing stimuli, to focus on those relevant for the task.
8. Development of verbal tools and concepts to help discrimination and memory of input stimuli.
9. Ongoing improvement in spatial orientation.
10. Growing need for precision and accuracy in data gathering.
11. Developing capacity for considering two or more sources of information at once and in an integrated manner.
12. Diminishing need for kinesthetic cues and concrete demonstration.

Elaboration Phase

1. Ability to enter into mental operations that are flexible and reversible.
2. Learning to sequence steps in problem solving.
3. Transition from dependence on the concrete to independent, abstract thinking.
4. Development of spatial orientation and stable systems of reference that later contribute to topological Euclidean organization of space.
5. Learning to ignore or go beyond initial, simple hypotheses and to attend to new, relevant stimuli.
6. Learning to deal with a problem that has no reference point in child's own life; lessening of egocentricity.
7. Becoming flexible in problem-solving approaches and learning to shift codes being used to represent the elements involved.
8. Increase in availability of vocabulary, images, schemes, and concepts to help memorize, reason, and problem solve, and in making a transition from images to concepts.
9. Moving in problem solving from the superficial to thoughtful analysis and looking "beneath the surface."
10. Expanding the mental field (aided by lessening of egocentric frame of reference) to focus attention on several attributes of an object or an event simultaneously in order to understand the relationships between dimensions.
11. Learning to process more than one kind of information at once.
12. Beginning to learn interiorization.
13. Beginning to learn how to transform stimuli mentally.
14. Beginning to learn inferential, hypothetical, "iffy" thinking and planning behavior.

Output Phase

1. Impulsive responding gradually replaced by reflection.
2. Beginning of projection of virtual relationships.
3. Curbing of trial-and-error responses as part of learning process itself.
4. Improvement in visual transport.
5. Learning to sequence responses.

DESCRIPTION OF MATERIALS AND PROCEDURAL GUIDELINES

The stencils used are from Feuerstein's (1979) adaptation of The Arthur Stencil Design Test (Arthur, 1930), but omitting the two most complex ones, numbers four and eight, for a total of 16. Feuerstein's (1979) practice designs are used for the present version for kindergarten–primary-age children, eliminating designs 13 and 16 since these would require stencils four and eight, respectively.

The procedure should first be modeled by the examiner. Then the child should practice by manipulation with a few designs different from those on the test and, next, do these same designs without concrete manipulation. An additional transitional step is to provide the child with the exact stencils required for the design. In the test itself, each design and its stencil choices should be on one page, reducing the need for a kind of visual transport not involved in the objectives for the instrument. Some children may go on to the regular Representational Stencil Design Test if they do the practice set without much difficulty.

TO BE RECORDED

The examiner should record all responses the child makes and determine the source of the emerging cognitive function difficulties.

Conclusions

Implementing effective research in dynamic assessment and cognitive modifiability remains a controversial subject. Although the underlying assumptions about children's cognitive development are quite different from those underlying psychometric testing and traditional teaching, theorists and practitioners in dynamic assessment often feel pressure to succumb to the usual type of predictability study. Then they often have difficulty finding a criterion for prediction, especially in the absence of the critical intervening variable of an appropriate educational program to bring about the predicted cognitive modifiability.

A straightforward procedure to test the effectiveness of the teaching process in Feuerstein's (1980) Instrumental Enrichment or the LPAD process itself in bringing about cognitive modifiability might be a retesting on the LPAD after a lapse of a few weeks. Improvement in performance after that period of time likely would reflect the effectiveness of the dynamic teaching or mediation process itself in improving various cognitive functions, rather than being attributable to maturation or school instruction, particularly since school curricula seldom deal with this content. Then, if improvement can be demonstrated, the next step would be to relate these cognitive functions to academic content and achievement.

REFERENCES

Arthur, G. A. (1930). *A point scale of performance tests:* Clinical manual (Vol. I). New York: Commonwealth Fund.

Berreuta-Clement, J., Schweinhart, L., Barnett, W. S., Epstein, A., & Weikart, D. (1984). *Changed lives: The effects of the Perry preschool program on youth through age 19.* Monograph of the High Scope Educational Research Foundation, #8. Ypsilanti, MI: High Scope Press.

Bruner, J. (1963). *The process of education.* Cambridge, MA: Harvard University Press.

Burgemeister, B. B., Blum, L. H., & Lorge, I. (1972). *Columbia mental maturity scale (3rd ed.)*. New York: Harcourt-Brace-Jovanovich.

Burns, M. S. (1980). *Preschool children's approach and performance on cognitive tasks*. Unpublished master's thesis, George Peabody College of Vanderbilt University.

Caldwell, B. M. (1973). Infant day care. In P. Roby & S. Chisolm (Eds.), *Child care: Who cares?* New York: Basic Books.

Clarke, A. D. B., & Clarke, A. M. (1976). *Early experience: Myth and evidence*. New York: Free Press.

Erikson, E. (1950). *Childhood and society*. New York: Norton.

Feuerstein, R. (1979). *The dynamic assessment of retarded performers: The learning potential assessment device, theory, instruments, and techniques*. Baltimore: University Park Press.

Feuerstein, R. (1980). *Instrumental enrichment: An intervention program for cognitive modifiability*. Baltimore: University Park Press.

Feuerstein, R., & Jensen, M. R. (1980). Instrumental enrichment: Theoretical basis, goals, and instruments. *Educational Forum, 5,* 401–423.

Ginsburg, H., & Gannon, K. (1985). *Cognitive style in the educational context*. Paper presented at the Society for Research in Child Development meeting, Toronto.

Gray, S. W., Ramsey, B. K., & Klaus, R. A. (1981). *From 3 to 20: The Early Training Project*. Baltimore: University Park Press.

Hobbs, N. (1975). *Issues in the classification of children*. San Francisco, CA: Jossey-Bass.

Hunt, J. McV. (1961). *Intelligence and experience*. New York: Ronald Press.

Hunt, J. MV. (1979). Psychological development: Early experience. *Annual Review of Psychology, 30,* 103–143.

Kamii, C. K., & Radin, N. L. (1966). *An application of Piaget's theory to a framework for a preschool curriculum*. Unpublished paper. Ypsilanti, MI: Perry Preschool Project.

Kessler, J. W. (1966). *Psychopathology of childhood*. Englewood Cliffs, NJ: Prentice-Hall.

Mussen, P. H., Conger, J. J., Kagan, J., & Huston, A. C. (1984). *Child development and personality (6th ed., pp. 218–264)*. New York: Harper and Row.

Palmer, J. (1983). *Psychological assessment of children*. New York: John Wiley Interscience.

Rey, A., & Dupont, J. B. (1953). Organization des graphes des points en figures géométriques simples. *Monographs de Psychologie, 3.*

Tzuriel, D., & Klein, P. (1984). *The assessment of analogical thinking modifiability among regular, special education, disadvantaged, and mentally retarded children*. Unpublished manuscript, Bar Ilan University, Tel Aviv.

10

Assessing the Young Child: Children's Analogical Thinking Modifiability

DAVID TZURIEL AND PNINA S. KLEIN

The dynamic approach to assessment of learning potential is a relatively new and promising field for clinical practice and empirical enquiry. A growing dissatisfaction with the use of static IQ tests as measures of intellectual functioning has derived from their inadequate indexing of learning potential and the insensitivity of these measures to learning processes and to optimal level of performance. However, few attempts have been made to develop dynamic measures and procedures for assessment of learning potential (Brown & Ferrera, 1985; Budoff, 1974; Feuerstein, 1979; Vygotsky, 1978). The most prominent and articulated contribution to the field is Feuerstein's development of the Learning Potential Assessment Device (LPAD), which is based upon the theory of structural cognitive modifiability (Feuerstein, 1979). Structural cognitive modifiability refers to a self-perpetuating learning process characterized by permanence, pervasiveness, and centrality of cognitive change (Feuerstein, Rand, Haywood, Hoffman, & Jensen, 1985).

According to Feuerstein, learning occurs either by direct exposure from the individual's encounters with random stimuli, or by a mediated learning experience (MLE) (Feuerstein & Rand, 1974) in which the child is exposed to information presented by an adult who interposes himself or herself between the child and the world and intentionally mediates the information to the child. MLE involves modification of the information in such a way that the learning individual can register it meaningfully. Mediational processes may begin by simply repeating an event and systematically shaping the intensity, context, frequency, and order of stimuli, while arousing in the child alertness, sensitivity, and awareness of its special characteristics. MLE also involves "filtering," selecting, organizing, and labeling of information as well as the teaching of abstract rules and higher order mental strategies for problem solving. MLE refers to the transcendence of concrete and discrete stimuli by formation of generalized rules, attachment of meaning and significance to

David Tzuriel. Hadassah–Wizo–Canada Research Institute, Jerusalem, Israel and School of Education, Bar Ilan University, Ramat Gan, Israel.

Pnina S. Klein. School of Education, Bar Ilan University, Ramat Gan, Israel.

learned material, regulation of behavior, mediation of feelings of competence, and mediation of sharing behavior (for a detailed description of MLE characteristics see Feuerstein & Hoffman, 1982; Feuerstein et al., 1985; Klein & Feuerstein, 1984; see also Chapter 14, this volume).

According to Feuerstein's theory, adequate MLE is necessary for an individual to benefit from new experiences. Lack of adequate MLE leads to impaired cognitive functions that may be related to perception, elaboration, and communication of information, and to impaired motivational and attitudinal factors that affect learning. Dynamic assessment is a procedure based upon the theory of MLE, which provides an active teaching process that attempts to modify the individual's cognitive functioning.

The assessment of cognitive modifiability bears special significance for both disadvantaged and special-education children whose abilities are often underestimated by static psychometric tests (Haywood, 1983). The low performance scores on static tests characteristic of children from disadvantaged homes can be related to impaired cognitive functions in the input, elaboration, and output phases of the mental act (Feuerstein, 1979), poor learning habits, attitudes that interfere with encoding and decoding processes, and lack of intrinsic motivation for encountering and coping with challenging tasks (Haywood, Filler, Shifman, & Chatelanat, 1975).

The LPAD (Feuerstein, 1979), which is one of the most comprehensive, theoretically anchored, and elaborated procedures available, is different from the psychometric static tests in four main characteristics: (a) the context of testing, especially the tester–testee interactions; (b) the focus of testing, which shifts from a product to process orientation; (c) the structure and type of tests chosen for the battery; and (d) the nature of the interpretation of results (for a detailed description see Feuerstein, 1979, and Chapter 1, this volume).

One of the basic assumptions of dynamic assessment is that the deficient functions found in the cognitive processes of input, elaboration, and output phases can be modified. Furthermore, these cognitive functions can be modified to some extent during an assessment procedure and thus provide indications about an individual's modifiability. Examples of deficient cognitive functions from the input phase are: unplanned, impulsive exploratory behavior; lack of or impaired verbal tools that affect discrimination; deficient need for precision; and lack of capacity for considering two or more sources of information. Examples from the elaborative phase include: lack of spontaneous comparative behavior, episodic grasp of reality, and impaired strategies for hypothetical testing. In the output phase, examples are: trial-and-error responses; impaired need for precision in communicating information; and impulsive, acting-out behavior. A detailed, although not conclusive, list is elaborated and discussed in Feuerstein (1979). Level of cognitive modifiability is inferred from the amount and type of mediation needed in the intervention process, the child's application of learned rules and concepts to more complex and/or novel problems, the centrality of modified impaired functions (i.e., how basic they are for cognitive performance), and the efficiency of learning.

Development of Dynamic Assessment for Young Children

Because the LPAD has been developed primarily for use with adolescents and school-age children, a growing need has emerged for preschool dynamic measures, especially since early educational decisions about children's learning potential may affect them throughout the rest of their lives. Lidz (1983), in her review and discussion of dynamic assessment for the preschool child, mentioned that there is, as yet, no existing standardized preschool dynamic measure that is well developed and satisfactory. The Children's Analogical Thinking Modifiability (CATM) instrument (Tzuriel & Klein, 1985) is one of the first dynamic measures designed for a preschool population that is based on Feuerstein's theoretical model. Previous attempts at developing dynamic measures for preschool children (e.g., Jedrysek, Klapper, Pope, & Wortis, 1972; Lambert, Wilcox, & Gleason, 1974; Stott, 1978) were not based on a systematic integrative approach such as the one suggested by the LPAD model. In applying the LPAD model to preschool children, we believed that some modifications were necessary to adapt testing instruments and testing procedures to the special needs and learning styles of such young children. Instead of using the two-dimensional mode of presentation of analogical problems as in the Raven Progressive Matrices and LPAD Set Variations (subtests in the battery that tap analogical thinking), the CATM instrument includes three-dimensional blocks that can be manipulated in solving the analogical problems. The game-like characteristics of the CATM instrument attract and maintain the child's attention and motivate the child to explore the dimensions of the problem. Despite the game-like nature of the blocks, however, the problems constructed are difficult, and some require high levels of abstract thinking. Our basic assumption is that 5- to 6-year-old preschool children can solve analogical problems that require simultaneous consideration of two or three dimensions provided they receive appropriate mediation and an opportunity to manipulate the elements making up the analogical problems.

Other attempts to design preschool dynamic measures have been suggested by Bryant, Brown, Campione (1983), and Burns (1980, 1983). Burns, for example, has adapted the Stencil Design Test (SDT) (Arthur, 1947) for use with young children in order to compare two dynamic assessment approaches: a graduated prompting assessment procedure (Brown & Ferrera, 1985) and a mediational assessment procedure based on LPAD principles and strategies (Feuerstein, 1979). The SDT was originally composed of 18 cardboard stencils that varied in color. Six stencils were in solid colors and 12 had various shapes cut out of them. The child was shown models, presented one at a time, composed of cutout stencils that were superimposed on a solid-color stencil. The task was originally designed so that the child had to reproduce the model by motorically manipulating the stencils that make up the model. In accord with the LPAD principles, however, a major modification was introduced by removing the opportunity for motoric manipulation of the stencils. Instead, the child had to represent the stencils mentally and act in a reflective way to reproduce the model. The rationale behind this change was to bring disadvantaged children or retarded performers closer to higher levels of functioning and to modify their representational ability rather than allowing reliance on the trial-and-error strategies and concrete impressions that characterize their performance style. Use of the concrete manipulative approach was found to affect the child adversely by inhibiting opportunities for reflective thinking. With young children, both Burns and the present authors recognized that a perceptual–manipulative approach was needed. The perceptual–manipulative approach had been found to have significance as a bridge toward learning of abstract rules and higher levels of functioning.

The graduated prompt assessment procedure was developed by Brown and her associates (Brown & Ferrara, in press) and is based on Vygotsky's theory of the proximal zone of development (Vygotsky, 1978) (Chapter 3, this volume). According to this approach, the child is presented with a task and then with a series of prompts or hints that increase in their level of explicitness. If the child fails to solve the task on his or her first attempt, he or she is given the prompts or hints in a graduated way. The prompts are designed in a structured, fixed order beginning from low to high levels of explicitness. Different studies suggest that the graduated prompt procedure can discriminate differences in learning abilities that are not identified using normative assessment measures (Brown & Ferrara, 1980; Bryant, 1982; Hall & Day, 1982). The SDT was also given to young children by Burns using the mediating procedure derived from the LPAD approach. Burns (1983) found the mediating procedure to be more effective, especially on transfer tasks, than the standard graduated prompt procedure. The greater effectiveness of the mediating procedure is attributed to the fact that it is designed specifically to deal with the individual's unique needs and cognitive deficiencies. This approach also permits the collection of a detailed description of the child's strengths and weaknesses.

Results from Burns' (1983) study with high-risk preschool children also indicated that children performed better when given dynamic assessment than they did when given static assessment. Mediated assessment was associated with higher performance scores on the SDT and higher transfer scores (using the Animal House subtest of the Wechsler Preschool and Primary Scale of Intelligence (WPPSI) as a transfer task) than was either the "graduated prompt" or static assessment procedure. Graduated prompt was associated with higher performance scores on the SDT, but not higher transfer scores, than was static assessment.

Thus, the limited evidence that is available supports the concurrent validity of a mediated learning assessment approach for young children. The rest of this chapter will describe the structure and procedures of the CATM approach designed by the authors, as well as an empirical study with four criterion groups.

The CATM Instrument

The CATM instrument consists of 18 colored flat blocks and three sets of analogical thinking problems designed for *preteaching, teaching,* and *post-teaching* phases. The test problems require the recognition and mastery of three dimensions: color (red, blue, yellow), shape (circle, square, triangle), and size (big, small). Alternate sets with different blocks using parallel elements were constructed for the pre- and postteaching phases of the assessment. Each set of problems consists of 13 items ascending in order of difficulty. Four levels of difficulty were constructed. On level I (items 1 and 2) one dimension changes while the other two are held constant. On level II (items 3–7) two dimensions change and one dimension is held constant. On level III (items 8–10) all three dimensions change. On level IV (items 11–13) two additional elements (blocks) are introduced, in addition to the three dimensions that are changing. Sample items are presented in Figure 10.1. In addition, the test includes a rectangular strip of cardboard divided into four equal parts upon which blocks are placed, a sample problem card, and recording sheets using two scoring methods. There are four phases of test administration: preliminary, preteaching, teaching, and postteaching.

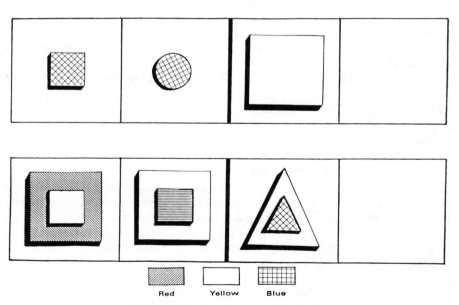

FIGURE 10.1   Sample items of the CATM.

Preliminary Phase

During this phase the examiner familiarizes the child with the specific features of the test materials and basic dimensions (concepts) involved in the test situation, and teaches the basic rules of solving analogical problems. This phase is critical for the establishment of a baseline mastery level for each child. Poor performance at this level requires further preparation of the child before moving to the next one. The child is asked through an inquiry process to construct a matrix using all the blocks (see Figure 10.2). The classification operation is repeated until the child reaches mastery of each category, i.e., color, shape and size. The intervention process involves labeling, focusing, probing, conflict arousal, rule teaching, and rewarding the child for correct classification.

The child is also taught to look for colors on both sides of the blocks. The use of different colors for each side of the block was introduced in order to reduce the total number of blocks used in the assessment from 36 to 18. Some deficient cognitive functions can be clinically identified at this phase (e.g. spontaneous comparative behavior, conservation of constancies—color, shape, size—across variations of other dimensions, simultaneous consideration of two or three sources of information, and impulsive acting-out behavior).

In the last steps of the preliminary phase an analogical problem is presented to the child. The tester places three blocks on the cardboard and asks the child to find a fourth block that goes with the other three. The child is then asked to explain his or her solution. Throughout the preliminary phase specific difficulties are recorded in order to compare performance deficiencies with those found in later phases. The preliminary phase may require between 10 and 20 minutes.

Preteaching Phase

This phase serves as a baseline for the assessment of analogical thinking. For each item in the preteaching phase the tester places the first three blocks on the cardboard and asks the child to find and add the missing last block. On items 11–13 two blocks are to be added in each part of the problem. The examiner places the blocks on the cardboard both to save time and to assure that the child focuses on the task. The cards are for the tester's use only. No intervention is given at this phase except for verbal response of "good" or "nice" following correct responses. The child's full response as well as any special behaviors are recorded on the answer sheet.

Teaching Phase

The objectives of this phase are to teach the child how to: (a) search for relevant dimensions required for the solution, (b) understand transforma-

FIGURE 10.2.   Classification matrix of CATM blocks—preliminary phase.

tional rules and analogical principles, (c) search systematically for correct blocks, and (d) improve efficiency of performance. The intervention strategies vary from nonverbal focusing, labeling, and "rhythmic intonation" of contents to direct teaching of classes and transformational rules.

For most problems there are two primary teaching strategies. The first is analytical; in this, each dimension (color, shape, size) is analyzed separately and then all the information is integrated. With some children we have found it useful to emphasize relations between blocks in a personified way: for example, "The red circle is a *friend* of the red square here [tester points to first two blocks], so who should be the friend of this red circle? [tester points to the third block]." The second intervention strategy involves the teaching of transformational rules. With this, it is emphasized that one or two dimensions change while the others stay constant. We have found it useful to use both approaches of teaching and to evaluate one child's preferences by observing the child's responses. Some children prefer the transformational strategy because they forget when working on the second or third dimension what they found on the first. Other children learn better by the personified style of finding "friends" or by the analytic way of finding one dimension after the other in an accumulative way.

A specific technique, *rhythmic intonation*, has been found particularly useful with the youngest children. The tester pronounces one dimension of the block loudly and the next of the same block softly (e.g., red–CIRCLE/ red–SQUARE//blue–CIRCLE/?), with a small pause between pairs of blocks. The rhythmic intonation can be used effectively on problems involving one or two dimensions. The teaching phase is longer than other phases and may take between a half and a full hour or more, depending on the child's level of functioning.

Postteaching Phase

The objective of this phase is to assess the final performance level, which is compared with preteaching performance. Both quantitative and qualitative aspects are taken into account. The amount of improvement for the whole test, as well as performance on specific items, serve as indications of the child's modifiability. The procedure for this phase is identical to the preteaching procedure. While a separation of 1 day is acceptable between the preteaching and teaching phases, the teaching and postteaching phases have to be completed at the same session, although a short break is possible between phases.

Recording and Scoring of Data

The examiner records the full verbal answer in each of the test phases using two scoring methods: all-or-none and partial credit. According to the first method each correctly solved *item* is given a score of 1; in items 11–13 the maximum score is 2 since there are two blocks in the solution. According to the partial credit method, each correctly solved *dimension* is given a score of 1. Thus, the maximum score possible for items 1–10 is 30 (3×10) and for items 11–13 is 18 (3×6). A total score is computed according to each scoring method for pre- and postteaching sets and a gain score is computed by deducting the preteaching score from the postteaching score. Separate scores for the difficult items 11–13 are also computed. Table 10.1 summarizes the CATM phases.

An Empirical Validation Study

Validation of the CATM was carried out by comparing the analogical cognitive modifiability of four groups of kindergarten children (Tzuriel & Klein, 1985): regular, disadvantaged, special education, and mentally retarded (MR). These groups were assumed to respond differentially to modification by a similar teaching process. We hypothesized that (a) the regular and disadvantaged children would show the highest modifiability scores following a teaching process, and (b) CATM scores (pre- and postteaching) would be significantly higher than scores derived from standard administration of the Raven Coloured Progressive Matrices (RCPM) (included as a static measure), and even higher than the difficult analogy items of B_8–B_{12}.

Subjects and Procedures

The sample was composed of 140 kindergarten children in the Tel Aviv area (70 boys and 70 girls) who were randomly selected from 10 kindergarten classes with a total enrollment of 300. The kindergarten sample included the following groups: regular children from middle-class families ($N = 71$), culturally disadvantaged children from low-socioeconomic-status (SES) families ($N = 51$) (these children came from a kindergarten labeled by the Ministry of Education as disadvantaged), and special education students (SPED) from programs in regular schools ($N = 18$). The middle-class parents had an average of 12 years of formal education as compared to the 8 years or less of the low-SES parents. The SPED parents were primarily of middle class and participated in the study because their children were previously identified as having learning difficulties, social maladjustment, and/or some emotional problem. The SPED group was heterogeneous, and the children in this group were not given any specific diagnostic label at such young age. The MR group (11 boys and 9 girls) was randomly selected from four institutions; their mental ages were between 5 and 6 years. The age of the kindergarten children ranged between 4:0 and 6:6 years and of the MR children between 10 and 16 years.

All children were given the CATM and the RCPM by two trained undergraduate students. Order of administration was counterbalanced. The CATM was administered as described above.

Results

ITEM ANALYSES
The Cronbach Alpha reliability coefficients for the pre- and postteaching tests were .72 and .90, respectively. Corrected item–total correlations of .10 to

TABLE 10.1. Summary of CATM Test Phases

Phase	Materials	Goals	Means of intervention
Preliminary	18 blocks (Color × Form × Size) Example item Cardboard divided into four parts	Familiarity Classification Test rules Rapport	Construction of matrices Mediation of dimensions (i.e., inquiry, labeling, focusing, conflict arousal, teaching of rules) Reinforcement and verbal feedback
Preteaching	18 blocks 13 problems	Assessment of analogical thinking	Solving problems with no intervention
Teaching	18 blocks 13 problems	Discovery of relevant dimensions Understanding of transformation and analogical rules Application of rules Search of correct element Efficiency in performance	Teaching of analogies using mediational processes Control of impulsivity Consideration of two or three sources of information Metacognitive means Pronunciation of rhythms (e.g., RED–blue–RED–blue) Reinforcement and verbal feedback
Postteaching	18 blocks 13 problems	Assessment of analogical thinking	Solving problems with no intervention

.64 were found for items in the preteaching test, and of .34 to .73 for items in the postteaching test.

ANALYSES OF VARIANCE

Two analyses of variance, one for each scoring method, of Group by Pre–Postteaching (4×2) were carried out on the CATM scores, the last factor being a repeated measure. Using the all-or-none scoring method, significant main effects were found for Group ($F_{3,148} = 44.11$, $p < .001$) and for Pre–Postteaching ($F_{1,148} = 159.30$, $p < .0001$). The results indicate that the regular children scored highest, followed by low-SES, SPED, and MR children, and that postteaching scores were significantly higher than preteaching scores. The main effects were modified by a significant interaction of the two variables ($F_{3,148} = 12.36$, $p < .0001$) as shown in Figure 10.3.

The highest gains were achieved by the regular and disadvantaged groups (4.6 and 5.0, respectively) whereas the SPED and MR groups' gains were small (.40 and .70, respectively). Application of the Newman–Keuls (.05) procedure revealed that on one preteaching test the regular group scored significantly highest (6.44), followed by the disadvantaged and SPED groups, who scored intermediately (5.20 and 5.11, respectively), and the MR group, who scored lowest (1.45). However, on the postteaching test the low-SES and regular groups scored highest (10.20 and 11.00, respectively), the SPED group intermediately (5.40), and the MR group lowest (2.15). Thus, the only

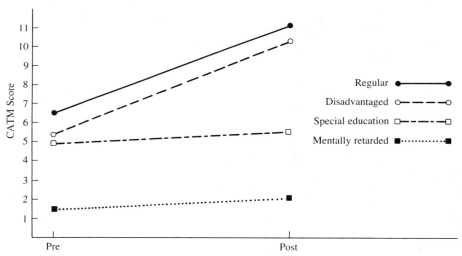

FIGURE 10.3.   CATM pre- and postteaching scores using the all-or-none credit scoring method. (From Tzuriel, D., & Klein, P. S. [1985]. Analogical thinking modifiability in disadvantaged, regular, special education, and mentally retarded children. *Journal of Abnormal Child Psychology*. Copyright © by American Psychological Association, reprinted by permission.)

group that had changed its position from low to high performance level following the teaching phase was the low-SES group.

Using the partial credit scoring method, significant main effects were found for Group ($F_{3,145} = 4.61$, $p < .01$) and Pre–Postteaching ($F_{1,145} = 27.00$, $p < .0001$), and a significant interaction of both factors was found ($F_{3,145} = 3.01$, $p < .05$). These results, using the partial scoring method (see Figure 10.4), are somewhat different from the results found using the all-or-none method (see Figure 10.3). When the partial credit method was used, the MR group showed gains similar to the regular and low-SES groups, despite overall low performance. The findings also indicated that the low-SES group scored higher than any other group and that the SPED group performance decreased from pre- to postteaching test. A detailed analysis revealed that this decrease was contributed mainly by levels III and IV of difficulty, whereas the increase in the other groups was similar across all levels of item difficulty.

COMPARISON OF CATM AND RCPM SCORES

Two RCPM scores were compared with the CATM pre- and postteaching scores: total RCPM score and a score composed of $B_8–B_{12}$ items (see Table 10.2). These items, which tap analogical thinking, were considered by Raven (1965) and Jensen (1969) to represent level II thinking, which is determined, according to their theoretical orientation, ultimately by hereditary factors and

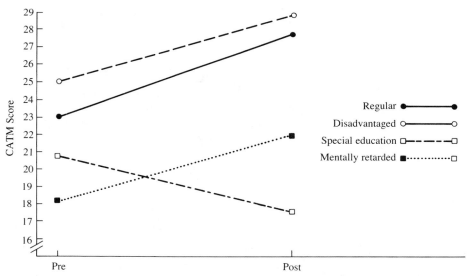

FIGURE 10.4.   CATM pre- and postteaching scores using the partial credit scoring method. (From Tzuriel, D., & Klein, P. S., [1985]. Analogical thinking modifiability in disadvantaged, regular, special education, and mentally retarded children. *Journal of Abnormal Child Psychology*. Copyright © by American Psychological Association, reprinted by permission.)

TABLE 10.2. Percentages of Correct Responses on the RCPM and CATM in Regular, Disadvantaged, Special Education, and Mentally Retarded Children

| | RCPM | | CATM | | | | | | | | |
| | | | Items 1–10 (levels I–III) | | | Items 11–13 (level IV)[a] | | | Total score | | |
Group	Total	B_8–B_{12}	Pre	Post	Gain	Pre	Post	Gain	Pre	Post	Gain
Regular	39.00	10.70	47.18	77.32	30.14	28.64	54.46	25.82	40.23	68.75	28.52
Disadvantaged	43.60	8.63	39.21	70.39	31.18	21.24	52.94	31.70	32.52	63.77	31.25
Special education	34.86	8.88	42.78	42.78	.00	13.89	20.37	6.48	31.94	34.37	2.43
Mentally retarded	16.41	2.00	12.50	16.50	4.00	3.33	8.33	5.00	9.06	13.44	4.37

Note: From Tzuriel, D., & Klein, P. S. (1985). Analogical thinking modifiability in disadvantaged, regular, special education, and mentally retarded children. *Journal of Abnormal Child Psychology.* Copyright © by the American Psychological Association, reprinted by permission.

[a] The range score for items 11–13 was 0 to 2; each of the two elements was given a credit of 1.

is conceived as untrainable (see Feuerstein, 1979, for counterarguments). Three CATM scores were compared: total score, score on items 1–10, and score on items 11–13. The last score represents a much higher level of complexity and abstraction than B_8–B_{12} items (see example in Figure 10.1). For a more convenient comparison, all scores were converted into percentages.

The total RCPM scores were lower than the CATM postteaching scores for all but the MR group. The B_8–B_{12} scores were lower than both pre- and postteaching CATM scores in all groups. The greatest differences between scores (B_8–B_{12} and CATM–Post) were found in the low-SES group (62%) and regular group (67%).

It is interesting to note that, whereas on items 1–10 the regular and low-SES groups had about equal gain scores (31.18% and 30.14%, respectively), on the difficult items 11–13 the low-SES group had higher gain scores (31.70%) than the regular group (25.82%).

CORRELATIONAL ANALYSES

In order to examine, on item level, whether gains differentiated between children with low versus high preteaching performance levels, correlation coefficients between pre- and postteaching scores were computed for each item. The correlations were computed for each criterion group separately. We reasoned that, whereas low, insignificant correlations would indicate a differential gain for different items, a low or high preteaching score does not necessarily mean a respective low or high postteaching score. Significant positive correlations, on the other hand, would indicate equal gains; low and high preteaching performers would achieve low and high postteaching scores, respectively. The results revealed that, for the regular group, nine (out of 13) correlations were significant ($p < .05$), ranging between .19 and .40, whereas for all the other groups, only one significant correlation was found.

An interesting result emerged from correlating the item difficulty with pre- to postteaching gain in each of the criterion groups. (Item difficulty was based on the mean item score for each criterion group.) This correlational analysis was based on the hypothesis that the more difficult the item (represented by low preteaching score), the more the child would benefit from the intervention aimed at improving the child's level of understanding and problem-solving skills. Significant correlations were found between item difficulty and gain score only for the regular children ($r = -.84$, $p < .001$) and special education children ($r = -.70$, $p < .01$). Pearson correlations of the low-SES ($r = -.40$) and MR ($r = -.30$) groups were not significant, although they were in the same direction.

ANALYSIS OF QUALITATIVE CHANGES

One of the main research questions posed in this study was to what extent performance on each dimension (color, shape, and size) improved in each of the four criterion groups. Analysis of variance of Group by Pre–Postteaching

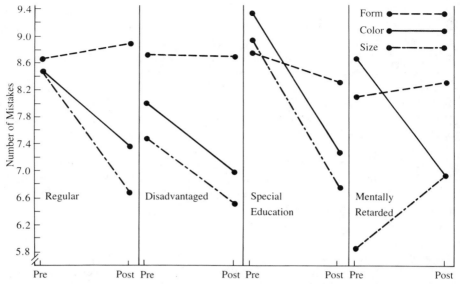

FIGURE 10.5.   Number of color, shape, and size mistakes in pre- and postteaching tests. (From Tzuriel, D., & Klein, P. S., [1985]. Analogical thinking modifiability in disdvantaged, regular, special education, and mentally retarded children. *Journal of Abnormal Child Psychology.* Copyright © by American Psychological Association, reprinted by permission.)

by Type of Mistake ($4 \times 2 \times 3$) was carried out with Group as a between factor and the other variables as within factors; the third was nested within the second. Significant main effects for Pre–Postteaching ($F_{1,148} = 11.43$, $p < .001$) and Type of Mistake ($F_{2,148} = 55.28$, $p < .001$) indicated that there were more mistakes in the pre- than in the postteaching test and that there were more mistakes of shape than of size. The main effects were modified by two- and three-way interactions. The interaction of Pre–Postteaching by Type of Mistake ($F_{2,148} = 16.08$, $p < .0001$) indicated that color and size mistakes decreased whereas mistakes of shape slightly increased from pre- to postteaching test. The interaction of all factors ($F_{6,148} = 3.35$, $p < .005$) is presented in Figure 10.5.

As can be seen in Figure 10.5, color mistakes decreased in all groups, mistakes of shape were at about the same level in all groups, and mistakes of size decreased in all groups with the exception of the MR group, where size mistakes increased.

Discussion

Dynamic testing of kindergarten children by the CATM has yielded a higher level of functioning when compared to static RCPM scores, especially for the low-SES and regular children. The results support our hypothesis that young children as well as older MR children can function on a higher level of thinking provided they are given adequate MLE. The MLE used in the intervention process was related to alleviation of cognitive deficiencies that were interfering with optimal learning, as well as teaching abstract rules of transformation and systematic strategies for efficient gathering of information, elaboration, and communication. The higher level of functioning on the CATM can be partially attributed to the specific characteristics of the instrument. The three-dimensional blocks allow manipulation and arouse interest. Consequently, the information required for correct solution is better articulated and attracts the child's attention more than a two-dimensional stimulus. Some of the problems on the CATM require a high level of abstraction (see Figure 10.1). The tangible and colorful blocks seem to be more functional for young children as a means of bridging between the concrete thinking level and the abstract level required in the correct solution. Further comparative research is needed in which mediational strategies will be used with two-dimensional problems versus problems requiring manipulation of three dimensions.

The improvements of the low-SES and regular groups on the CATM indicate, as expected, high cognitive modifiability. Of special interest is the finding that low-SES children have high gains on the difficult items (level IV) and close the gap between their performance and that of the regular group in the preteaching test.

The lack of improvement found for the MR and SPED groups (all-or-none scoring method) should not, however, be interpreted as an indication of lack of cognitive modifiability. It is expected that, with more appropriate intervention strategies compatible with unique individual needs and learning styles, their performance could be improved as well. It should be emphasized that for research purposes the intervention procedures were standardized for all children. These procedures were primarily aimed at modifying cognitive impairments characterizing low-SES or regular kindergarten children. In a clinical assessment session, however, the examiner usually deviates from a prescribed procedure whenever it is felt that the child has specific difficulties that need a different kind of mediation. The main difficulties characterizing the MR and SPED groups, as reported by the examiners, were such as required other interventional strategies. The main difficulties of the SPED group noted throughout testing phases were related to short attention span, distractibility, impairment in simultaneous consideration of more than one source of information, poor spontaneous comparative behavior, and impaired summative behavior. The last three cognitive functions were reported to be the most common in all criterion groups. In future research, attention should be given to the use of alternative teaching strategies with different criterion groups as well as different levels of task abstraction. In this way, the degree of modifiability for each of the group by teaching method by task abstraction conditions could be examined in detail. Variations in teaching approach should be related to graduated teaching strategies, elaboration of transformation principles, repetition of analogical problems, synthesis of a few sources of information, and improvement of performance efficiency in input, elaboration, and output phases of the mental act.

Using the two methods of scoring (all-or-none and partial credit) proved to be of great diagnostic value, especially in clarifying the functional difficulties underlying analogical thinking. Two intriguing results were found: (a) the MR children showed high improvement from pre- to postteaching phases, and (b) the low-SES group showed higher scores than the regular group in both testing phases. These two differences can be viewed as an outgrowth of understanding the analogical thinking process. Analogical problems require inductive reasoning composed of two complementary phases: *analytic* processing of the given information and *synthesis* or integration of the analyzed information. High modifiability was found in the MR group when partial solutions were credited as compared to no modifiability when a full solution (all dimensions are integrated) was required. The results might be explained by the MR children's impairment in the integrative–synthetic rather than analytic phase of the inductive process. The results of the disadvantaged group could also be explained using the analytic–synthetic phases explanation of the analogical thinking process. The disadvantaged children turned toward detailed analytic processing of information more than toward synthesis of information and therefore showed an overall higher performance than the regular group when the partial credit method was used. If they chose an incorrect block, at least one or two dimensions of the answers were correct. The regular children, on the other hand, were more proficient than the low-SES group in synthesizing a few sources of information and thus showed higher performance when the all-or-none method was applied. When choosing an incorrect block they tended to give a "full-blown" mistake.

The performance pattern of the SPED group revealed small gains according to the all-or-none method and a small decrease according to the partial credit method (see Figures 10.3 and 10.4). This pattern indicates that in the postteaching test there were slightly more correct integrative solutions than in the preteaching test (all-or-none credit method). However, when a wrong solution was given, they tended to give more "full-blown" mistakes in the postteaching test than in the preteaching test. In other words there were more wrong solutions in the preteaching phase but these mistakes were not as gross as in the postteaching test. Most of the "full-blown" mistakes were given in the postteaching test on the more difficult items (8–13, levels III and IV). This performance pattern might be attributed to factors such as task satiation, situation novelty, ability to concentrate and invest mental efforts, and resistance to mediation, which affect the SPED group more than other groups. Since the SPED group was heterogeneous, it is suggested that future research classify individuals more specifically according to source or nature of difficulty, and that different intervention strategies be applied in order to assess the modifiability pattern revealed by each group. A detailed behavioral observation during testing could provide important information when combined with information on cognitive performance.

Results of the correlational analysis throw light on some finer aspects of cognitive modifiability. Preteaching items were correlated with their parallel postteaching items for each group. Whereas in the regular group nine correlations (out of 13) were found to be significant, only one significant correlation was found in the other groups. Since the regular and disadvantaged groups have shown similar gains, one may infer that the gains were more or less equal for all children, whereas in the low-SES group, gains differed for high and low preteaching performers. The only significant correlation found for the MR and SPED groups seems to be due to the relative lack of gains rather than to differential gains within each group.

The qualitative analysis clearly indicates that mistakes of shape are most resistant to modification, whereas mistakes of color and size are relatively easy to modify. These results are congruent with developmental findings indicating color as the most perceptually primitive element (Pick & Pick, 1970; Zeaman & House, 1963). Size perception is developed later and shape is the most differentiated and therefore difficult to modify. Except for the theoretical implications of the qualitative results, these mistakes also have important implications for the dynamic assessment process and for intervention programs. More emphasis should be given to shape perception in teaching analogies than to size and color. The qualitative analysis also suggests that modifiability interacts with task and that any child's modifiability can only be assessed in the context of a specific situation.

The results of our study support our conviction of the need to develop both dynamic assessment measures and innovative intervention procedures specific to young children. Young children, especially those who come from a low-SES background or who are characterized by some cognitive handicap, are very susceptible to the pitfalls of conventional psychometric tests. Further research is needed, however, that compares dynamic assessment longitudinally with the effects of different types of educational interventions. The dynamic assessment of a learning potential approach as applied to the plasticity of young children and to their unique developmental characteristics would appear to be the optimal method in providing accurate predictions as well as efficient intervention strategies.

ACKNOWLEDGMENTS

This research was supported in part by the Internal Research Fund, Bar Ilan University. We wish to express our appreciation to the children and teachers who participated in this study, to Frida Spanier for her assistance in data collection, and to Steve Greenwald for data analysis.

REFERENCES

Arthur, G. (1947). *Manual of directions for the Stencil Design Test I.* New York: Psychological Corporation.

Brown, A., & Ferrara, R. (1980). *Diagnosing zones of proximal development: An alternative to standardized testing?* Paper presented at Conference on Culture, Communication and Cognition: Vygotskian Perspectives, Center for Psychosocial Studies, Chicago.

Brown, A. L., & Ferrara, R. A. (1985). Diagnosing zones of proximal development. In J. V. Wertsch (Ed.), *Culture, communication and cognition: Vygotskian perspectives.* New York: Academic Press.

Bryant, N. R. (1982). *Preschool children's learning and transfer of matrices problems: A study of proximal development.* Unpublished master's thesis, University of Illinois.

Bryant, N. R., Brown, A. L., & Campione, J. C. (1983). *Preschool children's learning and transfer of matrices problems: Potential for improvement.* Paper presented at the Society for Research in Child Development meeting, Detroit.

Budoff, M. (1967). Learning potential among institutionalized retardates. *American Journal of Mental Deficiency, 72,* 404–411.

Budoff, M. (1974). *Learning potential and educability among the educable mentally retarded.* (Final Report Project No. 312312). Cambridge, MA: Research Institute for Educational Problems.

Burns, M. S. (1980). *Preschool children's approach and performance on cognitive tasks.* Unpublished master's thesis, Vanderbilt University, Nashville, Tennessee.

Burns, M. S. (1983). *Comparison of "graduated prompt" and "mediational" dynamic assessment and static assessment with young children.* Unpublished doctoral dissertation, Vanderbilt University, Nashville, Tennessee.

Feuerstein, R. (1979). *The dynamic assessment of retarded performers: The learning potential assessment device, theory, instruments, and techniques.* Baltimore: University Park Press.

Feuerstein, R., Rand, Y.,Haywood, H. C., Hoffman, M., & Jensen, M. (1985) *The learning potential assessment device (LPAD). Examiners Manual.* Hadassah–Wizo–Canada Research Institute, Jerusalem, Israel.

Feuerstein, R., & Hoffman, M. B. (1982). Intergenerational conflict of rights: Cultural imposition and self-realization. *Journal of School Education, 58,* 44–61.

Feuerstein, R., & Rand, Y. (1974). Mediated learning experiences: An outline of the proximal etiology for differential development of cognitive functions. In L. Goldfein (Ed.) *International understanding: Cultural differences in the development of cognitive processes* (pp. 7-37). New York: ICP.

Hall, L. K., & Day, J. D. (1982). *A comparison of the zone of proximal development in learning disabled, mentally retarded, and normal children.* Paper presented at the Annual Meeting of the American Educational Research Association, New York.

Haywood, H. C. (1983). Dynamic assessment: The learning potential assessment device (LPAD). In R. L. Jones (Ed.), *Nondiscriminatory (high validity) assessment: A casebook.* Washington, DC: U.S. Department of Education.

Haywood, H. C., Filler, J. W., Jr., Shifman, M. A., & Chatelanat, G. (1975). Behavioral assessment in mental retardation. In P. McReynolds (Ed.), *Advances in psychological assessment* (Vol. 3, pp. 31–51). San Francisco: Jossey-Bass.

Jedrysek, E., Klapper, A., Pope, L, & Wortis, J. (1972). *Psychoeducational evaluation of the preschool child.* New York: Grune & Stratton.

Jensen, A. (1969). How much can we boost IQ and scholastic achievement? *Harvard Educational Review, 38,* 1–123.

Klein, P. S., & Feuerstein, R. (1984). Environmental variables and cognitive development: Identification of potent factors in adult-child interaction. In S. Harel & W. N. Anastasiow (Eds.), *The at-risk infant: Psycho/Socio/Mediational aspects* (pp. 369–377). Baltimore: Paul H. Brookes.

Lambert, N. M., Wilcox, M. R., & Gleason, W. P. (1974). *The educationally retarded child.* New York: Grune & Stratton.

Lidz, C. S. (1983). Dynamic assessment and the preschool child. *Journal of Psychoeducational Assessment, 1,* 59–72.

Pick, H. L., Jr., & Pick, A. D. (1970). Sensory and perceptual development. In P. H. Mussen (Ed.), *Carmichael's manual of child psychology* (pp. 773–848). New York: Wiley.

Raven, J. C. (1965). *Guide to using the Coloured Progressive Matrices, Sets A, Ab, and B.* London: H. K. Lewis.

Stott, D. H. (1978). *The hard-to-teach child.* Baltimore: University Park Press.

Tzuriel, D., & Klein, P. S. (1985). Analogical thinking modifiability in disadvantaged, regular, special education, and mentally retarded children. *Journal of Abnormal Child Psychology.*

Vygotsky, L. S. (1978). *Mind in society: The development of higher psychological processes* (M. Cole, V. John-Steiner, S. Scribner, & E. Souberman, Eds. and trans.). Cambridge, MA: Harvard University Press.

Zeaman, D., & House, B. J. (1963). An attention theory of retardate discrimination learning. In N. R. Ellis (Ed.), *Handbook of mental deficiency* (pp. 159–223). New York: McGraw-Hill.

11

The Preschool Learning Assessment Device: Extension of a Static Approach

CAROL SCHNEIDER LIDZ AND CATHERINE THOMAS

Dynamic assessment is a general model of examiner–examinee interaction, and is not tied to specific tests or age groups. The essential components of a dynamic assessment are a test–teach–retest framework, with the "teaching" involving mediation of cognitive functions by an examiner-as-teacher with an examinee-as-learner. The outcome is an indication of the modifiability of the learner as well as of the means by which such modifiability may or may not be induced (see Feuerstein et al. and Jensen and Feuerstein, Chapters 1 and 14, this volume, for further discussion). Both Feuerstein (1979) and Budoff (e.g., 1969; Budoff, Meskin, & Harrison, 1971) have focused on adolescents in developing their procedures. A number of contributors to this book describe their approaches for assessment of young children, and each of these procedures follows a somewhat different course. For example, Mearig (Chapter 9) describes a literal downward extension of Feuerstein's Learning Potential Assessment Device (LPAD); Campione and Brown (Chapter 3) interpret Vygotsky somewhat differently and present their young children with a set of graduated predetermined prompts; and Tzuriel and Klein (Chapter 10) use the LPAD as a model, but design entirely new tests for their young subjects.

What we offer in this chapter is yet another alternative for applying dynamic assessment to young children, a dynamic extension of an existing, normed, static test. In this approach, we address children of ages younger than those worked with by the other authors, attempting to go as low as age 3. This approach was chosen with some very practical ideas in mind. First, we view dynamic assessment as providing unique information and responses to referral questions, but not as providing all of the answers to all of the questions. That is, we are not willing to discard the baby with the bathwater and dismiss normed and criterion-referenced measures as useless. At the same time, the typical school psychologist serves a large number of pupils, and must complete assessments within a limited period of time. It thus seemed

Carol Schneider Lidz. Clinic Team Services, United Cerebral Palsy Association of Philadelphia and Vicinity, Philadelphia, Pennsylvania.

Catherine Thomas. Division of Special Education, New Jersey Department of Education, Trenton, New Jersey.

reasonable to proceed in the direction of extending a test that is likely to be administered to most or many of the children of the population we wished to address, namely, preschool children between the ages of 3 and 5. We therefore chose the Kaufman Assessment Battery for Children (Kaufman & Kaufman, 1983) as a well-standardized measure, appropriate to this age level with the advantage of subtests that approximate those used in the LPAD. Other advantages included prepared task analyses of the subtests and factor-analyzed groupings of subtests that would allow us to look at both intra- and interdomain transfer.

Why a Preschool Procedure?

There is more than a simple, obvious response to the question of why we need a preschool dynamic procedure. On the surface it hardly seems necessary to provide a rationale. As long as there are preschool children to assess, why not have dynamic as well as normed and criterion-referenced approaches in the assessment repertoire to respond to referral issues? Dynamic procedures provide unique responses to referral questions for young children just as they do for older ones. However, at a less obvious level is the issue of the appropriateness of this approach for use with young children. It is possible that a certain level of cognitive development is necessary before a dynamic procedure can be successfully applied, particularly if we think of dynamic assessment as involving executive processes and strategies.

Reviewers of the area (Etzel, 1978; Lidz, 1983) have noted both the seeming appropriateness of the dynamic model for use with preschool children, and, at the same time, the lack of truly dynamic procedures for this population. Lidz (1983) also cited evidence supportive of the need for a mediational procedure, in contrast to lack of success with mere provision of additional practice or opportunities for increased procedural familiarity with many low-performing learners (e.g., Oakland, 1972; Scholnick & Osler, 1969; Whitely & Dawis, 1974).

In addressing the issue of the appropriateness of a dynamic procedure for preschool children, Ballester and Lidz (in preparation) and Burns (1980) have demonstrated the observability and reliable scorability of many of the cognitive functions and deficiencies described by Feuerstein (1979, 1980) in children as young as 3 and 4 years old. Furthermore, Ballester and Lidz provide evidence of the relationship between some of these deficiencies (particularly spontaneous comparative behavior and impulsivity at output) and academic performance for 3- and 4-year-olds.

The Cognitive Functioning of Preschool Children

There is varied evidence and a variety of speculations about the emergence of metacognitive processes in young children (Siegler, 1983). Evidence for logical cognitive strategies has been claimed even for infants (e.g., Haake & Somerville, 1985), but it is a moot point whether what is being observed are strategies (behaviors en route to a final objective) or emergent cognitive processes per se. However, most agree that strategic skills are what pre-schoolers appear to lack (e.g., Brown & DeLoache, 1983); use of strategies requires both a high degree of conscious control and a repertory of experience that the young child has not yet developed or acquired. It is both coordination and control that appear to be difficult for the young child, rather than defi-ciencies of isolated skills (Brown & DeLoache, 1983; Case, 1978). Thus, such cognitive functions as the ability to deal with two or more stimuli at the same time (Feuerstein, 1979) would be considered an issue of development rather than of mediated learning experience at this age. That is, failure to find this ability in the child would not necessarily be attributed to inadequacies of mediation.

Early cognitive skills that are generally recognized to exist in the pre-school child include: recognition, visual scanning, categorical perception, learning, and intersensory integration (Siegler, 1983).

Most of what has been learned about the cognitive development of pre-school children has relied on communication abilities. The ability to com-municate, to understand communications, and to internalize language have all been closely associated with cognitive development (Flavell, 1977), but reliance on communication skills may also obscure cognitive functions that become apparent when alternative means of assessment are developed, as has been the case in infancy (Kogan, 1976). Also, more is often learned from the nature of children's "errors" than from what they are able to articulate verbally (Greeno & Simon, 1984). Findings from research on cognitive skills of young children, in addition to being limited by communication abilities, are also influenced by the fact that tasks are more likely to be novel to the young child (Brown & DeLoache, 1983; Kogan, 1976). Although performance in novel situations may be one of the best indicators of intelligence, this novelty is more likely to characterize the situation for the young child. It may therefore be the case that different abilities are being measured by similar tasks and that conclusions regarding deficiencies or deficits may reflect these experiential differences rather than cognitive abilities. For example, the de-velopment of abilities such as deductive reasoning appears to be related to certain kinds of educational experiences rather than to chronological age per se (Hawkins, Pea, Glick, & Scribner, 1984).

One executive-like function relevant to dynamic assessment that begins to develop in early childhood is self-control or self-regulation (Flavell, 1977). This function relates to the reflectivity–impulsivity dimension, which has received much attention in the cognitive-style literature and which, on the one hand, is an important differentiating factor between good and poor learn-ers, and, on the other hand, is susceptible to intervention and modification (see Chapter 17, this volume). It is the development of self-regulation that enables the child to be assessed by a predetermined procedure and not merely by observation of spontaneous behavior (Flavell, 1977).

Preschool children are also capable of abstraction and qualitative logic in the form of "identities" and "functions," which, although lacking quantitative precision (Flavell, 1977), permit comparative behavior, prediction of consequences, and beginning means–end analysis, cognitive functions important to dynamic assessment and to the differentiation of effective versus deficient learners (Feuerstein, 1979, 1980). According to Flavell (1977), a qualitative identify refers to the child's "cognitive isolation or differentiation of a permanent quality of an object, namely, its identity or 'same-thingness', from such potentially alterable and variable properties as the object's form, size, and general appearance" (p. 73). The idea of function involves notation of "simple functional relationships and recurrent covariations among observable events . . . [the ability] to say that changes in one thing tend to be associated with changes in another" (p. 76).

Other researchers see the preschool years as a harbinger of development of deductive reasoning skills. Hawkins et al. (1984) cited evidence of deductive reasoning ability in their 4- and 5-year-old subjects. According to Zaporozhets and Elkonin (1964/1971), "during the preschool age there is a shift from visual-motor thinking to visual-figurative, and, thereafter, to verbal thinking. The decisive condition for such a shift is the child's acquisition of experience of solving problems in terms of the visual-motor plan" (p. 231). They see the preschool years as the beginning of deductive reasoning that does not depend upon direct perception. Age 3 appears to be a time of emergence of deductive abilities, with major gains made during the fourth, and, especially, the fifth years (p. 242). However, according to Piaget, the child below age 5 would not be capable of the level of inference required to solve analogical reasoning problems (in Sternberg & Nigro, 1980). Sternberg (1979) concluded that a minimal age of 10 is required before "mapping" (linking the relationship between the terms of the analogy; i.e., between A and C of A:B::C:D) is possible, although he works with children as young as 7. In their research with children with an average age of 9 at the youngest level, Sternberg and Nigro (1980) reported a developmental trend of greater reliance of the younger subjects on "association between the last term of the item stem and the correct response option" (p. 34), rather than true reasoning by analogy.

One source of evidence supporting the existence of metacognition in preschool children derives from reviewers such as Wellman (1977), who concluded that children as young as 3 use mnemonic behaviors as aids in memory tasks. However, in the case of visual scanning strategies related to comparative behavior, children between the ages of 3 and 5 show restricted range, which results in insufficient information and frequent error (Vurpillot, 1968).

Another factor related to the functioning of preschool children and dynamic assessment is the need for a change in the types of tasks used for assessment. Feuerstein (1979) has emphasized the need for abstract, non-manipulable tasks, in order to force deficient learners to conceptualize in more abstract terms. However, in the case of the very young child, although it is still necessary to ask the child to reach to a higher conceptual level, there is a clear need to include more concrete manipulables in the assessment. Because the children are still more sensory–perceptually dominant than those studied by researchers working with older children, and because attention maintenance is a major factor at this age, it is necessary to use tasks that involve active object manipulation. This is supported by the research findings of Carlson and Wiedl (1980), who concluded that "the result indicating that the puzzle-form of the test was effective in its own right in improving performance of second-grade children over that obtained for the booklet-form demonstrates the value of providing younger children with materials which can be overtly manipulated, allowing actual physical activity and comparisons" (p. 316).

In studying strategic behavior of subjects ages 3 through 20, Weir (1964) found that 3- and 4-year-olds tended to employ what was called a "maximization" strategy, or what others might term perseveration; that is, repetition of a response previously emitted, unrelated to whether it was correct or incorrect. This suggests that children, especially at age 3, are responding more in terms of a response "set" (that is, structural demands) than in terms of actual experience. They are not yet maximally responsive to or modified by feedback—another aspect of metacognitive behavior.

In summary, much of the research on the development of cognitive skills in young children suggests that the age of 5 or 6 is a turning point during which the child becomes significantly more skilled in metacognitive/executive processes than at younger preschool ages. However, many of these processes are in partial evidence or emerging between the ages of 3 through 5, and their degree of operation may provide the basis for differentiation between the more and less competent learners even at this age, or as precursors to learning competence at older ages. If they are emerging, the structural capacity may be inferred, and enhancement, or development through mediation, remains a possibility. Luria's (1979) observations of the young child lend further credence to our efforts to apply dynamic assessment techniques to children within this age range:

> It is at this period [3½] that mylenization of the neurons of the frontal lobes begins to reach completion; and it is at this age that young children begin to control their behavior in accord with verbal instructions. In both cases, there is evidence that the complex organization of human consciousness depends critically on the operation of neurophysiological mechanisms in the frontal lobes. (pp. 164–165)

However, what may be least accessible to the child below 5 are the cognitive processes involved in analogical reasoning, which leads to some pessimism regarding the possibility of mediating this skill in children as young as those involved in the work to be described in this chapter.

Mediated Learning Experience and Dynamic Assessment

One of the dilemmas of designing a dynamic procedure within the Feuerstein model (1979) for any age level is the central role of the mediated learning experience (MLE) in assessment, combined with the impossibility of providing a completely standardized, step-by-step format for the MLE. The two are simply mutually exclusive. It is not possible to be a responsive mediator and at the same time follow a prescribed, standardized procedure. However, what can be done is to discuss the concept of the MLE in general, as well as in relation to the specific assessment tasks. The tasks of any procedure are chosen to elicit certain cognitive functions and to provide opportunities to observe the application of these functions and the corresponding deficiencies. It then becomes possible to offer suggestions for mediation, particularly as experience is accumulated in administering the tasks. However, there will always be the elusive elements of clinical judgment, inference, and artistry that will remain definitive of this approach. The ultimate test is not so much that all assessors are engaging in exactly the same behaviors during the course of the assessment, but that the conclusions and recommendations resulting from the assessment have demonstrated reliability and validity.

MLE is perhaps the most primary and central concept in Feuerstein's theory and proposals for assessment and intervention. MLE is described as the central causative factor in cognitive development and defines the nature of the interaction between examiner/teacher/parent and children during assessment, remediation, or child rearing. MLE is the primary agent not only of development, but of change and modification as well. Feuerstein (1980) defined MLE as "the way in which stimuli emitted by the environment are transformed by a 'mediating' agent . . . [who], guided by his intentions, culture, and emotional investment, selects and organizes the world of stimuli for the child" (pp. 15–16). Indeed, Wood, Bruner, and Ross (1976) suggested that such interactions are among the unique characteristics differentiating the human from other species. And White's (White, Kaban, & Attanucci, 1979) research would suggest that development of competence in young children relates strongly to the availability and quality of interaction with adults as resources, from which develops the child's ability to use the adult as a resource.

Central to our discussion in this chapter is Feuerstein's suggestion that "the more and the earlier an organism is subjected to MLE, the greater will be his capacity to efficiently use and be affected by direct exposure to sources of stimuli" (1980, p. 16). Clearly, earlier is viewed as better, and Klein (Klein, undated; Klein & Feuerstein, 1985) looked at MLE in infancy in her research with parents and children.

There are six published criteria of an MLE (Feuerstein, 1980; Klein & Feuerstein, 1985), and three that have recently been added (Feuerstein, personal communication).[1] These are as follows:

1. A tenth criterion of MLE has since been added; see Jensen and Feuerstein (Chapter 14, this volume) for full discussion and elaboration.

1. *Intentionality and reciprocity, or mutuality:* The mediator sets about influencing the child with conscious intent, and the child is a willing receiver and participant in the process. Without this reciprocity on the part of the child, mediation is not possible.
2. *Transcendence:* Connections are made by the mediator with events, objects, and concepts beyond the immediate and present; this is essential for the development of higher cognitive processes and abstract thinking.
3. *Mediation of meaning:* The mediator attributes meaning and value to and interprets events for the child; stimuli are not treated as equal or neutral, but are selected, highlighted, and evaluated. This is central to the passing on of culture.
4. *Mediation of a feeling of competence:* The mediator regulates environmental stimuli to enable the child to respond without becoming overwhelmed, and promotes feelings of mastery and competence with verbal comments, words of encouragement, or nonverbal gestures. This is a motivational variable.
5. *Mediated regulation and control of behavior:* The mediator helps the child to control and develop self-control over impulsivity. This relates to development of attentional skills that permit internalization of learning.
6. *Mediation of sharing behavior:* The mediator shares values, ideas, and feelings with the child, and encourages the child to do the same. This relates to mediation of meaning, but goes beyond attribution of meaning to include personal sharing of experiences and personal thoughts. This combines cultural transmission with self-regulation by promotion of identification with a valued model.
7. *Mediation of psychological differentiation:* Helping the child to differentiate between self and others, or between "me" and "you." Cognitively, this relates to a field-independent, analytic cognitive style. This also reflects the mediator's ability to separate the role of mediator from the child's role as learner; that is, the good mediator does not become overly involved in the task, but is concerned with helping the child learn and master a situation or task.
8. *Mediation of goal seeking:* Setting of goals and development of strategies and plans to reach the goals; helping the child to organize experiences and to determine the means by which goals can be reached. This is a central executive process.
9. *Mediation of challenging behaviors:* Enhancing the child's natural tendency to search for novelty and complexity by encouraging the child to strive and reach for higher levels of thinking.

   Specific behaviors the mediator may employ during a mediated learning experience might include any of the following: focusing, selecting, provoking, requesting, repeating, reinforcing, rewarding, inhibiting, controlling, providing, transmitting, sequencing, directing, deducing, confronting, organizing, and the like. However, these behaviors would not in and of themselves be MLEs unless in the service of the above criteria. The criteria, then, are the crux of what happens during the course of a dynamic assessment that attempts to follow the Feuerstein model. The specific behaviors emitted by the examiner, in the context of the learner's responses and nature of the tasks, compose what is recorded and discussed in the ensuing report and prescriptive suggestions. The superiority of this approach over static procedures for independent task performance and over both static and graduated prompt procedures for transfer has been shown by Burns (1985).

The Preschool Learning Assessment Device: Background

As indicated above, in pursuing our goal of developing a dynamic assessment compatible with Feuerstein's (1979) model for use with preschool children, we wished to be as practical as possible, and chose the route of developing a dynamic extension of an existing static test, the Kaufman Assessment Battery for Children (K-ABC) (Kaufman & Kaufman, 1983). It then becomes possible to administer the static measure first, to derive whatever information is meaningful for the child from that point of view, and then to use the next session or two for the dynamic extension (our procedure is best administered in one session of about 1½ hours).[2] Another advantage of this alternative is that the static measure can provide both pre- and posttest scores when doing research that compares static and dynamic procedures.

The next step was to design the dynamic extension to reflect Feuerstein's theory of MLE (1979, 1980) and to serve as a means of observing cognitive deficiencies. The Interpretive Manual of the K-ABC provides a task analysis for each subtest that includes some, or approximations of some, of the cognitive functions discussed by Feuerstein. Others were added as relevant to the particular tasks used. The task analyses were more useful to the first half of our procedure, which used the Triangles subtest of the K-ABC.[3] This subtest was selected because it provided many opportunities for mediation, while minimizing demands on verbalization and vocabulary knowledge. It also was appropriate for the older end of the age range we were addressing, and responded to our intent to use tasks that required the child to "reach" somewhat above the child's current cognitive level and therefore provide a need for mediation (Feuerstein, personal communication). The Kaufmans describe the Triangles subtest as permitting "direct observations of children's problem-solving strategies, their ability to benefit from feedback as they ma-

2. For "triangles" only—to be described.

3. We have since dropped the second half of the procedure. The Triangles subtest is the only pre-post assessment.

nipulate the puzzle pieces and compare their products to the models and their skill at applying rules learned in easy items to the more complex designs"— all compatible with dynamic assessment objectives (Interpretive Manual, p. 10).

For the second half of our procedure, the Matrices subtest was selected because of its similarity to one of the tests incorporated into the dynamic assessment procedures of older children by both Feuerstein and Budoff. However, in the case of Matrices, Sternberg (e.g., 1977; Sternberg & Rifkin, 1979) has produced such extensive research that it was decided to join his outline of processes with those to be derived from Feuerstein for the actual mediation. According to Sternberg's (1977) theory, the mandatory processes involved in analogical reasoning include encoding (translating the terms "into an internal representation"), inferring (the relationship), and application (stating the solution) (p. 355). There has been some success in training children to solve analogies, but none of these studies involved children as young as preschool age (reviewed in Sternberg & Rifkin, 1979). Nevertheless, there have been tests of analogical reasoning that have been designed for use with young children, and it is therefore of interest to determine both the ability of preschoolers to solve this kind of problem and their response to intervention.

The decision to use only two subtests, even with extensive intervention, represents a major reduction of tests and time, compared with Feuerstein's LPAD (1979). This direction was taken because of both the limited attention span of the young child and our expectations of difficulty maintaining the involvement of a child referred because of learning difficulties, as well as the practical limitations of the assessment situation for most psychologists. On the one hand, dynamic assessment requires an adequate amount of time to induce cognitive modification; on the other hand, no psychologist can realistically be expected to use this procedure within a school, clinic, or even private setting unless the time span involved is reasonable in terms of the parameters of that setting (e.g., chargeable hours). What needs to be determined is the least amount of time that is "sufficient," realizing that this will vary considerably for every child. The primary issues are to be able to derive information that is truly different from other procedures, that is, that informs intervention decisions, and to provide a *sample* insight into the modifiability of the child, realizing that the assessment is not the intervention, and that the child should be assessed periodically in order to provide ongoing input into the educational process.

In addition to outlining the general cognitive functions to address with MLE, we next needed to determine the exact tasks to use during the mediation phases of the assessment. We chose to use tasks both of inherent interest and relevance to the preschool child and that shared cognitive functions with the criterion test. In the case of Triangles, we selected draw-a-person,[4] block building of a stair from the Gesell tests, and parquetry designs (Playskool),[5] and determined mediation procedures for each cognitive function for each of these tasks, aiming for generalization of the cognitive functions that each shared from one task to the next, and, finally, to the Triangles posttest (see Appendix A for the entire procedure). To increase the information regarding modifiability, each of the mediation tasks involved its own pre–posttest format. The actual mediation is carried out in response to the child's deficiencies and is determined on the spot at the time of assessment. These deficiencies derive from observations of the child's performance on the Triangles and Matrices pretests, as well as from the mediation pretests within the Triangles subsection. Thus, the list of mediation procedures is suggestive and not mandatory for each child.

In the case of the Matrices mediation, this subtest did not lend itself as did the Triangles to the use of separate tasks that incorporated similar cognitive functions. Instead, mediation was designed to address each of the three major cognitive functions suggested as necessary for task solution by Sternberg (1977), translating these into Feuerstein's terms.

Several forms were then developed to facilitate recording and reporting of information from the Preschool Learning Assessment Device (PLAD). Figure 11.1 shows the recording options for the Triangles mediation, and Figure 11.2 shows the format for the recording of Matrices mediation. The examiner makes notations in each of the relevant boxes of the child's behavior in terms of observed cognitive deficiencies and adequacies, as well as of intervention successes and failures. The examiner needs to be familiar with Feuerstein's (1979, 1980) writings on cognitive deficiencies in order to carry out this assessment. Most of this information needs to be noted at the time of occurrence in order to prevent memory lapses, but some can be filled in and elaborated directly following the assessment. A good deal of management is required in order to maintain the flow of the assessment, regulate the child, make written notations, and decide what interventions to offer. At some points, it is simply necessary to tell the child to wait a moment to allow time for quick recording.

Following completion of the assessment, results are summarized and recorded on the Results Feedback Form, shown in Appendix B. This can be used as a partial report to serve as a basis for discussion with teachers and parents, or may be kept by the examiner merely to summarize the assessment,

---

4. This task has been shown by Leviton and Kiraly (1974) to be sensitive to enrichment efforts for young children.

5. Designs originally used are no longer produced; designs from Ideal will be substituted. The reader should also note that the PLAD is an experimental procedure and in the constant process of modification.

FIGURE 11.1. Recording sheet for Triangles test and mediation. Examiner records existence of deficiency, remediation, and response to remediation.

Deficiencies in:	Triangles present	Figure drawing	Block building	Parquetry	Triangles posttest
1. Visual-motor coord.					
2. Verbal concepts					
3. Color matching					
4. Spatial orientation					
5. Spontaneous comparison					
6. Part–whole analysis					
7. Comprehension of prob.					
8. Perception of figure gestalt					
9. Trial–error–impulsive responding					
10. Inflexible approach					
11. Other:					

FIGURE 11.2. Recording sheet for Matrix Analogies training. Examiner records specifics of child's strengths/weaknesses, interventions, response to interventions.

Recording Sheet for Matrix Analogy Training

Deficiences re:	Analogies pretest	Encoding mediation	Inferring mediation	Application mediation	Analogies posttest
Task comprehension					
"Reading" stimuli					
Noting relevant details					
Using cues to infer relationship					
Spontaneous reference to model					
Inferring relationships					
Development of strategy					
Development of hypotheses					
Appropriate vocabulary/ concepts					
Precise communication of responses					

to be incorporated into the larger report. The next and final step is to elaborate the findings of the assessment into an educational plan, illustrated in Figure 11.3. The format of the final plan may be modified to conform more closely to an individualized education plan, but the special components contributed by the PLAD as a dynamic assessment are represented in the categories incorporated into the format as outlined in the figure.

Examples of two cases that have been assessed and reported with the PLAD as a supplementary procedure, utilizing the above forms, are included in Appendices C (case W.F.) and D (case H.R.). These includes the final psychological report, the Results Feedback Form, and the objectives sheet.

The reader should now have an idea of our basic thinking and intentions in designing the PLAD, as well as the procedure to follow. We next turn to our preliminary attempt to research the effectiveness and validity of this new procedure.

Research on the PLAD

One of the most difficult issues in trying to assess the validity of a dynamic procedure concerns the criterion. Static IQ measures traditionally use school achievement as a criterion of predictive and concurrent validity, and are generally recognized as being the best predictors of this criterion. Those of us who support the need for development of dynamic approaches question the appropriateness of achievement as a criterion for the determination of validity of these procedures (Lidz, 1983). Feuerstein (1979) stated his position on validity in the following comments:

> The search for validity of the LPAD is not to be centered on the instruments of assessment but on the changes in the functioning of the individual following the intervention characteristic of the dynamic assessment. Extrinsic criteria can be used as a source of validation of the LPAD only in those cases in which the subsequently prescribed remedial strategies, resulting from the LPAD assessment, have been used. (p. 326)

In support of Feuerstein's position, both Camp (1973) and Carlson and Wiedl (1980) provided evidence of the relatively poor predictive validity of static IQ tests when the criterion is changed from achievement to response to adapted instruction, with the dynamic procedure used by Carlson and Wiedl outpredicting IQ for subjects experiencing adapted (individualized) rather than standard teaching conditions. Babad and Bashi (1975) and Budoff et al. (1971) also provided evidence to support the superiority of the results of dynamic assessment over IQ in predicting response to educational intervention. Therefore, what is ideally needed as a criterion measure for predictive validity is a measure of response of the subjects following exposure to an

Name: _____   Page: _____

Strengths/special behaviors	Cognitive deficiencies/ instructional objectives	Recommended interventions

FIGURE 11.3.   PLAD educational plan form.

educational program individualized on the basis of assessed cognitive functions and deficiencies.

But, what of concurrent validity? It may be that concurrent validity, as test–retest reliability, is not appropriately applied to dynamic assessment. Nevertheless, in our study of the validity of the PLAD, we did attempt to determine concurrent validity, partly for expediency, and partly to see if effects could be found. We strongly wished to avoid the traditional criterion of school achievement, and, instead, chose to respond to the observations of Mercer (1973) regarding the phenomenon of the "6-hour retarded child" (p. 89), and used adaptive behavior. We reasoned that adaptive behavior would more likely reduce the influence of background factors associated with the child's ability to cope with everyday experiences. However, also wishing to reduce the potential unreliability of parental reporting, we selected a measure that could be completed by teachers, the California Preschool Social Competency Scale (Levine, Elzey, & Lewis, 1969). We did not expect our dynamic procedure to outpredict IQ for the criterion of academic achievement, since these two measures share demands on cognitive functions, but we did see the possibility of dynamic assessment more accurately reflecting the child's social competency skills because of the reduced emphasis on cognitive functions that are directly related to classroom achievement, yet are part of the concept of intelligence.

The actual research study involved 60 children between the ages of 3 and 5 years who had been referred for special education services by their teachers. All of the children attended a preschool program for poverty-level children, and all came from urban, mostly black backgrounds. The children were randomly assigned to treatment and control groups, with the treatment group administered the PLAD, and the control group exposed to the same materials for the same length of time, but without the mediation of the PLAD. Each child was seen for two sessions.

In response to the emphasis placed on transfer tasks as measures of learning by Brown and Campione (1984), the children in this study were then tested with two additional subtests from the K-ABC: Face Recognition, representing across-domain transfer (within-domain transfer being simultaneous processing and across-domain being sequential processing), and Hand Movements, representing across-domain transfer. Finally, the classroom teachers were asked to complete the California Preschool Social Competency Scale, as the concurrent criterion measure.

What we were looking for in this study were several things. First, we looked for the extent to which something "different" was happening within the experimental versus control groups, in terms of the differences on the K-ABC posttest scores (i.e., was MLE doing anything for these children?). We expected the posttest scores of the experimental group to increase more than those of the controls in response to the training on related cognitive functions. Second, we looked at differences between the groups in relation to adaptive behavior, anticipating that the posttest results following mediation would outpredict the static posttest scores in relation to this criterion. As another indication of the effectiveness of mediation, we were interested in the extent of generalization as measured by the transfer tasks, expecting greater generalization for the experimental group, and, even for that group, greater within- than across-domain transfer.

The details of this study will be elaborated in a more traditional research journal–oriented manuscript (Thomas & Lidz, in preparation). To summarize the major findings, we first demonstrated that the experimental (E), or mediated, group achieved significantly higher gain scores on both the Triangles and Matrices subtests, whereas the control (C) group showed essentially no gain (Table 11.1). Furthermore, posttest difference scores between the E and C groups on both K-ABC subtests were highly significant ($p < .001$), in favor of the mediated subjects. We interpret this as an indication that the mediation was effective in producing a higher level of performance.

The concurrent validity data correlating Triangles and Matrices posttest scores with the scores of the measure of social competency yielded an r of .55 for E and .35 for C groups on the Triangles (a large, significant difference), and an r of .41 for E and .49 for C groups on Matrices (a nonsignificant difference). We interpret this as indicating that dynamic assessment with the Triangles portion of the PLAD was a significantly better predictor of adaptive

TABLE 11.1. Mean Gain Scores for Triangles and Matrices

		Experimental		Control		
Scale	N	Mean	S.D.	Mean	S.D.	t
Triangles	30	2.63	1.56	.16	.72	7.84*
Matrices	30	1.77	1.49	.03	.75	5.78*

*$p < .001$.

behavior than the static, unmediated, procedure, but that no difference was found for the Matrices portion. Thus, although mediation of both Triangles and Matrices resulted in higher levels of performance on these subtests, the concurrent validity of dynamic assessment using the PLAD with these subjects was demonstrated only for the first half of the procedure (Triangles).

Finally, regarding the issue of intra- and interdomain transfer using other K-ABC subtests, no differences between E and C groups were found. This is in accord with other existing research (see Chapters 2 and 3, this volume).

Future Directions

The study described in this chapter represents the very beginning of our investigations into the applications of dynamic assessment to preschool children as a general concern, and our specific interest in continued development of the PLAD. One area we will pursue is to refine and further operationalize the mediation procedure so that what is done during the mediation portion of the assessment can be communicated in as clear and replicable a fashion as is possible; however, as indicated above, it is not appropriate to strive for complete standardization. Klein (undated; Klein & Feuerstein, 1985) has made important inroads toward this objective, and we follow her lead in developing our own interpretations of MLE. Appendix E portrays a preliminary attempt by the senior author to develop an observational rating scale of MLE. This scale includes most, but not all, of the criteria described by Feuerstein. It was designed for observation of a 10-minute parent–child interaction. The criteria most appropriate to parent–child interaction, but also applicable to the PLAD tasks and that are most likely to occur within such a limited period of time, as well as the criteria attributed the greatest importance by Feuerstein, have been included. However, for use during assessment, it would be appropriate to add the "mediation of change" criterion. This scale is intended for use both in research and for parent and teacher training, and has been designed to provide a means of determining if an MLE process has indeed occurred. Other of the criteria may be included, depending upon the application of the scale. The scale itself will require research, particularly to determine interrater reliability. If this scale is found to be useful, valid, and reliable, it can then be used to investigate the MLE process itself;

TABLE 11.2. Interscorer Percentages of Agreement for MLE Rating Scale (within 1 Point, on Original Scale)

	1	2	3	4	5
1	—	98	95	88	88
2		—	90	92	92
3			—	88	80
4				—	95

for example, to look at the relative importance and contributions of the various components of MLE.

A preliminary attempt has been made by the senior author to determine interrater reliability of the rating scale, using two speech therapists and three psychologists exposed to 2 hours of training. The scorers rated five 10-minute segments of parents teaching their 4-year-old children how to build a dog with Bristle Blocks. The results are portrayed in Table 11.2. These results were calculated for agreement regarding each item on the scale for all five ratings (i.e., a total of 40 items).

Although we have begun research on the concurrent validity of the PLAD, much work remains to be done to further explore validity and reliability in terms meaningful for dynamic assessment (see Chapter 5, this volume). For example, the senior author is in the process of conducting a predictive validity study that compares the PLAD and the pre–posttest K-ABC subscale scores on the Triangles subtest (representing static versus dynamic) as predictors of the response of preschool children to a 10-month intervention program.

Both authors have expressed agreement about relatively greater satisfaction with the Triangles portion of the PLAD, and the research results certainly support this view. There are three routes that could be taken; first, to abandon the Matrices, should the Triangles section prove to be adequate in and of itself; second, to improve the Matrices mediation to increase access to the basic processes of this skill and to increase the meaningfulness of the procedure for the young child; or, third, to look at an alternative subtest for use as a dynamic extension. We hope that others will join us in developing research to inform these decisions.

REFERENCES

Babad, E., & Bashi, J. (1975). *Final report: An educational test of the validity of learning potential measurement.* Cambridge, MA: Research Institute for Educational Problems, Inc.

Ballester, L. E., & Lidz, C. S. *The relationship between specific cognitive strategies and learning in preschool children.* Manuscript submitted for publication.

Brown, A. L., & Campione, J. C. (1984). Modifying intelligence or modifying cognitive skills: More than a semantic quibble? In D. K. Detterman & R. J. Sternberg (Eds.), *How and how much can intelligence be increased* (pp. 215–230). Norwood, NJ: Ablex.

Brown, A. L., & DeLoache, J. S. (1983). Metacognitive skills. In M. Donaldson, R. Grieve, & C. Pratt (Eds.), *Early childhood development and education—Readings in psychology* (pp. 280–289). New York: Guilford Press.

Budoff, M. (1969). Learning potential: A supplementary procedure for assessing the ability to reason. *Seminars in Psychiatry, 1,* 278–290.

Budoff, M., Meskin, J., & Harrison, R. H. (1971). Educational test of the learning-potential hypothesis. *American Journal of Mental Deficiency, 76*(2), 159–169.

Burns, M. S. (1980). *Preschool children's approach and performance on cognitive tasks.* Unpublished masters thesis, George Peabody College for Teachers of Vanderbilt University.

Burns, M. S. (1985). *Comparison of "graduated prompt" and "mediational" dynamic assessment and static assessment with young children* (Technical Report No. 2). Nashville, TN: Peabody College, Vanderbilt University, John F. Kennedy Center for Research on Education and Human Development.

Camp, B. W. (1973). Psychometric tests and learning in severely disabled readers. *Journal of Learning Disabilities, 6*(7), 512–517.

Carlson, J. S., & Wiedl, K. H. (1980). Applications of a dynamic testing approach in intelligence assessment: Empirical results and theoretical formulations. *Zeitschrift für Differentielle und Diagnostische Psychologie, 1*(4), 303–318.

Case, R. (1978) Intellectual development from birth to adulthood: A neo-Piagetian interpretation. In R. S. Siegler (Ed.), *Children's thinking: What develops?* (pp. 37–71). Hillsdale, NJ: Erlbaum.

Etzel, B. C. (1978). *A review of intervention approaches based on learning-assessment (for early identification and treatment of at-risk preschool level children)* (ECI document No. 19). Lawrence, KS: University of Kansas, Kansas Research Institute for the Early Childhood Education of the Handicapped.

Feuerstein, R. (1979). *The dynamic assessment of retarded performers: The learning potential assessment device, theory, instruments, and techniques.* Baltimore: University Park Press.

Feuerstein, R. (1980). *Instrumental enrichment. An intervention program for cognitive modifiability.* Baltimore: University Park Press.

Flavell, J. H. (1977). *Cognitive development.* Englewood Cliffs, NJ: Prentice-Hall.

Greeno, J. G., & Simon, H. A. (1984). *Problem solving and reasoning.* (Code 442 PTJ, report No. UPITT/LRDC/ONR/APS-14). Arlington, VA: Personnel and Training Research Program, Office of Naval Research.

Haake, R. J., & Somerville, S. C. (1985). Development of logical research skills in infancy. *Developmental Psychology, 21*(1), 176–186.

Hawkins, J., Pea, R. D., Glick, J., & Scribner, S (1984). "Merds that laugh don't like mushrooms": Evidence for deductive reasoning by preschoolers. *Developmental Psychology, 20*(4), 584–594.

Kaufman, A. S., & Kaufman, N. L. (1983). *K-ABC. Kaufman Assessment Battery for Children. Administration and Scoring Manual, and Interpretive Manual.* Circle Pines, MN: American Guidance Service.

Klein, P. S. (undated). *Criteria for observation of mediated learning experience in infancy and early childhood.* Unpublished manuscript, Bar Ilan University, Department of Education, Tel Aviv, Israel.

Klein, P. S. & Feuerstein, R. (1985). Environmental variables and cognitive development: Identification of the potent factors in adult-child interaction. In S. Harel & N. J. Anastasiow (Eds.), The *at-risk infant: Psycho/Socio/Medical aspects.* Baltimore: Paul H. Brookes.

Kogan, N. (1976). *Cognitive styles in infancy and early childhood.* Hillsdale, NJ: Erlbaum.

Levine, S., Elzey, F. F., & Lewis, M. (1969). *Manual for the California Preschool Social Competency Scale.* Palo Alto, CA: Consulting Psychologists Press.

Leviton, H., & Kiraly, J., Jr. (1974). The effects of a short training program on the Draw-A-

Man Test scores of pre-school children. *Educational and Psychological Measurements*, *34*, 435–438.

Lidz, C. S. (1983). Dynamic assessment and the preschool child. *Journal of Psychoeducational Assessment*, *1*(1), 59–72.

Luria, A. R. (1979). *The making of mind—A personal account of Soviet psychology*. Cambridge, MA: Harvard University Press.

Mercer, J. R. (1973). *Labeling the mentally retarded*. Berkeley, CA: University of California Press.

Oakland, T. (1972). The effects of test-wiseness materials on standardized performance of pre-school disadvantaged children. *Journal of School Psychology*, *10*(4), 355–360.

Scholnick, E. K., & Osler, S. F. (1969). Effect of pretest experience on concept attainment in lower- and middle-class children. *Developmental Psychology*, *1*(4), 440–443.

Siegler, R. S. (1983). Information processing approaches to development. In P. Mussen (Ed.). *Handbook of child psychology* (4th ed.). *Volume I: History, theory, and methods* (pp. 129–211). New York: John Wiley.

Sternberg, R. J. (1977). Component processes in analogical reasoning. *Psychological Review*, *84*(4), 353–378.

Sternberg, R. J. (1979). Stalking the IQ quark. *Psychology Today*, *13*, 242–254.

Sternberg, R. J., & Nigro, G. (1980). Developmental patterns in the solution of verbal analogies. *Child Development*, *51*, 27–38.

Sternberg, R. J., & Rifkin, B. (1979). The development of analogical reasoning processes. *Journal of Experimental Child Psychology*, *27*, 195–232.

Thomas, C., & Lidz, C. S. The effects of mediation on the performance of disadvantaged preschool children. Manuscript submitted for publication.

Vurpillot, E. (1968). The development of scanning strategies and their relation to visual differentiation. *Journal of Experimental Child Psychology*, *6*, 632–650.

Weir, M. W. (1964). Developmental changes in problem-solving strategies. *Psychological Review*, *71*, 473–490.

Wellman, H. M. (1977). The early development of intentional memory behavior. *Human Development*, *20*, 86–101.

White, B., Kaban, B. T., & Attanucci, J. S. (1979). *The origins of human competence—The final report of the Harvard Preschool Project*. Lexington, MA: D. C. Heath and Co.

Whitely, S. E., & Dawis, R. V. (1974). Effects of cognitive intervention on latent ability measured from analogy items. *Journal of Educational Psychology*, *66*(5), 710–717.

Wood, D., Bruner, J. S., & Ross, G. (1976). The role of tutoring in problem solving. *Journal of Child Psychology and Psychiatry*, *17*, 89–100.

Zaporozhets, A. V., & Elkonin, D. B. (Eds.). (1971). *The psychology of preschool children* (J. Shybut & S. Simon, transl.). Cambridge, MA: MIT Press. (Original work published 1964)

Appendix A: PLAD Procedures

Triangles

Test

Administer Triangles subtest of K-ABC; observe for problems with:

- Visual–motor coordination
- Color matching
- Spatial orientation
- Part–whole analysis
- Comprehension of nature of problem
- Perception of figure gestalt
- Trial-and-error/impulsive responding
- Inflexibility of approach

Mediate

I. Administer figure drawing: ask child to "draw a picture of a child, a boy or a girl." Observe for problems cited above.
   A. Mediate for following deficiencies according to response of the child.
      1. *Visual–motor coordination:* Model, and have child practice drawing, vertical and horizontal lines, circles, triangles, and rectangles. Correct pencil grip and posture to optimize productions. Provide verbal labels to guide movements: "across and stop"; "down and stop"; "around and stop." (Use verbal directions to inhibit impulsivity.)
      2. *Spatial orientation:* Model and practice orientation of puzzle pieces, adding language to action of examiner. Review incorrect orientation to discuss why other orientation is better. With puzzle, teach vocabulary of up, down (e.g., "The head is up; the legs are down"), middle, on top, on bottom.
      3. *Part–whole analysis:* Use puzzle to discuss parts of body. Ask child to refer to self and examiner as reference points (promote comparison with model). Play game of "what's missing" by hiding pieces; let child do same for examiner.
      4. *Comprehension of nature of problems:* Help child verbalize what the task is, what needs to be done, at each step in the process.
      5. *Perception of figure gestalt:* With puzzle, reinforce what correct placement of figure is, and then play game of placing pieces in bizarre locations. Ask child "What's wrong?" and to correct. Encourage the child to use words to describe problem.
      6. *Trial-and-error/impulsive responding:* Restrain child's excessive movements with verbal cues (e.g., "wait") or hand restraint. Ask child how he or she plans to proceed—what will he or she do first, next? Guide into a sequential plan, reinforcing concepts of first, next, last. If child is unable to verbalize, provide the language she needs.
      7. *Inflexibility of approach:* If child drew a girl, ask to draw a boy, and vice versa; encourage to add more details ("What else?"). With manikin, when assembled according to one sequence, ask if there's another way to do it, and work with child to carry out an alternative plan. Whatever the child does, encourage additions or alternatives.
   B. Repeat initial request to draw a child.

II.   Administer block building design: Examiner builds a "stair" behind a screen as in the
      Gesell Preschool Test, tells child to look carefully, takes apart, and asks child to make one
      just like it (give same number blocks needed). Observe for above deficiencies.

A.   Mediate for following deficiencies according to response of child.
      1.   *Visual–motor coordination:* Help child pick up and place blocks with finger, hand,
           or arm placement modifications necessary to optimize performance. Encourage
           child to use both hands, one to place and one to stabilize.
      2.   *Spatial orientation:* Provide model for child, and discuss concept of "stairs," and
           orientation of gradations of steps (placement of whole figure, location of step
           side). Build two models and move one around in different orientations, getting
           child to compare and note differences; have child move one to match model.
           Refer to the model to help the child guide his or her movements.
      3.   *Part–whole analysis:* Help child focus on components of construction, on the idea
           of decrease by one block with ascent, *counting the number of blocks* required,
           and the need for a solid section to support the decreasing side.
      4.   *Comprehension of nature of the problem:* Help child to verbalize what he or she
           is to do; ask what figure looks like; reinforce concept of steps or stairs.
      5.   *Perception of figure gestalt:* Focus child's attention on critical features; make
           "wrong" constructs and help child discuss what's wrong (by means of comparison
           with model).
      6.   *Trial-and-error/impulsive responding:* Ask child for plan regarding how to proceed.
           Discuss pros and cons of plan, what first, next, last.
      7.   *Inflexibility of approach:* Whatever plan was used, ask for another (e.g., if pro-
           ceeded horizontally, push for vertically.)
      8.   If the child is unable to build stair, have the child repeat the procedure with a
           more simple block design:

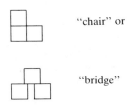

"chair" or

"bridge"

B.   Repeat request to build a 10-block stair.

III. Administer parquetry: Ask child to complete figure of girl design (of Parquetry Blocks
      and designs) with the design to his or her left as a model. (Provide blank sheet of paper
      on which to place pieces.)
      A.   Mediate on an alternate design for the following deficiencies according to the response
           of the child at initial presentation.
           1.   *Visual–motor coordination:* Help child find hand and finger positions to manip-
                ulate pieces optimally; encourage child to use two hands, one for manipulation,
                the other for helping or stabilizing.
           2.   *Spatial orientation:* Focus child's attention on matching shape positions to the

model; discuss where the point should be; have the child place pieces on top of the page to match model and then do it off the page.

   If the child is unable to build the design apart from the model, have him or her build the design on top of the model. Then, slide the model from beneath the design and ask the child to show where various blocks are in the model and in the design. Play "what's missing" by removing a piece from the model and asking the child to show what was taken on the design.

3. *Part–whole analysis:* Elicit association to what the design looks like as a whole (give name if necessary); discuss sections and give names for parts (e.g., house, rocket).

4. *Comprehension of nature of the problem:* Help child verbalize what needs to be done at each step of the process—even if it is one or two words.

5. *Perception of figure gestalt:* Make design for child with missing parts and have child tell what's missing (and add part). Make sure the child understands that all parts must touch in order to make the picture. (Similar to #2 above.)

6. *Trial-and-error/impulsive responding:* Encourage reference back and forth to the model; discuss a plan for proceeding with construction. Inhibit non-goal-directed manipulation of pieces. Verbally cue with "Wait; let's think."

7. *Inflexibility of approach:* Encourage alternative plan ("where else can we start; what other color can we use?")

8. *Color matching:* Focus attention on matching colors; assure child has correct names at least receptively; have child find color examiner points to.

B. Repeat initial request to complete figure of girl.

Test

Administer Triangles subtest of K-ABC. Observe for changes in success in constructions and for existence of changes in deficiencies.

Appendix B: Preschool Learning Assessment Device Results Feedback Form
(Blank Form)

Name: _____   Dates of Assessment: _____
Birthdate: _____   C.A.: _____
Examiner: _____   School/Program: _____

Pre–Posttest Information:

K-ABC   Pre   Post
  Triangles   Comments:
  Transfer tasks:
  Face Recognition
  Hand Movements

Pre–Post Changes in:
  Figure drawing—

  Block building—

  Parquetry—

Intervention Gradients:

Figure drawing	1	2	3	4	5	6
	min.					max.
Block building	1	2	3	4	5	6
	min.					max.
Parquetry	1	2	3	4	5	6
	min.					max.

Key (later steps include previous steps):

1. Sufficient to require only repetition of instructions or request to "do it again."
2. Requires rewording of instructions.
3. Requires breaking task down into simpler units; verbal restraint of impulsivity.
4. Requires simplification and verbal guidance of movements while working on task; may also require repetition of instructions and of task units.
5. Requires modeling; may require physical restraint of impulsivity.
6. Requires moving through the task.

Appendix C: PLAD: Sample Psychological Assessment

Case: W.F. (female)   Dates of Assessment: May, June, 1984
Date of Birth: 11/7/79   C.A.: 4–7

Reason for Referral

W.F. has been referred with concerns regarding both her speech and learning ability. Her speech is unclear; she has difficulty following directions, and she has not learned the content of her preschool curriculum. Speech and language assessment (4/84) finds normal articulation but moderate to severe language delays. W.F.'s mother describes a full term, normal pregnancy with birth weight of 6 lbs., 15 oz. Developmental milestones are recalled as fast for walking but slow for talking. At home, her mother notes slowness in school-related tasks but normal play. There are no health problems, but a vision checkup is pending. She is an only child. Her father died four years ago.

Findings

W.F. is a pretty, nicely dressed girl who is cooperative with the assessment. She moves and speaks slowly, with monotonic verbal expression and stiff muscle movements. She holds her eyes close to the pages of pictures, but appears to see well enough for the assessment. Most of her communication is in short phrases. She is not able to relate what she had eaten for the lunch which immediately preceded the testing session. Because of time restraints and absences, classroom observation was not possible.

   W.F. was administered three standardized cognitive measures and an informal test-teach-retest procedure (Preschool Learning Assessment Device/PLAD). Her teacher completed a questionnaire describing her social adjustment. Results of the standardized measures are as follows:

1. *Stanford-Binet Intelligence Scale:*
   IQ 72, MA3–9 (corrected MA 3–3); Basal age 3–0; Ceiling age 4–6.
2. *McCarthy Scales of Children's Abilities:*
   General Cognitive Index = 63 (MA 2–9).

Subtest	Scale Index	Age Equivalent
Verbal	36	3–6
Perceptual–Performance	23	2–6
Quantitative	24	2–6
Memory	39	3–6
(motor, omitted)		

3. *Developmental Tasks for Kindergarten Readiness*, by Lesiak: Norm ratings range A to D.

   Body concepts—   Color naming: below D
      awareness: B   Relational concepts: below D
      use: below D   Number knowledge—
   Auditory association: below D   counting: C (with help)
   Visual discrimination: D   use: below D
   Alphabet knowledge: D   naming: below D

4. *California Preschool Social Competency Scale:* Percentile score: 71.

W.F.'s current level of cognitive functioning is estimated within the "borderline deficient" to "deficient" range, or, educationally, within the "educable retarded" level. She shows relative strength with verbal and memory tasks; however, this verbal strength is for the more rote, imitative demands, as she has a great deal of difficulty answering questions, giving word meanings, and completing verbal opposites to the extent of showing a significant processing problem. While she shows adequate visual discrimination and only mildly delayed copying ability, she shows significant perceptual and spatial problems, again showing difficulty with processing the elements she appears to record accurately. Her attempts at block building are highly unusual in degree and nature of perceptual inaccuracy. For example, she attempted to build the following: ⊞ as ⊔⊔ and ⊔⊤ . Severe difficulty was also evident in other visual-perceptual-motor tasks such as puzzles and imitation of a sequence of taps, and she was totally unable to organize a recognizable drawing of a human figure (drew scattered circles), although was able to add some parts to an incomplete figure organized for her.

W.F. could answer some simple "what to do" types of questions involving her own activities, such as what to do when thirsty and what you do with books; however, her sentence construction suggested possible syntactical problems and she rarely used full sentences.

W.F.'s mastery of preacademic learning is also low for her age. She can identify most major body parts receptively, but not describe their use (eyes: "play with it;" legs: "broke it", and repeated "break" for the rest). She neither named nor receptively recognized any of the primary colors except blue, and, when rechecked on blue, she could not relocate this color. Her knowledge of basic concepts is poor. When asked to locate items on the page, she would often not respond to the instruction "show me", but would require the more explicit "put your finger on". She also tended to choose the first position among two or more choices and needed to be encouraged to look at all the choices. When counting, she would not spontaneously begin with "1" but, if started at 1 by the adult, she could rote count to 6. She did not show 1:1 correspondence, and could name no letters or numbers. She also gave her age incorrectly as 3. W.F. tends to nod her head "yes" when asked any question, apparently responding to the tone of voice or phrasing rather than the content, further suggesting a processing problem.

W.F.'s ratings on the social competency scale place her well above average; however, with the serious qualifications that some of the ratings appeared more positive than is actually the case of her behavior because of some inadequacies of the scale used and W.F.'s passivity and lack of responsiveness in class. For example, she was rated highly on the item tapping her ability to handle changes in routine, but the item choices were not appropriate, as W.F. tends to be nonresponsive to these changes rather than flexibly adaptive. Nevertheless, these results do contrast with her cognitive functioning and suggest that her social adaptation is at a higher level than her school-related learning.

W.F.'s response to the informal teaching procedure showed considerably more motivation and task involvement than was evident in any other circumstance, especially reports of classroom behavior. Her ability to improve her level of success on a test task from a deficient to average level suggests that she has potential for change. However, the great amount of teacher investment which was required to induce this change further documents W.F.'s need for a specialized, individualized instructional situation.

When W.F. was given the opportunity to move from a passive to active role in the learning situation, she brightened up, and, most importantly, showed long term retention (over the four days between sessions) of what she learned. This was carried out by showing her how to play a simple game (hiding her eyes, and then determining which body part of a puzzle was missing), and then having her take on the role of teacher, with the Examiner as student.

There were two incidents where W.F. showed initiative and revelation of higher order thinking skills than were otherwise characteristic of her functioning. The first occurred during instruction for the concepts of up/down, using arm positions of the human figure puzzle to illustrate these positions. After working on this for several minutes, W.F. suddenly placed the arms in a straight-out position and looked impishly up at the Examiner as if to say "now what; is this up or down?" The second example occurred during the "what's missing" game with the same puzzle, where W.F. broke the set established by the Examiner of hiding one part at a time, and hid several pieces at once. These two incidents were dramatic in their display of active thinking and initiative in the learning situation, behaviors which had never previously been noted.

W.F.'s areas of strength in the diagnostic teaching situation include her ability to work and attend for long periods of time without tiring. This makes her easy and pleasant to work with. She also shows flexibility in her problem-solving; that is, she does not get stuck on one solution in perceptual-motor tasks, but will explore a number of possibilities. Her cognitive deficiencies include her lack of basic concepts necessary to many age-level tasks, lack of spontaneous comparative behavior, impulsivity during task presentations, and perseveration in terms of difficulty with response inhibition. Remedial suggestions for each of these are elaborated in the attached IPP.

Recommendations

Programmatic recommendations include follow-up regarding W.F.'s pending vision evaluation, referral for language therapy when she enters kindergarten, and referral for the transitioning child project while in kindergarten so that her progress will be monitored and an individualized program will be written. W.F. shows considerable risk for learning disability, affecting both language and perceptual-motor-spatial areas. There is evidence that her potential is above her currently mildly retarded level, although it will require intensive and ongoing remediation to induce higher level functioning.

Appendix C: Preschool Learning Assessment Device Results Feedback Form

Name: _____WF (female)_____   Dates of Assessment: ___6/14, 6/18/84___
Birthdate: _____11-7-79_____   C.A.: ____4-7____
Examiner: _____C. Lidz_____   School/Program: _____Head Start_____

Pre–Posttest Information:

K-ABC:	Pre	Post
Triangles	6	9
Matrices	10	9
Face Recognition	5	7
Hand Movements	9	6

Comments:
scores recorded are
scaled scores; results
show intra, but not
inter-domain transfer.
Triangles training re-
sulted in significant im-
provement; matrices
training resulted in es-
sentially no change.

Pre–Post Changes in:

Figure drawing—number of features increased from 3 (head, feet, leg) to 4 (head, nose, hair, ears); or, alternatively, number of facial features increased from 0 to 4. Neither drawing is easily recognizable. Both show considerable organization, spatial orientation, and integration problems. The second has consid- erably increased perseveration.

Block building—Block construction changed from an unrelated at- tempt to one which duplicated the peripheral outline of the model; that is, the horizontal and vertical extremes. Her final product was still not an exact reproduction.

Parquetry—Parquetry improved regarding color match and spatial orientation of the rocket wings.[1] She continued to have a shape mismatch for the tail, and the interior remained correct.
1. A different parquetry set was used here. It is no longer manufactured.

Intervention Gradients:

Figure drawing	1	2	3	4	5 X	6
	min.					max.
Block building	1	2	3	4	X	6
	min.					max.
Parquetry	1	2	3	4 X	5	6
	min.					max.

1. A different parquetry set was used here. It is no longer manufactured.

PLAD Educational Plan

Name: __WF (female)__

Strengths/special behaviors	Cognitive Deficiencies/Instructional Objectives	Recommended Interventions
Shows flexibility in manipulation of materials. She will spontaneously move pieces around in a variety of orientations in an attempt to problem-solve. However, her moves tend to be trial and error rather than planned and anticipated. She showed two instances of initiative and spontaneity in her thinking, both when working with the human figure puzzle: 1. When reviewing up/down concepts re arm/hand placement, she placed the arms out straight, as if to challenge the Examiner to label that up or down. 2. When playing "what's missing", she broke the model set by the Examiner by removing one piece at a time and removed three at once. Shows increased affect and cognitive processing when she is in leader/teacher role in a game previously modeled for her. Showed improvement in spontaneous comparative behavior by the time of retest. Able to work for long periods of time (with activity changes) without tiring or losing attention (in one to one active intervention situation, can work for over an hour with little stress).	1. Lacks basic conceptual tools necessary for task— a. Needs to demonstrate knowledge of up/down. b. Needs to respond appropriately to questions involving "or" choices. c. Needs to demonstrate knowledge of names of primary colors and basic shapes. d. Needs to respond to "what" questions appropriately, and to differentiate between "what" and "where" questions. e. Needs to develop one to one correspondence in counting up to five and to answer "how many" questions to five.	1. Requires maximal cuing and much repetition, with demonstration and induction of action, in order to grasp concepts. "Or" choices: use snack food. Ask: do you want this one or that one. Ask her to draw a picture and choose between two colors. Emphasize: "no, just one" when she echoes both choices or tries to take both. Have her play teacher and ask questions re choices. Begin color and number concepts at matching level. Play follow direction games involving 1 and 2: hop on one leg; hop on 2 legs; raise two hands; touch one foot, etc. Introduce absurdities such as "touch 2 noses" and encourage creative problem solving (e.g., she can touch her nose and someone else's. Attach color concepts to food: yellow banana, red apple, etc. Play game with M&M's: "you may eat the red one"; if she misses, she doesn't get one.

Name: __WF (female)__

Strengths/special behaviors	Cognitive Deficiencies/Instructional Objectives	Recommended Interventions
	2. Lacks spontaneous comparative behavior, which relates to deficiencies regarding part/whole analysis, i.e. she doesn't look, so can't analyze. a. Needs to refer to model when copying a construction to guide construction activity and to check end product: will refer to model two or more times while building and at least once to check final product.	2. Play mirror game, taking turns re who is the mirror; i.e., imitate postures and body positions. This should also help problem with spatial orientation. Play imitation games with sequences of hand movements. Have her copy simple block constructions, parquetry designs, pegboard patterns; verbally describe to her the errors and how to correct them. Emphasize the need to look at the model; point out what to look at about the model. • Play "what's missing" games with pictures of common objects. Cover over or remove part of the object when her eyes are closed and ask her "what's missing". Let her play teacher role after the game is modeled for her.
	3. Impulsive at input stage; when asked to imitate sequence, will begin before model sequence is completed; when many materials are within reach, will begin to manipulate materials before the instructions are completed: will wait for completion of instructions before proceeding with task.	3. • Tell her to wait. • Rest hands on her to inhibit handling of materials and to signal "wait." • Use pointing to indicate "my turn" vs. "your turn." • Begin with any of above interventions, but drop them out after a while to see if she shows signs of self-inhibition. Reinstate if she loses control.
	4. Perseverative responses in drawings, which relates to impulsivity at output,	4. Teach her to verbalize to control actions as she draws: e.g., when drawing a cir-

lack of number concepts, and poor part/whole analysis:

- Will draw simple pictures of common objects (e.g. house, tree) and human figure with correct number of parts (correct according to model).

5. Difficulty with spatial orientation shown in shape placement and location of body parts in drawings:

   a. Will draw simple pictures of common objects and human figure with correct location of parts.

   b. Will correctly orient at least five major shapes to duplicate model.

cle, "around and stop."

- Review rote counting and 1:1 correspondence from 1 through 3.
- Teach her to verbalize to repetitive sequences, e.g. hand clapping and tapping: "1,2,3, stop."
- Have her copy simple drawings and model/coach re analysis of parts: e.g. draw a house; "Let's begin with a square. How can we draw a square? Where shall we put it? Shall we make it big or small? How many windows? Where do they go? Shall we use a circle or square for the windows? . . ."

5. With puzzle pieces of human body, assemble and discuss parts in terms of spatial orientation and location.

- Review basic concepts of up/down, top/bottom, etc. in following direction and movement games such as follow the leader and Simon Says. Reemphasize what is taught in group on an individual basis.
- Play follow direction game by taking turns telling where pieces should be, using puzzles or block designs, e.g. "put the square on top." "put the triangle on bottom." The goal is to get the new construct to look like the model with verbal direction only.

317

Appendix D: PLAD: Sample Psychological Assessment

Case: H.R. (male)   C.A.: 4 years 6 months

Reason for Referral

H.R. has been showing delays in all areas, particularly regarding language and visual–motor development. Assessment has been requested to estimate his levels of functioning, to determine areas of special need, and to provide recommendations for intervention. Unfortunately, H.R.'s program has been closed for several months because of asbestos problems. He was observed briefly in class, but the assessment was carried out by special arrangement with his mother while his center was closed. Audiometric testing found his hearing to be normal for speech and language development, but noted a history of chronic colds and upper respiratory infections. He has been receiving speech and language services. Between November, 1982 and October, 1984 assessments, his receptive and expressive language progressed from severely to moderately impaired; limited attention span was noted with occasional impulsivity. Occupational therapy assessment found delays in both fine and gross motor functions.

Findings

H.R. is a child of normal physical appearance. He speaks with a high-pitched, low-volume voice. His speech is at times indistinct, particularly when he doesn't know an answer. He has not established hand dominance, but shows some preference for his left hand. When he draws, he holds the pencil in a fist-like grasp midway up the pencil. Maintenance of attention and restraining impulsive interactions with materials are issues for him. He also tends to take a passive stance in all learning situations, to the extent of asking the examiner to do some of the work for him before he makes an initial attempt.

The following measures were administered:

1. *Stanford-Binet Intelligence Scale:* IQ 75; MA: 3.9 (Corrected MA: 3.3); Basal Age 3.0; Ceiling Age 5.0.
2. *McCarthy Scales of Children's Abilities:*

Subtest	Scale Index	Age Equivalent
Verbal	37	3.6
Perceptual–Performance	32	3.0
Quantitative	27	2.6
Memory	43	4.0

   General Cognitive Index: 68 (Age Equivalent 3.0).
3. *Developmental Tasks for Kindergarten Readiness* (normed ratings):

   Body concepts—
     awareness: below D
     use: below D
   Auditory association: below D
   Visual discrimination: B
   Visual motor: C

   Color naming: below D
   Relational concepts: below D
   Number knowledge—
     counting: B
     use: below D
     naming: below D
   Alphabet knowledge: D

4. *Woodcock–Johnson Scales of Independent Behavior* (short form): Age score: 5.1; Instructional range: 4.0 to 6.2.
5. Informal test–teach–retest procedure (Preschool Learning Assessment Device): results incorporated into interpretations.

Excerpt from Body of Report

Despite H.R.'s low level of performance, he demonstrated modifiability during a brief period of intervention. It is necessary to interpret his behaviors of echolalia, inattention, and mumbled speech as cues that the task is too difficult. As he has difficulty organizing many pictures or objects, tasks need to be structured for him, while teaching him how to organize and analyze the work for himself. To aid his delayed visual-motor development, he needs guidance regarding how to hold a pencil/crayon, experience completing drawings and copying from a model, as well as free and unstructured paper/pencil time.

H.R. needs to learn to refer to a model when he is copying and guidance to help him know what to notice when he is looking at the model. Because of his impulsivity, he often misses the message of directions. It is necessary to assure that he has heard the complete direction before proceeding and to teach him to wait and listen before manipulating the materials. Opportunities for success and independent task completion increase his willingness to work; it is important to assure him he is working on something he has a chance of doing well, to provide the appropriate guidance to ensure success, and, when possible, allow him to be the teacher.

Appendix D: Preschool Learning Assessment Device Results Feedback Form

Name: _____H. R._____   Dates of Assessment: ___2/25/85___

Birthdate: _____8/19/80_____   C.A.: _____4 yrs. 6 mos._____

Examiner: _____   School/Program: _____

Pre–Posttest Information:

K-ABC	Pre	Post	Comments: made
Triangles	2+ (9)	4+(11)	significant improvement
Matrices	not admin.		from pretest to posttest,
Face Recognition	not admin.		even though pretest was
Hand Movements	not admin.		average. Improved re

Comments: made significant improvement from pretest to posttest, even though pretest was average. Improved re comparative behavior and part–whole analysis. Important: on posttest, began to show verbalization to self to guide problem solution. Important: attitude change–at end said: ''I did a good job'' (compared to previous passivity).

Pre–Post Changes in:

Figure drawing—Change was minimal but in positive direction. Began with a single wiggly line; posttest was concentric circular scribbles. Problem in organizing the concept/percept for himself. Much better at adding missing parts when structure is begun for him. Shows deficiencies in motor execution, passivity, and impulsivity.

Block building—Showed originality in hiding game–took more than 1. This was the most difficult for him–very hard time with part–whole analysis, exacerbated by inattention and impulsivity. Improved re achieving more of a step–like construction, but still far from model.

Parquetry—Most successful of the tasks; responded quite well to having task broken down (covering over sections)–again suggests he has problem with part–whole analysis. Needs much structure to inhibit impulsive interaction with materials. Improved re adding tail and center pieces–moderate, not great, improvement.

Intervention Gradients:

Figure drawing
(min)	1	2	3	4	X̶	6	(max)

Block building
(min)	1	2	3	4	X̶	6	(max)

Parquetry
(min)	1	2	X	4	5	6	(max)

PLAD Educational Plan

Name: _____ H.R. (male)

Strengths/special behaviors	Cognitive deficiencies/instructional objectives	Recommended interventions
1. Despite difficulties, did respond to efforts to keep him involved with tasks for 1½ hours, with one break.	1. Short attention span/distractibility:	1. a. Interpret his echolalia, increased mumbling and loss of attention as a communication that the work is too difficult. State this observation to him and then work to modify or change the task.
2. Showed instance of original thinking in game where pieces of puzzle were hidden; examiner modeled hiding one piece; he initiated hiding two.	• Will maintain involvement with construction task up to 30 minutes aided, and 10 minutes, unaided.	b. Refocus his attention by calling his name or touching his arm.
3. Showed ability to be modified, and, particularly to transfer what he learned to criterion task. Level of modifiability was low–moderate, requiring great amount of structuring.	• Will attend to 5-minute story and be able to answer two questions concerning who the story was about and what happened.	c. Organize and structure tasks for him; when he can do work, increase information given to him—e.g., don't ask him just to "draw" a certain picture, but have him copy or complete a drawing, with the goal of having him do it without the model.
4. Most important gain was his spontaneous use of verbalization at the end to guide his actions in solving criterion task (posttest).		d. Have him take turns being the teacher once he knows what to do.
5. Showed ability to become more active and motivated; his passive, uninvolved attitude modified to the point where, at the end, he spontaneously said, "I did a good job!"		e. Provide contingency for task completion.
		f. Use tasks that can be completed within short periods of time.
		g. Involve visual–motor component when possible.
		h. Teach comparative behavior: to look at the model, and what to notice when looking.

Name: _____ H.R. _____

Strengths/special behaviors	Cognitive deficiencies/instructional objectives	Recommended interventions
	2. Impulsive interaction with materials: • will listen to directions before proceeding with tasks.	2. a. Limit materials available to those needed for task. b. Cue him to "wait and listen" before proceeding. c. Provide gentle physical restraint to inhibit touching materials. d. Ask him to tell what he will do before proceeding. e. Play games where he has to look and describe objects without touching them, e.g., "I spy," or "You're getting hot/cold"
	3. Difficulty with part–whole analysis and procedural planning for a task: • will complete age-appropriate visual–motor task without external structure; for example, drawing a picture of a person or building a block design from a model.	3. a. Model and teach him how to cover over parts of tasks so as to simplify. b. Talk with him about where and how to start and help him to keep to the plan. c. Help him see patterns to help structure the task, e.g., "Shall we do all the reds first?" d. Keep reminding him of the whole or of the end goal ("What are we making? Where are we going?").

4. Work in content areas of verbal–spatial concepts (e.g., up/down) and fine motor skill (has fist grasp; switches hands; has poor pencil control).

4.
a. Correct grasp.
b. Remind him to use preferred hand.
c. Remind him to hold the pencil at bottom for better control.
d. Be sure to give him thick pencils and crayons.
e. Try sloping the drawing surface.
f. Teach spatial concepts by having him follow one-step directions using the concept (put the arms up; move the pencil down).
g. Have him play game where he describes what he will do with an object, e.g., "I throw the ball up" (have children take turns with two or three concepts that have been modeled by teacher).

Appendix E: MLE Observation Form and Rating Scale—Revised*

Child's Name _____ Date: _____ Rater: _____

1. *Intentionality:* Mediator deliberately and actively assumes the role of teacher and tries to instruct and get the child to perform the task (scored within the first 5 minutes).
    - 0 = Not present
    - 1 = Fades in and out
    - 2 = Moderately engaged
    - 3 = Totally and consistently engaged

    Observation:

2. *Reciprocity:* Child responds to mediator in the role of learner (scored within the first 5 minutes).
    - 0 = Not present
    - 1 = Fades in and out
    - 2 = Moderately engaged
    - 3 = Totally and consistently engaged

    Observation:

3. *Mediation of Meaning:* Mediator helps child make sense out of task by attributing meaning to whole or parts, imparting values or affect; these must relate to the object or concept involved.
    - 0 = Not present
    - 1 = Labels parts
    - 2 = Refers to whole percept or concept
    - 3 = Adds activity, animation, elaboration to labels

    Observation:

4. *Transcendence (includes sharing):* Mediator relates task to experiences and concepts beyond the immediate situation, including relations with child's experiences, making inferences, determining cause and effect. If it relates to child's experiences, it is transcendence; if to mediator's, sharing.
    - 0 = Not present
    - 1 = Relates to a similar concept/percept
    - 2 = Relates to past or future experience
    - 3 = Promotes inferential thinking, cause/effect

*For use for parent–child interaction. Scale developed by C. S. Lidz, based on R. Feuerstein.

Observation:

5. *Mediation of feelings of competence:* Mediator regulates task to enable child to succeed, makes comments or nonverbal indications of encouragement or praise.
   a. *Task regulation:*
      - 1 = Not present
      - 1 = Passive intervention, e.g., holds object as only intervention
      - 2 = Offers explicit verbal instruction or gesture
      - 3 = Shows consistent flexible responsiveness to child's needs in determining input ("scaffolding")

   Observation:

   b. *Praise/encouragement:* (deduct 1 point for putdown, negative remarks) (2 and 3 include: makes reassuring remarks to prevent discouragement and preserve self-esteem).
      - 0 = Not present
      - 1 = Statement of "good," "fine," "OK," "right," etc.
      - 2 = Occasional praise includes information about the task
      - 3 = Frequent use of praise with information

   Observation: (Give a 2 if mediator makes remarks to prevent child's feelings of discouragement, in service of preservation of self-esteem.)

6. *Mediation of control of behavior:* Mediator regulates child to inhibit impulsivity and promote attention to task.
   - 0 = Not present
   - 1 = Occasional, but not frequent
   - 2 = Frequent
   - 3 = Frequent, plus includes information the child can use to develop self-regulation

   Observation:

7. *Mediation of goal directedness:* Mediator helps child to think in terms of the ultimate goal or percept and to plan the steps to achieve the goal; helps child to proceed systematically.
   - 0 = Not present
   - 1 = Nonverbal reference to model
   - 2 = Verbal reference to model
   - 3 = Verbal reference plus articulation of a plan

Observation:

8. *Mediation of psychological differentiation:* Mediator functions in a way to help the child deal with the task without becoming involved; that is, mediator separates himself or herself in an objective way from the task, does not become competitive with the child or a coparticipant; functions to enable the child to do or learn the task.
   - 0 = Not present
   - 1 = Task is mostly mediator's, occasionally child's
   - 2 = Task is mostly child's, with occasional lapses
   - 3 = Mediator shows high degree of ability to fade in and out as needed in service of enabling the child to do the task

   (deduct 1 point if mediator rejects child's efforts to become involved)

   Observation:

Total Score: _____
Summary of observations:

12

A Comprehensive Approach to Assessing Intellectually Handicapped Children

NANCY J. VYE, M. SUSAN BURNS, VICTOR R. DELCLOS,
AND JOHN D. BRANSFORD

The purpose of our chapter is to present some preliminary findings from our research on dynamic assessment. The research project has been in existence for a year and a half, and although the data do not address many points, they nevertheless provide an excellent context within which to discuss issues related to learning assessment.

Our research project, and hence our discussion, is organized around three topics: the utility of dynamic assessment for predicting learning ability, its utility for generating educationally relevant prescriptions, and factors associated with the implementation of dynamic procedures.

Our thinking on dynamic assessment has been influenced in fundamental ways by the ideas of Feuerstein (1979), Brown, Campione, and their colleagues (Brown & French, 1979; Campione, Brown, & Ferrara, 1982), and Vygotsky (1934/1962, 1978). It is beyond the scope of this paper to present the theoretical ideas of these authors in any detail. Instead, we refer the reader to relevant papers in this volume (see Chapters 1, 3, and 4). Let us say at the outset, however, that we are fully responsible for any departures from and/or misconstruals of this theory base.

Overview of Research Issues

When we first began thinking about how to give shape to a research project on dynamic assessment, it seemed important that our research address questions in the three broad areas of identification, prescription, and implementation. The identification area seemed important for several reasons: The first

Nancy J. Vye. Department of Psychology, University of Western Ontario, London, Ontario, Canada.

M. Susan Burns and Victor R. Delclos. Department of Education, Tulane University, New Orleans, Louisiana.

John D. Bransford. Department of Psychology, Vanderbilt University, Nashville, Tennessee.

related to our initial focus on preschool children. It is well documented that until children are about 5 years of age, static assessments of learning ability are relatively unreliable (Brown & Ferrara, 1980; Lidz, 1983; Reynolds & Clark, 1983; Simner, 1983). Thus, it seemed to us that dynamic assessment measures would meet an important need if, as suggested by our initial data and the data of others (Brown & Ferrara, 1980; Budoff, 1967), they proved to be a valid means of identifying young children with learning difficulties.

A second reason for focusing on the identification issue was to establish the relation between estimates of learning ability derived from static assessments and those derived from the dynamic assessments we had developed, and perhaps more importantly, to determine the validity of these dynamic estimates. Consider, for example, a situation in which a static measure of learning ability fails to predict children's performance in dynamic assessment. To what might this be attributable? One plausible explanation is that the inconsistency is due to the unreliability of one or both of the measures. We, of course, want to rule out such explanations. It seemed important, therefore, to begin investigating the extent to which dynamic assessment estimates were predictive of performance on tasks in both related and different domains.

A second area that we wished to address in our research was prescription. Although most would agree that it is important to go beyond mere classification, standardized diagnostic–prescriptive procedures are quite rare and the outcome data on those available have been disappointing (Arter & Jenkins, 1979). Although our work in this area is just beginning, our approach appears promising for several reasons. In a dynamic assessment, one is able to gather information about the effectiveness of various instructional manipulations. Furthermore, dynamic assessment emphasizes learning processes rather than underlying "abilities" or "traits." We assume that task-relevant knowledge and general and task-specific strategies can be assessed in dynamic assessment and are amenable to change, and that these changes will produce meaningful improvements in task performance. This information in turn might prove useful to teachers.

In the third area of implementation we have been addressing the question of whether there is an association between dynamic assessment and a change in perception about a child's abilities and potential. We have also been investigating whether teachers see the utility of information provided by a dynamic assessment, and, finally, ways to communicate dynamic assessment prescriptions to facilitate the likelihood of their implementation.

The theoretical rationale for our project revolves around a "continuum of assessment services" model. The continuum model involves initial screening by means of an individually administered intelligence test. Children whose IQ results are in or above the average range would not receive any further assessment, whereas those who scored more than 1 SD below the mean would receive "graduated prompting" dynamic assessment in each of the verbal, quantitative, and perceptual performance domains. (Graduated prompting is described below.) Children who are above criterion on these tasks would be viewed as responsive to instruction, and no further assessment would be provided. A young child who does poorly on static measures, but performs at high levels following graduated prompting, may well be a child whose primary need is an enriched learning environment such as that provided by a preschool experience. A school-age child who shows this profile may be one who could profit from the benefits of a resource person in addition to regular classroom instruction. Our assumption here is that these children are able to learn, but lack experience with the concepts and procedures or the motivation required to do well on intelligence tests.

Graduated prompting was placed second along the continuum because its instruction seems most similar to the type one might see in a classroom. If this assumption about graduated prompting is correct, then we would be justified in using it to predict the children who could profit from regular or enriched classroom experiences. From our perspective at least, the assumption has face validity. For example, graduated prompting instruction is only as explicit as needed, and classroom group instruction, by necessity, is often just sufficient to enable independent performance in most learners.

There are several additional reasons favoring the use of graduated prompting at this stage. It is a fully scripted procedure, and hence may not need to be administered by a professional. This may make it more cost effective and easier to implement on a broad scale. Furthermore, one can derive measures of learning speed (i.e., number of prompts to criterion) from graduated prompting, and learning speed may prove to be a particularly sensitive predictive measure.

Children who are below criterion following graduated prompting would next receive "mediation" dynamic assessment. (This procedure is also discussed more fully below.) Children who reach this final stage of assessment would presumably be those experiencing fundamental learning difficulties. The purpose of this assessment would be to determine the child's ability to profit from a period of intensive, contingent instruction, that is, instruction whose content is determined by the needs of the individual child. Another purpose would be to derive educationally relevant descriptions of learning processes. These descriptions—which we will discuss more fully below— would entail information about content and processes on which the child was experiencing difficulty, as well as effective remediation strategies.

Mediation Assessment

Our continuum assessment services model employs assessment procedures based on Feuerstein's mediation principles (i.e., mediation assessment) and Brown and Campione's zone of proximal development procedure (i.e., graduated prompting assessment). In order to make our research feasible, we were compelled to develop a brief form of Feuerstein's dynamic assessment.

His extended assessments can last from a number of hours to several days, whereas our mediation assessments last only about 30 minutes. Despite the brief nature of the assessment, our results confirm that a session of this duration can provide valuable information about children's learning. Where more in-depth information is needed, for example, about specific prescriptions and their implementation, we have used a series of mediation sessions (i.e., as in the case of the single-subject research described later).

Mediation procedures were developed initially for children of preschool age in the perceptual performance (PP) domain (Burns, 1985), and the task used was an adaptation of the Representational Stencil Design Task (Arthur, 1947; Burns, Haywood, Delclos, & Siewert, in press). Since then, we have designed tasks and procedures for young children for the quantitative (hereafter called quantitative task or QT) and verbal domains, and for middle school–age children in the core curriculum areas of mathematics (for both computation and word problems) and reading comprehension.

Consider for a moment the mediation procedure for the Stencil Design Task (SDT). On the SDT, the child is presented with an array of 18 colored cards. Twelve of the cards have a shape or pattern cut out of them ("cut-outs"); the remaining 6 cards are of a solid color ("solids"). The child's task is to place a cut-out on top of a solid to create a design that matches a model design. During mediation, the child receives training on four such designs. For research purposes, children are posttested on eight new designs that they are asked to complete without assistance from the examiner.

The components of the mediation assessment for the SDT are representative of those used in other task domains. Appendix A describes the structure of the assessment. Three general instructional components are included: familiarization of materials and basic cognitive functions, instruction on task-specific rules and procedures, and feedback. As illustrated in Appendix A, familiarization of materials for the SDT involves helping the child distinguish the relevant dimensions of color, shape, size, location, and orientation, whereas familiarization of basic cognitive functions involves encouraging the child to compare cards on the basis of these dimensions and to systematically search the entire array of cards. Feuerstein (1979) has suggested that children who have been deprived of sufficient mediated learning experiences are often deficient with respect to these fundamental learning processes, or what he calls "basic cognitive functions," and this in turn interferes with their ability to perform more complex cognitive operations. Thus, an important aspect of the mediation assessment is to encourage the child to engage in these behaviors, and for the examiner to communicate this expectation prior to specific instruction on the task.

Task-specific rule instruction involves teaching the child the need for two cards, the order for combining cards, the effect of combining different cards, and the use of the model. As we shall see, the graduated prompting procedure consists of instruction on these same rules, although the method of instruction differs.

The third component of the mediation assessment is feedback. After the child has completed a stencil design, the examiner draws the child's attention to and discusses both the errors and the correct aspects of the construction. The feedback portion of the assessment is perhaps the most informative with respect to diagnosing strengths and weaknesses in the child's approach and the child's response to different attempts at remediation.

Graduated Prompting Assessment

The procedures used in the graduated prompting assessment are based directly on the work of Brown, Campione, and associates (Brown & Ferrara, 1980; Bryant, 1982; Campione, Brown, Ferrara, Jones, & Steinberg, 1983). In graduated prompting, a series of prompts or hints is used to teach the rules needed for task completion. The prompts are ordered in explicitness, with general prompts given first and more explicit prompts later. One prompt is presented to the child each time he or she cannot complete the task.

The sequence of prompts developed for the SDT are contained in Appendix B. Notice that the initial prompts are very general; the child is first reminded about his or her previous construction. Subsequent prompts teach the two-card rule, then how to identify the solid and cut-out in the model, how to combine cards, how to search for cards in the array, and so forth. In our research using the SDT, graduated prompting is given on four designs and unassisted, posttest performance is assessed on eight designs. Thus far we have developed graduated prompting procedures for young children in the perceptual performance and quantitative task domains.

The Utility of Dynamic Assessment for Predicting Learning Ability

Comparison of Static and Dynamic Assessment

When we were initiating our work, the available research on dynamic assessment suggested that dynamic measures were capable of further discriminating differences in learning ability among children who had been homogeneously grouped on the basis of static intelligence scores (Brown & Ferrara, 1980; Budoff, 1967). The correlations that had been reported between various intelligence measures and learning measures (i.e., performance gains, learning speed, transfer) were either low or nonsignificant. However, full-scale IQ was typically the static measure employed, and it could be argued that the reported correlations were spuriously low because of the use of a global static measure (compounded in some cases by attenuation due to restriction of IQ range). We wanted therefore to establish the relation between dynamic measures and "nonglobal" (i.e., subscale) static measures. In addition, we wanted to extend the findings to our new tasks and dynamic procedures.

Thus far in our research we have not found evidence to suggest that the previously reported results are in any way spurious. In our first experiment (hereafter Study A), we calculated correlations between dynamic measures and full-scale and subscale scores. The McCarthy Scales of Children's Abilities (McCarthy, 1972) were used as static measures. The dynamic measure was children's unassisted performance on the SDT following graduated prompting. Table 12.1 contains the obtained correlations. The pattern of results is quite clear: Consistent with previous reports, General Cognitive Index (GCI) bears only a moderate relationship to measures on the SDT following dynamic assessment. Although the correlation did not achieve significance, we suspect that the obtained score is an underestimate that is most likely due to a restriction of range in GCI scores.

The correlations between the subscale and the dynamic measures were of particular interest in Study A, and inspection of Table 12.1 reveals that the correlation is significant when the task domain is the same (e.g., SDT and PP). Although this correlation is higher than the GCI/SDT correlation, it is clear that a subscale score would not be a very reliable indicator of the child's response to instruction.

A slightly different breakdown of Study A makes the point more forcefully. The 77 handicapped children—the number includes children from a second study (Study B) as well—were grouped according to GCI. Groups consisted of children whose GCIs were below 37, from 37 to 52, from 53 to 68, and from 69 to 108. The handicapped children in the 69–108 group are those children who have a 2-SD difference between subtests—many are from a school for learning-disabled children. Figure 12.1 represents the percentage of children in each GCI group who learned to do the SDT following dynamic assessment. As can be seen, a substantial number of children reached criterion on our brief dynamic assessment procedure: 36% of the children with IQs between 37 and 52 reached criterion; 53% of the children with IQs between 53 and 68; 82% of the children with IQs between 69 and 108; and even in

TABLE 12.1. Correlations between McCarthy Scores and Scores on Stencil Design Task following Graduated Prompting ($N = 44$)

	McCarthy Scales			
	General cognitive index	Perceptual performance	Verbal	Quantitative
Stencil design task	.18	.48*	−.05	−.15

*$p < .01$.

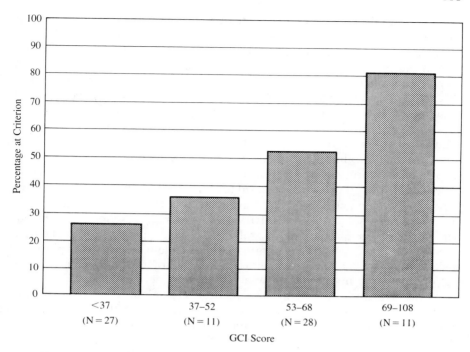

FIGURE 12.1. Percentage of children in each GGI group who reach criterion (≥ 75% correct on SDT).

our lowest IQ group (below 37), 26% reached criterion. In spite of their static classification, a sizable number of children in each group were responsive to instruction.

The results of Studies A and B point to several conclusions. Consistent with previous work, full-scale intelligence measures do not predict dynamic performance with any great precision. More significantly, the present research indicates that subscale measures increase prediction only slightly. A large proportion of our children would have been misclassified with respect to their ability to profit from instruction if static measures had been used as the basis for classification. It is also noteworthy that these results were obtained for the first time using our adapted mediation assessment and thus are an initial demonstration of the feasibility of the procedure.

The Relation between Dynamic Assessment and Within- and Across-Domain Transfer

Our long-range purpose in conducting experiments such as Study A and Study B is to investigate the predictive utility of dynamic assessment procedures.

We hope over the course of our work to demonstrate that dynamic assessment can serve as a valuable tool either alone or in combination with static, normative measures for estimating children's future learning on a task. A first step in the process is to establish that dynamic estimates are not redundant with static estimates (i.e., perfectly correlated). Studies A and B accomplish this goal. Although, strictly speaking, the low correlations that we reported could be attributed to the unreliability of either or both the static and dynamic measures, the consistency with which moderate correlations are observed argues against the unreliability hypothesis.

A second step in the process is to explore the relation between dynamic assessment performance and performance on transfer tasks within and across task domains. In other words, we need to assess the concurrent and predictive validity of dynamic measures. We have data from Study A and Study B and from two single-subject projects that begin to address these issues. Although some of our data analyses are in preliminary stages, particularly in the case of Study B, there is sufficient information available to suggest that performance following dynamic assessment is predictive of within-domain transfer performance, but not predictive of across-domain performance.

Consider Study A once again. The design is one in which children first receive a session of dynamic assessment on the SDT, either mediation or graduated prompting, followed by unassisted or independent performance (hereafter IP) on the SDT and on three within-domain transfer tasks. Table 12.2 contains children's scores on each of the tasks and illustrates the relation between performance following dynamic assessment and performance on the transfer tasks. Children who do well on the SDT, and by this we mean children who meet or exceed a criterion of 75% accuracy, also do well on two other stencil tasks (one involving stencils of animal shapes and the other involving

TABLE 12.2. Mean Independent and Transfer Performance (% Correct) following Dynamic Assessment

	Stencil design	Animal stencils	Reverse stencils	Animal house (mean raw score)*
Graduated prompting ($N = 15$)	37%	33%	49%	18.60*
Mediation ($N = 15$)	47%	51%	62%	18.33*
Children above 75% criterion on Stencil Design Task				
Graduated prompting ($N = 5$)	85%	73%	95%	29.80*
Mediation ($N = 4$)	75%	75%	78%	21.50*
Children below 75% criterion on Stencil Design Task				
Graduated prompting ($N = 10$)	13%	14%	26%	13.00*
Mediation ($N = 11$)	36%	42%	56%	17.18*

*Raw score.

the same geometric shapes as the SDT but in an appropriate figure–ground relationship), and the Animal House Coding Task (raw score). Similarly, children who do poorly on the SDT tend to do poorly on the transfer tasks.

The differences on transfer performance between above- and below-criterion children are statistically significant when considering the graduated prompt conditions. The transfer differences did not reach significance in the mediation groups, although the means are in the same direction. The mediation results are most likely due to the relatively good transfer performance of the below-criterion children, and suggest that mediation instruction promotes greater generalization. Although we have not examined our ideas empirically, we suspect that the mediation and graduated prompt procedures may differ in terms of the relative emphasis placed on metacognitive skills. The mediation procedure, for example, devotes instructional time to search and self-checking strategies. Transfer of strategies such as these may account for the better performance of the below-criterion mediation children over their graduated prompting counterparts. Before leaving this issue—we will return to it shortly—we should say that the observed differences in transfer performance do not imply that one procedure is "better" than the other; the value of each procedure is established by reference to the function it is designed to serve. As suggested earlier, the graduated prompting procedure may prove to be more valid than the mediation procedure when used to predict a child's response to classroom instruction, assuming that classroom instruction is more similar to the graduated prompting than the mediation type of instruction.

The results of Study A suggest that dynamic assessment, that is, instruction of a brief duration, may prove helpful for predicting how well children will perform on related tasks. We have also obtained similar results with more severely handicapped children. Because of the degree of handicap, we have used a single-subject research methodology, and have extended the mediation over a number of sessions. In the first experiment, baseline measures consisting of IP on the SDT and the two stencil transfer tasks were collected over a series of sessions (the actual number was staggered across the three children who participated). The mediation sessions followed, and continued until such time as an improved and stable level of performance was observed on the SDT (IP measures on SDT were taken at the end of each mediation session). At this point, mediation instruction was discontinued, and maintenance of learning was assessed over several more sessions. Figure 12.2 depicts the SDT results for the three children (fictitious names are used to protect the children's identities). The results of particular interest here are the transfer results. Independent performance on these tasks was assessed in a session following each of the mediation sessions. Figures 12.3 and 12.4, which depict SDT and transfer results of two of the children, show quite clearly the spontaneous transfer of SDT learning to the other stencil tasks. Again, this illustrates the correspondence between performance following dynamic assessment and per-

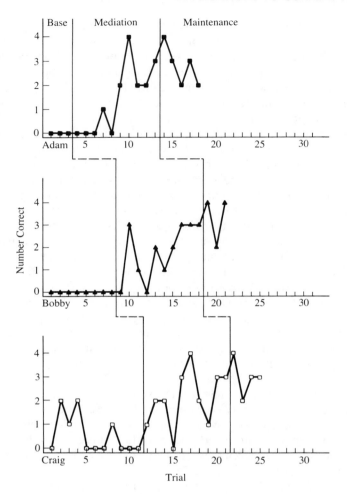

FIGURE 12.2.   Number of stencils correct on the SDT.

formance on related tasks. These results are in contrast to much of the training research conducted with mentally handicapped persons, wherein transfer of learning has been the exception rather than the rule. The present findings may be due in part to the multisession nature of our research design. There does seem to be a time lag between improvement on the criterial task and improvement on the transfer task. These latter improvements would be missed if, as is usually the case, only a single transfer session were used.

Having spoken about within-domain performance, let us address briefly the case of across-domain performance. We have conducted two experiments, Study B and a second single-subject design, that bear on this issue, and in both cases we looked at the correspondence between performance on a PP and a QT. In contrast to the results from within-domain tasks, we have not found evidence of spontaneous transfer. Nor have we found any evidence to suggest that responsiveness to instruction in one task domain predicts responsiveness to instruction in a second. That is, the children who achieve our learning criterion following dynamic assessment (either mediation or graduated prompting) on the SDT do not consistently achieve criterion following instruction on the QT, nor are the below-criterion SDT children always below criterion on the QT.

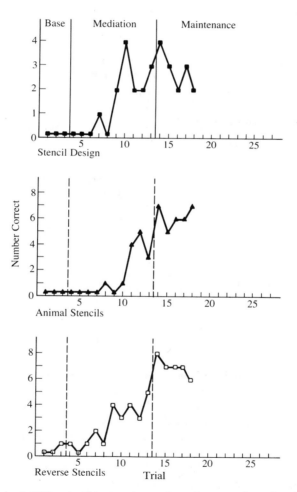

FIGURE 12.3.   Adam's SDT and within-domain transfer performance during baseline, mediation, and maintenance trials.

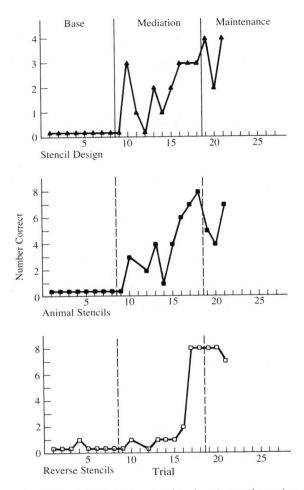

FIGURE 12.4.   Bobby's SDT and within-domain transfer performance.

To summarize, then, our work thus far suggests that there is a relation between performance following dynamic assessment and performance on tasks in a related domain. Study A showed that handicapped children who met a learning criterion tended to do well on a series of near-transfer tasks, whereas those children who did not meet the criterion did not transfer nearly as well. In contrast, we have not found evidence indicating across-domain correspondence. Study B failed to show that classifying handicapped and nonhandicapped children according to learning status on the SDT improved appreciably our ability to predict learning status on the QT. We should make the disclaimer, however, that we have yet to complete correlation analyses on Study B data;

what we have presented are the results of preliminary chi-squares. Nonetheless, we expect that this will leave our major conclusions unchanged.

The within-domain transfer observed in the single-subject experiment deserves further comment. At first glance it might seem as if the result contradicts our conclusion that performance following dynamic assessment helps us to predict performance on similar tasks, since the children, who were selected because of the severity of their handicap, showed evidence of spontaneous transfer. The result also seems to fly in the face of other reports (Belmont & Butterfield, 1979; Brown, Bransford, Ferrara, & Campione, 1984; Campione et al., 1983) indicating the utility of learning and transfer profiles for identifying children who are "truly" mentally handicapped. These notwithstanding, we suggest that our conclusion holds since the children did perform poorly at first both in response to mediation and on the transfer tasks. It was only after several intensive mediation sessions that children began to improve on the SDT, and the transfer effects were delayed by several more sessions. Nonetheless—and we wish to stress the point because we fear that it is often lost—the children did possess the ability to learn the task if provided with the appropriate intervention, and were able to transfer the acquired skills. Conclusions, ours and those of others, about "nonlearners" or "nontransferers" need to be interpreted cautiously, that is, in relation to the learning criteria and tasks selected by the experimenter and not in an absolute sense.

The Utility of Dynamic Assessment for Predicting Learning Ability: Directions for Future Research

Our research suggests several conclusions about the utility of dynamic measures. First, Studies A and B results indicate that static and dynamic measures do indeed produce different estimates of learning, and that this discrepancy is not an artifact of taking a full-scale rather than a subscale measure. Furthermore, there is an ever-increasing body of evidence that argues against the possibility that this discrepancy is attributable to the unreliability of either the static or dynamic measures. The stability of the static–dynamic correlations across replications weakens any claim about unreliability.

A second conclusion that emerges from our research relates to the validity of dynamic measures. (It is important, of course, to establish that the information derived from our dynamic assessments, its uniqueness and reliability notwithstanding, will help us to predict learning and performance.) The results of Study A indicate that responsiveness to instruction on the SDT is predictive of performance on transfer tasks, a striking correspondence in view of the fact all of the children had been below criterion during the first phase of the study and a correspondence that bolsters validity claims. Our single-subject work leads to a similar conclusion. The learning curves obtained from the mediation closely parallel (with a time lag) those obtained from untrained transfer measures, indicating that a child's response to instruction on one task is closely tied to uninstructed learning in another. Taken together, the data represent evidence of the concurrent validity of dynamic assessment.

The above-mentioned results were derived from tasks selected from the same domain, that is, the perceptual performance domain. The across-domain data suggest a different conclusion. We have not found evidence of between-domain transfer (between QT and PP domain) in our single-subject research. Nor do Study B data show a relationship between responsiveness to instruction in one domain and responsiveness in another. As far as we can tell, then, dynamic measures, if and when implemented, would need to be taken in each domain for which learning is to be predicted.

One final point deserves reiteration, and that is the relation between graduated prompting and mediation assessment. The data from Burns (1985), Study A, and Study B show that the two procedures do not produce different numbers of above- and below-criterion children, and therefore appear to be equally effective for teaching the task at hand. The mediation procedure does seem to be somewhat more effective for promoting transfer. We are doubtful, however, that this will prove to be an important factor in determining their relative predictive utility because what is important for prediction is a rank ordering of children's performance and not the absolute level of performance. As discussed earlier, we do believe that the two procedures may serve different assessment functions. The GP procedure by virtue of its scripted nature seems ideally suited for prediction. As suggested by the work of Brown and colleagues (Bryant, 1982; Campione et al., 1983), using a measure of the number of prompts needed to reach criterion in conjunction with static measures (instead of the pre- to postgain measures that we have been using because of the comparative nature of our research) may significantly improve the precision with which we can assess relative learning ability. Or, as suggested by the continuum model, a measure of number of prompts may be more feasible to use as a second stage in the process of assessing individuals who have already been identified as having possible learning difficulties. The mediation procedure, on the other hand, may prove to be better suited as a diagnostic–prescriptive device in view of what appears to be a relatively greater emphasis on contingency in instruction and metacognitive skills.

With this as background, we can consider suggestions for directions of future research. Generally speaking, further research is warranted on the concurrent and predictive validity of the measures, and, in view of our previous comments about prediction, it would seem to make most sense to focus efforts on the graduated prompting procedure.

One avenue that seems important to pursue is the relation between dynamic measures in the same task domain (given the evidence amassed thus far, the perceptual performance domain is the most logical initial choice). We have investigated the relation between dynamic assessment and static transfer and between dynamic assessment and spontaneous learning, but not between prompting on a predictor (i.e., SDT) and prompting on a transfer (i.e., Animal Stencils) task. We would hope, of course, that a rank ordering of children on the basis of their responsiveness to instruction would be similar across tasks.

As suggested earlier, an aspect that should be given consideration is that of using a measure of number of prompts to index learning rather than, or in addition to, a measure of gain. We are in the process of deriving this measure from the research we had already completed, and may well find that it represents a more sensitive estimate. Brown and colleagues, who routinely use this measure, have discussed the merits of the approach (see Brown & Ferrara, 1980), not the least of which is that it enables one to discriminate between children who show similar gains but who differ in the amount of instruction needed to make these gains.

The above-mentioned recommendations follow from studies already completed. Let us now consider the research agenda from a broader perspective. It seems clear we need to investigate other types of criterion measures in our validation studies. For example, we need to look at the extent to which dynamic measures can predict to classroom tasks, to learning in classroom environments, and to learning in response to interventions generated by the assessment. Ultimately, we would want to do this longitudinally as well as concurrently. Although field research seems somewhat premature at this point, one way to begin to address these issues might be to undertake instruction of a curriculum unit under laboratory conditions and look at the relation between dynamic measures and various criterion-referenced measures.

Another issue that has no doubt occurred to the reader is that the research conducted thus far needs to be extended to other task domains; our research has focused on perceptual performance and to a lesser extent on quantification, although work on developing dynamic procedures and criterion and predictor tasks in the verbal domain is ongoing. In addition, the research needs to be extended to older children, although, again, we have begun to develop procedures and tasks for elementary-age children.

Preliminary Findings on Dynamic Assessment and Educational Prescriptions

An issue of major concern to us has been the utility of dynamic procedures, in particular mediation, for deriving prescriptive information. The need for such measures goes undisputed. The available diagnostic tests are not very well standardized (Arter & Jenkins, 1979), nor do they provide information about a child's learning processes, that is, information about task-specific and general learning strategies or about remedial strategies. Dynamic procedures, on the other hand, would seem to be ideally suited for such purposes. Indeed,

Feuerstein's Learning Potential Assessment Device (LPAD) is in large part used to diagnose cognitive functioning.

Observations of Young Children's Learning

Our work on prescription has focused on observational measures of young children's general cognitive strategies. The long-range goals of this work are to identify a set of behaviors that can be coded reliably and that reflect cognitive strategies determined to underlie successful performance, and to identify instructional methods that will foster the development of such strategies (and eliminate the use of ineffective ones).

We should make it clear that our emphasis on general cognitive strategies does not imply that we believe that knowledge base and task-specific strategies are unimportant. To the contrary, we view assessment of these skills as equally critical. Out of necessity, however, we had to initially narrow our research focus, and both previous research and the age of our target population led us to choose general strategies as a starting point. Age entered into our decision in that we reasoned that knowledge base would be less of a factor for young children on the tasks we had selected than it would be for older children on school-like tasks. The use of an observational methodology does not imply an exclusive commitment. In fact, we are in the process of developing a scheme for analyzing the errors young children make during mediation. We hope that this will provide further information about "bugs" in a child's thinking.

The starting point for our studies on prescription was an investigation by Burns and colleagues (Burns et al., in press). Her study involved observing 4- and 5-year-old children as they performed a series of tasks (including the SDT). Observations were coded using the behavior categories contained in Table 12.3. A subset of these (the six categories marked with asterisks) were found to discriminate high from low test scores and/or the performance of low-socioeconomic-status (SES) from high-SES children. For four of the categories (the exceptions being Information Giving and Visual Scan) high frequencies were associated with poor and/or low-SES performance. For the two exceptions, low frequencies were associated with poor and/or low-SES performance.

The nature of the strategies presumed to underlie these categories deserves comment. In developing the coding scheme, Burns was influenced by Feuerstein's propositions concerning deficient cognitive functioning, as well as by other cognitive models, (Bransford & Stein, 1984; Brown & DeLoache, 1978; Brown et al., 1984; Flavell, 1979) emphasizing the importance of metacognitive skills such as planning and monitoring. For example, the Visual Scan, Looking at the Model, and Inappropriate Manipulation of Materials categories could be considered to be behavioral representations of Feuerstein's deficient cognitive functions of unsystematic search, lack of compar-

TABLE 12.3. Behavioral Categories and Brief Definitions[a]

- Attention—looks at experimenter or materials during instructions and/or looks at materials while performing.
- Attention & On-Task Manipulation—active contact, using hands, with the materials that the child is working with. This is applicable only when it is time to be manipulating materials.
- Off-Task Behavior—active contact, using hands, on the environment or body that is not part of the material in the study. This includes manipulating task materials when the child should be listening to instructions.
- Information Giving—explains what he or she is going to do before performing the task and/or explains intermediate steps. This information is specific in nature.[*]
- Visual Scan/Looking at Model—looks at model or head moves past the center line (imaginary) dividing the left and right sides of the materials.[*]
- Corrects Self—gives an answer and, without any intervention from the experimenter, changes the answer.[*]
- Confirmation Seeking, Helpless Gestures, & Verbalizations—looks to the tester while using the task materials or asks for help in a nonspecific request.[*]
- On-Task Comments—comments made by the child about the task that are not specific to the task completion.
- Inappropriate Manipulation of Stencils—the number of stencils that the child touches that are not a part of the model design that is being made.[*]
- Speaking Out before Instructions Finished—speaks, gestures, or starts the task before the instructions are finished.
- Used All Blocks—when making a block design, uses all nine blocks, even though none of the designs required using all of the blocks.[*]

---

[a] Adapted from Burns et al. (in press)

[*] Category was found to discriminate high from low test scores and/or the performance of low-SES from high-SES children.

ative behavior, and trial-and-error behavior, respectively. Other categories, such as Used All Blocks, Information Giving, and Corrects Self, appear to capture problem definition, monitoring, and planning strategies.

In all our research on dynamic assessment, we have videotaped the experimental sessions. These are then coded to derive measures on the behavioral categories described above. (It also provides a record of tester behavior that is coded to ensure that the tester has adhered to the prescribed dynamic procedure). We will discuss the results of two of our studies, Study B and a single-subject project, as they relate to prescription.

In Study B, handicapped and nonhandicapped children were assigned to either a mediation, graduated prompting, or static (i.e., task demonstration only) assessment condition. For part of the study, children received the following sequence of treatments: 1) pretesting on the SDT; 2) mediation, graduated prompting, or static assessment on the SDT; and 3) posttesting on the SDT. Observational data are available for all sessions, and thus far have been coded for the Corrects Self categories.

Our purpose in collecting these data was to investigate the degree to which dynamic assessment was helpful in teaching general strategies that facilitate performance. We wished to know whether our interventions could

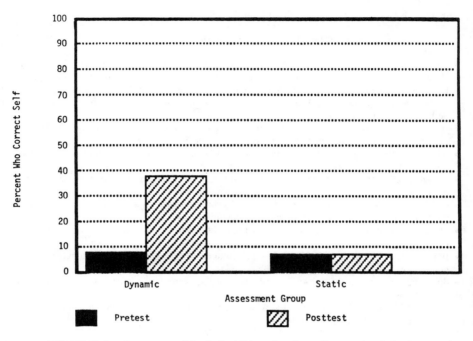

FIGURE 12.5.   Percentage of Study B children showing self-correction behavior.

positively influence strategy use, in which case this might be usefully communicated to teachers. Figure 12.5 depicts the changes observed in self-correction. As can be seen, dynamic assessment is generally effective for creating
change in strategy use for the SDT.

While the results of Study B are encouraging, it is nevertheless clear that
some handicapped children do not benefit from our interventions. This of
course makes it difficult to specify prescriptive information that might help
teachers help these students learn more effectively. To address this issue, we
undertook a series of longer term assessments. One of these was a single-
subject project whose performance data were mentioned earlier. What was
not discussed at that point was the nature of the mediation that we provided.
After the first sessions of mediation, we began to tailor the intervention to
address particular behavior categories. Using both behavior category frequencies from the first several sessions and examiner judgments, we identified
a strategy that appeared relatively problematic for the child. Following this,
all subsequent sessions emphasized remediation of the targeted behavior in
addition to the standard mediation interventions. Low frequencies of visual
scanning and self-correction were identified in Bobby and Adam, respectively
(see Figure 12.6).

FIGURE 12.6.   Frequency of strategy use and stencil performance data for Bobby and Adam.

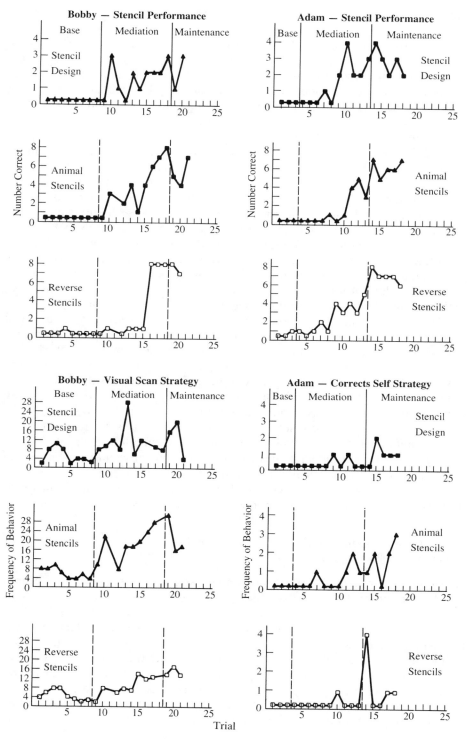

Consider the case of Bobby. This child was observed to search only a portion of the stencils before selecting one. To overcome the problem, the examiner first taught the child to use his "eyes" to look at all of the stencils. The examiner would model the behavior of using her eyes to look at each stencil. The looking was done in a much-exaggerated way, and the child was encouraged to imitate. The examiner next established the rule that the child was required to place his hands at the table's edge and to find the correct stencil using his "eyes" before selecting it. As the rule became more automatic and the frequency of scanning increased, the examiner occasionally used the verbal reminder to "first find it with your eyes." Of course, throughout the sessions the child received praise whenever he scanned appropriately.

Note what happened in the case of Bobby, whose tailored mediation commenced on trial 13. Referring to Figure 12.6, we can see that the examiner's interventions resulted in increased visual scanning on the SDT and on the transfer tasks as well. The improvement on transfer, although not as dramatic as that observed on the SDT, is nonetheless remarkable since the examiner did not intervene during performance on these tasks. Notice also that the point where the examiner begins to focus on visual scanning behavior is the point at which Bobby begins to evidence some consistency in improved performance on the SDT. In view of this, it seems worthwhile to consider modifying future designs in such a way as to allow determination of whether the observed improvements in performance are due to the tailoring, the standard mediation, or both. For example, for a child such as Bobby, it would mean using a control child who exhibited relatively little visual scanning behavior and who received only standard mediation.

To summarize, the results suggest that mediation is generally effective for remediating strategies that help children perform effectively. In addition, we have described the strategies we assess and our procedures for assessing them. Finally, we described a model for conducting longer term assessments that can be used when standard mediation is not sufficient and from which one can derive and test prescriptions that are tailored to the individual child.

The Utility of Dynamic Assessment for Generating Prescriptions: Directions for Future Research

Although our research is at a preliminary stage, it seems clear that even a relatively brief session of dynamic assessment can provide valuable insights into a child's cognitive processing. In our work with young children we have focused on the assessment of general cognitive strategies that reflect planning, monitoring, and so forth, whereas with older children—we regret that space does not permit detailed discussion of our work with these children—we have been more concerned with task-specific knowledge and strategies. Any prescriptive assessment will ultimately need to address all three aspects.

Another important aspect of research on prescription is the method by which the prescriptions are derived, and our work illustrates a number of the available options: observation, interaction, and error analysis. In each case, the requirement is that the method can reliably produce valid prescriptions. Although our work is just beginning, we feel we have made progress in this direction. For example, the observational measures that we have used with young children are easily derived, and the results of Burns et al.'s (in press) study and our single-subject project indicate that the behaviors are closely associated with task performance. We also suggested a methodology for establishing a more direct causal link between behavior and performance, one that could be easily applied to each of the behavior categories.

There are several other avenues of research that could be pursued. One that seems important is to establish the validity of the behavior categories for other tasks, in particular, tasks that a child might receive in school. A second, perhaps more basic, avenue would be to gather convergent and discriminant validity data on the strategies assumed to underlie the behavior categories.

Another important aspect of a prescriptive assessment is the nature of the instruction given to children. Our initial attempts at developing mediation for older children clearly demonstrated that the method of instruction influences the richness of the information that is generated about children's learning. Similarly, it appears from Study B that standard mediation, more so than graduated prompting, is an effective technique for changing strategy use.

It is a delicate balance indeed. It is necessary to find an instructional approach that makes the child's cognitive processes as explicit as possible and at the same time proves effective for remediation so that this information can be communicated to teachers.

Factors Related to the Implementation of Dynamic Assessment

Teachers are the ultimate recipients of information derived from dynamic assessment. For this reason we have been concerned with investigating a number of issues related to implementation: the association between observation of dynamic assessment and a change in a teachers' perceptions about children's abilities and potentials, teachers' evaluations of the utility of information provided by dynamic assessment, and the extent of interactions between judgments about utility and instructional orientation.

Overall, a review of the literature suggests two major conclusions. First, it appears that expectations can play an important role in a teacher's prescriptive planning for a child, and second, it appears that seeing positive change in a child's performance can help alter initially low expectations. These data support the idea that one important role of dynamic assessment may be to change the pessimistic attitudes of teachers toward handicapped children and to convince them that the children have more potential to learn than is traditionally thought.

In our first study, we compared the responses of teachers who viewed an interpreted segment of a standard, static assessment session with their responses following viewing of an interpreted segment of a dynamic assessment session on the same child. Assessment sessions were presented to the teachers via an interactive videotape system. Introductory material was the same across both conditions. Each taped segment was divided into several parts. Clarifying information (e.g., information that the child chose the correct solid card but the wrong stencil) was presented on the computer screen after each trial.

There were two treatment groups. Both groups saw one segment of a child participating in a static assessment session. Group 1 then a saw a second segment of the same child participating in another static assessment session. Group 2 saw a second segment of the same child participating in a dynamic assessment session. After viewing each assessment segment (either static or dynamic), each participant completed an 18-item questionnaire. The items on the questionnaire were grouped into three subscales: 1) Task Involvement (including items such as "Was the child attentive, persistent, interested in doing well?"); 2) Task-specific Knowledge and Strategies (with questions like "Did the child know the names of relevant shapes, look at all the materials, compare his work to the model?"); and 3) General Competence ("Was the child competent, successful, aware of his or her success/failure?").

In Figure 12.7, we see that all teachers viewed the children as moderately involved in the task in both the static and dynamic conditions (the ratings

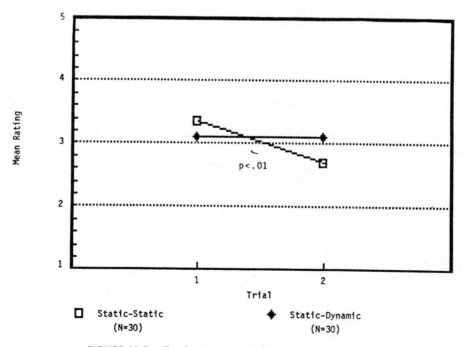

FIGURE 12.7.   Teachers' ratings of children's task involvement.

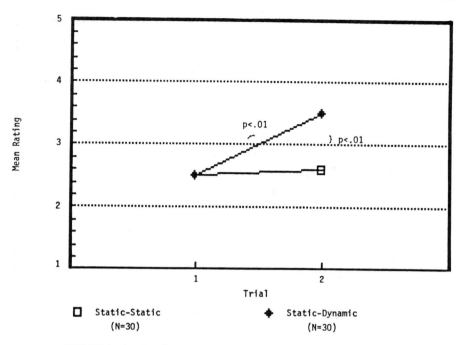

FIGURE 12.8.   Teachers' ratings of children's task-specific knowledge.

hover around 3, the midpoint of the scale), with a small decrease in the ratings from Trial 1 to Trial 2 in the group who saw two static sessions.

With regard to Task-specific Knowledge and Strategies (Figure 12.8), all teachers considered the children to be somewhat low (about 2.5) after viewing the first segment of static assessment, but those teachers who then viewed the same children during dynamic administration of the same task rated them much higher (about 3.5) than did those who viewed an additional segment of static assessment.

In Figure 12.9, we see an even more dramatic shift in judgments of the children's general competence (from 2.1 to 3.8) by the teachers who viewed dynamic assessment segments during Trial 2, as contrasted with those who remained firm in their low estimations of the children's competence after viewing two brief static assessment sessions.

Overall, then, teachers considered the child they observed to be using more task-appropriate strategies and to be generally more competent when viewed in a dynamic testing situation than when viewed in a static assessment session working on the same task. These effects held regardless of the level of training and experience of the teacher, although less-experienced teachers did tend to rate the children more positively across trials and assessment types.

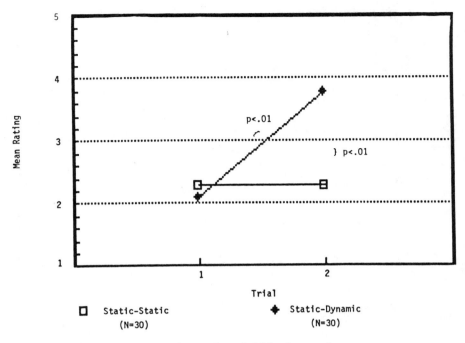

FIGURE 12.9.   Teachers' ratings of children's general competence.

The results we have just presented were based on the combined responses of 60 teachers, each of whom saw 1 of 2 children. We will now consider the responses to each of the children separately.

The videotapes used as the stimuli in this study depicted two very different children. It is instructive to compare the responses of teachers to the performance of each of these children on the two scales that showed significant effects of dynamic assessment: Task-specific Knowledge and Strategies, and General Competence.

Frank is 6 years old. He has been classified as mentally retarded–physically handicapped and attends a special school for multiply handicapped children. He scored in the mentally retarded range on the GCI of the McCarthy and his mental age (MA) was estimated to be 2 years, 10 months. He has poor muscle tone and has just begun to walk alone this year. His speech has been generally limited to one- and two-word utterances.

Gary is 5 years, 3 months old. He has been classified as mentally retarded–emotionally disturbed and attends a special education school. He also scored in the mentally retarded range on the GCI of the McCarthy and his MA was estimated at 3 years, 0 months. He is strong and big for his age. His speech is often difficult to understand. To summarize, Frank is older, smaller, and more retarded (based on intelligence test scores) than Gary.

All teachers rated Frank as relatively low (around 2) with regard to task-specific knowledge and strategy use after the first trial. Those who saw him in a second static session rated him somewhat higher, but those who viewed the dynamic session ranked him two full-scale points higher than they had after Trial 1 (see Figure 12.10). Teachers rated Gary higher than they did Frank after Trial 1, accurately reflecting his higher level of functioning as measured by the McCarthy. After Trial 2, teachers who saw more static assessment rated him significantly lower than they had earlier, whereas teachers who viewed him during dynamic assessment made no change in their rating (see Figure 12.11). It appears that the nature of this child's emotional disturbance may be a factor in the lower expectations of his performance on cognitive tasks as a function of getting to know him better—his poor prognosis as a learner may be perceived more as a function of his emotional disturbance than of his cognitive ability.

The same pattern is repeated on the General Competence Scale, with Frank being rated very low after Trial 1, but very high after the dynamic assessment session of Trial 2, an actual increase of 2.4 scale points (see Figure 12.12). On the same scale, Gary was again rated higher than Frank on first impression. On Trial 2 the static group rated his performance significantly

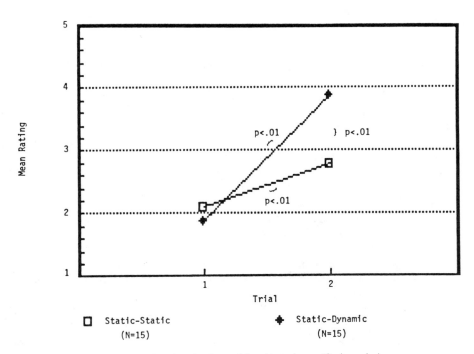

FIGURE 12.10.   Teachers' ratings of Frank's task-specific knowledge.

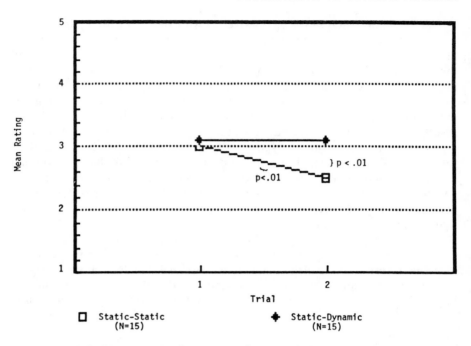

FIGURE 12.11.   Teachers' ratings of Gary's task-specific knowledge.

lower, whereas the dynamic group judged him to be significantly more competent (see Figure 12.13).

In summary, teachers' initial ratings of both children coincided with their relative standing as measured by a normative measure; Frank was viewed as less strategic and less competent than Gary. In addition, there were differential effects of static versus dynamic assessments for both children on both scales; all group differences on Trial 2 were statistically significant. The results also indicated that Frank's ratings improved in both testing conditions on Trial 2, but the dynamic assessment always produced far larger rating changes. Finally, Gary's ratings decreased over trials on both the Task-specific and General Competence scales after repeated static assessment, while they held or increased after dynamic assessment.

What does all of this say about dynamic assessment for young handicapped children? Taken in the context of the literature on the effects of expectations on teachers' behavior toward handicapped children, we believe our data demonstrate the potential benefits of including teachers in the dynamic assessment process. If, as the literature suggests, a teacher's expectation of a student's potential for learning has direct impact on the level and type of effort that teacher devotes to the child, then the effects of dynamic assessment on teachers' judgments of strategic ability and general competence

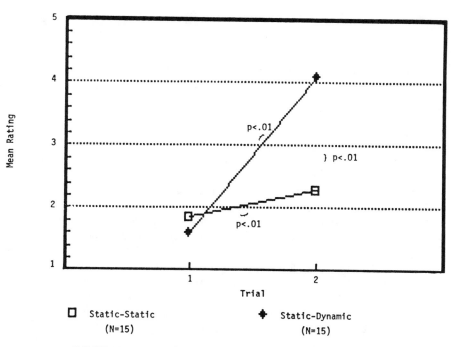

FIGURE 12.12. Teachers' ratings of Frank's general competence.

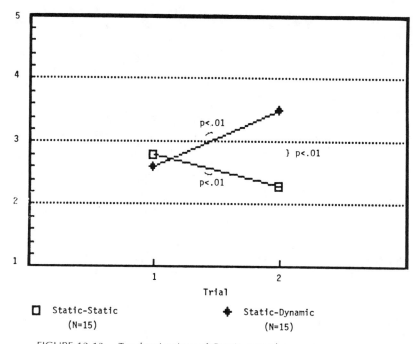

FIGURE 12.13. Teachers' ratings of Gary's general competence.

that we have demonstrated here have important implications for the way we should approach assessments of handicapped children.

Summary and Conclusions

Our research has focused on three major topics: the utility of dynamic assessment for predicting learning, the utility of dynamic assessment for generating educationally relevant prescriptions, and factors associated with the implementation of dynamic procedures. Although many interesting and important questions remain to be answered about these topics, our research offers several conclusions and suggestions for future research.

Consistent with earlier reports, our work indicates that static and dynamic measures do indeed produce different estimates of learning. A substantial number of our children learned to perform tasks when static measures suggested that they would do otherwise. Furthermore, we have demonstrated that this discrepancy is not an artifact of using full-scale rather than subscale static measures. Nor is the discrepancy likely due to any unreliability associated with the measures themselves.

The validity of dynamic measures is indicated by data from several experiments. It appears that, for handicapped and nonhandicapped children alike, responsiveness to instruction is predictive of within-domain transfer performance. On the other hand, there does not seem to be a strong relation between responsiveness to instruction across domains, suggesting that dynamic measures, if and when implemented, would need to be taken in each domain for which one wanted to predict learning.

In sum, it appears from research conducted thus far that dynamic assessment is useful for predicting learning. It seems clear, however, that we need to consider other criteria in order to broaden the base of our validation studies. For example, we need to look at the extent to which dynamic measures can predict to classroom tasks and to learning in classroom environments. Of course, we want ultimately to do this longitudinally as well as concurrently.

Our research on the topic of prescription has indicated that mediation assessment is generally effective for remediating strategies that help children improve their performance. Moreover, we are particularly encouraged by our experiences with extended mediation. Using observational information, we have tailored our mediation to the needs of individual children, which in turn has produced changes in the targeted strategies and improvements in task performance. The model of extended mediation is promising because it allows us to derive information about ineffective learning processes and to observe the results of our attempts to remediate these processes. Such information may ultimately be of value to teachers. However, research must begin to address the issue of the generality of the behavior categories, in particular for tasks a child might receive in school. As discussed earlier, future research also needs to consider the assessment of task-specific knowledge and strategies in addition to general cognitive strategies.

Finally, our research investigating the impact of implementing dynamic procedures illustrates that dynamic assessments can have important effects on teacher expectations. Although encouraged by this, we are nevertheless aware that changes in expectations will not necessarily produce changes in teaching behaviors, especially if teachers do not have a better idea of how to teach in ways that help various children learn. This is one of the reasons why we are placing more and more emphasis on using assessments to provide prescriptions for teaching.

We are greatly encouraged by the potential of dynamic procedures and their future role in psychoeducational assessment.

ACKNOWLEDGMENTS

Preparation of the chapter was supported by Grant G0083C0052 awarded to Vanderbilt University by the U.S. Department of Education, Office of Special Education, and by Grant T238Al awarded to the first author by the Natural Sciences and Engineering Research Council of Canada. The authors would like to acknowledge the other project investigators, Carl Haywood and Ted Hasselbring, and our research assistants, Keith Allred, Ron Buen, Randi Glorski, Judy Johnson, Stan Kulewicz, Tamara Ogan, Kim Sloan, Deborah Stephens, and Julie Tapp. Finally, we wish to thank all of the children who participated in this research.

REFERENCES

Arter, J. A., & Jenkins, J. R. (1979). Differential diagnosis—prescriptive teaching: A critical appraisal. *Review of Educational Research, 49*(4), 517–555.

Arthur, G. (1947). *A point scale of performance tests.* NY: Psychological Corporation.

Belmont, J. M., & Butterfield, E. C. (1979). The instructional approach to developmental cognitive research. In R. V. Kail, Jr. & J. W. Hagen (Eds.), *Perspectives on the development of memory and cognition.* Hillsdale, NJ: Erlbaum.

Bransford, J. D., & Stein, B. S. (1984). *The IDEAL problem solver.* NY: W. H. Freeman and Company.

Brown, A. L., Bransford, J. D., Ferrara, R. A., & Campione, J. C. (1984). Learning, remembering, and understanding. In P. H. Mussen (Ed.), *Handbook of Child Psychology.* NY: John Wiley.

Brown, A. L., & DeLoache, J. S. (1978). Skills, plans, and self-regulation. In R. Siegler (Ed.), *Children's thinking: What develops?* Hillsdale, NJ: Erlbaum.

Brown, A. L., & Ferrara, R. A. (1980, October). *Diagnosing zones of proximal development: An alternative to standardized testing.* Paper presented at the Conference on Culture, Communication, and Cognition: Vygotskian Perspectives, Center for Psychosocial Studies, Chicago.

Brown, A. L., & French, L. (1979). The zone of potential development: Implications for intelligence testing in the year 2000. *Intelligence, 3,* 255–273.

Bryant, N. R. (1982). *Preschool children's learning and transfer of matrices problems: A study of proximal development.* Unpublished master's thesis, University of Illinois.

Budoff, M. (1967). Learning potential among institutionalized young adult retardates. *American Journal of Mental Deficiency, 72,* 404–411.

Burns, M. S. (1985). *Comparison of "Graduated Prompt" and "Mediational" dynamic assessment and static assessment with young children.* Technical Report No. 2. *Alternative assessments of young handicapped children.* Nashville, TN: John F. Kennedy Center for Research on Human Development, Vanderbilt University.

Burns, M. S., Haywood, H. C., Delclos, V. R., & Siewart, L. (in press). Young children's problem solving strategies: An observational study. *Journal of Applied Developmental Psychology.*

Campione, J. C., Brown, A. L., & Ferrara, R. A. (1982). *Mental retardation and intelligence.* In R. J. Sternberg (Ed.), *Handbook of human intelligence.* New York: Cambridge University Press.

Campione, J. D., Brown, A. L., Ferrara, R. A., Jones, R. S., & Steinberg, E. (1983). *Differences between retarded and nonretarded children in transfer following equivalent learning performance: Breakdowns in flexible use of information.* Unpublished manuscript, University of Illinois, Champaign–Urbana.

Feuerstein, R. (1979). *The dynamic assessment of retarded performers: The learning potential assessment device, theory, instruments, and techniques.* Baltimore: University Park Press.

Flavell, J. H. (1979). Metacognition and cognitive monitoring. *American Psychologist, 34,* 906–911.

Lidz, C. S. (1983). Dynamic assessment and the preschool child. *Journal of Psychoeducational Assessment, 1,* 59–72.

McCarthy, D. (1972). *Manual for the McCarthy Scales of Children's Abilities.* New York: The Psychological Corporation.

Reynolds, C. R., & Clark, J. H. (1983). Assessment of cognitive abilities. In K. Paget & B. Bracken (Eds.), *The psychoeducational assessment of preschool children.* New York: Grune & Stratton.

Simner, M. L. (1983). The warning signs of school failure: An update profile of the at-risk kindergarten child. *Topics on Early Childhood Special Education, 3,* 17–27.

Vygotsky, L. (1962). *Thought and language* (E. Hanfmann & G. Vakar, Trans.) Cambridge, MA: M.I.T. Press. (Original work published 1934)

Vygotsky, L. (1978). *Mind in society: The development of higher psychological processes* (M. Cole, V. John-Steiner, S. Scribner, & E. Souberman, Eds. and Trans.). Cambridge, MA: Harvard University Press.

Appendix A: Mediation Procedure for the Stencil Design Test

Familiarizing the Child with Materials and Relevant Dimensions

1. Point out cut-outs (I CUT THEM OUT).
2. Label shapes. If there is resistance or difficulty learning labels, then tell the child the label, but go quickly to finding shapes that match and say FIND ALL THE CARDS LIKE THIS. Comment on the lack of labels in a report, but do not get bogged down—the matching encourages comparative behavior while establishing shape as a relevant feature.
3. Point out solids (NOT CUT-OUTS—NO HOLES). Note all are in bottom row, near child.
4. Label colors (see notes for label shapes).
5. Have child COUNT THE SOLIDS. Focus here is not on the ability to count, but on the child's conceptualization of "solid" or "not cut-out." If child counts correctly to 6, then the distinction is being made.

* * *   WARNING   * * *

If child cannot count all the solids, he or she needs more work on the preceding concepts.
6. Compare 2 circles (big, small)/2 white squares (straight, crooked)/2 blue cards (solid, cut-out)/2 yellow cards (solid, cut-out)/yellow and blue crosses (yellow, blue).
7. At some point, put solid and cut-out back in wrong place—again to gauge whether the discrimination is being made.

* * *   WARNING   * * *

If child cannot see that you put solid back in wrong place, he or she needs more work on preceding concepts.

Combination Rules

1. Demonstrate what happens when a green circle is placed on a yellow solid. Point out 2 colors, made from 1 ± 1.
2. Change solids, showing that the *inside* color changes by changing *solids*. Allow child to try 1 or 2 color changes. Emphasize that it is *solid* that is changing.

* * *   WARNING   * * *

If child cannot change the color of the solid, he or she needs more work on the preceding concepts.
3. Use white solid with green circle. Change cut-outs (don't reproduce any of the upcoming designs). Show that *outside* color changes by changing cut-outs.
4. Put solid on top of cut-out and establish necessary order rule and reason. Have child repeat the rule "I put a cut-out on top of a solid and the color of the solid is in the middle."
5. End with the sample design formed from stencils, then introduce the sample design model.

Helping the Child Reproduce the Model

1. Display model while reproduction is still on the table, discussing how a picture was made of it. Point out that there are *2* colors in the picture and *2* colors in the reproduction, but only *1* color on each separate card.
2. Put stencils back in place and request reproduction. Teach search pattern over cut-outs and over solids. Have child say "Is it this one?"
3. When production is made, encourage checking back to model. Go over what is *right* and what is *wrong* about the production.

* * *   WARNING   * * *

If the child's production is wrong, he or she needs more work on the preceding concepts. Refer to any errors made in route to a correct answer (spontaneous corrections) and discuss why they were wrong. Alternate the correct one and the wrong one. Always end with the correct solution.

4. Repeat Step 3 with each of the remaining training models.

Appendix B: Graduated Prompting Procedure for the Stencil Design Task

1. DO YOU REMEMBER HOW YOU DID IT WITH THE LAST ONE? If so, HOW DID YOU DO IT? If not, point out and label the solid cards and the cut-outs, then explain that a solid and a cut-out are put together to make one that looks just like the model.
2. LOOK AT ALL THESE CARDS (point out each card individually; a pencil is useful for this). EVERYTHING YOU NEED TO MAKE THIS ONE IS HERE. SEE IF YOU CAN MAKE ONE THAT LOOKS JUST LIKE THIS ONE.
3. SEE THIS MODEL (point to the model)? DOES ONE OF THESE (point to stencils) LOOK JUST LIKE THE MODEL? If child responds no, say RIGHT, NONE OF THEM LOOKS JUST LIKE THE MODEL. If the child responds yes, say NO, NONE OF THEM LOOKS JUST LIKE THE MODEL. Then say, YOU SEE IN THE MODEL WE HAVE A (point out and name the color) SOLID AND A (point out and name the color) CUT-OUT. YOU NEED TO PUT SOME OF THESE TOGETHER (point to solids and cut-outs) TO MAKE ONE THAT LOOKS JUST LIKE THE MODEL. SEE IF YOU CAN MAKE ONE THAT LOOKS JUST LIKE THIS MODEL.
4. LET'S LOOK AT THESE AGAIN. THESE ARE THE SOLID COLORS (point). DOES EACH SOLID HAVE ONE COLOR OR TWO COLORS? LOOK AT THIS ONE, FOR EXAMPLE. (Hold up white solid, #5.) If child does not respond correctly, give correct answer.

   THESE ARE THE CUT-OUTS (point). DOES EACH CUT-OUT HAVE ONE COLOR OR TWO COLORS? LOOK AT THIS ONE, FOR EXAMPLE. (Hold up red cut-out, #17.) If child does not respond correctly, give correct answer.

   DOES THE MODEL HAVE ONE COLOR OR TWO COLORS? LOOK AT THIS ONE, FOR EXAMPLE. (Hold up red-over-white sample model). If child does not respond correctly, give correct answer.

    YOU NEED ONE SOLID AND ONE CUT-OUT TO MAKE ONE THAT LOOKS JUST LIKE THE MODEL (point). SEE IF YOU CAN MAKE ONE THAT LOOKS JUST LIKE THIS MODEL (point to item model).

5. LET'S LOOK AT THE MODEL AGAIN. POINT TO (or NAME THE COLOR OF) THE PART THAT LOOKS LIKE IT COMES FROM A SOLID. Point if the child responds incorrectly. POINT TO (or NAME THE COLOR OF) THE PART THAT LOOKS LIKE A CUT-OUT. Point if the child responds incorrectly. NOW SEE IF YOU CAN MAKE ME ONE THAT LOOKS JUST LIKE THE MODEL.

6. LOOK AT THIS MODEL. (Show red-over-white sample model.) LET'S SEE WHAT SOLID I NEED TO MAKE THIS ONE. IS IT THIS ONE? Explore the other solids and whether they are correct. LET'S SEE WHAT CUT-OUT I NEED TO MAKE THIS ONE: IS IT THIS ONE? Explore the cut-outs up to the correct one. LOOK AT WHAT HAPPENS WHEN I TAKE A WHITE SOLID AND I PUT A RED CUT-OUT ON TOP OF IT. PART OF THE WHITE SOLID GETS COVERED UP. THAT IS HOW I MAKE ONE JUST LIKE THIS MODEL. (Point to original model.) If the child uses the correct solid, skip prompt 7 and use prompt 8.

7. LOOK AT THIS MODEL. WHICH SOLID COLOR DO YOU NEED TO MAKE THIS MODEL? If the child does not answer say, SHOW ME ON THE MODEL. Demonstrate if child responds incorrectly. THESE ARE THE SOLID COLORS (point). PICK ONE OF THESE. AND SEE IF YOU CAN MAKE ONE THAT LOOKS JUST LIKE THE MODEL.

8. THIS (<u>name the color of the solid</u>) ONE IS PART OF THE MODEL. (Place the correct solid in the center of the board if it is not already there.) LOOK AT THIS PART OF THE MODEL (point to part that looks like a cut-out.) FIND A CUT-OUT FROM HERE (point) THAT LOOKS JUST LIKE THIS PART OF THE MODEL. SEE IF YOU CAN MAKE ME ONE THAT LOOKS JUST LIKE THE MODEL.

9. PUT THIS (name color) CUT-OUT ON YOUR SOLID COLOR. SEE, YOURS LOOKS JUST LIKE MINE.

13

Assessing Deaf Children

KEVIN J. KEANE

Historically, deaf persons have suffered, at best, from what Moores (1978) describes as "benign neglect" by society at large. Classified as mentally defective or "incapable of reason" (Hodgson, 1953), both civil and religious liberties were denied to deaf individuals in many cultures (Bender, 1960). Twentieth-century concepts have, of course, altered these points of view and most researchers and educators of the deaf would agree that the intellectual endowment of the deaf population is similar to that of the hearing population (Quigley & Kretschmer, 1982). However, this similarity represents an implicit criticism against psychological and educational practitioners, since performance characteristics of the deaf indicate a potential that is far from realized. As Levine (1981), in her description of the "average" deaf group, noted:

> The average group encompasses the deaf-at-large. The chief handicaps are scholastic retardations, linguistic deficiencies, and related conceptual gaps and limitations. Nevertheless, innate mental endowment is average and not infrequently better than average. The bulk of the group represents education's failures. (p. 157)

It would appear from this description that our present assessment and educational practices are limited in their ability "to fully help deaf people develop and use their abilities" (Quigley & Kretschmer, 1982, p. 63). Acknowledgment of this inability has led a number of researchers to investigate, at least in the area of cognitive assessment, alternate, nontraditional procedures. The purpose of these alternative approaches is to assess more accurately the potential of this population, and, thereby, promote changes in the educational environment of the deaf population. This does not imply that the task of maximizing the potential of deaf individuals is a simplistic one. As in any other human endeavor it is highly complex. However, it is certainly a task that is worth investigating when one considers that a viable resource is not being fully developed.

Characteristics of the Deaf Population

In order to consider fully the current practices used with the deaf population, it is necessary to describe the parameters of this group. Deafness refers to

Kevin J. Keane. Private practice, New York, New York.

the degree of auditory loss suffered by a person. Educationally, deaf persons are defined as individuals whose hearing impairment is so severe that their hearing is nonfunctional for the purposes of educational performance (Public Law 94-142). Audiometrically, individuals manifesting a hearing loss greater than 90 dB (profound) are considered deaf; those in the range above 70 dB (severe) are classified as being in a "transitory category between hard-of-hearing and deaf" (Quigley & Kretschmer, 1982, p. 3).

To define this population further, clarification of certain major impacting variables is necessary. One variable is the age of onset of loss; prelingual deafness refers to a loss encountered prior to the establishment of language (usually 2 or 3 years of age). A second variable is the etiology of the loss. Deafness may be caused by either endogenous or exogenous factors. Heredity, syndromes, and blood incompatibilities are examples of endogenous etiologies, whereas accident, drugs, and bacterial infections are examples of exogenous etiologies (Quigley & Kretschmer, 1982). Many of these causative factors may impart other handicapping conditions along with deafness. Quigley and Kretschmer (1982) posited the hearing status of the parents as another intervening variable. Deaf children with hearing parents compose 90% of the deaf population. Research concerning performance characteristics of deaf children with deaf parents indicate significant group differences, compared with deaf children of hearing parents, along a number of academic, behavioral, and cognitive parameters (Brill, 1969; Conrad, 1979; Meadow, 1980; Ray, 1979; Schlesinger & Meadow, 1972; Vernon & Koh, 1970). The studies reviewed in this chapter, in general, refer to prelingually deaf individuals (severe to profound loss) with mixed etiologies from homes with deaf or hearing parents.

Manifest Functioning of the Deaf

Research into the effects of auditory deprivation on speech, linguistic, and academic abilities provides clear-cut evidence that deafness detrimentally affects development in these areas for most deaf individuals (Bonvillian, Charrow, & Nelson, 1973; Furth, 1966; Goetzinger & Rousey, 1959; Lane, 1976; Levine, 1981; Meadow, 1980; Moores, 1970, Stuckless & Birch, 1966; Tomlinson-Keasey & Kelly, 1978; Trybus & Karchmer, 1977; Vernon & Koh, 1970). With regard to performance on traditional intelligence measures, the deaf perform similarly to the hearing population (Anderson & Sisco, 1977; Quigley & Kretschmer, 1982; Ray, 1979). However, investigations using cognitive tasks such as those delineated by Piaget have been, at best, inconclusive. Although similarities in performance on certain cognitive tasks between deaf and hearing populations do exist, marked differences on other tasks are also evident (Ottem, 1980).

With regard to social and behavioral functioning, research shows that, as a group, the deaf manifest higher degrees of impulsivity, egocentricity, dependency, lack of reflectivity, and rigidity than the population at large (Altshuler, Deming, Vollenweider, Rainer, & Tender, 1976; Harris, 1978; Levine, 1976, 1981; Myklebust, 1960). In a cross-national study, Meadow and Dyssegard (1983) reported that teachers of deaf children in both America and Denmark tended "to see their students (at both young and older age levels) to be lacking in motivation, independence, and initiative" (p. 347). In another study that asked educators of the hearing impaired from elementary to postsecondary programs to prioritize the personal and social needs of their hearing-impaired students, results indicated that acceptance of responsibility for one's actions was the most deficient competency (White, 1982). This behavior is related to locus of control, and concurs with other studies (Dillon, 1980; Harris, 1978) that indicate that the deaf manifest a more external locus of control—that is, as as group, there is a greater perception that external forces exert more control over one's life than internal factors; that life is not a consequence of one's own actions (Bodner & Johns, 1977).

Intelligence Testing with the Deaf

Because of the concomitant English linguistic deficit accompanying deafness, performance-type intelligence tests are the preferred measures used to assess the intellectual abilities of deaf persons (Brill, 1962; Levine, 1974; Sullivan, 1982), with the Wechsler Intelligence Scale for Children (WISC) Performance scale (now the revised WISC-R) being the most frequently administered (Levine, 1974). Along with the Hiskey–Nebraska Test of Learning Aptitude, which was standardized on deaf children, the WISC also has deaf norms (Anderson & Sisco, 1977). Other performance tests that are used frequently, such as the Leiter International Performance Scale, were not standardized on the deaf, and thus are not normed for this population. Gerweck and Ysseldyke (1975) have questioned the validity of using many of these popular performance measures with deaf populations because of a difference in the acculturation of the deaf from that of the hearing groups on which the tests were standardized and because the instructional communication of the tasks varies so widely among psychologists serving the deaf.

Although results of performance tests are used for important decisions concerning programming and placement of deaf children (Levine, 1974), the utility of these measures for purposes other than classification is questionable. Generally, correlations between these tests of intelligence and achievement have not been high for this population (Childers, Lao, & Lingerfelt, 1979). In fact, Joiner, Erikson, Crittenden, and Stevenson (1969) found that self-concept of academic ability appeared to be a better predictor of achievement than intelligence test scores. Also, as product-oriented ability measures, these instruments are limited in their implications for pedagogical or habilitative intervention (Feuerstein, 1979; Glaser, 1981).

Dynamic Assessment with the Deaf

Disenchantment with traditional psychometric approaches and instruments has been noted among researchers who serve the general hearing population. Certain researchers, such as Garcia (1981) and Olmedo (1981), have questioned the use of traditional measures with populations whose cultural, linguistic, economic, or social background differs from that of the mainstream society. This concurs with Gerweck and Ysseldyke's (1975) criticism of such instruments with the deaf population, as previously noted. Furthermore, research on the impact of nonintellective forces, such as affective–motivational factors, on cognitive functioning has led some to consider that cognitive and social competencies are reciprocal in nature (Scarr, 1981; Ziegler & Trickett, 1978). Traditional cognitive–intellective assessment procedures fail to take nonintellective factors into account, and therefore may "often yield insensitive indicators of cognitive level" (Dillon, 1979, p. 364). Out of concern regarding the manifest social–behavioral characteristics found in the deaf population, as well as the acculturation differences of this population, some researchers have investigated the use of nontraditional and more "dynamic" approaches in assessing the cognitive–intellective level of members of this population.

Dillon (1979) described two approaches that were designed to enhance the accuracy of cognitive assessments with deaf individuals. Both approaches involved learning tests and "require that the individual being tested be actively engaged in the testing situation" (p. 364). The first approach was referred to as a "testing-the-limits" procedure and the second involved learning potential assessment. For the studies to be discussed below, differentiation will be made between those using Feuerstein's (1979) Learning Potential Assessment Device and another using a different learning potential assessment paradigm.

Testing-the-Limits Procedures

Carlson and Dillon (1978) and Dillon (1979, 1980), in a series of studies, utilized a testing-the-limits paradigm to assess the intellectual capabilities of hearing-impaired children. This paradigm involves "the integration of standardized procedures of intervention into the testing situation itself" (Carlson & Dillon, 1978, p. 217). Dillon (1979) indicated that this procedure has more utility over a learning potential assessment approach in that it does not require training or practice outside the actual testing situation. She contended that the testing-the-limits procedure is better suited for "routine psychoeducational assessment" (p. 364).

The testing-the-limits paradigm involves a series of six elaborative conditions. The research investigated the effects of these conditions on the cognitive performance of hearing-impaired individuals. A description of the six test administration conditions is found in Dillon's (1979) study:

1. standard condition
2. simple feedback concerning correctness or incorrectness of response
3. child's "verbalization" of solution strategies following each choice
4. child's "verbalization" during and after solution of each item
5. elaborated feedback by examiner as to reason for correctness of each choice
6. examiner verbalization during and after solution coupled with elaborated feedback (p. 364)

In the Carlson and Dillon (1978) study, 70 deaf children, ranging in age from 6:1 to 10:11, with a mean IQ of 98.3 as tested on the Leiter International Performance Scale (mean IQ on the Leiter is 95), were administered the puzzle and booklet forms of the Raven Coloured Progressive Matrices (RCPM). Five conditions were delineated in this study, from a standard condition to a "performance dialogue," where elaborated feedback was given to the subject and the subject was asked to give a rationale for his or her choice of a particular item. If the choice was incorrect, the subject was asked to choose again. Regardless of condition, only the first response by the subject was scored. Interaction in all of the studies cited was carried out in Total Communication (i.e., simultaneous verbalization and signing). The results of this study indicated that the nonelaborative conditions, (i.e., the standard and simple feedback conditions) did not lead to higher levels of performance. However, each elaborative condition resulted in increased levels of performance. No difference was found between the two forms of test (puzzle or booklet) administered. With regard to the increased performance due to elaborative conditions, the authors cautioned that the results "cannot be attributed to a relatively simple learning process" (p. 222), but rather that some sort of "activation process," such as focusing the child's attention, which in turn led to solution strategies, was probably involved.

Another study by Dillon (1979) with a larger sample of deaf subjects ($N = 120$) essentially corroborated the study described above. Using the RCPM and a Piagetian battery involving order of appearance, multiplicative classification, and asymmetrical seriation, with the six conditions previously described, subjects in the more fully elaborated conditions performed significantly better on all tasks. Dillon (1979) did note that the conditions where the subject "verbalized" alone after a response or during task performance were "more likely to facilitate the development of appropriate solution strategies for those children (hearing as well as hearing impaired) having better language skills" (p. 369). The results of using testing-the-limits procedures, as reported here, support the use of this paradigm over a standard format in that greater cognitive potential may be realized in the deaf child.

Learning Potential Assessment

Koehler (1977) investigated the effects of training specific cognitive processes on a sample of deaf students. The subjects in this study ranged in age from

6:7 to 10:7; all subjects tested within the average or above-average intellectual range as measured by the Leiter and the Hiskey–Nebraska Test of Learning Aptitude. Using the RCPM in a test–train–retest format as designed by Budoff (1972), she concluded that treatment through learning potential assessment did not significantly improve performance on the RCPM. Koehler attributed the nonsignificant results to the possibility of a ceiling effect on the instrument since an unusually large proportion of the population sample scored "above average" on the initial administration of the RCPM.

Feuerstein and the LPAD

Feuerstein's (1979) approach to assessment differs from other learning potential assessment paradigms in both theory and practice. Chapters 1 and 14 of this text provide an explanation of this approach to dynamic assessment. To date, a few studies with deaf individuals have been conducted using the Learning Potential Assessment Device (LPAD) designed by Feuerstein (1979).

Katz (1984), in a single case study design, administered seven instruments from the LPAD battery to a 14-year-old deaf girl with a WISC-R Performance score of 85. Using Feuerstein's (1979) procedure of observing deficiencies at the input–elaboration–output phases of the mental act, Katz found the LPAD to be a useful tool in delineating cognitive deficiencies, strengths, and potential. He further stated that his observations seem "to support the notion that mediational deprivation is contributory or causally related to poor performance of some deaf children on many achievement and intelligence measures" and "that the effects of mediational deprivation can be reversed" (p. 105). Katz supported the value of the LPAD process-oriented approach in that it provides the examiner with more of an opportunity to generate prescriptive recommendations for instructional planning.

Feuerstein (1979) noted in his studies that mediational intervention through LPAD results in higher gains for low achievers than for high achievers. Huberty and Koller (1984) investigated this premise in a study comparing deaf and hearing subjects. The sample consisted of 40 hearing subjects with a mean age of 12:11 and 28 deaf subjects with a mean age of 13:6. For the hearing group, those who scored in the top 25% on the Stanford Achievement Test (SAT) were classified as high achievers and those in the bottom 25% as low achievers. For the deaf group, those who scored in the 65th percentile or better on the SAT hearing-impaired version were designated as high achievers, and those at the 35th percentile or lower were grouped as low achievers. Subjects in each group were then randomly assigned to either training or nontraining groups.

One LPAD instrument, the Representational Stencil Design Test (RSDT), was used in this study. The RSDT is a variation of the Grace Arthur Stencil Design Test (Arthur, 1947) in that the same stencil designs are used; however, they are not manipulated. In the RSDT, the subjects must mentally project the stencils in the appropriate order for completion of a design. Because of the complexity of this task, the training and nontraining groups were further broken down into input and noninput groups. Those receiving input were informed as to the numbers of the stencils needed to complete a design; the noninput group did not receive this information.

The results of this study indicated that: 1) low achievers performed as well as high achievers with training, regardless of hearing ability; 2) input manipulation had a powerful effect on the ability of hearing and deaf students to solve a cognitive task; 3) there were no differences in the ability of hearing and deaf students to learn complex problem-solving skills with proper training, input, and control of language variables; and 4) learning potential procedures could be effectively used with the deaf (Huberty & Koller, 1984, p. 27). The finding that input manipulation served to "equalize performance across all experimental conditions" indicated "that the deaf may have more difficulty with initial input of information than do hearing persons" (Huberty & Koller, 1984, p. 26).

In conclusion, Huberty and Koller (1984) contended that, although there were practical limitations, learning potential approaches could be useful in terms of research and application for both deaf and hearing persons. Furthermore, they stated that "if deaf persons do not perform well on cognitive tasks, it may be that deafness has contributed to the development of deficient functions, and remediation efforts may be indicated" (p. 27).

Keane (1983) and Keane and Kretschmer (submitted for publication), in agreement with the above statement, suggested that beyond the practical utility of LPAD with deaf persons, Feuerstein's (1979, 1980) mediated learning experience construct may provide a framework for understanding the manifest functioning of this population. In their research, they attempted to apply Feuerstein's (1979) "mediated learning" theory to the deaf population. This research will be discussed following a description of Feuerstein's theory of mediated learning.

MEDIATED LEARNING THEORY[1]

Grounded in cognitive psychology and social learning theory, Feuerstein's (1979, 1980) theory is that development beyond the biological–physiological level is affected by two modalities of learning: direct experience and mediated experience. Direct experience learning refers to the learning that occurs from the earliest stage of life through direct contact with stimuli that impinge upon the child. In mediated exposure, however, direct experience with stimuli is altered through the action of an "experienced, intentioned, and active human being" (Feuerstein & Rand, 1977, p. 110). By situating himself or herself

---

1. *Editor's note:* The concept of mediated learning experience is reviewed in a number of chapters throughout the book. Because each author relates the concept in his or her own way to the chapter content, this redundancy is viewed as necessary.

between the stimulus and the individual, this caring human "mediates the stimuli (verbally and nonverbally) in such a way that each stimulus is changed as it reaches the organism" (Feuerstein & Rand, 1977, p. 110). Through a repertoire of actions, such as selecting stimuli for exposure, framing environmental events, focusing the individual in terms of salient aspects, provoking anticipatory behaviors, and feeding back environmental experiences, the experienced person transmits appropriate learning sets and habits to the developing individual (Feuerstein, 1979).

Central to mediated learning experience is the "intentionality" of the intervening person. By intentionally mediating the meaning of experience, the specific content of an action is transcended, and over time a process for learning is established. In this way, the intentioned adult orients and organizes the phenomenological world for the child. Such mediation "occurs at a very early stage at the preverbal level and continues into early childhood on verbal levels in those areas that are novel to the organism" (Feuerstein & Rand, 1977, p. 110).

In this theoretical approach, both modalities of learning, (i.e., direct learning and mediated learning) are perceived as essential to development. However, the contention is that, through mediated learning, the ability of the individual to benefit from direct experience is enhanced, and that mediation is essential for continued direct exposure learning. The importance of mediated learning experience is underscored by Feuerstein (1979) as a "prerequisite to effective, independent, and autonomous use of environmental stimuli by the child . . . and to the development of an attitude toward thinking and problem solving that is actively and efficiently involved in organizing the world of stimuli impinging on the individual from both internal and external sources (pp. 71–72).

Insufficient mediated learning experience results in cultural deprivation (i.e., an alienation from one's own culture), marked by a significant reduction in the ability of an individual to adapt and become modified by his or her own culture. This alienation may be produced by a number of determinants, including sociological, geopolitical, psychophysical, and cultural conditions (Feuerstein, 1979). Feuerstein (1979) stressed that the concept of cultural deprivation in this framework "refers to an intrinsic criterion of the specific culture itself: *intergenerational transmission*" (p. 39), and thus emphasis is placed upon the intergenerational communication or transmission of culture as opposed to popular notions of culture involving group organizations and the by-products (artifacts) of that culture.

Feuerstein and Rand (1977) offered two factors to explain lack of mediated learning: 1) an environment that fails to mediate the world to the child, and/or 2) a child who himself or herself produces barriers to attempts at mediation. Regardless of the causative aspects of insufficient mediated learning, the most salient result is that it leaves the individual a passive receiver of information, an individual centered primarily with an external locus of control, and one who has a "limited capacity to become modified through direct exposure and experience, perceptual, motor, and emotional" (p. 111). In observing the manifestations of the mental actions of individuals who are mediationally deprived, a host of cognitive deficiencies may be observed at the input, elaborational, and output levels of the process. However, Feuerstein (1979) contended, and has found support in his research, that "a great part of the low performance manifested by [mediationally] disadvantaged populations does not reflect poor elaborative thought processes but is determined by other variables such as deficient functioning at the input or output phases" (p. 306). For this reason it may be possible to observe dramatic positive changes in performance through a relatively short intervention involving mediational interaction.

Mediated Learning and the Deaf

Scarr (1981) used the term "intellectual competence" to refer to the structural ability to adjust and adapt to life situations, such as schooling, and later on in vocational or occupational pursuits. Investigations with deaf populations indicate that they meet with difficulties with regard to the development of this competence. As noted previously, problematic social–behavioral characteristics occur more frequently in the deaf than in the hearing population. Academic retardation has also been cited as a significant problem with this group (Furth, 1966; Levine, 1981; Tomlinson-Keasey & Kelly, 1978; Trybus & Krachmer, 1977), along with occupational underachievement for deaf adults (Schein & Delk, 1974). The above characteristics are similarly found in culturally (mediationally) deprived populations (Feuerstein, 1979, 1980).

It is critical to recognize, however, that the performance characteristics cited are evident only when the deaf population is viewed as a group. Levine (1981) noted that "a common misconception about prelinguistic deafness is that it reduces all its victims to one common denominator. This is not the case; far from it" (p. 155). The fact that many profoundly deaf individuals demonstrate high levels of cognitive functioning as measured by the culture at large attests to a potential that is not precluded by the sensory loss alone and, thus, suggests that in large measure the sensory impairment itself may be a distal rather than a proximal etiology, as suggested by Feuerstein.

Over 90% of deaf children are born to hearing parents. For a majority of these parents, it is their first encounter with the handicap of deafness (Schlesinger & Meadow, 1972). Mindel & Vernon (1971) cited guilt, anger, grief, and repression as stages through which parents normally pass in coping with the reality of having a hearing-impaired child. As the nurturing agents in the environment of the deaf child, the nature of the parents' coping mechanisms may cause a significant disruption or reduction in the mediational learning process, that is, a situation where the organization of environmental stimuli is not adequately interpreted for the child. Also, as a hearing person, the adaptative response to the environment is through an integrated sensory network with audition playing a central role in the orienting framework. Hearing parents are faced with a dilemma of trying to mediate the world to their deaf child visually when they are not singularly visually oriented themselves.

In general, hearing parents of deaf children exhibit a greater degree of trauma then deaf parents in accepting their deaf child, more conflict concerning child-rearing practices, and significantly more difficulty in establishing a communication system (Schlesinger & Meadow, 1972). Studies focusing on comparative aspects of deaf children born to deaf parents and deaf children born to hearing parents indicate lower performance levels in written language, reading, vocabulary, and fingerspelling for the latter group (Quigley & Frisina, 1961; Stuckless & Birch, 1966; Vernon & Koh, 1970). In contrast to deaf children of deaf parents, deaf children of hearing parents also demonstrate comparative weaknesses in the areas of positive self-image and social adjustment (Meadow, 1980), exhibit less impulse control (Harris, 1978), and manifest lower scores on traditional tests of intellectual ability (Brill, 1969; Conrad, 1979; Ray, 1979).

In applying Feuerstein's (1979) theoretical construct of mediated learning to the deaf population as a whole, it would appear that hearing parents may be more disadvantaged than are deaf parents in terms of intergenerational transmission. This difference may be so not only because of a communication facility and a better acceptance of the condition of deafness, but also because deaf parents would be more adept at visually orienting the mediational aspects of learning for their children. Feuerstein and Rand (1977) stated that mediated learning experience was not limited to specific language or content; rather, it was the intentionality (i.e., the transcendence of the specific task itself) on the part of the mediator that played the key role.

The comparative performance characteristics between deaf children of hearing parents and deaf children of deaf parents lend support to a hypothesis suggested by Meadow (1980) and Levine (1981) that deafness causes the "caring others" in the environment to react in such a way as to promote a more maladaptive interaction pattern between hearing parents and their deaf children, thus causing a disruption in cultural transmission. As Chess (1975) indicated, "the deaf child is doubly deprived, the first deprivation arising from his deafness and the second from the effect of his handicap upon the environment" (p. 150). To translate this statement into Feuerstein's terms, by virtue of sensory deprivation, the deaf child faces a barrier to attempts at mediation that in turn promotes an environment that is incapable of mediating the world of objects and events in the most beneficial way to the deaf child. Thus, the causative factors of cultural deprivation would appear cyclical in nature in relation to the deaf child and the environment.

As the deaf child's world expands into the realm of schooling, the causative factors of cultural (mediational) deprivation may persist. Levine (1981) stated that deaf children were more dependent upon formal schooling than hearing children because they had less access to informal out-of-school input. However, she criticized formal education of the deaf for its limitations "in opportunities for independent thinking and for developing mental initiatives and controls" (p. 142). Levine's view is supported by interaction studies (Craig & Collins, 1970; Wolff, 1977) that indicate an inordinate amount of time spent in teacher-dominated talk with the level of questioning remaining primarily at a fact-response level. Meadow (1980) indicated that teachers tended to lower their expectations for their deaf students and, according to Liben (1978), restricted the levels of experience available to them. Such an environment may serve to reinforce such behaviors as passive acceptance of certain kinds of information, dependency, and lack of responsibility for one's own behavior, which are associated with the syndrome of cultural (mediational) deprivation.

Study of Mediated Intervention with the Deaf

Based on the contention that mediated learning may be a powerful factor in the ontology of development in the deaf child, and that impoverishment in mediated learning experiences tends to mask cognitive potentials, Keane (1983) and Keane and Kretschmer (submitted for publication) investigated the cognitive modifiability of a sample of deaf children when exposed to mediated intervention. Using a multigroup pretest–posttest design, 45 pre-lingually deaf subjects between the ages of 9 and 13, with hearing parents, were randomly assigned to one of three test–treatment conditions prior to testing. These test–treatment conditions consisted of one experimental group, an "investment" condition, and two comparison groups: a "standard" and an "elaboration" condition. The mean WISC-R Performance score for each group was 91.3, 94.6, and 99.8, respectively. The three conditions varied in the nature of the examiner–examinee interaction in each, and in the alteration of one set of stimulus materials. All groups received both the training and the assessment sections of each of the LPAD instruments.

In the experimental condition, 15 subjects received the battery of LPAD tasks as designed by Feuerstein (1979). In the standard condition, 15 subjects received the same instruments as the experimental group; however, for one of the tasks, this group received a motor-manipulative form of the test. Interaction between the examiner and examinee followed standard psychometric practice. In the second comparison group, the elaboration condition, 15 subjects received the same test instruments as the standard group; however, the examiner–examinee relationship was altered. Because Dillon (1979, 1980) and Carlson and Dillon (1978) demonstrated that elaborated feedback (testing-the-limits procedure) during testing improved performance of deaf subjects on certain cognitive–intellective tasks, this group served to compare the effect of a "testing-the-limits" procedure with mediated exposure. Using Dillon's (1979) format, in this condition the examiner provided feedback to the examinee as to the correctness or incorrectness of response, requested the examinee to articulate a rationale for each response, and, if the response was incorrect, explained the underlying premise of the task item, although the alternate correct response was not provided.

Prior to actual treatment, a test for differentiation of interaction type was conducted. This was done to ensure that a clear demonstration of interaction type was evident among the three treatment conditions. Three naive raters, given a written description of each type of interaction, observed a videotape of 10 randomly assorted segments of interactions and rated each segment as to whether it belonged to an investment, standard, or elaboration condition. Results of this procedure indicated that, within the 10 segments, differentiation of interaction type was possible 100% of the time among the three raters.

Six instruments from the LPAD battery were administered to each group. Following is a description of the instruments used.

1. Raven Coloured Progressive Matrices (RCPM) (Raven, 1956) and LPAD Set Variations I. These two instruments involve figural analogies. The LPAD Set Variations I is similar in construct to the latter portion of the RCPM. The Set Variations consists of five sets of analogies; each set contains six analogies, the first of which is used for training purposes; the five other analogies function as variations of that training analogy.

2. Organization of Dots (Rey & Dupont, 1953). This task consists of amorphous arrangements of dots that have to be organized according to an imposed geometric structure. This instrument consists of two parts, the first of which is used for training purposes and the second for assessment.

3. Plateau Test (Rey, 1950). This is a positional learning task that involves a projection from a three-dimensional to a one-dimensional frame of reference, and a mental transformation of learned positions through various rotations. The training phase of the Plateau Test occurs during the practice in learning the initial positions of four stationary items.

4. Associated Recall Test (Rey, 1966). This is an associative memory task that taps the capacity of an individual to use increasingly reduced visual cues to remember 20 figures. Because of the nature of this task, all subjects received this test under the same format.

5. Grace Arthur Stencil Design Test (SDT) (Arthur, 1947) and Representational Stencil Design Test (RSDT) (Feuerstein, 1979). The RSDT, as previously noted, is a procedural variation of the SDT in that the motoric manipulation of the stencils is removed. The ex-

perimental group received the RSDT and the two comparison groups received the SDT. All groups received a set of training/practice stencils and a set of test stencil designs.

The nonverbal battery of the Cognitive Abilities Test (CAT) (Thorndike & Hagen, 1979), which consists of three subtests (Figure Classification, Figure Analogies, and Figure Synthesis), served as a pre–post measure and was administered to all three groups under standard psychometric conditions. The Kohs Block Design (Kohs, 1923) was also administered as a pretest–posttest measure. Since impulsive responding was overtly treated in the experimental condition where necessary, the block design served as a device to measure change in "planning" behavior, that is, the number of trials attempted to successfully complete a given design in the test. The purpose of administering both measures was to observe any transfer effect along cognitive and/or behavioral dimensions that might occur from treatment.

The results indicated a significant main effect for treatment for five of the treatment instruments. Post hoc analysis for contrasts indicated that the experimental group performed significantly better ($p<.01$) than the two comparison groups. The subjects in the elaboration group performed better than those in the standard group, and two of the tasks resulted in a significant ($p<.05$) difference between the two comparison groups. The only task that did not indicate a significant main effect was the Associated Recall Test. Because of the nature of this instrument, all three groups were administered this task in the same way. Therefore, this instrument served as an internal check with regard to interaction effect.

Results of performance on the CAT also indicated a significant main effect for treatment. Post hoc analysis for contrasts indicated a significant difference ($p<.001$) between the experimental condition and the standard, and a significant difference between the two comparison groups ($p<.01$) in favor of the elaboration group, but no significant difference between the experimental and elaborative conditions.

For the Kohs Block Design, a nonparametric sign test was performed on: 1) the pre- to posttest increase in the number of designs successfully completed by each individual in each group, and 2) the number of trials from those designs successfully completed on the pretest versus the same designs completed on the posttest. The results of the sign test for design completion indicated a significant increase in the number of designs successfully completed for the experimental group ($p < .01$, $N = 14$) but no significant increase for the comparison groups. In terms of number of trials, the sign test indicated a significant decrease in the number of trials used for the experimental group ($p < .05$, $N = 13$) but no significant decrease in trial performance for the two comparison groups.

One limitation was noted in Keane (1983) and Keane and Kretschmer's (submitted for publication) study, and that is that only one examiner provided treatment across the three groups. This was a necessary limitation because of a lack of examiners who were (a) trained on the LPAD tasks and (b) conversant in manual communication. To adjust for this, the pretest and posttest measures were counterbalanced, as well as internally checked for reliability, by two examiners. Keane (1983) noted that the posttest results mitigate examiner bias in the treatment conditions. Krapf (personal communication), in an ongoing study using the LPAD with deaf adolescents, noting the above limitation, utilized two examiners to observe the effect of examiner bias on treatment. In his study, no examiner effect for treatment was noted.

The findings of Keane (1983) and Keane and Kretschmer's (submitted for publication) studies indicate that there is a great deal of cognitive potential within this sample of deaf individuals that is obscured by both traditional psychometric approaches and "testing-the-limits" procedures. The pretest–posttest results indicate that qualitative interactive feedback is a variable in transfer of learning to novel but comparable cognitive tasks, with mediated feedback producing more statistically significant learning transfer. Furthermore, the significant performance for the experimental group on the Kohs Block Design indicates that mediated interaction can affect behavior outside of the treatment itself, at least for a limited time period. The authors interpret the preceding results as supportive of the relevance of Feuerstein's (1979) theory of mediated learning for the deaf population. In addition, the results support Feuerstein's notions that: (a) mediated learning is not a simple variant of direct learning and (b) increased cognitive performance is not simply a function of providing positive feedback and/or practice. These data suggest that cognitive functioning seems to be, in part, the result of specific active intervention on the part of a caring adult. In other words, the adaptive cognitive functioning of individuals, including deaf individuals, seems to be partially a function of a specific kind or quality of adult–child interaction rather than its sheer quantity.

Conclusion

The studies cited here with regard to dynamic assessment with deaf populations indicate that greater cognitive potential is evidenced through these approaches than through standard, traditional procedures. Furthermore, a number of researchers state that dynamic, process-oriented approaches to assessment offer much information with regard to prescriptive, diagnostic habilitation and also curriculum development. Theoretically, further research concerning Feuerstein's developmental foundations could demonstrate its value as an orientation for serving this population both educationally and psychologically, in that it provides a framework for understanding manifest functioning while providing mechanisms for change. It is important that professionals understand but then look beyond certain manifest functioning in the deaf population and "intentionally" move toward effecting change. By merely listing or observing manifest behavior, there is a tendency to maintain a status quo or, at worst, promote a self-fulfilling prophecy of failure.

As noted, successful adaptation in modern society requires the potential to change and modify oneself to a variety of situations. Continued research that investigates the interaction of assessment for potential and educational/ habilitative programming could serve to actualize such a potential in deaf individuals. That there is a capacity for change within this population is evidenced by how, as a group, the deaf have dealt with society's treatment of them over time. As Best (1943) stated, the deaf are "the most misunderstood sons of men but the gamest of them all" (p. 15).

REFERENCES

Altshuler, K., Deming, W., Vollenweider, J., Rainer, J., & Tender, R. (1976). Impulsivity and profound early deafness: A cross cultural inquiry. *American Annals of the Deaf, 121*(4), 331–339.

Anderson, R., & Sisco, F. (1977). *Standardization of the WISC-R performance scale for deaf children* (Series T, No. 1). Washington, DC: Gallaudet College Office of Demographic Studies.

Arthur, G. (1947). *A point scale of performance tests: Clinical manual*. New York: Commonwealth Fund.

Bender, R. (1960). *The conquest of deafness*. Cleveland: Western Reserve University Press.

Best, H. (1943). *Deafness and the deaf in the United States*. New York: Macmillan Co.

Bodner, B., & Johns, J. (1977). Personality and hearing impairment: A study in locus of control. *Volta Review, 79*, 362–372.

Bonvillian, J., Charrow, V., & Nelson, K. (1973). Psycholinguistic and educational implications of deafness. *Human Development, 16*, 321–345.

Brill, R. (1962). The relationship of Wechsler IQ's to academic achievement among deaf students. *Exceptional Children, 28*, 315–321.

Brill, R. (1969). The superior I.Q.'s of deaf children of deaf parents. *The California Palms, 15*, 1–4.

Budoff, M. (1972). Measuring learning potential: An alternative to the traditional intelligence test. *Studies in Learning Potential, 3*, 39.

Carlson, J., & Dillon, R. (1978). Measuring intellectual capabilities of hearing impaired children: Effects of testing the limits procedures. *Volta Review, 80*, 216–224.

Chess, S. (1975). Behavior problems of children with congenital rubella. In D. Naiman (Ed.), *Needs of Emotionally Disturbed Hearing Impaired Children*. New York: New York University School of Education, Health, Nursing and Art Professions.

Childers, J., Lao, R., & Lingerfelt, M. (1979). *A report of some non-traditional psychological and academic measures among hearing impaired residential students in three southeastern states*. Paper presented at the Southeastern Psychological Association Meeting, New Orleans.

Conrad, R. (1979). *The deaf school child*. London: Harper & Row.

Craig, W., & Collins, J. (1970). Analysis of communicative interaction in classes for deaf children. *American Annals of the Deaf, 115*, 79–85.

Dillon, R. (1979). Improving validity by testing for competence: Refinement of a paradigm and its application to the hearing impaired. *Educational and Psychological Measurement, 39*, 363–371.

Dillon, R. (1980). Cognitive style and elaboration of logical abilities in hearing impaired children. *Journal of Experimental Child Psychology, 30*, 389–400.

Feuerstein, R. (1979). *The dynamic assessment of retarded performers: The learning potential assessment device, theory, instruments, and techniques.* Baltimore: University Park Press.

Feuerstein, R. (1980). *Instrumental enrichment: An intervention program for cognitive modifiability.* Baltimore: University Park Press.

Feuerstein, R., & Rand, Y. (1977). *Studies in cognitive modifiability: Redevelopment of cognitive functions of retarded early adolescents.* Jerusalem: Hadassah–Wizo–Canada Research Institute.

Furth, H. (1966). A comparison of reading test norms of deaf and hearing children. *American Annals of the Deaf, 111,* 461–462.

Garcia, J. (1981). The logic and limits of mental testing. *American Psychologist, 36,* 1172–1180.

Gerweck, S., & Ysseldyke, J. (1975). Limitations of current psychological practices for the intellectual assessment of the hearing impaired: A response to the Levine study. *Volta Review, 77,* 243–248.

Glaser, R. (1981). Education and thinking—the role of knowledge. *American Psychologist, 36,* 1103–1111.

Goetzinger, C., & Rousey, C. (1959). Educational achievement of deaf children. *American Annals of the Deaf, 104,* 221–231.

Harris, R. (1978). The relationship of impulse control to parent hearing status, manual communication, and academic achievement in deaf children. *American Annals of the Deaf, 123,* 52–67.

Hodgson, K. (1953). *The deaf and their problems: A study in special education.* London: Watts Pub. Co.

Huberty, T., & Koller, J. (1984). A test of the learning potential hypothesis with hearing and deaf students. *Journal of Educational Research, 78,* 22–27.

Joiner, L., Erikson, E., Crittenden, J., & Stevenson, V. (1969). Predicting academic achievement of the acoustically-impaired using intelligence and self-concept of academic ability. *Journal of Special Education, 3,* 425–431.

Katz, M. (1984). Use of the LPAD for cognitive enrichment of a deaf child. *School Psychology Review, 13,* 99–106.

Keane, K. (1983). *Application of mediated learning theory to a deaf population: A study in cognitive modifiability.* Unpublished doctoral dissertation, Columbia University, New York.

Keane, K., & Kretschmer, R. The effect of mediated learning intervention on cognitive task performance with a deaf population. *Journal of Educational Psychology.* Manuscript submitted for publication.

Koehler, L. (1977). *Learning potential assessment of a hearing impaired population.* Unpublished doctoral dissertation, University of Kansas, Kansas.

Kohs (1923). *Intelligence measurement.* New York: Macmillan.

Lane, H. (1976). Academic achievement. In B. Bolton (Ed.), *Psychology of deafness for rehabilitation counselors.* Baltimore: University Park Press.

Levine, E. (1974). Psychological tests and practices with the deaf: A survey of the state of the art. *Volta Review, 76,* 298–319.

Levine, E. (1976). Psycho-cultural determinants in personality development. *Volta Review, 78,* 258–267.

Levine, E. (1981). *The ecology of early deafness.* New York: Columbia University Press.

Liben, L. (Ed.). (1978). *Deaf children: Developmental perspectives.* New York: Academic Press.

Meadow, K. (1980). *Deafness and child development.* Berkeley: University of California Press.

Meadow, K., & Dyssegard, B. (1983). Social-emotional adjustment of deaf students. Teachers' ratings of deaf children: An American-Danish comparison. *International Journal of Rehabilitation Research, 6*(3), 345–348.

Mindel, E., & Vernon, M. (1971). *They grow in silence.* Silver Spring, MD: National Association of the Deaf.

Moores, D. (1978). *Educating the deaf: Psychology, principles, and practices.* Boston: Houghton Mifflin Co.

Moores, D. (1970). Psycholinguistics and deafness. *American Annals of the Deaf, 115*, 37–48.

Myklebust, H. (1960). *The psychology of deafness.* New York: Grune & Stratton.

Olmedo, E. (1981). Testing linguistic minorities. *American Psychologist, 36*, 1078–1085.

Ottem, E. (1980). An analysis of cognitive studies with deaf subjects. *American Annals of the Deaf, 125*, 564–575.

Quigley, S., & Kretschmer, R. (1982). *The education of deaf children: Issues, theory, and practice.* Baltimore: University Park Press.

Quigley, S., & Frisina, D. (1961). *Institutionalization and psychoeducational development of deaf children.* Urbana, Illinois: CEC Research Monograph.

Raven, J. (1956). *Guide to using the Coloured Progressive Matrices, Set A, AB, and B.* Dumfries, England: Grieve and Sons.

Ray, S. (1979). *An adaptation of "Weschler Intelligence Scale for Children–Revised" for deaf children.* Unpublished doctoral dissertation, University of Tennessee, Knoxville, Tennessee.

Rey, A. (1950). *Six epreuves au service de la psychologie clinique.* Brussels: Establissements Bettendorf.

Rey, A. (1966). *Les troubles de la memoire et leur examen psychometrique.* Brussels: Charles Dessart.

Rey, A., & Dupont, J. (1953). Organization des groupes de points en figuires geometriques simples. *Monographs de Psychologie Appliqué, 3.*

Scarr, S. (1981). Testing for children: Assessment and the many determinants of intellectual competence. *American Psychologist, 36*, 1159–1166.

Schein, J., & Delk, M. (1974). *The deaf population in the United States.* Silver Spring, MD: National Association of the Deaf.

Schlesinger, H., & Meadow, K. (1972). *Sound and sign: Childhood deafness and mental health.* Berkeley: University of California Press.

Stuckless, E., & Birch, J. (1966). The influence of early manual communication on the linguistic development of deaf children. *American Annals of the Deaf, 111*, 452–460, 499–504.

Sullivan, P. (1982). Administration modifications on the WISC-R performance scale with different categories of deaf children. *American Annals of the Deaf, 127*, 780–788.

Thorndike, R., & Hagen, E. (1979). *Cognitive abilities test.* Hopewell, NJ: Houghton Mifflin Co.

Tomlinson-Keasey, C., & Kelly, R. (1978). The deaf child's symbolic world. *American Annals of the Deaf, 123*, 452–459.

Trybus, R., & Karchmer, M. (1977). School achievement scores of hearing impaired children: National data on achievement status and growth patterns. *American Annals of the Deaf, 127*, 62–69.

Vernon, M., & Koh, S. (1970). Effect of manual communication on deaf children's educational, achievement, linguistic competence, oral skills, and psychological development. *American Annals of the Deaf, 115*, 527–536.

White, K. (1982). Defining and prioritizing the personal and social competencies needed by hearing impaired students. *Volta Review, 84*, 266–274.

Wolff, S. (1977). Cognition and communication patterns in classrooms for deaf students. *American Annals of the Deaf, 122*, 319–327.

Ziegler, E., & Trickett, P. (1978). IQ, social competence, and evaluation of early childhood intervention programs. *American Psychologist, 33*, 789–798.

ISSUES AND IMPLICATIONS

14

The Learning Potential Assessment Device: From Philosophy to Practice

MOGENS REIMER JENSEN AND REUVEN FEUERSTEIN

Disenchantment with traditional testing practices and growing interest in the possibility that higher levels of cognitive functioning, or intelligence, can be taught have caused many psychologists to reconsider fundamentally the role of assessment in decision making and program planning for the low-functioning child, adolescent, and adult. If intelligence is not an immutable, reified substance but rather a capacity that can be targeted for development, then consideration must be given to supplanting the passive acceptant approach to intelligence testing with an active modification and dynamic approach that can produce the prescriptive information required to forge its enhancement. In the search among alternatives to meet this need, increasing attention is being given to the Learning Potential Assessment Device (LPAD) (Feuerstein, 1979; Feuerstein, Miller, Rand, & Jensen, 1981; Feuerstein, Rand, Jensen, Kaniel, Tzuriel, Schachar-Segev, & Mintzker, 1986). For most professionals, however, this approach is completely novel and, although its general concepts may elicit interest and support, many professionals are at a loss for conducting rigorous conceptual analyses of the LPAD and hence for determining the extent to which this dynamic approach may help articulate and meet their assessment needs. The only integrated conceptual framework available is often the one underlying traditional testing practices and, in spite of the criticisms leveled against it, this is frequently the framework professionals attempt to use when evaluating the LPAD. The purpose of this chapter is to assist the reader in developing an understanding of the LPAD as a conceptually coherent and clinically rigorous approach to the dynamic assessment of the low-functioning individual.

Philosophy

The assumption guiding the development of the LPAD is not merely that the individual is active in registering, selecting, processing, and communicating stimuli from both the external and internal environments—a defining char-

Mogens Reimer Jensen. Department of Psychology, Yale University, New Haven, Connecticut; and Hadassah–WIZO–Canada Research Institute, Jerusalem, Israel.

Reuven Feuerstein. Hadassah–WIZO–Canada Research Institute, Jerusalem, Israel; and School of Education, Bar Ilan University, Ramat Gan, Israel.

acteristic of the paradigm adopted for much of modern psychology—but, rather, that the individual is an *open system* susceptible to influences that can produce *structural* changes in cognitive functioning. The dynamic assessment of learning potential targets the modifiability of the capacity to undergo such structural changes as a capacity that exists above and beyond any specific change or inculcation of skill. Conceptualizing and dealing very specifically with the process of change, the LPAD neither produces an inventory of what the examinee knows, nor produces a stable product such as an intelligence quotient. The LPAD rather seeks to identify the causes that prevent the examinee from functioning at higher levels and, through an assessment of the learner's modifiability, to produce information about the type, amount, and nature of investments that may be required to remove, by-pass, or overcome these obstacles and permit the examinee to accede to higher levels of functioning.

The Theory of Structural Cognitive Modifiability

The Role of the Mediated Learning Experience

The LPAD is based upon the theory of structural cognitive modifiability. The theory attempts to account for the differences in the capability of individuals to benefit from both formal and informal opportunities to learn. Feuerstein (Feuerstein, 1980; Feuerstein, Jensen, Hoffman, & Rand, 1985) has argued that a universal modality of learning is represented by the direct exposure of the individual to sources of stimuli, but that this modality alone can account neither for the observed differences in intellective functioning nor for the phenomenon of culture and the fact that people invest themselves in need systems only remotely related to their biological survival.

The theory presumes that the crucial determinant of the development in humans of higher levels of cognitive functioning depends upon the growing child's opportunity to benefit from mediated learning experiences (MLE). In this second modality of learning—and contrary to the fragmented, disassociated, and even random fashion in which stimuli reach the organism's systems through direct exposure experiences—stimuli are selected by a mediator; their appearance is scheduled in time and organized in space; and they are framed by goals and attributes, regulated in intensity through repetition, and enhanced through being connected by purpose and imbued with meaning. The mediator serves as a powerful filter, assisting the child in structuring his or her experience, expanding experience to areas inaccessible to the learner through the sheer activation of sensorial systems, thereby instilling and enlarging need systems.

Mediated Learning Experiences and the Transmission of Culture

Feuerstein posits a very close relationship between the processes of mediation and the transmission of culture. By mediating such processes as focusing and systematic exploration; selection of stimuli; imitation; reinforcement and reward; verbal stimulation; inhibition and control; short- and long-term recall; transmission of past and representation of future; discrimination and sequencing; cause–effect relationships; deductive, inductive, and inferential thinking; need for logical evidence; and need for precision, the MLE effects the induction of the child into his or her own particular culture. The MLE-deprived child is perceived as culturally deprived in the sense that the child has been deprived of his or her *own* culture.

Mediated Learning Experiences and Prerequisites of Thinking

Although the MLE is seen as a primary vehicle for the process of intergenerational transmission within all cultures, this form of learning may also be viewed more formally for its contribution to the establishment of prerequisites necessary for the development of higher levels of thinking. These prerequisites include a series of what we have termed cognitive functions, as well as mental operations and learning sets reflecting factors of self-perception, affect, and motivation.

The individual who has been the recipient of MLE is characterized by a high degree of modifiability when exposed to a need for change, whereas the individual who has not received adequate MLE reveals rigidity and a lack of plasticity in the face of such needs. Deficient cognitive functions, fragile or nonexistent mental operations, an eroded sense of self, passivity, and deficient need systems are seen as resulting from a disruption of those processes of mediation that normally ensure the cognitive development of the human being.

Investigations with the LPAD have revealed that the lack of adequately mediated learning experiences may result in cognitive deficiencies across three broad phases of the mental act, including the initial investment to gather information about problems (input), the mental transformation of collected information (elaboration), and the communication of the results of the mental activity (output).

Among the cognitive deficiencies affecting the initial investment and collection of information are: inadequacies in the perception and definition of a problem as a result of a lack of need to invest in the perceptual process and to search for and establish relationships between the elements of a task; inability to select relevant cues as a result of an inadequate goal orientation of the cognitive process; inadequate investments in the perceptual process resulting in blurred and sweeping perception; impulsive and unsystematic exploratory behavior produced by a limited awareness of the need for information required to produce an appropriate answer; impaired verbal tools affecting discrimination; difficulties with spatial and temporal relationships resulting in impaired representation of relationships between objects and events; impaired conservation of constancies affecting the conservation of identity; deficient need for precision and accuracy; and an impaired capacity for the simultaneous consideration of two or more sources of information.

Inadequately mediated learning experiences may produce a series of deficiencies affecting the mental elaboration of stimuli. These include a lack of spontaneous comparative behavior; a narrowness of the mental field that limits the number of pieces of information that can be coordinated and combined; an episodic grasp of reality causing objects and events to be perceived as dissociated, unrelated, and fragmented across time and space; impaired need for summative behavior that may affect the grouping and classification of objects and events; impaired need for pursuing logical evidence; impaired inferential hypothetical thinking; impaired planning behavior; impaired interiorization reflected in the limited use of symbols, signs, and concepts; and nonelaboration of cognitive categories reflected in the absence of the organization of gathered data into superordinate categories.

Cognitive deficiencies affecting primarily the communication of responses include: egocentric communication modalities as revealed in inadequate consideration of the listener's need for information to achieve comprehension; difficulties in applying recognized relationships to new situations (the projection of virtual relationships); a tendency to block in response to failure; difficulty in relating antecedent behaviors to outcomes (trial-and-error behavior); and deficiencies in visual transport (attempts to carry mental images) as a result of the vulnerability of the cognitive support system available for perceived elements.

The deficient cognitive functions along with the passivity, motivational deficits, and negative self-perception produced by mediational deprivation are considered to be the immediate causes accounting for an individual's low level of manifest behavior. These immediate causes have been found with the LPAD to be broadly shared among those who, for a great variety of reasons, have been deprived of adequate mediated learning experiences. The dynamic assessment of learning potential focuses upon these immediate causes. Through a highly focused and intensive MLE, the trained professional seeks to determine the nature, type, and amount of investment required to remediate the cognitive deficiencies and produce affective and motivational support for improved levels of functioning.

Dynamic Assessment and Distal Etiological Reasons for Inadequate Mediated Learning Experience

Reasons for the inadequate provision of MLEs may vary greatly and range from obstacles to mediation produced by the organism (e.g., hereditary, organic, or temperamental factors) to conditions in the family and environment (e.g., emotional difficulty or apathy in the parents, low parental maturational level, low socioeconomic status, cultural difference). Whenever factors such as these (exogenous or endogenous) result in the inadequate provision of MLEs, subnormal, low levels of functioning are anticipated because of the resultant underdevelopment of the prerequisites of higher levels of thinking. On the other hand, if ways are found to bypass or overcome either endogenous or exogenous obstacles to provide the individual with the requisite MLE, the theory predicts that the resultant enhancement of modifiability will permit normal learning and both autoplastic and alloplastic adaptation to occur.

With the LPAD the search for possibilities to produce structural enhancement of the individual's modifiability is undertaken irrespective of three parameters often assumed to impose firm upper limits for structural change: age, etiology, and severity of condition. Although each of these factors necessitates a very careful consideration of the impact upon the individual's experiential repertoire and possibilities for interacting with stimuli, the use of the LPAD represents a commitment to challenge the perception that these factors must automatically be perceived as constituting immutable barriers that *necessarily and unavoidably* prevent the attainment of higher levels of functioning. Rather, the dynamic assessment is required to determine the modifiability of dimensions affected by these factors and the degree to which the nature, extent, intensity, and type of intervention may be varied to produce meaningful change.

The Proposed Learning Paradigm

The paradigm that guides the theory of structural cognitive modifiability in general and the LPAD in particular is presented in Figure 14.1. It highlights the role of the human mediator (H) and the presumed significance of mediated learning for the instillment of those prerequisite cognitive functions and need systems that will permit the individual subsequently to benefit from direct exposure and to function in an autonomous and independent way. The par-

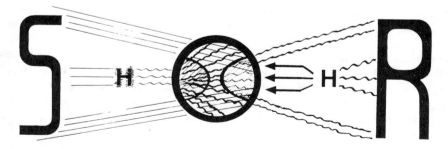

FIGURE 14.1.   The mediated learning experience model. The mediator (H) selects stimuli from the environment (S), transforming them according to purposes and goals before they reach the systems of the learner (O). The mediator (H) selects responses produced by the learner (O) shaping and transforming them to develop response modalities (R). Following mediation the learner (O) is able to interact effectively with the environment (S → O → R) without mediation.

adigm in Figure 14.1 sets the theory of structural cognitive modifiability apart from both the behavioral stimulus (S) → response (R) paradigm and the Piagetian S → learner (O) → R paradigm.

LPAD Techniques and Instruments

In order to carry out the dynamic assessment of retarded performers with the LPAD examiners must be thoroughly familiar with the philosophy underlying this active modification approach, the theory of structural cognitive modifiability, the MLE, and the deficient cognitive functions. In conjunction, these elements orient the examiner to the goals and purposes of the dynamic assessment. They identify mediated learning as the basic modality through which the attempt first to produce and then to assess change is carried out. Moreover, they point to the deficient cognitive functions and the attitudinal and motivational deficits as the target areas for mediated learning.

A thorough knowledge of the above factors is combined for the LPAD examiner with knowledge of the specific techniques of mediation, the rationale for the construction and use of the LPAD tools, and knowledge pertaining to the interpretation of results. These areas are discussed below.

The Examiner–Examinee Relationship

Emphasizing comparability of individual respondents as a necessary if not always sufficient condition for predictability, the conventional psychometric approach standardizes the test situation and the examiner–examinee relationship. Conceptually consistent with the view that intelligence represents an immutable, reified substance, the standardization is intended to ensure that capacity rather than contingencies of the examiner–examinee interaction, or test administration, is measured: The examiner is permitted to record and catalogue responses with minimal freedom to explore the circumstances and reasons for failures and successes alike.

The examiner–examinee relationship appropriate for traditional psychometric assessment is sharply contrasted with the relationship between examiner and examinee in the dynamic assessment of learning potential with the LPAD. Viewing the individual as an open system, accessible to structural changes in cognitive functioning, the LPAD focuses the assessment upon the identification and removal of the obstacles that presently may prevent the individual from functioning at higher levels. In the LPAD the examinee's manifest level of functioning, as evidenced by low IQ and achievement scores and often convincing observational data, is not denied. Rather, to the contrary, such data may constitute global evidence of the presence of cognitive and motivational deficiencies that may have resulted from the inadequate mediation of learning experiences. In the LPAD the examiner–examinee relationship is structured to help the examiner determine as precisely as possible (a) what the specific deficiences are, and (b) the amount and nature of the investment that may have to be offered to the examinee to overcome them.

Searching for deficient functions and inadequate mental operations, the LPAD examiner functions as a specially trained mediator. In remediating cognitive deficiencies and in producing positive motivational and attitudinal support for higher levels of functioning, the mediator seeks to prevent failure and indeed provides the child with help needed to overcome inadequacies in functioning. To attempt to forge the enhancement of modifiability through remediation of deficiencies, the examiner–examinee relationship becomes a highly focused, intensive, and interactive MLE characterized by the following 10 characteristics.

INTENTIONALITY AND RECIPROCITY

The LPAD mediator/examiner must be animated by an intentionality to interact in a meaningful way. The presence of such an intentionality ensures that the interaction will be endowed with purposes and goals to shape and guide the experience. Animating the mediator, the intentionality affects the LPAD examiner's face, eyes, and voice, making them conspicuous and generating an orienting response and a state of vigilance in the examinee. Such a state of vigilance may be necessary both to produce in the low performer a readiness to focus and to ensure acuity of the perceived and experienced. The examinee's reciprocation enables the mediator/examiner to determine the rate at which the interaction should progress, producing a readiness to slow down if necessary, to frame stimuli, to exaggerate movements and to model parts of whole sequences of behaviors as needed by the examinee. Intentionality and reciprocity ensure the existence of a bond between the examinee and the mediator.

TRANSCENDENCE

This characteristic of the examiner–examinee relationship identifies the goals of the mediated interaction to be beyond—or even to be totally unrelated to—the requirements and needs of the specific task, or materials. The goal is the remediation of deficiencies within the examinee's cognitive structure and the tasks of the LPAD are merely the tools through which such goals may be reached. The materials of the LPAD therefore do not embody the goals of the examiner–examinee interaction, but are used by the examiner to assess and to remediate the prerequisites of higher levels of functioning. The LPAD materials, as will be discussed below, have been specially selected, or constructed, to permit the examiner to register deficiencies, provide opportunities for remediation, and subsequently, record the extent to which this mediation may have been helpful in strengthening both cognitive functions and mental operations targeted for such intervention. The property of tran-

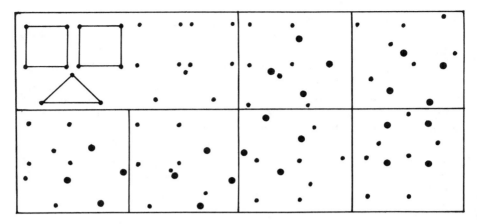

FIGURE 14.2.   The Organization of Dots and the principle of transcendence. With proper mediation the task of connecting the dots to form the model figures can be utilized, among many
possible transcendent goals, to restrain impulsivity and regulate behavior, to institute modalities
of thinking such as the search for and use of relevant information, to enhance the projection of
virtual relationships, and to develop comparative behavior.

scendence may be illustrated by the instrument Organization of Dots (see
Figure 14.2).

A goal frequently targeted by the LPAD examiner using this tool is the
resetting of the three phases of the mental act (regarding regulation of behavior, see also below). The normal flow of the mental activity of problem
solving is initiated by the perception of a disequilibrium, or problem, and a
need to search for clues for its articulation that produces an investment in
the perceptual process. This, in turn, yields information that is transformed
and elaborated, depending upon goals, leading to the output, or communication, of the results of the mental activity. A tendency, frequently a result
of mediational deprivation, to activate fragments of the mental act out of
sequence (e.g., the individual elaborates without input, moves directly from
input to output, or fails to communicate even adequately elaborated responses) may completely disrupt the normal rhythm and flow of the mental
act.

The regulation of behavior—only one of many goals that can be reached
with this instrument—is completely unrelated to the manifest task of the
Organization of Dots, which involves the connection of the dots within each
frame to reproduce model figures of a square and a triangle. The transcendent
goal can be reached only by the trained examiner through the intentional
selection and framing of stimuli in conjunction with additional techniques of
mediation to be described in the following.

MEANING

The mediation of meaning is considered necessary, along with intentionality
and transcendence, for mediated learning to occur. In the LPAD the examiner

detects the changes that are taking place in the examinee's performance and attributes meaning to these. Meaning cannot be grasped by the senses alone and its mediation is required both for the enhancement of the energetic and motivational component of the examinee's performance and for the development of insight. The mediation of meaning thereby permits experience to be the point of departure in the formation of more robust propensities within the individual to apply acquired cognitive functions and mental operations as components of need systems that may go far beyond those elicited by the specific task.

REGULATION OF BEHAVIOR

The LPAD mediator/examiner carefully regulates the examinee's behavior. The low-functioning student, because of deficient cognitive functions, the lack of required mental operations, or the contribution of affective and motivational factors, will frequently evidence both minute and gross disjunctions in the application of the broad phases of the mental act (input, elaboration, and output).

A large number of cognitive functions are involved in maintaining the normal rhythm and flow of the mental act. The LPAD examiner, through such behaviors as modeling and focusing, seeks to establish within the learner the propensities (a) to gather data through properly oriented and adequately timed investments in the perceptual process, (b) to elaborate and transform stimuli following their careful registration, and (c) to impose the necessary latencies to permit registration and elaboration of stimuli as well as the selection of proper communicational modalities to take place. To assist in this task the LPAD examiner may also target the development of systematic exploratory behavior, need for precision and accuracy at both input and output levels, and need for logical evidence (at the elaboration level), among others.

MEDIATION OF A FEELING OF COMPETENCE

The LPAD mediator/examiner, by ensuring conditions for successful interaction, creates a climate wherein a feeling of competency follows successful mastery. In order to enlist impulses of mastery and a motive to achieve, the LPAD examiner organizes opportunities for success, and through the mediation of a feeling of competence following mastery, produces within the individual the expectancies of success that will enhance the learner's ability to effect transfer. The mediation of a feeling of competence provides a motivational enhancement to seek mastery of increasingly complex and difficult tasks and is necessary to secure the development of autonomous, independent functioning.

SHARING

An important source for the development of output functions (and of social behavior), the mediation of sharing is in some respects a primary criterion of the MLE; sharing represents the energetic component that, through examiner–examinee eye contact, pointing, and tracking, enables the mediator to impart stimuli selected by intent. "Sharing behavior is thus the spearhead of the mediation which, by virtue of its affective, emotional quality ensures the effectiveness of the mediator in his or her mediational interactions with the child." (Feuerstein, Jensen, Hoffman, & Rand, 1985, p. 49). The mediation of sharing in the LPAD examiner–examinee interaction contributes to the establishment within the examinee of need systems to communicate with others and the propensity to search for the appropriate tempo and modality to overcome egocentricity.

INDIVIDUATION/PSYCHOLOGICAL DIFFERENTIATION

Whereas in vivo the mediation of sharing in the neonate originates with the earliest forms of "co-vibration" and imitative behaviors, the mediation of individuation/psychological differentiation addresses the child's capacity for and right to a dualistic organism–world relationship. In the LPAD the examiner assesses the student's locus of control and provides mediation to establish an internal locus along with the regulation of behavior, mediation of competence, and strengthening of both cognitive functions and mental operations that may be required to maintain it.

GOAL SEEKING, GOAL SETTING, AND GOAL ACHIEVEMENT

Assessing the modifiability of the examinee's cognitive structure through the mediated provision of intensive, focused learning experiences, the examiner seeks to forge conditions for the establishment of goal-seeking, goal-setting, and goal-achieving behavior. "The orientation toward goal-oriented and purposeful behavior is to a large extent the product of a mediational process, especially in areas that transcend the individual's immediate elementary and cyclic needs for which there is no biological support in the organism" (Feuerstein, Jensen, Hoffman, & Rand, 1985, p. 50). The examinee's episodic grasp of reality and difficulty with the representation of and projection into the future may have to be targeted for mediation along with planning behavior and hypothetical types of reasoning. However, following the development of the necessary prerequisites, the LPAD examiner mediates goal-seeking behavior by relating it to contingencies of awareness, need systems, attitudes, and values. Similarly, the subordination of means to goals is mediated to produce in the examinee the criteria for the selection and sequencing of requisite behaviors for goal achievement.

CHALLENGE

Although drawing upon the mediation of a feeling of competence, the mediation of challenge is targeted separately by the LPAD examiner. The development through mediation of the propensity to seek out tasks for their novelty and complexity is required above and beyond the mediation of competence to overcome the insecurity and anxiety associated with the unfamiliar.

This is even more so because involvement with the unfamiliar will often necessitate a temporary acceptance of incompetence before mastery of the novel task is gained.

CHANGE

The mediation of change is also attended to within the LPAD examiner–examinee relationship. The mediation of change is related to the feedback techniques used with this dynamic assessment: Constant and fine-grained feedback regarding performance is continually offered by the examiner. Failure is acknowledged but limited in its import to the specific behaviors or deficient functions that produced it. Successes are amplified and attributed to the examinee's growing mastery.

> Feedback is essential for the low-performing subjects inasmuch as their capacity for self-correction is limited, not only because they lack the knowledge and standards with which to compare results, but also because they lack both the need and the propensity to compare. Without feedback, subjects may not attempt to correct a task in which they have failed and may not be able to modify their behavior in the tasks presented to them. (Feuerstein, Haywood, Rand, Hoffman, & Jensen, 1985, p. 41)

The mediation of change is undertaken to equip the child with insight into his or her growing proficiency, thereby permitting the establishment of internalized expectancies for reinforcement and reward. The meaning attributed to the successful application of a mental operation, for example, changes with the development of efficiency. Once it has become established, the application of the mental operation will become detached from the positive feedback that characterized its emergence. The mediation of change both forges and supports the incremental widening of applications for newly acquired modalities of functioning through appropriate revisions of the import of both success and failure.

The LPAD examiner–examinee relationship, in sum, is structured to enable the examiner to identify deficiencies and produce changes. Regulating behavior to control impulsivity and inhibit passivity; modeling his or her own behavior; preparing the examinee for more complex levels of functioning by establishing prerequisites; providing corrective feedback; and creating the conditions for insight and the formulation of principles, rules, and methods, the LPAD examiner–examinee relationship is designed to produce changes that will enhance the examinee's capacity to approach new tasks successfully.

The Construction of LPAD Materials

Assuming that intellective functioning is immutable, traditional psychometric tests seek to identify stable, individual differences that can be used for purposes of comparison and classification. In developing these tests, careful statistical analyses are performed to ensure that retained items contribute reliably to the discrimination among respondents.

Tests developed in this manner are not appropriate for the assessment of structural cognitive modifiability. Demanding instruments, or tools, rather than tests, the LPAD offers to the trained examiner an extensive set of materials that give the examiner a greater range of functioning. First, the examiner can access the examinee's cognitive structure. The need to gain access to the cognitive structure necessitates that the LPAD include tools that employ modalities that are unlikely to elicit rejection and premature motivational closure. Modalities such as the verbal or numerical may, especially in the early part of the assessment, produce rejection as a result of association with past experiences of failure. To gain access to the cognitive structure the LPAD must also include tasks of low complexity, low abstractness, and very limited verbal requirements to ensure that even the functionally illiterate examinee will be able to perform and thus permit the examiner to make observations and begin the process of remediation.

Second, the examiner can ascertain the status of cognitive functions, mental operations, and nonintellective factors. This implies that the LPAD tools must present the examinee with tasks that provoke the activation of the examinee's cognitive structure in such a way that the examiner will have the opportunity to determine the deficient and efficient parts within it. This goal is met partly by the use of unfamiliar and varying task modalities and partly by careful variation of the complexity of materials. This, in addition to the intentional framing and selection of stimuli by the LPAD examiner, permits rich opportunity to determine quite precisely the status of the cognitive structure.

Third, the examiner can offer focused MLEs as needed. In order for an instrument to be effective for purposes of the assessment of structural cognitive modifiability, it has to offer *opportunity for learning that will affect learning capacity*. The LPAD instruments therefore must not only permit the examiner to register responses and offer global feedback, but also, must enable the examiner to modify the examinee through mediation. The instruments must therefore permit the kind of learning to occur that will affect the way in which the individual learns. Items involving sheer knowledge of factual content (e.g., "Who is the President of the United States?") are not useful for this purpose because of the limited information about changes in learning capacity revealed either by knowledge of the answer, or the retention or nonretention of the answer following its provision.

Fourth, the examiner can observe the extent to which the mediation provided has benefited the examinee. LPAD instruments typically consist of two parts. In the first part the LPAD examiner observes and remediates cognitive functions, offers verbal tools and operations, and ensures appropriate communication modalities among many possible mediations. Using the second part, the examiner obtains information about the extent to which the mediation may have resulted in improved performance. Here the examiner will intervene as little as possible and only as much as necessary to maintain motivation, prevent or overcome blocking, and derive insight from failure if incurred. Although within each instrument Part II employs the same modality as Part I, the materials in Part II are typically more complex and, hence, were it not for the mediation, would place more pressure on the examinee's cognitive structure.

To enable the examiner to observe the extent to which mediation may have affected learning capacity, LPAD instruments must be *sensitive to change*. The LPAD materials therefore must function as detectors of newly acquired functions, operations, vocabulary, attitudes, and motivation. Moreover, a fairly high degree of precision and sensitivity to change must be ensured by the instruments, inasmuch as the changes at first often will be small. Early detection is necessary to permit the examiner both to produce further amplification and to ascribe to the change the proper interpretation and meaning for the modifiability of the examinee, especially in light of the short time period for the dynamic assessment (see also "Interpretation of Results" below).

Finally, the examiner can offer opportunities for successful interaction. Since the LPAD also examines the modifiability of attitudinal and motivational factors in an attempt to enlist their support for the development and maintenance of higher levels of functioning, it is important to construct instruments that provide the examinee with opportunities for successful interaction and experiences of growing competence. Materials must be available that balance familiarity with complexity to produce appropriate challenges enabling mastery to occur. Securing competence within specific types of tasks, the LPAD materials are also constructed with enough similarity among them to make transfer possible. With mediation of deficiencies this permits the examinee, often within a short period of time, to function quite autonomously on extremely complex tasks, often including tasks employing verbal and numerical modalities.

Figure 14.3 presents examples of the LPAD tools to illustrate the characteristics of these materials.

Process Orientation

In contrast to traditional psychometric testing, the dynamic assessment of learning potential is not concerned with the measurement of a specific entity such as the "IQ," but rather seeks to determine and to modify the reasons responsible for failure, thereby changing the *processes* whereby the individual registers, elaborates, and communicates information.

The examiner is aided in this undertaking by a thorough knowledge of the cognitive map. The cognitive map consists of seven parameters that are

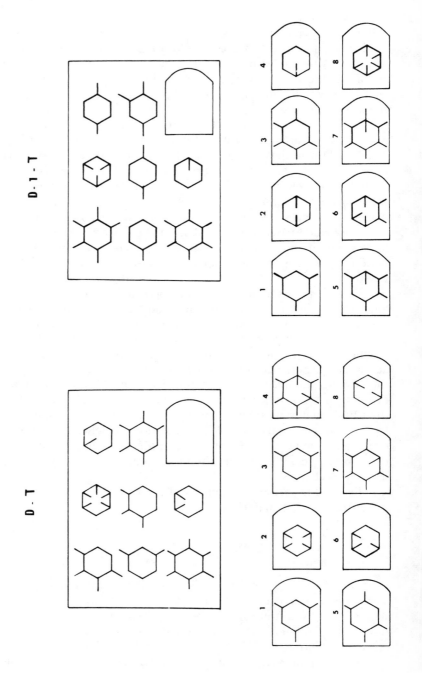

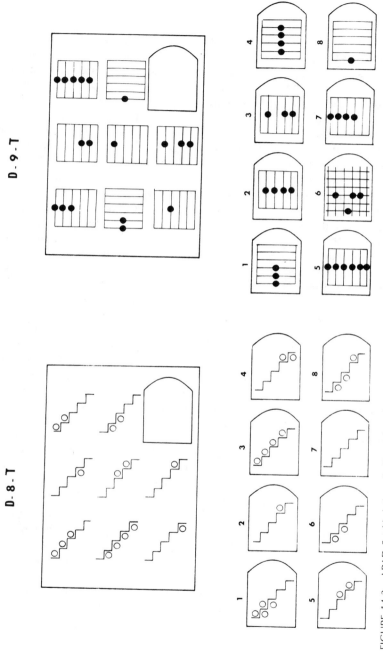

FIGURE 14.3. LPAD Set Variations II. Examples of tasks from the LPAD that can be utilized to provide mediation and subsequently assess modifiability. The mediated interaction seeks to equip the learner with awareness of a principle that transcends the particular task, establishing within the learner the prerequisites that will enable a successful approach to similar and progressively more difficult tasks.

systematically varied by the LPAD examiner both to identify the locus and clarify the examinee's deficiencies and to determine their modifiability.

Equipping the examiner with the conceptual apparatus to assess the nature and extent of the examinee's deficiencies, the cognitive map orients the examiner to the possibility that failure may be due to: (a) unfamiliarity with the particular contents of a task; (b) the language, or modality, employed in the presentation of the task (e.g., figural, verbal, numerical); (c) the absence, or fragility, of cognitive functions and mental operations needed to solve the task; (d) the possibility that the complexity of the task exceeds the child's present capacity; (e) the possibility that the level of abstractness is too high; or (f) simply impaired or underdeveloped efficiency, although the prerequisites in fact are available within the examinee's cognitive structure.

Using the techniques of mediation and with systematic variation of the parameters of the cognitive map, the examiner employs the LPAD materials to conduct a multitude of small, controlled experiments to identify and remediate areas of deficiency. For example, observing failure, the examiner may determine that it was due in whole or in part to a lack of spontaneous comparative behavior. By selecting and framing stimuli the examiner will attempt to target this function for remediation using Part I of the instrument where the failure was first identified and analyzed. In Part II the examiner will observe to what extent the deficiency may have been overcome by the mediation provided. Subsequently, the examiner shifts tools and then watches to see if performance within the new modality is again characterized by a lack of comparative behavior or whether this function is spontaneously applied. If it is applied, the examiner may concentrate on other deficiencies. If comparative behavior still is deficient, more mediation in Part I of the second tool will be offered. This is followed by observations on Part II of the second instrument and subsequently by mediations and observations on other LPAD materials that expose the function in different constellations with other functions and mental operations and across levels of increasing complexity and abstractness. The examiner registers changes in the efficiency of the examinee, provides feedback, and mediates competence and insight in order to instill and enlarge need systems to apply the previously deficient function.

Familiarity with the LPAD tools; knowledge of the cognitive map, the deficient functions, and mental operations; and skill as a mediator are all involved in the redevelopment of the variety of components that may be deficient for any particular examinee. The selection and specific sequencing of materials depends upon the examiner's choices in response to the needs of the examinee. Of the more than 15 tools available, the experienced LPAD examiner will on average use between five and seven instruments. Substantial variability among the needs of examinees contributes to the variation in both the number and the specific instruments actually used, and it is not uncommon to deviate from this average.

Interpretation of Results

Concerned with the creation of a global index of mental functioning, traditional psychometric testing ignores the occasional, rare, or isolated response of exceptional quality. These responses, whether exceptionally good or exceptionally dysfunctional, are given very little attention because they do not represent the predominant mode of the individual's functioning.

The dynamic assessment of learning potential does not seek to produce a global index of functioning (or of modifiability) but seeks to determine the type and intensity of interventions that have to be offered to the examinee to produce a realization of that potential for change that may become revealed with the LPAD. To derive these estimates and to prescribe specific interventions, the LPAD examiner continually interprets results from observations and mediations carried out during the assessment. In contrast with traditional testing, the LPAD examiner pays particular attention both to the unusually dysfunctional and the unusually functional response. In this way working hypotheses may be formulated that consider both the areas in greatest need of remediation and the best ways to provide it. Materials may be selected that permit deficiencies to be targeted while enabling the mediation to draw on functions that may already be in the repertoire. In this way the mediation of the deficiency may be quite focused and at the same time lead quite rapidly to the development of mastery and a feeling of competence. The LPAD continually seeks to provide opportunity and encouragement for peak responses to appear in order to create hypotheses to guide the search for the deficiencies that at present may prevent the child from functioning more generally at the level indicated by the peaks.

The assessment is terminated when the examiner is satisfied that a sound professional judgment can be derived with regard to the structural cognitive modifiability of the examinee. This usually includes knowledge of the deficient cognitive functions that may account for the examinee's present level of functioning and knowledge of the amount and type of investments necessary to remediate them. Inspecting results across the instruments employed, the examiner assesses the efficiency, generalizability, and stability of the examinee's cognitive functions and mental operations across levels of increasing complexity and abstractness, ascribing to each change the proper meaning in terms of its significance for additional future developments that may be anticipated with intervention. The changes observed in such areas as locus of control, achievement motivation, need for mastery, level of aspiration, awareness of own improvements, fear of failure, pleasure in success, frustration tolerance, constructive self-criticism, task motivation, and ability to work independently and autonomously are all integrated in the interpretation of results and in the development of recommendations.

The need for carefully trained examiners is underscored by the fact that the information produced by the dynamic assessment of learning potential itself cannot be considered evidence of immutable and fixed characteristics even to the extent that no claim can be made that the examinee's modifiability will remain stable. To the contrary, the indicators of modifiability obtained during the assessment constitute a reduced form of what can be expected with intensive and appropriately focused investment. This includes also the rate of observed change, which itself may undergo meaningful change in the direction of both higher and more rapid modifiability following intervention. The recency and relative fragility of the examinee's acquisitions in the context of a comparatively brief, albeit intensive, dynamic assessment produces evidence of modifiability that may become much more enhanced with consolidation, crystallization, and habit formation, which may be achieved with intervention over a period of time. This circumstance necessitates that LPAD examiners receive careful training in the interpretation of results. Professionals with experience in the administration and interpretation of traditional psychometric tests should not assume that they can either undertake or supervise dynamic assessment without such training (see also "Case Management and the Role of the Professional," below).

The LPAD Tools

The LPAD tools are divided into three broad classes. Both supervised training and experience with these materials are necessary for the examiner to learn how to use each tool efficiently for the redevelopment of the cognitive structure of the low-functioning examinee.

The first broad category includes instruments that draw upon *visual–motor and organization* tasks: Organization of Dots, Complex Figure Drawing, The Diamond, Representational Organization of Complex Figures, and Human Figure Drawing. In all of these instruments the perceptual and motor component is of much less interest than the cognitive and nonintellective factors whose contribution to performance represents the major target for the provision of MLEs.

The second class of LPAD materials includes tools that involve *higher cognitive processes and mental operations:* Raven Coloured Progressive Matrices, LPAD Set Variations B^8–B^{12}, Set Variations I and II, Representational Stencil Designs, The Organizer, Propositional Reasoning, Numerical Progressions, and Verbal Analogies. Higher cognitive processes and a large number of mental operations can be assessed and modified using these tools. They include analogical reasoning, logical multiplication, seriation, inferential hypothetical modes of thinking, deduction and instantiation, induction and generalization, and syllogistic thinking. All these tools permit the examiner to access and to modify the area of abstract thinking and representational behavior. They all possess a relatively high degree of complexity and represent tasks that, under normal circumstances, are rarely if ever offered to the low-functioning individual.

The third class of LPAD materials includes tools involving *memory with a learning component:* The Plateaux, Five by Twenty-Five, Associated Recall (Part–Whole and Functional Reduction), and Word Memory. Containing memory tasks based almost exclusively on a learning component, the cognitive components rather than simple fixational memory again play the central role. The search is for the production of changes in the capacity to consolidate and retrieve using mnemonic processes. Many of these instruments involve representational thinking and allow the examiner to focus on the modifiability of the examinee's capacity to benefit from symbol-formation processes and metacognitive support systems for the enhancement of memory. An example of this type of material is presented in Figure 14.4.

Active Modification Approaches and Dynamic Assessment: Some Implications

Viewing the individual as an open system and employing an active modification approach for assessment and intervention necessitates changes both in the roles of professionals and in the way educational systems are structured.

Case Management and the Role of the Professional

In traditional psychometric testing in the schools the role of the examiner is frequently limited to a "hit-and-run" approach whereby the examiner catalogues the respondent's manifest level of functioning on a series of standardized measures. Equating manifest with potential level of functioning, the task of case management often becomes one of identifying the stable environment that is most suitable to the child. The lower the functioning of the child is found to be, the lower the expectations should be in the stable environment. Selections are typically made from options including, among others, resource room, learning-disabilities class, self-contained classes for the "educably mentally retarded," and classes for the "trainable mentally retarded." Following placement, case management (and systems accountability) is maintained by retesting after a time lapse to ascertain the continued appropriateness of the placement.

Adopting an active modification approach that targets the development of the capacity to change necessitates a reformulation of the goals of case management and the role of the professional. Beginning with the assessment and lasting over a period of time, the LPAD examiner must often function as an ombudsman for the examinee. Frequently the only one to have seen what the examinee is capable of with appropriate mediation, the examiner must attempt to forge the conditions and provide the necessary interventions

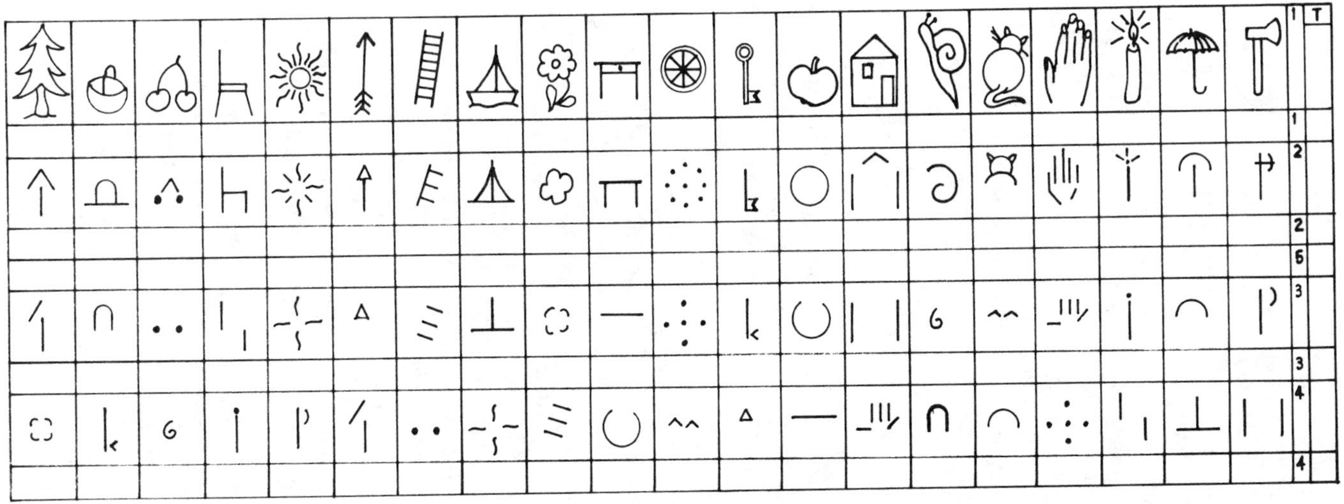

FIGURE 14.4. Associative Recall: Part–Whole Reduction. The tool enables the examiner, among other goals, to assess the examinee's capacity to retrieve objects stored visually and verbally by association under conditions of reduced cues and changed order. The cognitive process involves the use of substitute representations as a support for remembering a learned object.

to realize the documented potential for change. Even more important, since the proper intervention may produce changes that may make the individual accessible to both areas and levels of functioning that could not be specifically predicted from the initial assessment, it is important that the examiner continue to monitor, interpret, and produce support for the examinee.

In this undertaking the LPAD examiner will often attempt to enlist the support of teachers, social workers, and parents. Instrumental Enrichment (e.g., Feuerstein & Jensen, 1980; Feuerstein, Jensen, Hoffman, & Rand, 1985) was designed as a sister-program to the LPAD and is offered to the trained classroom teacher as a tool to remediate cognitive and motivational deficiencies in low-functioning students. In the absence of an appropriate thinking skills program, the LPAD examiner must frequently attempt to orient the teacher to the role of a mediator and, together, they may examine the available opportunities and curriculum materials for purposes of remediation of the individual's deficiencies. This collaboration is frequently initiated by the teacher's participation as an observer during the dynamic assessment and it may extend for a while also to the participation of the examiner in classroom learning activities.

Social workers and, when convenient, parents, also participate as observers in the dynamic assessment. This permits them to see for themselves what is involved in producing the enhancement of the examinee's functioning and thus be in a better position to formulate with the examiner the appropriate agenda for intervention. Through creative use of existing, nonstigmatizing frameworks in both school and community, the social worker is often able to recommend opportunities for involvements that may produce and support the development of need systems for the examinee to engage in those higher levels of functioning that become available with the focused investment provided by the teacher. Parents, similarly, may be oriented to the possibilities of mediating to the examinee in the context of the family and home environment. Since the provision of mediated learning does not depend upon the availability of specific materials, but, rather, is dependent upon attitudes (intentionality) and goals (e.g., the mediation of a feeling of competence, the mediation of goal-setting behavior, the mediation of change; see above) the possibilities are very rich for the receptive parent to play a very meaningful role in the realization of the child's potential for change.

Case management for the LPAD examiner, in sum, consists of attempts to enlist the support and forge the development of a collaborative coalition among those with interest in and responsibilities for the well-being of the examinee. The LPAD presents and sequences the specific goals that should become the targets of this collaborative work. The LPAD examiner, moreover, can make substantive suggestions about the preferential ways for reaching these goals and can set fairly accurate expectations with regard to the amount of investment that may be required for these goals to be reached.

The LPAD examiner will often assess the child again briefly from time to time to ascertain that the desired progress is being accomplished or to help teachers overcome a particularly difficult and resistant element in the child's cognitive structure through the provision of a focused intervention.

The Structure of Educational Systems

In order for educational systems to be effective in the enhancement of modifiability as a capacity that exists above and beyond the inculcation of specific skills, it is necessary that they be perceived and shaped as fundamentally open systems.

A commitment to the development of the capacity to change is consistent with the increasingly rapid and discontinuous changes that characterize modern society. These changes not only encompass the quickly changing body of knowledge that may be relevant for adjustment to life, but also affect the ways in which knowledge is developed, stored, retrieved, and communicated. The development of the capacity to change may thus increasingly constitute a general educational goal. If the school wants to address this goal, the implication is that it no longer can meet the needs of its students by structuring itself as a closed system that seeks to impart a specific body of content knowledge. Moreover, the degree to which students are seen to be able to fit the values of the school system can no longer be measured by a passive–acceptant registration of IQ and standardized achievement test scores leading, for the low-functioning student, to placement in classes where lowered expectations previously were seen to enlarge the perception of student–school system fit.

Abandoning the passive–acceptant approach, the school system must become structured to permit support services to be rendered in accordance with the needs of the student who experiences difficulty in functioning. The highly standardized approach to testing that allocates a specific amount of time per student regardless of the problem must be rejected in favor of permitting the professional the opportunity to conduct a sensitive and careful search for the problems that remediation must address. Especially when a full dynamic assessment is called for, this may require a substantially longer time investment than psychometricians currently are allotted. On the other hand, time is often saved later when the individual no longer has to be retested time and time again throughout his or her school career. Costly special education time is also saved once the school system is able to target the development of those prerequisites of reasoning (the first R) that may be necessary to avoid the failure and frustration that currently characterize the teaching of the traditional three Rs even in those special education classes that supposedly should make this possible.

The LPAD and the theory of the MLE lend themselves easily to use both as a prereferral and as a general counseling model. Although this application of the model requires considerable skill, it often does not require a great expenditure of time. The dynamic assessment of structural cognitive modifiability, finally, can also for certain purposes be carried out in a group format. Although the mediation offered here is much less specific, the group format mimics more closely the normal conditions in a classroom. The changes indicated by the group format to be possible can therefore be considered within reach with very limited investment. The individual LPAD is indicated for those who are not found to benefit from the group mediation, because their condition may require more specialized intervention. Overall, the application of active modification approaches does not produce a hopeless backlog of cases. To the contrary: In comparison with current systems where assignment to special services often continues until the end of the student's school career, the active modification approach holds the promise that time in special services will be reduced for many students.

The important issue of systems accountability undergoes significant change once the individual is perceived as an open system and active modification approaches to both assessment and intervention are implemented. Whereas accountability in the present school system can be maintained by retesting every so often and finding that the child constantly functions at the same level (the more constant the data the more the confidence in them), such a finding will be a cause for concern in any system that targets the development of the capacity to change.

Differential Application of the LPAD

Although the LPAD can be utilized with low-functioning individuals, the active modification and dynamic approach is useful also with slow-learning and learning-disabled children, adolescents, and adults. The dynamic approach of the LPAD, by making a clear distinction between the input, elaboration, and output phases of the mental act, can also be used with benefit for many handicapped individuals (such as the deaf, the blind, and those with cerebral palsy) whose handicaps mainly may affect the input and output levels. The active modification approach with the LPAD is also used to guide rehabilitation work for individuals with traumatic brain dysfunction and children and youth with Down syndrome. Used partly as an assessment device and partly as a counseling device, the LPAD, with Instrumental Enrichment, is also used in work with delinquent (incarcerated) youth and for the retraining of workers where changes in life conditions or economic situations may necessitate employment in new and unfamiliar sectors of the economy. Dynamic assessment with the LPAD has also found use among professionals concerned with the culturally different or bilingual individual who may score low on standardized psychometric tests and yet, unless cultural difference is compounded with MLE deprivation, may be found to possess an intact cognitive structure once investigated with the LPAD. The LPAD group test can be utilized to screen large groups of children for class placement based upon their modifiability and needs for specific forms of intervention. The group test can also be used as a screening device to identify gifted children among socioeconomically disadvantaged and culturally different youth.

The LPAD should not be used to develop an alternative source of labeling or classifying individuals and should not be used in general unless there is a commitment in both principle and practice to search for and attempt to remove the obstacles that may prevent the individual from functioning at higher levels. Misuses in the administration, in the interpretation of results, and in case management tend to accompany the use of the LPAD for other than its intended purposes.

REFERENCES

Feuerstein, R. (1979). *The dynamic assessment of retarded performers. The Learning Potential Assessment Device, theory, instruments, and techniques.* Baltimore: University Park Press.

Feuerstein, R. (1980). *Instrumental enrichment: An intervention program for cognitive modifiability.* Baltimore: University Park Press.

Feuerstein, R., Haywood, H. C., Rand, Y., Hoffman, M. B., & Jensen, M. R. (1985). *Learning potential assessment device: Manual.* Unpublished manuscript, Hadassah–WIZO–Canada Research Institute, Jerusalem, Israel.

Feuerstein, R., & Jensen, M. R. (1980). Instrumental enrichment: Theoretical basis, goals, and instruments. *The Educational Forum, 44,* 401–423.

Feuerstein, R., Jensen, M. R., Hoffman, M. B., & Rand, Y. (1985). Instrumental enrichment, an intervention program for structural cognitive modifiability: Theory and practice. In J. W. Segal, S. F. Chipman, & R. Glaser (Eds.), *Thinking and learning skills, Vol. I, Relating instruction to research* (pp. 43–82). Hillsdale, NJ: Erlbaum.

Feuerstein, R., Miller, R., Rand, Y., & Jensen, M. R. (1981). Can evolving techniques better measure cognitive change. *Journal of Special Education, 15,* 201–219.

Feuerstein, R., Rand, Y., Jensen, M. R., Kaniel, S., Tzuriel, D., Ben Schachar-Segev, N., & Mintzker, Y. (1986). Learning potential assessment. *Journal of Special Services in the Schools, 2/3,* 85–106.

15

The Training of Dynamic Assessors

JOEL MEYERS

This book documents much of the exciting work in dynamic assessment that has been taking place in recent years, spanning three continents. The result has been an extensive body of knowledge that has the potential to stimulate profound changes in the conduct of psychological assessment by professional psychologists. Whereas, traditionally, most assessment and diagnostic procedures have been designed to provide a diagnostic label and to help make placement decisions, dynamic assessment has direct implications for intervention. In the hopes of facilitating change in this direction, this chapter will illustrate some approaches to training psychologists to perform dynamic assessment. Training is crucial in promoting change since neophyte psychologists are likely to rely on those techniques that they have learned to use during training.

The training procedures delineated in this chapter have been developed from the author's efforts to implement alternative approaches to assessment within the context of two different training programs designed to prepare professional school psychologists. Although it borrows many ideas from dynamic assessment as discussed by Feuerstein (1979), this training program does not focus specifically on the Learning Potential Assessment Device (see Chapter 14, this volume, for a discussion of training linked to the Learning Potential Assessment Device). Instead, the goal is to provide training in an alternative approach incorporating many concepts that are consistent with dynamic assessment as a model. This approach is also referred to as "process assessment," and it has been described in some detail elsewhere (Meyers, Pfeffer, & Erlbaum, 1985). It is based, in part, on four conceptual issues that will be elaborated later in this chapter: (a) that there must be a link between assessment and intervention, (b) that assessment must be tied closely to the environment, (c) that assessment must be focused on the processes as well as the products of behavior, and (d) that assessment must involve a process of generating and testing hypotheses.

Process assessment is conceptualized broadly here as an approach focusing on cognitive functioning and social–emotional behavior, and includes academic content such as reading and math as well. This model bridges both

Joel Meyers. Department of Educational Psychology and Statistics, State University of New York, Albany, New York.

dynamic assessment as conceptualized in other chapters of this book, and diagnostic teaching approaches. Since it has been implemented within the context of programs designed to train professional school psychologists, the assessment strategies have been implemented primarily with school-age children. Therefore, the assessment of children is the focus of the training procedures described in this chapter. Although process assessment has been implemented with schoolchildren who have either *learning* or *adjustment* problems, this chapter considers primarily the dynamic assessment of learning problems. *Throughout this presentation the term "dynamic assessment" will refer to this model of process assessment.* Finally, it is important to clarify a distinction between the approach to process assessment that underlies this presentation, and Feuerstein's approach to dynamic assessment. Whereas Feuerstein makes the assumption that is is possible, and indeed a desirable goal, to change the client's underlying cognitive processes, this chapter makes no such assumption. Process assessment simply makes the assumption that by gathering data focused specifically on the client's *learning processes* it is possible to develop meaningful intervention plans to influence learning. Although the orientation uses techniques derived from Feuerstein, it is possible that this conceptual difference leads to some variations in assessment strategy and, therefore, some differences in training procedures.

The chapter is divided into three sections:

1. A brief outline of the model of process assessment that forms the basis for the training procedures presented in this chapter.
2. A discussion of the key dilemmas in professional training that have particular implications for dynamic assessment.
3. A delineation of specific techniques and approaches that can be useful in training professionals in dynamic assessment.

An Overview of Process Assessment

Process assessment is rooted in a rationale that emphasizes three issues: (a) the *link between assessment and intervention*, (b) the *link between assessment and the environment*, and (c) *examination of the processes* as well as the products of behavior. Although traditional norm-referenced approaches to assessment may answer questions about selection, prediction, and diagnosis/labeling, they are inadequate in determining specific intervention strategies. Including intervention as part of the assessment process can help to overcome this limitation. When interventions are tried out during assessment, there can be a meaningful data base to support the specific recommendations resulting from assessment. Although evaluation of the environment also helps to develop relevant recommendations, most assessment techniques focus on the characteristics of the person while essentially ignoring the environment. In contrast, process assessment seeks to observe key environments as well as observing the child in various environmental conditions (i.e., the assessment–environment link). This facilitates the development of recommendations focused on environmental modifications. Finally, cognition has been described as a process that continues to develop through interaction with the environment rather than remaining static (Feuerstein, 1979; Piaget, 1971; Vygotsky, 1978), and it is important for assessment strategies to examine this dynamic process. Particularly relevant to assessment is the increasing evidence that children's strategies and learning styles can have a significant effect on learning (e.g., Brown, 1975; Brown, Campione, & Murphy, 1977; Meichenbaum, 1980; Weinstein & Mayer, 1986). Consequently, there is a potential to increase the utility of diagnosis by developing and using assessment techniques designed to determine *how* a person learns rather than being restricted to assessing the outcomes or products of learning (i.e., to examine the processes of behavior). Data indicating how the person learns are important in facilitating the development of recommendations that facilitate the learning of individual children.

The Assessment Model

The model for process assessment that forms the basis for the training procedures discussed in this chapter is based, in part, on a systematic focus on the *task*, the *child*, and the *environment*. This model suggests that, first, data must be gathered that describe adequately each of these three factors. Once data have been gathered, the primary goal is to *assess the interactions* between them. Techniques such as trial interventions, diagnostic teaching (which includes task-analysis procedures), and ethologically based observation techniques are among the techniques that can be used to assess task–child–setting interactions. Moreover, this implies the need for nonstandardized use of various standardized assessment instruments, and this means that testing the limits would be used systematically during assessment. A more detailed description of this model can be obtained in other sources (Meyers, Pfeffer, & Erlbaum, 1985; Smith, 1980).

Training Dilemmas

It is not easy to train neophyte professionals, and many training dilemmas occur in all areas of professional training (see Keys, 1983). This is due partly to the fact that, regardless of the field, there is always considerable substantive knowledge as well as professional procedures that would be desirable for beginners to learn. There is always more to learn than can be taught effectively within the time limitations of a finite training program. Furthermore, dynamic assessment presents unique dilemmas since it frequently involves unlearning old concepts and techniques, while acquiring new theories and approaches. This section considers some of these dilemmas and their implications for training. Some of these address the major changes required by dynamic assessment as discussed in Chapters 1, 14, and 16 of this volume, but will be dealt with here in terms of implications for training.

Freedom Versus Constraint

Professional training is always marked by tension regarding the degree to which trainees should be allowed the freedom to experiment, learn for themselves and develop their own style. Although such freedom is desirable, it is important also to provide structure and limits to the learning experience. Not only does this make a training program manageable with groups of trainees, but it also helps to ensure that certain important components of training are provided to all trainees. Both freedom and constraint can be valuable during training, and yet, these approaches can conflict. It is important for any program providing training in dynamic assessment to strike a balance between the two, so that the use of constraints does not prohibit the possibility of providing appropriate freedom for the trainee. For example, a structured training program can help to provide the conceptual framework and the basic skills involved in dynamic assessment (i.e., techniques for introducing the environment and interventions into assessment while evaluating the process of learning). Nevertheless, an effective component of training is to encourage the trainee to experiment with these ideas, developing unique ways to implement, adapt, and further develop these concepts during assessment, rather than depending solely on the specific approaches presented by the trainer. This is particularly important in dynamic assessment, which is a new field that can benefit from innovation.

Scientists Versus Practitioner

Another dilemma in professional training concerns the degree of emphasis to place on the scientific bases for practice versus the degree of emphasis to place on training practitioner skills. A focus on the scientific bases provides the knowledge base that is necessary for professional practice. Without this knowledge base it may not be possible to use professional skills and techniques in an informed and flexible manner; with this knowledge base the neophyte professional can begin to develop the capacity to solve a variety of professional problems in a flexible manner. The knowledge base allows the professional to practice without being dependent upon a particular skill that may be irrelevant to the presenting problem or that may become obsolete.

Although a scientific focus clearly can be important, a focus on practitioner skills has significant advantages, as well. In most professional fields it is difficult to obtain and keep an entry-level position without a minimal degree of competence in certain professional skills. For example, for a school psychologist to obtain an entry-level position in the schools, the psychologist must have sound skills in traditional diagnostic techniques such as norm-referenced measures of intelligence, academic performance, and social–emotional behavior. Although the underlying knowledge base may be useful, the crucial prerequisite often will be implementation of these particular skills. Furthermore, since structured training with close supervision providing specific feedback may be necessary to the development of many professional skills (e.g., see Kuehnel & Kuehnel, 1983), professional training programs must provide training and feedback in the skills and techniques that will be a requirement for effective professional practice.

Clearly there is a rationale for training to focus both on practice and its scientific bases. Yet, given the finite time available to most training programs, it is difficult to achieve the desirable balance between these two factors. This represents a particular problem for training in dynamic assessment because it is based on several principles as well as techniques that are entirely different from traditional approaches to assessment. On the one hand, implementation of dynamic assessment simply requires more time than static procedures, and, on the other hand, it places more demands on clinical judgment and inference, which are difficult to teach.

Label Versus Intervention

Traditional approaches to cognitive assessment are designed primarily to help develop a diagnosis of the problem. For schoolchildren, the purpose of the diagnostic effort is generally to predict the likelihood of the child succeeding in a regular school placement. In those instances when it is predicted that the child is highly unlikely to succeed, the assessment helps to determine the most appropriate educational placement. Generally, this results in a "differential diagnosis" (mentally retarded, emotionally disturbed, learning disabled, etc.) that is based on assumptions about the underlying causes for the problem. For example, if the cause is viewed as intellectual inability, the youngster is·placed in a classroom for the educable mentally retarded; if the cause is viewed as a perceptual deficit or a specific disability in an academic subject, then the youngster is placed in a classroom for the learning disabled; and finally, if the cause is emotional problems, the youngster would be placed in a class for the emotionally disturbed.

Although traditional approaches to assessment have focused primarily on prediction of behavior, diagnostic labeling, and placement decisions, they have not been designed to help develop specific intervention plans or remedial strategies. Yet, if assessment is to be used to its fullest potential, then techniques must be developed that lead clearly to specific intervention approaches. Since traditional approaches have not been designed to achieve this goal, new assessment approaches are needed, and dynamic assessment represents one promising example. A strength of dynamic assessment is that, by focusing on the environment and the process of learning, and by including trial interventions as a part of assessment, there are clear implications for specific interventions that have the potential to remediate the observed cognitive and/or academic limitation. This presents a dilemma for training. Should dynamic assessment procedures be emphasized instead of traditional approaches? If so, a body of data must be developed indicating the predictive validity of dynamic assessment techniques in answering questions relevant to prediction, diagnosis, and placement, since these latter questions remain important in education. At present, this data base is not sufficient to support training in dynamic assessment while excluding traditional norm-referenced techniques. Consequently, professional training programs have the dilemma of determining the degree to which each type of approach should be stressed.

Presently, there is too great a focus on traditional approaches and too little focus on dynamic assessment. Although it is clear that there should be a shift in emphasis toward dynamic assessment, it is not clear how this should be accomplished. Should both approaches to assessment be incorporated into courses on cognitive and academic assessment? Should there be separate courses representing each orientation? And, which approach should receive more attention in professional training programs? Currently there is no empirical answer to these questions, and this should be a focus of future research. Nevertheless, training programs will need to make some of these decisions before the desired data base is available. Clearly there is a need for training programs in professional psychology to find ways to increase training in dynamic assessment, and this will require decisions to cut or deemphasize other areas of training. Which areas to reduce and exactly how to incorporate dynamic assessment will probably vary from program to program. For example, plausible arguments can be made to incorporate dynamic assessment throughout all of the training in assessment, and equally plausible arguments can be made to provide courses focused particularly on dynamic assessment. In making these decisions it will be critical that careful attention is maintained on the scientist versus practitioner dilemma so that this change in orientation does not dilute the scientific component of training.

Process Versus Product

Norm-referenced approaches to assessment produce scores reflecting the products of learning or development, reported as IQ scores or some standardized measure of absolute achievement such as a percentile. These approaches are based on an assumption that learning is best assessed as a summative product, and this may imply that there is little opportunity to influence learning. Dynamic assessment requires that professionals learn to challenge these basic assumptions, adopting instead the viewpoint that learning, like all human behavior, can change in response to environmental input. This assumption requires a shift in the focus of assessment from an almost exclusive examination of the products of learning to the *processes of learning*.

An understanding of the learning process can lead to strategies with the potential to promote learning. Since process has not been incorporated systematically into training programs focused on diagnostic and assessment techniques, it is important to shift in this direction. However, the dilemma faced by training programs is to determine how much of this shift to make and precisely how to do this. Moreover, in many instances a shift toward the processes of learning may require a radical conceptual shift as well. Rather than viewing learning behavior as fixed and unchangeable, this framework views learning behavior as modifiable.

Observer Versus Teacher

Dynamic assessment requires a dramatic shift in conceptualization of the roles of both the examiner and the examinee. In marked contrast to traditional approaches, dynamic assessment assumes that both the examiner and the client must be actively involved. In the case of schoolchildren this includes the parent(s) as well. Rather than simply responding passively to interview questions, a variety of techniques would be used to increase the parent's involvement with assessment (e.g., having the parent observe parts of assessment in order to obtain feedback from the parent regarding their perceptions of their child's performance). Similarly, the child would no longer be limited to a role of passively answering questions posed by the examiner. Instead, the child might be asked to explain solutions to various problems and/or might be asked to try out a particular intervention.

Just as the child is asked to assume the role of learner at some points during assessment, at these times the examiner must assume the role of teacher. This represents a dramatic shift. Traditionally the examiner is expected to be a neutral observer whose behavior is kept under control so that it does not influence the child's responses. (See Schafer, 1954, for an excellent discussion of this viewpoint as well as some of the problems associated with implementing this approach). However, when assuming a teaching role, the examiner makes direct attempts to modify the behavior of the child. This provides the empirical basis for recommendations resulting from the assessment.

The increased active involvement of both examiner and client has dramatic implications for training. Traditionally, considerable time and effort were devoted to teaching the examiner how to be a neutral observer, and how to keep personal reactions and behaviors from influencing the youngster being assessed. Although these skills are still important for some aspects of assessment, as the examiner learns to be a ''teacher,'' it is necessary for him or her to learn teaching techniques that can be in opposition to this neutral stance. This basic training dilemma occurs because assessment requires both skills on the part of the examiner. Therefore, training programs must find ways to provide training in both skills despite their derivation from concepts that appear to be contradictory. A major dilemma for training in dynamic assessment is to determine how much training to devote to each of these two approaches, and to do so in a way that maintains competence in these potentially conflicting skills.

Real Versus Ideal

This volume demonstrates a growing research base supporting the variety of dynamic assessment techniques, and documents that this approach is being used increasingly in practice. Nevertheless, dynamic assessment is not yet accepted broadly by practitioners, and it is not yet implemented on a sufficiently large scale. Consequently, at the present time there is rarely external pressure or support for beginning professionals to use dynamic assessment. Moreover, because it is so different and because it can be time consuming, there may be many settings where this approach is received with suspicion and antagonism. This has significant implications for training. First, in addition to teaching professionals how to conduct evaluations using dynamic assessment, it is important to provide training in techniques that can be used to communicate to clients, other professionals, and the public that dynamic assessment can be a useful approach. In this connection, it may be effective for professional trainees to learn program evaluation techniques that can be used to help document the potential advantages of dynamic assessment. However, if dynamic assessment is not specifically taught by the professional training institutions, it is unlikely to be adopted as a significant element in practice and will fail to develop sufficient credibility among professionals to become an established part of the assessment repertory.

Dynamic assessment requires a substantial time commitment, which is significantly longer than expected in most work situations. This can present a problem, since training creates standards that often are not realistic for the demands of professional practice. Unfortunately, "productivity" is defined, too often, as the number of evaluations completed within a set time period, rather than a more meaningful criterion like change in learning behavior or usefulness to the teacher. This problem is not unique to dynamic assessment, since any thorough orientation to training would suggest assessment procedures that take longer than is typically expected or desired in practice. However, this is a particular problem for dynamic assessment, which is focused on the development of specific interventions, and which sometimes can take even longer to implement because trial interventions are used.

The dilemma between real versus ideal assessment practices is a particular challenge for training in dynamic assessment. One responsibility of training programs is to exert influence on the field to maintain the highest possible standards for practice. This implies that dynamic assessment should be taught in its ideal format. Then, to help trainees cope with future job situations, the training program can present additional information about the real demands of practice as well as strategies for dealing with these realities.

Training Techniques

A variety of techniques can be used to facilitate training in dynamic assessment. Because there is not sufficient space to delineate each specific technique, this chapter will describe the major categories of training procedures that have been useful for training in dynamic assessment. Six different categories of training procedures are discussed in this section, which, despite some overlap, are useful in conceptualizing training programs for dynamic assessment. Also, the reader should note that the section on training dilemmas has additional implications for training procedures.

Stages of Skill Training

Kuehnel and Kuehnel (1983) have summarized the literature on skills training and concluded that, despite the variety of literature in this area, there is general support for a series of stages for training most professional skills. These include (a) detailed instructions, (b) modeling, (c) behavioral rehearsal, and (d) in vivo practice. These stages provide a systematic way to address the dilemma of "freedom versus constraint" as they move toward increasing responsibility and active participation by the trainee. In the first two stages the trainee receives input directly from the trainer, and in the last two stages the trainee becomes increasingly active and responsible in using the skill— first in rehearsal, and later in application with real clients. In addition, as Ford (1977, 1978) has pointed out, during those parts of training that require performance by the trainee (i.e., either behavioral rehearsal or in vivo practice) it is crucial to use systematic feedback. Two types of feedback are useful in training. Initially, during stages 3 and 4, it is important to provide *immediate feedback*. However, in the later phases of these stages, it is important to provide *delayed feedback*, since this helps to prepare trainees for the real world of professional practice where feedback is not available on an immediate basis, if at all.

STAGE 1: DETAILED INSTRUCTIONS

The dynamic assessment of cognitive and academic behavior requires the use of numerous specific assessment techniques. In addition to understanding the entire model, the examiner must know how to use each assessment technique, and how to determine which technique(s) to use in specific cases. *Detailed instructions are a necessary first step in learning to implement any of these procedures.* For example, one approach to assessing the process of learning is to use "think-aloud" procedures, and the first step in training professionals to use this approach would be to provide detailed instructions about how to implement think-aloud procedures with a particular assessment task such as the block design subtest from the Wechsler Intelligence Scale for Children–Revised (WISC–R). These instructions might include:

1.   Define thinking aloud as a process in which all of the child's thoughts are described while trying to solve the block design task.
2.   Explain that the goal is to learn about the child's unique problem-solving strategies.
3.   Provide a metaphor that can help the child understand what is meant by thinking aloud (e.g., "Just like a sports broadcaster, I want you to provide a play-by-play account of each of your thoughts as you try to solve the problem.")
4.   Inform the child that some of the block design problems may be difficult and that the examiner is particularly interested in learning about the child's thoughts and problem-solving strategies in these instances.
5.   The examiner must learn a reliable system for coding the think-aloud responses prior to assessment.
6.   The coding system is used to determine what responses need to be followed with a question from the examiner.
7.   The examiner must be knowledgeable about responses from a normative sample of children so that the "think-aloud protocol" (see Lytle, 1982) can be interpreted.

Although this does not present an inclusive list of all the steps needed to implement think-aloud procedures, it helps to demonstrate the complexity of this task.

STAGE 2: MODELING

The second important step in training a professional skill is to model the procedure for the trainee. This can be done in two effective ways, and whenever possible it is suggested that both approaches to modeling be used. One effective approach to modeling is to present a videotape of an examiner implementing the procedure. The trainees are encouraged to observe the videotape actively in an effort to observe the steps implemented by the examiner and to consider the strengths and weaknesses of the examiner's efforts. These observations are then compared to the instructions that were provided earlier to the trainee in order to determine the model's adequacy. By referring back to the instructions in this manner, modeling helps to reinforce the trainee's learning of these procedures.

For example, a program for training learning potential assessment was developed by John Manni for the New Jersey State Department of Education; he developed a videotape using the Raven Progressive Matrices as the assessment device (Manni, 1981). The tape is excellent as a demonstration of the use of the Progressive Matrices to observe some of the key problem-solving strategies that are important to the child's performance on this task. In addition, it demonstrates the examiner's approach to developing intervention strategies that are practical to use during dynamic assessment.

Although videotape demonstrations provide an effective training procedure, they are not always available. Moreover, it can be important for the trainer to model the procedures being taught. This can increase the credibility of the trainer and increase the motivation of the trainee to implement the new procedure. Role-play techniques can be used in which the trainer demonstrates the procedure with one or more of the trainees in the role of examinee. However, it is also effective to demonstrate assessment procedures with an actual client. Similar to the videotape, the trainer's demonstration would be used to stimulate discussion with the trainee(s) to determine the strengths and weaknesses of the trainer's approach and to determine how the trainer followed the detailed instructions.

Stop-action techniques provide an effective strategy to use as an adjunct to modeling. This involves stopping the demonstration at key points designed to facilitate discussion concerning critical events illustrated in the demonstration. This can be done with videotapes by having predetermined points at which the trainer will stop the tape to stimulate discussion. In addition to stopping action at predetermined points the trainer can choose such moments spontaneously as well as suggesting that the trainees choose these points.

STAGE 3: BEHAVIORAL REHEARSAL

There are two basic approaches to behavioral rehearsal that are applicable to training in dynamic assessment. The first involves brief role plays of particular components of the assessment process in which the trainer or one of the trainees plays the role of the person being assessed while one of the trainees practices the assessment technique. The second approach to behavioral rehearsal involves practice of one entire technique with a client. This approach does not involve a client who is referred for help with a real problem, and generally only one technique is used rather than conducting a complete assessment. The first approach to rehearsal will be referred to as "rehearsal based on partial role play," and the second approach will be referred to as "rehearsal based on simulation."

During rehearsal based on partial role play the trainee tries out a specific aspect of dynamic assessment in a short time period (e.g., 5 minutes or less). The purpose is to provide practice with a specific skill component of dynamic assessment, to present the trainee with situations which may be experienced later during professional work, and to facilitate a particular aspect of skill development. During this process, the trainer takes an active role *providing specific feedback* to the trainee, and, when appropriate, the trainer would offer suggestions to promote skill development.

This component of training is ignored frequently, and yet it can promote effective training in dynamic assessment. For example, rehearsal based on role play can be used with considerable effectiveness as an adjunct to training professionals to use think-aloud approaches in assessment. When learning to use these approaches, it can be particularly difficult for the examiner to learn effective ways to teach the examinee how to think aloud, because this is so different from other approaches to assessment. Consequently, brief rehearsals of the beginning phase of think-aloud approaches in assessment can facilitate the development of this skill. For example, it was noted earlier in this chapter that think-aloud procedures can be used to assess the problem-solving strategies children use to solve block design tasks. Brief rehearsals of the instructions provided by the examiner can be role played in which the examiner is asked to provide instructions covering the following points: (a) provide a definition of "thinking aloud," (b) indicate that the purpose is to determine the child's problem-solving strategies, (c) indicate that the examiner and the child will work together to learn this information, (d) provide a metaphor to help the child understand what is meant by thinking aloud, (e) indicate that some of the block design problems will probably be difficult to complete since they are designed for older children, and (f) state that there are no right or wrong answers. An adjunct to this technique is to have the person playing the role of the child ask questions and make responses designed to facilitate certain aspects of the training. For example, children in sixth or seventh grade often feel uncomfortable stating all their thoughts out loud since they feel this is like talking to themselves. The person playing the role of "child" can be instructed to say: "It seems foolish to talk to myself." This places the "examiner" in a difficult situation that demonstrates a response that may be needed to use later when using this technique with real clients.

There are an infinite number of ways this technique can be used to facilitate training in dynamic assessment. One additional example would be to practice administration of any technique where the child's response may be difficult to score and the examiner needs to make a decision whether to query. This is particularly important when using think-aloud approaches since queries have the potential to influence the child's responses unnecessarily. Pursuing the use of think-aloud techniques with block design, the person role playing the child could be instructed to provide an ambiguous think-aloud response. For example, one frequent strategy is to visualize the discrete blocks in the picture of the design before putting the blocks together. It is difficult to determine whether or not this strategy is being used when the youngster makes a response like: "First I look at the picture to visualize where the blocks go." Under these circumstances it would be important for the examiner to query in a way that minimizes any potential influence on the child's response. Feedback would be given to the trainee based on whether the examinee is asked for further information, and whether this query is sufficiently neutral to minimize interference.

STAGE 4: IN VIVO PRACTICE

Probably the most important part of training focused on the skills involved with dynamic assessment is practice using this approach with clients presenting real problems. This most closely approximates the way in which dynamic assessment will be used later in the trainee's professional work. Initially, during training, this is conducted most effectively by providing close supervision, including careful planning with a supervisor prior to conducting the assessment, observation of the assessment followed by detailed feedback from supervisor to trainee, and careful planning following each assessment session to interpret the results of the evaluation and to determine the next steps or recommendations. Supervision would be reduced later during training when independent practice becomes the goal, and delayed feedback would be provided at this time. During this stage, rather than being observed by the supervisor, the examiner might be instructed to observe his or her own performance and bring those observations to the supervisory meeting. Also, at this stage, the supervisory discussions would focus more on the trainee's questions about the case and possible procedures, rather than relying on direct input from the trainer. During this phase of training one important issue will be to consider how to implement this approach given the real demands for service that will be made once the trainee moves to a work setting.

Technology and Skills Training

There are several technological innovations that have the potential to facilitate skills training in dynamic assessment; these include the use of videotape and microcomputer equipment. It has been noted earlier in this chapter that videotape techniques can be used to model the skills being taught. In addition, videotape techniques can be used to facilitate feedback during the behavioral rehearsal or in vivo practice stages of training. This would be done by videotaping the trainee's performance during each of the above stages of practice. Then, the videotape is played back for the trainer and trainee, and stop-action procedures are used by the trainer to provide feedback at key points in the trainee's performance. This allows an opportunity to provide detailed and specific feedback since the trainee observes his or her own performance directly, and therefore has the greatest opportunity to understand any feedback that is provided.

Microcomputer technology also has the potential to facilitate training in dynamic assessment. However, it is understood that this is only a *potential* asset at present, since computer programs would need to be written for this purpose. There are several promising areas for the development of computer programs that could facilitate training in dynamic assessment. For example, for learning potential assessment using the Raven Progressive Matrices, computer programs can be developed to assess the trainee's ability: (a) to determine the examinee's problem-solving strategies on the Progressive Matrices, and (b) to determine what intervention strategies to try during the "teaching" portion of assessment. The development of computer programs to assist training in dynamic assessment is suggested as an important area for future work. Computers may also contribute by being used for some of the more traditional, static aspects of assessment, thus freeing the examiner for the more clinically sensitive dynamic procedures.

Training in the Scientific and Conceptual Rationale

The techniques discussed in the prior section on the stages of training are focused particularly on skills training. In an effort to be certain that training focuses also on the scientific bases for practice, training should begin by providing the conceptual rationale and the scientific data base that support the use of dynamic assessment. It is only after the trainee understands the conceptual framework that guides process assessment that skills can be implemented in a professional manner. Much of the material presented throughout this volume can be used as a basis for developing this didactic presentation. In particular, this presentation would emphasize both how and why dynamic assessment focuses on the learning process, the link between assessment and intervention, and the link between assessment and the environment. This presentation could emphasize the scientific aspects of dynamic assessment by illustrating how the examiner works as a "scientist" who generates hypotheses about the case and then sets up miniexperiments during assessment to determine the validity of these hypotheses.

Didactic presentation of information is not the only way to provide training regarding the conceptual rationale and scientific bases for dynamic assessment. The clinical components of training can also be focused toward this goal by utilizing techniques that emphasize professional judgment and problem-solving skills for trainees rather than rote learning of isolated assessment techniques. Two particular approaches to this goal are useful for training in dynamic assessment. The first approach is to include trainees as active participants in research investigating some aspect of dynamic assessment. For example, when the trainee is involved in the process of explaining to an institution such as a school why it should participate in a research project on dynamic assessment, the trainee is essentially forced to learn the scientific and conceptual rationale in a more detailed and more meaningful way. Similarly, by gathering data regarding process assessment, by participating in the project as an examiner, and by helping to analyze and interpret results from the study, there is a potential for in-depth learning of the theoretical orientation, while practicing some relevant skills.

The second approach to clinical training that can be used to reinforce the conceptual basis is to encourage the trainee to conduct dynamic assessment without using any specific assessment techniques or tests. The trainee would be instructed to gather data that can be used to solve the referral problem using the dynamic assessment framework but without using any preprepared materials. This requires the trainee to rely on ingenuity to develop assessment procedures that may be relevant to the referral problem. This is an exercise that is best used in the later phases of training. Not only does this help to reinforce the trainee's understanding of the conceptual framework of dynamic assessment, but it also helps to demonstrate that no single assessment technique is as important as the theoretical framework used by the examiner. Furthermore, this training technique increases the probability that the trainee will be capable of developing additional techniques, which is important since this is an evolving field that needs continued input from researchers and practitioners to achieve its potential.

Training for Intervention during Assessment

One radical change that is reflected in dynamic assessment is that intervention is incorporated into assessment. This is done in two basic ways. The first is to use test–teach–retest approaches and the second is to use trial interventions during assessment.

Test–teach–retest approaches include the basic approaches to learning potential assessment that have been described by Feuerstein (1979) and Budoff (1975) (see Chapters 1 and 2, this volume). They have used primarily nonverbal measures of intelligence, such as the Raven Progressive Matrices, that provide a good opportunity to observe problem-solving skills. First, a pretest is conducted to determine the youngster's score on the measure as well as to provide an opportunity to observe the child's problem-solving skills. Then, based on observed strengths and weaknesses in problem-solving skills, the examiner teaches the skills necessary to solve the problem. Following this "teaching" there is a posttest to determine the impact of teaching. Budoff has developed some norms with the Progressive Matrices to help determine how much of a change from pre- to posttest may be significant.

This same process can be applied with any nonverbal or verbal problem-solving task; one example that may be particularly pragmatic for practicing psychologists is to use the block design subtest from the WISC-R. Furthermore, this same basic process can be used with any academic test to assess academic skills. The basic idea of trying interventions during academic assessment and evaluating their effects on the child's learning has been referred to previously as diagnostic teaching (Meyers, Pfeffer, & Erlbaum, in press; Smith, 1980; see the Introduction to this volume and Chapter 1 for a discussion of the difference between dynamic assessment and diagnostic teaching.) Test–teach–retest procedures can be used specifically with academic tests such as the Woodcock–Johnson Psycho-Educational Battery, the KeyMath Diagnostic Arithmetic Test, and the SPACHE Diagnostic Test of Reading. Just as was described with block design, there would be a pretest on the particular measure to be used. Then trial teaching would be conducted based on information generated from the test and other components of assessment. Following the trial teaching, a posttest on the relevant test would be completed. Change in performance from pretest to posttest would be used to help to determine the validity of the teaching procedures that were used during assessment.

Training in the use of test–teach–retest procedures needs to focus on several issues. First, the examiner must be proficient in administration and interpretation of whatever test is used whether it be a cognitive measure such as the Raven Progressive Matrices or an academic test such as the Woodcock–Johnson Psycho-Educational Battery. This includes proficiency maintaining the role of neutral observer during assessment, which can be particularly difficult for trainees to accomplish during the posttest after the examiner has worked with the child in the role of "teacher."

Second, the examiner must know how to work with the child in the role of teacher. It was already noted that this can present a problem to the trainee because the role is so different from and may conflict with the traditional diagnostic role of neutral observer. However, this is also a critical focus of training. In effect, professionals who conduct dynamic assessment must have expertise in two areas that traditionally have been conceptualized separately: diagnosis and intervention. Therefore, training must include practice generating intervention plans, and this can be done effectively in training by suggesting that the trainee brainstorm alternative intervention plans.

The last component of training specifically designed for test–teach–retest procedures has to do with interpretation of the posttest results. Unfortunately, at the present time there are no norms available to help the examiner interpret any change in performance from pretest to posttest. (The current exceptions to this problem are noted in this volume.) Training needs to emphasize this point and to help trainees develop a basis for interpreting pre–post changes, and this training must emphasize the importance of conservative interpretation on the part of the examiner, since some change in performance might be expected simply as a function of the posttest alone. Training a conservative approach to interpretation might include an orientation toward multiple sources of data prior to concluding that a technique is effective. For example, the examiner might hypothesize that impulsivity interferes with performance on a variety of cognitive and academic tasks. Under these circumstances the examiner would teach a simple technique designed to control impulsivity, and would use a test–teach–retest model on at least two different tests. If the expected improvement in performance is obtained in both instances, then the examiner might conclude that impulsivity is a significant factor and that the teaching procedures used are likely to be effective intervention plans for this child. In addition to conservative interpretation of assessment data, professionals need to develop norms to help interpret any pre–post changes that are observed.

Trial intervention approaches include any efforts to intervene during assessment that are independent of specific test–teach–retest procedures.

Trial interventions may be attempted by the examiner during assessment (e.g., modification of the seating arrangement, the visibility of test materials, the examiner's tone of voice), or by a caregiver outside of the testing situation (eg., the parent or teacher). Similar to test–teach–retest procedures, training for trial interventions needs to focus on a variety of teaching techniques. The trainee must learn to translate general intervention techniques into procedures that can be implemented in a brief time span with visible results. This will help the examiner to develop intervention plans that can be assessed adequately during the assessment process in order to estimate their likely efficacy over time in the child's day-to-day environment. In addition, training for trial interventions needs to focus on techniques for working effectively with parents and teachers, since it is not always easy to enlist their cooperation in implementing interventions. This requires training in consultation skills (see Alpert & Meyers, 1983; Parsons & Meyers, 1984).

Training to Assess the Learning Process

Whereas traditional assessment focuses on the products of learning, dynamic assessment focuses on the processes of learning so that effective intervention ideas can be developed. Training in dynamic assessment must focus particularly on techniques to assess process since these skills are not likely to have been developed previously and they are not likely to be part of other aspects of training. Several different techniques can be used to assess the learning process, and each of these should receive attention during training. In addition to receiving didactic input regarding the variety of available approaches to assessing process, the trainee should have opportunities to practice each approach. Test–teach–retest techniques provide one way to assess the learning process, and since these were discussed in the previous section they will not be discussed further here. The second approach to assessing the process of learning is to observe the child's behavior carefully during learning or problem-solving situations. This is a skill that requires much practice, and the examiner needs to learn to take detailed process notes so that all pertinent observations can be recorded carefully. In addition, the trainee needs to learn how to judge what behaviors are important to observe, and which ones are less significant. One guideline that can be useful to trainees is to pay careful attention to those behaviors exhibited by the youngster when having difficulty or experiencing frustration with a problem-solving task. Feuerstein's (1979, 1980) list of cognitive deficiencies and Lidz's chapter in this volume (Chapter 17) provide additional guidelines for the assessor and trainer with regard to what processes to observe and to train. A third approach to assessing the learning process is to ask the child how he or she solved the problem. This allows the examiner to learn about those learning strategies that are clearly under the conscious control of the child. Frequently, this will suggest different strategies from those that are observed, since observation techniques often focus attention on strategies that are not under the conscious control of the

youngster. A fourth approach to assessing process is to ask the child in ret-
rospect to describe what his or her thoughts were while solving the problem.
The fifth approach to assessing the learning process is to ask the child to think
aloud while solving a particular problem. Similar to observation techniques,
think-aloud strategies are most likely to elicit information about problem-
solving strategies that are not typically under the child's conscious control.

Think-aloud approaches have great potential for the assessment of problem-solving strategies and the process of learning, and they have only recently
been considered as alternative approaches to assessment. Earlier sections of
this chapter have discussed the use of think-aloud strategies while using the
block design subtest from the WISC-R. However, in addition to such cognitive
tasks, think-aloud procedures can be used to assess problem-solving strategies
in a variety of academic and interpersonal situations. Although the assessment
of interpersonal factors is beyond the scope of this chapter, it is useful to
consider the use of think-aloud procedures in assessing problem-solving strategies on academic tasks. Examples might include performance on both mathematics and reading tasks, and there have been beginning efforts to apply
this approach to the assessment of reading comprehension strategies (Lytle,
1982).

The use of think-aloud approaches in assessing comprehension strategies
is similar to the procedures described for block design. The major distinction
is that the child is asked to read one sentence at a time and to think out loud
after reading each sentence. The task begins with all of the sentences covered,
and they are then uncovered one sentence at a time until the entire story is
uncovered. After the story is completed the youngster is asked to summarize
the story and then to describe the strategies that were used to help understand
the story. Training procedures are similar to those that have been described
previously in this chapter. Training would begin by presenting the conceptual
rationale, followed with the stages of skill development (detailed instructions,
modeling, behavioral rehearsal, and in vivo practice). In addition, training
would break down the think-aloud procedure into its basic components: (a)
instructing the client in think-aloud techniques; (b) learning a system for
coding think-aloud responses; (c) determining when to query and how to do
so while minimizing interference with the client's responses; (d) learning to
record the client's think-aloud responses to produce a precise, word-for-word
protocol of the client's responses; and (e) learning how to interpret responses
obtained on a think-aloud protocol. Training will require instructions, modeling, and opportunities to practice each of these components of the skill.

Training for Environmental Assessment

This chapter has discussed how dynamic assessment includes the environment
as a key factor. This must be addressed during training, since it is frequently
a weakness in the training of professional diagnosticians. The environment

can be used systematically during assessment in three ways: (a) observation of the key settings that relate the referral problem (e.g., the home or the school); (b) observation of the child's learning behavior in the different key environments; and (c) manipulating environmental factors to induce change.

Observation of key environmental settings is potentially an important aspect of almost any approach to assessment, as well as dynamic assessment. Nevertheless, it is often ignored in training. Therefore an important aspect of training in dynamic assessment is simply to emphasize the importance of including the environment in assessment as crucial to developing a meaningful understanding of the problem. Trainees need practice in making detailed, descriptive notes of home settings and various school settings. They need to know what aspects to observe and how these can relate to outcome. One of the most difficult aspects of training for this assessment is to help trainees develop observation techniques while minimizing the impact of their presence as observers. This means that they must learn to avoid interaction with any people who are present in the environment during observation, and it means that, in effect, they must find ways to make themselves "invisible" during observation. Detailed instructions, modeling, and behavioral rehearsal are useful in developing this skill.

Descriptive process observations are not the only way to observe learning environments. A variety of systematic and empirical observation systems are available. For example, behavioral observation systems can be used to assess the degree of reinforcement, punishment, and ignoring of learning behaviors that occurs in the environment. These include measures of teacher–student interaction such as the Flanders Interaction Analysis Categories (Flanders, 1970) and the Dyadic Interaction Analysis System (Good & Brophy, 1973) and measures of teacher discipline strategies (i.e., Kounin, 1970). In addition to learning the conceptual bases for these observation systems and the definitions of terms used during observation, training requires opportunities to practice using the system so that reliable observations and reliable scoring can be achieved.

The second way in which the environment is brought into assessment is by observing the child's learning behavior in different environments. This is a radical shift from norm-referenced approaches to assessment, which seeks to minimize the impact of the environment so that general conclusions can be made about the child's cognitive or academic behavior independent of the environment. In contrast, dynamic assessment seeks to learn about the ways in which the environment affects the child's behavior and, therefore, it does not make the assumption that generalized statements about the child's cognitive or academic behavior are applicable. To determine how behavior varies as a function of the environment it is necessary to sample the child's behavior in different settings. This can be done by having two different teachers or a teacher and a parent each administer the same type of learning task to determine how the child's behavior varies in these different situations. Thus in addition to the observation skills noted above, dynamic assessment requires training in the techniques required (a) to determine which environments are relevant for observing a particular behavior, and (b) to interpret results obtained under different environmental situations. Like many aspects of dynamic assessment, systematic norms are not available to assist with these decisions. Therefore, training has to focus on a conservative approach to interpretation based on the need for multiple observations to make a single conclusion. Training must also focus on strategies for developing local norms to assist in decision making based on such data.

Training for the Evaluation of Assessment

A requirement for the long-term acceptance of assessment techniques is to evaluate the efficacy of these techniques. Yet, training rarely focuses specifically on evaluation techniques that can be used to determine the effectiveness of assessment strategies. Evaluation of assessment techniques can be conceptualized as two distinct types: formative evaluation and summative evaluation. Formative evaluation is designed to determine the degree to which the expected steps in assessment are followed, and summative evaluation is designed to determine the outcome of assessment.

Formative evaluation is important for training in two ways. First, it is an important skill for professionals to use later in their career. By recording the use of various steps in the assessment process and various assessment procedures the examiner can develop a data base to help maintain a high level of performance. For example, if the examiner keeps a record of those procedures used to assess the process of learning, the environment, and trial interventions, it is more likely that the examiner will resist any pressures to perform assessments that do not examine each important aspect of behavior. In addition, formative evaluation can be used during training to keep a record of the degree to which each important aspect of dynamic assessment is implemented by the trainee. An effective training assignment is to have the trainee develop a Dynamic Assessment Checklist. Figure 15.1 includes a partial example of such a checklist. However, it is useful to have trainees develop their own checklists. This helps consolidate some of the earlier learning and maintains the trainee's active involvement in the learning process. After the checklist is developed, the trainees are given the assignment of using the checklist to evaluate their own performance when conducting an assessment.

Summative evaluation techniques are important for the long-term acceptance of alternative approaches such as dynamic assessment, since positive outcome data will help to demonstrate the utility of the technique. Dynamic assessment lends itself readily to outcome evaluations focused on change in the learning behavior of the client rather than relying on gross measures such as the number of evaluations, the numbers of children placed in different

Dynamic Assessment Checklist

	Implemented satisfactorily	Implemented unsatisfactorily	Not implemented
1. Techniques to assess the learning process: _____ _____			
2. Techniques focused on the assessment/ environment link: _____ _____			
3. Techniques focused on the assessment/ intervention link: _____ _____			

FIGURE 15.1. Dynamic assessment checklist

special education settings, and the like. Summative evaluation in dynamic assessment is developed easily based on the goals of intervention attempted during assessment. These goals would be expanded into long-term goals following evaluation, and they could be evaluated by repeating certain components of the assessment at the end of a time period that is reasonable for observing change in the expanded behavioral goals.

Conclusions

Training is a key factor in expanding the practice of dynamic assessment, and will be important also in developing research that deals with the practical realities of implementing dynamic assessment. For example, it is crucial that practitioners and researchers develop efficient ways for implementing dynamic assessment to facilitate a broader acceptance of this approach by practitioners. Training is a key factor in developing such efficient approaches. For example, much of the work in learning potential assessment that has been conducted by Feuerstein, Budoff, Haywood, and others has used nonverbal measures of cognitive performance such as the Raven Progressive Matrices. Presumably this has been done because these nonverbal measures provide an excellent opportunity to observe the child's problem-solving strategies and because these measures have been found to be more susceptible to intervention than others (e.g., verbal measures). Nevertheless, the Raven Progressive Matrices are not used routinely by most child diagnosticians, and tying learning potential assessment to this technique may decrease the probability of its use in practice. This chapter has suggested that training in learning potential assessment should focus on more frequently used nonverbal tests of cognitive performance such as the block design subtest of the WISC-R. For example, Lidz and Thomas (Chapter 11, this volume) take the approach of tying their dynamic assessment procedures to a frequently used preschool measure. If it is possible to demonstrate the utility of such tasks for dynamic assessment, it will be more likely that practitioners who are pressured to use traditional approaches to assessment may more readily incorporate dynamic assessment techniques into their practice.

There are many other factors that can be emphasized during assessment to increase the probability of implementing dynamic assessment. For example, practitioners are more likely to implement assessment techniques that incorporate intervention if the format of diagnostic reports is changed to include a specific section focused on the efficacy of trial interventions. This section of the report can be labeled "The Potential for Learning." Similarly, training clinics attempting to implement dynamic assessment may have to require trainees to use at least one technique to focus on each of the primary factors underlying this approach to assessment (i.e., at least one test–teach–retest procedure, one environmental assessment, and one assessment of learning process). Also, since this approach views intervention as an integral part of assessment, it may be necessary to require at least two feedback sessions for the relevant caregivers.

This chapter has discussed how training in dynamic assessment can focus both on the scientific–conceptual factors that underlie this framework for assessment and on the development of specific skills needed to implement dynamic assessment. In particular, it has focused on techniques for training focused on the link between assessment and intervention, the link between assessment and the environment, and assessment of the learning process. Although it is hoped that this will be an effective step in facilitating the implementation of dynamic assessment, the reader must maintain caution about these techniques. There is not yet a sufficient data base to justify the uncritical use of these techniques, or to justify the use of these techniques to replace other approaches to assessment. At the present time the framework can be used to conceptualize the assessment process, and the specific techniques associated with dynamic assessment should be used as an adjunct to traditional assessment approaches. In addition, it is crucial for the field that research programs be implemented to demonstrate the utility of various dynamic assessment techniques.

REFERENCES

Alpert, J. L., & Meyers, J. (Eds.) (1983). *Training in consultation*. Springfield, IL: Charles C Thomas.

Brown, A. L. (1975). The development of memory: Knowing, knowing about knowing and knowing how to know. In H. W. Reese (Ed.), *Advances in child development and behavior* (Vol. 10). New York: Academic Press.

Brown, A. L., Campione, J. C., & Murphy, M. D. (1977). Maintenance and generalization of trained metamnemonic awareness by educable retarded children. *Journal of Experimental Child Psychology*, *24*, 191–211.

Budoff, M. (1975). Measuring learning potential: An alternative to the traditional intelligence test. In G. R. Gredler (Ed.), *Ethical and legal factors in the practice of school psychology*. Harrisburg, PA: Department of Education.

Feuerstein, R. (1979). *The dynamic assessment of retarded performers: The learning potential assessment device, theory, instruments, and techniques*. Baltimore: University Park Press.

Feuerstein, R. (1980). *Instrumental enrichment: An intervention program for cognitive modifiability*. Baltimore: University Park Press.

Flanders, N. A. (1970). *Analyzing teaching behavior*. Reading, MA: Addison-Wesley.

Ford, J. (1977). Training in clinical psychology. A reappraisal based on recent empirical evidence. *The Clinical Psychologist*, *3*, 14–16.

Ford, J. (1978). Training in environmental design. In L. Krasner (Ed.), *Handbook of environmental design*. New York: Pergamon Press.

Good, T., & Brophy, J. E. (1973). *Looking in classrooms*. NY: Harper & Row.

Keys, C. B. (1983). Graduate training in organizational consultation: Three dilemmas. In J. L. Alpert & J. Meyers (Eds.), *Training in consultation*. Springfield, IL: Charles C Thomas.

Kounin, J. S. (1970). *Discipline and group management in classrooms*. New York: Holt, Rinehart & Winston.

Kuehnel, T. G., & Kuehnel, J. M. (1983). Consultation training from a behavioral perspective. In J. L. Alpert & J. Meyers (Eds.), *Training in consultation*. Springfield, IL: Charles C Thomas.

Lytle, S. L. (1982). *Exploring comprehension style: A study of twelfth-grade readers' transactions with text*. Doctoral dissertation, University of Pennsylvania.

Manni, J. (1981). *Learning potential assessment: A demonstration video-tape*. Sewell, NJ: Educational Improvement Center South, New Jersey State Department of Education.

Meichenbaum, D. (1980). A cognitive-behavioral perspective on intelligence. *Intelligence*, *4*, 271–283.

Meyers, J., Pfeffer, J., & Erlbaum, V. (1985). Process assessment: A model for broadening assessment. *Journal of Special Education*, *19*, 73–89.

Parsons, R. D., & Meyers, J. (1984). *Developing consultation skills*. San Francisco: Jossey-Bass.

Piaget, J. (1971). *The psychology of intelligence* (6th ed.). London: Routledge & Kegan Paul.

Schafer, R. (1954). *Psychoanalytic interpretation in Rorschach testing*. NY: Grune & Stratton.

Smith, C. R. (1980). Assessment alternatives: Non-standardized procedures. *School Psychology Review*, *9*, 46–57.

Vygotsky, L. S. (1978). *Mind in society: The development of higher psychological processes*. Cambridge, MA: Harvard University Press.

Weinstein, C. E., & Mayer, R. E. (1986). The teaching of learning strategies. In M. C. Wittrock (Ed.), *Handbook of research on teaching* (3rd ed.). New York: Macmillan.

16

Dynamic Assessment as a Nondiscriminatory Procedure

TREVOR E. SEWELL

A fundamental principle underlying the assessment process is the requirement that tests should be selected that are not racially or culturally discriminatory. In the context of the psychometric tradition, the question of bias in the assessment of minorities has emerged as being centrally important to the general issues of testing and equality of opportunities. From a historical perspective, the concerns over bias in psychological assessment of American minorities stimulated an extensive examination of the theoretical and practical factors associated with test construction and educational uses. In addition, these concerns provided the legal basis for the involvement of the courts in the application of psychological tests to educational practice. However, if testing or assessment were conceived with the central purpose of contributing to instructional strategies rather than selection or classification, perhaps issues such as "nonbias" and "nondiscriminatory" concerns would not be at the core of this enduring controversy.

The discriminatory implications of IQ tests in psychoeducational assessment serve as the basis in this chapter for an examination of dynamic assessment as a nondiscriminatory procedure. The initial focus in this chapter on IQ-related issues within the legal scrutiny of minority testing and the programmatic needs of retarded children highlights the pressing need for a reconceptualization of the purpose of assessment and further suggests that dynamic assessment might be explored in the search for viable alternatives or supplements to current psychometric approaches.

Issues in Psychometric Assessment of Minorities

The issues embedded in the assessment of minorities are integrally related to the broader issues of social justice and equality of educational opportunities. The observation that "until a decade or so ago, the measurement of intelligence was generally considered to be one of psychology's major success stories" (Tyler, 1973, p. 13) reflects a shift in perception perhaps attributable

Trevor E. Sewell. College of Education, Temple University, Philadelphia, Pennsylvania.

to the growing suspicion that IQ testing of poor and minority children perpetuates social and economic injustices (Gould, 1981; Kamin, 1974). Much of the highly acclaimed contribution of psychology to education centers around the implementation of intelligence testing in schools. Paradoxically, it is precisely this psychometric contribution that is undoubtedly linked to educational policies that are perceived as restricting the educational opportunities of minorities.

Gordon and Rubian (1980) have highlighted the contradiction in the dual concern for social justice and psychometric integrity. They contend that the standardized nature of test construction is consistent with the integrity of the psychometric tradition but "inconsistent with social justice when the criteria for a just society are fairness (i.e., appropriateness of background), sensitivity to differential attributes and conditional or pluralistic standards" (p. 350).

No amount of optimism could lead one to the conclusion that the elimination of the use of IQ tests with minority populations will markedly impact on the variety of factors associated with social justice in the broad society. Perhaps, however, the defense of IQ testing on the basis of its scientific merits independent of the social and political issues constitutes a major barrier to a more meaningful focus on strategies that are more likely to contribute to the educational process. If one assumes that the central purpose of testing is selection and classification, then scientific support for the IQ test is impressive. The technical adequacy of the IQ test for predicting school-related performance justifies the contention that the test is valid for all segments of the population (Cleary, Humphreys, Kendrick, & Wesman, 1975; Jensen, 1980). However, if the quality of educational programming becomes the conceptual basis for testing, the science of the psychometric tradition conflicts with the practical issues of testing, thus presenting a complex and confusing picture.

Given the relatively poorer academic performance of minority children, assessment dictated by academic problems and geared to provide diagnostic information to guide the teaching–learning process is vitally necessary. The glaring lack of support for existing testing instruments that in terms exemplify the accomplishments of scientific psychology is unquestionably linked to adverse social and educational consequences, particularly for minority children. It is within this professional and social framework that the question is asked: How can the social concerns of restricted educational opportunities and disproportionate representation of minorities in "stigmatizing" classes for educable mentally retarded (EMR) students be disentangled from IQ tests despite their impressive scientific and technical qualities?

The notion that alternatives to IQ testing could potentially be harmful to the educational aspirations of minority children seems unconvincing in light of the legal, social, and philosophical issues raised by the use of IQ tests. Nevertheless, support for IQ testing is usually built on the claim that "Testing on a broad scale was adopted by the schools to improve the opportunities of lower-SES and minority children for selection into educationally and occupationally advantaged positions and to reduce the pervasive class and ethnic biases of personal [judgment]" (Scarr, 1981, p. 4). In a balanced presentation of issues centered around the use of IQ tests, Travers (1982) highlighted the proponents' position that IQ tests offer the best chance for individuals of disadvantaged background to achieve competitive advantage in occupational selection, thus ensuring economic success. In line with this position, the subjective and qualitative assessments associated with teachers' ratings have been persistently depicted as potentially more discriminatory than tests. This line of reasoning presents a rather striking conceptual confusion because of the failure to differentiate between testing for instructional purposes and testing to determine eligibility for occupational selection. Whereas opponents point to the well-documented undesirable outcomes of testing minority children such as tracking and special class placement in addition to occupational selection, the proponents of standardized testing argue that the social concept of equality of educational opportunities is best served by the excellent predictive validity of tests. Even when the distinction between the purposes of testing is not fully explicated, the critics have argued that differential socioeconomic circumstances make the tests inherently biased against low-income and/or minority children and consequently negatively affect educational opportunities and career success.

It is perhaps this recognition that negative outcomes are indeed associated with current testing practices that motivated Messick (1980) to argue that the statistical and empirical evidence of test validity should not obscure the need to examine the social consequences of testing. In this light, the objective scientific analysis of testing minority children cannot ignore the moral and emotional implications of the contention that these tests perpetuate the belief system of the genetic inferiority of blacks to perform intellectually. The well-articulated view that minorities are hindered by genetically dictated limitations in mastering higher level conceptual tasks based on test-related evidence must be seen as potentially capable of adversely affecting educational outcomes regardless of the specific purpose of testing (Jensen, 1969; Terman, 1916). In the context of these persistent views, unfounded or not, Scarr (1978) is possibly quite correct in her assertion that "abandoning the tests cannot make the society more pluralistic, [ensure] equal rights or redistribute social and economic benefits" (p. 340). But if there are aspects of both comedy and tragedy in the legal play over IQ testing, as she contended, for those who advocate abandoning the tests because they perpetuate social myths and injustices in educational and occupational opportunities, there is a growing perception that their continued use with poor and minority children is more of a tragedy. Given the perplexing nature of the theoretical and empirical evidence in which IQ testing is embroiled, the attempts by the courts to provide some professional guidance might shed light on the merits, pitfalls, and possible alternatives to testing minority children.

Nondiscriminatory Assessment: The Legal Context

The requirement that testing be nondiscriminatory is one of the important features of Public Law (PL) 94-142. This public policy provision, supported by judicial opinion suggesting that IQ tests have a discriminatory impact, is perhaps the basis of a seemingly unresolvable controversy among measurement experts. Although several models of test bias have been advanced (Peterson & Novick, 1976), there is no acceptable agreement as to what constitutes a fair test. Thus, Ysseldyke's (1978) observation that "[t]here is little agreement on the concept of non-discriminatory assessment" (p. 150) reflects the complexity of the current state of affairs. From the psychometric perspective, however, the reliance on predictive validity to justify the nonbias argument has been supported by considerable empirical evidence (Jensen, 1980). The data on which this evidence is based are primarily derived from research in which achievement tests serve as the criterion. Given the lack of a clear distinction between the abilities involved in the IQ test and the achievement criterion in that both have a common source of bias (Mercer, 1975), the soundness of this scientific stance has been strongly challenged.

Despite the elegant statistical methodology on which IQ tests have been established as unbiased predictors of academic performance, in the Larry P. case the school system as defendants acknowledged the culturally biased nature of IQ tests but advanced the notion that their continued use is justified on the basis of the lack of acceptable alternatives. Interestingly, the court recognized the need for identifying children in need of remedial services but contended that the use of "irrational" means such as the IQ test was not acceptable despite the lack of suitable alternatives. Thus, the biased conception of intelligence tests was a crucial issue in the challenges to IQ testing of minorities, but the related issues of EMR placement and the preeminent role of the IQ test in the placement process were the practical concerns embedded in the constitutional question of educational equality.

Prior to the legal focus on the implications of the use of IQ tests for EMR placement, precedent-setting litigation in *Hobson v. Hansen* (1967) questioned the use of group tests to place children in ability tracks. Based on the disproportionate representation of black students in the lower academic tracks and whites in the upper tracks, questions as to the constitutionality of the tracking system and the issues related to psychological tests were raised. It is noteworthy that ability grouping did not rely solely on psychological tests as the only source of information. It was acknowledged, nevertheless, that "the proper operation of the track system practically demands reliance on test scores" (*Hobson v. Hansen*, 1967, p. 475). In *Hobson*, several significant conclusions of the court supported the unconstitutional discriminatory impact of psychological tests. The findings that approximately 820 of 1,272 children were misclassified on the basis of group tests must have profoundly influenced the court's decision. More importantly, however, the relegation of a disproportionate number of black children to classes in which restricted resource allocation and diminished educational opportunities ultimately rendered them inferior and stigmatized was a direct violation of constitutional safeguards. According to Bersoff (1981), "*Hobson*, when read in its entirety, represents the justified condemnation of rigid, poorly conceived classification practices that damage the educational opportunities of minority children" (p. 1047). Thus, although the validity of the individual test was not in question, the conditions were established for continued examination of the adverse impact of psychological tests on the assessment and placement process.

The continued legal attack on the discriminatory impact of intelligence tests in the context of classification and placement of minorities in special education is exemplified in both *Diana v. State Board of Education* (1970) and *Guadalupe v. Tempe Elementary School District* (1972). The central issue in both cases was the overrepresentation of bilingual children in special education classes based on the plaintiff's contention that the use of intelligence tests was an invidious factor in the denial of equal educational opportunities. In what must be considered an explicit failure of IQ tests to differentiate validly the learning ability of minority children, several thousand minority children were returned to regular classes. The similarity of this finding to that reported in the *Hobson* case, in which two thirds of the children in the special education track were assessed as being not genuinely retarded, is quite noteworthy. The consent decree issued by the court in both the *Diana* and *Guadalupe* cases substantially restricted the use of IQ tests as the primary instrument for classifying children as mentally retarded. Again, the implication of overrepresentation of minority children in special classes was addressed within the framework of the constitutional issue of equality of access to educational opportunities.

Despite considerable prior legal scrutiny, the *Larry P. v. Wilson Riles* (1979) litigation provided the most in-depth analysis of the use of intelligence tests as a primary determinant of special class placement of minority children. *Larry P.* was initiated as a class-action suit filed on behalf of black children placed in programs for mildly retarded children. Focusing on the issues of cultural bias in intelligence tests and the questionable efficacy of special classes, the court ruled that the constitutional guarantee of equal protection had been violated. Thus, the outcome of *Larry P.* was to enjoin the defendants permanently "from utilizing, permitting the use of, or approving the use of any standardized tests . . . for the identification of black EMR children or their placement into EMR classes, without first securing approval by [the] court" (p. 989).

Before the full impact of the *Larry P.* decision was evident in professional practice, an opposing decision on the use of IQ tests with minority children was rendered in *PASE* (Parents in Action in Special Education) *v. Hannon*

(1980). In contrast to *Larry P.*, in which the discriminatory impact of the IQ test was dramatically highlighted, Judge Grady in *PASE v. Hannon* was unimpressed with expert witnesses and ruled that intelligence tests such as the Wechsler scales and the Stanford–Binet, if used appropriately under conditions established by PL 94-142, do not discriminate against black children. By rejecting professional expertise and characterizing the testimony as often reflecting "the result of doctrinaire commitment to [a] preconceived idea [rather] than the result of scientific inquiry" (*PASE v. Hannon*, p. 836), Judge Grady's opinion, rendered from the perspective of his unique analysis, failed to match the judicial credibility of *Larry P.* Thus, although the favorable ruling on the discriminatory issue was applauded by the defendants, according to Bersoff (1981), "the method by which Judge Grady reached that [judgment] is embarrassingly unsophisticated and ingenuous" (p. 1049). Interestingly, Judge Grady's ruling upholding the validity of IQ tests for minority children was based on his perception that only eight items on the Wechsler Intelligence Scale for Children–Revised (WISC-R) were actually discriminatory. Despite this conclusion, he apparently perceived the need to couch his opinion in terms of the nondiscriminatory clause of PL 94-142 in which a single instrument, even if it is discriminatory, would not render the multidisciplinary assessment system invalid. From this viewpoint, he evidently ignored the evidence that the IQ test continues to be a causal variable of inordinate importance in the placement decision (Berk, Bridges, & Shih, 1981).

Since much of the litigation involving the educational use of IQ tests centers around the educational outcome for minority children, there seems to be a need for a redirected focus on the quality of instruction resulting from IQ-generated inferences about learning ability. Despite the contradictory judicial resolution, the courts have consistently noted that EMR placement was of questionable educational benefit. To depict an educational program as "totally harmful" and "inferior" is to cast considerable doubt not only on the related issues of assessment but on the scientific assumptions on which such programs are built (*Larry P. v. Wilson Riles*, 1979).

If the controversial debate on the practical implications of testing is refocused to emphasize educational outcome, then the long-standing position of minorities (Bernal, 1975; Jackson, 1975) that the central concern is the negative impact on the rights of minorities to be fully educated will fit that perspective. Reflecting a similar perspective, Mercer (1975) eloquently argued that changes in classification procedures of exceptional children was not an issue that evolved from professional dissatisfaction with the present system. This fact, she contended, "signifies that the central issues are conceptual and ethical rather than technical and empirical" (p. 131). Perhaps a disproportionate representation in self-contained classes of a segment of the population that is performing poorly in school would be highly desirable if there were evidence that such programs facilitated learning. Consequently, an analysis of the educational outcome of special class placement should provide the fundamental reasons for a reconceptualization of the assessment process and its contribution to instruction.

Effectiveness of Special Classes for the Mildly Retarded

The classification and placement of children in special classes is a professional decision based on the implicit assumption that available special resources, specialized curricula, and individualized teaching strategies within these programs will directly benefit the student. In an extraordinarily perceptive analysis of the special education efficacy issue, Glass (1983) indicated that treatment efficacy merits serious attention since it is intertwined with questions of diagnostic validity. If the effectiveness of special education cannot be demonstrated, the examination of the educational setting and related instructional issues will inevitably raise questions as to the prescriptive contribution of the diagnostic process. A key factor in the evaluation of special programs is the possibility that the multiple causes advanced to account for retarded performance will not be recognized as being linked to diversity in the learning characteristics of EMR children. If the efficacy studies then fail to examine the extent to which the individualized instructional programs are linked to the assessment process, it may be implicitly assumed that testing was conceptualized as a means of determining eligibility for placement rather than for providing instructional guidance.

Unfortunately, the classroom settings have been the central focus of efficacy studies (Heller, 1982). Consequently, not only are the different educational approaches ignored to a large extent, but studies of the effectiveness of specific instructional strategies derived from diagnostic and placement decisions are virtually nonexistent. The noted exceptions have evaluated instructional models based on the underlying assumption that the differential diagnosis of psycholinguistic and perceptual–motor abilities can provide the prescriptive teaching directions for academic remediation. Reviewing the research on the effectiveness of perceptual–motor training, Glass (1983) noted that "the 637 effect size measures present an unbroken vista of disappointment, no positive effect; nothing; a complete washout" (p. 71). Similarly, the research on psycholinguistic training shows a disappointing failure to enhance academic performance (Kavale, 1981; Hamill & Larsen, 1973, Newcomer & Hammill, 1976).

If the attempts to teach specific but narrowly defined psychological processes are a dismal failure, the general educational teaching models in classroom settings have not shown much promise either. Despite the glaring methodological problems noted by Heller (1982), efficacy studies have received considerable attention. In addition to studies motivated by earlier concerns over the segregation of minority children in self-contained classes, PL 94-142 has stimulated renewed interest in the differences attributable to self-contained versus mainstreaming practices in special education. Although self-contained special classes and the practice of mainstreaming mildly retarded children in the least restricted environment are assumed to be desirable and beneficial, the empirical support for these practices is embarrassingly limited.

To conclude, as Carlberg and Kavale (1980) did, that "special class placement is an inferior alternative to regular class placement in benefiting children removed from the educational mainstream" (p. 304) is to imply that the disproportionate placement of minority students in such classes is indeed discriminatory. The indication that special classes fail to provide tangible academic benefits raises two compelling questions:

1. If special class placement conveys limited educational benefits, on what scientific or philosophical grounds do we justify the preeminent role of the IQ in the assessment process?
2. Given the evidence of the negative educational outcome of special class placement, should not the assessment issue be shifted from classification to pedagogical concerns, thus raising the question as to what extent testing facilitates effective learning by providing some instructional guidance?

By shifting the focus of testing from selection, assessment would be geared to meet the instructional needs of students regardless of the educational setting. The traditional use of the IQ test, however, is rooted in the conception that it was designed to sort and classify those who cannot profit from regular class instruction. From a practical, professional perspective, its potential to contribute to remedial instruction is indeed questionable. In this context, the measurement issues centered around psychometric theory are of no particular value if the IQ test cannot demonstrate a beneficial link to instructional outcome. This link is clearly in doubt, and the scientific merits of the IQ tests as demonstrated by technical adequacy are encountering perplexing questions concerning their educational utility. It is this conflict between the need to recognize the scientific merits of IQ tests and the clinical demands to contribute to remedial instruction through assessment procedures that remains an unsettling issue for practitioners. Moreover, many of the scientific issues that are core factors in the IQ controversy, such as "innate" potential, cannot be translated into meaningful instructional strategies. How then should the assessment process be reconceptualized? The conceptual model guiding the assessment process should satisfy the fundamental requirement of identifying deficient cognitive processes so that the instructional needs of the individual may be served in a nondiscriminatory context. Dynamic assessment has embraced this theoretical and practical objective.

Dynamic Assessment and Conceptual Framework

The judicial scrutiny that has provoked concerns over issues of constitutional rights and the empirical findings questioning the efficacy of special class placement are forces giving impetus to the search for alternative assessment approaches. Neither of these forces, however, seems to have provided any conceptual guidelines for the emerging trends in the assessment of retarded performers. A focal point in the stream of controversies surrounding IQ testing is the need for instructionally relevant information. The notion that information derived from tests should inform instruction has provided the central factors in developing models of assessment in which the conceptual framework shifts the purpose of testing from one of classification to an approach designed to facilitate the instructional needs of the student. Within this theoretical context, the *dynamic* or *process* model of assessment, with its diagnostic and remedial objectives, has emerged.

In contrast to the psychometric model, which identifies global levels of functioning, the dynamic-oriented assessment procedure pinpoints the underlying mental processes related to academic difficulties. The concept of dynamic assessment is rooted in the theoretical notion that intelligence is a dynamic entity. It is unlike the traditional psychometric models that emphasize the products of intellectual performance achieved from a static measurement format, which do not adequately reflect learning potential. Feuerstein (1980) argued that fundamental to the conceptual framework of dynamic assessment is the thinking that the intellectual performance of retarded performers is modifiable and "the individual's manifest level of performance at any given point in his development cannot be regarded as fixed or immutable" (p. 2). With the notion that modifiability is central to the theoretical conception of intelligence, assessment, and intervention, dynamic assessment involves the direct measurement of learning potential, which is facilitated by a focused intervention in the assessment process. Consistent with the theoretical model that the cognitive performance of retarded children can be improved, Feuerstein (1979) stated that

> Static measures completely neglect separate assessment of the dimension of modifiability because they equate the measure of manifest functioning with the true and immutable capacity of the individual. The dynamic approach does not deny the fact that the functioning of the individual, as observed in his level of achievement or his general behavior, is low; but by considering his level as pertaining only to the manifest repertoire of the individual, it takes into consideration the possibility of modifying this repertoire by appropriate strategies of intervention. (p. 95)

In contrast to the recent efforts to apply dynamic assessment to educational problems, cognitive psychologists, for several decades, have advanced the theoretical model for assessment of learning ability by directly measuring the child's ability to profit from systematic intervention in the assessment process. The rationale for a shift from the psychometric emphasis on the quantitative factors of assessment to qualitative analysis for determining learning potential and to infer a degree of modifiability has its roots in the longstanding notion that psychometric instruments do not address the cognitive processes underlying learning difficulties (Vygotsky, 1934/1962).

The focus on the assessment of modifiability by direct measurement of learning from a structured learning experience minimizes the impact of several theoretical issues that have been at the forefront of the discriminatory testing controversy. If the primary purpose of assessment is to determine learning potential for instructional purposes, the emphasis on stable individual characteristics that reflect prior learning experiences will be rendered meaningless. Such an emphasis will likely perpetuate the issues underlying cultural bias without enhancing the strategies for cognitive change. A direct implication for minority assessment is that the radical shift in the conception of intelligence should probably highlight the irrelevance of the enduring genetic arguments within the context of schooling. Finally, the conceptual model of dynamic assessment has not embraced, in a traditional manner, the highly acclaimed value of validity and reliability on which the scientific foundation of the psychometric approach putatively rests. The distinction between the two approaches in this critical issue of testing is based on the unambiguous psychometric procedure of utilizing an individual's current level of cognitive performance to predict future learning. The sharply defined contrast of assessing modifiability by evaluating change during the assessment procedure has led to the assertion that "[i]mproved techniques for raising the levels of test reliability and validity cannot be considered relevant if our goal is to change cognitive functioning, not to stabilize it" (Feuerstein, Miller, Rand, & Jensen, 1981, p. 204).

Dynamic Assessment Procedure

The Learning Potential Assessment Device

Feuerstein (1979, 1980; see Chapter 1, this volume) has developed a model of dynamic assessment that is currently the most comprehensive approach in that it links assessment practices to intervention at both a theoretical and clinical level. His Learning Potential Assessment Device (LPAD) constitutes a battery of tests and training procedures that were derived from his extensive research and clinical involvement with disadvantaged children (see Chapters 1, 7, and 14, this volume). It is precisely this factor, the commitment to identify strategies for improving academic competence of culturally disadvantaged and retarded children, that has promoted a model of assessment and intervention that minimizes, if not eliminates, charges of discriminatory practices that infringe on the constitutional right of equality of educational opportunities.

The dynamic assessment model's emphasis on understanding the principles underlying the processes of thinking and behavior rather than on assessing global levels of functioning by IQ tests requires the following four fundamental changes in the assessment procedure (Feuerstein, 1979):

THE STRUCTURE OF THE TEST

The testing instrument must be constructed to enable an examiner to probe cognitive processes in a test–teach–retest format, thus generating hypotheses as to the individual's problem-solving skills, the individual's preferences for various modalities of presentation, and the differential effects of the teaching process on the capacity for cognitive change. By changing the nature of the testing instrument, the critical issue of the sociocultural factors impacting on content familiarity in conventional IQ tests is minimized, and the issue of cultural bias, from a practical perspective, is defused.

EXAMINATION SITUATION

The second area of significant change centers around the examination situation. The interactive approach to the examiner–examinee relationship in the test–teach–retest paradigm of the dynamic assessment procedure presents the most striking contrast to psychometric testing procedures. Unlike the standardized procedure of IQ testing, in the test–teach–retest paradigm,

> the examiner constantly intervenes, makes remarks, requires and gives explanations, whenever and wherever they are necessary, asks for repetition, sums up experiences, and creates reflective insightful thinking. . . . He is vibrant, active and concern[ed] instead of aloof, distant, and neutral, and gives the examinee the feeling that the task is important, difficult, and yet quite manageable. (Feuerstein, 1979, p. 102)

It is widely assumed that anxiety and motivational difficulties are deeply embedded in the performance of cognitive tasks as a result of persistent academic failure and/or other cultural factors. For minority children whose performance is usually associated with motivational problems, the interactive process of dynamic assessment provides the opportunity for selective feedback and specific problem-solving instructions, thus ensuring successful learning experiences in a context that promotes a transformation of behavioral patterns.

THE ORIENTATION OF THE TEST

The orientation of testing must be viewed in the context of the purpose of assessment. The goal of testing in the dynamic approach is to explore the nature of learning, with the objective of collecting information to bring about cognitive change and to enhance instruction. Viewed from this perspective, the orientation of the test has shifted from the objective of determining the static characteristic of the child to a more process-sensitive method of assessing cognitive skills and learning strategies.

INTERPRETATION OF RESULTS

The standard procedure of comparing an individual's performance to normative data is in diametrical opposition to the practice of dynamic assessment, in which performance peaks are interpreted as estimates of cognitive potential rather than measurement errors or random fluctuations. From a psychometric perspective, the validity of interpreting an "uncharacteristic excellent response" as reflecting learning potential is clearly questionable. On the other hand, from a clinical perspective, the privilege to probe and to provide detailed feedback and inquiry enhances the understanding of performance levels and helps to establish remedial goals. If one assumes that cultural factors may have differential effects on patterns of cognitive performance, then dynamic assessment has provided a key conceptual framework for capitalizing on the strengths of disadvantaged children reflected in single unique responses as a basis for determining learning potential.

Within the subjective dimensions of task analysis in the dynamic assessment approach, the LPAD is guided by a cognitive map that clearly delineates the potentially deficient functions within three phases of mental activity: input, elaboration, and output. It is within the established seven parameters of the cognitive map that the cognitive tasks are analyzed. The sensitivity of this process to environmental, motivational, and cognitive problems is a decisive factor in making this assessment process an attractive alternative for testing the culturally different child. Two of the parameters in which cognitive activities are analyzed, content and modalities, are of particular importance to the assessment of minorities. Learning, regardless of the content, is usually mediated by experiential and cultural factors. Given the analytical framework of the process-oriented approach, the diversity in cultural experiences that gives rise to charges of cultural bias would conceivably play a less significant role in determining learning potential. Additionally, the requirement that tasks would be presented on different modalities that constitute the language of instruction is a key factor in pinpointing specific strengths and weaknesses. By deliberately shifting the modality of task presentation within the wide boundaries of verbal, pictorial, numerical, and figural modalities, the dynamic assessment approach provides differential information for prescriptive directions.

Test—Train—Retest

Arguing that the cognitive performance of children from poor and/or minority backgrounds on IQ tests does not reflect their problem-solving capability, Budoff and associates (Babad & Budoff, 1974; Budoff & Freidman, 1964, see Chapter 2, this volume) have devised a learning potential assessment strategy that is cast in the conceptual mold of the test—teach—retest paradigm of dynamic assessment. In line with the views of other proponents of dynamic assessment, the primary theoretical and professional issue underlying Budoff's work is the observation that experiential factors are implicated in the assessed low performance of minority children. Issues such as content familiarity, lack

of motivation, and inadequate examiner–examinee interaction in the traditional testing procedure are assumed to contribute to a level of performance
that is not reflective of the cognitive strengths of individuals from impoverished backgrounds. The human mediating factor in the training procedure
that stresses task analysis and motivation is the critical condition that generates
clinical information indicating the differential effects of training. Noting the
beneficial impact of the procedure for children of "poor and/or nonwhite
background," Babad and Budoff (1974) suggested that the "training helps
the child to narrow the cognitive gap between previously learned problem
solving strategies and those implicit to the problems he must ordinarily solve
on the middle-class bias tests he encounters" (p. 440). Budoff categorized
those individuals showing substantial improvement following training as
"gainers" and those for whom the impact of training was minimal as "nongainers." Focusing on the differential training effects, Budoff has consistently
found that training results in a substantially greater level of improvement for
low-socioeconomic-status children. Arguing that the experiental background
of middle-class children contributes to an apparent optimal level of performance on IQ tests, Babad and Budoff (1974) pointed out that the category of
gainers is significantly related to lower-class status.

IQ Testing and Low Socioeconomic Status

Evidence that the IQ test is not an unbiased index of learning ability for low-
socioeconomic-status children has been accumulating for some time. Studies
that have focused on the comparative merits of assessment procedures using
intelligence and laboratory-based learning tasks such as paired associates have
provided impressive empirical data to cast considerable doubt on the validity
of the IQ test (Green & Rohwer, 1971). In addition to having the child engage
directly in learning in order to assess his or her learning ability, others have
asked whether the child's learning ability could improve as a function of
training. In both cases, the wide disparity between socioeconomic classes in
measured intelligence is not reflected in an equally discrepant learning ability
when learning is measured directly by performance on paired-associate tasks
(Rohwer, 1971). The implications seem clear: whatever measure of direct
learning ability is used to assess the learning potential of low-socioeconomic-
status children, the comparative results suggest that inferring learning ability
by measuring past learning has profound limitations for psychoeducational
decisions.

The Validity of Dynamic Assessment as a Nondiscriminatory Procedure

Relative to the impressive scientific support for the predictive validity of IQ
testing and other technical features, the learning potential assessment pro-

cedure has been subjected to considerably less research. Nevertheless, the available empirical evidence offers strong support for the potential to aid in the development of diagnostic and remedial objectives, particularly with children from disadvantaged backgrounds. Feuerstein's (1979, 1981) experimental studies address the assessment of minority children. Focusing on culturally different children, he was able to identify children who demonstrated significantly higher levels of learning potential than would have been inferred from their IQ-defined mentally retarded status by using a dynamic assessment procedure.

Strikingly similar results on the differential effects of training among children of different social class backgrounds were reported by Babad and Budoff (1974). Comparing the performance of children in the subnormal (mean = 72), low-average (mean = 88), and high-average (mean = 113) IQ ranges, they reported that a substantial number of EMR children performed in line with their nonretarded peers following training in the context of the test–teach–retest paradigm of dynamic assessment.

Given the impressive quantitative data on which the validity claims of intelligence tests are established, there seem to be compelling reasons to inquire into the extent to which the professional perspective advanced by dynamic assessment is informed by the science of psychological measurement. From another perspective, it is also reasonable to question whether or not validation data on the learning potential measure should be pursued modeling the traditional psychometric emphasis on prediction (see Chapter 5, this volume). If, indeed, validity determination should be expanded beyond the technical factors of prediction to include social consequences, as Messick (1980) suggested, then Feuerstein (1979) was correct in suggesting that the achievement attributable to the use of the learning potential assessment method for returning "masses of adolescents previously placed in special schools, classes and institutions for the retarded . . . into regular education framework, in agricultural, vocational and academically oriented high schools" (p. 327) is perhaps the crucial evidence of validity.

Consistent with the notion that change is the sine qua non of assessment, Feuerstein (1979) refocused the measurement of validity from the instruments to the evidence of change following intervention. Accordingly, if a substantively higher degree of modifiability can be demonstrated than is usually expected from a given diagnostic label, quantitative evidence of validity is of considerably less importance. Similarly, Swanson (1984) argued that the undue emphasis on validity and reliability of tests is myopic given the failure of existing theoretical models to guide assessment practice.

Nevertheless, the principle of evaluating and selecting assessment instruments on the basis of their technical qualities of reliability and validity is deeply entrenched in educational and psychological practice. Consequently, despite the radically different conceptual basis of the dynamic assessment approach, the challenge to demonstrate its technical adequacy is of significant

professional and scientific interest. In view of the persistent interest in evaluating the claims of dynamic assessment by the scientific technical standards
of psychometric testing, I have explored the differential predictive effectiveness of dynamic assessment and IQ tests (Sewell, 1979; Sewell & Severson,
1974). In emphasizing the need to develop assessment techniques that provide
diagnostic information related to cognitive modifiability, learning styles, and
personality–performance interaction, I have observed that the clinical data
derived from dynamic assessment contribute substantially to the teaching–
learning process (Sewell, Winikur, Berlinghof, Berkowitz, & Miner, 1984).

In terms of motivational factors, the enthusiastic involvement of examinees in a dynamic assessment testing situation was unparalleled. Test-taking
behavior of minority and/or lower-class pupils in the dynamic assessment
situation decidedly contradicts the findings that indicate that they experience
diminished motivation and are discouraged from learning. Instead, they become invested in the quality of their performance (Samuda, 1975).

Focusing on the relative merits of dynamic assessment, experimental
learning tasks, and IQ tests in predicting scholastic achievement of children
of markedly different experiential background, I have found that the IQ test
provides a more valid estimate of learning ability for middle-class children
under varied learning conditions than for children of lower socioeconomic
status (Sewell, 1979). Using the dynamic assessment procedure, I have reported consistent evidence showing posttest performance to be the best predictor for lower-class black children. Strikingly similar results were reported
by Babad and Budoff (1974). They found posttest learning potential correlations with achievement to be superior to IQ predictors for children of subnormal intellectual classification. The failure of the posttest to improve on
the predictive power of the pretest for middle-class children suggests that, on
static measures of ability, middle-class children were already performing near
their optimal level of learning ability on the pretest; thus, the impact of the
posttest following training was negligible.

The reason for the improved correlation between achievement and posttest performance after change produced by training is not clear. Presumably,
the brief intervention strategy in the assessment process results in a change
in the level of problem-solving ability—the magnitude of which produces
differential effects in the relationship to achievement. What is clearly evident
from these results is that the initial levels of performance were distinctly
different from those that were assessed following training, suggesting that the
test–retest comparisons in the dynamic assessment paradigm would produce
low correlations.

Summary

The many scientific and professional issues intertwined with the disproportionate placement of minority children in special classes by assessment ap-

proaches that have been adjudicated as discriminatory will not be resolved by dynamic assessment. In fact, Reschly (1984) shared the belief of many that "the new direct measures of learning, for example, the Learning Potential Assessment Device, are highly unlikely to significantly alter present classification practices, or, for that matter, educational programming" (p. 15). Nevertheless, optimism regarding the prospect of dynamic assessment adding meaningfully to the assessment and intervention policies in special education is gaining widespread practitioner appeal (Barnett, 1983; Lidz, 1981; Manni, Winikur, & Keller, 1984). The increasing focus on dynamic assessment to supplement, if not substitute for, the IQ test may be attributed to the following factors. First, although the dynamic assessment procedure does not deal with the issue of which curriculum is most appropriate to meet instructional needs of minority children, it raises crucial questions concerning the practices of testing children on materials where the possibility of content irrelevance is considerable and where historical experiences have poorly equipped the child to deal with standardized tests. Furthermore, the emphasis on cognitive modifiability provides the basis for speculation that, if a mentally retarded child shows impressive cognitive changes attributable to training, then the academic expectations, social responsiveness, and educational programming of the child may be revised substantially with the possible eventual outcome of improved performance.

Second, the well-developed conceptual model presented by Feuerstein (1979), with an emphasis on the interaction between cognitive processes and motivational factors, satisfies both the theoretical and practical perspectives for linking assessment to the prescriptive and instructional needs of retarded performers. This specific orientation of emphasizing treatment goals may conceivably have the salutary effect of counteracting the historical tendency to attribute the low functioning of minority children on IQ tests to irreversible cognitive deficits.

Finally, given the sensitivity of the dynamic assessment procedure in differentiating individual differences in learning ability, it should not be assumed that the high potential of any low-socioeconomic-status child, determined by the degree of modifiability considered feasible, will be necessarily translated into school achievement. If this is not happening, that is, if those children with demonstrated capability of learning are not learning, the focus of assessment should be redirected from the child to the instructional program, the family, the community, and, not least of all, to the social system where social and political ideologies often determine educability as well as retardation.

REFERENCES

Babad, E., & Budoff, M. (1974). Sensitivity and validity of learning potential measurement in three levels of ability. *Journal of Educational Psychology, 66*, 439–447.

Barnett, D. (1983). *Nondiscriminatory multifactored assessment*. New York: Human Sciences Press, Inc.

Berk, R., Bridges, W., & Shih, A. (1981). Does IQ really matter? A study of the use of IQ scores for the tracking of the mentally retarded. *American Sociological Review*, *46*, 58–71.

Bernal, E. (1975). A response to "Educational uses of tests with disadvantaged subjects." *American Psychologist*, *30*, 93–95.

Bersoff, D. (1981). Testing and the law. *American Psychologist*, *36*, 1047–1056.

Budoff, M., & Freidman, M. (1964). "Learning potential" as an assessment approach to the adolescent mentally retarded. *Journal of Consulting Psychology*, *28*, 433–439.

Carlberg, C., & Kavale, K. (1980). The efficacy of special versus regular class placement for exceptional children. A meta-analysis. *Journal of Special Education*, *14*, 295–309.

Cleary, T., Humphreys, L., Kendrick, S., & Wesman, A. (1975). Educational uses of tests with disadvantaged students. *American Psychologist*, *30*, 15–41.

Diana v. State Board of Education. C-70 37 RFP District Court for Northern California, 1970.

Feuerstein, R. (1979). *The dynamic assessment of retarded performers: The learning potential assessment device, theory, instruments, and techniques*. Baltimore: University Park Press.

Feuerstein, R. (1980). *Instrumental enrichment: An intervention program for cognitive modifiability*. Baltimore: University Park Press.

Feuerstein, R., Miller, R., Rand, Y., & Jensen, M. (1981). Can evolving techniques better measure cognitive change? *Journal of Special Education*, *15*, 201–219.

Glass, G. (1983). Effectiveness of special education. *Policy Studies Review*, *2*, 65–78.

Gordon, E.W., & Rubin, R. (1980). Bias and alternatives in psychological testing. *Journal of Negro Education*, *49*, 350–360.

Gould, S. J. (1981). *The mismeasure of man*. New York: Norton.

Green, R., & Rohwer, W. (1971). SES differences on learning and ability tests in black children. *American Educational Research Journal*, *8*, 601–609.

Guadalupe v. Tempe Elementary School District. District Court for Arizona, 71-435. January 1972.

Hammill, D., & Larsen, S. (1974). The effectiveness of psycholinguistic training. *Exceptional Children*, *41*, 5–14.

Heller, K. (1982). Effects of special education placement on mentally retarded children. In K. Heller, W. Holtzman, & S. Messick (Eds.), *Placing children in special education: A strategy for equity*. Washington, DC: National Academy Press.

Hobson vs. Hansen, 269 F. Supp. 401 (D. D.C. 1967).

Jackson, G. (1975). On the report of the Ad Hoc Committee on Educational Uses of Tests with Disadvantaged Students. *American Psychologist*, *30*, 88–92.

Jensen, A. (1969). How much can we boost IQ and scholastic achievement? *Harvard Educational Review*, *38*, 1–123.

Jensen, A. (1980). *Bias in mental testing*. New York: Free Press.

Kamin, L. J. (1974). *The science and politics of IQ*. Potomac, MD: Erlbaum Associates.

Kavale, K. (1981). Functions of the Illinois Test of Psycholinguistic Abilities (ITPA): Are they trainable? *Exceptional Children*, *47*, 496–510.

Larry P. v. Wilson Riles, N. CO-71-2270 RFP, U.S. District Court for Northern District of California, 1979.

Lidz, C. S. (1981). *Improving assessment of school children*. San Francisco: Jossey-Bass.

Manni, J., Winikur, D., & Keller, M. (1984). *Intelligence, mental retardation and the culturally different child*. Springfield, IL: Charles C Thomas.

Mercer, J. R. (1975). Psychological assessment and the rights of children. In N. Hobbs (Ed.), *Issues in the classification of children* (Vol. I). San Francisco: Jossey-Bass.

Messick, S. (1980). Test validity and the ethics of assessment. *American Psychologist*, *35*, 1012–1027.

Newcomer, P. L., & Hammill, D. D. (1976). *Psycholinguistics in the schools*. Columbus, OH: Charles E. Merrill.

PASE v. Hannon, 506 F. Supp. 831 (N. D. Ill. 1980).

Peterson, N., & Novick, M. (1976). An evaluation of some models for culture-fair selection. *Journal of Educational Measurement, 13*, 3–29.

Reschly, D. (1984). Beyond IQ test bias: The National Academy Panel's analysis of minority EMR over representation. *Educational Researcher, 13*, 15–19.

Rohwer, W. (1971). Learning, race and school success. *Review of Educational Research, 41*, 191–210.

Samuda, R. (1975). *Psychological testing of American minorities*. New York: Dodd, Mead & Co.

Scarr, S. (1978). From Larry P., or what shall we do about IQ tests? *Intelligence, 2*, 325–342.

Scarr, S. (1981). Dilemmas in assessment of disadvantaged children. In M. Begab, H. C. Haywood, & H. Garber (Eds.). *Psychological influences in retarded performance*. Baltimore: University Park Press.

Sewell, T. E. (1979). Intelligence and learning tasks as predictors of scholastic achievement in black and white first-grade children. *Journal of School Psychology, 17*, 325–332.

Sewell, T. E., & Severson, R. (1974). Learning ability and intelligence as cognitive predictors of achievement in first-grade black children. *Journal of Educational Psychology, 66*, 948–995.

Sewell, T., Winikur, D., Berlinghof, M., Berkowitz, C. S., & Miner, M. (1984). *Cognitive modifiability of retarded performers: The effects of intervention on cognitive and academic performance*. Paper presented at the Annual Conference of the National Association of School Psychologists, Philadelphia.

Swanson, H. L. (1984). Process assessment of intelligence in learning disabled and mentally retarded children: A multidirectional model. *Educational Psychologist, 19*, 149–162.

Terman, L. (1916). *The measurement of intelligence*. Boston: Houghton Mifflin.

Travers, J. (1982). Testing in educational placement: Issues and evidence. In K. Heller, W. Holtzman, & S. Messick, (Eds.), *Placing children in special education: A strategy for equity*. Washington, DC: National Academy Press.

Tyler, L. E. (1976). The intelligence we test—an evolving concept. In L. B. Resnick (Ed.), *The nature of intelligence*. Hillsdale, NJ: Erlbaum.

Vygotsky, L. (1962). *Thought and language* (E. Hanfmann & G. Vakar, Trans.). Cambridge, MA: M.I.T. Press. (Original work published 1934).

Ysseldyke, J. (1978). Implementing the "Protection in evaluation procedures." Provisions of Public Law 94-142. In L. Morra (Ed.), *Developing criteria for the evaluation of protection in evaluation procedures provisions*. Washington, DC: Bureau of Education for the Handicapped.

17

Cognitive Deficiencies Revisited

CAROL SCHNEIDER LIDZ

In order to conduct a dynamic assessment, it is necessary to observe and analyze the child's performance across a variety of domains and derive hypotheses about the child's adequate and deficient cognitive functions. This analysis is followed by a sampling of interventions in order to generate information regarding promising remediations. It is therefore a prerequisite of a dynamic assessment to have a coherent notion of the cognitive functions expected to be involved in the solution of tasks selected for inclusion in the assessment, as well as a working list of possible deficiences.

Feuerstein (1979, 1980) and his colleagues have provided the most explicit listing of such deficiencies, based on an input–elaboration–output model of the mental act (Appendix A). They have also delineated the types of interventions to be involved, based upon their descriptions of mediated learning experiences (Feuerstein, 1979, 1980; Feuerstein & Hoffman, 1982).

Efforts to relate theories of cognitive functioning to actual task solution tend to involve two approaches: first, the determination of basic, prerequisite cognitive functions, and second, determination of differences between successful and unsuccessful problem solvers. Sternberg (1984d) emphasized the former and has developed a curriculum to enhance the thinking skills of all learners. Feuerstein and his associates have stressed the latter, that is, characterizing the problem-solving approaches of unsuccessful problem solvers, and have developed a curriculum to remediate the cognitive functioning of these deficient performers (Feuerstein, 1980). Feuerstein and his associates derive their conclusions from direct experience over many years with adolescents who are described as culturally deprived in the sense of lacking exposure to adequate mediated learning experiences.

This chapter attempts to clarify some of the mixtures of concepts apparent in Feuerstein's listing of cognitive deficiencies, to reconceptualize the list in terms of current cognitive theories and research, and, from this, to develop a revised guideline for analyzing the child's performance during the course of a dynamic assessment. This is approached from the point of view of a practitioner trying to make sense of the extensive and often confusing literature on cognitive functioning.

Carol Schneider Lidz. Clinic Team Services, United Cerebral Palsy Association of Philadelphia and Vicinity, Philadelphia, Pennsylvania.

Specific clarification is needed regarding such concepts as cognitive structure, mechanism, style, process, operation, strategy, and—intermingled with all of these—motivation and need. Such clarification is necessary in order to determine the nature of deficiencies to be included in any guideline; that is, it is necessary to respond to the question of deficiency of what (style? structure? strategy?). Review of Feuerstein et al.'s very extensive and almost exhaustive list reveals a mixture of these varying concepts, often addressing need rather than function, and spontaneous use rather than capacity (see items in parentheses in Appendix A). Indeed, the issue of the differentiation between spontaneous use and capacity is critical to conceptualizations of mental retardation (Bransford, 1979; Bransford et al., 1982; Butterfield & Belmont, 1977), and needs to be addressed as well.

First, the specific concepts will be reviewed, and, finally, the concepts will be integrated into a general guideline to be applied to dynamic assessment. This review is intended to be representative rather than exhaustive, and is approached with the ultimate objective of application to an assessment situation.

In this discussion, the term "cognitive functioning" is essentially equated with intelligence, and intelligence is defined in a very general way as "the capacity of the individual to use previous experience in his adaptation to new situations" (Feuerstein, 1979, p. 95), or, more specifically, "the use of information obtained through . . . transformational procedures in order to plan and structure behavior effectively for goal attainment" (Das, Kirby, & Jarman, 1975). Essential to the conceptualization of intelligence is the hypothesis of modifiability and the notion of dynamic development, that is, the idea that intelligence is an ongoing product of the dynamic interaction between an individual's response capabilities and a responsive, mediating environment, with response capabilities at any point in time reflecting the results of this interaction. This does not suggest that the individual is a tabula rasa, to be written upon by the environment, but emphasizes the importance of interactional processes. Whereas the above definitions of intelligence cut across specific domains, Feuerstein (1979, 1980) elaborated his ideas of the components of intelligence in terms of a cognitive map that represents an outline of the parameters of the "mental act." Such an approach contrasts with that of Gardner (1983), which is domain specific. Thus, Feuerstein's model can be characterized as "horizontal," in contrast to Gardner's more "vertical" approach. Both approaches to intelligence emphasize problem-solving skills and knowledge acquisition. However, Feuerstein proposes not so much a theory of intelligence as an approach to remediation, whereas researchers such as Gardner (1983) and Sternberg (1977, 1984a) explicitly strive for a theory of intelligence per se. Nevertheless, even an approach to remediation rests on a theory of intelligence, and it remains to be seen whether the evidence supports the more vertical or horizontal theory. For the purposes of this discussion, intelligence is viewed in its more global aspects, as internalizing mechanisms that adapt the organism to environmental demands, but without necessarily assuming the validity of "g," or a general intelligence, factor.

Before proceeding further, it is also necessary to discuss the concept of deficiency. The implication is that there is a lack or failure to use a prerequisite function, skill, or strategy that is necessary for successful problem solving. In his work with older children and adolescents, Feuerstein implied that there is primarily a failure (although sometimes a lack) of spontaneous use. In the younger child, the differentiation between lack and failure to use is less clear, and more dependent upon developmental level. According to Feuerstein's point of view, deficiencies result from inadequacies in mediated learning experiences (MLEs) (see Chapters 1 and 14, this volume, as well as Feuerstein, 1979, 1980, and Feuerstein & Hoffman, 1982, for discussion), attributable either to deficiencies in the caretaker's proficiency or to failure to devise MLEs sufficient to overcome conditions or characteristics of the learner that increase the barriers to profiting from both direct experiences and MLEs. Exactly what it is that the child lacks is the primary focus of this chapter. The focus, nevertheless, and by choice, is on the learner. This does not assume cause of deficiency within the learner, but simply represents the learner as the locus of deficiencies that result from inadequacies of MLE as primary cause, and a variety of social–environmental–biological conditions as distal cause. Nevertheless, it is the learner who needs to adapt. Although the value of adapting may be questioned, and interventions may need to be applied to aspects of the learning situation other than the learner, the stress to cope is on the individual.

Although the emphasis on deficiency may appear negativistic on the surface, it must be kept in mind that what has been devised is a diagnostic–remedial approach. Each negative statement of deficiency implies its converse, a positive function. Thus, the deficiency of impulsivity implies the positive function of reflectivity to which remediation is geared. What ultimately needs to be done in devising such a system is to attempt a delineation of prerequisite cognitive functions, determine which deficiencies (and functions) are critical for specific tasks, and demonstrate that remediation of the deficiency results in successful task performance. The diagnostic effort relies on such demonstrated connections. Thus, another focus of this chapter will be to present research evidence supportive of or relating to these associations between cognitive functions and achievement.

Mechanism and Structure

The term "mechanism" is used here as a general term to indicate explanatory substrata of observed performance. Mechanism encompasses not only the location of a process, but a description of how the process works (Flavell, 1984; Kessen, 1984). Since questions of mechanism involve the what, where, and how of cognitive performance, both structure and process are included in this concept. The difference between structure and process has been described as the difference between what (structure) and how (process) (Phillips, 1982), or between the hardware and the program (Rowe, 1985).

Although structure can in its most general sense include "everything the individual has learned" at any point in time (Klausmeier & Allen, 1978, p. 1) and is not readily distinguishable from process (Sternberg, 1981), the term "structure" is used here in its most concrete sense as the anatomical and physiological (including neuronal, chemical, electrical) representations in the nervous system of the observed behaviors (Simon, 1976), in this case, behaviors attributed to the cognitive domain. Although any such distinctions are imposed and not "real," they remain useful to attempts to understand and manipulate behavior or, in this case, to devise an outline to guide dynamic assessment. Despite the actual or potential observability of structure, its relationship to performance relies on inferential association with observed behaviors. The assessment of structure lies primarily within the provinces of neurology (within the medical sciences) and neuropsychology (within the behavioral sciences), and is not the primary focus of the dynamic assessment procedure. Nevertheless, the topic of structure is relevant to both the theory and practice of dynamic assessment. First, Feuerstein (1980) described structural cognitive modifiability as the central goal of his remedial approach of Instrumental Enrichment: "The essential feature of this approach is that it is directed not merely at the remediation of specific behaviors and skills, but at changes of a structural nature that alter the course and direction of cognitive development" (p. 9). Second, some of the inferences made from the child's performance during the course of a dynamic assessment are likely to have structural implications, and the examiner needs to be aware of this possibility in drawing conclusions and in making recommendations.

Feuerstein (1980) defined the concept of structural cognitive modifiability as "changes in the state of the organism" (p. 9). Writing with Hoffman (1982), he characterized structural changes "by their *part–whole relationship*, in which a change in a part affects the whole; by *transformation*, in which parts of the structure are conserved while other parts change; and by *self-perpetuation*, in which schemata continue to develop, expand and adapt" (p. 7). These ideas reflect Piagetian conceptualizations of structure; however, although Piaget and Piagetians have been explicit in their use of the term structure, they have not been clear in their descriptions and definitions (Siegler, 1983). Piaget (1970) defined structure as "a system of transformations [that] . . . involve laws . . . the notion of structure is comprised of three key ideas: the idea of wholeness, the idea of transformation, and the idea of self-regulation" (p. 5). Piaget clearly stated his position that "structures are inseparable from performance" (p. 69), but elaborated his concept of structure in terms more suggestive of process than of structure, as used in this chapter. To the extent that the nervous system provides principles and laws of operation (Fischer & Silvern, 1985), these are accepted here as structural elements, but, for the most part, Piaget's view of structure, which he located "somewhere between the nervous system and conscious behavior" (p. 138), is not directly useful to the dynamic assessor.

Structure determines such things as how events are recorded, what events are recordable, sequences of development, organization of information entering the system, response repertories, and speed of processing. Functionally, structure relates to capacity. Most theorists in this area appear to agree that there is a significant degree of plasticity and flexibility to cognitive development, even at the structural level. It is this plasticity that interventions such as those devised by Feuerstein specifically address. Although not explicitly the concern of dynamic assessment, some deficiencies observed during the course of the assessment may be structural. That they are structural does not imply that they are not modifiable. That they are modifiable by any direct means is unlikely, certainly not within the context of the assessment. What is likely is that modifiability can be achieved through manipulation of experiential routes involving processes and strategies.

In order for a process to develop, the structural capacity must be present. Development of such capacities has been described in terms of dynamic mechanisms that, although representing "givens" in the nervous system, depend upon active self-construction for their realization (Case, 1978; Piaget, 1970). The same structures and capacities are not equally well developed at all ages. For example, Case (1984) observed that control structures only begin to emerge at about age 4 years and are not well integrated until about age 6. On the other hand, it is not always structure that characterizes developmental differences. For example, the memory capacity of adults and children over 6 appears to be about the same (Case, 1984); it is primarily content and executive strategies that differ (Brown & DeLoache, 1978).

The difficulty for the assessor is that any observed deficiency may reflect structure, process, or strategy (or style, or motivation . . .) deficits, each of which involve to varying degrees both biological and experiential aspects (Torgesen, 1979). Intervention usually begins at the level of strategy, which allows observation and inference regarding process, and, at times, regarding structure. Inferences regarding structure can be derived from observations of the child's response to remedial efforts, that is, from degree of modifiability. However, even this is not free of attitudinal and motivational factors. As a general guideline and hypothesis, given a reasonably motivated child who is trying to respond to the examiner's attempts at intervention, it is suggested here that there may be a continuum of modifiability that relates to a continuum of structure–process–strategy, with deficiencies at the structural end being the most resistant to attempts at modification (Borkowski & Konarski, 1981).

The difficulty of separating structure and process becomes evident as soon as an attempt is made to list either. On the one hand, the structural aspects of many processes have not been fully worked out. On the other hand, it is not appropriate for the psychological assessor to become entwined in the neurological convolutions of learning when it is really the functional aspects that are of primary concern. Therefore, the listing of structural aspects of the learner's performance will include some unavoidable redundancy with process, although the assessor may conclude that it is either the process or the structural level that appears dysfunctional.

Appendix B presents a summary review of the literature in order to abstract structures for the dynamic assessment outline. In order to facilitate reading, this review is presented in tabular format. These various proposals for structural mechanisms are summarized in the following functional, and unavoidably process-like terms, which are still able to be conceptualized within the broader input–elaboration–output model proposed by Feuerstein et al.:

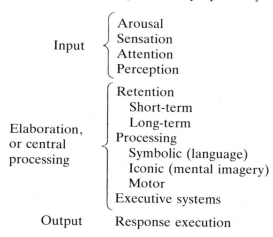

It is hardly necessary to point out that the sequencing of the list is not meant to be a strict representation of the sequencing of a cognitive event, since the executive systems would play a regulating function relating to all of the structures and processes. In very general terms, the existence of structure implies selection, recording, organization, and response. How this is all done is a matter of process, style, and strategy.

Process and Function

The terms "process" and "function" are often used interchangeably in the literature, and represent the activities of the structures of the nervous system. At times, the term "operation" is equated with process, although operations are usually more task specific and include such activities as addition, subtraction, transportation, substitution (Berlyne, 1965), and seriation (Carlson & Wiedl, 1980). These operations will not be included as processes in the outline, but will be left to be specified by a procedure designer as aligned with the specific content of the task.

Cognitive processes serve to internalize environmental information, and allow self-regulation of the organism. It is this internalization that can be viewed as the hallmark of learning and adaptation, and, therefore, of intelligence (Brown & Campione, 1984). Because of its relevance, this discussion will emphasize information-processing theories and research as the most satisfactory approach to explanation of cognitive functioning (Sternberg, 1984c). However, it is not possible in this chapter to do justice to the information-processing literature. The venture is too complex and unresolved. It is therefore not possible to present any final or ultimate listing of processes. What can be done at this time is to review some representative thinking in the area, and to select a listing of processes of promising usefulness to the purposes of dynamic assessment. The specifics of any such list would be expected to change. The general outline should remain relevant and applicable.

Processes can be described as both general and specific. One general dichotomy includes excitatory and inhibitory mechanisms (Berlyne, 1965), which allow the organism to respond as well as to select and reject information so as not to be overwhelmed. These mechanisms (with structural and process properties) allow for response regulation and to a great extent contribute to the phenomenon of attention. A process such as detection would involve both excitation and inhibition since both response and selection/rejection are simultaneously involved. Other general dichotomies or classifications of processes include analysis and synthesis, proposed by Carlson and Wiedl (1980); assimilation and accommodation, described by Piaget (e.g., 1970); differentiation/integration, referred to by Flavell (1977); and simultaneous and successive synthesis, discussed by Luria (1966) and further elaborated by Das, Kirby, and Jarman (1975, 1979).

Cognitive processes are assumed to be universal and not culture specific (Berry, 1981). It is primarily their application as expressed in characteristics such as style that accounts for many group differences (Cole & Scribner, 1974).

Although specific processes can be viewed in terms of their inhibitory versus excitatory aspects, in terms of their contributions to assimilation versus accommodation, or as simultaneous versus successive in nature, for the purposes of dynamic assessment it is more useful to delineate specific processes, and then to evaluate the general functioning of the learner in terms of the more general processes if and when patterns appear. It could then be determined if the child is a more successful assimilator or accommodator, or if inhibitory processes appear to be lacking, or if it is simultaneous rather than successive processes that appear more deficient.

The review of the literature on processes to be suggested for the dynamic assessment outline (Appendix C) is presented in tabular form, as were the structures, to facilitate reading. From the multitude of processes enumerated and elaborated by the many researchers cited in this list derives the listing of processes in Table 17.1, which will be suggested for adoption for the ultimate

TABLE 17.1.   Structures and Processes

	Structure	Process (specific)
Input	Arousal Sensation Attention Perception	Stimulus detection (orientation) Decoding (simple comprehension) Encoding (transformation) Intersensory integration Discrimination Comparison Pattern detection
Elaboration	Retention Short-term Long-term	Memory storage Memory retrieval (including the content of long-term storage of relevant knowledge and skill components, related to the task)
	"Processing"	Conceptualization processes Abstraction and combination (analysis and synthesis) Categorization/classification Induction Deduction/rule generation/inference Elaborative associations
	Executive systems	Responsiveness to feedback Awareness of processes Selection of processes and allocation of resources Monitoring processes Planning processes Prediction of consequences; determination of means/end Evaluating results of actions Decision making
Output	Response execution	Performance processes: implementation in verbal, written, gestural, motoric, figural communication modalities.

Process (general)
Excitation/inhibition Assimilation/accommodation Simultaneous/sequential Differentiation/integration

purpose of guiding dynamic assessment. These processes will have to be more clearly operationalized into observable behaviors in order to be used for an actual assessment.

Cognitive Strategies

A strategy is both the most observable aspect of a learner's performance and the aspect most accessible to intervention and modification. There is accumulating evidence that modification of strategies can increase learner performance (Belmont & Butterfield, 1971; Danserau et al., 1979; Kaufman & Kaufman, 1979; Lloyd, 1980; Lloyd & de Bettencourt, 1982; Lloyd, Saltzman, & Kauffman, 1981; McKinney & Haskins, 1980), and that spontaneous employment of strategies accounts for a good deal of the difference between developmental levels that differentiate both retarded from nonretarded performance as well as children of varying chronological ages (Belmont & Butterfield, 1971; Brown & DeLoache, 1978; Case, 1978; Chi, 1978).

Swanson and Watson (1982) provided a representative definition of strategy as "an organized sequence of responses by a child made in an effort to achieve the solution to a problem . . . a plan representing stages of information gathering . . . and information process" (p. 114). Stated another way, strategic knowledge, as a component of cognitive activity, "includes processes for setting goals and adopting general plans or methods in working on a problem" (Greeno & Simon, 1984, p. 2), or assemblage of operations or processes for a specific task (Posner & McLeod, 1982). These definitions imply the existence of several aspects of strategies: organization (planfulness), goal directedness, observability, and inferential relatedness to process. Posner and Snyder (1975) also characterized strategies as being under the conscious control of the learner.

The specific strategies employed by a learner, and those that are/are not successful, vary with the task situation (Bruner, Goodnow, & Austin, 1981) as well as the learner (Snow, 1982). That is, there is no one-to-one necessary connection between a task and a strategy; and both personal characteristics and strategic alternatives intervene to produce a successful or unsuccessful result (Gagné, 1984).

Bruner et al. (1981) proposed three criteria for evaluation of a strategy: the extent to which the information gathered is appropriate to the goal or nature of the task, the extent to which the cognitive strain on information assimilation is reduced, and the extent to which elements of risk are controlled. Loper (1980) also suggested that, in order to be effective, a strategy must help the learner to differentiate relevant from irrelevant information. Loper made the further point that the application of a strategy is only sufficient if the learner is able to profit from its application.

Thus, we have an idea of what a strategy is, as well as of what a good strategy is. Enumerations of specific strategies are many. Much of the literature in this area deals with memory strategies, and there is a great deal of attention to prototypical problem situations such as the Tower of Hanoi, as well as situations requiring more prolonged planning and decision making. Some researchers have specifically addressed academic domains, but this area has been relatively neglected (Willows, Borwick, & Butkowsky, 1983) (see Chapter 3, this volume). Some general findings include the observation that the more specific the strategy that is taught the less the interdomain transfer to be expected (Wagner & Sternberg, 1984). Wagner and Sternberg also suggested that the greatest transfer or generalizability is induced by meta-cognitive training (accessed via strategy?). This conclusion is also supported by Brown and Campione's (1978) review of research, which noted the effectiveness of "training children to stop, check, and self-question before responding" (p. 146), and Zelnicker and Jeffrey's (1976) conclusion from modification studies that it is training in systematic search strategies that reduces errors from impulsive responders, not instruction simply to slow down. Gagné (1984), in fact, equates cognitive strategies with executive control processes.

A number of authors have investigated or summarized literature regarding effective strategies. These are reviewed in tabular format in Appendix D, as was done in other sections.

The bridge between strategy, structure, and process is suggested by Phillips (1982): "the relation between strategy and structure may depend upon the ability of structures to process information in particular ways. Through experience individuals may learn to recognize which strategy is most appropriate for a particular task and be able to shift input to the appropriate processing structure" (p. 18). What the mediator attempts to do during the course of a dynamic assessment is to provide precisely the type of "experience" that will induce this relationship, with the ultimate result of successful task solution, but, even more importantly, also attempting to equip the learner with the ability to apply problem-solving skills in situations not directly mediated by the assessor, thus resulting in a learner who can successfully generalize and transfer.

There appears to be agreement among researchers that clear problem definition–representation, and systematic application of processes are important to the problem-solving process in many (e.g., Posner, 1973), although not all (e.g., Rogoff, 1984), cases. However, it is not only the use of a strategy that is important, as well as the obvious point of the use of a task-relevant strategy; it is the flexible adaptation and application of a strategy that often distinguishes successful from unsuccessful problem solvers (Rowe, 1985). The assessor needs to ask not only whether a strategy is applied and whether the strategy is relevant and potentially effective, but whether the learner shows flexibility in the selection and application of strategies.

In considering the issue of strategies, another factor is the developmental level of the child. Although all learners can be described in terms of structure and process—that is, those structures and processes characteristic of their developmental level—the determination of strategies may not be meaningful until after the age of 5 (Siegler, 1978; Vurpillot, 1968); however, there is evidence that strategies may emerge and become susceptible to educational influence by the age of 4 (Siegler, 1978).

The dynamic assessor thus would seek to determine the existence, appropriateness, and flexible use of strategies, as well as effectiveness in terms of criteria such as those suggested above by Bruner et al. (1981). Because any number of strategies might be appropriate for any single task, and effectiveness is not only task but learner related, there can be no exhaustive listing of strategies that would be applicable to all situations. Depending upon the specific tasks used for the dynamic assessment, the procedure designers would need to work out a suggestive listing of strategies that have been found to produce success; but any single assessor with any single learner would need to discover what is promising for that particular individual. What would be generally applied is the idea of generating a planful approach, inducing in the child both a concern for development of strategies that are potentially generalizable across domains, and recognition of when such a planful approach is appropriate.

It might also be argued that all strategies should be considered as a function of executive processes. This would at least be the case for the selection of a strategy. However, in the outline presented, the strategies have been more widely distributed and assigned to the processes they appear to serve. However, with further evidence and discussion, this is likely to be modified, and perhaps, in the final analysis, regrouped under executive processes.

A suggestive listing of strategies as derived from the researchers cited above is given in Table 17.2. Evidence for the relationship between strategy training and reading is provided by Brailsford, Snart, and Das (1984). Lloyd (1980) also found that the use of systematic strategies, active involvement,

TABLE 17.2.   Strategies Outline

	Process
Input	Visual scanning
	Scanning in response to hypotheses
	Concentration management
Elaboration	
Memory	Rehearsal
	Grouping
	Visual imaging
	Development of acronyms and acrostics
	Linkage to stored information
	Use of cues
Processing	Application of logic
Executive	Problem identification and definition
systems	Reduction to simpler units
	Identification of assumptions
	Goal and subgoal determination
	Scheduling
	Means–end analysis
Performance	Paraphrasing
	Outlining
	Summarizing

and covert verbalization were effective in reducing impulsivity and in increasing academic success.

Cognitive Style

The concept of cognitive style is one of the most confusing issues to be discussed. Style can characterize perception or cognition, as well as have implications for personality. Style can apply to both processes and strategies, and many of the specific styles elaborated in the literature are overlapping and appear tied to specific methods of measurement (Coop & Sigel, 1971; Cronbach & Snow, 1977; Santostefano, 1969).

Most investigators agree that style has to do with intraindividual consistencies and preferences for a particular mode of response or conceptual organization both within and across tasks (Blackman & Goldstein, 1982; Coop & Sigel, 1971; Kagan, Moss, & Sigel, 1973; McDermott, 1979–1981, Serafica & Sigel, 1970; Witkin, 1973). It is often suggested that the concept of style is relevant to education because, first, some styles appear better than others for certain tasks; second, style is modifiable through educational interventions; and, third, the matching of teacher and pupil styles appears to enhance learning (e.g., Berry, 1981). Style describes the individual's unique and characteristic approaches to a task's demands on process and structure. Whereas process refers to the repertory of operations or functions required for successful task-relevant problem solution that an individual may or may not have or may or may not apply, style refers to the intraindividual consistencies of problem-solving approach actually used by the learner. It is a combination of selection of strategies, employment of processes, knowledge base, and style variables, within the context of needs and motives, that contributes to differentiation of one learner's performance from another's (Keating, Keniston, Manis, & Bobbitt, 1980). However, research results have been inconsistent, and the concept of style is not universally acknowledged as meaningful (Cronbach & Snow, 1977). Nevertheless, style factors are discussed widely as relevant to educational assessment, and account for many of the functions and deficiencies referred to in accounts of cognitive deficiencies such as Feuerstein's.

The most frequently described and researched styles include field dependence/independence, with field independence defined as attending "to relevant cues" and discarding "the irrelevant," and reflection/impulsivity, with reflection defined as "careful attention to, and monitoring among, stimuli. The reflective individual works slowly and produces few errors" (Blackman & Goldstein, 1982, p. 107). Blackman and Goldstein (1982) noted the greater relative success in modifying impulsivity than field dependence. Researchers have also found the relevance of these two style dimensions to vary with the task; for example, Brannigan, Ash, and Margolis (1980), using the Wechsler Intelligence Scale for Children–Revised (WISC-R) subtest scales, found reflection/impulsivity, as measured by the Matching Familiar Figures Test, to relate to the attention/concentration subtests, but not to verbal comprehension.

Coop and Sigel (1971) provided the most complete listing of styles, associating each with their primary researchers:

- Field independence (analytic) and dependence (global): Witkin
- Conceptual versus perceptual dominance: Broverman
- Leveling versus sharpening, field articulation, equivalence control: Gardner
- Functional–concrete versus abstract attitude: Bolles
- Focuser versus scanner: Bruner
- Descriptive versus relational versus categorical: Kagan, Moss, Sigel
- Cognitive tempo dimensions of reflective versus impulsive: Kagan
- Convergent, divergent, evaluative: Guilford

Meltzer (1984), in applying the concept of style to problem-solving strategies, condensed the above list into four categories: impulsivity versus reflectivity, trial-and-error versus systematic hypothesis testing, fixation on detail versus generalization, and erratic solutions versus consistent self-monitoring. These all suggest strategic applications of executive processes.

Goldstein and Blackman (1977) provided a listing of styles similar to that of Coop and Sigel, and, in a later publication (1978), which reviews and summarizes the research literature, concluded that cognitive styles are:

a. reliable over short periods of time
b. reflect developmental changes to some extent
c. show mixed findings regarding consistency across situations
d. do not appear to reflect a unitary dimension, although some overlap
e. show a lack of consistent relationships among measures of cognitive complexity, integrative complexity, and field dependence
f. show low significant correlations with intelligence in most cases, with the highest association between intelligence and field independence
g. present problems because of differences in measures between studies
h. show relationships with child rearing practices.

The trend in the cognitive style research is supportive of the positive association between achievement and both field independence and reflectivity (Barrett, 1977; Blackman & Goldstein, 1982; Maccoby, Dowley, Hagen, & Degerman, 1965; Schwebel, 1966; Weithorn, Kagan, & Marcus, 1984; Zelnicker & Jeffrey, 1976). Both sex and SES differences have been found (Witkin, 1973); for example, Barrett (1977) found the error score of impulsivity to predict achievement for boys, whereas response latency predicted achievement for girls, and the positive association between reflectivity and achievement, evident for most of their subjects, did not characterize their low-socioeconomic-status (SES) grade 5 and 6 subjects.

Kagan's (1965) evidence supports the conclusion of a negative relationship between impulsivity and academic achievement, with subjects high in impulsivity making more reading errors. He observed that style dimensions appear to play a significant role in academic achievement between the time of mastery of the rudiments of a new skill and automatization of the skill. Kagan et al.'s (1973) discussion allowed inference that places the reflection/impulsivity dimension within the context of antecedents of an analytic attitude, which involves "the ability to inhibit motor discharge; the ability to modulate behavior in the face of irrelevant stimulation that tempts reactivity; the ability to reflect in situations that elicit alternative response tendencies" (p. 110). It is through this relationship with analytic attitude that impulsivity/reflectivity may influence achievement. A suggestion of just why there should be this relationship between a reflective style and analytic attitude (and higher achievement) is provided by the evidence cited by Messer (1976), which indicates that reflectives engage in more glances at the task stimulus and generally were found to gather more information, more looks, more coverage, and more comparison, and to engage in more systematic information gathering. That is, something is happening while the learner pauses to reflect; it is not the pause that is significant in and of itself.

In discussing the style of impulsivity, it is important to note the dual aspects of the traditional definition of impulsivity in terms of response time *and* error rate (Messer, 1976); that is, impulsive equals fast plus wrong. This definition presents difficulties for research that attempts to establish relationships between impulsivity and any particular competency because of the problem of independence of measurement. If a subject is both fast and wrong, there is a built-in necessary negative association between the two variables, since, by definition, it is impossible to be fast and correct and be called impulsive. Thus, impulsivity must be associated with poor performance. Researchers have tried to circumvent this dilemma by using measures that are relatively independent of the experimental task, but the extent to which these measures are truly independent might be questioned (Mumbauer & Miller, 1970). It would appear to be a more promising approach to remove the "wrong" aspect of the definition and apply other criteria to characterize learner response, such as responds before instructions are complete or proceeds in trial-and-error fashion, or, alternatively, to operationalize the definition in terms of a specific task such as draw-a-line-slowly (see Ballester & Lidz, in preparation). Messer's (1976) observation of stability of response time but instability of errors for school-age children, and of relatively higher correlations between IQ and Matching Familiar Figures Test errors compared with response time, would support these observations.

For the purpose of this chapter, style dimensions will be adopted primarily from the Blackman and Goldstein (1982) and Meltzer (1984) descriptors, and will be listed as generalized terms that can be applied to any level of an individual's functioning, that is, input, elaboration, or output, and at any stage of the problem-solving process. These styles are as follows:

- Impulsive versus reflective
- Trial-and-error versus systematic
- Detailed versus global
- Field dependent versus field independent
- Abstract versus concrete

What we have now is a means for conceptualizing and analyzing the characteristics of any individual's functioning and the ability to describe strengths and deficiencies of performance, that is, in terms of structure, process, strategy, and style (Table 17.3). What is needed to increase the relevance of the assessment for the educational setting is to extend this conceptualization beyond the characteristics of the learner to include the problem situation (Bransford, 1979). One way of doing this is to outline the major steps of a typical problem-solving situation. Once this is done, it becomes possible to conceptualize the outcome of the assessment in terms of the characteristics of the learner on one axis and the steps of the problem-solving situation on the other.

The Dynamic Assessment Situation

Following Rogoff's (1984) view of thinking as "a practical activity which is adjusted to meet the demands of the situation" (p. 7), that is, the importance of thought plus content, a two-dimensional model of the dynamic assessment process is proposed, a model descriptive of both the learner and the problem situation. Within this model, the learner will be describable in terms of structure, process, strategy, style, and attitudinal/motivational states, as outlined above. Each of these categories, of course, subsumes the learner's history of mediated learning experiences and the knowledge/skill base vis-à-vis the specific problem situation.

Expanding upon Forbes and Greenberg's (1982) outline of planning (formulation of a goal, formulation of strategies, continuous evaluation of strategy effectiveness, and alternations in plans as needed), and Glass, Holyoak, and Santa's (1979) outline of the components of a problem (the problem, operations for solution, and the solution), the proposed outline for the problem situation is as follows: problem recognition, problem definition, knowledge/skills necessary for problem solution, proposals and executions of solutions, and evaluation of results. Each of these outlines can be put on an axis, with specific functions used or not used but necessary at each stage filled into the appropriate spaces (Figure 17.1). The assessor would begin with the presentation of a "standard" problem situation, and analyze the learner's performance at each stage of problem resolution. This analysis is applied both at the time of pretest and at the time of posttest, with the examiner intervening in an attempt to induce appropriate processes, strategies, styles, and attitudes

TABLE 17.3. Structure–Process–Strategy–Style Outline

Structure	Process	Strategy	Style
Input			
Arousal	Stimulus detection (orientation)	Visual scanning	Impulsive versus reflective
Sensation	Decoding (simple comprehension)	Scanning in response to hypotheses	Trial-and-error versus systematic
Attention	Encoding (transformation)	Concentration management	Detailed versus global
Perception	Intersensory interaction		
	Discrimination		
	Comparison		
	Pattern detection		
Elaboration			
Retention	Memory storage	Rehearsal	Field dependent versus independent
Short-term	Memory retrieval	Grouping	Abstract versus concrete
Long-term		Visual imaging	
		Development of acronyms and acrostics	
		Linkage to stored information	
		Use of cues	
Processing	Conceptualization processes	Application of logic	
Symbolic (language)	Abstraction and combination		
Iconic (mental imagery)	Categorization/classification		
Motor	Induction		
	Deduction/rule generation		
	Elaborative associations		
Executive systems	Responsiveness to feedback	Problem identification	
	Awareness of processes	Reduction to simpler units	
	Selection of processes	Identification of assumptions	
	Monitoring of processes	Goal and subgoal determination	
	Planning processes	Scheduling	
	Prediction of consequences; determination of means/end	Means–end analysis	
	Evaluating results of actions		
	Decision making		

459

TABLE 17.3. Structure–Process–Strategy–Style Outline (Continued)

Structure	Process (specific)	Strategy	Style
Output Response execution	Performance processes: implementation in verbal, written, gestural, motoric, figural communication modalities Process (general) Excitation/inhibition Assimilation/accommodation Simultaneous/sequential Differentiation/integration	Paraphrasing Outlining Summarizing	

relevant to successful problem solution. In proceeding along this outline, the examiner poses the following questions:

- Can the learner recognize and define the problem? If not, what is interfering with this?
- Does the learner have the necessary prerequisite knowledge and skill to deal with the problem? If not, what is interfering with this?
- Can the learner determine and carry out relevant solutions to the problem? If not, what is interfering with this?
- Can the learner analyze and evaluate the successes and failures of the problem-solving situation? If not, what is interfering with this?

Responses to the questions of what is interfering will come from hypotheses derived from experimental attempts within the assessment situation that aim to modify and improve the learner's performance. The responses will be in terms of specific processes, strategies, and styles, as well as motivations and attitudes.

The final outcome of this test–intervene–retest dynamic assessment can then be summarized as responses to the following questions:

1. To what extent was the learner modifiable by the interventions?
2. What aspects of the learner's functioning appear to account for difficulties within the problem-solving situation?
3. What aspects of the learner's performance responded or failed to respond to intervention?
4. What interventions worked or failed to enhance learning?
5. To what extent did the learner transfer newly acquired functions to other activities?
6. To what extent were newly acquired processes/strategies applied spontaneously in novel situations?
7. What intensity of effort was required to induce change?

The answers to these last three questions help to define the concept of modifiability. Earlier in the chapter, it was suggested that degree of response to intervention would be expected to correlate with level of functioning along the structure–process–strategy parameter, and would also contribute toward inferences about modifiability of the learner. Other aspects of the learner's performance, such as flexibility of applications of strategies, ability to spontaneously apply newly learned strategies, and ability to transfer these strategies, would also contribute to this definition. However, the assessment situation can only provide a limited amount of information, even if significantly extended beyond the average time of a static approach. Even dynamic assessment remains a mere sampling of behavior, and all the answers to all the questions, considering all the possibilities, would lie beyond the capabilities of even the most astute and well-practiced assessor. What is offered here is an attempt to think about as many aspects of the assessment situation as

462

Matrix of Guide Dynamic Assessment
The Problem Situation

The Learner	Problem recognition	Problem definition	Knowledge/skills	Execution of solutions	Evaluation of results
Structures					
Processes					
Strategies					
Styles					

Comments re needs/motives/attitudes:

FIGURE 17.1. Matrix to guide dynamic assessment.

possible, realizing that any single assessment cannot possibly provide responses to every detail and item mentioned.

It is also relevant to note that any conclusions from the assessment can be reported only in terms of the parameters of the specific task situation involved in the assessment. The more the task characterizes representative learning situations to which the learner is exposed, the greater the potential generalizability. However, in the case of dynamic assessment in contrast to diagnostic–prescriptive teaching (in which the examiner may also wish to engage) (see Chapter 15, this volume), it is the prerequisites to learning that need to generalize, not merely the content—that is, retrieval strategies or analytic processes, for example, perhaps in relation to numerical content, but not just in terms of the multiplication tables. It is at this point (as well as at the time of design of procedures) that Feuerstein's (1979, 1980) cognitive map is most relevant.

What remains is to describe some relevant research which deals with the relationships between specific cognitive functions and deficiencies and achievement.

Research on Cognitive Deficiencies

Feuerstein's (1979, 1980) listings of cognitive deficiencies derive primarily from the observations by him and his colleagues of the performance of adolescents during the course of administration of the Learning Potential Assessment Device (LPAD). There are others who have worked in the area of cognitive intervention who have derived similar observations, which provide confirming and supportive evidence for the Feuerstein et al. conclusions (e.g., Frankenstein, 1979; Meltzer, 1984; Sternberg, 1984b; Stott, 1978). However, what remains necessary is to establish both the occurrence and observability of such dysfunctions for children of varying ages and varying learning abilities, as well as to provide evidence of the relationship of such deficiencies to cognitive performance (and, ultimately, of their correction to cognitive success) (Bradley, 1983). In this section, both of these issues will be addressed.

It has already been mentioned above that spontaneous use of strategies and other indices of executive functions have been found to differentiate good from poor learners (e.g., Baumeister & Brooks, 1981; Belmont & Butterfield, 1971; Bransford, 1979; Bransford et al., 1982; Butterfield & Belmont, 1977; Chi, 1978). It was also mentioned that instruction in these abilities has been found to induce effective learning (e.g., Belmont, Butterfield, & Ferretti, 1984; Brown & DeLoache, 1978; Zelnicker & Jeffrey, 1976). Most learners do not differ so much in terms of the existence of structure or process, but more in terms of applications of process, strategy, style, and efficiency of functions. Differences in efficiency, which have not been given much attention so far, have been found to be a significant differentiating factor between good and poor learners (Brooks & McCauley, 1984; Case, 1978; Das et al., 1975).

Such differences, also discussed in terms of automatization, would help to increase memory capacity, which in turn would help to establish an adequate knowledge base (Glaser & Pellegrino, 1984)—assuming exposure to sources of knowledge and mediation (Glaser & Pellegrino, 1984; Sternberg, 1984a).

Content in terms of knowledge base also has been emphasized by researchers as an important distinguishing factor between good and poor learners (Chi, 1978; Greeno & Simon, 1984; Siegler, 1983). Other factors such as flexibility (Battig, 1975; Rowe, 1985) and field independence, reflective cognitive style, and active involvement (Bransford et al. 1982) have also been associated with successful academic achievement. Approaching effective learning with college students from a slightly different angle, that is, following remediation, Bloom and Broder (1950) found the differences between successful and unsuccessful learners to include: careful attention to directions to understand the problem, development of hypotheses before proceeding, active versus passive attitude, use of a systematic approach, more objective involvement, and more concern with adequacy of logic and solutions. Research results are generally supportive of the following summary of the characteristics of a good learner:

1. Has an adequate knowledge and skill base relevant to the task.
2. Spontaneously selects and applies the strategies and processes relevant to the task, adequately monitoring and evaluating the results of efforts.
3. Has good memory storage and retrieval.
4. Applies strategies and processes in a flexible way.
5. Inhibits impulsivity to allow for adequate comprehension, processing, and development of hypotheses.
6. Functions in an efficient manner, involving automatization of subskills and fast speed of processing.
7. Employs a reflective, field-independent, analytical cognitive style.
8. Proceeds with a systematic, strategic approach, when appropriate.
9. Shows active involvement in learning.
10. Shows concern with adequacy of solutions.

It has become a truism that middle-class children perform better on academically related tasks than children from low-SES backgrounds. The important issue is to determine why this should be so. Researchers are beginning to find evidence that suggests that it is cognitive functions and deficiencies such as those discussed in this chapter that may account for these differences, because low- and middle/high-SES groups have been found to differ on variables such as use of spontaneous comparative behavior (Burns, 1980; Heber, 1977), control of impulsivity (Burns, 1980; Schwebel, 1966), and use of systematic strategies and precision and accuracy in data gathering (Burns, 1980).

However, in order to be able to conclude that these cognitive functions and deficiencies mediate the connection between SES and academic performance, it is necessary to investigate the link between cognitive functions and deficiencies and academic performance more directly. This was the focus of the research carried out by Ballester and Lidz (in preparation; see also Ballester, 1984). In this study we focused primarily on two issues: first, to determine if the cognitive deficiencies observed by Feuerstein et al. could be operationalized as observable, recordable behaviors and if these could then be observed in children as young as ages 3, 4, and 5 years; and second, to investigate the relationship between cognitive deficiencies and academic (in this case, "preacademic") performance. The study involved 44 nonexceptional low-SES, urban, black boys between the ages of 3 years 8 months and 5 years 0 months who were in their second year of attendance at a full-day preschool program. All of the children were determined to have normal adaptive behavior. The children were observed as they worked on a series of cognitive tasks and rated from videotapes on a scale of cognitive functions and deficiencies selected as relevant to the age group and the tasks. These functions were able to be reliably scored and were found to vary with success on the cognitive tasks. Of most consequence was the significant negative correlation between the total deficiency score and the academic measure, with spontaneous comparative behavior and spatial orientation contributing the most to the deficiency score, and spontaneous comparative behavior and impulsivity at output, after age, serving as the best predictors of academic performance. The significance of these findings is particularly impressive in view of the fact that these children were all normal learners, as evidenced by their average-level performance on the academic measure; that is, even with relatively narrow variance on the academic measure, a significant association between cognitive deficiencies—specifically the one given particular emphasis by Feuerstein (spontaneous comparative behavior)—was substantiated.

REFERENCES

Ballester, L. E. (1984). *Feuerstein's model of cognitive functioning applied to preschool children: A study of the relationship between specific cognitive strategies and learning.* Unpublished doctoral dissertation, Temple University, Philadelphia.

Ballester, L., & Lidz, C. S. The relationship between specific cognitive strategies and learning in preschool children. Manuscript submitted for publication.

Barrett, D. E. (1977). Reflection-impulsivity as a predictor of children's academic achievement. *Child Development, 48,* 1443–1447.

Battig, W. F. (1975). Within-individual differences in "cognitive" processes. In R. L. Solso (Ed.), *Information processing and cognition: The Loyola symposium* (pp. 195–228). Hillsdale, N.J.: Erlbaum

Baumeister, A. A., & Brooks, P. H. (1981). Cognitive deficits in mental retardation. In J. M. Kauffman & D. P. Hallahan (Eds.), *Handbook of special education* (pp. 87–107). Englewood Cliffs, NJ: Prentice-Hall.

Belmont, J., & Butterfield, E. C. (1971). Learning strategies as determinants of memory deficiencies. *Cognitive Psychology, 2,* 411–420.

Belmont, J. M., Butterfield, E. C., & Ferretti, R. P. (1984). To secure transfer of training instruct self-management skills. In D. K. Detterman & R. J. Sternberg (Eds.), *How and how much can intelligence be increased* (pp. 147–154). Norwood, NJ: Ablex.

Berlyne, D. E. (1965). *Structure and direction in thinking*. New York. John Wiley.

Berry J. W. (1981, December). *Comparative studies of cognitive styles: Implications for the education of immigrant students*. Paper presented at the conference "The Educator of Ethnic Minority Immigrants," Florida International University.

Blackman, S., & Goldstein, K. M. (1982). Cognitive styles and learning disabilities. *Journal of Learning Disabilities, 15*(2), 106–115.

Bloom, B. S., & Broder, L. J. (1950). Problem-solving processes of college students. *School Review and Elementary School Journal, 73*. 1–103.

Borkowski, B. S., & Konarski, E. A. (1981). Educational implications of efforts to train intelligence. *Journal of Special Education, 15*(2), 289–305.

Bradley, T. B. (1983). Remediation of cognitive deficits: A critical appraisal of the Feuerstein model. *Journal of Mental Deficiency, 27*, 79–92.

Brailsford, A., Snart, F., & Das, J. P. (1984). Strategy training and reading comprehension. *Journal of Learning Disabilities, 17*, 287–290.

Brannigan, G. G., Ash, T., & Margolis, H. (1980). Impulsivity-reflectivity and children's intellectual performance. *Journal of Personality Assessment, 44*(1), 41–43.

Bransford, J. D. (1979). *Human cognition: learning, understanding, and remembering*. Belmont, CA: Wadsworth Publishing Co.

Bransford, J. D., & Stein, B. S. (1984). *The IDEAL problem solver: A guide for improving thinking, learning and creativity*. New York: Freeman.

Bransford, J. D., Stein, B. S., Vye, N. J., Franks, J. J., Suble, P. M., Mezynski, K. J., & Perfetto, G. A. (1982). Differences in approaches to learning: An overview. *Journal of Experimental Psychology–General, 111*(4), 190–198.

Brooks, P. H., & McCauley, C. (1984). Cognitive research in mental retardation. *American Journal of Mental Deficiency, 88*(5), 479–486.

Brown, A. L., & Campione, J. C. (1978). Permissable inferences from the outcome of training studies in cognitive development research. *Quarterly Newsletter of the Institute for Comparative Human Development, 2*, 46–53.

Brown, A. L., & Campione, J. C. (1984). Modifying intelligence or modifying cognitive skills? More than a semantic quibble? In D. K. Detterman & R. J. Sternberg (Eds.), *How and how much can intelligence be increased?* (pp. 215–230). Norwood, NJ: Ablex.

Brown, A. L., & DeLoache, J. S. (1978). Skills, plans, and self-regulation. In R. S. Siegler (Ed.). *Children's thinking: What develops?* (pp. 3–35). Hillsdale, NJ: Erlbaum.

Bruner, J. S., Goodnow, J. J., & Austin, G. A. (1981). *A study of thinking*. New York: John Wiley.

Butterfield, E. C., & Belmont, J. M. (1977). Assessing and improving executive cognitive functions of mentally retarded people. In I. Bialer & M. Sternlicht (Eds.), *The psychology of mental retardation: Issues and approaches* (pp. 279–305). New York: Psychological Dimensons, Inc.

Burns, M. S. (1980). *Preschool children's approach and performance on cognitive tasks*. Unpublished master's thesis, George Peabody College for Teachers of Vanderbilt University.

Carlson, J. S., & Wiedl, K. H. (1980). Applications of a dynamic testing approach in intelligence assessment: Empirical results and theoretical formulations. *Zeitschrift für Differentielle und Diagnostische Psychologie, 1*(4), 303–318.

Case, R. (1978). Intellectual development from birth to adulthood: A neo-Piagetian interpretation. In R. S. Siegler (Ed.), *Children's thinking: What develops?* (pp. 37–71). Hillsdale, NJ: Erlbaum.

Case, R. (1984). The process of stage transition: A neo-Piagetian view. In R. J. Sternberg (Ed.), *Mechanisms of cognitive development* (pp. 19–44). New York: Freeman.

Chi, M. T. H. (1978). Knowledge structure and memory development. In R. S. Siegler (Ed.),

Children's thinking: What develops? (pp. 73–96). Hillsdale, NJ: Erlbaum.

Cole, M., & Scribner, S. (1974). *Culture and thought.* New York John Wiley.

Coop, R. H., & Sigel, I. E. (1971). Cognitive style: Implications for learning and instruction. *Psychology in the Schools, 8,* 152–161.

Cronbach, L. J., & Snow, R. E. (1977). *Aptitudes and instructional methods—A handbook for research on interactions.* New York: Irvington Publishers, Inc.

Dansereau, D. F., Collins, K. W., McDonald, B. A., Holley, J. G., Diekoff, G., & Evans, S. H. (1979). Development and evaluation of a learning strategy program. *Journal of Educational Psychology, 71*(1), 64–73.

Das, J. P., Kirby, J., & Jarman, R. F. (1975). Simultaneous and successive synthesis: An alternative model for cognitive abilities. *Psychological Bulletin, 82*(1), 87–103.

Das, J. P., Kirby, J. R., & Jarman, R. F. (1979). *Simultaneous and successive cognitive processes.* New York: Academic Press.

Estes, W. K. (1981). Intelligence and learning. In M. P. Friedman, J. P. Das, & N. O'Connor (Eds.), *Intelligence and learning* (pp. 3–22). New York: Plenum Press.

Feuerstein, R. (1979). *Dynamic assessment of retarded performers: The learning potential assessment device, theory, instruments, and techniques.* Baltimore: University Park Press.

Feuerstein, R. F. (1980). *Instrumental enrichment: An intervention program for cognitive modifiability.* Baltimore: University Park Press.

Feuerstein, R., & Hoffman, M. B. (1982). Intergenerational conflict of rights: Cultural imposition and self-realization. Viewpoints in teaching and learning. *Journal of School of Education* (Indiana University), *58*(1).

Fischer, K. W., & Silvern, L. (1985). Stages and individual differences in cognitive development. *Annual Review of Psychology, 36,* 613–648.

Flavell, J. H. (1977). *Cognitive development.* Englewood Cliffs, NJ: Prentice-Hall.

Flavell, J. H. (1979). Metacognition and cognitive monitoring—A new area of cognitive-developmental inquiry. *American Psychologist, 34*(10), 906–911.

Flavell, J. H. (1984). Discussion. In R. J. Sternberg (Ed.), *Mechanisms of cognitive development* (pp. 187–209). New York: Freeman.

Forbes, D. L., & Greenberg, M. T. (Eds.). (1982). *New directions for child development: Children's planning strategies, No. 18.* San Francisco: Jossey-Bass.

Forrest-Pressley, D. L., & Gillies, L. A. (1983). Children's flexible use of strategies during reading. In M. Pressley and J. R. Levin (Eds.), *Cognitive strategy research-Educational applications* (pp. 133–156). New York: Springer-Verlag.

Frankenstein, C. (1979). *They think again—Restoring cognitive abilities through teaching.* New York: Van Nostrand Reinhold Co.

Gagné, R. M. (1984). Learning outcomes and their effects: Useful categories of human performance. *American Psychologist, 39*(4), 377–385.

Gardner, H. (1983). *Frames of mind.* New York: Basic Books.

Glaser, R., & Pellegrino, J. (1984). Improving the skills of learning. In D. K. Detterman & R. J. Sternberg (Eds.), *How and how much can intelligence be increased* (pp. 197–212). Norwood, NJ: Ablex.

Glass, A. L., Holyoak, K. J., & Santa, J. L. (1979). *Cognition.* Reading, MA: Addison-Wesley.

Goldstein, K. M., & Blackman, S. (1977). Assessment of cognitive style. In P. McReynolds (Ed.), *Advances in psychological assessment* (pp. 462–525). San Francisco: Jossey-Bass.

Goldstein, K. M., & Blackman, S. (1978). *Cognitive style - five approaches and relevant research.* New York: John Wiley & Sons.

Greeno, J. G. (1978). Nature of problem-solving abilities. In W. G. Estes (Ed.), *Handbook of learning and cognitive processes. Volume 5: Human information processing* (pp. 239–270). Hillsdale, NJ: Erlbaum.

Greeno, J. G., and Simon, H. A. (1984). *Problem solving and reasoning* (Code 442PTJ, report No. UP ITT/LRDC/ONR/APS-14. Arlington, VA: Personnel Training Research Program,

Office of Naval Research.

Hall, R. J. (1980). Cognitive behavior modification and information-processing skills of exceptional children. *Exceptional Education Quarterly, 1*(1), 6–15.

Heber, M. (1977). The influence of language training on seriation of 5–6 year old children initially at different levels of descriptive competence. *British Journal of Psychology, 68,* 85–95.

Kagan, J. (1965). Reflection-impulsivity and reading ability in primary grade children. *Child Development, 36,* 609–628.

Kagan, J., Moss, H. A., & Sigel, I. E. (1973). Psychological significance of styles of conceptualization. In J. C. Wright & J. Kagan (Eds.), *Basic cognitive processes in children* (pp. 73–112). Chicago: University of Chicago Press.

Kaufman, D., & Kaufman, P. (1979). Strategy training and remedial techniques. *Journal of Learning Disabilities, 12*(6), 63–66.

Keating, D. P., Keniston, A. H., Manis, F. R., & Bobbitt, B. L. (1980). Development of the search-processing parameter. *Child Development, 51,* 39–44.

Kessen, W. (1984). Introduction: The end of the age of development. In R. J. Sternberg (Eds.), *Mechanisms of cognitive development* (pp. 101–139). New York: Freeman.

Klausmeier, H. J., & Allen, P. S. (1978). *Cognitive development of children and youth—A longitudinal study.* New York: Academic Press.

Lloyd, J. (1980). Academic instruction and cognitive behavior modification: The need for attack strategy training. *Exceptional Education Quarterly, 1*(1), 53–63.

Lloyd, J. W., & De Bettencourt, L. J. Y. (1982). *Academic strategy training: A manual for teachers.* Charlottesville: University of Virginia Learning Disabilities Research Institute.

Lloyd, J., Saltzman, N. J., & Kauffman, J. M. (1981). Predictable generalization in academic learning as a result of preskills and strategy training. *Learning Disability Quarterly, 4,* 203–216.

Loper, A. B. (1980). Metacognitive development: Implications for cognitive training. *Exceptional Education Quarterly, 1*(1), 1–8.

Luria, A. R. (1966). *Human brain and psychological processes.* New York: Harper and Row.

Luria, A. R. (1973). *The working brain—An introduction to neuropsychology* (B. Haigh, Trans.). NY: Basic Books.

Maccoby, E. E., Dowley, E. M., Hagen, J. W., & Degerman, R. (1965). Activity level and intellectual functioning in normal preschool children. *Child Development, 36,* 761–770.

McDermott, P. A. (1979–1981). *Styles of learning among young school children: The Philadelphia–Phoenix project.* Unpublished manuscript, University of Pennsylvania, Philadelphia.

McKinney, J. D., & Haskins, R. (1980). Cognitive training and the development of problem-solving strategies. *Exceptional Education Quarterly, 1*(1), 41–51.

Meltzer, L. (1984). Cognitive assessment in the diagnosis of learning problems. In M. D. Levine & P. Satz (Eds.), *Middle childhood: Developmental dysfunction.* Baltimore: University Park Press, 131–152.

Merrifield, P. (1981). A tetrahedral model of intelligence. In P. Merrifield (Ed.), *New directions for testing and measurement: Measuring human abilities, No. 12* (pp. 87–99). San Francisco: Jossey-Bass.

Messer, S. B. (1976). Reflection-impulsivity: A review. *Psychological Bulletin, 83*(6), 1026–1052.

Mumbauer, C. C., & Miller, J. O. (1970). Socioeconomic background and cognitive functioning in preschool children. *Child Development, 41,* 471–480.

Phillips, K. (1982). Investigating psychological dysfunction: Problems and prospects. In A. Burton (Ed.), *The pathology and psychology of cognition* (pp. 8–23). New York: Methuen.

Piaget, J. (1970). *Structuralism* (C. Maschler, Trans. and ed.). New York: Harper and Row.

Posner, M. I. (1973). *Cognition: An Introduction.* Glenview, IL: Scott Foresman.

Posner, M. I., & McLeod, P. (1982). Information processing models—In search of elementary operations. *Annual Review of Psychology, 33,* 477–514.

Posner, M. I., & Snyder, C. R. R. (1975). Attention and cognitive control. In R. S. Solso (Ed.), *Information processing and cognition: The Loyola symposium* (pp. 55–85). Hillsdale, NJ: Erlbaum.

Rogoff, B. (1984). Introduction. In B. Rogoff & J. Lave (Eds.), *Everyday cognition: Its development in social context* (pp. 1–8). Cambridge, MA: Harvard University Press.

Rowe, H. A. H. (1985). *Problem solving and intelligence.* Hillsdale, NJ: Erlbaum.

Santostefano, S. (1969). Cognitive controls versus cognitive styles: An approach to diagnosing and treating cognitive disabilities in children. *Seminars in Psychiatry, 1*(3), 291–317.

Schwebel, A. I. (1966). Effects of impulsivity on performance of verbal tasks in middle- and lower-class children. *American Journal of Orthopsychiatry, 36,* 13–21.

Serafica, F. C., & Sigel, I. E. (1970). Styles of categorization and reading disability. *Journal of Reading Behavior, 2,* 105–115.

Siegler, R. S. (1978). The origins of scientific reasoning. In R. S. Siegler (Ed.), *Children's thinking: What develops?* (pp. 109–149). Hillsdale, NJ: Erlbaum.

Siegler, R. S. (1983). Information processing approaches to development. In P. Mussen (Ed.), *Handbook of child psychology* (4th ed.), *Volume I: History, theory and methods* (pp. 129–211). New York: John Wiley.

Simon, H. A. (1976). Identifying basic abilities underlying intelligent performance of complex tasks. In L. B. Resnick (Ed.), *The nature of intelligence* (pp. 65–85). Hillsdale, NJ: Erlbaum.

Simon, H. A. (1979). Information processing models of cognition. *Annual Review of Psychology, 30,* 363–396.

Snow, R. E. (1982). The training of intellectual aptitude. In D. K. Detterman & R. J. Sternberg (Eds.), *How and how much can intelligence be increased?* (pp. 1–37). Norwood, NJ: Ablex.

Stake, R. E. (1958). *Learning parameters, aptitudes, and achievements.* Princeton: Educational Testing Service and Princeton University.

Sternberg, R. J. (1977) *Intelligence, information-processing, and analogical reasoning: A componential analysis of human abilities.* Hillsdale, NJ: Erlbaum.

Sternberg, R. J. (1981). Cognitive-behavioral approaches to the training of intelligence in the retarded. *Journal of Special Education, 15*(2), 165–183.

Sternberg, R. J. (1984a). A theory of knowledge acquisition in the development of verbal concepts. *Developmental Review, 4,* 113–138.

Sternberg, R. J. (1984b). Mechanisms of cognitive development: A componential approach. In R. J. Sternberg (Ed.), *Mechanisms of cognitive development* (pp. 163–186). New York: Freeman.

Sternberg, R. J. (1984c). Preface. In R. J. Sternberg (Ed.), *Mechanisms of cognitive development* (pp. vii–ix). New York: Freeman.

Sternberg, R. J. (1984d, August). *Workshop on How to Increase Children's Intellectual Skills.* Annual Convention of the American Psychological Association, Toronto.

Stott, D. H. (1978). *The hard-to-teach child: A diagnostic–remedial approach.* Baltimore: University Park Press.

Swanson, H. L., & Watson, B. L. (1982). *Educational and psychological assessment of exceptional children.* St. Louis: Mosby.

Torgesen, J. K. (1979). What shall we do with psychological processes? *Journal of Learning Disabilities, 12*(8), 514–521.

Vurpillot, E. (1968). The development of scanning strategies and their relation to visual differentiation. *Journal of Experimental Child Psychology, 6,* 632–650.

Wagner, R. K., & Sternberg, R. J. (1984). Alternative conceptions of intelligence and their implications for education. *Review of Educational Research, 54*(2), 179–223.

Weithorn, C. J., Kagan, E., & Marcus, M. (1984). The relationship of activity level ratings and cognitive impulsivity to task performance and academic achievement. *Journal of Child Psychology and Psychiatry, 25*(4), 587–606.

Werner, H. (1937). Process and achievement—A basic problem of education and developmental psychology. *Harvard Educational Review*, *7*(3), 353–368.

Willows, D. M., Borwick, D. M., & Butkowsky, I. S. (1983). From theory to practice in readying research: Toward the development of better software. In M. Pressley & J. R. Levin (Eds.), *Cognitive strategy research—Educational applications* (pp. 157–187). New York: Springer-Verlag.

Witkin, H. A. (1973). *The role of cognitive style in academic performance and in teacher-student relations* (Research Bulletin RB-73-11). Princeton: Educational Testing Service.

Zelnicker, T., & Jeffrey, W. E. (1976). Reflective and impulsive children: Strategies of information processing underlying differences in problem-solving. *Monographs of the Society for Research in Child Development*, *41* (5, Serial No. 168).

Appendix A: Feuerstein's List of Cognitive Deficiencies (Feuerstein, 1980, pp. 73–74)

Input

1. Blurred and sweeping perception (style).
2. Unplanned, impulsive, and unsystematic exploratory behavior (style).
3. Lack of or impaired receptive verbal tools that affect discrimination: objects, events, relationships, etc. (content).
4. Lack of or impaired spatial orientation and the lack of stable systems of reference that impair the establishment of topological and Euclidean organization of space (structure/process).
5. Lack of or impaired temporal concepts (content).
6. Lack of or impaired conservation of constancies or factors such as size, shape, quantity, orientation, etc. across variations of other dimensions of the perceived object (process).
7. Lack of or deficient need for precision and accuracy in data gathering (motivation/ style).
8. Lack of capacity for considering two or more sources of information at once, which is reflected in dealing with data in a piecemeal fashion rather than as a unit of organized facts (process).

Elaboration

1. Inadequacy in the perception of the existence and definition of an actual problem (process).
2. Inability to select relevant vs. nonrelevant cues in defining a problem (process).
3. Lack of spontaneous comparative behavior or limitation of its application by a restricted need system (process/motivation).
4. Narrowness of the mental field (process/style).
5. Episodic grasp of reality (process/style).
6. Lack of or impaired need for pursuing logical evidence (motivation).
7. Lack of or impaired interiorization (process).
8. Lack of or impaired inferential, hypothetical, "iffy" thinking (process).

9. Lack of or impaired strategies for hypothesis testing (process/strategy/content).
10. Lack of or impaired planning behavior (process/strategy).
11. Nonelaboration of certain cognitive categories because the verbal concepts are not a part of the individual's repertoire on a receptive level or are not mobilized at the expressive level (content/process).

Output

1. Egocentric communicational modalities (process/style).
2. Difficulties in projecting virtual relationships (processes).
3. Blocking (motivation/process).
4. Trial-and-error responses (process/strategy/style).
5. Lack of or impaired verbal tools for communicating adequately elaborated responses (process/content).
6. Lack of or impaired need for precision and accuracy in communicating responses (motivation/style).
7. Deficiencies in visual transport (process).
8. Impulsive, acting-out behavior (style/process).

Appendix B: Structures—Literature Review

Author	Structures discussed
Baumeister & Brooks (1981); Rowe (1985); Siegler (1983); Simon (1976), 1979)	Sensory register, short-term store, long-term memory, attentional mechanisms.
Borkowski & Konarski (1981)	An architectural system "characterized by perceptual efficiency in the speed of encoding and decoding information" (p. 290), and an executive system, which includes control processes, metacognition, regulatory, mediational, and retrieval functions.
Brooks & McCauley (1984)	Perceptual and memory systems and attentional processes.
Luria (1966, 1973); Das et al. (1975)	Arousal and attention (reticular formation, limbic cortex, hippocampus); processing—including input, storage and recording (occipital, parietal, frontal/temporal), and planning/programming (frontal lobe).
Posner & McLeod (1982)	Language (symbolic), mental imagery (iconic), and enactive (motor) systems.

Appendix C: Processes—Literature Review

Author	Processes discussed
Baumeister & Brooks (1981)	Defined cognitive processes as "internalized events that mediate stimulus-response linkages"

Appendix C: Processes—Literature Review (continued)

Author	Processes discussed
	that involve "the detection, analysis, coding, transformation, and retrieval of information" (pp. 93–94).
Brooks & McCauley (1984)	Discussed executive processes, defined as "awareness of, monitoring of, or attention to one's own sets of cognitive operations and strategies" (p. 480).
Brown & DeLoache (1978)	Enumerated six executive processes: prediction of consequences of actions or events, checking the results of actions, monitoring one's own activities, reality testing, coordination, and control of problem-solving behaviors.
Butterfield & Belmont (1977)	Specified three memory functions: acquisition, retention, and retrieval.
Chi (1978); Greeno & Simon (1984); Klausmeier & Allen (1978); Siegler (1983)	All provided reminders of the importance of a knowledge base and stored skills repertory.
Cronbach & Snow (1977)	Described observational and analytical skills as well as arousal phenomena and mediational activities that include " 'comprehension' of instruction, including verbal coding, induction, and other elaborative processes," adding conclusions from research on "organizing, recalling, and reasoning from stored knowledge" (p. 342).
Estes (1981)	List of cognitive activities included: "perceiving relationships, comparing and judging similarities and differences, coding information into progressively more abstract forms, classification and categorization, memory search and retrieval" (p. 117).
Flavell (1977)	Listed three general interacting "psychological processes": thinking, perceiving, and remembering, involved in the operations of constructing, receiving, transforming, storing, retrieving.
Flavell (1979)	Specified four classes of metacognitive phenomena: knowledge ("stored world knowledge"), goals ("objectives of a cognitive enterprise"), and actions and strategies ("employed to achieve the objectives") (pp. 906–907).
Glaser & Pellegrino (1984)	Identified six general abilities from studies on inductive reasoning: encoding, inference, rule assembly, comparison, discrimination, and decision/response processes.
Glass et al. (1979)	Listed three processes: perceiving, remembering, and reasoning.
Greeno (1978)	Described three types of problems, each of which required different processes for solution: 1) problems of inducing structure (require understand-

Appendix C: Processes—Literature Review (continued)

Author	Processes discussed
	ing); 2) problems of transformation (require planning based on means–end analysis); and 3) problems of arrangement (require constructive search).
Hall (1980)	Specified acquisition, retention, and transformation as the three essential components of information processing.
Kagan et al. (1973)	Cited five basic cognitive processes: recognition, memory, convergent thinking, divergent thinking, and evaluation.
Luria (1973)	Described perception as a complex and active process "of searching for the corresponding information, distinguishing the essential feature of an object, comparing the features with each other, creating appropriate hypotheses, and then comparing these hypotheses with the original data" (p. 229). Thinking, in contrast, involves analysis and generalization (p. 325). Luria's listing of cognitive functions included: analysis and synthesis of extero- and proprioceptive stimuli; combined working of analyzers; maintenance of the general tone of the cortex; and analysis of information regarding the performance of actions, and comparing this with anticipated results (p. 36). Luria aligned his proposal of three functional units with structural areas of the brain as follows: reticular formation (regulating tone or waking), posterior regions of cerebral hemispheres (reception, coding, processing, storing), and anterior regions of cerebral hemispheres (programming, regulating, verifying).
Merrifield (1981)	Listed short- and long-term memory processes: recognition, recall, storage, and retrieval. His list of processes also includes evaluating, generating, and transforming.
Posner (1973)	Outlined three geneeral categories: abstraction of information from sensory to semantic structure and coding information in condensed form; generation or elaboration of information; and combination of information in arithmetic or logical form (p. 94).
Siegler (1983)	In his literature review, mentioned: recognition (encoding and retention), visual scanning, categorical perception, learning, intersensory integration, memory scanning, retrieval, and choice processes.
Simon (1976)	Cited sensation, perception, memory. In relating processes to specific problem-solving tasks, Simon

Appendix C: Processes—Literature Review (continued)

Author	Processes discussed
	listed two involved in the solution of sequential pattern problems: discovery of the pattern (detect periodicity, determine the rule, test inferred rule to check correctness of prediction), and performance of the extrapolation (inference).
Simon (1979)	Elementary information processes: retrieval from memory, scanning down lists in memory, comparing simple symbols. Higher mental processes: problem solving and concept attainment.
Stake (1958)	Listed memory functions: memory, perception, symbolization, reasoning, and learning.
Sternberg (1977)	Using the word component, he specified three kinds: metacomponents ("higher order control processes . . . used for planning . . . for making decisions . . . for answering the reassessing the success"); performance components ("used in the execution of problem-solving strategy"); and acquisition components ("involved in learning new information") (1981, p. 166). These are further elaborated in Sternberg (1984b). In reviewing the many developing information-processing theories, Sternberg (1984a) cited the commonalities across theorists and researchers in terms of: specification of processes for encoding and restructuring information acquisition, processes for combining disparate pieces of information, and processes for relating new information to old.
Werner (1937)	Viewed the relationship between achievement and underlying processes as "one of the most significant problems of genetic psychology as well as of the theory and practice of education" (p. 353), and cited abstraction as a particularly important mental function.

Appendix D: Strategies—Literature Review

Author	Strategies discussed
Bransford & Stein (1984)	Externalization of memory; breaking the large and complex down into simpler units; working backward; focus on a simple specific instance; familiarization with concepts developed by others; identification and definition of the problem; redefinition of the problem in a way to suggest a strategy; identification of implicit assumptions; application of logic; removal of emotional investment. Memory strategies: rehearsal of both single pieces

Appendix D: Strategies—Literature Review (continued)

Author	Strategies discussed
	as well as grouped information; organization of information into conceptual categories; linkage of meaningless with meaningful stimuli; development of acronyms and acrostics; formation of rhymes and codes; visualized walk-throughs.
Bruner et al. (1981)	Conservative focusing (successive elimination of single attributes); focus gambling (choices of attributes are varied, and more than one are compared at a time); simultaneous scanning (development of a simple hypothesis based on the first positive instance), and successive scanning (trial-and-error hypotheses).
Brown & DeLoache (1978)	Extracting the main idea; visual scanning; retrieval from memory storage. Strategies to maximize trans-situational transfer: predicting consequences of actions and events, checking the results of actions, self-monitoring of activities, reality testing, and coordination and control of problem-solving attempts.
Chi (1978)	Memory strategies: rehearsal and grouping.
Dansereau et al. (1979)	Executive strategies used to train college students: set the mood, understand, recall, digest, expand, and review. Recall strategies: paraphrase, develop imagery, networking to develop linkages, diagnosis, development of hierarchies, and analysis of key ideas. Retrieval strategies: set mood, understand requirements, recall main ideas, detail main ideas, expand into outline, and review. Support strategies: goal setting, scheduling, concentration management, and monitoring.
Forest-Pressley & Gillies (1983)	Strategies for academic content: (reading)– rereading, skim reading, paraphrasing, and summarizing. Executive strategies: determine the appropriate strategy, apply executive controls of selection, monitoring, and modification.
Greeno & Simon (1984)	Means–end analysis, determination of subgoals when the goal cannot be directly achieved; for problems of design or arrangement: narrow down possibilities; for induction problems: focusing and scanning strategies, and forming and evaluating of hypothesis.

CONCLUSION

State of the Art and Future Directions

JOHN D. BRANSFORD, VICTOR R. DELCLOS, NANCY J. VYE, M. SUSAN BURNS, AND TED S. HASSELBRING

In her introduction to this volume, Lidz notes that the concept of dynamic assessment—an approach to assessment that provides individuals with an opportunity to learn—is finally being taking seriously. Some individuals believe that dynamic assessment has the potential to reveal important information about processes of learning and to provide insightful suggestions for teaching. Lidz provides an excellent historical account of work in the area of dynamic assessment. In addition, although she is optimistic about the possible benefits of dynamic assessment, she emphasizes potential dangers. For example, she cites (p. 3), an article by Bradley (1983), who warns about "the danger of faddism, of a quick rise in interest, failure to take hold and infiltrate the establishment, followed by demise."

Lidz's warning of danger is extremely important. Many educational programs have seemed promising yet have disappeared because of failure to provide solid information about the conditions necessary to use them effectively (e.g., see Mann, 1979). It is fitting, therefore, that the present volume begins with Lidz's call for well-articulated theories and for careful research.

The emphasis on research—and especially on research from a variety of theoretical perspectives—makes this a landmark volume. To our knowledge, it represents the first time that people from many different research groups have joined together in a discussion of theory and data relevant to the topic of dynamic assessment. It has been a privilege to read and compare the papers. Clearly, we cannot hope to discuss all issues that are raised by this volume's

John D. Bransford. Department of Psychology, Vanderbilt University, Nashville, Tennessee.

Victor R. Delclos and M. Susan Burns. Department of Education, Tulane University, New Orleans, Louisiana.

Nancy J. Vye. Department of Psychology, University of Western Ontario, London, Ontario, Canada.

Ted S. Hasselbring. Department of Special Education, Vanderbilt University, Nashville, Tennessee.

Much of our knowledge of dynamic assessment stems from opportunities to work with Dr. Reuven Feuerstein and his colleagues. We are extremely grateful for these opportunities. It is important to note, however, that Feuerstein and his colleagues may disagree with many of the points made in this paper.

authors. Our goals are more modest. We propose to: (a) highlight issues that we feel are particularly important; (b) compare the approaches and findings of various authors that are relevant to these issues; and (c) provide suggestions for future research.

Different Approaches to Dynamic Assessment

The contributors to this volume provide a healthy diversity of views about the concept of dynamic assessment. There are several issues that highlight these differences of opinion. Three areas that seem particularly important are: (a) the nature of the tasks chosen for the assessment; (b) the nature of the teaching component of the assessment; and (c) assumptions about uses of dynamic assessment.

The particular tasks selected for testing and training during dynamic assessment have been chosen by each research group with a great deal of thought. Although most tasks have some elements in common (e.g., a requirement of general reasoning skills such as induction, analogy, and part–whole analysis), they also vary in a number of important ways. Some choices of task are made on the basis of theoretical considerations. Feuerstein and his colleagues select tasks from domains that are not likely to be threatening to students who have a history of failure in traditional academic areas in order to circumvent the motivational factors they consider to be very important in learning (e.g., see Chapters 10 and 14, this volume). Likewise, Budoff and colleagues have emphasized the importance of using *nonverbal* tasks in order to tap the reasoning abilities of children who have not grown up in a rich verbal environment (Chapters 2 and 6, this volume).

Other choices concerning the type of task to be used in dynamic assessment are based on more practical concerns. For example, researchers who have focused their work on very young children have stressed the importance of using manipulable materials, both to engage the child and to allow for analysis of the ways the child approaches reasoning tasks (e.g., Burns, 1985; Chapters 9 through 12, this volume). Another practical concern that has driven the selection of tasks is the degree to which the materials chosen are similar to those found in standardized tests of ability and achievement (e.g., Chapters 11 and 15, this volume). The reasoning is that assessors will be more likely to use dynamic assessment techniques if tasks that are familiar to them from standard testing situations are also used in dynamic assessment.

In addition to differences in tasks, dynamic assessment researchers use different forms of teaching during their assessments. Here again, we find decisions regarding the nature of the instruction based on both theoretical and practical concerns. In their zone of proximal development procedure, for example, Campione and Brown (Chapter 3, this volume) use hints, ordered in their level of explicitness, as the teaching phase of their assessment. This choice stems from their reliance on the Vygotskian notion of the social nature of cognitive development (see Chapter 4, this volume, for more detail). Campione and Brown describe their procedure as an attempt to capture the gradual transfer of control of thought from adult to child in the zone of proximal development.

In contrast to Campione and Brown, proponents of Feuerstein's notion of cognitive development attempt to provide an intensive mediated learning experience during the teaching phase of the assessment. Here we find instruction that is based on certain theoretical principles, yet closely linked to the performance of each individual child. Even within the group of researchers who rely heavily on Feuerstein's theories we find differences in instruction based on practical concerns. Burns (1985), Tzuriel and Klein (Chapter 10, this volume), and Vye et al. (Chapter 12, this volume) have employed carefully scripted versions of mediated teaching in efforts to standardize treatment for research purposes and to simplify procedures for easier training and widespread use by a variety of assessors. Others (e.g., Chapter 7, this volume) have used scripted procedures in the group administration of the Learning Potential Assessment Device. At the same time, Mearig (Chapter 9, this volume) argues strongly for the necessity of flexibility in the mediated teaching phase and believes that "scripting" is not compatible with the concept of mediated learning procedures.

Each of these approaches to the teaching component of dynamic assessment has potential advantages and disadvantages, and each may be suited to different goals or purposes. Effects of these differences in teaching on the degree of childrens' learning and transfer will be discussed later in this chapter. For present purposes it is sufficient to note that such differences exist.

Contributors to this volume also make differing assumptions about the roles of dynamic assessment in educational settings. For example, some investigators focus mainly on issues of classification. Their intention is to use dynamic procedures to improve the validity of classification. They are concerned with identifying children who have been erroneously classified as mentally handicapped (Chapters 2 and 6, this volume), or with the early identification of children who may be at risk for academic failure (Chapter 3, this volume). Other investigators focus on the role of dynamic assessment in developing diagnoses and prescriptions for teaching. They wish to use the assessment to derive diagnoses about deficient cognitive processes (Chapter 11, this volume) and/or to derive information for teachers about specific tasks and instructional methods that best meet the needs of individual children (Chapter 12, this volume). We discuss these differences in more detail later. First, it is helpful to consider ways in which the book's contributors agree.

Dissatisfactions with Traditional Assessment Techniques

Despite a number of differences in assumptions about dynamic assessment, the contributors to this volume all agree that static, standardized assessment techniques leave much to be desired. The dissatisfaction with traditional assessment tools, especially standardized tests of intelligence, is most often grounded in one or more of three basic arguments:

1. Traditional assessments deal only with the products of learning, disregarding learning processes.
2. Traditional assessments do not address the responsiveness of a child to instruction.
3. Traditional assessments do not provide prescriptive information regarding potentially effective intervention techniques.

Regarding the first argument, dynamic assessment researchers question the utility of using products of cognitive performance (e.g., test scores and solutions to problems) to predict and classify the ability to learn. Since the critical elements of cognition have to do with how children acquire, store, and utilize information, it is argued that the best way to assess cognitive ability is to directly assess those processes of thought that are involved in arriving at the products of cognition.

On the issue of the child's responsiveness to instruction, most question a basic tenet of traditional assessment: that the best predictor of future learning is prior learning. The argument is that this assumption depends on the equality of the prior learning experience and that, in reality, there are large and systematic inequalities in the prior learning experiences of minority children, physically and mentally handicapped children, and children who are normally developing and without special needs. Because the products of different qualities of learning experiences will most likely be different, it becomes important to examine *how* a child learns in a positive learning environment before we can hope to categorize his or her ability to learn. Haywood, Filler, Shifman, and Chatelanat (1975) provided a detailed discussion of these points. In addition, Embretson (Chapter 5, this volume) provides an excellent discussion of the many changes in psychometric assumptions that are necessary to effectively analyze change.

With respect to the third argument above, many authors find that traditional assessment techniques are not suited to the goal of providing specific instructional prescriptions. The prescriptions that are typically generated from static assessment reports are either broad generalizations from past clinical experiences or they are of the "general ability" variety, for example, prescriptions that are generated from tests of the differential diagnosis–prescriptive teaching genre (see Arter & Jenkins, 1979). What is desired by these authors are specific, individualized prescriptions that will directly address the learning problems of individual children.

Roles for Dynamic Assessment in Educational Practice

Many authors in this volume argue that the use of dynamic assessment techniques can fill some of the gaps left by traditional assessments and thus supplement those techniques in important ways. Other professionals have also expressed concern about gaps in current assessment practices. A recent report from the National Research Council (Heller, Holtzman, & Messick, 1982), entitled *Placing Children in Special Education: A Strategy for Equity*, provides an excellent context for discussing some possible supplemental roles of dynamic assessment. Heller et al. postulated that the main function of assessment should be to improve the quality of instruction and learning for individual children (see also Hobbs, 1975; Chapter 16, this volume). They suggested a preliminary, Phase I level of assessment that focuses on the ability of the current educational intervention the child is receiving to meet the needs of that particular child. This notion changes the focus of the search for causes of learning problems from sources within the child (e.g., mental retardation, learning disability) to the instructional environment in which the child is failing to learn. Two key issues arise from this redefinition of the role of assessment: How can we improve: (a) the quality of the instruction that children receive and (b) the validity of the referral and assessment procedures used to classify children? In the discussion that follows we try to clarify how dynamic assessment might be used to address these issues. We rely on data as much as possible, and we also discuss areas where there is a need for more research.

Information About Responsiveness to Instruction

As noted earlier, most contributors to this volume argue that dynamic assessment can provide information that is not necessarily available from traditional assessments. The results of several studies suggest that dynamic assessment can be used to correct misclassifications that have resulted from the use of traditional tests.

The research project reported by Budoff (Chapters 2 and 6, this volume) includes an impressive array of studies that focus on issues of classification. Budoff's program of research has been guided by the assumption that mentally handicapped children who can perform a task at the level of their nonhandicapped peers following a brief period of training are not "mentally" handicapped. He suggests that it would be better to consider these children as "educationally" handicapped, meaning that inadequate family and school experiences have left them ill-prepared rather than incapable of doing academic tasks.

In general, Budoff's research results show that children who perform competently following dynamic assessment (these children initially scored well or made large gains in performance) also do better in other learning and social situations. For example, Budoff, Meskin, and Harrison (1971) showed that the posttest performance of special education students of high learning potential status is indistinguishable from that of regular class control students following instruction on a curriculum unit of elementary science (verbal demands of the instruction were minimized). The educational relevance of the classification scheme is further indicated by the results of a study by Budoff and Gottlieb (1976) that investigated the effects of learning potential status and mainstreaming on achievement and self-concept. In this study students with high learning potential status (regardless of class placement) had higher achievement scores than those who did not profit as much from dynamic assessment. In addition, high learning potential students who had been reintegrated into regular classes reported feeling that other students regarded them more positively when they were mainstreamed than when they were segregated. The reverse was true for students of lower learning potential status.

The above results are important for several reasons. First, they illustrate differences in performance among children who were previously thought to be homogeneously grouped and of low learning ability. Second, these differences are educationally meaningful; that is, they are related to aspects of school performance and success.

Other contributors to this volume also present research findings showing differences in learning after dynamic assessment. For example, in our research with young handicapped children we have found sizable numbers of children in each General Cognitive Index group who reach our learning criterion on a perceptual performance task following dynamic assessment (see Figure 12.1 of Chapter 12, this volume). Furthermore, children's performance following dynamic assessment is predictive of performance on within-domain transfer tasks. In addition, Lidz and Thomas (Chapter 11, this volume) demonstrate the responsiveness of preschool special education referrals to the instruction provided in the Preschool Learning Assessment Device. Although they did not find evidence of transfer, one could argue that it might be more appropriate to consider their posttest measure as a near-transfer task. When one does, there is indeed evidence of transfer. A final illustration of the important information provided by dynamic assessment is taken from Brown and Ferrara (1980). They reported that, although learning and transfer performance following graduated prompting is related to static classification, many children's performance profiles are inconsistent with their static assessment classification. Dynamic assessment would therefore seem to be a particularly promising way to obtain information about children that goes beyond static assessment.

At first glance, Tzuriel and Klein's results (Chapter 10, this volume) are a notable exception to the above conclusion. Recall that they found that static assessment grouping was highly related to dynamic assessment performance; the special education group made very modest gains in comparison to other groups. We must keep in mind, however, that these are *group* comparisons, and that if one were to look at the performance of *individuals* within groups there would no doubt be some children who showed exceptional performance, even in the lowest functioning group.

Effects of Dynamic Assessment on Expectations

An assumption that underlies all forms of dynamic assessment is that performance failures can be attributed, at least in part, to deficient instructional procedures and experiences (e.g., Feuerstein's mediated learning experience) rather than to primary, causal deficits within the child. To the extent that cognitive deficiencies are implicated in poor performance, the origins of these deficiencies are themselves traced back to poor instruction. Good instruction is viewed as a means of overcoming these deficiencies. It is essential to communicate this fundamental assumption of the central role of instruction in cognitive development to the consumers of dynamic assessment information. Without this basic point of view, teachers cannot be expected to use dynamic assessment information to individualize teaching.

Evidence that a child can learn quite effectively in a dynamic assessment context can go a long way in convincing a teacher or parent that the child's major problem is the quality of the instruction received in the past rather than a lack of ability. Several authors in this volume suggest that dynamic assessment is most effective in a clinical setting when the parent or teacher of the child observes the actual assessment session. Rand and Kaniel, for example, address the importance of changing attitudes and expectations (Chapter 7, this volume). They report clinical experiences in which the inclusion of the parent or teacher as an observer in the dynamic assessment session has resulted in higher expectations and better instruction (they even suggest that these adults try to do the tasks themselves to experience their difficulty). Jensen and Feuerstein (Chapter 14, this volume) also note the value of including teachers in dynamic assessment sessions, and Mearig (Chapter 9, this volume) suggests that it may be desirable for the teachers themselves to perform the actual assessments, at least when dealing with very young children. Clinicians who advocate the use of dynamic assessment in this way attempt to capitalize on the dramatic and unexpected performance changes that often occur during the assessment as a means of convincing the observers of the potential of the child.

There is also some experimental evidence that dynamic assessment can affect teachers' opinions about the learning potential of a child. For example, Delclos, Burns, and Kulewicz (1985; see also Chapter 12, this volume) have presented data demonstrating that viewing a videotape of a dynamic assessment session can have a meaningful, positive impact on teachers' reports of their expectations of the performance of handicapped children. There are also data in the labeling effects literature that illustrate how information about children's abilities to learn has important effects on teachers' and parents' expectations about potential to learn (Aloia & MacMillan, 1983; Cooper, 1979). The ability to shift the teacher's conceptualization of the locus of failure from the child to the instructional techniques is an important first step toward changing the educational assessment and delivery system and can be seen as one valuable role of dynamic assessment.

In our research we have seen that dynamic assessment can be effective in changing teachers' attitudes about the learning ability of their students when the assessment information is communicated through *videotaped* demonstrations of the child's performance. Contributors to this volume have also noted numerous clinical reports that suggest that this same effect can be obtained when teachers and parents actually sit in on the assessment session. However, data reported by Hoy (1983) suggested that this kind of effect may be contingent on the method of presentation of the dynamic assessment findings. Teachers in her sample reported that they found information in written reports based on traditional assessment measures to be more useful for planning instruction than were written reports based on dynamic assessment measures. These data suggest careful attention to and further research on the method of providing dynamic assessment information to consumers.

The Importance of Different Types of Instruction

Although the preceding evidence on changes in expectations as a function of dynamic assessment is quite strong, we doubt that a mere change in expectations is sufficient to have a powerful impact on the quality of the instruction received by students. We suspect that teachers need more systematic prescriptive information about the kinds of tasks and teaching strategies that seem most useful for individual students.

Earlier, we mentioned the recommendations of the National Research Council Panel concerning the need to evaluate instructional quality (Heller et al., 1982). We suggested that these recommendations seem to be especially important, yet could be difficult to implement because of different definitions of quality. Several of the research projects discussed in this volume show that relatively subtle changes in quality can have strong impacts on the degree to which learning and transfer occur.

As an illustration of the importance of quality of instruction, consider Keane's research comparing the relative effects of mediational versus testing-the-limits instruction (Chapter 13, this volume). Testing-the-limits instruction involves a form of teaching that is less extensive than mediation. It does not, for example, provide elaborate explanations of correct and incorrect aspects of children's responses. These qualitative differences between mediation and testing-the-limits are reflected in learning and transfer. Overall, Keane finds that the performance of individuals receiving mediation is consistently superior to the performance of no-treatment control individuals. In contrast, individuals in the testing-the-limits group are only sometimes better than the controls. We have found a similar outcome in some of our recent research at Vanderbilt. This research examines the effects of instruction that includes a general description of task rules and a demonstration on one item. Even under this relatively minimal "demonstration" level of instruction, some handicapped preschoolers show improvement on the task. Nevertheless, the improvement is not as great or as pervasive as that observed following mediation or graduated prompting.

The preceding studies suggest a gradient or instructional quality, ranging from demonstration through testing-the-limits to mediation. But what about children who do not profit from even the more intensive mediation procedure?

Should we conclude that they are unable to learn? We would say no. We have found, for example, that multiply handicapped children who do not initially respond to our scripted mediational assessment and who are then given instruction that is more tailored to their individual needs do learn to skillfully perform the criterion and transfer tasks (see Chapter 12, this volume). Tzuriel and Klein also point out that the scripted nature of the Children's Analogical Thinking Modifiability instrument instruction (scripted for group research purposes) makes it likely that the instruction will be less than optimum for some children (Chapter 10, this volume).

The above discussion focuses primarily on the effects of different types of instruction on initial learning. It is possible that two instructional procedures could have comparable effects on children's ability to reach a learning criterion, but different effects on transfer. Research by Burns (1985) and by our group at Vanderbilt suggests that this may be the situation for graduated prompting and mediation. Although the two methods produce comparable learning, mediation seems to be associated with better transfer. This raises a question about which instructional approach is most appropriate to use, particularly since the choice has profound implications for our assessments of individual children. We suggest that the choice is best made by considering the *purpose* of the assessment. We find that mediation is well suited for our goal of discovering information about effective instructional strategies for individual children. Graduated prompting, on the other hand, may be better suited to address issues related to classification (e.g., Bryant, 1982). In any event it is clear, and Campione and Brown (Chapter 3, this volume) echo the point, that it is because one does not obtain the same degree of transfer that one needs to worry about the issue of instructional quality.

Assumptions about the Generality of Findings from Dynamic Assessment

The preceding data illustrating the effects of quality of teaching on transfer are encouraging because they suggest that many individuals might be able to benefit considerably from appropriate instruction. With respect to the National Research Council report (Heller et al., 1982), the data suggest that relatively subtle differences in teaching can have important effects. Nevertheless, it is also important to note that the preceding studies involve transfer tasks that are relatively closely related to tasks involved during training. For example, in the studies by Burns (1985) and Vye et al. (see Study A, Chapter 12, this volume) the training tasks involving problem solving on perceptual performance tasks involving shapes and colors, as did the transfer tasks. What would happen if one changed to a different domain, for example, to a quantitative domain?

Data discussed in Vye et al. (Chapter 12, this volume) suggest that transfer across domains often does not occur. Recall that we discussed the results of two studies investigating transfer across the perceptual performance and quantitative domains. We did not observe transfer in either study. To illustrate, consider the findings of one of the studies (see Study B). Groups of children were given a static pretest on the Stencil Design Test and our Quantitative Task. They then received either graduated prompting or mediation on the Stencil Design Task followed by a static posttest on tasks in the two domains. Although each of the instructed groups improved on the stencils, there was no evidence that the effects of the stencil training transferred to the quantitative task.

Findings indicated a lack of transfer across domains (e.g., from perceptual performance to quantitative domains) raise a number of important questions. These questions involve issues such as one's theory of performance difficulties and one's choice of assessment tasks. Both of these issues are discussed below.

Theories of Performance Difficulties

Consider first the issue of theories of performance difficulties. A number of contributors to this volume focus on the list of "deficient cognitive functions" that has been developed by Feuerstein and his colleagues as an explanation for performance deficits (Chapters 7, 10, and 14, this volume). Several authors have even reworked this list so that it will be more useful in dealing with young children (Chapter 9, this volume) or more comprehensible to practicing clinicians (Chapter 17, this volume).

Sternberg (1985a) provided a useful analysis of these deficiencies by grouping them into several broad areas of cognition such as *cognitive styles* (e.g., unplanned, impulsive, and unsystematic exploratory behavior); *knowledge base* (e.g., impaired verbal tools for communication); *motives* (e.g., lack of need for precision and accuracy); *metaprocesses* (e.g., inability to select relevant from irrelevant cues in defining a problem); and *processing capacity* (e.g., narrowness of the mental field).

Sternberg's analysis is helpful because it provides a bridge between Feuerstein's theory and other cognitive literature on thinking, intelligence, and problem solving (e.g., Bransford, Sherwood, Vye, & Rieser, in press; Sternberg, 1985b). In addition, this analysis highlights the fact that Feuerstein's theory involves more than an emphasis on "general strategies" that operate in any content domain. In particular, Feuerstein emphasizes the role of the knowledge base in successful performance (e.g., "lack of verbal tools") and the need for efficiency in accessing and utilizing appropriate knowledge (e.g., "inability to select relevant cues when defining a problem") (Feuerstein, 1979). This focus on the importance of knowledge and efficiency of access in addition to general strategies suggests that we should not always expect automatic transfer from one set of tasks to another. In many cases, successful performance depends on a rather lengthy process of perceptual and procedural learning in order to develop the knowledge and efficiency of access that is necessary in order to come to grips with the task (Anderson, 1983; Bransford et al., in press; Simon, 1980).

A Demonstration Experiment

As an illustration of the role of knowledge in problem solving, consider a simple memory problem that is illustrated in the following exercise (see Bransford, in press). In this exercise, please spend no more than 4 seconds reading each of the sentences listed below, and read each one only once. Most importantly, try not to use any fancy strategies such as generating elaborate images, rehearsing to yourself, and so forth. These are *effortful* strategies. Try to react to each sentence as *effortlessly* as you can.

- John walked on the roof.
- Bill picked up the egg.
- Pete hid the axe.
- Jim flew the kite.
- Frank flipped the switch.
- Alfred built a boat.
- Sam hit his head on the ceiling.
- Adam quit his job.
- Jay fixed the sail.
- Ted wrote the play.

Now try to answer the following questions without looking back at the preceding sentences.

- Who built the boat?
- Who picked up the egg?
- Who walked on the roof?
- Who quit his job?
- Who flew his kite?
- Who fixed the sail?
- Who hit his head on the ceiling?
- Who wrote the play?
- Who flipped the switch?
- Who hid the axe?

Most people have a very difficult time remembering who did what despite the fact that each statement was comprehensible. If you really approached these sentences in a relatively "effortless" manner, you probably could remember only two or three at most. In order to remember these sentences you would have had to use very effortful, sophisticated strategies such as thinking of someone you know with a particular name (e.g., a friend of yours named John) and making an image of him walking on the roof.

Sentences similar to those presented above become much easier to remember if our knowledge base can do much of the work for us. As an illustration, spend approximately 4 seconds reading each of the sentences presented below. As in the earlier task, do not attempt to use any effortful, sophisticated strategies. Instead, react to each sentence as effortlessly as you can.

- Santa Claus walked on the roof.
- The Easter Bunny picked up the egg.
- George Washington hid the axe.
- Benjamin Franklin flew the kite.
- Thomas Edison flipped the switch.
- Noah built the boat.
- Wilt Chamberlain hit his head on the ceiling.
- Richard Nixon quit his job.
- Christopher Columbus fixed the sail.
- William Shakespeare wrote the play.

Now answer the following questions without looking back at the list.

- Who built the boat?
- Who picked up the egg?
- Who walked on the roof?
- Who quit his job?
- Who flew the kite?
- Who fixed the sail?
- Who hit his head on the ceiling?
- Who wrote the play?
- Who flipped the switch?
- Who hid the axe?

Most people find that it is much easier to remember the second set of materials (about Nixon, Columbus, etc.) than the first (about John, Robert, etc.). The second set of materials is designed to activate knowledge that, without much effort, permits a number of elaborations that make the problem of remembering quite easy to solve. For example, you have probably not heard the exact statement that "George Washington hid the axe," but your knowledge of George Washington is rich enough to easily generate elaborations such as "it was the axe used to chop down the cherry tree—a tree he was not supposed to chop down." Similarly, for the sentence "Richard Nixon quit his job" you probably found yourself thinking that the job was the presidency that he was forced to resign, and so forth. Because of the richness of your knowledge, a number of elaborations almost automatically come to mind. This perspective on the role of knowledge in cognitive performance suggests caution in the interpretation of the "peaks of performance" observed in dynamic assessment.

Research on the Role of Knowledge

There is a wealth of research suggesting that the nature and organization of specific knowledge plays an extremely important role in problem solving.

Discussion in Bransford et al. (in press) represents a case in point. They noted that an emphasis on the role of knowledge has had important implications for theories of development and of individual differences. For example, earlier theories of development such as Piagetian stage theories (e.g., Piaget, 1970) assumed that development consists of the addition of capacities to the child's repertoire. Newer views of development also acknowledge that children become more effective at organizing information, solving problems, and so forth (e.g., Brown, Bransford, Ferrara, & Campione, 1983). However, theorists who are exploring these newer views hypothesize that many of these abilities emerge simply from the acquisition of new knowledge. This is different from the assumption that general "logical capacities" have been added to the child's repertoire of skills.

Consider first some of the developmental research on strategies and memory. In the memory literature, it is frequently argued that individuals at different developmental levels have different capacities for short-term retention, and utilize different strategies for rehearsing information, organizing it, and so forth (e.g., see Brown et al., 1983). Several studies suggest that the knowledge available to the learner plays an important role in memory performance and in the strategies that are used. For example, Chi (1978) demonstrated that 10-year-old chess enthusiasts who received a test of short-term memory for number strings performed at a level that was considerably below college students. However, when asked to remember the positions of chess pieces on a chess board, the performance of the children exceeded the performance of the college students (the latter were not experienced at playing chess). Similarly, Lindberg (1980) found that children show more evidence of clustering in a recall task than do college students when the information is especially meaningful to the children. These data suggest that processes such as clustering are often a relatively automatic consequence of previously acquired knowledge.

The availability of relevant knowledge has also been shown to affect children's abilities to conserve number and volume, to make inferences and take nonegocentric perspectives, and to select task-appropriate strategies. For example, Price-Williams, Gordon, and Ramirez (1969) and Adjei (1977) studied the conservation of clay by children of pottery-making parents. These children were advanced in this task, possibly because their familiarity with the medium reduced attentional demands; they therefore had enough attentional resources to notice simultaneous changes in length, width, and thickness. Gelman's (1969) classic work on number conservation provides additional information about children's abilities to decentrate and coordinate information. These abilities are evident for small numbers of items. When the latter become too large, the information-processing requirements seem to overwhelm children's abilities to perform number conservation tasks.

Other researchers have explored the conditions under which children can make transitive inferences and take multiple perspectives. Bryant and Trabasso (1971) demonstrated that young children could perform transitive inference problems when the relational terms used in the problems were well learned. Similarly, Rieser and Heiman (1982) found that 1- to 3-year-olds are not destined to be slavishly "egocentric" or bound by "rote learning" when given tasks involving spatial knowledge. In addition, Donaldson (1978) reported studies indicating that young children can take the perspective of other, hypothetical observers when the spatial layout is kept simple and meaningful. Finally, Siegler and Shrager (1984) provided an elegant analysis of how differences in the representation of knowledge affect children's decisions to use different strategies such as counting on their fingers or attempting to retrieve information directly from memory, and Carey (1985a, 1985b) provided important insights into ways in which children's developing knowledge of science information affects their performance on a variety of tasks.

Overall, the "new look" in developmental theory is providing important information about relationships between specific knowledge and activities such as inferencing, organizing, conserving, decentrating, and so forth. These advances suggest that thinking abilities are not simply added on top of existing domain-specific competencies. Instead, competencies in a domain and the ability to think about that domain seem to develop hand in hand.

An implication of this view is that changes in a few general strategies such as "becoming less impulsive" and "searching more systematically" will usually not be sufficient to produce powerful gains in classroom achievement. These strategy changes can provide a useful beginning, but there will also be a need to work closely with the child in order to develop domain-specific knowledge and skills. And, as Feuerstein and his colleagues emphasize, there is a need to help students become *efficient* in their ability to access relevant knowledge and skills. Otherwise they will be overwhelmed by new tasks because of attentional constraints.

Decision about Choices of Assessment Tasks

An emphasis on domain-specific knowledge and skills has implications for the types of tasks one uses in dynamic assessment. It is easy for people to confuse the general concept of dynamic assessment with the use of a particular set of tasks and procedures such as the Learning Potential Assessment Device (LPAD) (Feuerstein, 1979). For example, Reschly (1984) argued—quite appropriately, we believe—that the LPAD may not be the best procedure for finding specific teaching recommendations that are useful for the classroom teacher who is teaching traditional subjects. A major reason for Reschly's concern is that the tasks used in the LPAD are far removed from specific academic content areas such as reading, science, or math.

It is helpful in this context to note that the LPAD is just one example of the general concept of dynamic assessment. Feuerstein and colleagues use their cognitive map (e.g., see Chapter 14, this volume) as a guide for constructing assessment tasks. Furthermore, they note that the choice of tasks depends on one's ultimate goals. If we accept the goals espoused by the members of the National Research Council Panel (Heller et al., 1982), then it becomes important to use information from dynamic assessment to improve classroom teaching. From this perspective, it seems logical to construct tasks that provide more information about the types of domain-specific knowledge and skills that students need.

Campione and Brown (Chapter 3, this volume) provide an excellent illustration of assessment within the context of a specific task that is important for school achievement. They focus on the area of reading comprehension, and they use a reciprocal teaching format that encourages students to act as teachers during part of the instruction. An important advantage of the reciprocal teaching format is that, with the child generating questions and summaries, the teacher can more easily diagnose problems with each child's approach. The kinds of comprehension problems that become apparent in this context are more specific to reading than one would expect to find if the dynamic assessment task involved organization of dots, matrices, and other tasks that are not specifically related to reading comprehension (e.g., see Palincsar & Brown, 1984). Therefore, the choice of task has important effects on the suggestions for teaching.

In our research program at Vanderbilt, we are also finding that it is important to use tasks that are closely related to particular content areas. For example, in part of our research we are working with fourth- and fifth-grade students who are seriously delayed in mathematics. Part of their problem is that they have been unable to learn basic math facts such as $7 + 8 = 15$. This is embarrassing to them and prompts them to attempt to avoid situations where they have to do math. The students also have an extremely difficult time solving word problems. They simply grab for numbers rather than trying to understand the nature of the problems that they are being asked to solve.

In our work, we are finding that assessments that clarify reasons for problems in mathematics suggest specific teaching strategies, and that the use of these teaching strategies is having positive effects on the learning of most of our math-delayed children (e.g., see Bransford, Delclos, Vye, Burns, & Hasselbring, 1986, for more detail). As in the case of reading comprehension, however, we cannot expect to generate specific suggestions for teaching mathematics by restricting our assessment to tasks involving dots or inductive reasoning. Instead, we need to assess the domain-specific concepts and strategies that are necessary for effective mathematical performance. Note that this move to domain specificity by no means diminishes the importance of dynamic assessment. Indeed, it increases its importance by extending its applicability to a variety of new domains.

It is important to note, however, that a danger of working in specific content domains is that teaching may become purely task oriented with no emphasis on general principles of mediation such as those discussed by Feuerstein (see Chapter 14, this volume). These principles of mediation can be used to transform fact-oriented instruction into lessons involving thinking. As an illustration, consider a case discussed by Hasselbring, Goin, and Bransford (1985). They worked with math-delayed fifth and sixth graders on arcade-like software designed to give them practice at basic addition problems such as 7 + 8. The arcade program awarded points for speed and accuracy. All the students wanted to increase their scores. However, most had little idea of how to "debug" their current approaches to the game. For example, the vast majority paid little attention to the fact that they often counted on their fingers and hence could not significantly increase their speed until they moved from productive to reproductive strategies (Greeno; 1978). Furthermore, students knew the answers to some problems (e.g., 5 + 5) and hence needed to memorize answers to only a subset of the problems. Nevertheless, they did not spontaneously attempt to identify the set of problems that would be most beneficial for them to practice at home. With specific guidance from the teacher, the students were prompted to view the arcade game as a problem-solving situation, and they were helped to debug their current approaches to the problem of increasing their scores. Without the teaching, it is doubtful that the students would have taken a "higher order thinking" approach to the development of "lower order" skills.

Summary

In summary, it has been extremely valuable to us—and, we hope, to the reader—to have had the opportunity to read the chapters in this volume. Each author has pointed to important problems with current approaches to assessment, and each has provided excellent suggestions for ways that these problems might be addressed.

At the beginning of this chapter, we applauded the fact that contributors to this volume represent a variety of theoretical approaches. It has been very helpful to us to see this multiplicity of views. What emerges most strongly for us is the idea that dynamic assessment is a general concept rather than a specific set of tasks and procedures, and that initial data suggest that the concept has a great deal of potential. Particularly exciting is the prospect of using dynamic assessment both in the context of general problem-solving tasks and in the context of domain-specific activities such as reading, mathematics, and science. All of these activities are important for adaptation in our society, yet many students have difficulty becoming proficient in them. With teaching suggestions that are guided by task-appropriate dynamic assessments, there is a strong possibility that many of these difficulties can be overcome.

ACKNOWLEDGMENTS

Preparation of this paper was supported by Grant No. G0083C0052 awarded to Vanderbilt University by the U.S. Department of Education.

We wish to acknowledge the assistance of our research assistants, Brigid Barron, Ron Buen, Randi Glorski, Laura Goin, Rich Johnson, Stan Kulewicz, Kim Sloan, Deborah Stephens, and Julie Tapp, and the staff and children of the Metropolitan Nashville Public School System.
We would also like to thank the other members of our research group, H. Carl Haywood, Robert Sherwood, and Susan Williams. We are indebted to Jackie Welch for her editorial help.

REFERENCES

Adjei, K. (1977). Influence of specific maternal occupation and behavior on Piagetian cognitive development. In P. Dasen (Ed.), *Piagetian psychology*. New York: Gardner.

Aloia, G. F., & MacMillan, D. L. (1983). Influence of the EMR label on initial expectation for regular-classroom teachers. *American Journal of Mental Deficiency, 88*(3), 255–262.

Anderson, J. R. (1983). *The architecture of cognition*. Cambridge, MA: Harvard University Press.

Arter, J. A., & Jenkins, J. R. (1979). Differential diagnosis–prescriptive teaching: A critical appraisal. *Review of Educational Research, 49*(4), 517–555.

Bradley, T. B. (1983). Remediation of cognitive deficits: A critical appraisal of the Feuerstein model. *Journal of Mental Deficiency Research, 27*, 79–92.

Bransford, J. D. (in press). *Enhancing thinking and learning*. New York: Freeman.

Bransford, J. D., Delcos, V. R., Vye, N. J., Burns, M. S., & Hasselbring, T. S. (1986). *Improving the quality of assessment and instruction: Roles for dynamic assessment*. (Working Paper No. 1, Alternative Assessments of Handicapped Children). Nashville, TN: John F. Kennedy Center for Research on Education and Human Development, Vanderbilt University.

Bransford, J. D., Sherwood, R., Vye, N. J., & Rieser, J. (in press). Teaching thinking and problem solving: Suggestions from research. *American Psychologist*.

Brown, A. L., Bransford, J. D., Ferrara, R. A., & Campione, J. C. (1983). Learning, remembering and understanding. In J. H. Flavell & E. M. Markman (Eds.), *Carmichael's manual of child psychology* (Vol. 1). New York: Wiley.

Brown, A., & Ferrara, R. (1980). *Diagnosing zones of proximal development: An alternative to standardized testing?* Paper presented at Conference on Culture, Communication, and Cognition: Vygotskian Perspectives, Center for Psychosocial Studies, Chicago.

Bryant, N. R. (1982). *Preschool children's learning and transfer of matrices problems: A study of proximal development*. Unpublished master's thesis, University of Illinois.

Bryant, P., & Trabasso, T. (1971). Transitive inferences and memory in young children. *Nature 232*, 456–458.

Budoff, M., & Gottlieb, J. (1976). Special class EMR children mainstreamed: A study of an aptitude (learning potential) × treatment interaction. *American Journal of Mental Deficiency, 81*, 1–11.

Budoff, M., Meskin, J., & Harrison, R. (1971). Educational test of the learning-potential hypothesis. *American Journal of Mental Deficiency, 76*, 159–169.

Burns, M. S. (1985). *Comparison of "graduated prompt" and "mediational" dynamic assessment and static assessment with young children* (Technical Report No. 2, Alternative Assessments of Handicapped Children). Nashville, TN: John F. Kennedy Center for Research on Education and Human Development, Vanderbilt University.

Carey, S. (1985a). Are children fundamentally different kinds of thinkers and learners than adults? In S. F. Chipman, J. W. Segal, & R. Glaser (Eds.), *Thinking and learning skills: Current research and open questions* (Vol. 2). Hillsdale, NJ: Erlbaum.

Carey, S. (1985b). *Conceptual change in childhood*. Cambridge, MA: M.I.T. Press.

Chi, M. T. H. (1978). Knowledge structures and memory development. In R. S. Siegler (Ed.), *Children's thinking: What develops?* Hillsdale, NJ: Erlbaum.

Cooper, H. M. (1979). Pygmalion grows up: A model for teacher expectation communication and performance influence. *Review of Educational Research, 61*(3), 389–410.

Delclos, V. R., Burns, S., & Kulewicz, S. J. (1985). *Effects of dynamic assessment on teachers' expectations of handicapped children* (Technical Report No. 3, Alternative Assessments of Handicapped Children). Nashville, TN: John F. Kennedy Center for Research on Education and Human Development, Vanderbilt University.

Donaldson, M. (1978). *Children's minds.* New York: Norton.

Feuerstein, R. (1979). *The dynamic assessment of retarded performers: The learning potential assessment device, theory, instruments, and techniques.* Baltimore: University Park Press.

Gelman, R. (1969). Conservation acquisition: A problem of learning to attend to the relevant attributes. *Journal of Experimental Child Psychology, 7,* 167–187.

Greeno, J. G. (1978). Indefinite goals in well-structured problems. *Psychological Review, 83,* 479–491.

Hasselbring, T., Goin, L., & Bransford, J. (1985). *Dynamic assessment and mathematics learning.* Paper presented at 109th annual meeting of the American Association of Mental Deficiency, Philadelphia, PA.

Haywood, H. C., Filler, J. W., Jr., Shifman, M. A., & Chatelanat, G. (1975). Behavioral assessment in mental retardation. *Advances in Psychological Assessments, 3,* 96–103, 113–120.

Heller, K. A., Holtzman, W. H., & Messick, S. (Eds.). (1982). *Placing children in special education: A strategy for equity.* Washington, DC: National Academy Press.

Hobbs, N. (Ed.). (1975). *Issues in the classification of children* (Vols. I & II). San Francisco: Jossey-Bass.

Hoy, M. P. M. (1983). *The perceived value of the standard psychological report compared with the Learning Potential Assessment Device report.* Unpublished doctoral dissertation, University of Iowa.

Lindberg, M. (1980). The role of knowledge structures in the ontogeny of learning. *Journal of Experimental Child Psychology, 30,* 401–410.

Mann, L. (1979). *On the trail of process: A historical perspective on cognitive processes and their training.* New York: Grune & Stratton.

Palincsar, A. S., & Brown, A. L. (1984). Reciprocal teaching of comprehension-fostering and monitoring activities. *Cognition and Instruction, 1,* 117–175.

Piaget, J. (1970). Piaget's theory. In P. H. Mussen (Ed.), *Carmichael's manual of child psychology* (Vol. 1). New York: Wiley.

Price-Williams, D., Gordon, M. W., & Ramirez, M. (1969). Skill and conservation: A study of pottery-making children. *Developmental Psychology, 1,* 769.

Reschly, D. J. (1984). Beyond IQ test bias: The National Academy Panel's analysis of minority EMR overrepresentation. *Educational Researcher, 13*(3), 15–19.

Rieser, J., & Heiman, M. (1982). Spatial self-reference systems and shortest-route behavior in toddlers. *Child Development, 53,* 524–533.

Siegler, R S., & Shrager, J. (1984). Strategy choices in addition and subtraction: How do children know what to do? In C. Sophian (Ed.), *The origins of cognitive skills.* Hillsdale, NJ: Erlbaum.

Simon, H. A. (1980). Problem solving and education. In D. T. Tuma & R. Reif (Eds.), *Problem solving and education: Issues in teaching and research.* Hillsdale, NJ: Erlbaum.

Sternberg, R. J. (1985a). Instrumental and componential approaches to the nature and training of intelligence. In S. F. Chipman, J. W. Segal, & R. Glaser (Eds.), *Thinking and learning skills: Research and open questions* (Vol. 2). Hillsdale, NJ: Erlbaum.

Sternberg, R. J. (1985b). *Beyond I.Q.: Toward a triarchic theory of intelligence.* Cambridge, MA: Harvard University Press.

Index